KENYA

GUIDE

BE A TRAVELER ~ NOT A TOURIST!

OPEN ROAD TRAVEL GUIDES SHOW YOU
HOW TO BE A TRAVELER – NOT A TOURIST!

*Whether you're going abroad or planning a trip in the United States, take Open Road along on your journey. Our books have been praised by **Travel & Leisure, The Los Angeles Times, Newsday, Booklist, US News & World Report, Endless Vacation, American Bookseller, Coast to Coast**, and many other magazines and newspapers!*

Don't just see the world – experience it with Open Road!

ABOUT THE AUTHOR

Born in Kenya of British parents, Elise Vachon proudly traces her ancestry to the famous explorer, Dr. David Livingstone. It is from him that she inherits her passion for travel and adventure. After growing up in Kenya, her love for the wilds of Africa remains deeply entrenched. With relatives and friends still living in Africa, Elise maintains her ties. Elise had the opportunity of living in and visiting much of the world owing to her father's career with the United Nations as a Ph.D. in plant physiology. After traveling the globe, Elise picked charming Marietta, Georgia to call home since 1987. She is a freelance writer and photographer and is a published magazine and newspaper writer; *Kenya Guide* is her first book. For more information, see *www.mindspring.com/~rvachon* or e-mail *rvachon@mindspring.com*.

BE A TRAVELER, NOT A TOURIST - WITH OPEN ROAD TRAVEL GUIDES!

Open Road Publishing has guide books to exciting, fun destinations on four continents. As veteran travelers, our goal is to bring you the best travel guides available anywhere!

No small task, but here's what we offer:

• All Open Road travel guides are written by authors with a distinct, opinionated point of view – not some sterile committee or team of writers. Our authors are experts in the areas covered and are polished writers.

• Our guides are geared to people who want to make their own travel choices. We'll show you how to discover the real destination – not just see some place from a tour bus window.

• We're strong on the basics, but we also provide terrific choices for those looking to get off the beaten path and experience the country or city – not just see it or pass through it.

• We give you the best, but we also tell you about the worst and what to avoid. Nobody should waste their time and money on their hard-earned vacation because of bad or inadequate travel advice.

• Our guides assume nothing. We tell you everything you need to know to have the trip of a lifetime – presented in a fun, literate, no-nonsense style.

• And, above all, we welcome your input, ideas, and suggestions to help us put out the best travel guides possible.

KENYA
GUIDE

BE A TRAVELER - NOT A TOURIST!

Elise Vachon

OPEN ROAD PUBLISHING

To my family

2nd Edition

Text Copyright ©2000 by Elise Vachon
Maps Copyright ©2000 by Open Road Publishing
- All Rights Reserved -

Library of Congress Catalog Card No. 99-74390
ISBN 1-892975-15-7

Front cover photo © FPG International, New York. Top back cover photo courtesy of Elise Vachon. Bottom back cover photo © Andy Rouse/EarthWater. Maps by James Ramage.

TABLE OF CONTENTS

MAPS

SIDEBARS

SIDEBARS

1. INTRODUCTION

When Americans think of Kenya, they usually think of romantic adventure, great safaris, and vast savannahs where all manner of wild beasts roam. Not only will you unlock the secrets to one of Africa's most interesting countries with this detailed book, but you'll find out just how much more the astonishing, vibrant nation of Kenya has to offer.

I'll tell you the best places to find the "big five" - elephant, lion, rhino, buffalo and leopard, for up-close and personal viewing. Count on discovering the finest conservation areas on the continent, where large herds of zebra, gazelle, and long-necked giraffes run free.

When Johann Ludwig Krapf first traveled to equatorial Africa in 1849 and sighted the snow-clad tips of Mount Kenya, he intended for others like you to follow in his footsteps and experience these breathtaking twin peaks. I'll be your guide around the heart of these shining jewels while explaining the history of the country as well, from the discovery of early man to the influence of the British settlers.

You'll find pristine coffee and tea plantations and tour the Great Rift Valley and its amazing lakes. Discover legendary Lake Victoria (one of the country's borders), where the pink flamingos give spectacular water performances. If beaches, fishing, or sailing are more to your liking, then follow my directions to Kenya's tropical shores, where white sand, crystal blue waters, and sunny skies await.

I'll tell you how to avoid the crowds and where to find premium shopping bargains. If you want to be pampered with hot water, a bathtub, and fresh flowers in your tent, I'll tell you how to arrange that too! Or take a cold safari shower under the stars, ride a camel through the desert, or dig your own long-drop – you'll find tips on these and everything in between.

My goal has been to show the very best of Kenya so that you can have the trip of a lifetime. I hope it will help you enjoy, preserve, learn, and appreciate one of the last Gardens of Eden left on the planet. I trust you will leave a piece of your heart in Kenya while bringing home cherished memories to last a lifetime.

2. OVERVIEW

Jambo (hello) and *karibu* (welcome) to Kenya – a country of dreams, explorers' legends, and adventure. It is a land of contrast with hot dry deserts, snow-capped mountains, deep valleys, lush forests, slow mysterious rivers, picturesque lakes, rolling plains, palm fringed coastlines and incomparable game.

Here in Kenya you can experience those fantasies and quests that are still a part of Africa. Sleep under the stars beneath a canvas canopy, watch the sun set over **Mount Kilimanjaro**, behold the endangered wildlife as it struggles to survive or relax in a hammock on a pristine beach.

NAIROBI

To begin your safari try the largest city in East Africa – **Nairobi**. Many people are advised not to stay in Nairobi any longer than they have to; I must disagree. Here in the city and its environs there are many exciting things to see and much to learn about the people who make up this fabulous country.

One of my favorite sights is **Daphne Sheldrick's Animal Orphanage**, where you can greet a yearling, orphaned elephant by receiving a light puff of air into your face from a bristly but supple trunk. Blow gently back into the snout offered up to you and rest assured you're acquaintances for life. Neither of you will ever forget the special moment.

The **City Market**, where one could venture into the main hall to the perfume of fresh roses, orchids, guavas, mangoes and pineapples delighting the senses, is not what it used to be. The top floor has rows of souvenir stands, while the lower floor features fresh food, including meat and fish. You can still get in with no problem, but the smells are not as appealing as they once were. Behind the market, near the mosque, city officials chose to burn down an impromptu market that stood there for years. In its place will be a parking lot.

Along with the sweet aromas in the larger markets, the smell of meat and fish will prevail. Keep wandering, and you'll find the bargains you

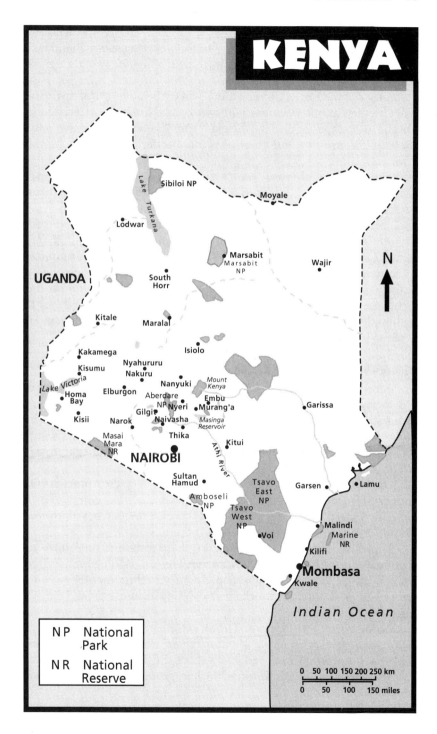

KENYA

Sibiloi NP

Moyale

Lodwar

Marsabit
Marsabit
NP

Wajir

N

UGANDA

South
Horr

Kitale

Maralal

Kakamega

Isiolo

Kisumu

Nyahururu

Nakuru

Nanyuki

Mount
Kenya

Lake Victoria

Homa
Bay

Elburgon

Aberdare
NP Nyeri

Embu

Murang'a

Garissa

Kisii

Narok

Gilgi

Naivasha

Masinga
Reservoir

Masai
Mara
NR

Thika

Kitui

NAIROBI

Sultan
Hamud

Tsavo
East
NP

Garsen

Lamu

Amboseli
NP

Tsavo
West
NP

Voi

Malindi
Marine
NR

Kilifi

●Mombasa

Kwale

Indian Ocean

NP	National Park
NR	National Reserve

0   50 100 150 200 250 km

0   50   100   150 miles

came for. With a little haggling, Kisii soapstone carvings, colorful sarongs, impressive ebony woodcarvings, paintings, menacing spears, hand made shields and other souvenirs are yours to take home. Beware though, the Africans are skilled salespeople.

A tour of the **Karen Blixen Home**, where the novel *Out of Africa* took place, depicts another era when life was simpler but more of a challenge. On the lush tropical grounds, the giant Candelabra Cactus is just one of the many impressive and colorful plants bordering the thick, verdant lawn.

At the **Railway Museum**, have fun climbing on the rail car used in the movie *Out of Africa*. Climb on the countless old trains and carriages and investigate their interiors. Feel free to revert back to your childhood days and pretend you are on a runaway commuter train! The centerpiece of the Railway Museum is the locomotive that enlivened the writing of *The Man Eating Lions of Tsavo*. During the laying of the railway lines that opened up Kenya, the lions in the Tsavo district developed a taste for human flesh. After the African cats killed many of the Indian workers, they set their sights on the white hunter who became the hunted, dragged out the window by a king of the jungle, the hunter was never seen alive again. This is all on display here.

NORTHERN FRONTIER DISTRICT

After the bustle and dust of Nairobi, a respite in the far reaches of the **Northern Frontier District** provides a stark change. The wild scrub deserts of the North are roughly two-thirds of this forbidding, exciting, and isolated country. A trip here is for the very adventurous, but it is worth it to see **Samburu National Reserve** or one of the other eight **game parks** in the area.

Dramatic rock formations, high mesas, and deep escarpments make the occasional thread of green along a river bank look like emeralds in the sun. The *doum* palms and spindly acacias throw a few patches of welcome shade.

Hippo, crocodile, elephant, buffalo, plains game and small birds and mammals survive by staying close to water. Three intriguing species found only in this region are the pin-striped Grevy's zebra, the delicate long-necked gerenuk antelope which feeds standing on hind legs, and the blue-legged Somali ostrich.

At **Ol Malo** (The Place Of The Greater Kudu), you can stay in the picturesque guest cottages and enjoy the separate thatched living and dining areas perched on the edge of a sheer cliff. A view of 5,000 acres of vast semi-desert, with **Mt. Kenya** in the background, unveils the very face of Africa.

I don't know which is more impressive at Ol Malo: the free form swimming pool with its overflow cleverly giving the impression that it courses over the edge of the precipice, or the irregular lurch of a ride on the back of a one-humped camel. Both the camel ride and a swim in the pool filled by a deep borehole are just a small part of the many treasures Kenya holds in store for you.

THE RIFT VALLEY

The Rift Valley offers a stunning and surprising view to the first-time visitor. After a drive through thick conifer forests, the vista abruptly opens up and before you is the edge of the Rift. The Rift is really a continental fault system stretching from Mozambique all the way to the Dead Sea, with a series of lakes scattered in between making this the greatest valley in the world.

At the top of the lake sequence is jade-colored **Lake Turkana** and at the bottom is blindingly white **Lake Magadi**. **Lake Baringo** and **Lake Naivasha** hold fresh water and the others are all shallow white soda lakes with distinctive features. Dozens of extinct volcanoes form giant calderas and semi-submerged islands conjure a furtive sense of mystery.

The vast flocks of bright pink flamingoes and 350 species of other birds that live on these lakes are the main attraction. There is, however, a growing population of toothy pink-mouthed hippo, magnificent leopard and lion, and many varieties of waterbuck and kudu.

A visit to **Meru National Park** offers you a chance to see the home and terrain that Joy Adamson (author of *Born Free*) loved so deeply. **Elsamere** is now a residential conservation center where visitors are welcome.

For those who are into adventure, try a little fly fishing for colorful trout in a refreshing stream, take a day or overnight safari where fourteen oxen pull you in an open-sided wagon through the game-filled valley, or build up an appetite as you swim with (supposedly) harmless crocodiles.

WESTERN KENYA

Western Kenya is often mistakenly overlooked as a tourist attraction. The fertile Western Highlands are home to never-ending green fields of coffee and tea. It is worth a visit to see the pickers in thick aprons surrounded by chest high bushes quickly filling baskets with prime pickings.

Take a trip to the only remaining section of primeval jungle still standing in **Kakamega Forest**. In the dark, moist tropical reserve there are multitudes of mammals and plants found nowhere else in the world. Look for colobus and blue monkeys and dazzling turaco birds hiding in the massive hardwood trees.

A hike through the **Cherangani Hills** or a visit to **Mt. Elgon** will afford you an eye-full of dramatic scenery of high and forested mountains. The famous **Kitum Caves** are a must for visitors. Thousands of bats live in the domed roof and the elephants pick their way over miles of rocky paths and steep trails to dig and eat the natural salts and minerals. It is an amazing sight to see the deep furrows left by the pachyderm's tusks as they mine the vital treats.

CENTRAL HIGHLANDS

Snow capped **Mount Kenya** in the **Central Highlands** is among the world's largest free-standing volcanic mountains and is waiting for you to tackle one of the eight routes up and around its peaks. Local outfitters will prepare you for the five-day walk.

The fertile foothills of Mt. Kenya play host to abundant wildlife and herds of cattle in perfect harmony with nature and each other. As wildlife allows the horses to get so close, the game viewing from horseback is spectacular. You can almost touch the Grevy's zebra, reticulated giraffe, amusing warthog and agile impala as they go about their daily lives. This is eco-tourism at its best.

Leopard, buffalo, rhino, elephant, lion and antelope inhabit the volcanic massif of the **Aberdare National Park**. There are streams for fishing, waterfalls, magnificent views and game watching both during the day and at night.

And you don't want to miss the "equator crossing experience." The local population loves enthralling tourists with a captivating demonstration of water flowing through a funnel. With two jugs (one filled with water) the friendly locals illustrate how the poured liquid swirls in different directions down the spout. Depending on where you stand in relation to the equator and the gravitational pull of the earth, the gyrating water changes its rotation from clockwise to anti-clockwise.

SOUTHERN KENYA

On the famous African plains in **Southern Kenya** there are many fascinating and uniquely African experiences to enjoy with a knowledgeable guide. Learn to make fire with a stick; shoot an authentic bow and arrow, or discover medicinal and practical plants (such as those used as a toothbrush). Take the time to look for ancient artifacts; explore the home of the village chief's first wife, and listen to mesmerizing Swahili songs. Spend the days shopping at a colorful local market but most of all enjoy the teeming wildlife.

As you bump and jolt along the wide open plains in your Land Cruiser there are many splendid sights. You might see a spectacular cheetah with her kill or a 30 count pride of lions, including a magnificent black-maned male resting in the heat of the day. The silly grunting wildebeest (also known as gnu) preparing for its famous migration and the comical warthogs with their tails straight up in the air will keep you laughing. Large numbers of dainty, leaping Grant's gazelle are too numerous to keep up with – it's all great fun!

Further to the East, within view of the soaring peaks of **Mount Kilimanjaro**, stay at a luxury lodge with a swimming pool, or, at the other end of the spectrum, opt for a rugged tented camp where naturalists focus on conservation efforts between wildlife and Masai cattle and people.

The outdoor shower is common in Kenya and can effuse rustic charm or be perfectly civilized. On the rough side, look for a small gnarled tree enclosed by a six foot tall screen of flimsy hand woven reeds supporting a five gallon bucket on a rope. To release the water, simply turn the tap on the bucket.

Most celebrated of the National Reserves is **Masai Mara**. No matter how hard anyone has tried to describe the Mara, no one ever comes close to giving this extraordinary ecosystem the glorious credit it deserves. To cut out a visit to this area would be a sad error which this book will help you avoid. If you have come to Kenya to see wildlife, this is the place to be. The air is alive with birds, the rivers are awash with hippo and crocodile, and the plains remain filled with game concentrations much the same as those seen by early explorers.

Southern Kenya also boasts **Amboseli** and **Tsavo National Parks**, which offer their own versions of Africa's diverse animal population. It might be rather exciting to see furry hyena, jackal, kudu, lion and elephant from the lofty height of a hot air balloon with a romantic champagne breakfast afterward.

THE COAST

As a final destination before returning for a day of shopping in Nairobi, try the picture perfect **Kenya coast**. The famous shore, renowned for its superb beaches with dazzling white sand and crystalline waters, is a great place to get away from it all.

A walk along the white powder-fine sand on **Diani Beach** with the warm Indian Ocean lapping at your feet, the unique Arab style architecture and furnishings, fragrant gardens filled with sweet coconuts and monkeys outside the window make staying at the beach exceptional. The open, airy construction is warm and welcoming and the friendly dogs add to the feeling. Sitting on the verandah having "caught-that-day" fresh seafood for dinner, enjoying the music from the ocean waves while the bush babies chatter in the trees, is like being in a scene from a movie.

If you like water sports, at low tide the **snorkeling** is worth the effort. There are plenty of brightly colored fish darting in and out of the coral. The partially submerged **coral caves** are home to bats and swallows who escape the heat of the day in the cool eerie rooms.

In the town of **Mombasa**, a visit to **Fort Jesus**, one of East Africa's oldest habitations, explains the history of how the country was founded and influenced by the Portuguese and the Arabs. The aromatic spice market, kaleidoscopic cloth shops, hand woven rug stores, plentiful fruit stalls and the constantly moving, multicolored crowds make this a great place to see.

ENJOY KENYA!

The Kenyan experience has fired the imagination of countless people ever since the intrepid early explorers told of the drama and magnificence of this dynamic country. There is no finer place to go through your own personal experience of discovery, whether it is white water rafting, trout fishing, horseback or camel riding, mountain climbing, golfing, ballooning or game viewing than Kenya. Pack your bags; let's go and enjoy the *safari* (journey)!

3. SUGGESTED ITINERARIES

In preparing for your trip, bear in mind that most tour operators in Kenya are willing to fit their schedules to whatever you want to do. If you work with an operator like this, the possibilities are limited only by time and money. There are also many affordable and gratifying itineraries to choose from in which the schedules are fixed with little room for change.

Kenya is a diverse country with much to do and see. Short of living there for months, it is impossible to experience it all in a short vacation. My proposed travel schemes will vary depending on your arrival time in Kenya and how you choose to move about within the country (car, plane, etc.).

The nine, eleven, and thirteen day itineraries I've put together are for someone like myself who plans everything down to the last detail and fits in as much as possible. I have seen the things I listed here in the time allocated below, but it took some careful organizing. If you prefer to take things a little more slowly, cut out a couple of items and do it your way. Most of all, remember to have a good time!

NINE DAY SAFARI
Day 1
Travel to **Nairobi**.
Check into the elegant Grand Regency Hotel with its soaring atrium.

Day 2
Savor the local fresh fruit breakfast in the 24-hour hotel coffee shop.
Hand-feed the endangered Rothschild giraffe at the educational Langata
    Giraffe Center.
Tour the original Karen Blixen House and part of the 360 acre estate's
    tropical gardens.
Lunch of tasty Lancashire Hot Pot at Karen Blixen Coffee Garden.

Climb on the countless old trains and carriages at the historic Railway Museum.

Tea with scrumptious homemade Hazelnut Dream Torte at Orna's; a local favorite.

Enjoy bargaining for anything from pineapples to baskets at the City Market.

Dinner at Haandi, where the Indian food is authentically cooked in clay ovens.

Day 3
Early breakfast of scrambled eggs and bacon.

Travel to the **Central Highlands**.

Check in and enjoy the up-country colonial elegance of the Outspan Hotel.

Swim in the heated pool.

On the terrace choose from an assortment of local dishes offered on the lunch buffet.

Visit the lush tapestry of a coffee plantation and take a peek at shy colobus.

Take a nature walk/hike and enjoy the panoramic vistas of Mt. Kenya.

Tea and scones on the verandah with brightly colored birds.

Afternoon game drive in search of elephant herds.

Dinner off the set-menu in the plush dining hall.

Day 4
Early breakfast of bacon and fresh eggs.

Travel to **The Rift Valley**.

Check in at the charming Lake Naivasha Club, which was Kenya's international airport after WWII.

Lunch buffet on the lawn under the spreading yellow fever trees.

Ferry over to Crescent Island; the outer rim of a submerged volcano.

Tasty tilapia for dinner in the bright dining room surrounded by panoramic garden views.

Day 5
Pancakes and honey for breakfast as you watch the grazing waterbuck.

Drive to Lake Nakuru to see the brilliant fuschia flamingoes and sleek leopard.

Lunch at Lake Nakuru Lodge where the "view terrace" offers stunning landscapes.

Head out in search of a family of endangered black rhino.

Fresh vegetables, potatoes and lamb for dinner on the verandah at Lake Naivasha Club.

Day 6
Early breakfast of toast, sausage and scrambled eggs.
Travel to **Southern Kenya – Masai Mara**.
Check into the simple thatched cottages decorated with animal art at
  Rekero Farm.
Spicy curried chicken lunch under overhanging trees.
Relax on your verandah and read about the animal wonders of Kenya.
Set off in search of ferocious Cape buffalo, pink ostriches and grunting
  wildebeest.
Settle into a director's chair for tea and chocolate cake under an acacia
  tree on the plains.
Roam around in search of the elusive cheetah, Burchelle's zebra, and
  eland.
Sundowners (cocktails) on the plains as the orange sun quickly slides over
  the horizon.
Lentil soup and chicken with rice for dinner by the crackling fire in the
  family dining room.

Day 7
Early game drive in search of hunting lion prides and Masai giraffe.
Breakfast on hot wheat porridge with brown sugar while feeding happy,
  chattering birds.
Take a hike, learn how to make a fire with sticks and shoot an authentic
  bow and arrow.
Picnic lunch of egg salad and sausage sandwiches under the shade of an
  acacia tree.
Visit a Masai manyatta (village) and take a look inside a genuine mud and
  dung hut.
Drive down to the river for a peek at the noisy hippo and twelve foot crocs.
Relax on the verandah with a view of the watering hole, a cup of tea, and
  a novel.
Dinner of spicy pasta under the stars.

Day 8
Bacon, poached eggs and toast for an early breakfast.
Travel to **Nairobi**.
Check into the Mayfair Court Hotel for a room reminiscent of an English
  country inn.
Delve into the ancient origins of man at the National Museum.
Light lunch on the terrace of the tree-lined coffee shop at Utamaduni
  Kenyan cooperative.
Shop for ebony masks, colorful fabrics, and souvenirs at Utamaduni.

Dinner at the Mischief Bar & Grill surrounded by interesting memorabila. Test your fortune with a little gambling at the Mayfair Casino & Club.

Day 9
Depart for home.

ELEVEN DAY SAFARI

Day 1
Travel to **Nairobi, Kenya.**
Check in at the Nairobi Hilton; a tall, circular landmark.

Day 2
Early breakfast of omelet and cheese.
Travel to **Southern Kenya – Melepo Hills.**
Check in at distant Sirata Suruwa luxury tented camp (shower al fresco!).
Picnic lunch with ham sandwiches and freshly baked bread.
Game drive in search of the elusive long-necked gerenuk and the elegant eland and zebra.
Tea in the thatched open verandah with gingerbread and wild honey.
Afternoon nature walk to a lofty ridge with majestic eagles.
Try the local posho or ugali (corn) for dinner as the stars shine brighter than ever.

Day 3
To start the day, an early nature walk to find the abundant and colorful wildflowers.
Breakfast of pork sausages, toast and scrambled eggs.
Join in the fun of a morning game count (see how many you can spot!).
Picnic lunch with salami sandwiches, fresh salad and fruit.
Explore a Masai settlement and welcome the curious children as they enjoy your company.
Tea with chocolate brownies and a view of snow-capped Mt. Kilimanjaro.
Kick back and enjoy the sunset and vista with binoculars.
Learn to play an old African board game, before a dinner of spiced chicken and rice.

Day 4
Early breakfast of cereal and fresh fruit.
Travel to **Northern Frontier District** (Samburu).
Check in to Ol Malo (Place of the Greater Kudu) on the very edge of a steep escarpment.
Lunch of home made pizza with breathtaking view of the animal watering hole below.

Swim in the large free-form pool perched cliffside.
Tea with chocolate cake on the terrace with a tame kudu.
Visit a Samburu settlement and have a lesson in authentic spear making.
Dinner of potatoes and lamb in the open thatched dining room with fine linen and silver.

Day 5
Early breakfast on your patio; watch the cute rock hyrax scurry below.
Nature walk over the semi-desert terrain and camel rides to the river.
Picnic in the bush with Mt. Everest salad, fresh fruit, and locally made cheese.
Drive back for tea while game viewing (spot a rare kudu or klipspringer).
Relax in the warmth of a huge stone bath before a dinner of Shepherd's pie.

Day 6
Early breakfast of sticky buns and omelets.
Travel to **Southern Kenya – Masai Mara**.
Check into the comfortable oasis of the Mara Intrepids Club.
Outdoor buffet lunch of cold meats and salad while watching playful monkeys and birds.
Relax and swim in the rustic pool surrounded by interesting rocks.
Tea in the traditional outdoor safari experience.
Afternoon game drive into the Mara to catch a glimpse of "the big five" – lion, elephant, rhino, buffalo, and leopard.
Candlelight dinner of pork chops and scalloped potatoes in the open sided dining tent.

Day 7
Early game drive over the plains in search of cape buffalo, elephant, and giraffe.
Breakfast of French toast (with noisy baboons and bright birds) overlooking the river.
Continue over the Mara looking for lion, wildebeest, cheetah, and light-footed gazelle.
Lunch buffet of cold meats, fresh warm breads, salad and fruit.
Relax by the pool with a good book and some sun screen.
Afternoon of watching wildlife videos with munchies and drinks in the rustic bar.
Barbecued ribs for dinner in the "cluster club" tent.

Day 8
Breakfast of eggs, bacon, and toast served in your tent.

Cross the suspension bridge to watch the graceful hippo maneuver in the river.
Make your own sandwiches for lunch from a delectable buffet selection.
Relax by the pool or take a short walk until it's time for tea.
Crumpets for tea under the shade trees.
Set off to find more Grant's and Thompson's gazelle, zebra, lion and if you're lucky, rhino.
Candlelight dinner of fresh trout almondine.
Watch from the wooden deck over the river as the leopard comes to feed on floodlit bait.

Day 9
Sunrise breakfast of pancakes and bacon.
Travel to **Nairobi**.
Check into The Norfolk Hotel where Teddy Roosevelt stayed.
Corned beef sandwich for lunch at Orna's – save room for desert!
Compare blue and pink ostriches at the Ostrich Farm; stand on a giant egg and shop, shop, shop.
Visit the cool interior of Karen Blixen's House and the lush grounds.
Tea and a great selection of pastries in the nearby Karen Blixen Coffee Garden.
At the Railway Museum, imagine riding on the cowcatcher at the front of a train.
All you can eat game meat cooked to your liking for dinner at the Carnivore (vegetarians, go to the Nairobi Tamarind Restaurant).

Day 10
A quiet breakfast of hot cinnamon porridge and fruit at the Norfolk's courtyard terrace.
Browse among the colorful wares in the City Market.
Picnic lunch of local Sambusas and fresh pineapple from the market.
Feed the giraffe at eye level at the Langata Giraffe Center.
Savor the historic, homey atmosphere with tea at the hotel's swank Lord Delamere Terrace and Bar.
Wander through the rambling gardens, walks, and aviaries.
Dinner in the candlelit Ibis Grill as the pianist plays your favorite songs.

Day 11
Depart for home.

THIRTEEN DAY SAFARI

Day 1

Travel to **Nairobi**.

Check into the New Stanley Hotel; a favorite of young Ernest Hemingway.

Day 2

Breakfast of paw paw, muffins, and a poached egg in your room.

At the Karen Blixen Museum, see the clothes worn by Meryl Streep in *Out of Africa*.

Meet an elephant up close and personal at Daphne Sheldrick's Animal Orphanage.

Fish-and-chips for lunch at a roadside stall.

Climb aboard the relics of the "Lunatic Express" at the Railway Museum.

Sip tea and read messages tacked to the live acacia tree at The New Stanley's Thorn Tree Cafe.

Listen to the cacophony of sounds as the locals shop in the City Market.

Try a genuine Kenyan buffet for dinner at Swara Restaurant.

Day 3

Early breakfast of oatmeal with syrup and fresh pineapple.

Travel to **Western Kenya**.

Check into Lokitela Farm, an up-country farm house with stunning Nandi Flame trees.

Farm fresh produce and fish cakes for lunch.

Visit Mt. Elgon National Park, one of the loveliest and most undiscovered areas of Kenya.

Savor a nice cup of tea and view the game around splendid Mount Elgon.

As part of the family dinner, savor a juicy steak and home-grown corn.

Day 4

Sunrise breakfast of cereal and fresh milk (milk the cow yourself!).

Visit Kakamega Forest and see the scaly-tailed flying squirrel or a host of monkeys.

Enjoy salami sandwiches on a picnic lunch among some rare and varied bird life.

Look for the unique hammer-headed fruit bat or bush-tailed porcupine.

Roast beef, gravy and baked potato dinner under the stars.

Day 5

Early breakfast of bacon, fruit and just-laid eggs.

Travel to **Northern Frontier**.

Check into the fantasy tree house of the Samburu Intrepids Club.

Outdoor buffet lunch with an enticing view of the flowing river.
Set off in the cool of the afternoon to discover any shy gerenuk or long-
legged ostrich.
Swim away the dust in the attractive pool or recline under the shade
creepers.
Evening game drive in search of giraffe, fierce lion, cape buffalo and
handsome kudu.
Moonlight bush barbecue with all the trimmings.

Day 6
Late breakfast of omelets and granadilla in the four-poster bed.
Clamber onto a camel for a special game-finding safari.
Cold meat and cool potato salad picnic lunch on the savagely beautiful
and arid plains.
Trek over the northern desert with a birds-eye-view of the animals.
Sundowners and mutton dinner lit by hanging gourds.

Day 7
Early breakfast of kippers and eggs by the river.
Opt for a nature and bird walk with an informative and entertaining
guide.
Travel to the **Great Rift Valley.**
Warm greetings await you at check in after a 20 minute canoe ride to
magical Island Camp.
Pasta salad and fish for lunch in the main thatched dining area at tree top
level.
Walk to hot springs and enjoy the bright lizards and exotic vegetation.
Take time to marvel at the scores of different birds.
Tea and oatmeal cookies with other guests in an intimate thatched
lounge.
Sundowners on a neighboring island as the crocodiles slither into the
water.
Starlit barbecue dinner of roast beef and baked potatoes.

Day 8
Daybreak breakfast of baked fresh fruit compote.
Junket in the marsh where the hippo will show you enormous pink
mouths and beady eyes.
Pool-side lunch of club sandwiches and banana pineapple sherbet.
Lounge in the shade until tea time and be mesmerized at the play of light.
Visit a Njemps village for exotic traditional dances.
Candlelight dinner of steak and kidney pie with live music from a Njemps
reed pipe.

Day 9

Cheery breakfast of eggs baked in bacon rings.

Travel to **Masai Mara**.

Check in at Mara Serena Lodge and step into the daydream world of a Masai village.

Cool lunch buffet of iced poached shrimp and mocha gelatin.

Take all the pictures you can while visiting the captivating Masai tribal dance performance.

Simple tea with sponge cake as you revel in the panoramic scenery.

Learn all about the "big five" and other game from a fascinating wildlife film.

Cool off in the pool and read a relaxing novel or walk among the luxurious flower beds.

Broiled sausages and sautéed mushrooms for dinner amid sparkling lights in hanging pots.

Day 10

Breakfast of orange sections and French omelet at the hippo pool where the show goes on.

Venture out into the Mara where you're bound to see giraffe, hyena, lion, and topi.

Lunch outdoors with paella and flan with fruit.

Relax by the pool until tea with cheese cake is served.

Set off again into the wilds and catch one last glimpse of the animals as they settle in.

Dinner of braised oxtail and carrots vichy by candlelight.

Day 11

Marvel at the expanse below from a hot air balloon over the plains.

Champagne breakfast will be waiting when you land.

Take a nature walk or visit a local village.

A game drive in the late afternoon is your last chance to see the wildlife you've missed.

Farewell dinner of roast stuffed turkey under the burnished moon bids you adieu.

Day 12

Creamed chipped beef with tea served for breakfast.

Travel to **Nairobi**.

Check into the plush, plant-filled Serena Hotel.

Seafood curry lunch at The Mandhari Restaurant and a panoramic view of the city skyline.

A quick trip to the Bomas of Kenya where you will enjoy cultural dances
and native songs.
The National Museum will satisfy your questions about mammals, birds
and tribal cultures.
Tea back at the hotel in Cafe Maghreb where tapestry screens add privacy
and class.
Next, have fun shopping in the local market.
As a grand finale to your safari, Italian dinner at the popular Trattoria.

Day 13
Depart for home.

MOMBASA EXTENSION

If you wish to extend your stay in Kenya for a little longer, I strongly
urge you to take in a special treat on the coast. You will find nothing more
gorgeous than the fine ivory sand and the warm **Indian Ocean** to lull you
into thinking you've found paradise. Let the fragrance of frangipani and
the gratifying flavor of coconut juice soothe away the thoughts of the long
trip home.

Day 1
Travel to **Mombasa**.
After an intriguing ferry ride, check in to Diani House; a taste of colonial
Kenya.
Casual lunch of freshly baked fish-cakes and chips outdoors on the cool
verandah.
Go for a relaxing swim in the Indian Ocean or try your hand at
windsurfing.
Take a stroll along the beach and feel the sand squish between your toes.
Visit colorful markets where locals buy clothes and staples (try crispy roast
corn on the cob!).
Listen to the sounds of the ocean and savor fresh sushi at a candlelight
dinner.

Day 2
Special breakfast of baked ham and diced potato cakes in your room.
Camel ride on the beach.
Snorkeling at Tiwi Beach where layers of coral and seaweed are home to
colorful fish.
Swim in underwater caves at low tide; see fruit bats and swallows living in
the coral cliffs.
Lunch of garnished English mixed grill under the majestic old baobab
tree.

By boat, visit nearby lush tropical islands and investigate the world-famous fishing.

Fresh tuna sashimi and prawns tempura for dinner with candles and chopsticks.

Day 3
Juicy mango, whole wheat toast, ham and scrambled eggs for breakfast on the open porch.
Full-day exhilarating Arab dhow safari to Kisiti Marine National Park.
Guided snorkeling on Wasini Island.
Refreshing cucumber sandwiches, crab salad and seafood lunch.
Late dinner of flambeed lobster and chilled white wine under the huge shimmering moon.

Day 4
Early breakfast of tropical fruit and hot porridge.
Drive to Mombasa and take in the unusual architecture and colorful locals along the way.
Visit historic Fort Jesus where you'll learn all about Kenya's blood-filled history.
Live seafood selections at the Tamarind guarantee freshness for your exotic lunch.
Walk around the maze of narrow streets in fascinating Old Town.
Visit lively markets where delicate fabrics, strange spices and unfamiliar fruit abound.
Back at Diani House, dinner of succulent oysters and crab bisque are ready when you are.

Day 5
Early breakfast of bacon, eggs and market-fresh bananas.
Travel to **Nairobi**.
Rest in The Jacaranda Hotel with attractive gardens and a swimming pool.
Shop in Westlands.

Day 6
Depart for home.

4. LAND & PEOPLE

THE LAND

Kenya is located on the east coast of Africa alongside the Indian Ocean. It is bordered in the north by Ethiopia and Somalia, in the south by Tanzania, and Uganda to the west. The 225,000 square miles of deserts, mountain glaciers, savannahs, forests and numerous lakes is all but cut in half by the equator. It is roughly the size of Texas.

Roughly divided into the Rift Valley, central highlands, western Kenya, remote north and northeast Kenya, and the southeast coast, the terrain varies greatly as you travel from one end of the country to the other. Every topographic characteristic and terrain in the world can be found somewhere in Kenya.

The main geographical features are the parched volcanic lowlands around Lake Turkana and the isolated mountains of the north; the dry thorn-bush covered plains and deserts in the east; the fertile central highlands and western Kenya, and semi-fertile coastal region.

The southwestern area holds 85 percent of the country's population and it is here that the economy flourishes. The vast plateaus of the west are fertile and stretch around the remarkable **Mount Elgon** where agriculture dominates the landscape. Known to the Masai as *Ol Doinyo Igoon* (The Mountain of the Breast) Mount Elgon has spectacular cliffs, deep valleys, ambrosial lagoons and hot springs. Of its many peaks, **Table Rock** is the most popular near the edge of the caldera.

Lake Victoria is a vast and popular freshwater body of water in the west of Kenya. Located outside the Rift Valley, Lake Victoria shares only a small portion of its shore with Kenya. Ideally suited for growing tea, this area has consistent rainfall formed by a unique local climate. As the sun evaporates Victoria's water, the clouds formed meet cold air flowing in from the mountains causing heavy precipitation.

LAKE VICTORIA

Lake Victoria is the world's second largest fresh water lake and the third largest of all lakes. Crocodiles living in the lake sometimes crawl off the beach and take themselves into the urban area. This causes little alarm to the citizens who proceed with their normal daily routines, but it might shake you up a bit!

Dramatically, the **Great Rift Valley** cuts a 3,280 foot trench through a 10,800 foot raised plateau in the Central Highlands and Rift Valley region. After the oceans, the Great Rift Valley is perhaps the single most dramatic feature on earth. Coursing along the land of the Masai, the Rift Valley boasts roughly 30 semi-dormant and dormant volcanoes, bubbling hot springs, and the famous soda and freshwater lakes.

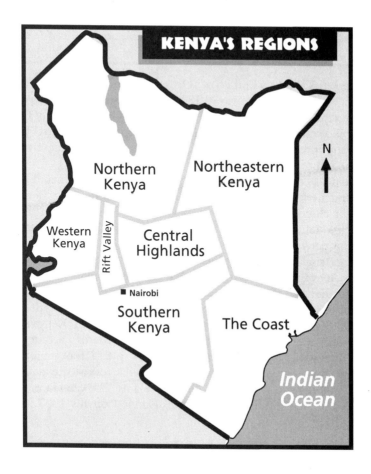

KENYA'S REGIONS

Northern Kenya

Northeastern Kenya

N

Western Kenya

Rift Valley

Central Highlands

■ Nairobi

Southern Kenya

The Coast

Indian Ocean

One such lake is called *En-aiposha* (the lake) in the Masai language. The name En-aiposha has become distorted over the years as Europeans try to speak the African language. Today it is pronounced **Naivasha**. Just south of Lake Naivasha, the numerous hot springs have been harnessed at the expansive **Olkaria** geothermal power station.

The lake's waters irrigate thousands of acres of fertile land. Here the carefully tended vineyards produce vintage Naivasha wines. During the high season, millions of colorful flowers are grown in the area. The bright bouquets are exported to countries in the grips of winter.

ELSAMERE

*It was on the shores of Lake Naivasha that Joy Adamson raised Elsa, the native born lion and her cubs. (A native born lion was born in the local bush – not one brought in from somewhere else or raised with people or in a zoo.) The author of Born Free was brutally murdered in 1980 in northern Kenya. Her home, **Elsamere**, is a living memorial to her and the wildlife education center is dedicated to continuing the legacy Joy left behind.*

The Rift Valley is a hotbed of volcanic activity just under the earth's surface. The last eruption was in 1899 when **Mount Teleki** spewed lava and ashes into the atmosphere. As late as the 1960s, the crater of **Central Island** billowed ash but never actually erupted. In the last 400 to 600 years, other eruptions at **Menengai** and **Longonot** remind us these massive giants lie temporarily dormant beneath the valley floor.

The peaks of **Mount Kenya** (including Nelion, Lenana, and Batian) bordering the valley to the east at 17,056 feet, very rarely poke their heads out of the clouds to show their icy glacier caps. This is the world's most perfect model of an equatorial mountain with its eternal string of glistening glaciers. The lower slopes of this range are heavily cultivated in coffee, tea, sisal, pyrethrum, pineapples, cotton, tobacco and sugar cane.

The **Aberdare Mountain** range soars to a lofty height of 12,125 feet a little further east in the valley, and offers some of Kenya's most scenic views with its thickly forested emerald slopes. In the Aberdares the broad mooreland plateaus and deep ravines offer some of Kenya's most spectacular waterfalls. **Gura Falls**, high in the Aberdares, cascades 1,000 feet to the pools below. **Thompson's Falls**, a 273 foot waterfall in **Nyahuru** ("where waters run deep"), is a popular tourist site and a high altitude training spot for Kenya's Olympic teams. The **Chania** waterfalls at 82 feet is where Winston Churchill camped on his 1907 journey through Kenya.

Lake Turkana in the north is the largest of the soda lakes covering 2,500 square miles. The other rich soda lakes are **Elmenteita, Nakuru,** and **Magadi.** Rainfall is rare in this area leaving the wild bush and scrub to be grazed by thin cattle. This part of Kenya is untouched by the modern world and fascinatingly wild.

Kenya has many seasonal rivers that spring up during the rains and run their course to the ocean. During the dry season, these rivers disappear leaving only a trickle of water or a sandy bed to remind us they will be back. These can be dangerous places as they give little warning when they are about to fill with rushing water.

Six permanent rivers course along Kenya's terrain. The **Ewaso Nyiro, Yala, Tana, Nzoia, Mara** and **Athi/Galana** offer life-giving water to the entire country. The most impressive is the Tana, which is born as a torrent in the Central Highlands and slowly loses strength during its course across the eastern lowlands. Eventually it ends up at the Indian Ocean and runs through a break in the coral reef and out to sea.

This invaluable reef protects the crystalline waters and bleached sands running roughly 300 miles along the seacoast. This exceptional area is a vast commercial gateway to the interior of Africa, with the second largest port on the east coast after Durban in South Africa.

The **Lamu Archipelago** and the Tana River estuary are part of a small coastal belt where the land is fertile enough for agriculture. Mangoes, passion fruit, jojoba, and castor oil are a few of the riches produced here and exported by multinational companies. A few miles inland beyond this strip is the **Taru Desert** – a major deterrent to early settlers and explorers.

The vast salt **Chalbi Desert** is an ancient lake bed. In this remarkable arid land rain comes once every fifty years. Chalbi floods and becomes a shallow inland sea covering several thousand square miles.

SINGING WELLS OF ULANULA

As with most of Kenya's inhabitants, the desert people hold their animals in the highest esteem. Rather than risk their herds dying in the Marsabit's (a forested mountain oasis) frosty night air they elect to walk 45 miles to the warmth of the desert floor. The nomads return to the oasis in a couple of days to water their beasts at the Singing Wells of Ulanula.

Each morning the men make a human ladder into the 15 to 50 foot wells. The persons at the top dig a small canal in the dirt under the quick-drying sun. Stitched giraffe hide buckets full of water feed the trough. As the precious liquid runs along in rivulets, the women catch it in clay jars. As the livestock eagerly gorge on the elixir of life, everyone sings while they work, giving the wells their name.

Like its people, Kenya's landscapes are characterized by diversity. From the lavish coast to the vast deserts, Kenya offers a taste of every possible landscape in the world. It is the planet in miniature.

PEOPLE

There are roughly seventy tribes dispersed around Kenya. They are made up of three primary groupings. The **Bantu**, who since 500 BC, have been drifting to Kenya from West Africa; the **Nilotic** tribes who arrived from Sudan and Egypt around 1000 BC; and the **Cushites** who made an entrance about 2000 BC from Somalia and Ethiopia. These groups make up approximately 98 percent of Kenya's population. Within the groups there are many sub-tribes too numerous to mention.

In Kenya your tribal affiliation is what is important to the people. The government has encouraged the alliance of all tribes for the national good and has succeeded to a certain extent. But, while the people are indeed proud of being Kenyans, nationality doesn't count as much to them as do tribal ties. When two people meet for the first time, part of their introduction includes what tribe they belong to.

The life style among the tribes is as varied as Kenya itself with hunter-gatherers, settled farmers, fishermen and nomadic herders. Intermarriage and community living have eradicated much of the original tribal stock, blurring both territorial frontiers and physical features. In spite of the minimal differences, which are almost completely linguistic, there is a constantly changing set of tribal hostilities brewing as overcrowded clans spill into adjoining lands.

The population growth in Kenya is one of the highest in the world. The economy is stretched to the limit as it tries to provide educational facilities and other services to the expanding populace. Many inhabitants are giving up life in the bush for an easier existence and more job opportunities in the cities and towns. From those continuing to live and work outside the cities, there is tremendous pressure exerted on the government to increase land being grazed and cultivated. Who will win and at what expense remains to be seen.

The Bantu

Among the Bantu, the largest tribal groups are the Kikuyu, Meru, Gusii, Embu, Akamba, Luyha (or Luyia) and Mijikenda. The Bantu are industrious farmers who have become the most prolific and wealthiest of the three tribal groups. All told, the Bantu make up two-thirds of the citizenry.

THE EMBU

Living on the southern slopes of Mount Kenya are the Embu tribe, noted for their bee-keeping skills. Not only renowned for their bees and honey, they are also fond of dancing. The Stilt Dance is performed by men clad in ominous looking black coats and white masks atop tall wooden stilts.

The largest tribal population is made up of the **Kikuyu,** who number approximately seven million. At the heart of Kikuyu civilization lies a complex system of land ownership organized around the family.

Perhaps better than any other tribe, the Kikuyu adapted to the challenge of Western culture. Today, convoys of trucks and pickups stream in nightly from the Kikuyu farmlands providing the bulk of the fresh produce sustaining Nairobi. Coffee, tea, and other crops grown by the Kikuyu largely feed the rest of Kenya and are exported throughout the world.

Living mostly along the shores of Lake Victoria are the farming and fishing **Luo** people. They belong to the Bantu group and have the second largest tribal population in Kenya with over four million in number. Their territory ranges from the Central Highlands to the coastal wilderness and the Tana River area.

The Luo people are known for their use of basket traps and gill nets spread across the mouth of a river. This is their traditional manner of fishing for tilapia and other fish. But perhaps the Luo tribes are best noted for their rustic boats. For poling in shallow water, the tribesmen build crafts out of papyrus and for deeper water their hollowed out logs serve them well.

Recognized for their stoicism, the Luo have learned patience in dealing with the adverse farming conditions surrounding their home. Rainfall either doesn't come at all or floods the growing fields, causing famine and disease. The tenacious people manage to hang on.

THE LUO

*Music is important to the Luo who produce haunting melodies on a one stringed lyre named **orotu** or an eight-stringed instrument called **thum.** The Luo have a wide range of skills, which include boat building, basketry, and pottery making. It is not uncommon to see tribespeople smoking indigenous tobacco from creatively formed home-made pipes.*

Nilotic Tribes

Nilotic tribal groups consist of Masai, Turkana, Samburu, and Kalenji (the Kalenji consist of the Pokot, Kipsigs, Nandi, Tugen, Marakwet, Keiyo, Terik, and Sabaot). The most famous of these are of course the **Masai** (in the south of the country), the **Samburu** (in the center of Kenya) and the **Turkana** (in the northwest). There are less than a million people in these three groups combined in Kenya, but their colorful and decorative lifestyles have immortalized them.

PRESIDENT MOI

*President Daniel Toroitich arap Moi is a **Tugen**, a sub-group of the **Kalenji** and a part of the larger Nilotic tribal group. He was born in the tiny village of Kurieng'wo in Sacho, Baringo District, in 1924. Because of his elevated position in Kenyan life, the Kalenji have become a powerful political force.*

The **Masai** are herders of cattle and goats. A very proud and beautiful people, the Masai enjoy adorning themselves with loads of beads and dressing in red colorful cloth. The women do all the day to day work, including building houses, while the men tend the cattle and make tribal decisions.

Cattle not only represent wealth by serving as currency for fines, marriage, and sacrifices but also supply food in the form of meat, milk, and blood and leather for beds and sandals. Cattle are the single most important part of Masai life. The people talk and sing to their cattle as they tend them every day.

Despite government driving the Masai to join the modern world, they have managed to hang on to the their nomadic traditions. Life for the Masai youth as they grow and mature is a series of ceremonies and celebrations. The process for a young man will begin with junior warriorhood, to senior warriorhood, junior elder, and finally senior elder. This process often takes years and years to achieve.

Samburu number less than 90,000 and live in mostly arid and often mountainous parts of the country, where survival is definitely only for the fittest. The Samburu dwell in small settlements called *manyatta*. The first wife's hut is always to the right of the main cattle entrance. If water and pasture for the livestock are depleted, they pack up and move on. Samburu tribes-people take great pride in their appearance and adorn themselves lavishly and in great detail with beads, feathers, and copper.

AMUSING PREOCCUPATION

The Samburu tribes find the western preoccupation with time to be somewhat amusing. To make fun of what they consider unnecessary, they wear bracelets in the shape of a watch. It is not uncommon for them to tell time to within half an hour just by the position of the sun. They reckon this is close enough when you have no appointments to keep.

Once upon a time the **Turkana** were a wild and dissident tribe. Traditional weapons used were eight foot spears with leaf-shaped points, fighting sticks, wrist knives and stretched hide shields. They pushed other tribes out of their lands during the 19th century until they were finally subdued by the British and began to settle down.

Following several droughts the Turkana resumed their expansive wandering. These nomads think nothing of a 25 mile walk in one day. Before the days of telecommunications, a runner would take a message in a cleft stick and cover 70 miles with no problem.

As with most African tribes, milk and cattle blood, tapped from the jugular vein of a bullock or cow, is their main diet. Fresh milk is dried on skins for later consumption. Wild berries are crushed and mixed with blood or ground into a dried meal. In the rainy season, the women cultivate gourds and millet to supplement their diets. Camel milk is often used to feed babies as it is low in fat and easily digestible.

As with all tribes, the Turkana men have many wives. The three year wedding ceremony is designed to ensure the ritual, social, and spiritual well being of those involved. A wedding ceremony cannot be completed until the first child is weaned. They live in temporary huts covered with cow skins and sleep on hide mats. The main entrance of a Turkana home faces east towards the sacred mountain. The chief wife has a day hut and night hut, both located to the right of the entrance.

THE TURKANA

Turkana are no longer a war-like people, but the occasional skirmish does occur. For the most part they continue the traditional cattle, sheep, and goat herding of their ancestors. Their reputation is one of skilled herdsmen and fearless watchmen.

Cattle rustling among all the tribes is as much a sport as soccer is elsewhere in the country. To this day, disputes are settled by spear with rare interference from formal law enforcement. Most of the time law officials are nonexistent in the bush. Everyone relies on the tribal elders for arbitration.

Cushites

The **Cushites**, a tiny portion of the country's population, consist of such tribes as El Molo, Somali, Boran, Burji, Dassenich, Gabbra, Orma, Sakuye, Boni, Wata, Yaaka, Dahalo, Rendille and Galla. Most Cushite tribes eke out an existence along the fringes of the northern and coastal deserts. They are barely clinging to survival in this region of wind-swept lava and sun-scorched desert. Out of these, the Somali are the most populous with just a few thousand.

Often touted as the smallest tribe in Kenya, both in number and stature, the **El Molo** claim a population of about 500. The El Molo hunt crocodiles and an occasional hippo for food, but fresh or dried fish is the staple diet. Legend has it that once upon a time they herded hippopotamuses, crocodiles, and turtles. Like camels and cattle they were bled and milked for food. Today, children live side by side with goats and seaweed-fed scrawny cattle.

Their basket-like homes are as flimsy as their bowed frail legs. The dome shaped circular huts are built of interlaced acacia branches and covered with palm leaves, reeds, grass or other vegetation and held down with stones against the prevailing winds. Inside, woven palm leaves are used as sleeping mats.

To fish and travel between islands, the El Molo build rafts made out of doum palm. If they are dry, the rafts are capable of holding three or four adults. Unfortunately, the palm wood quickly becomes water logged which limits the use of the raft to a few hours at a time. Two of these rafts are traditionally part of the price for a bride.

Not to be outdone by other tribes, although they are not quite as colorful, the El Molo enjoy collecting ornaments, such as strings of ostrich eggs and glass beads. Multiple metal wrist and elbow bracelets are worn by both men and women.

AN EL MOLO BELIEF

Legend has it the El Molo once lived at the furthest northern tip of Lake Turkana. One day the men went on a fishing expedition to find food for the tribe. When they returned, their village had been ransacked and their women and animals killed by the spears of bloodthirsty raiders. Afraid and sorrowful, the men set off to find a new home. Eventually they arrived and settled at their present site.

The **Somali** are entirely dependent on the precarious grazing and water in the semi-desert where they live. Their large herds of camels, cattle, sheep, and goats can wreak havoc on the ecological balance.

Overgrazing by livestock decimates what is left of the scrubby grass, leaving behind serious soil erosion.

Somali tribes are ethnically different from most other tribes in Kenya. An extremely well-spoken and politically cognizant tribe, the Somali are united equally by family allegiance and formal political treaties. Clusters of their rough grass huts surrounded by cattle or camels are a common sight in northern Kenya, where they compete with their neighbors for the same inhospitable grazing lands. In contrast with the rustic abodes, their carved headrests and woven artifacts are unmatched in careful detail and quality.

Other Groups

The remaining two percent of Kenya's population consists of **Arabs** (Swahili), **Europeans**, and **Asians**. This contingent of people may be small but is important to the retail and farming communities. The Arabs (about 40,000) tend to be localized around the coast, while the Asians (about 80,000) and Europeans (about 40,000) live and work in tight inland communities.

Along the coast the given name to the mix of people is **Swahili**. These people have been mixing, intermarrying, and trading with settlers from abroad for hundreds of years. Basically descendants of Arab and Persian immigrants, they are distinguished in their shipbuilding and woodworking skills. The famous ocean-going *dhows* with their unique triangular sails still cruise up and down Kenya's coast.

The Asian community largely comes from the 32,000 indentured laborers brought in to build the cross-country railroad. When their contracts expired, many of these people settled down in Kenya. Life has not been easy for this group. The Asian populace today is largely Indian with a small mixture of East Asians, mostly Chinese.

Over the years the Asian immigrants have had their businesses confiscated, been refused trading permits in rural areas and been persecuted or even killed by local tribes. Today, the animosities have largely been put aside. Many small hotels, book, and textile shops are owned by these astute business people. The local populace accepts that this important fragment of Kenyan society is here to stay.

As each year passes, the unique melting pot of communities and cultures mix and blend, allowing Kenyans to live together in relative harmony. Distinct cultural lines become less distinguishable with the passing of time as people get on with the daily chores of their chosen lifestyles. While Kenya is not without its population problems, its peaceful example stands out among the countries of the world.

CULTURE & CUSTOMS

Since before the 7th century, Kenya has been infiltrated by a mix of Arabs, Persians, Chinese, Indians, Africans and Europeans. Each group has left its mark on the civilization of today and creates one of the most fascinating cultures in the world.

It is important to remember the conduct and ideals of the Kenyan tribespeople are completely different to what we are used to in Western society. Visitors, often unprepared for certain behaviors, are taken aback. Polygamy, circumcision rituals, nudity, and unsanitary living conditions are a small sample of what you will notice in their normal everyday lives. They are content and accepting of the situation and you should be also.

All tribes share a basic outlook on life. At the same time, however, they are distinctly different from each other. Their manner of dress, language, and physical features vary widely. They are an extremely proud people who cling to the old ways of large families and herds of animals. Few Africans are willing to give up their wealth in cattle, camels, goats, and sheep for currency. Although money is used we must bear in mind that the barter system was around long before Europeans introduced currency.

The **tribal elders and chiefs** are due a great deal of respect in Kenya. Their word is law and they have the authority to act as guide, judge, jury, and intermediary. No one dares contradict, argue or go against an edict passed down from a supreme council. In many tribes, the members still vote according to the wishes of their chief. At all times, show these people the utmost respect and courtesy.

Among the local people, loyalties to family are strong. Although identity is associated with tribal ties, there is nothing stronger than the unity between a man and his wives and children, and to brothers and sisters by the same mother. Secondary loyalty lies with siblings by another mother then to the extended family, and finally the clan and tribe. It is considered proper for a man to help his kin first.

The laws concerning land are essential among those who cultivate it or have grazing animals. Most Africans have a little land even if it is only a garden plot which is passed down from generation to generation and subdivided among the male children. There are strict laws defining inheritance and ownership within each cultural group.

Because there is less and less land to support the ever increasing population, the question of to whom the land belongs at times results in escalating tensions. To try and ease the impending trouble, the Kenyan farms are tended primarily by the wives and children as the men go into the city to find work.

The concept of equality for women is totally alien in Kenya. The vast majority of hard labor is performed by the female segment of society. This includes running the home and family, cooking, cleaning, getting water and firewood, building the houses and farming. A woman is expected to obey the decisions made by her husband. If she is sent back to her family or returns on her own, her husband may remarry. She will face the consequences of being ostracized by her family and will get no further support from them or her husband. Education for women is of the most basic kind if they get any at all.

Tourists who are women enjoy a somewhat elevated status and are treated with respect by the local men. Considered an "honorary man," female tourists are positioned somewhere between local women and men. The local people will view you with a great deal of curiosity. To them you might as well come from Mars.

Getting too friendly with an African man can put a woman in an unpleasant situation. He will not know how to treat a foreign female tourist and as such an uncomfortable predicament may develop if he makes unwelcome advances. What is acceptable at home in regard to innocent friendliness can be totally unacceptable in Kenya.

THE PRICE OF A BRIDE

As a youngster traveling with my two sisters and parents on a camping vacation, we came across a Masai traveling the same road. We stopped the car and got out to take some photos and to chat. The handsome man fell in love with my ten year-old sister. He offered several goats in exchange for her hand in marriage. Without wanting to offend the Masai, my father politely declined, saying she was already spoken for!

Unfortunately, it is becoming more and more customary in Kenya for common folk to hassle tourists. Harassing visitors to purchase a souvenir or begging them to part with a few dollars is annoyingly common. Expect it and don't be taken by the contrived stories you will be told. Giving will generally not alleviate the plight of the individuals in question. If you donate to one, shortly there will be ten more to take his place.

When shopping, unless you really want to buy, don't encourage the locals to bargain with you.

It is not uncommon to see two men holding hands in Kenya. This is not a sign of homosexuality but rather a sign of friendship and trust between two men. The Africans have a tendency to touch each other and may possibly touch you as a sign of goodwill. Shaking hands is customary when meeting and leaving a gathering.

Kenyans are for the most part an extremely mannerly society. They think nothing of cordially extending an offer of hospitality and are quick with a friendly smile. It is important to address a man as *Bwana* (mister) and a woman as *Mama* (madam) as a sign of respect and to ask after their health. If you are invited into a village home, be prepared to eat and live as the family does or decline in the most polite way possible. A gift of some sort is always perceived as an excellent gesture of goodwill.

Circumcision in boys and clitoridectomy in girls are widely practiced ceremonies and rites of passage to adulthood. The custom is being discouraged but is still rampant, particularly in the more remote regions. Unless the individuals are prepared to leave their tribe or remain unmarried, there is no way to get around this time-immemorial tradition. As you are taken around to visit local *bomas* – traditional Kenyan homesteads – the conversation will invariably turn to such matters. Be prepared to handle the situation tactfully if you are embarrassed by the often frank and explicit discussions.

It is common in Kenya to have multiple servants. This is the norm among the local people but can be unsettling for newly arrived tourists. A cook, driver, and three or four others to set up camp, collect firewood and perform other duties is customary. The Africans consider these to be excellent jobs and compete intensely to attain them. They will stay on duty until you go to bed and will rarely refuse anything you ask. Be considerate and polite, but not condescending.

NARCOTICS

The use of drugs in Kenya is common among some of the tribes, as they claim it keeps them awake during the night while they watch over their herds. It is common knowledge the effects of the drugs can lead to severe sleep deprivation.

*There are two kinds of grass used by the local youth called **bhang** and **miraa**. These drugs are legal throughout the country. Both herbs grow wild and are either chewed or smoked to give the effects of a mild stimulant. In some of the wilder towns, there are gangs of intoxicated adolescents roaming the streets.*

It is customary in Kenya for the shops to close for the lunch hour. If you are planning on doing some shopping in the commercial center, make sure and check on the store hours. This practice is becoming less and less common as the competition for tourist dollars grows, but it does still happen. The shops that close do so anywhere from half an hour to a couple of hours.

Due to the British influence, Kenya has developed and continues to develop many of the customs imported by the early settlers. One of these customs is to have tea in the early afternoon. Usually tea is served hot and milk and sugar are mixed in to taste. There are always cakes or cookies of some sort to accompany the tea. The African tea (*chai*), as opposed to the English tea, is made with the milk and sugar already added. In my opinion, chai is too sweet and too milky – but this you'll have to find out for yourself.

You will notice a picture of President Moi in every store. It is a presidential decree that all shops must have a photograph of the ruler prominently displayed. The photo should be in a high place looking down so no one is above his image. The picture that is on display is always that of a much younger president. This sometimes prompts ridicule of Moi by those who don't favor him.

RELIGION

There are any number of churches, temples, and mosques scattered throughout Kenya, but are generally found around the towns. There is no lack of representation in the religious arena with cross-sections of Catholics, Hindus, Sunnis, Lutherans, Seventh Day Adventists, Protestants, Pentecostals and Weslyans vying for position with the Africans.

If you are interested in attending church services, check the local papers for a listing of worship times and locations. This can be a very captivating experience, as no one puts quite as much effort into worship and song as do Africans.

Total freedom of worship allows all sects and doctrines to celebrate and observe religious holidays. The government however, keeps an eye on what they might consider radical religious movements with an eye to preventing any possible repercussions affecting the governing powers.

Christian missions are generally found in the more isolated districts. The spread of religion by missionaries is and was mightily enhanced by the fact that if you wanted an education or some medical attention, the evangelists were the only ones who provided the otherwise nonexistent services.

Over time, many of the local beliefs have become intertwined with Christian doctrine forming an intricate system of communication with deity. As with Christianity, in many of the tribal religions there is only one god. Ancestors are asked to intercede with god on behalf of the people in much the same way as Catholics use their saints.

The coastal tribes and Somalis are affiliated with the Muslim faith of one sect or another. Most Muslims belong to the Sunni branch and have been fortunate enough to attract funding for schools, hospitals, and the like from Saudi Arabia. In Nairobi, the **Jamia Mosque** holds worship services for a small but devotedly patriotic part of the Kenyan community.

This large group of people play an important social and economic role in the country's development.

The local **witch doctor**, or **medicine man**, is still very much a part of the local way of life within a tribe. It is believed that bad things happen because the gods are offended, a curse has been called forth, or because of an unprovoked attack from an evil spirit. The people are convinced hexes can be placed upon someone or something.

SUPERNATURAL POWERS

It is not uncommon in Kenya to hear stories of people's staggering exploits while under the influence of the medicine man's magic. The trance-like state in which the medicine man operates along with the skins, mask, and feathers he wears can look extremely intimidating.

In many instances, a curse of death placed on a perfectly healthy man will result in death within a few days. Tribal Kenyans fervently believe this to be true. In effect, their belief kills them. The psychology at work here is very powerful. I have actually seen this happen. The man in question simply stopped eating and gave up the will to live after being cursed by a witch doctor.

The medicine men base their healing methods on the assumption that most, if not all, illnesses are caused by supernatural power and that supernatural powers are required to cure them. It is the task of the witch doctor to diagnose the disease or sorcery using divinatory techniques and then to apply the spiritual remedy. The remedy can take such forms as retrieval of lost souls, removing a disease-causing object, or exorcising an evil spirit. Sometimes the use of medicinal herbs and massage are also included in the rituals.

Using his magic, this powerful man or occasionally woman is consulted about curses, health, and crop-related issues. The tribal chiefs place a great deal of faith in the word of the witch doctor and follow his advice down to the last detail.

Justice is administered by the chief and the witch doctor as they see fit. Punishment for an accused person might include lacing locally made brew with poison. During the circumcision rituals, the witch doctor might cunningly put a dab of venom on the tip of his knife to get rid of a rival's son or a perceived enemy.

LANGUAGES

English, to some degree or another, is widely spoken throughout Kenya. Even in remote parts, you should be able to find someone who can communicate with you in English, even if it is on a very basic level. In all the tourist areas the people you will come in contact with will be able to understand what you want.

The official language in Kenya is **Swahili**, which is a blend of Arabic, Bantu, and English. To speak to each other, Africans use Swahili, although there are between forty and fifty tribes with their own particular languages, along with many other secondary dialects.

It is well received if you show some attempt to speak the local language. They may not understand your pronunciation, but at least you will know you gave it a sincere effort by the encouraging giggles and laughter.

To that end, here is a list of some useful phrases and words, first in English and then in Swahili:

Common Words & Phrases

Welcome	Karibu
Hello	Jambo
How are you?	Habari? (What's your news?)
Very well	Mzuri sana
Fine	Sawa
OK	Sawa sawa
Bad	Mbaya
Goodbye	Kwaheri (singular) Kwaherini (plural)
Yes	Ndiyo
No	Hapana
Mister/Sir	Bwana
Lady/madam	Mama or memsahb
I don't understand	Sielewi
Do you speak English?	Unasema Kingereza?
Excuse me	Samahani
Thank you	Asante
Please	Tafadhali
Thank you very much	Asante sana
How much?	Bei gani?
Money	Pesa

Other Words & Phrases

Baby-sitter/nanny	Ayah
Shop	Duka
Staple corn food	Posho or ugali
fenced compound	Boma
Thatched hut/room	Banda
Expensive	Ghali

Here	Hapa
Bug/insect	Dudu
Pole	Slow
Danger	Hatari
Bathroom	Choo
Let's go	Twende
Mini-van	Combie
Sleep	Lala
Sleep well	Lala salama
No problem	Hakuna Matata
Cloth worn around waist	Kikoi
Drugs	Quat

Food & Drink

Water	Mai or Maji
Beer	Pombe
Cold	Baridi
Ice	Barafu
Hot	Moto
Coffee	Kahawa
Tea	Chai
Sugar	Sucari
Food	Chakula
Eat	Kula

*To order a cold drink, add *baridi sana* to your order.

Numbers

One	Moja
Two	Mbili
Three	Tatu
Four	Nne
Five	Tano
Six	Sita
Seven	Saba
Eight	Nane
Nine	Tisa
Ten	Kumi

Whose English Is It, Anyway?

The British influence in Kenya is still extremely evident and shows itself in the English accents of the local European community. Many of the words, phrases, idioms, and spellings are a throwback to the time when Britain ruled this land. Kenyans are very proud of their heritage and still view the UK with much pride and attachment, continuing to use the British names for everyday items. Here is a list of a few of those words to help you in communicating:

American English	Kenyan-UK English
Cookies or small cakes	Biscuits
Flashlight	Torch

American English	Kenyan-UK English
Diaper	Nappy
Traffic circle	Round-about
Chips	Crisps
Corn	Maize
Gasoline	Petrol
Elevator	Lift
Mail box	Letter/post box
Mail	Post
Trunk	Boot
Hood	Bonnet
Glove box	Cubby box
Windshield	Windscreen
Napkin	Serviette
Truck	Lorry
Bathroom	WC, Loo, long drop (outdoor hole in the ground)
Dessert	Pudding
Candy	Sweets
Cocktails	Sundowners
Bathing suit	Swimming costume
Snorkeling	Goggling
Closet	Cupboard

5. A SHORT HISTORY

IN THE BEGINNING

Kenya, the "Cradle of Humankind," holds the world's oldest noted record of life on earth. Written into the ancient volcanic rocks is the story of creation. The chronicles of evolution in these stones stretches back 25 million years. Virtually all stages of life's growth and change within that span are preserved as fossils.

Many millions of years ago, Kenya's form was drastically reshaped. Sloping east to the Indian Ocean, its ancient plateau wrenched apart and strained upwards in massive earth movements and volcanic eruptions. Tremendous volcanoes formed out of molten lava.

Swelling, the land split from north to south, forming a great depression in the west. This giant basin eventually filled with water to become **Lake Victoria**. This second largest fresh water lake in the world featured prominently in the early explorer's search for the source of the Nile.

The main crevasse is the **Great Rift Valley**, running from the Dead Sea to Mozambique. In Kenya, the valley forms a great rift through the middle of the country. Streams from the high ground on both sides of the fault flowed into this giant depression, forming a series of lakes that rose and fell with the rainfall. Two of these lakes (Naivasha and Baringo) are fresh; the others are shallow soda lakes.

The new highland mountains created rain shadows on their leeward sides. Because of this, the forests in the lower and hotter sections of the valley began to disappear and Savannah grasslands formed.

In the Rift Valley, the **Leakey** family led the famous paleontological expeditions into man's past. **Dr. Louis Leakey** and his spouse **Mary Nicol Leakey** brought to the surface an assortment of fossilized remains. Uncovered ancient campsites disgorged the leavings of animal meals and handmade stone tools from a time long ago.

A GREAT LOSS

On December 9, 1996, at the age of 83, Mary Leakey died peacefully after more than half a century of dedication to paleolothic archaeology. She was a highly respected and ardent contributor to her field.

In time, as the land changed, families of apes made their homes on the shores of the Rift Valley's lakes and streams. These ape species evolved into an early form of hominid – ancestral apeman.

On the shores of **Lake Turkana**, a fossilized skull called "1470" was the first discovery since the initial hesitant footsteps of Homo Erectus. Nairobi's **National Museum** now displays this amazing and priceless artifact. The two to three million year old skull belonging to "Handy Man," Homo Habilis, represents the oldest known ancestor of modern man.

The very first true humans to occupy Kenya did so between five and ten thousand years ago. They were simple hunter-gatherers, living in small isolated groups spread far across the land. These people are the ancestors of the Boni, Wata, and Wariangulu wanderers of the bush.

The arrival of a group of Cushitic shepherds from southern Ethiopia around 2000 BC interrupted the dominance of these simple people. The first of many migrants, they introduced their domesticated animals such as cattle, goats, and sheep.

Eastern **Cushites** followed one thousand years later and brought new languages and farming skills. They tilled the soil and made pots from lava and pumice that they found in abundance. Cultivation of crops such as sorghum was introduced by the Cushites about 2000 BC. A tall, lean nomadic people, the Cushite characteristics of time past are noticeable in the Kenyan people of today. Their more enduring legacy however, is that of the irrigation systems which still exist along with many of the deep wells and large dams found in remote northern Kenya.

Subsequently, the Nilotic-speaking cultures from the west and Bantu-speaking people from the south arrived. Nourished by the fertile soil and watered by the sweet waterways, these wandering people decided to make Kenya a permanent home.

The more skillful **Bantu** introduced iron-working. Their simple but effective metal implements cleared larger tracts of land for agriculture. By 1000 AD, Kenya moved into the Iron Age.

During the trans-African migration and inter-tribal unions, Kenya remained a mystery; protected from the outside world by its natural barriers. Just inland were the **Taru Desert** and the **Rift Valley**, which only the foolhardy and the brave were tough enough to tackle. The desert was all but impossible to cross due to the vast stretches of parched and sizzling sand. As for the valley; the steep cliffs, thick vegetation, dangerous wildlife, hostile tribes and razor sharp rocks were too much to contend with.

THE COAST

Development differed considerably along the coast. Around 110 AD, the very first European visitors spent time traveling up and down Kenya's shores. At different times, two Greek merchant/geographers named **Diogenes** and **Ptolemy** visited the Kenyan coast from their homes in Egypt. Both men wrote of the wealth found along the coast. Olives, adzes (an ax-like tool), iron, copper, brass, glass, cloth, ivory and rhinoceros horn are just a few of the riches they saw loaded onto ships from the island of **Mombasa**.

Around the ninth century, a millennium later, a steady trickle of Arabs intermarrying among the Bantu tribes introduced **Islam**. This was the beginning of a glorious golden age which created a spectacular architectural and cultural heritage.

Persian and Arab settlers developed the coastal and caravan trade, established commercial centers and made great contributions with new literature, colorful crafts and splendid architecture. Coral and "rags," an unusual mixture, were the construction materials of the day. A house was framed with small tree trunks and long poles felled from nearby standing timber. Walls were then filled in with blocks carved from large chunks of coral stuck together with mud. Small chips of coral (the rags referred to above) were used to fill in the smaller cracks and crevices along with more mud. Homes built in this style can still be seen all around Mombasa.

The elaborate mosques, ornate monuments, and elegantly carved balconies, windows and doors are remnants of the Arab influence. Much of this traditional style is still in use today. The ornately hewn doors with their brass and copper ornaments and the unique window style adds a definite charm to the narrow streets of the Old Town.

The **Swahili** culture emerged around the fourteenth century. This mixture of African and Arab civilizations is predominant and most evident in the cities today. The name Swahili comes from the Arabic plural of *Sahel*, meaning coast. **Kiswahili**, the language of the Bantu, became their legacy to Kenya.

Mombasa's wealth in gold, ivory, and other riches came to the attention of the Portuguese, who decided they should get in on the action in the late 15th century. King John of Portugal ordered **Vasco da Gama**, his greatest navigator, to find a way around the Cape of Good Hope to India. En route, Mombasa was the reward.

The Arabs living in Mombasa repulsed the Portuguese fleet on several occasions. One strategy they used was to cut the fleets' anchor ropes. This tactic forced da Gama to sail on to **Malindi** where the ruling sultan, who was feuding with the ruler of Mombasa, welcomed him warmly.

The king of Portugal did not give up his attempts to conquer the coast. He was determined to share in the riches he saw were readily available. Two years after the monarch's last defeat, he sent **Cabral** to ransack Mombasa. Five years later, in 1505, another Portuguese mariner, **Francisco d'Almeida**, plundered the city once again. The pillaging sailors of **Nuna da Cunha** followed twenty-three years later and again wreaked havoc on the coast. With each attack the damage was great, but residents repeatedly avoided being defeated. Eventually however, the Portuguese persistence prevailed and they occupied Mombasa.

In 1593, the building of **Fort Jesus** began. Overlooking the entrance to the old harbor, it took a total of five years to complete and bears witness to the town's violent history. The fort was built in the shape of a human body with a trunk, two legs, and two arms. This shape allowed for a more efficient defense system.

REPRESENTATIVES OF CHRIST

Fort Jesus was so named because the Portuguese sailed under the flag of the Order of Christ. The sailors regarded themselves as representatives of Christ first and Portugal second. During this time there was little else more powerful than the church and what it exemplified.

Not all members of the local Arab populace were happy with the Portuguese rulers. Rebellious uprising was common and often strong. Their attacks from the sea and land were frequent and fierce. However, even with support from the troops of Ali Bey, a Turkish buccaneer, they were unable to rid themselves of the unwavering Portuguese for a significant interval.

The brutal centuries following the Portuguese conquest earned Mombasa its name of "Island of War." Between 1631 and 1875 the fort endured fifteen battles, overthrows, and mutinies. The blood of thousands of people was spilled in the constant struggle for power.

On March 15, 1696, a historically important and decisive battle began with the siege of Fort Jesus. Barricaded inside the fort were 50 ruling Portuguese and 2,500 loyal Arab locals. Those entrenched here survived attacks, famine, and disease with an uncanny will to survive. When their food reserves ran low during the fighting, these people existed for months on short rations smuggled in at night. Fresh water came from a deep well inside the fortress. Eventually, with the help of a passing Welsh sea captain and his crew, the revolutionary Arabs finally climbed over the fort's walls and regained what was theirs. Of the original number inside the citadel, only eleven men and two women survived.

Despite almost three centuries of occupation, the unwanted Portuguese left for good in 1729. From 1895 to 1958 the fortification was run by the government and used to house prisoners. After 1958 the fort, a major landmark in the history of East Africa, became a popular museum.

In spite of all the horrors, the Portuguese rulers emphatically changed the course of history for Kenya. They introduced a legacy of maize (corn), cassava, cashews, tomatoes and tobacco from the recently discovered Americas.

Around the 16th century, while all this was going on at the coast, the Nilotic-speaking **Luo** began to drift down from southern Sudan. The Maa-speaking **Masai** and **Samburu** followed not long afterwards.

The Luo took control of the western Lake Victoria region, while the Masai and Samburu moved southward, establishing themselves in the more central areas. Kenya was becoming more and more populated as these tribes made claims on the lands they settled.

THE ARABS RETURN

Once again the coastal towns were subject to Arab rule. But the rival **Omani dynasties** were constantly fighting in much the same way as they did at home. This led to the downfall of the prosperous trading that brought them to Kenya's coast in the first place.

In 1805, **Bey Saidi Sultan Sayyid Said** stabbed the current ruler in Oman and seized power. After seventeen years he became secure in his throne and decided to send an army to subdue the islands of Penba, Pate, and Mombasa which were under the rule of **Mazruis**.

During that time, the British ship *HMS Leven* was visiting Mombasa. Mazruis begged **Captain Owen** to help him in his battle against the ruler of Oman. The British officer agreed, and proclaimed Mombasa a protectorate of Britain on February 7, 1824. In exchange, Mazruis reluctantly resolved to abolish slavery.

Captain Owen assigned his first officer, **Lieutenant J.J. Reiz**, as proconsul before continuing on his voyage. He left behind an interpreter, four sailors and four marines. Satisfied he had done his Christian duty he sent word to London and India asking for the sanction of his covenant.

Two months later, Reitz died from malaria leaving his deputy, **Lieutenant Emery**, to assume the role of governor. Three years later the British refused Owen's protectorate agreement.

For the next fifty years sultan Sayyid Said prospered with his trails of slavery running as far as **Lake Victoria**. He began to dream of an African empire.

Britain noticed the power and wealth of the Omani government now headquartered in Zanzibar. The British government wanted to stop the slave trading and put a great deal of pressure on the Arab rulers. In 1845, Said unwillingly agreed to a treaty that severely compromised slaving.

EXPLORERS & COLONIALS

In 1844, a German missionary, **Johann Ludwig Krapf**, arrived in Kenya and established a mission at **Rabai**, just a few miles from Mombasa. Along with his associate, **Johannes Rebmann**, Johann traveled far inland to spread Christianity while at the same time trying to end the slavery trade.

By 1850 the Dutch, English, and French had successfully established trade routes leading from the coast deep into the interior and the question of East Africa became a hotbed in the European political arena. There was much passionate argument to avoid involvement in the "Dark Continent" but in the end, scientific curiosity prevailed and the British entered the fray. Many missionaries and explorers set off to record the terrain of Kenya and outlined the first maps and land characteristics.

After negotiations with the Germans and the Kikuyu among others, Kenya was eventually assigned to the British as a **protectorate** in 1895.

During the latter half of the 19th century, civil wars raged among the many tribes. The disputes were mainly about land takeovers by the British. The Masai were particularly aggressive. They disrupted trade, threatened missionaries, and drove back early explorers.

The Masai were no match for the British Army who hastily arrived to deal with the problem. Brutally subdued, some tribes submitted. Others organized their feared warriors and antagonized the British for years.

The British decided the construction of a railway line, the **Uganda Railway** from Mombasa on the coast to Lake Victoria in western Kenya, was a necessary move. The rail would allow them to reach strategically important Uganda and have control of the Nile before the Germans arrived from the south. Other secondary benefits were the possible eradication of slave trade and the opening up of Kenya's interior.

Opposition to the railway was extreme. The resistance group in parliament felt it was a monumental waste of time and money. They called it a "lunatic line to nowhere," hence the nickname the **Lunatic Line**. The natives also had a nickname for the train – "iron rhinoceros" and would have little to do with it. As a result of the local disinterest, **32,000 Indians** arrived from India's Gujarat and Punjab provinces to replace the local laborers who did not want to work on the railway.

Construction of the railway began in 1893. Despite the poor conditions in the East African Protectorate, Nairobi became the inland railhead. The land was a disagreeably damp, malodorous swamp plagued with disease and a variety of pests such as mosquitoes and snakes. The man-eating lions, cholera, and precipitous terrain did not stop the railway from being completed five years later.

At a cost of five million pounds (a king's ransom!) the seeds for Kenya's future development were irrevocably sown. This incredible train journey across 1,000 miles of desert, grass plains, mountains and forests crosses the equator and displays every facet of Africa's geography and climate.

THE LUNATIC LINE

A short poem by **Labouchere Henry du Pre** *(1831-1912), British journalist and radical political leader, printed in the London magazine* Truth *expressed the prevailing sentiments concerning the railway:*

What will it cost no words can express;
What is its object no brain can suppose;
Where will it start from no one can guess;
Where is it going nobody knows;

What is the use of it none can conjecture;
What it will carry there's none can define;
And in spite of George Curzon's superior lecture,
It is clearly naught but a lunatic line.

The Lunatic Line was a great success despite all the negativity surrounding it, and remains one of the great railways of the world. Kenyans use it to travel from one end of the country to the other in the old colonial style.

Europeans settled anywhere along the line the land permitted ranching or farming. The Catholic fathers at **St. Austin's mission** planted coffee. On the wooded uplands of **Limuru**, near the Rift Valley, farmers cultivated tea. These became two of Kenya's major income producers.

In 1916, spurred on by the governor, more settlers set off in ox-wagons to stake claims on the finest agricultural lands in Kenya. Sisal, pineapple, and cereals grew in what the people classified as the "White Highlands." **Hugh Cholmondeley**, better known as **Lord Delamere**, lost a fortune as he experimented and often failed in farming ventures. His sheep died of foot rot and the abundant wildlife enjoyed his initial cereal crops. He never gave up. History justly credits him for initiating much of Kenya's current farming industry.

The native population moved from the fertile land they originally claimed to specially created, overcrowded preserves. Those allowed to remain in their homes paid rent and hut taxes, which they raised by working for their new masters.

During this period, white settlers wiped out indigenous wildlife and cleared vast tracts of ancient forest to make way for agriculture. Elsewhere in the country the Asian population busily monopolized retail outlets, developing small industry and related services.

With the advent of the First World War, over 200,000 conscripted African soldiers joined the British Army. Marching into Tanganyika, they fought hard and took heavy casualties. Victorious in war, the vanquishing black army returned home to mixed fortunes.

To encourage settlement and amass revenues for the governor's coffers, **Sir Edward Northey** rewarded the white veterans with new land rights. Massive immigration began by British ex-servicemen taking advantage of the offer of cheap land.

This "Soldier Resettlement Scheme" in the new Crown Colony, caused great bitterness as the Africans returned to impoverished lives. The general circumstances motivated a number of political associations to spring up. Supported by and chiefly made up of Kikuyu ex-servicemen, these groups began a series of protests and rallies, reaching a peak in 1921 when the disturbances forced the governor to take action.

The greatest threat seemed to come from a group calling itself the East African Association, led by a government clerk, **Harry Thuku**. As a result of the protests he led, Thuku was arrested and imprisoned where he remained for seven years. Without leadership, the Africans were once again defeated.

In 1923, a government White Paper stating the principle of "Africa for the Africans" was revived and was to be enforced. Essentially this was a Bill of Rights for the African people. Her Majesty's Government felt the interests of the African native must come first. The worried immigrant races were of secondary importance.

AFRICAN BILL OF RIGHTS

The British government declared "... the interests of the African native must be paramount, and that if and when those interests and the interests of the immigrant races should conflict, then the former should prevail."

After this decree, many Africans, especially the adaptable Kikuyu, found work in the fast growing city of Nairobi. They refused however, to give up their farms (*shambas*) in the highlands and left their senior wives at home. This would ensure upkeep of the farm and continued crop harvests.

Bending to demand and eager to regain its previous acceptance, the authorities allowed the Asian community two seats on the legislative council, which they later increased to five. As a goodwill gesture they included one Arab seat. None of these token actions were a problem for the 11 majority European seats.

During the 1920's and 1930's, the white settlers enjoyed an unmatched interval of good fortune. The lush forested **Wanjohi** valley of the **Aberdares** became infamous for the lascivious behavior of the upper social bracket. *White Mischief* and other books depict the exploits at what became known as "Happy Valley." This gaiety was not to last, as the Africans were becoming more disgruntled every day with their European leaders.

Establishing separate Kikuyu schools quieted the unrest temporarily and overcame attempts to deny Africans an education. English was just one of various subjects taught to the youngsters.

Among the aspiring pupils was **Johnstone Kamau** who would eventually move to Britain to complete his education. Kamau was an orphan raised and influenced by missionaries during his early years. He later changed his name to **Jomo Kenyatta**, and became one of the most influential personalities in Kenyan history. As a leading member of the Kikuyu Central Association and initiator of other organizations, he planned several African rights movements. On a visit to London in 1931, Kenyatta presented his people's case. This was the beginning of fifteen years of self-imposed exile in the Western world.

Just as the white population adjusted slowly to inevitable changes, Italian-held Ethiopia declared war on Kenya. The Second World War reached Africa.

Pushed by publicity showing Hitler as the latest racist threat to world peace, and assured of favorable changes, the Africans quickly and voluntarily joined the **King's African Rifles**. The fighting in North Africa, Burma, and the Middle East helped the African soldiers gain a sense of power as they realized the Europeans in Kenya were human and vulnerable.

At the end of the Second World War, promises of improvements once again went mostly unfulfilled. As if to add insult to injury, more white immigrants arrived laying claims to new tracts of land. Anger and resentment among African ex-servicemen ran deep.

THE MAU MAU UPRISING

While on his sojourn in England, Jomo Kenyatta got married. In the polygamous fashion of the Kikuyu, his English companion Edna Clarke was the second of his wives. This was one more annoyance for the British when in 1946, Kenyatta returned to Kenya after fifteen years and received a hero's welcome.

In 1947 he was chosen President of the **Kenya African Union** (**KAU**) by a landslide. It was widely acknowledged that Kenyatta was the only man who could unite the different political and tribal groups under one common voice with one common goal.

As discontent spread throughout the country, Kenyatta energized the rapidly growing KAU. A series of illegal underground movements formed and "oathing ceremonies" began, wherein the pledges swore loyalty to African political objectives such as freedom and independence.

Many Africans did not want violent change. They saw savagery as a last resort and sought a middle of the road approach to political, economic, and social equality. This was not to be however, and in 1948 the **Mau Mau** organization was born.

SOCIAL RIFTS

There was much division within the ranks of the settlers and the locals. Blacks and whites often found themselves on the same side opposing violent change and the oaths of aggression. Many inhabitants, including African chiefs and villagers, knew peaceful reform was on the way, albeit slowly. Violence was seen by black Christians as something near sacrilege. Missionaries, colonials, and those Africans who would not join the movement were targeted and many were killed.

Many British-trained African ex-soldiers provided the core of the guerrilla-type operations. Operating from hidden camps in the highland forest, the members started waves of violence. African chiefs were murdered, settlers' property was destroyed, and anyone loyal to the government was attacked.

Despite Kenyatta's denied involvement, he was arrested on October 20, 1952. Convicted along with five of his colleagues, he was sent to prison. Kenyatta's influence was still strongly felt throughout the years of rebellion as he tried to control the escalating violence.

The administration declared a state of emergency banning all political organizations and rounding up all known leaders. Additional British forces arrived in Kenya and an unwavering military campaign began to deal with the rebellion.

Africans suspected of harboring or assisting the guerrillas were arrested and moved to "protected villages," which were essentially concentration camps. Many lost their homes and their land. Throughout this policy of "villagization," up to one-third of the entire adult Kikuyu population – approximately 30,000 – were detained.

Eventually, the British succeeded in wounding, capturing and finally hanging the Mau Mau commander in chief, **Dedan Kimath**. The rebellion collapsed. At its conclusion, 32 white settlers and over 13,000 Africans lost their lives.

FREE AT LAST

Fearing further unrest, the administration hesitantly conceded that white domination was coming to a close, and began to prepare for majority rule. White settlers, worried about their futures, moved out of the country if they could.

Two newly formed African organizations, the **Kenya African National Union** (**KANU**) and the **Kenyan African Democratic Union** (**KADU**) began jostling to fill the vacuum of power.

After nine years of imprisonment Jomo Kenyatta was released. As the newly elected leader of KANU, Kenyatta led the party to a decisive victory in what was the country's very first one man, one vote general election.

INDEPENDENCE

On December 12, 1964, seventy-one years after Kenya became a protectorate and forty-four years after it became a colony, Kenya won independence. The bonds that now united Kenya and Britain were those of admiration and affection. While there certainly was some animosity on both sides, most Kenyans were not interested in violence and the peoples of Britain and Kenya respected each other and remain fond of each other. The ties are deep and, I believe, unbreakable, particularly for the older folks who remember those times.

The Union Jack came down for the last time. In its place the new green, black, red, and white flag of Kenya ran up the flag pole. The green represents the land, the black represents the people, and red represents the blood that was shed in the fight for freedom. The British influence in Kenya is still tremendous and there remains a great deal of regard for how life once was and the legacy left behind. The Queen was then and is still today a very revered personality among the Kenyans, and Her Majesty's picture can be seen in many business establishments.

In May 1963, Jomo Kenyatta became the first Prime Minister of the Republic of Kenya, and in December 12, 1964, he became President at independence. He held the office until his death at Mombasa on August 22, 1978.

Urgent issues of land reform, the release of detainees, and the dissolution of KADU – the main opposition to his ruling party – were high on the agenda. The settlers, who had carved their farms from the bush and who struggled to survive against all odds, were of no mind to give it all up. During negotiations with Kenyatta, the final outcome decreed land sold by willing sellers would go to willing buyers. This avoided a threat by the settlers to leave behind a "scorched earth" as they left their farms and more possible bloodshed.

Now seeing Kenya as a model state, Britain helped finance resettlement of the Africans back into the fertile highlands. Within five years of independence, more than 45,000 families were resettled. Approximately 2.3 million acres transferred back to Africans. The land was often acquired by successfully run, small-holder cooperative societies.

Over the next ten years there were many changes and good and bad times for the growing equatorial country. In 1974, **Kiswahili** became the official language of government. There were political assassinations, corruption in the government, and internal unrest, but through it all Kenyatta managed to carry the presidency for a full ten years. With help from large grants and loans from the United States and Great Britain, Kenya prospered. The national income doubled, education was free up to the first four grades, tea production tripled, coffee crops increased by fifty percent, prejudice was largely eradicated and medical care on an outpatient basis was free.

After continued failing health, Kenyatta died in Mombasa in August 1978. The legacy of freedom and stability were his gift to the land he loved so ardently. He was deeply mourned throughout the world and respected for his humanity and statesmanship. Many Kenyan's felt as though they lost a father.

What is Kenyatta's legacy? Mixed, as is the case with most leaders, but mostly good. During his time in office he did much for the country of Kenya. He loved both Kenya and the diverse population. Yes, he did crack down on his competition and got rich along with his cronies and family, but he also did so much for his people. He reconciled the country's rival ethnic groups. He developed the economy along capitalist lines. He advanced African business interests. His rule was filled with tactical flexibility and sometimes ruthlessness. Kenyatta mostly emphasized industrial hard work and communal values. To date, he has been the best leader in any African nation, keeping the peace and the people united behind him.

HARAMBEE

During his inaugural address, Kenyatta invited Europeans, Asians, and Africans to work together in the spirit of harambee (pulling together) to build a republic. Kenyatta's legacy of harmabee still stands and is now part of the country's coat of arms. It is this inheritance that has made Kenya one of the most prosperous and peaceful African nations.

His successor, **Daniel Arap Moi**, promised great reorganization, eagerly eradicating corruption in the bureaucratic civil service and freeing unconvicted political prisoners. Still in power today, though, Moi's government is now filled with crooked politicians, and bribery and theft are rampant.

Initial efforts to stamp out tribalism and corruption were well received but short-lived. A reawakening unrest culminated in a badly organized and unsuccessful attempted coup, in August 1982, by an organization called The People's Redemption Council. For a period of 24 hours during the confusion, Africans ran across the countryside, directing much of their anger and resentment against the minority Asian community. Shops were vandalized, looting was rampant, homes were burned and women were raped.

The coup, led and supported by many Air Force personnel, was put down by the army and a specially trained security force. The official unsubstantiated death toll was 159, including many students.

What happened? Moi got caught up in the glitter, glitz, wealth, and power and soon became corrupt. Today he is not too well liked by many Kenyans who regard him as a dictatorial thug. Kenya is still one of the most prosperous and peaceful countries in Africa, however, despite the problems caused by Moi. He started out with great intentions, but somehow along the way lost sight of his goals.

PRESENT DAY

Politically organized along Westminster (parliamentary) lines, Kenya is a multiparty state. KANU (Kenya African National Union) is currently the ruling party. A single legislative assembly contains 188 members (176 are elected) led by the President, who is also commander-in-chief of the armed forces. The president's cabinet is accountable to parliament, which approves all government expenditures. There are 28 ministries, each headed by a senior minister, two assistant ministers, and a permanent secretary.

Kenya has eight provinces, each overseen by a provincial commissioner, and 41 districts headed by a district commissioner and several assistant officers. An additional number of chiefs and their supporters work at a sub-district level.

Every five years there are elections. The change from secret balloting to public "be seen and counted system" where voters line up behind their chosen candidate, has led to inevitable charges of intimidation.

Based on the English system, the judiciary consists of a High Court presided over by a chief justice, a Magistrate Court, and finally a Court of Appeal. It is the general opinion that it is not effective because of the president's power to dismiss any unfavorable judge without recourse to a tribunal.

Studies made by Amnesty International repeatedly highlight Kenya's poor human rights record and have prompted the cancellation of ongoing Western aid programs. Undeterred, President Moi continues to persecute outspoken dissenters, regularly accusing foreign powers of "mischief making."

There will always be two schools of thought, those who see the corruption and dissension and those who see the impressive progress Kenya has made in a relatively short period of time. No other nation on the African continent has maintained democracy, law, and order, and managed to make great economic and social progress.

Kenya is the world's third-largest producer and second largest exporter of both tea and coffee. The "star of Africa" is the third largest producer of pineapples and is self sufficient in the production of maize, the staple food. Kenya is also the leading sports nation of developing countries, dong itself proud with many Olympic gold medals for events such as running and boxing.

Tourism, the number one industry, brings in over two hundred million dollars annually for Kenya. Approximately five hundred thousand visitors each year enjoy this unique nation from the lush west to the pristine beaches of the east. These facts speak loudly for Kenya as a fascinating and safe vacation destination.

6. PLANNING YOUR TRIP

WHEN TO GO

When you choose to visit Kenya is entirely dependent on what you will be doing while you are there and how particular you are about the weather. If you plan on staying at the beach and fishing, taking a camel trek in the northern desert regions, or enjoying a safari through the game parks, you should vary your arrival time accordingly for the best possible conditions. There are pros and cons to just about all travel periods.

Most game park visitors arrive in January through March, trying to escape the worst of the winter at home. A second shorter peak season occurs in July and August. At these times you can usually expect warm and dry weather in Kenya. These are the busiest time of the year and you certainly need to make reservations well in advance if you plan on arriving during the peak periods.

Towards mid-March, the humidity begins to increase and many local people elect to stay indoors; creating the impression it is a bad time to visit. This interval is busiest around the beach and coastal areas where inviting swimming pools beckon. This hot spell precedes the long rains which tend to come between late March and June.

September and October are also considered excellent months to visit the coast just before the short rains in November and December. You might see an increase in the amount of seaweed on some beaches and a little less sun for sunbathing during a rainy spell at the coast.

When the rains arrive, the parks, hotels, and lodges are less busy. Some take advantage of the seasons and use this opportunity to do any necessary remodeling and maintenance to their establishments. Others prefer to remain open but drop their prices considerably. This is a good time to go if you are willing to gamble on having good weather.

Between March and June you can often pick-up great discount tours and bargain rates to Kenya. Tour companies advertise cheap rates and book enough business to keep them going in the off season. In my opinion this is the time to go.

If you are on a standard safari, the minibuses won't be nearly as prolific or as crowded. You will end up getting a better quality and more personal tour without having to pay an exclusive outfitter's prices. Besides, the dust which is inevitable and unavoidable in the high season becomes less of a nuisance if you travel in the wet off-season.

All in all, I really don't think there is a bad time to see Kenya. The rains do tend to make travel a little more difficult as the roads can often turn into impassable mud craters. But if you weigh this against having more of Kenya to yourself, it may be a fair trade.

The rains can sometimes be exaggerated. The picture painted is one of endless torrents of rain and monsoon conditions. In actual fact, it is more like several sudden daily outbursts or heavy showers that don't last too long. The downpours have a cleansing effect on the air and make everything greener and more luscious.

As always there are many sides to any argument. As the wildlife areas green up and food becomes more plentiful, the animals are inclined to disperse, making them harder to find and photograph. My advice is to select the time of year that best suits your itinerary, budget, and your climatic preference. With a little patience and careful planning, Kenya, a land of great contrasts, is more than able and willing to accommodate you.

CLIMATE & WEATHER

The previous section gave you a general sense of when to travel to Kenya. This section will provide you with some more detail.

The fact that the equator runs through the middle of the country explains why Kenya has no defined seasons but rather a pleasant climate all year round.

As mentioned above, there are two rainy intervals in Kenya; the long rains from March to early June and the short rains in October and November. Depending on where you are in the country, you will be able to experience just about any kind of weather you choose – from snow to desert and anything in between.

It is important to allow your body time to acclimatize to the high altitude. If you begin to suffer from headaches, nausea, shortness of breath, vomiting and dizziness these may be symptoms of altitude sickness. Visitors attempting to climb any of the numerous mountains in Kenya need to bear this in mind. Even those who are physically fit suffer from this strange phenomenon.

WEATHER CONVERSION CHART
degrees F = (1.8 x degrees C) + 32
1 inch = 25.4mm

Kenya has an undeserved reputation for being extremely hot, when in fact quite the opposite is true. For the most part, the temperatures remain relatively constant along with the 6:00 am to 6:30 pm daylight hours. Altitude and rainfall are the determining factors when it comes to temperature.

At zero altitude along the coast it is generally humid and hot all year round but it appears cooler because of the sea breeze gently caressing the land. From November through June the north-easterly monsoon winds blow and for the rest of the year the residents count on south-easterly winds to sweep in from the ocean.

The highlands and Rift Valley are warm during the day and cool at night. The residents consider winter to be in the months of July and August when the temperatures drop slightly and the skies get a little gray. It does feel a little nippy and I must confess to wearing a warm sweater, especially at night.

In most houses and some hotels in Kenya there are fires burning in cozy fireplaces to counter the evening chill. There are no central heating systems anywhere in the country. Building a wood fire is a normal part of the staff's training and very much taken for granted by the local populace. It is a real treat to come back to your room and find a crackling blaze glowing in the hearth.

There is nothing I dislike more than getting into cold bedclothes before slumber. Therefore, one of the charms of Kenya that I always enjoy is the ritual of the hot water bottle. Each cold night, an oddly shaped, flat, rubber receptacle filled with steaming water, is placed between the sheets at the foot of the bed. I am always so appreciative of the warmth against my toes!

Up on Mount Kenya, the statistical low temperatures are equivalent to those in the arctic. The snow is constant and so is the freezing climate. Between December and March the sun is on the north face of the mountain. The south side is then experiencing its "winter." Rock and ice climbing are popular pastimes.

Around Mount Kenya and the Aberdares regions the rainfall is heavy. It is from this part of Kenya that the rest of the country gets most of its water. Rivers start out here as tumbling streams and end up converging as raging and powerful torrents coursing through the ancient river beds.

Eventually the waterways calm down into sinuous rivers as they become the country's main watershed.

Western Kenya has a tendency to be warm, humid, and fairly wet all year round. The highest rainfall occurs during the month of April and generally in the evening. Lake Victoria influences the temperatures in the west depending on how much moist air sweeps off its waters.

MAGIC WATER

At the equator the locals stand by to show visitors an entertaining phenomenon. On one side of the sign marking the equator they pour water through a funnel. The water swirls clockwise which seems perfectly normal. They will then take you about fifteen feet on the other side of the equator sign and pour the liquid through the funnel again.

Here the water swirls counter-clockwise. As the tourists gasp and giggle in surprise the proud guide explains this fascinating phenomenon is due to the changing gravitational pull of the earth. Notice which way the way the water goes down the drain in your hotel sink and which way it swirls as you flush the toilet. When you stay at your next hotel check to see if the water has changed directions.

The desert lands in the northern reaches of Kenya are hot, dusty, and dry all year round. There are some desert regions such as the Central Highlands that can have extreme lows at night and highs during the day. Flourishing here and there in this desolate area are pockets of thick forest. The trees and animals manage to survive not due to any rainfall but because of the mist and clouds providing moisture around the mountains.

In the past these general weather patterns have applied but more and more the climate is becoming unpredictable. This year the wet and dry climatic norms were completely turned around. There was rain when there should be none and dry spells when it should be wet. Many of the wheat and potato crops failed because of the odd weather. The temperatures were unusually cold.

WHAT TO TAKE

The most important thing to remember is that Africa is a very relaxed place. The people here don't take life too seriously. The pace is casual and the people friendly and fun-loving.

Tour operators, particularly if you are on safari, ask that you bring a medium sized soft duffel bag that weighs no more than 30 to 40 pounds when it is full. Expect your luggage to be weighed at all airports regardless of whether you will be going on a small plane or a large one. The weight restrictions are enforced with a fixed dollar amount for every pound the suitcase is overweight.

Traveling light is very important if you are going to use any of the small commuter planes. The room in the small crafts is limited and stashing a large hard suitcase is difficult. You will be asked to leave luggage behind in storage if the planes weight limits are exceeded. (These storage compartments are not always watertight. You might find damp or wet gear at the end of your trip.)

Vacationing with one suitcase should not be a problem as **laundry** services are fast and efficient in Kenya. You will notice that your clothing disappears from the ever present straw hamper and reappears the next day freshly washed and pressed.

It is recommended that you take care of washing your own undergarments. In some hotels soap powder is provided in a bottle next to the basin. Sometimes there is a clothes line in the bathroom; if not, drape your laundry around the room. It doesn't take too long to dry in the warm air.

All laundry in Kenya is done by hand and often with a scrub board, so if you have anything that can't take the rough handling or will shrink in hot water, don't send it to be washed. The laundries are not used to taking care of delicate fabrics and silks or other sheer fabrics, which may very well be damaged.

When the clothes are returned to your room, they will be immaculately pressed and folded. As you wander around the grounds of your hotel you will see the wash being line-dried and perhaps catch a glimpse of the traditional charcoal-heated iron being used to smooth out the wrinkles in all your apparel. I have never seen such meticulously ironed and folded T-shirts!

It is strongly suggested that while on safari you wear neutral colors. White and bright colors tend to alert wildlife and attract bugs. Because of this and the ever-present dust, the best color to wear is **khaki**.

It is wise to dress according to your temperature preference. During the day, the temperature will vary from 70 to 90 degrees Fahrenheit. At night it tends to get a little cooler, with the temperatures ranging from 50 to 60 degrees.

For **day wear**, the following items should be more than adequate: two to three pairs of shorts; five or six short sleeve shirts; one bathing suit; five or six pairs of underwear; four pairs of socks and one comfortable pair of walking shoes.

For **night wear** bring: one light jacket (waterproof); one sweater or sweatshirt; two cotton turtleneck sweaters; two casual evening outfits (khaki pants or a dress); two pairs of jeans, a night gown, and one pair of casual dress shoes.

As far as shoes go, it all depends on what kind of trip you will be on. If your trip includes a walking safari ,you will need hiking boots to protect you against the penetrating acacia thorns and any snakes you mistakenly disturb. If you will be in a vehicle the entire time then I'd say keeping your feet cool would be the priority. Most of all it is important to take comfortable shoes that won't give you blisters.

Other **miscellaneous items** that you will find useful on the trip are: sunglasses; sunscreen; a small lightweight flashlight; a hat or baseball cap; a fanny pack; laundry detergent (woolite); a Swiss army knife; a sewing kit, binoculars, a journal, one empty duffel bag to bring your "treasures" back in, a couple of plastic bags to pack your dirty clothes and muddy shoes, and a sense of humor.

Casual is the name of the game at the beach in Mombasa. For your stay at the coast you might want to dress like the locals and wear a pretty and practical caftan or sarong (the prices on these items are very reasonable in the local markets).

Along much of the coast, where the people are Muslim, it is frowned upon to expose too much skin; this includes legs and arms. Conservative attire will get you more respect from the locals, particularly in Lamu. As a courtesy to the inhabitants whose country you are visiting, try to keep yourself covered. Men should not wear shorts and women should cover their knees and shoulders.

A jacket and tie may be worn at the deluxe hotels in Nairobi, but for the most part it is not necessary. At some of the fancier establishments, like the **Mount Kenya Safari Club**, a coat and tie are required. Traveling with these bulky things is cumbersome, however, so design your trip with this in mind.

Depending on what kind of vacation you plan, your clothing should be arranged accordingly. If you will be golfing, caving, camping, diving or fishing inquire from your tour operator as to what is appropriate. Most equipment can be rented from local outfitters but it may take time. Organize equipment rental well in advance to avoid rushing at the last minute.

The following companies should be able to provide what you need:
• **Atul's**, *Biashara Street in Nairobi, Tel. 225 935*
• **Yare Safaris**, *PO Box 63006, Nairobi, Tel. 214 099, Fax 213 445*
• **Safaris Unlimited**, *PO Box 24181, Nairobi, Tel. 891 168*
• **Special Camping Safaris Ltd.**, *PO Box 51512, Nairobi, Tel. 338 325*

Your backpack or day pack is strictly a personal choice as is a tent, stove, pots, pans and foam mat. It all depends on how much comfort you want and how much you are willing to carry.

I cannot stress enough the importance of a good pair of **sunglasses**. The glare can be really troublesome when you are squinting to spot an animal on the horizon. The sun at the high altitudes in Kenya is strong and I often find my eyes get sunburned when I make the mistake of forgetting my dark glasses. I prefer to travel with a cord attached to my sunglasses. If I need to take a photo or look through my binoculars, I can just drop the glasses and not worry about putting them down somewhere safe.

This is not the United States, with a pharmacy at every corner, and it doesn't hurt to go prepared with a small assortment of **medical supplies**. The most useful basics are: eye drops; extra contact lenses or glasses and cleaner; pain relievers; Band-Aids; antihistamine; insect repellent; diarrhea medication; antacids and anti-malaria medication.

As far as repellent goes, take something to spread on your exposed skin during the day and for nighttime take mosquito coils. The small, green, round coils burn all night while giving off their smoky mist; the mosquitoes hate it! I prefer the coils for two reasons: I have used them all my life and kind of like the smell; and by using these repellents, I avoid smearing myself with some greasy, malodorous substance that will only rub off on my sheets.

PASSPORTS & VISAS

All visitors are required to have a passport that is valid for at least six months. It is important to allow plenty of time (up to six weeks) for a visa to be processed. If you need to get a passport, I suggest getting it well ahead of time. It will be necessary to send your passport along with your application to the Kenyan embassy, as your visa is stamped directly into your passport.

The visa application form looks a little intimidating. A list of requirements on the back of the form seems impossible to fulfill. Don't be disturbed. As long as you send in your valid passport(s), two photos (each), a copy of your itinerary, a stamped, self-addressed return envelope, and your cashiers check or money order you shouldn't have any trouble.

It is necessary to send in one form per person. The fee is $30 dollars per person. Send your forms via certified letter to make sure it gets where it's going and also make the return envelope certified. This will make things easier. Visa requirements vary from time to time, so if you are in any doubt call the nearest Tourist Office or preferably the Kenyan embassy or consulate:

• **Kenyan Embassy**, *2249 R Street, NW, Washington DC 20008. Tel. 202/ 387-6101*
• **Kenyan Consulate**, *424 Madison Avenue, New York, NY 10017. Tel. 212/ 486-1300*

• **Kenyan Consulate**, *9150 Wilshire Boulevard, Suite 160, Beverly Hills, CA 90212. Tel. 310/274-6635*

If for some reason you need to extend your stay once you are in Kenya, it is possible to obtain an extension from the immigration department. The cost is $8 for a single re-entry permit and $40 for a multiple-entry permit. In the past no shillings were accepted as payment, but ask, as this may have changed in recent reforms.

While in Nairobi, contact **The Immigration Department**, *Nyayo House, Kenyatta Avenue, PO Box 30191, Tel. 332 110.* In Mombasa, the immigration office is at *PO Box 90284, Tel. 311 745.*

GETTING TO KENYA

The airports in **Nairobi** and **Mombasa** handle 90 percent of all arrivals in Kenya. The other ten percent arrive by land, rail, and boat. If you fly in (which most of us do) allow at least one and a half days of travel time. Usually you will have to fly through London, Paris, or Belgium and pick up a connecting flight there. The stopover can be from a few hours to a full day.

Many of the smaller airlines only open their offices if they have a flight arriving or departing. In order to make travel changes or confirm your bookings, make certain the offices are open or call the information/ reservation number.

It is possible with a lot of hard work to arrange to travel into Kenya from Pakistan or the Gulf on a *dhow.* This will take a great deal of time and you must travel from October through March, when the northeast monsoon winds blow. I don't suggest this method of arrival unless you have unlimited time and a very flexible schedule.

If you don't have to stick to a rigid itinerary or flight schedule, you can often buy your airline tickets by checking the travel section in the Sunday paper. Being adaptable to sudden and frequent date and time changes can be stressful if you are not accustomed to traveling this way, but going this route to get bargain prices will make your vacation more affordable. On the west coast try the *Los Angeles Times* or *San Francisco Examiner-Chronicle*; on the east coast look in the *New York Times.*

I have found that for me, the discount travel agents or brokers work out well. Sometimes the trip takes a little longer with a couple of extra stops, but to save $600.00 it's worth it to me. Check you local paper in the back of the travel section. I try to make my reservations 30-35 days in advance and so far, have had no problems.

A round trip ticket from the US to Nairobi will cost about $1,200 but can run up to $6,000 depending on when you book it and what time of year you plan to travel. During the off season, September 15 to November 30 and February 1 to May 14, you will find the lower fares and special package deals.

If you are the daring sort, try buying your ticket through the advanced purchase program. Using this method you will end up saving between 30 and 40 percent off the regular economy fare. Naturally, to get such a great deal you'll have to put up with the restrictions. Read the fine print and ask questions before you pay for the ticket. Usually you have to stay for a minimum of 14 days and return within 180 days. If you must change your travel dates or destinations expect it to cost you dearly with advanced purchases. The only other restriction I know of is the 21 day advance purchase requirement.

For those under the age of 26 or students, ask your travel agent if there are any reduced fares available. To find a special price as a student you may have to travel during the off season, change planes several times, or fly a less direct route. It all depends on how much you are willing to sacrifice for savings.

CUSTOMS

When you arrive, you will be required to go through customs but usually this is just a formality and should not concern you. The customs officers have the right to inspect your luggage and to detain you if they find anything illegal.

Your personal effects, camera, and video equipment will be allowed in duty free. A refundable assessment may be required for radios, tape recorders and musical instruments. It is understood these items are for your personal use and should not be sold during your visit.

It is also permissible to bring in perfume, cigarettes, cigars, cheroots, tobacco, wine and liquor all within reasonable quantities. Plants and plant materials are prohibited for obvious reasons.

Firearms must be brought in with a special import permit issued ahead of time by the **Central Firearms Bureau**, *PO Box 30263, Nairobi.*

HOTEL BASICS

Hotels usually do not have street addresses, and street signs are few and far between. In this book, you'll notice that outside of Nairobi, most hotels do not have local addresses and phone numbers; the reservations are handled in Nairobi and sometimes abroad.

There are few telephones and they work intermittently (the country does not yet have touch-tone service, which renders communication such as automated voicemail systems etc., a thing of the distant future). When you call information in Nairobi, you hear the one operator on duty put down her receiver and thumb through the phone book. The system is primitive. The more remote hotels only have radio phones which turn on for emergencies and for communication for an hour each evening (this is when the generator is running). I often and specifically mention using the telephone (with a phone card) at the local post offices because phones are not common.

Usually the smaller hotels or lodges are owned by colonials who live in Nairobi and they handle all business dealings, including reservations, from their Nairobi address. They have a permanent African staff staying at their lodge for when guests arrive. Many of the larger resorts are owned by corporations, such as Block Hotels, who also do their bookings from a central office in Nairobi. Unless specified otherwise, the phone numbers are for the hotels themselves as opposed to a Nairobi booking office. If the telephone listings do not include an area code, they are local numbers. If the numbers are for reservations outside the area, I give the appropriate area code.

When planning a trip, visitors should always make reservations before leaving North America or Europe. From my descriptions, you should get a pretty good idea of where to go and stay. The next step is to contact the office of the lodge in question, make reservations, and arrange to be picked up. If tourists want pictures, the hotels may have a brochure they are willing to part with. It is not usually a good idea to arrive in Africa without having planned for a place to stay. This is particularly true during the peak seasons at the beach.

I strongly suggest getting a driver when visitors rent a car. It is cheaper to get a driver with the car than to pay for the insurance, gas, etc. The drivers are trained to know where everything is. Towns and cities are so small, getting to know the locations of restaurants and hotels is quite simple for the guides/drivers. I also mention, when tourists are venturing out into the bush, it is not wise to travel alone but instead take a guide – these people always know where everything is.

If tourists fly to the remote lodges, the hotels arrange to pick up their customers and drive them around. It isn't too common for guests to have to find their own way in Kenya because it is impractical and unsafe. Taxis, drivers, and labor in general are very inexpensive, so people make use of the plentiful help.

HOTEL RATES & CAMPING

You will be pleased to know that Kenya has something for every budget imaginable. The hotel rates can be as low as $3 on up to $500 per person per night. Obviously, the more you pay, the better your accommodations are likely to be.

When making arrangements to go on safari, your tour operator will take care of all your accommodation needs. If this is your first time to Kenya, it might be a good idea to use one of these booking agents to do everything for you. They know all about the fees for getting into the parks, game drive fees, airstrip transfers, and other small details that can detract from your visit if they are left for the last minute. An agent might cost a little more but you will be sure and have a more pleasant safari. The second time you go, plan and book your own itinerary.

HOTEL RATING PROCEDURES

The government's official grading process is quite strict and involves inspecting and judging the entire facility. Some of the considerations are: the number of public restrooms; the number of bathrooms compared to the number of bedrooms; the quality of furnishings and equipment throughout; the cleanliness and sanitation services; amenities in the rooms and recreation areas; food preparation and structural integrity.

The Hotel and Restaurant Authority places all hotels into one of four categories. The line-up consists of town hotels, vacation hotels, lodges, and tented camps. In each class, the accommodations are grouped from one (lowest) to five (highest) stars, or from D (lowest – which would be any non-tourist establishment) to A (highest).

For most coastal hotels, check out time is 11 am. In the city and at the safari lodges check out time is 10 am. Depending on what period of the tourist season you are in and how busy the hotel is, you might be able to ask for an extension to your check out time. If you feel you really need the room for a considerable part of the next day, the manager may give you a special day rate.

Real bottom of the range hotels serve as brothels first and hotels second. These places are very cheap; $1.50 for a single and $3 for a double room. If you don't mind the noise and general air of sleaze, they will (barely) pass for a place to stay.

You will have to check the room first and make sure it has clean sheets and see if you can stand the smells. Occasionally, you might find such an establishment that is actually cheap and not a bad place to stay. Don't write this kind of accommodation off entirely if you're looking for the absolute cheapest way you can stand to see Kenya.

Don't be embarrassed if the person renting you the room inquires as to why you want it for the whole night. Usually they are rented by the hour and the questions will be a matter of curiosity. If you happen to be by yourself, be prepared for even more quizzical glances. Be polite but don't let them get too nosy.

If a clean room with a private bath, towels, soap and clean sheets is the only acceptable accommodation for you, a few more shillings ($4 for a single and $6.50 for a double room) will have to part company with your wallet. It really isn't much more money but it is definitely worth the upgrade. On the down side, if you are a light sleeper you can expect a noisy restaurant and bar below to keep you up well into the night.

HOTEL RESERVATION AGENCIES

To make reservations, try any of the following excellent services:

Micato Safaris: *15 West 26th Street, New York, New York 10010, Tel. 212/545 7111, Fax 212/545 829. PO Drawer 43371, Nairobi, Kenya, Tel. 226 944 or 226 6944, Fax 336 138*

Bush Homes Africa Safaris: *750 Piedmont Avenue, Atlanta, Georgia 30308, Tel. 404/8880909, Fax 404/888-0081, e-mail safari@bushhomes.com*

Abercrombie & Kent Ltd.: *PO Box 59749, Nairobi, Tel. 228 700, Fax 215 752*

Hilton Hotels: *PO Box 30624, Nairobi, Tel. 334 000, Fax 339 462*

Prestige Hotels: *PO Box 74888, Nairobi, Tel. 335 208, Fax 217 278*

Block Hotels: *c/o UTC, PO Box 40075, Nairobi, Tel. 335 807 or 540 780, Fax 543 810*

Sarova Hotels *(New Stanley Hotel): PO Box 30680, Nairobi, Tel. 333 248, Fax 211 472*

Lonrho Hotels: *PO Box 58581, Nairobi, Tel. 216 940, Fax 216 796, E-mail: lonhotke@form-net, web: www.lonrohotels.com*

In the next hotel category things will improve drastically. At a rate of $15 to $25 you will get a private bathroom with the rudimentary comforts of home. Hot water, toilet paper, a table, chair and perhaps a phone and room service are options in this range.

If you are interested in meeting travelers such as yourself, a youth hostel might be the place for you. Most of the larger towns have hostels but they may not be easy to find. To stay here you will need to be a member. Join at home before you go. At roughly $5 for a dormitory bed, you will have company throughout the night. In Lake Naivasha and Mount Kenya the youth hostels are exceptional.

In Nairobi, another couple of clean and inexpensive options are the **YMCA** or the **YWCA**. You will find these to be a perfectly safe place to spend the night. If you are interested in a working or study tour, where they may choose to stay at a Y, try **TST Tours**, *PO Box 50982, Nairobi, Tel. 791 227, Fax 780 461,* which offers a wide range of selections.

Kenya is really just one big camp site with plenty of room to pitch a tent. Camping is certainly a viable option and will save you money. You can either join a camping safari or set off by yourself. Basic camp sites are accessible in every game park and national reserve but the facilities are rudimentary. You might find a water tap and a couple of long-drop toilets. You'll almost certainly have the place to yourself with the exception of wild animals.

MAPS

*Maps can be obtained from any good book store in Nairobi. Try **Nation Bookshop** in the New Stanley Building or the **Book Corner** on Mama Ngina Street, or perhaps **Westland Sundries** in the New Stanley Hotel. Check to see when the maps were updated last as sometimes they can be rather old. Bartholomews, Macmillan, and Nelles offer good country maps. Perhaps the best map is the A to Z: Guide to Nairobi by D. T. Dobie – Kenway Publications.*

While it is best to get your maps before leaving home, the selection isn't always as good. Sometimes maps can be bought at the main entry to a reserve or game park. They are more expensive here than in town but will do in a pinch. If you are shopping for some sort of fieldguide to wildlife that will help you identify the game you see, these bookstores carry selections that ought to do the job.

The freedom is exhilarating if you are on your own, but be careful and know where you are going. Don't camp without either a guide or a good map and, as an extra precaution, letting someone know your schedule.

You can rent any kind of camping equipment in Nairobi, but it would be cheaper to bring the basics from home; it all depends on how much in the way of supplies you are willing to lug half-way around the world. Next to the essential four-wheel drive vehicle, I'd include a tent, hammer, sleeping bag, pillow, grill, cooking utensils, stove, opener, lamp, matches, cups and water container.

There are **private tented campgrounds** that offer more in the way of facilities but they are a little less common and harder to find. There are also mobile sites that move to a new spot with each season or each new group of visitors. These places tend to be a little more rustic because they are portable and cannot put up permanent facilities. The purpose is to give the guest a more realistic safari experience.

Tented camps in the game parks are not necessarily an economical alternative. In the luxury tented campgrounds ($150 to $500 per night), the walls are canvas but there are four-poster beds, flush toilets, and a roof. The service at these establishments is usually excellent.

Along the coast camping is not safe, particularly on the beaches. It is not unheard of for campers to get mugged by local thugs. Even though campers would seemingly not have much to offer a thief, a foreign backpacker has more wealth than some of these people will see in a lifetime. As an enterprising camper you may be able to ask permission and pitch your tent on the grounds of a hotel or find a small local campsite.

At the coast, take a look at renting a cottage. If you are traveling with your family, this is an excellent way to save a little money on your trip. The house will have all the comforts of home, a maid and for a little extra money ($2 to $7 a day) a cook. Unless you ask, this option is not always forthcoming from your travel operator.

Bandas, a form of thatched hut, are a preference of the Kenyan middle class when they go camping. These cabins are usually only one or two rooms with the most basic of furnishings. You will need to bring your own bedding, food, and anything other than water. The facilities will vary from a gas stove to an outside campfire. If you want to stay in a banda, book well in advance during the high season and ask what comforts you can expect.

If you are on your own and haven't made reservations ahead of time just ask any local for the nearest old **colonial hotel**. The colonial hotels are a throwback to more glorious times, but you will find the rooms clean and comfortable. Many of these three star hotels prefer to cater to locals and don't bother posting non-resident rates. If you can get a room, this is often the most value for your money at $30 to $50 per night.

At the top end of the price scale you will find the customary chains of hotels. The prices start at $150 for a single and go up from there to about $500. The **resort hotels** and the **lodges** in the preserves and along the beach fall into this category. Safari or game lodges tend to be small hotels constructed and decorated in creative and resourceful ways.

Expect to be charged a cancellation fee if you either reduce the number of days in your stay or cancel altogether. At the coastal hotels or lodges, the fee is ten percent of your room rate for every night canceled between 20 or 30 days before your intended stay; 25 percent if you cancel between 19 and 10 days; and 35 percent if you cancel between nine and two days. Any cancellation under 48 hours is charged full value and considered a no-show.

In Nairobi they are not quite so rigid and will only charge you if you cancel nine days or less before your stay. The fees charged are the same as for the coast or lodges.

TREE-HOTELS

Tree-hotels are lodges whose accommodations are built into the trees high off the ground. Sometimes they are built in the tops of the trees themselves and sometimes they are on stilts. Often the different rooms of the hotel are connected by open rope or wooden walkways suspended high above the earth. They are often considered too dangerous and confining for small kids.

GETTING AROUND KENYA

Kenya is the epitome of getting back to nature and is not without its problems when it comes to getting around. Take note that this is still a third world country and you will face the challenges that go with that status. As long as you have an open mind and don't expect it to be like home, things will be fine.

By Air

With the variety of schedules and the reasonable airfares, you will be able to get from place to place within the country with little inconvenience. I suggest this as the best way to travel to your destination in a short period of time. There are many partial or total air-safaris, where the worst parts of the trip are covered by small plane.

The view from the plane is often a bonus if the pilot can fly low. If the weather is clear, the panorama is spectacular and will give you a great feel for Kenya's terrain.

The two major airports are: **Wilson Airport**, *PO Box 19011, Tel. 501 941,* in Nairobi and **Moi International**, *PO Box 98498, Tel 433 211,* in Mombasa. The other two smaller airports are **Kisumu Airport**, *PO Box 12, Tel. 40125,* in Kusumu and **Malindi Airport**, *PO Box 67, Tel. 20981,* in Malindi. Most towns and major game parks have their own comparatively small airfields. A fee of $2 (cash) per passenger is charged at all domestic airports as a departure tax in addition to the ticket price.

There are daily scheduled flights to Masai Mara, Samburu, and Amboseli from Nairobi. Lamu, Nanyuki, Nyeri, and Eldoret are also on the flight schedule with private operators but not with as much frequency.

Kenya Airways, the national carrier, runs services to about 30 destinations. Their locations include: *Barclays Plaza, Loita Street, PO Box 41010, Nairobi, Tel. 229 291, Fax 336 252; Jomo Kenyatta International Airport, Tel. 822 171/822 288; Savani House, Mombasa, Tel. 21251; Moi Airport, Mombasa, Tel. 433 211; Malindi, Tel. 20237, and Kisumu, Tel. 44056.*

Air Kenya, *Wilson Airport, PO Box 30357, Nairobi, Tel 501 421, Fax 500 845*, offers flights across the country. This airline runs flights to Nyeri, Nanyuki, Masia Mara, Lamu and anywhere in between. The airlines enforces a strict weight restriction on luggage.

If you can get enough people together and hire a charter plane it makes the trip more affordable. To find the best deal, try one of the main private air carriers, including: **Eagle Aviation**, *Tel. 606 015*, **Skyways Airlines**, *Tel. 506 018*, **Equator Airlines**, *Tel. 501 360*, and **Prestige Air Services**, *Tel. 501 212*.

To make sure your seat is held for you, reconfirm at least 48 hours in advance. It is not uncommon for passengers to be bumped off a flight if they have not confirmed their booking. The airlines have a tendency to overbook, and those who do not reconfirm can find themselves sitting at the airport waiting for the next available flight.

By Bus

In the main cities the buses offer cheap and relatively reliable transportation. Departure time is as soon as the bus is packed full. If a city bus normally holds 45 to 50 people, you can easily expect the number of passengers to be at least double.

The worst time to ride is during rush hour and around lunch time when the buses are loaded with as many people as the interior can hold. Occupants are not limited to people. You could find yourself sitting next to some form of domestic animal. In the peak hours, you will have to battle your way off.

The buses tend to be rather run down as they are used so heavily with little maintenance. During the rains, they are covered with mud from one end to the other and the interior is not much better. For a short distance it might be worth the experience, but be prepared for a rough ride.

For a bus trip out of town, there are many privately owned operations. The advantage here is that buses run during the day and offer a view of the countryside. For a long journey, it is worth paying a little extra to get a seat on one of the better motor coaches. The recommended companies are **Malindi Bus**, *Tel. 229 662*; **Goldline**, *Tel. 225 279*; and **Coastline Safaris**, *Tel. 214 819*.

By Car

Driving is not a bad way to get around if you don't need to go a great distance or if you have ample time. You will certainly get to see Kenya in a personal way providing you can cover enough ground.

Because of the costs of up-keep, renting a car in Kenya is terribly expensive. The rates will include Collision Damage Waiver (CWD), theft protection and compulsory Third Party Insurance (TPI). A 15 percent

VAT will apply on the final bill. In order to rent a vehicle you must be over 23 years of age and under 70.

Vehicles are not permitted for use north of Samburu Game Reserve or Maralal due to poor road infrastructure, and lack of adequate auto services and phone lines. In case of theft or damage to a rented vehicle, the charge will be about $364 for the first three categories of cars and $909 for the last cars listed in the following sidebar.

APPROXIMATE CAR RENTAL RATES

The daily rates include 31 miles; the weekly rates include 311 miles.

	Daily Rates	Weekly Rates	Per extra mile
Daihatsu Charade *G1004 door, 1000 c.c. Inside city limits only*	$47	$282	.20
Nissan *4 door 1300 c.c. Not for game parks*	$55	$355	.25
Suzuki Sierra-Maruti *1000 c.c., 4 x 4, 2 door*	$58	$390	.27
Mitsubishi Pajero *4 x 4, 2600 c.c.*	$104	$724	.58

The driving standards in Kenya are appalling and great caution is advised if you decide to drive yourself around. Driving is on the left, but it is not uncommon for the vehicles to avail themselves of the best stretch of road no matter what side it is on. It will appear as if the other driver is playing a game of "chicken" and it can be very dangerous. Serious accidents are common, particularly when it comes to the Matatu buses.

The speed limit throughout Kenya is 62 miles per hour (100 kph) on the main roads, 31 miles per hour (50 kph) in the towns and 19 miles per hour (30 kph) on secondary roads. It is not uncommon to have two or three speed bumps ("sleeping policemen" or "rumble strips") at any given interval. There is no warning that the bumps are coming up and they are often difficult to see.

Driving at night is a bad idea. Depending on where you are, there may be bandits waiting to prey on unsuspecting passersby. Besides the dangers of highway robbers, many vehicles belonging to locals have no working headlights. In the dark these cars are impossible to see until it is too late.

The law requires drivers turn on their headlights at 6:30 pm but this is not enforced.

If you look like a tourist or easy prey, be prepared for any number of ingenious scams. For example: a local will pour oil on your tires and explain to you that something is seriously wrong with your differential or bearings. Of course, he happens to have a friend in a nearby garage that will "fix" the leak at a special price for you.

To drive in Kenya, a valid driver's license from the US is acceptable for 90 days. In theory your license requires endorsement at the Road Transport Office, Nyati House, Kenyatta Avenue, Nairobi or at Provincial Headquarters in Mombasa. No one seems to enforce this policy or worry about it too much. If you possess an international driver's license, this law does not apply.

The roads in Kenya are a heated topic of conversation. Depending on where you are going, what time of year it is and the maps you use, getting around can be a challenge. A map might or might not show airfields, railroads, highways, main roads and minor roads. If there is only one road marked it usually is the main thoroughfare but don't count on it being in great condition. It could be a dirt track and still be the main route.

There are many well maintained asphalt roads leaving Nairobi and Mombasa. Once you leave these however, the condition of the roads declines the further out you go. In some places the route can be barely more than a track. If you don't know your way around or have a competent guide, it is easy to get lost. Giving directions can be a bit tricky as sign posts are rare. Maps can be unreliable because things change quickly. There are some good main roads like the A2, A109, A104, A3 and A1 that traverse the country, but that's it. Once you get off the main "highways," a typical set of directions might include: left at the fork in the road, 1/2 mile down the dirt trail, right at the rotting tree stump... The ruts that serve as roads in the countryside change after each rainy season and are difficult to find, much less follow. For that reason, it is important to get good directions and pick up reliable road maps (see *Maps* sidebar above).

The roads, particularly in the rainy season, can turn into one giant mud hole. For touring in the bush, a four-wheel-drive vehicle is essential. A lengthy journey might look relatively simple on a map but it could take four hours or four days depending on the weather. In many places the black cotton soil is a nightmare to drive in when wet as it gets thick and very sticky. It feels like you are driving on ice with the added challenge of bog-like mires.

To ensure a safe trip it is best to take a few precautions before you drive off in your newly rented vehicle. Check to see that you have a spare tire in reasonably good condition and that it is inflated. Make sure the jack is actually in the car and that it has all the necessary working parts. Try out the lug wrench to see if it indeed fits the nuts on your particular car. Finally, check your oil, water, and tire pressure. Please, don't take any of these things for granted!

Gasoline is available at nearly all game lodges and in most towns, but it isn't a bad idea to carry a full five gallon can just to be on the safe side. If you should run low and the gas station is closed, it might get you to the next town. As of this writing, gasoline is $6 per gallon.

Before you leave the lot, let the booking agent record the mileage on your contract and also write down what grade of gasoline is required. Agree on either regular or super and that you will be charged for one or the other. This can sometimes turn in to an argument at the end of your trip if the agent tries to charge you for premium when you used regular. Avoid vehicles that run on diesel, as it is hard to find out in the bush.

TRUSTWORTHY CAR RENTAL AGENCIES

Abercrombie & Kent Ltd., *6/7 Floor Bruce House, Standard Street, PO Box 59749, Nairobi. Tel. 228 700, 334 955, Fax 215 752*

Concorde Car Hire, *PO Box 25053, Nairobi. Tel. 448 953, 448 954, Fax 448 135*

Hertz, *(United Touring Company & Block Hotels), Muindi Mbingu Street, PO Box 42196, Nairobi. Tel. 531 322, Fax 216 871*

The Car Hire Company, *Standard Street, New Stanley Hotel, PO Box 56707, Nairobi. Tel. 225 255, Fax 216 553*

The small fee the rental agency charges for a driver is money well spent. To hire a driver for normal working hours in the city will cost $8 a day. During normal working hours for an out of town journey, the daily cost is roughly $13. Anything outside of normal working hours is $1.45 per day for a driver. If you go this route, you won't have to pay the Collision Damage Waiver or insurance. In addition, your driver will no doubt be an excellent tour guide, animal spotter, and tire changer. (Yes, count on having several flat tires!)

Finally, a last word of caution. Dogs, sheep, cows, and humans are commonly seen walking along the roads and it is your responsibility to avoid hitting them. In many areas wildlife such as giraffe and zebra are seen wandering along the roads. Please go slowly when you encounter them and remember they *always* have the right of way.

By Matatu

These small brightly colored vans and trucks are everywhere. They are a way of life for the local people. The drivers are required to put in long work hours and are pressured by owners to make as much money as possible. Because of this, the conductor packs an unimaginable number of bodies into the vehicle and the driver moves wildly at demented speeds.

The Matatu driver's have a bad habit of stopping in the middle of the road to let passengers off. When traffic is snarled up, more often than not it is because of a stationary Matatu. Blaring horns and curse words follow these vehicles around wherever they go. It is a very cheap way to get around if you have the internal fortitude to be crushed at every turn, withstand the odor of your fellow friendly passengers and watch as the conductor hangs precariously on the outside.

Because they are privately owned and try to cover for the shortage of city buses, the fixed fare is usually 50 cents or 50 cents higher than the regular bus. You as a tourist can be sure you will not be charged more than other passengers.

By Taxi

Prices on taxis are negotiable and should be agreed upon before you get going. You will be told the cars are metered but if they do actually have a meter, it is generally not working. Porters at the hotels and your tour operator should be able to give you a pretty close approximation of the price for your destination.

There will be at least one taxi outside all the larger hotels and on the main streets at designated taxi stands. You will find the usual collection of decrepit cars for hire but these seem to be on the decline around the cities. My preference is the London taxis which offer a safer and more comfortable trip. Besides, it is rather fun to ride in a cab that came all the way from London and has the clever fold-down seat facing backwards.

TAXICAB SCAMS!

Cabdrivers are notorious for trying to pull a fast one on innocent tourists. The most common scam is to claim they have no change. This is their problem, not yours. If you think about it and would rather avoid the hassle, take smaller denominations with you. If you don't have lesser bills, don't be bullied into giving the driver an outrageous tip. Insist on their getting the necessary change. Another ploy is to get you into the cab after you agree on a rate and when you arrive at your destination, they will try to tell you that the price was per person. If there are two of you, the driver will quickly double his take for your trip. Don't be fooled by this clever trick!

By Train

If you have the time, this is a wonderfully scenic way to see Kenya. This breathtaking route covers 585 miles, giving you a glimpse of Kenya's beauty as it takes you across the Tsavo Plains, into the Central Highlands, through the vast tea plantations, and across the Rift Valley. There is nothing quite like watching the graceful impala graze on the plains as the sun goes down.

There is only one train a day each way between Mombasa and Nairobi and Kisumu and Nairobi. There used to be a slower train departing at 5:30 pm but this no longer runs. It was rumored to stop 43 times during the trip and the service was not up to par.

The outstanding overnight service between Nairobi and Mombasa departs at 7:00 pm and is a delightful method of experiencing the Kenya of days past. Passengers board in the evening and begin to soak up the ambiance. Dinner is worthwhile not only for the four-course meal but also for the style in which it is served. The china, cutlery, and linens make you feel a little like royalty. Try to choose the second seating so that you can linger at the table and finish your coffee and conversation. The price for dinner is roughly $3 and breakfast is $2. For children's portions the prices are between $1 and 75 cents. Paying for an all inclusive ticket, which can include dinner and/or breakfast, at the start of your journey is an option you might consider. If you selected breakfast as part of your trip, it is served just before arrival at the intended destination.

After the evening meal, retire to the comfort of a sleeping car that is well equipped with clean toilets, washbasins, and cooling fans. Bedding,

---

WINSTON CHURCHILL'S AFRICAN JOURNEY

In 1908, Winston Churchill had the thrill of riding on a "garden seat" attached to the train's cowcatcher. He describes the East African Railway as the most romantic in the world in his book, My African Journey:

"The plains are crowded with animals. From the windows of the carriage the whole zoological gardens can be seen disporting itself. Herds of antelope and gazelle, troops of zebras – sometimes four of five hundred together – watch the train pass with placid assurance, or scamper a hundred yards further away, and turn again. Many are quite close to the line. With fieldglasses one can see that it is the same everywhere, and can distinguish long files of black wildebeeste and herds of red kongoni – the hartebeeste of South Africa – and wild ostriches walking sedately in twos and threes, and every kind of small deer and gazelle. The zebras come close enough for their stripes to be admired with the naked eye."

which includes a mattress, sheets, pillows and a blanket can be had from the conductor at the beginning of your trip for a small fee. You can also include them in the price of your fare or you can bring your own. A sleeping bag always works well.

It is best to book the **express train** (leaves at 7:00 pm) at least one week in advance in order to get a comfortable berth in first or second class. Second class has four berth cabins and first class has two, so book ahead. In third class, the hard seats are all there is and it can be an uncomfortable way to travel, especially for an overnight trip. It is a good idea to reconfirm your bookings several times. The trains have a tendency to fill up quickly. If you have to get on the train and don't book ahead, you will end up riding on an uncomfortable bench in third class.

Return tickets are valid for three months. If you cancel your journey, be sure and do so 24 hours prior to the time you were supposed to depart. Otherwise you might find the ticket agent not too willing to refund or exchange your ticket.

When time is no object and you want to get to the towns of Malaba, Naivasha, Nakuru, Eldoret, Webuye, Bingoma, Tororo, Iganga, Jinja, Kawolo and Kampala, there is overnight rail service available. This train runs once a week leaving Nairobi station on Tuesdays and arriving in Kampala on Wednesday. The return trip leaves Kampala on Wednesdays and arrives in Nairobi on Thursday.

These trains traveling to the smaller towns do not have the same wonderful reputation of cleanliness and the service leaves something to be desired. If you are feeling adventurous give it a try. Perhaps things have improved since their new schedules have been implemented.

RAILWAY TIMETABLE

Fares include both meals and bedding; the prices are for non-resident round-trip fares.

Destination	Departure time	Arrival time	1st, 2nd & 3rd Class
Nairobi-Mombasa	7:00 pm	8:05 am	$50, $35, $9
Mombasa-Nairobi	7:00 pm	8:40 am	
Nairobi-Kisumu	6:00 pm	7:10 am	$35, $24, $7
Kisumu-Nairobi	6:00 pm	6:20 am	
Nairobi-Kampala	Tues. 10:00 am	Wed. 8:55 am	$80, $64, $19.50
Kampala-Nairobi	Wed. 4:00 pm	Thur. 2:45 pm	

Please note that theft can be a problem on board so keep a close eye on your valuables and if possible keep them inside your shirt or touching your skin. It is always a good idea to lock your berth if you can when you are not there.

The door and windows of the overnight train are always locked to prevent thieves from jumping on at stops along the route. It would be circumspect to ask the porter if the keys are handy. Then in the event of an accident, these emergency exits could be opened quickly.

On March 24, 1999 a passenger train carrying foreign tourists and Kenyans to the coast derailed. Sadly, many were killed. A similar accident also took place in January 1993. I thought therefore I should comment on the aspect of train safety in Kenya. (Oddly enough, there were also two serious train wrecks with fatalities in the US around the same time).

As the trains have a tendency to break down, and this one in March did so several times during the night, the driver was trying to make up for lost time by going too fast. I still think however, that train travel in Kenya is relatively safe. Train travel is still a viable mode of transport for the local European population who continue to get to Mombasa this way. We can only hope that the engineers driving the trains have learned a valuable lesson – it is better to be late than not arrive at all.

The **Nairobi Station** is located on Station Road; **Mombasa Station** is on Haile Selassie Avenue; and **Kisumu Station** is on New Station Road. *For more information, call 221 211, extension 2700/1/1 in Nairobi.*

PHOTOGRAPHY

In 1977, Kenya banned all hunting. This of course encouraged the tourism industry to diversify and come up with an alternative – photography. Kenya naturally lends itself to creating the photographer's dream. The light is usually perfect and the abundance of colorful subjects will keep you taking frame after frame. Most of your game viewing while on safari will be in the early morning and late afternoon. This is when the game is active and therefore the best time to be driving around.

Two to three rolls of film (100 speed) for every game run is probably about average. Just in case of a low-light day, be prepared with some 400 speed film. To avoid missing the perfect photo opportunity, it is wise to come well prepared with a suitcase full of film and batteries. If you can't or don't use them, you can always take them home.

The prices for film are roughly the same as at home. A roll of 36 exposure Ektachrome 100 (color slide film) speed will cost about $9 and a roll of Kodak 200 speed 36 exposure color print film is roughly $6. I prefer to use 400 speed Fujichrome (slide film), which is a little harder to find.

Film and batteries are available in most of the small towns and of course in Nairobi and Mombasa. You won't be able to buy either of these items in the bush. Camera batteries may be more difficult to purchase than film. If your equipment requires special batteries, carry extras at all times. This is of particular importance in the higher altitudes, where you will notice the charge in your batteries does not last as long. It can be very annoying to hear your shutter speed slowing down at the most inopportune moment!

As you will probably be taking pictures from your safari vehicle, many people recommend a cushion or bean bag to steady your camera. I find this to be one more piece of junk I have to carry and keep up with. In my opinion this also applies to tripods and flash equipment. If you have to spend time carrying these around and making sure they are safe, it can distract you from what you are there to do – enjoy yourself. Opt to travel light.

PHOTO TIPS

Always ask before photographing native people. Generally they will expect you to pay them or offer a gift. The going rate seems to be under one dollar or KSh 10 or 20, but in the crowded tourist areas some tribes have been known to charge up to $10. It is up to you to decide if the photo is worth it or not.

Do not take pictures of military installations, police stations, airports, soldiers, police or border posts. If you are caught, at the very least they will confiscate your film and at the very worst you could end up in jail.

If you are using a 35mm camera and are taking pictures of people or scenery, I suggest a lens such as a fixed 50mm or a 35 to 135mm telephoto lens for your average photo taking opportunities. This lens selection allows you to take close-up shots of people, plants, buildings, scenery and anything other than wild animals.

To get up close and personal with the wildlife in Kenya, it is advisable to take a minimum of a 300mm lens. With anything under a 300, your photos will end up with the lion, elephant, or cheetah as a disappointingly small speck in the distance. It is very frustrating to be so close and yet so far when you have a lens that doesn't quite reach.

The dust can get rather tiresome while you are out in the bush. It has a tendency to get in the cracks around everything, including camera equipment. Bring adequate cleaning supplies to service your camera between outings. Lens covers help to protect equipment when not actually in use, as will a case or sealing plastic container of some kind.

The best advice I can give you when taking photos of wildlife is – be prepared. The animals are furtive and do not particularly like to pose for photos. You might only have a fraction of a second to get that shot of the leopard as he trots through the bush.

If you can't wait to get home to see your pictures, there are places in Nairobi that can develop your film in 24 hours. On the corner of Mama Ngina is the **Pioneer Cine Services Ltd.**, *Tel. 226 846*, and **Woolworth's**, *Tel. 335 011*, also advertises this service. On Kimathi Street across from the Thorn Tree Cafe, try the **Elite Camera House**, *Tel. 226 234*, for excellent services or **Expo Cameras**, *Tel. 221 797*, and **Camera Experts**, *Tel. 337 750*, on Mama Ngina. At any of these places you can rent or buy anything you need.

RECOMMENDED READING LIST

Glossy

Serengeti – Mitsuaki Iwago
African Ark – Angela Fisher
Africa Adorned – Angela Fisher
End of the Game – Peter Beard
Vanishing Africa – Mirella Riccardi
Visions of a Nomad – Wilfred Thesiger
An African Experience – Simon Combes

Animals

Almost Human – Shirley Strum (baboons)
Elephant Memories – Cynthia Moss (elephants)
A Field Guide to the Birds of East & Central Africa – John G. Williams

General

Nine Faces of Kenya – Elspeth Huxley
The Africans – David Lamb

Novels & Autobiographies

Out of Africa – Karen Blixen
My Pride & Joy – George Adamson
Snows of Kilimanjaro – Ernest Hemmingway
Flame Trees of Thika – Elspeth Huxley
West With Night – Beryl Markham

Historical

Lunatic Express – Charles Miller
Blue Nile – Alan Moorehead

White Nile – Alan Moorehead
Facing Mt. Kenya – Jomo Kenyatta
Kenya Vol. I and II – Elspeth Huxley

SAFARI CHECKLIST

Clothing
Tennis shoes
Hiking boots
Rubber thongs
Hats
Windbreaker/Jackets
Pullover sweater/sweatshirt
1 pair safari pants
1 pair jeans
3 pairs safari shorts
4 pairs sports socks
3 short sleeve shirts
2 long sleeve shirt
6 T-shirts
Pajamas
Swimsuit
1 pair dress shoes
2 casual evening outfits
6 sets of underwear
Belt

Toiletries
Malaria prophylactics
Motion sickness pills
Insect repellent
Sun screen
Lip balm
Shampoo
Conditioner
Deodorant
Toothpaste
Toothbrush
Dental floss
Hair brush
Comb
Razor

Emery board
Tweezers
Hand lotion
Feminine hygiene supplies
Toilet paper
Soap powder
Band-Aids
Antihistamine
Diarrhea medication
Antacids
Eye drops
Pain relievers

Sundries
Empty duffel bag
Passport
Health cards
Air tickets/vouchers
Money pouch
Credit cards
Travelers checks
Calculator
Sunglasses/case
Books/journal/maps
Binoculars
Flashlight
Sewing kit
Scissors

Camera Equipment
Camera body
Extra batteries
Telephoto lens (300)
Cleaning equipment
Film
Zip lock bags
Camera case

7. BASIC INFORMATION

BANKING & MONEY

The Kenyan currency is **shillings** (KSh), also called "Bob" as a slang term. It is divided into 100 cents and based on the decimal system. Shilling notes are in denominations of 10, 20, 50, 100, 200 and 500. Coins are denominated in 5, 10, and 50 cent pieces. Finally, there are 1 and 5 shilling coins. The 5 and 10 cent pieces are copper, while the 50 cent piece and the 1 and 5 shilling coins are silver. To check the most current exchange rate try *www.xe.net/currency* on the web.

"**Tourist prices**" are Kenya's non-resident rates for hotels, museums, game parks, and safaris. To pay the resident rates for entry to tourist attractions and parks, a valid Kenya driver's license as an ID is all that is required. Outside of this two-price policy and excluding gasoline and car rental, Kenya is comparatively cheap.

Travelers checks are readily accepted in Mombasa and Nairobi, but you might have trouble changing one if you are in a local market or the bush. It is best to plan ahead and cash a few checks before you leave for your rural destination. Any amount of travelers checks can be brought into the country and there is no limit on how much you can spend.

To change travelers checks or money up until about a year ago, you needed a currency declaration form. You were given one when you arrived and if one wasn't offered, it was best to ask for one. This form was needed in order to buy international airline tickets in Kenya and was collected at departure time by the customs agents. This is no longer the case. In an effort to improve relations with tourists and reduce the hassles at departure time, officials have seen fit to eliminate this policy.

EXCHANGE RATE

As of this writing, the exchange rate was 64.87 shillings to the US dollar. In other words, $1.00 US = 64.87 KES.

As a precaution, when changing money always get a receipt and keep it until you have safely left Kenya. If there should be any question about how much money you brought in, you'll have proof that should be good enough to dissuade any official from pursuing the matter.

Generally changing money is no problem at all. There are many exchange booths prominently advertised wherever there are tourists to be found. These small cubbyholes are referred to as **Bureau de Change** or exchange counters. If you can't find an exchange counter to do business with, there should be a bank around somewhere. At least one bank in the smaller towns will happily change US dollars. In the larger cities of Nairobi and Mombasa most banks will handle foreign exchange. The rate of exchange should be the same everywhere, as it is set daily by the Central Bank of Kenya.

Banks are open 9 am to 2 pm Monday through Friday. On the first and last Saturday of each month, the banks open from 9 am to 11 am. You will find the airport exchange desks open 24 hours a day in Mombasa and Nairobi.

The larger hotels and inns exchange money for their guests but may have a limit of $100. In the game parks there are no banks, so while on safari, you will have no choice but to use the lodges for exchange purposes. Most shops in the tourist areas will accept foreign currency at the going rate of exchange.

All good hotels, restaurants, nightclubs, and shops will take your credit cards. Visa and MasterCard are the two most widely accepted. Before you pay with a credit card, make sure no additional charges will be added for its use.

Except for a couple of shillings, the official word is that no local currency can leave the country. Upon leaving, you can change your local Kenyan currency back into US dollars at the airport bank if you have the receipts showing your original exchange transactions. Expect the rate to be low and also expect to be charged a steep commission. You are better off not converting too much money at once unless you're sure it will be spent by the end of your stay.

At the airport each individual will have to pay a **$20 departure tax**. Up until a year ago, the only currency that was not accepted was Kenya shillings. This foolish policy has been changed to include shillings. Travelers checks will not be accepted. For a quick departure, it is best to have exact change ready.

Finally, it is considered a serious offense to destroy or mutilate Kenyan currency in any way. The people feel that by defacing the picture of the president on the money, you are insulting the position he represents. Perhaps this is a silly notion, but the local officials can make your stay very miserable if they choose to do so.

BUSINESS HOURS & ETIQUETTE

Most businesses are open from 8 am to 1 pm and 2 pm to 5 pm during the week. You will find a few individual businesses open on Saturdays from 8:30 am to 12:30 pm. If you need a pharmacy, they generally are open from 8 am to 8 pm, and you should be able to find at least one open later than that.

Dealing with local business people can be a frustrating and lengthy process. The promises will be sincere and the smiles genuine, but quick action may not be forthcoming. Hopefully this won't be the case if you follow a few simple guidelines.

If you need to meet with someone, make an appointment and reconfirm. If you have a set time and place to meet you will have a better chance of actually hooking up with the person you need to see. As Kenyans have a tendency to run late or not show up at all, polite reconfirmation will serve as a good reminder.

Always shake hands at the start and finish of every meeting. A handshake is considered basic good manners in Kenya and will buy you trust. A handshake acts as a seal on a deal or is seen as a gesture of goodwill.

Before jumping into the business at hand, Africans like to have a social chat. It is considered polite to inquire about their health and their families. The conversation does not need to get too detailed or lengthy. Show you are interested in their well being. In the long run, you will get more accomplished if you follow this general rule of etiquette.

Networking in Kenya is a very valuable resource. If you are a member of any kind of club (such as the Lions Club) or organization that has a membership in Kenya, use the contact to your advantage. If not, a great place to meet business people is at the larger and central pubs and bars. In Mombasa, try the **Castle Hotel** and in Nairobi the **Norfolk**.

COST OF TRAVEL

Transport Costs

The price of car rentals in Kenya is expensive. You can count on $300 to $750 per week for a four-wheel drive (4WD). In addition, there is a 20 cent per mile charge for anything over 300 miles. For a more compact vehicle, count on at least $300 per week. The bad news is that this price will not include taking the vehicle into the bush.

Public transportation is reasonably priced and usually runs on a fairly regular basis. When one bus is full, they send another one along. The average person in the street does not own a car and must rely on this mode of transport. Buses going around town are cheap but can be a less than pleasant experience. The custom is to pack as many people as possible into the bus. This might be up to 80 people on a bus that should only hold 40.

The trains offer a great opportunity to see Kenya if you have the time. To get from Mombasa on the coast all the way across Kenya to the western border will only cost around $50 in first class and $35 in second class. In the third class compartments it will be roughly $10. This is a wonderful way to travel and you should take advantage of the option if you can.

Park Entry Fees

If you are venturing off on your own and have a car which you want to take into the reserves or parks, you will have to pay an entry fee. The fee is roughly $27 per person plus a few dollars for the vehicle itself. If you plan to spend the night, add another five dollars or so to your budget.

Safari Costs

Safaris fluctuate widely in price and what they include varies just as much. A standard safari of nine nights and ten days with a group of six to eighteen people costs around $2,480 per person. The rates go up from there. This is an average price for a reasonably good view of Kenya and includes airfare, transport, food, tents, entry fees to the parks, guides and a cook.

Food & Drink Costs

Soft drinks and beer prices were regulated by the government up until not that long ago. At a Class D establishment (any non-tourist hotel), the local beer (Pilsner, Tusker, and Whitecap) is about $1.20 to $1.85 and sodas (Coke, Pepsi and Fanta) are 75 cents.

If you find one café in a town, you have usually found them all. For not much more than you would pay at home you can try a delicious traditional meal surrounded by the local residents who also frequent these restaurants. In an establishment patronized by the general public, you can count on the food being reasonably priced as well as tasty.

The Indian restaurants seem to be the greatest value and the most consistent in quality. The quantities served by these restaurants are generous with one portion being enough for two people. After lunch at one of these places, you'll be satisfied for the rest of the day. All this will cost you anywhere from $4 to $15.

Lodging Costs

Lodging in Kenya is easy to find and usually adequate. Often in the cheaper places you will share a bathroom (toilets and showers). In the establishments that are priced at rock bottom, you sometimes may not get soap and towels but you can always count on clean sheets.

Prices start at $1.50 for a single and $3 for a double and go up from there. If you are uncomfortable about sharing a bathroom, and are willing to pay for your privacy, the prices go up from $4 single and $6.50 double on up to $500. Accommodations in Lamu, along the coast, cost less than in either Mombasa or Nairobi.

ELECTRICITY

In most places the power supply is fairly reliable, but there are periods when blackouts occur. It has been this way for a long time and there isn't much anyone can do about changing the way the system runs. It is best to take it in stride and eventually the power will come back on.

In instances when the power fails due to a storm or excessive demands, it is smart to have a flashlight as a backup. As you unpack your suitcase, strategically place your flashlight within reach. If you get caught in the dark, you will know exactly where to find the light. (Due to the altitude, batteries have a tendency not to last as long so carry a few extras in your luggage. It never hurts to be prepared.)

Electricity is 220 volts. If you plan on bringing electrical equipment, make sure you bring along adapters or converters. Personally I find this to be more trouble than it's worth and would rather do without while I'm in Kenya.

The lodges and safari camps always have their own generators as there is no other source of power around. Be prepared to have the lights turned off at about 10 pm. If you want to read or move about in your room, ask for a lantern or bring a flashlight adequate enough to do the job.

HEALTH CONCERNS

Compared to many other countries in the world, Kenya is a relatively healthy country to visit. As always, use common sense and listen to your body. If it is telling you it is thirsty – drink! While the list of potential dangers may seem quite daunting, with a few precautions and adequate information you should have no trouble at all. Only a few of the hundreds of thousands of visitors each year have health emergencies and those usually don't have anything to do with the fact they are in Kenya.

When you return home at the end of your safari, if you start to feel ill in any way, it is strongly recommended that you visit your doctor and inform him you have been traveling in Kenya. This will allow him to look for possible illnesses that he would not normally look for.

Rather than tell you all manner of woes from travel in the tropics, I will cover the most obvious and common health problems found in Kenya. I also suggest you contact the Centers for Disease Control &

Prevention (CDC) (*(888) 232-3228, www.cdc.gov*), chase any of the excellent books on tropical travel ava book is Open Road Publishing's *CDC's Complete Guide to*

Pharmacies

Pharmacies, or **chemists** as they are called in Kenya, are found ju about everywhere, except the smaller villages and of course, game parks. You'll be surprised to find their prices reasonable and their selection of goods more than adequate.

Many of the chemists are open 24 hours in case you should have a minor emergency. There is no problem trusting whatever the pharmacist recommends, as they are usually well trained professionals much the same as at home.

If you require special or continuing medications, you are better off bringing your own sure supply. However, many drugs that are available at home only with a prescription can be purchased over the counter in Kenya. As a precaution, check the expiration date on anything you buy.

Medical Facilities

Main towns around Kenya have good health care facilities and in the rural areas, there are basic hospitals, clinics and local missions. During your trip, the closest of these places will take care of any urgent and immediate medical needs but insurance of some kind is advisable (see the section ahead on Flying Doctors).

Nairobi has a reputation for excellent specialist medical facilities. These operations are often staffed by American and British trained doctors and dentists who are equipped to handle any problems you might come up with.

If you choose to go to any of the premium private clinics the cost will increase significantly but the drugs, service, and equipment will be more like what you are accustomed to at home. These clinics are run by Asians and chiefly service their own communities in Kenya.

Most major hotels and resorts have some sort of medical officer. If you need help, check in with this person first. If he is not equipped to handle the problem he will get you to the nearest medical agency.

The best hospitals in the country are:
- **Nairobi Hospital**, *Argwings Kodhek Road, Nairobi. Tel. 721 160, Fax 728 003*
- **The Aga Kahn Hospital**, *3rd Avenue, Parklands, Nairobi. Tel. 740 000*
- **Mombasa Hospital**, *Tel. 312 190*

These hospitals will provide excellent care. If you feel the need for a more comprehensive list, check the yellow pages or *What's On* magazine.

on for two months, visitors can enjoy
ying Doctors' Society of Africa (FDSA).
sly ill person to free emergency evacua-
,ya to Nairobi and care once they arrive.
en days a week, the non-profit FDSA has
providing health care to tourists and rural
fully equipped medical rescue aircraft on
aff are all highly qualified physicians, nurses
a..

The ..., .n arrange to have their patients transferred
from a hospital in ... to Jomo Kenyatta International Airport and on
to the US in a commercial or chartered aircraft. If requested, a flight nurse
will escort the patient to their destination.

For more detailed information and an application, contact :
• **The Flying Doctors' Society of Africa**, *PO Box 30125, Nairobi. Tel. 501
3001/2/3 or 500 508, Fax 502 699*

AIDS

There are over 750,000 people in Kenya between the ages of 20 and
40 with AIDS. If you were to take the enormous risk of sleeping with any
of the numerous partners available, have the good sense to use a condom.

If you need a blood transfusion, contact the American Embassy.
There is a list of donors who are not infected and may be able to give blood
on your behalf. It may even be possible to get blood from a local supply
stored in a blood bank.

Inoculations

Certificates of inoculation against yellow fever and cholera are
advised by the US Health Department but are not mandatory when
traveling from the United States. If you are coming from the Far East
where cholera may be a problem, or from Central America or other
regions of Africa where yellow fever are found, it may be mandatory to
have inoculations and the certificates to prove it.

The charge for both the yellow fever and cholera inoculations in the
US will run you about $40 each if you decide to get them before you fly.
The inoculations must be administered al least two weeks before your trip
and cannot be given at the same time. Apparently there can be negative
reactions if they are dispensed together. Allow at least two months to get
the full set of inoculations as the shots cannot all be given at the same time.

When you apply for your Kenyan visa, make your trip arrangements
with a travel agent or purchase your ticket from the airlines, check to make
sure the rules regarding health inoculations have not changed.

Malaria

Malaria seems to be the biggest worry for tourists in Kenya an so, as it can be a killer. Malaria is endemic to many parts of the co but is more prevalent in low lying areas, the most affected areas being coast and Lake Victoria where there is a lot of standing water an swampland. There is generally no risk in Nairobi and areas above 2,500 meters.

It is a wise precaution to start taking anti-malaria prophylactics two to six weeks before arriving. This treatment must continue throughout your stay and go on for four weeks after leaving. The CDC recommends undertaking chemoprophylaxis with mefloquine.

A drug commonly used is **Paludrine**. It is not available in the US, but in Kenya it can be purchased over the counter. The adult dose is 200 milligrams per day, usually taken with food. For children 33 pounds or less, half a tablet a day; under 66 pounds, one tablet a day; and under 100 pounds, one and a half tablets a day.

Larium has surfaced as the latest in medication for the possible prevention of malaria. In my experience, it does more harm than good. The stories of people getting deathly ill after taking Laruim for a few weeks are common. Even if your physician strongly suggests you take it, I would think twice.

For more and detailed information on preventive malaria medications and advisories call the **CDC** (Center for Disease Control) *(888) 232-3228*, or try their web site at *www.cdc.gov.*

BILHARZIA PARASITE WARNING

*Avoid swimming in lakes or slow-moving water, particularly **Lake Victoria**, where the parasite **bilharzia** is prolific. This tiny parasite is carried by a particular species of freshwater snails. The snails release microscopic worms into the water. These worms must then find a host to burrow into in order to survive. After painfully tunneling their way in, the worms attack and destroy the larger organs such as the liver. Once you have acquired the parasite, there is no guarantee of a cure from this agonizing and debilitating disease.*

The best way to avoid malaria is to avoid the mosquito that carries it. Use the net over your bed, at night wear long sleeves if possible, and use insect repellent with DEET.

Malaria can be cured if it is caught soon enough. If you so much as suspect you have it and are feeling flu-like symptoms, even months after your trip, get to a doctor quickly.

very deceptive and can cause severe burns if you
ared. The high altitude and closeness to the
n faster. Even an overcast day will not prevent
burned. Plan on covering yourself with a high
This is not only true at the coast but also while
of Kenya.

...ly important to protect your eyes. I learned the hard way
that my light colored eyes have a tendency to get burned. The red stinging
sensation I endured for days could easily have been avoided if I had used
sunglasses!

Water

In Nairobi and most municipal areas, the water is generally drinkable.
As a tourist however, it may be better to stick to bottled water to avoid the
possible upset stomach from having to make the adjustment to local
water. Anywhere outside the city, the water should be boiled.

Sometimes when you are on safari, drinking contaminated water may
be the only choice you have. If you are going to travel, this is a risk you
must be willing to take but there is no reason you shouldn't be prepared.
Sterotabs, Halazone, and Potable Aqua are just a few of the brand name
water purifying tablets on the market today. These are fine for some water
but will be ineffective against hepatitis and amoebas. Instead, I recommend that you carry a 2 per cent tincture of iodine. Add five drops to a
gallon of clear water or ten drops in a gallon of cloudy water and wait thirty
minutes. This should solve all your water drinking problems.

With the European influence in Kenya, you will notice very few
people, other than American tourists, using ice in their drinks. It is the
custom here to have drinks warm. If you are unable to adapt to this, it is
advisable to find out what kind of water was used to make the ice in your
drink.

Most hotels and lodges provide bottles or flasks of filtered drinking
water in guest rooms. Both local and imported mineral water can be
purchased in supermarkets, kiosks, and hotel shops. While on safari, it is
probably a good idea to use this water when you brush your teeth even if
you don't plan on swallowing it. Why take the chance?

Dehydration

Because of the high altitude, heat, sun and plane travel, dehydration
can be a problem. Take water with you whenever you plan on being on
the road for any length of time. Dehydration can happen quickly when
you don't drink enough and often catches you off guard. If you begin to
have headaches, feel dizzy or nauseous, start drinking. These symptoms

may be caused by something other than dehydration so if they persist after you rehydrate, check in with a doctor.

Altitude

If you are planning on climbing any of the mountains in Kenya, particularly Mount Kenya, it is advisable to use caution. Anywhere above 11,000 feet you will notice the effects of the altitude in the form of mountain or altitude sickness.

The symptoms to look for are nausea, loss of appetite, sleeplessness, swelling, mood swings and headaches. To help prevent becoming a victim, take time during your ascent to allow your body to acclimatize to the thin air, altitude, and temperature. Youth, strength, and fitness make no difference with altitude sickness.

This illness can be fatal if not dealt with immediately. The results of continued climbing will be pulmonary oedema or waterlogged lungs, and cerebral oedema, also known as waterlogged brain which ultimately results in death.

HOLIDAYS

• **December 26**, Boxing Day
• **December 25**, Christmas Day
• **December 12**, Jamhuri Day (Independence/Republic Day)
• **October 20**, Kenyatta Day (Anniversary of the day Kenyatta was arrested)
• **October 10**, Moi Day (President Moi's inauguration day)
• **June 1**, Madaraka (self-rule) Day
• **May 1**, Labor Day
• **March/April**, Good Friday/Easter Monday
• **January 1**, New Year's Day

For public holidays falling on a Sunday, the following Monday is observed as the official holiday.

There are various festivals celebrated at different times of the year but these are local affairs and shouldn't affect your stay. The two largest are **Idd-Ul-Fitr** and **Maulidi** which mark the end of the month in which the Prophet was born. Both are held at different times each year for the Muslim population. The Maulidi festival at Lamu is akin to the pilgrimage to Mecca, with thousands of people parading and dancing in the streets.

POST OFFICES

The post offices are open from 8 am to 5 pm Monday through Friday and from 8 am to 1 pm on Saturdays. As a whole, the postal system is reliable but slow. Letters eventually arrive but packages or money tend to disappear. The method of *poste restante* (where you sort your own mail from the pile) is often the norm at the post office. In this way, people receiving letters get some relief from the feeling that their mail is in the wrong pigeon hole.

When sending mail to Kenya, make sure you write clearly and underline the last name as sorting can be less than perfect if they have any doubt about which letter of the alphabet to file under. A letter back to the US from Kenya will cost you about 97 cents and usually take roughly seven days to arrive at its destination.

If you find yourself with excess baggage at the end of your trip or you just don't want to carry it all, consider the parcel post. It will take four or five months to arrive, but it will get there and save you the trouble of trekking around with extra stuff. Do not wrap your parcel until it has been examined by the post office custom's official.

SHOPPING

Shopping hours are usually 8:30 am to 5:30 pm Monday through Saturday. Be prepared to take a break during the lunch hour from 1 pm to 2 pm as many of the shops are closed.

The two main shopping areas are **Nairobi** and **Mombasa**. This is where the most people are concentrated and eventually where the tourists must pass through on their way to or from anywhere. Shopping selections in these two cities is great but if you miss the opportunity, don't panic. Wherever you go there will be at least one shop with a few souvenirs and trinkets.

Shopping in Kenya is a fun experience as there is always much to choose from. As soon as you are recognized as a potential sale, a crowd will form around you and the sales pitch begins. It is sometimes difficult not to feel sorry for them and buy things you don't really want. If you cave in, you'll end up with more baubles than you know what to do with.

The first price tossed your way will usually be whatever they think they can get away with. As an American you automatically have the wrong

STOLEN COPPER

Common items for sale along your safari route will be bracelets, earrings, and bangles made from shiny copper-wire. These trinkets are pretty and make lightweight gifts for friends at home. Bear in mind, the next time you can't make a telephone call, where the copper-wire came from – the copper wire used in the telephone lines is often stolen by the Kenyan tribespeople, as it makes great jewelry.

accent. Obviously, anyone with an American accent must have money! With this being the general impression of Americans, the cost of the item in question will at least double.

The **baskets** in Kenya are an excellent purchase. Generally made by Africans for Africans, the straw baskets can take much abuse and are very well made. Sisal **kiondos** are often popular as handbags. The array of choices both as far as color and size can be overwhelming. You will find laundry baskets, handbags, jewelry boxes, trays, placemats and all sorts of other colorful woven goods to take home.

Wood carvings are found all over Kenya. The **makonde** statues are very popular with tourists. These usually depict groups of people sometimes carved in abstract forms. Napkin rings, salad utensils, bowls, different sized animals, masks, statues and swizzle sticks are just a few other items you'll see. There is always a wide price range for these souvenirs depending on what kind of wood was used. The shopkeepers

SOUVENIR PRICE CHART

A friend of mine living in Nairobi told me something I'll never forget – "if you see a souvenir you like and it's worth the asking price to you, then buy it." This is how I feel about shopping in Kenya. If you think something is pricey then it's not worth it.

The quality and size will play a considerable part in the prices of souvenirs, but as a rough guide here are what you should aim for when bargaining:

Bow – $20

Arrows (4) – $15

Quiver – $15

Long throwing spear – $100

Gourds – $5 to $25

Clubs – $3 to $10

Sisal baskets – $4 to $25

Kikoi – $2 to $5

Shuka – $4

Soapstone (small) –$.50 to 10

Wood carvings of people – $15 to $25

Masks – $75 to $400

Beaded leather (cushions) – $25 to $250

Leather ottomans – $50 to $100

Three legged stools – $10 to $25

Earrings – 50¢ to $3

will tell you it is the well known and expensive ebony but don't take their word for it. Instead, use a fingernail to scratch the base of the carving. If it is a fake, the shoe polish will come off under your nail and the light color of the sham wood will show under your scratch.

Two of my favorite items are the **leather goods** and the cleverly made **earrings**. Cushions, three legged Masai stools with leather seats, and **poufs** (ottomans) are hand made out of cow hide. Colorful beads are carefully sown onto the leather in flattering designs and combinations. The earrings, which come in all lengths and creations are usually hand made and one of a kind.

It would be hard to mention every shop, stand, market and stall in Kenya as there are hundreds. All it takes for a shop to open is for someone to throw down a blanket and cover it with trinkets. The tour guides often have a pre-arranged deal with certain shops and will guide you that way.

If the first stop on your Kenya tour is Nairobi, a word of caution is in order. Don't buy everything here. While you are on safari, there will be many opportunities to buy from the local craftsmen at what may be better prices. You can always stop back here on your way out of the country.

TELEPHONES & FAXES

Local and trunk calls are quite straightforward. In most towns you will find phone boxes just about everywhere which stay in working order. Sometimes the lines of people waiting to use the phone can be four or five deep but generally this is not a problem.

An efficient subscriber trunk dialing service (STD) is available for sending faxes and for making local and international calls. The lodges are all connected to their head offices by radio and also to the post office radio telephone system.

To make arrangements with tour operators, hotels and safari outfitters from the US it is easiest and quickest to send faxes. You will find that the response time is fast and you will get your bookings done in record time. To send a fax from the US, dial the **country code 254 2** and the number. To send faxes from Kenya to the US is also a quick way to communicate but may cost a little more.

If you are out in the countryside and need to make a call, find the telephone lines and follow them to their source; usually a shop. Be courteous to the owner and try to negotiate some arrangement whereby you can use his phone.

To use the phone to make a local call, make sure and insert a KSh 1 coin first, regardless of what you put in after that, or you may have trouble making the call. The phones will only accept either a KSh 1 or 5 coin. For long distance calls, you can either go through the operator or dial the number yourself using a **phone card**. Phone cards are available from the post office in denominations of KSh 200, 400, or 1000. After each call, a display will show how much credit you have left on your card. For $3.70, you will get about a three minute call to the US. Telephones that accept phone cards are available at the **Extelcom** building on Haile Selassie Avenue in Nairobi and the main post offices.

IMPORTANT NUMBERS

To call from the US, initiate the call with 011 then Kenya's country code – 254 – and your city code (2 for Nairobi) and the number.
International Dialing Code for Nairobi : 254 2
Operator: 900
Placing a call & International Information: 0191
Directory Assistance: 991
International STD: 000 or 001
International Operator: 0196
Fax: (to send a fax to Nairobi, dial 254 2 and the number)
Police, Fire, Ambulance: 999

International calls are fairly easy to make from Kisumu, Mombasa, and Nairobi. In other towns, you may want to use an operator connected call from the post office. It is important to note that the Extelcom's office (for operator assisted calls) in Nairobi is only open from 8 am to midnight.

If you are making a call from one of the larger hotels in Kenya, be prepared to pay a 50 to 100 per cent surcharge. You are better off calling from the **Kenyatta Conference Centre** (City Square, Nairobi), where it is relatively quiet and has an international call office in the lobby.

TIME

Kenya is 7 to 8 hours ahead of Eastern Standard Time, depending on daylight savings time. When it is noon in Kenya, it is 4 am in New York and 1 am on the West Coast of the US. Time is Greenwich Mean Time (GMT) plus three hours all year round. If it is April 15, 1999, 11:00 am in Atlanta, in Kenya it is April 15, 1999 6:00 pm. A good web site for more detailed international time information is *www.swiss.info.net*.

As Kenya is on the equator you can count on the sun setting rapidly. Sunrise and sunset vary only by thirty minutes for the entire year. Sunset is at 6:30 pm and sunrise is 6:30 am. Twelve hours of daylight is consistent year round. It is best not to be caught outside near sunset as it can be dangerous after dark, both from the point of view of four footed and two footed animals.

TIPPING

Unlike the US, Africans regard tipping as more of a gift than wages earned. If you wish to show your gratitude for good service, by all means leave an extra tip.

Tipping is often optional in Kenya as a 10 to 15 percent gratuity is usually built into hotel and restaurant bills. Most of the time this information isn't forthcoming, so it is best to ask before you leave an additional tip. A small stipend ($1) is adequate for luggage handling and other such aid. Taxis and bar services do not require a tip.

When your safari experience is over, leave a good tip; $5 per person per day for your guides/drivers is adequate, if your staff served you well. A good tip will be a great motivator to continue to do an excellent job.

In order that you don't end up tipping twice, check to make sure your tour operator hasn't taken care of the gratuities already. In some instances, the compensation may have been added to the original purchase price of your tour.

While traveling on your own or out in the more rural areas, take along cigarettes, ball-point pens and/or cheap digital watches to use as "gifts" in exchange for a photo or some necessity. The Africans always welcome a gift as a sign of trust and friendship. You will get what you want more quickly if you show this courtesy.

WHERE TO GET MORE INFORMATION

The only tourist offices in Kenya are the ones in Mombasa and Nairobi. In Nairobi the **Kenya Tourist Development Corporation** on City Hall Way is near the Hilton Hotel. *For information, write to PO Box 30471 Nairobi, or call 21855.* The hours are from 8:30 am to 12:30 pm and 2:00 pm to 5:00 pm Monday through Saturday.

If you have Internet access try the following addresses for weather updates, daily news and other information: *www.kenyaweb.com, www.bwanazulia.com, everythingafrica.com, www.seekenya.com, www.nationaudio.com, www.abercrombiekent.com, www.hotelstravel.com/kenya.*

The **Mombasa Information Bureau** is located on Moi Avenue next to the giant elephant tusks. Business hours are from 8:00 am to 12 noon and 2:00 pm to 5:00 pm Monday through Saturday. *For information, call 311 231 or 225 428.*

In spite of these two information offices, it will be surprising to you how little tourist information there is in Kenya. The three booklets below are free and offer some interesting local information. Pick them up at any of the major hotels or bookstores but don't expect the facts to necessarily be up to date. Data includes a list of car rental agencies, safari organizers, major hotels, train schedules, ferry schedules and notable airlines.

The three are:
- **Tourist's Kenya** (weekly), *PO Box 40025, Tel. 337 169*
- **What's On** (monthly), *PO Box 49010, Tel. 728 290/7*
- **Tourists Index** (monthly), *PO Box 9165, Tel. 26206*

In the US, there are two **Kenya Tourist Offices**:
- *9100 Wilshire Boulevard, Doheney Plaza, Suite 111, Beverly Hills, CA 90121*
- *60 East 56th Street, New York, NY 10022*

US citizens are encouraged to register with the **US Embassy**. To fax information, passport data and itinerary *(254 2) 743 204, 749 590 or 749 892*. In Kenya, the US Embassy is located at the *USAID Building, PO Box 30137, The Crescent, Nairobi, Kenya, Tel. (254 2) 751-613*. For after-hours emergency situations, the Embassy duty officer can be contacted at *(254 2) 751 871*. If you have serious trouble, contact the embassy and they should be able to offer you good advice and perhaps get you out of a jam.

Because of the bombing of the embassy which took place in August of 1998, the numbers and address are temporary. The services offered are only emergency consular services until it is determined when routines can be resumed. The design and rebuilding of the embassy will take four to five years. The Kenya government has allocated Washington a site in Nairobi's industrial area district.

The bomb site has remained vacant and will be turned into a memorial garden for the 250 bomb victims.

Two books that can be of service to you either before you get to Kenya or while you are there are: *The Camping Guide to Kenya* (Bradt), is a comprehensive guide to all the camp sites in Kenya; both in the cities and parks. It's full of information for backpackers who wish to venture off the main tracks by themselves. *Mountain Walking in Kenya* (Robertson-McCarta), offers a wide selection of easy strolls or mountain expeditions all over Kenya. Included are maps, and equipment suggestions.

In Kenya there are several international organizations that may be of service if you need it. There is a **United Nations Complex** at Giri, about seven miles from the center of the city. In the complex you'll find the **United Nations Environment Programme** (UNEP), *Tel. 333 930*, and the **United Nations Centre for Human Settlements** (HABITAT), *Tel. 332 383*. Other helpful organizations are the **World Health Organization** (WHO), *Cathedral Road, Tel. 720 050*, and the **United Nations Educational Scientific and Cultural Organization**, *Tel. 25861/2/3/8*.

There are three major English language newspapers in Kenya; *The Nation*, *The Standard*, and the *Kenya Times*. All three come out on a daily basis. Of the three, the one that will supply you with the most information is probably *The Nation*.

The government-owned **Kenya Broadcasting Corporation** runs the main English language radio station and the only nationwide TV station. If you are within the Nairobi environs you will be able to pick up a TV channel which is partly owned by CNN and offers superior programming.

SAFETY

As you read this section on safety keep in mind that most of these warnings are extreme. Don't let the words of caution scare you or stop you from coming to this natural wonderland. Kenya is a fabulous country and, unless you are very unlucky or take unnecessary risks, you will have one of the most wonderful experiences of your entire life. Use common sense as you would if you were in any foreign country in the world and you will be fine.

In Cities & Towns

Some people in Nairobi are very good at playing on a tourist's emotions and gullibility. Crowds have a tendency to form rather quickly and you will hear every sob story from the "sick mother" to "someone stole my bus ticket." It may seem harsh but it is best to ignore all these requests for money.

Kenya does not lend itself to expensive jewelry or fancy baubles. Unless you plan on going out to dinner at a very fancy restaurant or someone's house, leave these at home. You will save yourself the worry of keeping up with them and using a hotel safe.

If you decide you can't part with your jewels, lock them in a strongbox when you don't have them on. It is also best not to put valuables in your suitcase when you travel as they sometimes disappear.

It is not uncommon to find pick-pockets in crowded public places or to have your purse snatched by a quick thief. A money belt worn around your neck or waist inside your shirt will avoid the risk. Fanny packs are a little safer but slashing the belt is not a problem for practiced thieves.

Don't take more money than you need when you go out for a day of sightseeing. With this precaution, if you are robbed you can part with the money without ruining your vacation. If you do find yourself in this predicament, give up the money. It is not worth the risk of being hurt if you refuse.

Should you become an unfortunate victim and require the assistance of the police department, be prepared to face a long drawn-out procedure. The results will probably not be to your satisfaction and it is best not to expect too much. Unless you need a police report for your insurance company, I recommend not involving the local police at all.

DIRE CONSEQUENCES

If you yell "thief" the consequences can be serious for the perpetrator if he is caught. The crowd has a tendency to go crazy and sometimes inflicts serious harm on the robber. One of the more ghastly forms of punishment a wild crowd will administer is to pin the thief in a car tire, pour gasoline all over him, and set him on fire!

If you find yourself out at night, don't walk, even if it is just a few blocks. It is not worth ending up in a hospital or worse. Muggings are not very common, but they have been known to happen.

In rural Kenya, the problem is bandits or **shifta**. These are generally refugees who have nothing and were forced to flee from neighboring Uganda, Somalia, Sudan, or Ethiopia. The famine, war, and drought has taken a heavy toll on the lives of these people and forced them into exile.

The Kenyan government is doing everything it can to ensure the safety of tourists. Tourism supports a large part of Kenya's economy and as such vacationers are highly valued. You will see the local police or **askari** patrolling the roads and sometimes the game parks and preserves.

It is very common to see road blocks on all well-traveled roads. There are two or three policemen in uniform inspecting randomly selected cars as they drive by. They are checking to make sure the inspection stickers are valid and that the car is not stolen. The check points consist of two strips of wood about five feet long and a foot wide staggered so as to allow a car to pass between them. The wooden boards are covered with ten inch long nails. The sharp end of the nail sticks up into the air and will certainly ruin any tires that dare run over them.

If you plan on going off on your own, inquire carefully and listen to what the locals and police say about the unsafe areas. While on the road at dusk, find a safe place and stop for the night. Resume your journey the next day.

In The Bush

The animals you see are in no way, shape, or form tame and should be treated for what they are – wild. In the national parks you will be shown around by a guide and asked to follow a few rules. These may seem silly to you but they will keep you safe.

Some basic rules of survival are:

When you are with a guide follow his instructions to the letter. If he tells you not to run, don't; it may save your life. He knows this bush and can spot an animal long before you can. Don't question his decisions.

Always shake out your shoes and sleeping bag before putting in your feet. This is a favorite place for snakes and scorpions. Remember to do this if you get up in the middle of the night for a bathroom visit.

If you should be bitten by anything, seek medical attention immediately. The venom of some of Kenya's poisonous snakes will kill within 30 minutes. Scorpion bites are painful but you will not die from one. Get a rabies and tetanus shot along with other treatment. As you walk around, keep an eye on where you put your feet. The more noise you make the more likely you are to scare away any snakes. (Unfortunately, this will also scare away any wildlife you are trying to catch a glimpse of). If you sit on a rock or the ground check around carefully. Wear hiking boots in the bush; if you step on a thorn or a snake they might offer some protection.

Don't ever feed the animals. This teaches them to be dependent on humans and can cause problems when no one feeds them. These creatures are wild and unpredictable and will bite for no apparent reason. Monkeys are some of the worst offenders when it comes to begging or stealing food. Don't encourage it.

Stay in your car unless you are told by your guide to get out. Animals may not seem to be aware of you, but they are. If they feel threatened in any way, they will turn from docile to fierce in no time at all. This is particularly true if there are young in the area.

WEIGHTS & MEASURES

The metric system is the accepted form of weights and measure in Kenya. Pounds are converted to kilograms and ounces are converted to grams. Multipy the ounces or pounds by the corresponding number of grams or kilograms and to convert the other way, divide.
• **1 ounce** (oz) = 28.35 grams (g)
• **1 pound** (LB) = 0.454 kilograms (kg)

CONVERSION TABLE

From	To	Multiply By
Miles	Kilometers	1.6090
Acres	Hectares	0.4047
Gallons	Liters	3.785
Inches	Centimeters	2.54
Feet	Meters	0.3048
Yards	Meters	0.9144

To convert the other way around, say from kilometers to miles, divide instead of multiply.

8. ECO-TOURISM & KENYA'S WILDLIFE

GOING ON A TOUR

If this is your first trip to Kenya, I suggest you use a reliable tour organizer and allow them to plan much of your trip for you. If there is anything in particular you have read or heard about and want to see while traveling, let the travel agent know and they can find a tour that includes your selections.

Most safari operators have standard tours already put together for tourists. Competition is very healthy for your tourist dollar and everyone is willing to bend over backwards to give you what you want. Usually all you have to do is ask.

As always, the pleasure and uniqueness of your visit, no matter where you journey, will go up in proportion to the money you spend. The second most crucial factor after money is time. The more time you have to see the myriad of sights in Kenya the more you will enjoy the trip.

It is best to book your tour well in advance especially during the peak season between Christmas and Easter and in August. If your tour operator is worth his salt, you will spend most of your visit seeing the things you want to see and not much time backtracking. Your stay will be arranged so you really shouldn't have to worry about getting around, accommodations, or finding the best attractions. A pre-planned excursion is truly the hassle-free vacation.

The minivan has taken over Kenya when it comes to showing tourists around. The cheaper your tour, the more people in the ever present minibus. I would not recommend a safari where there are more than six passengers in the customized nine-seater bus. The view may be obstructed by other people as you won't always have access to a window.

If you are physically disabled and want to go on safari or vacation in Kenya, it is possible to accommodate your needs even if it means being carried when necessary. As there is no shortage of manpower in Kenya this can be arranged. With a few generous tips and advanced planning nothing is impossible.

At all major airports there are washroom facilities for those who are wheelchair bound. At the Hilton and the New Stanley hotels in Nairobi; Diani Reef and Jadini hotels in Mombasa; and the Keekorok Lodge in the Mara there are accommodations for the handicapped. For more information, contact the **Association for the Physically Disabled**, *PO Box 46747, Nairobi, Tel. 224 443.*

WHAT'S A SAFARI?

Safari is the old Swahili word for travel or a hunting expedition. Today the word is used more by tourists to describe a trip to Kenya to see wildlife. Safaris range from group package deals to small personalized trips through the bush.

MAKING YOUR OWN ARRANGEMENTS

Planning and organizing your own trip might save you a little money, but be prepared for a lot of hard work and research. Thanks to the modern technology of fax machines in Kenya, the relatively easy part will be choosing your trip requirements and making bookings at a particular camp or hotel. You just have to research the places you select to make certain they will be what you expect.

The harder part will be making reservations for local commuter plane travel, remembering to get a confirmation voucher for each leg of the journey, paying park entry fees, and arranging transportation between the airports and lodges. This can get quite complicated without the added task of working with a foreign currency.

Keep in mind car rental is expensive. With your own car you will be left to your own devices but it might not be the best choice as a first time visitor. Cars have a tendency to break down and get stuck in the middle of nowhere. This can ruin your entire trip if you are somewhere where no one speaks English or if there's no auto mechanic in the vicinity.

The bottom line is, it all depends on what will make you happy. If you want to go on a camel safari, ride the colonial train, hike the scenic mountains, go fly fishing or sit on the picturesque beaches, it's all there for you.

As the distances between hotels in Kenya are so great, the costs are often all-inclusive. At the very least your meals will be included with your accommodations. Additional fees to look for are: local transportation, guided wildlife viewing, and park entry fees.

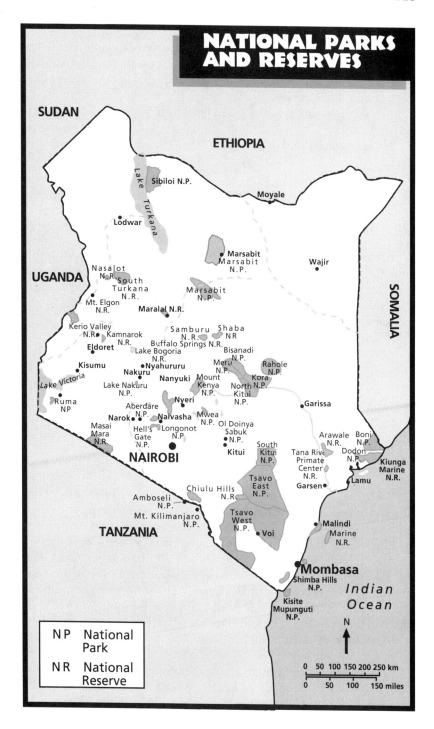

NATIONAL PARKS AND RESERVES

SUDAN

ETHIOPIA

Lake Turkana

Sibiloi N.P.

Moyale

Lodwar

Nasalot N.R.

UGANDA

South Turkana N.R.

Mt. Elgon N.R.

Marsabit Marsabit N.P.

Wajir

Marsabit N.P.

SOMALIA

Maralal N.R.

Kerio Valley N.R. Kamnarok N.R.

Eldoret

Samburu N.R. Shaba NR

Buffalo Springs N.R.

Lake Bogoria N.R.

Bisanadi N.P.

Kisumu

Nyahururu

Nakuru

Meru N.P.

Rahole N.P.

Lake Victoria

Lake Nakuru N.P.

Nanyuki Mount Kenya N.P.

Kora

North N.P.

Kitui

Ruma NP

Aberdare N.P.

Nyeri

Garissa

Narok Naivasha

Mwea N.P.

Masai Mara N.R.

Hell's Gate N.P.

Longonot N.P.

Ol Doinya Sabuk N.P.

Arawale N.R.

Boni N.P.

NAIROBI

Kitui

South Kitui N.P.

Tana River Primate Center N.R.

Dodon N.P.

Kiunga Marine N.R.

Lamu

Chiulu Hills N.R.

Tsavo East N.P.

Garsen

Amboseli N.P.

Mt. Kilimanjaro N.P.

TANZANIA

Tsavo West N.P.

Voi

Malindi Marine N.R.

Mombasa

Shimba Hills N.P.

Kisite Mupunguti N.P.

Indian Ocean

N

| NP | National Park |
| NR | National Reserve |

0 50 100 150 200 250 km

0 50 100 150 miles

TOUR OPERATORS

Tourism in Kenya is a very important source of income. Because of this, there are some excellent travel organizers ready to plan a unique safari adventure especially for you. The number of operators is endless, so I organized a select list.

Any of the tour operators listed below will certainly put together a quality vacation:

Micato Safaris, *15 West 26th Street New York, NY 10010, Tel. 1 800 642 2861 & Fax 212 545 8297. In Nairobi – View Park Towers, Uhuru Highway, PO Drawer 43374 Tel. 226 994, Fax 336 138.*

In 1967, Felix and Jane Pinto decided to take their many years of experience in Kenya and their devotion to the country's wildlife and turn it into Micato Safaris. From their homes and offices in Kenya and New York the Pintos are constantly in touch with their guests to ensure a distinct and special safari. Micato also has a great reputation in dealing with cruise line safaris. Responsible tourism is their motto as they share one of the world's most fragile eco systems with welcome travelers. Micato Safaris is a class act.

Abercrombie & Kent Ltd., *PO Box 59749, Nairobi, Tel. 228 700 or 334 955, Fax 215 752.*

Abercrombie & Kent has been around since 1962. They are extremely knowledgeable and professional in the services they provide. The company offers experienced tour services all over the world. You will be in good hands with everything involving your trip, including car rental. With A&K, you can count on some of the most entertaining and sophisticated tours anywhere in Kenya.

Bush Homes Africa Safaris, *750 Piedmont Avenue, Atlanta, Georgia 30308, Tel. 404 888 0909, Fax 404 888 0081, E-mail: bushhomes@africaonline.co.ke.*

With this tour operator, privacy is the name of the game. Bush Homes offers an intimate opportunity to view East Africa from the perspective of European settlers. Guests stay on exotic estates all over the country where wildlife prevails and many choices of entertainment are always yours.

African Adventures L.C., *Tim Lapage, 10 Claimjumper Court, Park City, UT 84060, Tel. 435 649 4655, www.safariexpert.com, safari@sisna.com.*

Tim Lapage, President of the Lewa Wildlife Conservancy, offers a custom made safari to fit your needs. A native Kenyan, Tim keeps his finger on the pulse of Africa and takes his safaris to exciting destinations.

Kingdoms of Africa, Inc., *Richard Salmon Safaris, PO Box 1035, Cumming, Georgia 30128, Tel. 770/889-5833.*

Richard will arrange your trip from the US and offers reasonable rates and reliable safaris. Kingdoms of Africa will guide you towards the best areas and include a cross-section of animal and bird life.

Yare Safaris Ltd., *PO Box 63006, Nairobi, Tel. 213 445, Fax 214 099.*

In the language of the Samburu, *Yare* means quest and this is exactly what Yare Safaris is all about; their quest to give you the holiday of a lifetime. Specialists in camel safaris, this outfitter will take you from half a day to ten days into the bush with a professional English speaking guide. If you are interested in mountain climbing, big game safaris or doing a stint on the beach, Yare Safaris will prepare everything for you including a shower and a cook.

Safari Camp Services Ltd., *PO Box 44801, Nairobi, Tel. 228 936 or 330 130, Fax 212 160.*

This tour operator offers a dozen different collections of safaris put together by Dick Hedges. All the tours depart from Nairobi every week of the year with a wide price range of top-value and economy vacations. They are particularly famous for the "Turkana Bus," which takes you on a relatively inexpensive bus ride to Lake Turkana with camp accommodations and food included.

United Touring Company Ltd., *(UTC) PO Box 42196, Nairobi, Tel. 331 960 or 331 973, Fax 216 871.*

This is one of the largest tour operators in Kenya. They are Thomas Cook representatives and include Hertz Cars and Block Hotels. The range of tours available through them will accommodate anything from mid-range on up.

Tony Mills Safaris, *PO Box 122, Kitale, Kenya, Tel. 884 091 or 882 160, Fax 325 20695 or 882 723.*

As I was born in Kitale, I feel a certain kinship with this outfitter and can vouch for an unforgettable out-of-the way safari. Tony puts together a small, personalized adventure, tailor-made to meet your expectations. In groups of one to six, Tony Mills Safaris will pick you up at the airport and start you off on a comfortable but authentic tented safari.

Cheli & Peacock, *PO Box 39806, Nairobi, Tel. (254 2)748 327 or (254 2) 748 633, Fax (254 2) 750 225, E-mail: chelipeacock@attmail.com, www.chelipeacock.com.*

As a small family-run business this operator offers unique, private, and superior tented safaris. As owners of Tortilis Camp they have won a prestigious *British Airways Tourism for Tomorrow Award* for excellence in eco-tourism. Outstandingly presented and operated you will experience the sights and sounds of the African bush, sleep under the stars beneath a canvas canopy, and enjoy abundant wildlife and dramatic scenery.

Concorde Safaris Ltd., *PO Box 25053, Nairobi, Tel. 643 304 or 743 316, Fax 748 628 or 448 135.*

Concorde extends arrangements for accommodations as well as car rental for visitors to Kenya. Concorde will provide a way for you to experience the joys and frustrations of offbeat Africa.

African Tours & Hotels Ltd., *PO Box 30471, Nairobi, Tel. 336 850, Fax 218 109.*

As owners of at least nine lodges and hotels, African Tours has been in the business for years. They will take care of all your needs as you enjoy a visit to Samburu National Park, Mount Kenya, and the exquisite Kenya coast. (Note: this outfitter has a recent reputation of having let its lodges and hotels get a little run down.)

Recently (1998) the **Kenya Professional Safari Guides Association** was formed to try and ensure quality among safari guides. Clients might be wise to ask any safari company or camp in Kenya if their guides have qualified and become KPSGA members.

If you feel that the list of tour operators above is not extensive enough or that you want to contact the other 589 possible agents available, you can supposedly obtain a list from the **Kenya Association of Tour Operators** (KATO), *PO Box 48461, Kaunda Street, Nairobi, Tel. 225 570.* I have not managed to get a response from them up until now, so good luck!

Most tour operators know each other in Kenya and sometimes you will see one company using another agency's vehicles if their own are not serviceable. It is probably impossible for you to tell who is who, but watch out for the safari companies who are actually only agents. They end up giving the bulk of your money to the actual safari outfitter and charging you a commission to do so.

Outfitters will do their best to ensure you have a memorable vacation but sometimes such things as flat tires (which are common), stuck, or inoperable vehicles are beyond their control. After all, this is the wilds of Africa where these things are not as easy to deal with as on an interstate highway at home. To improve your odds against this happening, do your homework when making safari arrangements; go with realistic expectations and an open mind.

WILDLIFE & CONSERVATION

The most common phrase you will hear while on safari in Kenya is "the big five." **Rhino, leopard, lion, elephant** and **buffalo** were the five most coveted trophies of game hunters and now have become the most important animals to spot while on safari.

No one will dispute they are magnificent and it would be a shame to miss any of them, but there are at least 165 other beasts in the bush that are just as spectacular and intriguing. If you don't see one of the "big five" (rhinos are very rare and leopards are very shy, so if you do get a glimpse of these two count yourself lucky) it should not detract from you trip.

The danger of a wild beast attacking you is very slim. The wildlife knows people mean trouble and prefer to get as far away as possible. If you come across an animal unexpectedly it's better not to run. Instead, back away slowly if you can or gradually head for the nearest tall tree (this obviously won't help with anything that climbs!).

While out looking for game, stay as far away as you reasonably can while still getting a good view. If you notice the animal getting angry, back off. The usual cautions, such as check your shoes for any unwelcome intruders before you put them on and watch where you walk, apply.

Kenya can be the most delightful place on earth if you relax and enjoy what it brings you. With any luck at all you should spot between 30 and 40 species of mammals on a well organized safari. It would be impossible for me to list every animal this wildlife Mecca has to offer, so I put together an abbreviated list below.

Conservation Efforts

Before I go any further in discussing wildlife, I think a word on the conservation efforts in Kenya is warranted. In the short term, Kenya is being saved from destruction by tourism. Without tourism, there would be no game parks and the wildlife would have been sacrificed to feed livestock and grow crops.

WILDLIFE IN THE SUBURBS

*While you are in Nairobi keep an eye open for the array of wildlife that lives in the suburbs. It is not uncommon to see a leopard sitting off in the distance with city buildings in the foreground. In **Nairobi National Park**, you can quickly be surrounded by a troop of greedy baboons.*

Tourism however, has brought on a whole new set of problems starting with the underwater enthusiasts who uncaringly tamper with the delicate coral reefs (which sometimes take hundreds of years to repair themselves) and ending with the extensive damage swarms of vehicles produce in the national parks. Kenya's ecology is precariously balanced on the edge of a razor blade.

There is tremendous pressure between wildlife and the local people who are vying for survival on what is left of the fertile land. Due to overgrazing and cultivation the soil will no longer support the ever growing population, which is quickly becoming dependent on relief aid.

Africans resent that the land taken from them is being used to make money for those in charge. In many cases the parks are barely tolerated and the resentments scarcely hidden. As a possible solution, it is becoming more common for outfitters to employ mostly local tribespeople and to give them a portion of the take. This, however, is luring the tribes away from their traditional ways of life. Sacrificing culture may be the lesser of the evils.

Long term projects include conservation education, research, and animal rescue. It is a common sight to see school children in trucks or buses out on field trips. These children are Kenya's future. The government recognizes the importance of teaching them the value of the land and the animals.

In many small pockets of the African landscape, the nomadic peoples are settling. Neighboring European homesteaders are working with the family chiefs to teach them how best to use their land, both in terms of wildlife management and grazing livestock. It's more and more common to see zebra and Grant's gazelle mixing with local cattle herds. The tribes are slowly learning that together, conservation techniques and domestic herds can provide adequate incomes with all concerned coming out as winners.

The ecological problem in the fertile mountains seems to be one of too much water. Rain sweeps the productive top layer of soil down into the rivers and out to the ocean. Just the opposite is true on the plains, where severe escalating droughts and strong winds are also causing serious soil erosion. Through the efforts of national and international conservancies, understanding and preservation efforts are slowly beginning to take hold.

If you are interested in joining the burgeoning membership of ecology minded organizations, write to **East African Wildlife Society**, *PO Box 20110, Nairobi, www.e-volve.com/hirolaf/help.html*. Most of the people in Kenya who can afford it join this reputable group and display the member's sticker proudly. This is the only way to conserve the delicate balance of nature between animals, plants, and people, which is in serious jeopardy today.

In 1961 Amboseli was turned over to the Masai and in 1970 a sanctuary around Lake Amboseli was created for wildlife only. In 1977 the area became a national park. Thirty years ago, a lady by the name of Cynthia Moss, left a promising career at *Newsweek* and set off to study elephants in Africa. In 1972 she founded the **Amboseli Elephant Research Project**. Over the years it has become the longest-running African elephant research project in the world.

From her camp in the shadow of Mt. Kilimanjaro, Cynthia studies over 1,600 elephants. She dutifully records the births, deaths, social relationships and other dramas of the elephant's lives. With her presence and help from the Masai this group of elephants represents the largest group in Africa with an intact social structure. Her contributions are invaluable in educating the world.

She is affiliated with the and sponsored by the **African Wildlife Foundation** (*1400 Sixteenth Street, N.W., Suite 120, Washington D.C. 20036, Tel. 888/4-WILDLIFE, 202/939-3333, Fax 202/939-3332, E-mail: africawildlife@awf.org, www.awf.org*). For those whose hearts are touched by the plight of the animals in Kenya, I would strongly suggest joining and contributing to this very worthwhile organization. It was founded in 1961 and is the leading international conservation organization working solely in Africa. Based in Washington D.C. AWF supports more than 35 field projects in Africa.

There is also the **Lewa Wildlife Conservancy** (*10 Claimjumper Court, Park City, Utah, 84060, Tel. 435/649-4655, http://aazk.epower.net/lewa, www.safariexpert,com, safari@sisna.com*) which is one of the most well-respected not for profit, conservation efforts in Kenya. Located on Lewa Downs (See *Where to Stay*, Isiolo/Central Highlands). Their focus is on all wildlife, but particularly rhinos. I love getting their newsletters and finding out for example, that prior to November 1998 six baby rhinos were born. Tim Lapage, their president, spends his time between Utah and Kenya and enjoys spreading the conservation word about Ngare Sergoi Rhino Sanctuary.

KENYAN WILDLIFE

Lions

In the animal kingdom, the predators seem to draw the most attention. The most famous in this category is the regal lion. The largest of the great cats in Africa, they spend a great deal of time resting in the shade. When the pride hunts at dusk or dawn, the males drive their prey towards the concealed females who do the actual killing. Living on the savannahs in prides of one to three males and up to 15 females, lions look like docile cats stretched out in the sun.

Cheetahs

The cheetah is legendary for its speed. With tawny black spots and a striped muzzle, it is one of the most sleek and captivating, though shy, cats in the world. They live in small groups on the savannahs and while hunting in the early morning or late evening can get up to speeds of 70 miles per hour for short bursts of up to 130 feet.

Leopards

The graceful leopard lives a solitary life except during the mating season. The beauty of the dark spots against the rich gold background belie the power these cats can muster if necessary. Generally considered nocturnal, the best place to find them is in rocky hills, high in tree branches or in the thick woodland brush. As one of the most adaptable of the predators, they will eat almost anything (rodents and monkeys) to continue to survive as a species. As agile as a common cat, they drag their kill to the top of a tree where they can rest assured scavengers will be less likely to find it.

Jackals

There are three species of nocturnal jackal living in small packs on the Kenya savannah. Their color varies from yellowish gray to brown with three differentiating markings; the **black-backed** (with a black back), the **side-striped** (with a white stripe down their side) and the **golden**. These common small fox-like animals scavenge off the kills of other predators and hunt small insects and mammals to survive.

GAME BOOKS

There are many books with excellent descriptions and pictures of Kenyan wildlife available in Nairobi bookstores. Try Collins' **Fieldguide to the Larger Mammals of Africa** *or Karmali's* **Beautiful Birds of Kenya***. It is a good idea to have along a pen so you can make notes and check off the wildlife you see. This is a nice keepsake in addition to your pictures.*

Hyenas

After the lion, the **hyena** is perhaps the most well known African animal because of its eerie laugh and piercing scream. The loud noises are heard particularly around the mating season. As an African predator and scavenger, the hyena serves a crucial function in cleaning up the savannahs. The scruffy coat with blackish spots along with a steeply sloping back and short legs makes the hyena look ungainly; but it is perfectly capable of bringing down a large antelope. This large dog-like creature is largely nocturnal and lives in small packs in burrows beneath the ground's surface.

Baboons

In the Kenyan primate world, the most common animals are the **yellow** and **olive baboons**. They live in large troops on the ground or in caves along rocky cliffs. They spend their days searching for food such as insects and eggs. With their brown coats and square dog-like faces they tend to be rather homely looking, but don't be fooled, as their large teeth can be very dangerous.

Monkeys

The **black-and-white colobus monkey** is by far the prettiest of the primates. It has a white fringed cape across the back of its jet black body, a white plume at the end of its tail, and an impish white muzzle. Living in troops of up to twelve animals, they rarely leave the safety of the treetops. Found only on Mount Kenya and Mount Elgon, and in the Saiwa Swamp and the Aberdares, they are difficult to see but are an impressive sight when spotted.

The **vervet monkey**, unafraid of people, often hangs around hotels and campsites where it might get a bite of food. In groups of 20 or 30 they are unabashed about moving into your tent or car in search of a tasty morsel. The vervet is the smallest and most common of Kenya's four main species of primates. It has a brown back with light beige stomach and its dark face is tasseled with white bangs.

Elephants

The elephant can live to the ripe old age of 100 and will eat vast amounts of green material to survive each day. Elephants are found roaming in close knit herds with the matriarch in charge. Older and younger bulls can be found wandering alone and tend to be rather on the cranky side. These large beasts flap their ears to keep from overheating. The large appendages carry a great deal of blood and act as an air-conditioning unit to cool the fluid and in turn the animal. When ear flapping is combined with snorting however, it's usually a sign of agitation.

In 1987, two-thirds of Kenya's elephants had been brutally killed and butchered for their ivory. Poachers went unrestricted despite a ban on hunting. As the herd numbers plummeted into the hundreds it was time for desperate action. A shoot to kill policy for military rangers with appropriate training and equipment was enacted and enforced. Poachers were and still are killed on sight. The ban on ivory hunting was celebrated with an enormous ivory bonfire and a plea to the world not to support the ivory traders. The tactics worked. Today less than 20 elephants are lost each year.

Elephant herds vary from family groups of five all the way up to 50. As the world's largest land mammal with superior intelligence and sophisticated social behavior, elephants communicate with each other with any number of sounds. It has been written that when poaching was rampant, elephants learned they could hide family members with large tusks in the center of a large crowd. Elephants can quickly adapt from open plains to thick forests and are constantly on the move depending on where food and shelter are found.

Rhinos

There are two species of rhinoceros, the **black** and the **white**. The black rhino is smaller with a pointed upper lip. The coloration for the black and white rhino is actually a dark gray. Both species are extremely rare and tend to prefer living either alone or in pairs. Their habitat varies from dense forest to open scrub where they feed on the leaves of bushes and trees. What they lack in good eyesight they more than compensate for with excellent senses of smell and hearing. If startled, they will try to flee from danger, but have been known to attack when they or their young feel significantly threatened.

Buffalo

The African buffalo has a reputation of having a bad temper if disturbed. These huge ox-like creatures carry heavy, dangerous looking horns which they are willing to use to get rid of any pests. They can usually be found near water. Their dark brown hides, which they love to coat in thick mud, offer protection from biting insects. Large herds of up to 100 gather on open grasslands and smaller groups tend to congregate in thick forests.

Giraffes

The most common of the three giraffe varieties is the **Masai giraffe** with its light tan coat and smudged irregular brown spots. The **Rothschild giraffes** are very rare and found in the west of Kenya. The males of this group have four horns while both males and females "wear" white socks and have a pronounced bump on their foreheads. As a separate species, the **reticulated giraffe** has a much paler undercoat with crisply defined reddish-brown patches all over its tall body.

Hippos

Spending their days in lakes, ponds, and rivers, the **hippopotamus** comes out to eat at night. Their short legs can only withstand the enormous weight of their large heads and fat bodies for a short time. They are generally huddled in sociable groups of up to 30 with only their eyes and ears visible above the surface of the water. If riled, the hippo's normally amiable demeanor can quickly flare into an ugly tantrum. Just about every hippo you see has the scars to prove it.

Zebras

The popular zebra has two species to its credit. The **Burchell's zebra** is the more common of the two and can be found in large numbers. Its broad uneven stripes are easily distinguished from the thin symmetrical stripes of the **Grevy's zebra**. As opposed to the Burchell's zebra, Grevy's has large rounded ears, a white belly, and is found only in the Samburu region. Mixing in abundant herds on open grassland, both species are outgoing and affable but do not breed outside their own kind.

NATURAL ADAPTATION

*Each species of herbivore in Kenya selects a specific grass or leaf to feed on and over the centuries has evolved physically to accommodate their eating habits. The **gerenuk**, a small gazelle that often stands on its hind legs to reach a tasty leaf, has developed an elongated neck for eating from overhanging branches. The **giraffe**, with its long neck, finds little competition for the tender leaves at the top of the acacia tree.*

Warthogs

Amusing to watch as they run with their tails straight up in the air are the ungainly warthogs – one of my favorite animals. The most common of several wild pigs, they live off grass, roots, and bark. Their small upwardly curving tusks draw your attention away from their lumpy wart-covered snouts and beady eyes. All warthogs have grayish brown skin with long manes matted down the length of their backs.

Wildebeests

The humble wildebeest or **gnu** is renowned for its legendary migration. Searching for grazing, herds number in the millions. Clumsy looking and with huge heads they are known for eccentric behavior, including head tossing, grunting, and running in circles for no apparent reason. With a straggly mane and beard and small thick horns meeting across their foreheads, they appear to be a cross between a horse, ox, and antelope.

THE FAMOUS MIGRATION

Steady columns of two million wildebeests are given a secret and unknown signal to begin their annual trek to or from the Serengeti or Masai Mara. The wildebeests are single minded in their migration. If a baby loses its mother it cannot stop to say goodbye. If a fence crosses their path or any other obstacle halts their progress, they will either stop and often die or try to force their way through. At the river crossing, thousands lose their lives through drowning, crocodiles, or simply the struggle to climb over each other. It is an awesome but disturbing spectacle.

Gazelles & Antelopes

The largest of Kenya's gazelles is the **impala** living in large herds all over the country. It is nothing for these athletes to reach speeds of 60 miles per hour or jump ten feet into the air. Looking much like a north American deer, they have black stripes on their behinds and tails and a dark strip along their noses. The males have long easily identifiable horns.

The huge and fairly common **eland** is found in the reserves in herds of six to twelve. About the size of a cow, the eland has a black strip of hair across its back and down its belly. Both female and male eland have long horns that face backwards and have an odd looking spiral at the base. A strict hierarchy is followed within the larger herds as they forage for grass and leaves in the late evening and early morning.

Other notable antelopes are the **bushbuck, dik-dik, gerenuk, hartebeest** and **Grant's gazelle**. These are just a few of the more common gazelles you are likely to encounter as you enjoy your safari. Make it a game to see how many you can actually identify with your essential fieldguide.

While walking in the wilds of Africa, you will come across small mounds of droppings from the tiny **dik-dik**. These graceful little creatures have a habit of doing their bathroom business all in the same spot. Legend has it that one day a family of dik-dik was happily wandering along in the bush and tripped over a pile of elephant dung; their feelings were hurt. Ever since then, they have been accumulating their droppings to try to trip up the elephant!

Birds

I would be remiss if I did not mention the variety and number of the bird population in Kenya. Just as there are hundreds of diverse habitats there is an equally impressive number (over 1,000) of bird species. An adequate identification guide to take along is Collins' *Field Guide to the Birds of East Africa*.

Depending on the time of your visit, you will see an assortment of migrating birds as well as the local feathered residents. Many tour operators offer exclusive bird-viewing safaris which can be rewarding for twitchers.

A permanent inhabitant of the grasslands is the ever present **vulture** with several species to its credit. It is hardly likely that you will get too close to a vulture, but if you do, be prepared for the ever-present stench of rotting flesh. The vultures perform a valuable service as they clean up carcasses already picked over by other meat eaters.

One of the most fascinating of the bird family in Kenya is the **ostrich**. The bird is easily recognized by its very long legs and neck, which are covered with pink or blue skin depending on the species. In the mating season, this pink skin turns bright red in males.

Ostriches tend to be loners who gather in groups of no more than six. To compensate for their flightlessness, ostriches are very fast runners and have a dangerously powerful kick. When feeding on flowers, leaves, seeds, and grass they accumulate it in their throats and eventually pass it downward to their stomachs. It is entertaining to watch these lumps move along their long skinny necks.

OSTRICH TRIVIA

One male ostrich will mate with more than one female during the breeding season. The female first approached will build a nest for her eggs. All the other mated females will lay their eggs, up to five, in that same nest and then have nothing more to do with any aspect of chick hatching or rearing. Up to 30 baby ostriches can hatch out of one nest and will be cared for by the number one female and her mate. The babies, about the size of an adult chicken, are surprisingly small compared to their parents.

Flocks of up to two million **greater** and **lesser flamingoes** mixed in with pelicans make a breathtaking sight as you visit the brackish soda lakes of the Great Rift Valley. These pink colored waterbirds prefer the level of the lakes low and the salinity high. Feeding through a sensitive and complicated filtration system in their beaks, the flamingoes sweep their heads from side to side to gather minute organic particles along with algae and mollusks. They tend to move from lake to lake depending on the water level. No matter which lake they are on, the viewing is best in January and February.

Kaleidoscopic birds such as **bee-eaters** and **sunbirds** will enhance your visit tremendously. There are many other feathered friends that are just as impressive. A short list includes the **lovebird, flycatcher, kingfisher, golden** and **crimson weaver, woodpecker, turaco, secretary bird** and the notable **Marabou stork.** Many of these birds tend to congregate around the freshwater lakes such as Naivasha and Nakuru, where food is plentiful.

Snakes

Along with all the other thrilling forms of wildlife, Kenya has 169 species of venomous snakes and an interesting collection of reptiles. There are any number of snake or reptile farms around the country which allow you to see and often hold these denizens of the dirt.

For the most part, snakes will avoid contact with humans if at all possible. If they hear you coming they will hide or get out of the way. The only possible danger is if they are asleep and caught off guard.

Pythons are the largest and most dramatic of the snakes and may reach up to twenty feet in length. Fortunately they are not poisonous but rather constrict to kill their food. The biggest of these reptiles can eat a gazelle with no problem.

A common snake is the short, sluggish camouflaged **puff adder** which is the most dangerous of all Kenyan snakes and the most difficult to see. The adder won't usually try to get away if it hears someone coming but rather waits for the person to avoid them or strikes. Puff adders like to warm themselves on sun-soaked rocks and live in large holes nearby. While hiking through the warmer regions of Kenya, keep a sharp look out for these very deadly snakes.

The **spitting cobra**, on the other hand, tries to escape if it thinks there is danger. At the first sign of a predator, the cobra turns in the other direction and keeps going until it feels safe. If it senses a threat it will throw venom at the face of its assailant. No one knows for sure if it actually aims or if this is just a myth.

If you are visiting heavily forested areas, the tree dwelling **boomslang** or the deadly **gaboon viper** are probably in residence. The boomslang is venomous but its poison fang is far back in its throat making a deadly bite difficult. The gaboon viper, however, is one of the most dangerous snakes alive, often inflicting a lethal bite.

Crocodiles

The prehistoric crocodile is a part of everyday life in many parts of East Africa. Relying on the heat of the sun to keep their reptilian bodies warm, they lie on sand bars along the edges of rivers and lakes in the afternoon and morning sunshine. Crocs are easily missed or mistaken for a fallen log or a rock as the gray color of their skin blends well with the environment. Signs saying "Beware of crocodiles" are scattered all over Kenya. The crocodile will not hesitate to take anything that moves down into the deep recesses of its larder; including unwary humans. It is not uncommon for the disappearance of an African to be blamed on this cold-blooded killer.

Lizards

Chameleons and **geckos** are seen throughout Kenya and are looked upon as benevolent do-gooders. The two lizard species keep African houses free of mosquitoes and other troublesome insects. Most Kenyans encourage the reptiles to move in and ignore them as they scurry about in the rafters.

TERMITE MOUNDS

*The enormous **termite mounds** scattered across the dry grasslands can get up to an impressive 10 feet across and 13 feet in height. Made from up to 3 tons of red mud, there is a main shaft going down into the ground to a wet spot where the workers gather water. The water is used to maintain an essential humidity and temperature level.*

To relieve pressure created by the social organization of millions of termites living below, the mounds are built with ventilator shafts at strategic points. You can feel and hear the warm air rushing out of these vents as they keep the temperature constant.

After foraging through underground tunnels for food such as decayed animals or plants, the termites return to excrete and regurgitate the mixture so others can feed. After the meal has been eaten twice, it is used to harden the walls of their home.

In the center of the hill, a large queen spends her life laying one egg every two seconds.

The chameleon is represented by several varieties and is known for its ability to change color and blend with the background. When challenged, some species of chameleon will open their mouths and emit a rather scary hiss as a warning. While they are basically harmless, they have been known to give a sharp bite to anyone getting too close.

The unobtrusive gecko has suction pads on its feet allowing it to scamper up and down ceilings and walls in pursuit of a tasty bug. The delicate gray-brown lizards are quite gentle and completely harmless to humans.

PLANT LIFE

Europeans found that East Africa's varied climatic regions would support any kind of plant life. They used this to their advantage to avoid the feelings of homesickness by bringing a sampling of plant life, such as roses and daisies, from home. In the process, these avid gardeners got carried away and happily inundated Kenya with the colorful splendors from gardens all over the world.

Africans in general are not too interested in the flora growing in and around Kenya unless it is in some way practical to them. This is understandable as they are busy trying to survive and don't have much time for such things as flowering bushes and trees.

The latest industry in Kenya, which is beginning to rival tourism as a profitable venture, is that of flower and vegetable growing. Flowers like roses and carnations and vegetables such as brussel sprouts, peas, green beans and carrots are grown in long rows of green houses. There are hundreds of acres of these white low buildings taking over the Kenyan landscape.

With growing lights extending the growing time to more than twelve hours, these commodities are packaged, priced, and shipped to the UK and other European markets overnight. The produce arrives on the shelves fresh and ready for consumers the next day.

Useful and practical crops such as maize (corn) and potatoes came from the Americas. All over Kenya are small plots of maize being grown for local consumption. This maize has become the staple of the African diet. It is cooked into an interesting concoction called **posho**.

STAPLE DIET

*A firepit surrounded by stones in the middle of the floor of a small mud hut serves as the "kitchen." Here you will find **posho** being cooked twice a day. The corn, ground to the consistency of grits, is slowly added to an eight inch iron bowl full of boiling water straddling the fire. A large wooden spoon is used to stir the corn until it is cooked into a thick dough-like consistency. Each person in the household is served a heaped cereal bowl full of the mixture by the matriarch/cook. Occasionally the meal is supplemented with cow's blood mixed with cow's urine and cow's milk. Fingers are the utensils for the meal.*

Other imports which have taken off in Kenya and supply some of the most delicious fare are citrus from China and coconuts from the Polynesian islands. At the coast, the coconut has been incorporated into African life where every part of it is used for something.

The bright orange **paw paw** (papaya) is served for breakfast almost everywhere you go. The tree grows abundantly in the fertile soils of Kenya and is a deliciously refreshing and healthy fruit. It is said that seven paw paw seeds (pips as the locals call them) a day will keep arthritis away.

Forests grown for their timber consist largely of eucalyptus from Australia and imported pine. The most common tree found throughout Kenya is the amazing flat-topped **acacia** (*tortillis* in Swahili). There are several varieties that grow in the many different terrains. Acacias are popular with all forms of wildlife. Giraffes eat from the top of the tree, gerenuk eat from the lower branches, and ants form a symbiotic relationship with the fascinating trees.

In the bush, there are many medicinal and practical plants. For example there is the **toothbrush bush** which serves for exactly that –

THE SACRED BAOBAB TREE

The baobab tree is revered by Africans and has many legends and superstitions surrounding its creation. The story goes that the gods were angry at the tree and so planted it upside down as punishment. If you take a good look at a baobab, it does look as if the roots are sticking straight up in the air.

The large trunk of the baobab tree stores water which can be life-saving in the parching heat of the dry season. The heavy fruit it bears contains cream of tartar and the edible leaves are considered to have medicinal properties. The Africans use the tree bark to make rope and baskets.

toothbrushing. You will often see the local people walking along with a stick in their mouths which they chew and rub along their gums to keep their teeth in good shape. Around the northern Samburu regions, there is a small shrub which is used to cure skin cancer. If it is rubbed on the affected skin, some suggest all signs of the cancer generally disappear within two weeks.

Each level of altitude has its own specific indigenous plants. At 10,000 feet there is wonderfully aromatic heather and giant groundsel mixed in with gladioli and dazzling delphiniums. Between 5,000 and 8,000 feet of elevation the slow-growing forests of hardwoods like mahogany, teak, and ebony find themselves at home. Many of the lower level forests have been felled for timber.

Once up into the higher regions, the forests turn into a private garden show. Flowering vines intertwine with the ancient looking lichen and pale green bamboo shelters delicate orchids from the sun. The bright purple **African Violets** bloom in tiny clusters along the ground adding one more reason to take a stroll through the Kenyan bush.

On the savannahs, which range from 4,000 to 5,000 feet, the vegetation is unique and lovely in its own way. Only the famed **yellow fever tree** and **prickly cactus** survive the long droughts and hot equatorial sun. Amid the tough grass the fleshy aloe plant is just one of the more than 40 species of vegetation growing here. The yellow fever trees got the name because the early settlers set up their camps under the wide sheltering branches and soon after came down with yellow fever. They thought it was something contracted from the beautiful light green trees.

The brightly painted **geraniums** which are native to South Africa grow to an amazing size in Kenya. Left outside all year long in the perfect climate for perennials, the rounded and irregularly lobed leafed shrub will grow nine feet tall. Their white, pink, and red blooms are seen everywhere enhancing the natural beauty of the country.

At the coastal levels, the brilliant red, pink, and white of Brazilian bougainvillea turns gardens into a haven. Up and down the shore, twisted roots of slow growing mangroves offer sanctuary to young fish as they escape wily predators.

The streets of Nairobi come alive with the purple jacaranda and scarlet flame trees imported from South America and Madagascar respectively. Perhaps my favorite is the creamy white and yellow flowers of the fragrant frangipani tree.

9. SPORTS & RECREATION

When people hear the mention of Kenya, they think of wild game safaris with lions and elephants. This image is well earned and is definitely a large part of what attracts visitors to this unique equatorial country. Kenya however, is paradise for any of the myriad of activities it offers. There is trout fishing, camel riding, and mountain climbing year round. Most recreations enjoyed in the Western world are found here also. The trick is knowing where to find them.

BALLOONING

This is the way to go if you want to see the golden savannahs and the unequaled wildlife from a completely different perspective. Once you are off the ground, the breathtaking views will capture your heart and soul.

While this is an expensive way to see Kenya (about $350 per person), there is no more spectacular scene of a hidden cheetah planning a kill or a mother elephant showing her young how to knock down a tree.

SPORTS CALENDAR OF EVENTS

January: Seven-day International; Bill Fish Competition – Malindi
February-March: Fishing Festival – Mombasa; Delaware Cup; Mnarini Fishing Club – Kilifi
March: Kenyan Open Golf Championship
April: Safari Rally
May: Kenyan Two Thousand Motor Rally
June: Nakuru Agricultural Show
August-September: International Agricultural Show – Mombasa
September-October: Nairobi International Agricultural Show
October-November: Seven-day Sea Fishing Festival

Hot air balloon trips operate in the **Masai Mara, Taita Hills**, and **Tsavo** game parks. The excitement begins well before dawn as the twelve man basket lifts off with a roar from the burners. Included in the price is a classy champagne breakfast served on the plains at the end of your trip. For more information contact:

- **Abercrombie & Kent**, *PO Box 59749, Nairobi, Tel. 228 700, Fax 215 752*
- **Block Hotels**, *PO Box 47557, Nairobi, Tel. 335 807*
- **Balloon Safaris**, *PO Box 43747, Nairobi, Tel. 502 850, Fax 501 424*
- **Hilton International**, *PO Box 30624, Nairobi, Tel. 334 000*

BIRDING

One of the lesser known delights in Kenya is its birds. If you want to study one species or just get a detailed overview of all birds in Kenya you have only to ask and your tour will be organized accordingly.

On the western shore of **Lake Baringo** the profusion of gorgeous wild birds (over 300 species) is astounding. The **Lake Baringo Club** has the perfect set-up for anyone interested in our feathered friends. The resident ornithologist will introduce you to the area's birds.

In the trees around **Saiwa Swamp National Park** are some of the loveliest birds you will ever see. Several varieties of turaco are likely to be included in your viewing.

A small cross-section of the once vast African rainforest, **Kakamega Forest**, is well worth a visit for the spectacular and rare bird species, such as the blue-headed bee eater. Here you will also find over 200 species of diverse and colorful butterflies.

For more information on birding tours contact: **East African Ornithological Safaris**, *PO Box 48019, Nairobi*; or **Tony Mills Safaris**, *PO Box 122, Kitale*.

CAMEL SAFARIS

This once in a lifetime thrill is worth the hardships you will endure as part of the experience. When making your booking, be sure to read the fine print. With some camel safaris you walk while the camel carries your gear. With other tours you actually ride the camel. No matter which version you choose, you will work hard and end up having a sore back and rear. Don't be discouraged as this is an excellent way to get to know your camel, driver, and the local customs. You will really see Kenya up close and personal.

Camel safaris can vary in length to suit your needs and your pocket-book. Prices vary from $150 to $500 per person per day. These safaris are usually offered only in the drier northern parts of Kenya and are suspended during the rains.

For more information on camel safaris contact:
- **Simon Evans Ewaso River Camel Safari Bookings Ltd.**, *PO Box 56707, Nairobi, Tel. 225 255, Fax 216 553*
- **Yare Safaris**, *PO Box 63006, Nairobi, Tel. 214 099, Fax 213 445*
- **Desert Rose Camels Ltd.**, *PO Box 44801, Nairobi, Tel. 228 936, Fax 212 160*
- **Kenya Camel Safaris Let's Go Travel**, *PO Box 60342, Nairobi, Tel. 340 331, Fax 336 890*
- **Safaris Unlimited**, *PO Box 24181, Nairobi*
- **Special Camping Safaris Ltd.**, *PO Box 51512, Nairobi, Tel. 338 325*

OX-WAGON SAFARIS

This is truly a dizzying experience. You will go back in time to an era when this was the mode of transport of the day. Sixteen oxen with enormous horns slowly draw a replica of a pioneer wagon through the Kenyan bush. In the evening, dinner is served on fine china at your luxurious tented camp at **Crater Lake**.

For more information on ox-wagon safaris contact: **Safaris Cordon Bleu**, *c/o UTC, PO Box 42196, Nairobi.*

A 1920S TRIP THROUGH KENYA

*An excerpt from **Marjorie Pharazyn's** writings as she experiences a 1920s journey to Nairobi:*

"A trip to Nairobi was a major enterprise. By mule cart to Eldoret, then by trotting ox-cart service we travelled through the dark night, stopping every ten miles to change oxen and drivers, to Londiani, where we transferred to the Uganda Railway. The old fashioned carriages were roomy and one took one's bedding if one wanted any. When the train stopped at mealtimes all the passengers got out for delightful meals served in the station dining room of fresh eggs, tea, bread and butter and jam, and much chat with one's fellow travellers."

HIKING, BIKING & MOUNTAIN CLIMBING

Mt. Kenya should be the first choice for any visitor who wants to climb in Kenya. Skill and determination are essential to complete this challenge. Remember that just about all the walking will be at high altitudes that can seriously affect your performance, no matter what kind of shape you may be in.

Mt. Elgon in western Kenya near Kitale, offers exhilarating mooreland scenery (swampy wasteland but very beautiful nonetheless) and distant views. The two hour hill hike will take you to the crater of the mountain. Other excellent selections where you will find some of the most scenic hiking in Kenya are in the **Aberdares**, the **Cherangani Hills**, or the **Ngong Hills** close to Nairobi.

Walking or biking through bush and game country really puts you in the thick of things. These walks are designed to show you the best of Kenya's wildlife and scenery. Tour operators offer several safari options with trucks, horses, and camels as a back-up in case you are unable to go on. An average fitness level will allow you to enjoy any of these unique adventures. Rates for the trip can range from $38 to $1,000 per person depending on the comfort level and services provided.

For more information, contact:

- **Tropical Ice Ltd.**, *PO Box 57341, Nairobi, Tel. 740 811, Fax 740 826*
- **The Mountain Club of Kenya**, *PO Box 45741, Nairobi, Tel. 501 747*
- **Naro Moru River Lodge**, *PO Box 18, Naro Moru, Tel. (0176) 62622, Fax (0176) 62211,* also headquarters to the Warden of the Mountain National Parks and the Guides and Porters Association
- **Hiking & Cycling Kenya Ltd.**, *PO Box 39439, Nairobi, Tel. 218 336, Fax 224 212*
- **Off The Beaton Path**, *with Ron Beaton, Bush Homes Africa Safaris, PO Box 56923, Nairobi, Tel. 506 139, Fax 502 739 REKERO*
- **Tribal Treks & Wildlife Walks Kentrak Safaris Ltd.**, *PO Box 47964, Nairobi, Tel. 441 704, Fax 441 690*
- **Yare Safaris**, *PO Box 63006, Nairobi, Tel. 214 099, Fax 213 445*
- **Gametrackers**, *PO Box 62042, Nairobi, Tel. 338 927, Fax 330 903*
- **Bike Treks: Walking and Cycling in Kenya**, *PO Box 14237, Nairobi, Tel. 446 371, Fax 336 890*
- **Hiking & Cycling Kenya Ltd.**, *PO Box 39439, Nairobi, Tel. 218 336, Fax 224 212*

CAVING

Near **Kitale** around **Mount Elgon** there are cave sites you should include if time allows. **Kitum** is renowned for elephant and antelope who visit the caverns. The animals enjoy the minerals and salt they dig from deep inside the chambers. Over the years the game has enlarged the cavities significantly.

All across Kenya there are extensive caves and lava tubes to explore. A few others worth mentioning are **Makingeny**, **Mt. Susa**, and the **Chyulu Hills**. For more information contact: **Cave Exploration Group of East Africa**, *PO Box 46583, Nairobi.*

HORSEBACK SAFARIS

This a really lovely way to see Kenya, as wildlife is much more accepting of a horse than a human on foot. The ride safaris are for people with experience, but if you wish to ride for relaxation, there are ranches and homestays which offer this as an aside.

The rides always start first thing in the morning with stops for bathroom and drink breaks and of course, lunch. You will arrive at your destination to find the camp set up and tea ready.

There are grooms hired especially to take care of your horses until you are ready to set off again the next day. Some of the less expensive saddle safaris offer a "no frills" version where the guests actually help take care of the horses or perform other camp chores. Generally included in the price are tents, horses, food, and equipment.

All riders must have their own medical insurance in case of an accident and come prepared with adequate riding attire. This includes a rain coat or poncho and warm clothing.

For exquisite views of the Rift Valley and a ride through **Ngong Hills** and Kitengela Reserve, I suggest you try a three day horse safari. Ngong Hills is the area where many white settlers built their colonial farms and houses. The lush English gardens and colorful flower beds transport you back in time.

For more information contact:

• **Safaris Unlimited (Africa) Ltd.**, *PO Box 24181, Nairobi, Tel. 891 168, Fax 891 113*
• **Richard Bonham Safaris Ltd.**, *PO Box 24133, Nairobi, Tel. 882 521, Fax 882 728*
• **Equitor Worldwide Riding Holidays**, *Bitterroot Ranch, PO Box 807, Dubois, Wyoming 82513, Tel. 800/545-0019, Fax 307/455-2354*
• **FITS Equestrian**, *685 Latin Road, Solvang, California 93463, Tel. 805/ 688-9494, Fax 805/688-2943*
• **Offbeat Safaris Ltd.**, *PO Box 56923, Nairobi, Tel. 506 139, Fax 502 739*
• **Special Camping Safaris Ltd.**, *PO Box 51512, Nairobi, Tel. 338 325*

GOLF TOURS

Add a few yards to your shot at the high altitude Kenya golf courses. Although they are a relatively little used source of entertainment, the golf courses in Kenya are very well maintained.

You may be surprised not to find golf carts anywhere but don't worry; caddies are the norm. Relax and enjoy the wildlife along the route. Don't be astonished if a nearby hippo keeps an eye on your golfing efforts.

There are at least six outstanding 18-hole courses around Nairobi. The best is **Windsor Golf** that meets professional international standards. Another excellent course is the **Country Club**.

KENYA'S UNIQUE GOLF RULE

Kenya is one of the only places in the world where the rules of golf state: "If a ball comes to rest dangerously close to a hippopotamus or crocodile, another ball may be dropped at a safe distance, but no nearer the hole, without penalty."

Many of the courses outside Nairobi were built by the colonials and offer spectacular settings. In the **Rift Valley**, **Central Highlands**, and **Limuru**, at least ten courses are open to visitors at a day membership fee.

For more information contact:
- **Kenya Golf Union**, *Muthaiga, PO Box 49609, Nairobi, Tel. 763 898*
- **The Windsor Golf Hotel**, *PO Box 45587, Tel. 802 206/8/10, Fax 802 188*
- **UTC**, *PO Box 42196, Nairobi, Tel. 331 960, Fax 216 871*

TENNIS, SQUASH, & TABLE TENNIS

With traditional hospitality and first class facilities, tennis, squash and table tennis can be found at any of the sports clubs and hotels along the coast. Up until independence these sports were exclusively played by Europeans. Now both Africans and Asians play enthusiastically. In 1987, Kenya won two gold and one silver medal in the Fourth All African Games.

For more information on facilities for tennis, squash, cricket, football and hockey contact: **Impala Club**, *Tel. 568 684*; **Nairobi Club**, *Tel. 725 726*; **Nairobi Gymkhana**, *Tel. 742 804*, and **Parklands Sports Club**, *Tel. 742 938*.

HEALTH CLUBS & GYMS

Costs are fairly competitive with those at home if you want to stay fit while on vacation. You will be able to avail yourself of saunas, masseurs, and exercise equipment. The facilities are often offered in the larger hotels and resorts for a membership fee, but don't overlook the local gyms. Try those listed above under *Tennis, Squash, & Table Tennis*.

DARTS, BILLIARDS, POOL & SNOOKER

Almost exclusively found in sports bars and clubs, billiards, pool, and snooker are popular among the local people. Kenyans also love to play darts. You will find hotly contested tournaments in local night spots where alcohol distillers spend large amounts of money to encourage the sport.

SWIMMING

It is not advisable to swim in the rivers and lakes in Kenya, as crocodiles and the parasite bilharzia are present. Most good hotels have swimming pools, and if you feel the need to swim they will accommodate you for a small fee. A popular pool is the one at the **YMCA** (on State House Road) which has a modest charge.

The Indian Ocean is warm and inviting all the way down the coast and is pleasant for swimming. Keep your eyes open for sea urchins that are painful if stepped on, and man-o-war which will give you a very nasty sting. Sometimes you will find a lot of seaweed, but it is generally harmless. The currents can get strong so be sure you don't swim alone.

DHOW TRIPS

Wooden carved African boats, or **dhows**, with their triangular sails have been trading along the coast for over 1,000 years. Sizes vary from a humble two person craft to a large elegant vessel. A dhow tour with a little sightseeing, history, sailing, fishing and sunning is certainly an unrivaled adventure.

Fish oil is used to condition the wood so be prepared to smell a bit fishy when you finish the tour. Don't let this deter you from taking the expedition as a quick bath will take care of the scent.

Just off the coast in **Lamu**, operators offer a lazy, relaxing trip from half a day up to several days. Sailing up and down the scarcely populated shore and its quiet islands is irresistible. You can live off your fresh daily catch and hear wild stories around the campfire at night, and tour the **Takwa** ruins and swamps around **Maboko** during the day.

RENOWNED TAMARIND DHOW

*Enjoy an enchanting evening aboard the acclaimed **Tamarind Dhow**, which appears to be out of the romantic myths of Sinbad the Sailor. This traditional dhow has been transformed into a floating seafood restaurant with a magical ambiance.*

In Mombasa, the dhows offer several singular tour choices. Visit the floating craft market enjoy a luscious lobster dinner under the stars, or try a fresh seafood lunch. The operators will pick you up and return you to your hotel. Book the tours through any Mombasa hotel or call **Jahazi Marine**, *Tel. 472 213 or 471 895*, **Kenya Marineland Dhows**, *Tel. 485 248/ 886/7738*; **Tamarind Dhows**, *Tel. 20990,* or **Pilli-Pipa**, *PO Box 84045, Mombasa , Telefax 0127 2401.*

FISHING

The best deep sea fishing is from November through March, but this is not to say other months won't yield a bountiful catch. For deep sea game fishing the best places to go are **Diani Beach**, **Shimoni**, **Lamu Archipelago**, **Malindi**, **Watamu**, **Kilifi** and **Mombasa**.

Kenya offers some of best trophy fishing in the world. Success will bring in species such as dorado, barracuda, marlin, and sailfish in record sizes. If you use the standard catch and release approach, your reward is a photo and certificate. The fish lives to fight another day.

For more information, contact:
- **Sea Adventures Ltd.**, *PO Box 56, Shimoni, Tel. Shimoni 12 or 13*
- **Hemingways**, *PO Box 267 Watamu, Malindi, Tel. 32624, Fax 32256*
- **James Adcock Fishing Ltd.**, *PO Box 95693, Nyali, Mombasa, Tel. 485 527*
- **Carr Hartley Safaris**, *PO Box 59762, Nairobi, Tel. 882 453, Fax 884 542*
- **Marajani Tours**, *PO Box 86103, Mombasa, Tel. 314 935/312 703, Fax 312 879*

For fresh water fishing, the places to go are lakes **Turkana** or **Victoria**. At either of these, the Nile perch can reach 220 pounds and the tiger fish put up a good fight. You might try the **Lake Turkana Fishing Lodge** or the **Oasis Lodge** for a comfortable stay at Lake Turkana.

On Lake Victoria there are also lodges catering to fishing enthusiasts. **Rusinga** and **Mfangano Islands** offer exclusive fishing resorts. To get to Mfangano, you will have to coordinate with the ferry schedule or fly in as most people do. Rusinga is connected to the mainland by a causeway but again, most visitors fly in.

For more information, contact:
- **Kericho Sotik Fishing Association**, *PO Box 281, Kericho*
- **Bookings Limited**, *Nairobi, Tel. 220 365 or 225 255*
- **Governors Camp**, *Mfangano, PO Box 48217 Nairobi, Tel. 331 871, Fax 726 427*
- **Lonrho**, *Rusinga, PO Box 58581, Nairobi, Tel. 216 940, Fax 216 796*

BEST FISHING SEASONS

Black Marlin	*January thru March and July thru December*
Blue Marlin	*Feb. thru March and July thru October*
Striped Marlin	*January thru March and December*
Sailfish	*January thru March and Nov. thru December*
Mako Shark	*Feb. thru March and June thru October*
Yellowfin Tuna	*June thru October*

PRIMEVAL FISHING

Mfangano Island is a center of history where the locals practice their own art of primeval fishing. Casting a kerosene lamp out from the shore after sundown and hauling it in slowly lures a bountiful catch of squirming freshwater shrimp (dagga) into waiting nets.

In western Kenya in the **Cherangani Hills**, **Aberdares**, and **Mau Escarpment** you will find mountain streams notable for fly-fishing. The **Marun River** is fairly accessible where the road crosses the river at Cheranganis. In most cases, there are no organized facilities and you will have to provide your own equipment.

At **Kenya Trout and Salmon Flies Limited**, *Kikuyu Road, Nairobi, Tel. 569 790*, you can choose from a tremendous variety of hand tied fly-fishing lures. The factory is a major manufacturer and exporter of trout and salmon lures the world over. Prices are a fraction of those at home. Place an advanced order for a few dozen Royal Coachmen, Kenya Bugs, Mrs. Simpson's, or Adams Irresistible's. Newly tied, they'll be ready for your fishing adventure in a couple of days.

Information on locations of fishing camps off the main roads is obtainable from the Fisheries Department. You must work out your own transportation and reservations are not an option. Licenses are required for all freshwater fishing and are available from the **Fisheries Department**, *PO Box 58187, Nairobi, Tel. 743 579*.

DIVING & SNORKELING

Malindi and **Watamu** are the locales for scuba diving. Diving is from a boat or a dhow just off the coast. Visibility sometimes is only fair because of the plankton in the water. There are plenty of colorful fish and the coral is spectacular.

The season is from April to October with drift diving being the norm. Take your certificates or be prepared to take a test. The reefs are superb and are accessible by glass bottom boat. Some coral gardens can be reached on foot at low tide for snorkeling (known as **goggling** in Kenya).

For more information, contact:
- **The Crab Diving School**, *PO Box 454, Ukunda, Mombasa, Tel. 3431/2118, Fax 2218*
- **One Earth Tours and Expeditions**, *PO Box 82234, Mombasa, Tel. 471 771, Fax 471 349*
- **Scuba Diving Kenya Ltd.**, *PO Box 160, Watamu, Tel. 32099, Fax 32430*

WINDSURFING

Most of the resort hotels south and north of **Mombasa** have windsurfer rentals. The waters are sheltered by the offshore reef preventing annoyingly high waves. The breeze is usually strong and steady.

For more information, contact **Harald Geier's Windsurfing School**, *Surf and Safaris Ltd., Turtle Bay Beach Hotel, Watamu, Tel. 32622, Fax 32268.*

HANG GLIDING

The **Gliding Club of Kenya** has its headquarters in **Mweiga** near Nyeri in the Aberdares. Flights are available every day except for the months of July and August. The great cliffs and thermals of the Rift Valley attract world-class gliders hoping to break a world record.

For more information, contact:
• **The Gliding Club of Kenya**, *PO Box 926, Nyeri, Tel. 2969*
• **The Aero Club of East Africa**, *Wilson Airport, PO Box 40813, Nairobi, Tel. 501 772*

BEACHES

One of Kenya's great allures is the exquisite beaches that delineate the coast. It is easy to stay longer than expected. The perfect water temperature, dazzling white sand, and palm trees make for the consummate vacation spot.

There are several magnificent options. An excellent choice is **Diani** if you don't mind other resorts along the shore. For beach camping, try **Twiga Lodge** at **Tiwi beach** where life is more laid back.

WHITE WATER RAFTING

The **Athi** or **Tana** and **Ewaso Nyiro** rivers are usually where you'll put in. You can book a one day or a week long trip depending on what you're looking for and how much you want to spend. The trips can go from 40 miles to 400 miles and can be combined with caving and game drives.

White water rafting adventures can vary significantly according to the water levels. The options range from roughing it to showers and wine with dinner. As far as the ride itself goes, you can choose slow limpid drifting all the way up to Class 5 rapids, chutes, and waterfalls.

For more information on rafting, contact: **Savage Wilderness Safaris Ltd.**, *PO Box 44827, Nairobi, Tel. 521 590, Fax 501 754.*

CAR RACING

The **555 Safari Rally** is the longest endurance feat and the main event in the international car race. The event covers some of Kenya's worst dirt roads and tracks. Broadcast around the world, it is fun to watch as the drivers battle thick dust, unpredictable wildlife, and each other. The three-day rally is held over Easter weekend every year.

Other smaller rallies used to determine "Motorsportsman of the Year" take place throughout the year. They include road safety, training, economy-run, national rallies and go-cart races. An all time favorite is the **Rhino Charge** that raises money for Kenya's sadly dwindling rhino population.

Each year preparations get underway for the famous "Rhino Charge". The cross-country endurance rally is great fun for those involved and the spectators encouraging their teams to win. For the past two years in a row, the lovely bronze casting of a black rhino, which is the winners trophy, sat on the bar of Cheli & Peacock's Tortillis Camp. I cannot say enough about this worthwhile effort of raising money. All the funds raised go to the fencing project at **Aberdare National Park** to protect the resident elephant and rhino populations.

For more information about these rallies, contact:
- **East Africa Motor Sports Club**, *PO Box 42786, Nairobi*
- **Safari Rally Ltd.**, *PO Box 59483, Nairobi*

THE CAMEL DERBY

An increasingly popular day of unadulterated pandemonium is held at the end of September each year. The race is known unofficially as the **Camel Derby** *and officially as the* **Maralal International Camel Derby***. Participation is open to all who care to take a chance on the back of a rented camel. Hosted by the Yare Safaris Hostel, the participants range from professional jockeys to greenhorns. Great fun is had by all!*

HORSE RACING

The races are held on Sunday afternoons at the **Ngong Racecourse** on Ngong Road in Nairobi. There are no races in August and September or on most public holidays. You will delight in an engaging afternoon at one of the world's prettiest racecourses. The amenities and caterers tend to be exceptional.

The racing is popular and well run with bookmakers, tote facilities, a qualified handicapper, and stewards. The eight-race card races are inexpensive and wholly gratifying.

For more information, contact the **Ngong Racecourse** or the **Jockey Club of Kenya**, *PO Box 40373, Nairobi, Tel. 566 108.*

For the first time in the history of the sport, there was a "men versus horse" race featuring the 4 x 400m relay team of internationally acclaimed

Kenyan track stars. Believe it or not, the men overwhelmingly won this race that had the crowds on their feet cheering.

BOXING

The number two sport after athletics (track and field), boxing has rewarded Kenya well in the international arena. With over twenty-five gold, silver, and bronze medals to its credit, Kenya enthusiastically encourages continued excellence in the boxing ring.

SOCCER

Soccer is considered Kenya's national sport and passions run strong. It is played in most villages and all the way up to the national level. While the **Harambee Stars**, the national team, are winners in Africa, they still rank rather low worldwide. The two top teams are **AFC Leopards** and **Gor Mahla**. Matches between the two rivals can be counted on to be colorful and entertaining, with bands and cheerleaders egging on the crowd.

Each weekend, hundreds of thousands of spectators and football fans cram the stadiums to see their favorite teams in action. The entertainment is appealing and the price fair.

For more information, contact **The Kenya Football Federation**, *PO Box 40234, Nairobi, Tel. 226 138.*

PALEOANTHROPOLOGY & ARCHAEOLOGY

Visiting ancient ruins and digs may not exactly be a sport, but it certainly is a leading recreational activity for tourists in East Africa. Kenya is distinguished for its ancient fossils and prehistoric remains. In **Sibiloi National Park**, Richard Leakey and his teams unearthed some of the most remarkable hominid finds. The makeshift museum at **Koobi Fora**, a sliver of sand at **Lake Turkana**, shows some of these remarkable items.

There are several hundred sites that are worth touring to see the vast array of stone age artifacts. To visit these areas it is best to obtain permission in advance from the **National Museum of Kenya**, *PO Box 40658 Nairobi, Tel. 742 131, Fax 741 424.*

Along the coast, there are 31 sites with at least 53 standing ruins of mosques dating back to the tenth century. To some, these are just a pile of rubble, but to others they represent a rich inventory of African past. The ancient city of **Gede**, located near **Malindi**, is one of the most dramatic sites uncovered. The population once stood at roughly 2,000.

The town of **Lamu** within the Lamu Archipelago will transport you back in time. The people still live in houses made of coral bricks set on a labyrinth of streets. They are not accustomed to tourists, so when you arrive be conservative in your dress and act as inconspicuously as possible.

ANCIENT GAMES

The age-old African game of **Bau** *is played on a board into which parallel rows of holes are symmetrically carved. Two players move pieces of stone, seeds, or pebbles from one hole to the other in an elaborate game. The objective is to take as many markers as possible. If betting is involved, there is generally an exchange of cattle or women.*

Other notable archaeological remains on the islands of **Paté** and **Manda** are **Kitau** and **Takwa**. Established in the first half of the 14th century, it is speculated that these served as religious retreats.

Forty miles outside of Nairobi is **Olorgesailie**, a prehistoric hunters' camp. With the help of a knowledgeable guide, you'll see excavated ancient fossils, tools, weapons, and bones. This place is not difficult to get to as the roads are pretty good almost all the way. It is worth a visit if you have time.

Hyrax Hill near Nairobi offers a New Stone Age settlement dating about 1000 BC. At this site, archaeologists discovered an Iron Age cemetery directly above a much older Neolithic one. No one can explain why they both chose to bury their dead at exactly the same spot.

TEA & COFFEE TOURS

Unusual and vast tea and coffee plantations are worth the time it takes to tour. In **Limuru** the lush hills are clothed with conifer, banana, and eucalyptus forests between the tea and coffee plantings. Located just north of Nairobi, any of the tea or coffee factories will gladly show you around and answer your questions.

Plan on a full day's tour if you want the works at **Mitchell's Kiambethu Tea Farm**, *Tel. (0154) 40756*. The package includes a forest walk to observe the colobus monkeys, drinks, and a scrumptious lunch with several courses. Make arrangements before going up there and you will be introduced to the entire fascinating process of tea production.

10. TAKING THE KIDS

Kenya is a "state of the art" country only as far as Jomo Kenyatta International Airport and some of the five star resorts. You must be willing to take your children back to a more primitive time, or Kenya is not generally considered as a vacation spot for anyone under the age of eight. This is not to say a holiday with offspring is impossible or that families with small children are not welcome, but flexibility and adaptability are a must!

Kenyans are amazingly friendly people and they love kids. A wide and winning smile from local youth soon eliminates the language barrier for visiting youngsters. If you ask, the local children might even include your kids in one of their ancient games.

There are no store-bought diversions, but rather the children use their imaginations to create new fun. It is amazing how much you can do with a few sticks and some mud. Creative African pastimes for children have been handed down from generation to generation for centuries. Long ago, "board games" chiseled into large rocks allowed the shepherd boys to while away the hours as they watched their grazing herds. The carvings are still found all over Kenya.

SAD REALITY

African families are too poor to afford any luxuries for their children. Life for the majority of kids is hard. They start working in the fields or taking care of the cattle almost as soon as they can walk. As a large portion of Kenya's population is under fifteen, it is a common sight to see children toiling in the sun alongside their mothers.

KID-FRIENDLY HOTELS

Generally, the tree-hotels don't accept children under the age of age of seven due to the possible dangers presented. When you are making your reservations, check with your travel agent or the hotel booking service to make sure children are admitted.

A member of the **Block Hotel** chain, **Ol Tukai Lodge**, *Tel. 540 780, Fax 545 948,* in the heart of **Amboseli National Park** welcomes children of all ages. Most of their bedrooms are easily large enough to accommodate an extra bed. A children's menu and early supper is available and security guards allow parents to enjoy their dinner by listening for pillow fights or a wakeful baby.

At the coast, located 60 miles from Mombasa, **Hemingways**, *Tel. 225 255, Fax 216 553,* offers windsurfing, sailing, snorkeling, swimming and diving for families of all ages. Opened in 1988, this quality family hotel is situated on some of the finest stretches of pristine beach in Kenya. Children will be looked after by the hotel staff and can be entertained in the lounge/video room built for kids. Here, children over the age of 13 are classified as adults and will be charged accordingly.

Prestige Hotels Limited, *Tel. 335 208, Fax 217 278,* which include **Mara** and **Samburu Intrepid Clubs** and **Ziwani Camp** also welcome children to their classy tented facilities located about Kenya. These luxury tented lodges have all the comforts of home while providing a wilderness experience in natural and often majestic settings. Each of the Intrepid Clubs has refreshing swimming pools and comfortable common areas. Children's rates are only applicable between the ages of two and twelve when they share accommodations with an adult. Infants under the age of two stay free.

CURIOUS KIDS

Kenyan children are fascinated by tourists and often want to hold your hand, look at your watch, and hold your camera. I often let them look through the lens of my camera and push the auto focus button. It is amazing how quickly they learn even with the language barrier. Don't be afraid to have them touch you, they are just being curious children and want to see what unusual things travelers carry. With a friendly smile and shy eyes, they will flock around you, perhaps asking if you have any pencils they can have for school.

All hotels outside of Nairobi will have an interesting feature that will be fun for the kids – **mosquito nets**. Used as a precaution against mosquitoes carrying malaria, these nets are draped around the beds every evening just before the sun goes down. Sleeping under a net gives the feeling of sleeping in a home-made fort and adds a sense of adventure.

Most resort hotels have baby-sitting facilities which they offer during the day and in the evening. Many hotels have swimming pools which entertain youngsters and keep them cool during the long hot afternoons. In the traditional colonial fashion, children in Kenya are expected to be seen and not heard. Kids go quietly off to bed or play after dinner, leaving the evening for adults. In many places the children are served their supper before the adults.

OTHER LODGING OPTIONS

If you plan on staying in Kenya for more than a couple of nights, take a look at the option of renting a cottage or a bungalow. If you make your travel arrangements through a tour operator, they may not offer you this alternative. You will have to ask. The cottages are a particularly nice choice along the coast and will save you a fortune in hotel and food expenses. You can shop like the local people and eat at home.

Camping is a pretty good choice if you have children with you and are trying to save money. Be sure and know where you are going and have some good maps handy. Camping equipment can be rented in Nairobi, but you are better off bringing the basics with you. I would suggest making reservations in advance. When you arrive at your site, keep a very close eye on your kids. Traveling this way will be cheap and rustic.

KIDS & TRAINS!

Train travel in Kenya is a pleasant experience. The old colonial style of travel is not likely to be found anywhere else in the world. If you have the time and are going to the coast, this is something the kids will thoroughly enjoy. (See Chapter 6, *Planning Your Trip*, for more details).

If a trip to the beach is part of your desired itinerary but flying is not an option for you because of the expense, try the train. The long journey to the coast will be more fun than it could ever be in a car. Moving about is not a problem and much of the travel is at night while the kids are asleep.

MUDDY DELIGHT

As children in Kenya, my sisters and I loved to play in the sticky black cotton soil when it rained. Today, this is still very much an acceptable pastime for the local children. It is not uncommon for small kids to be seen in their yards covering each other from head to toe in thick mud. The whites of their eyes and their happy smiles tell the rest of the story. I can vouch for the unadulterated pleasure of this delightful game!

PARKS & RESERVES

While there is no restriction on children visiting the reserves or national parks, there may be age limits for the longer or more dangerous tours. Check with the tour operator when booking your trip.

While on safari, it is strongly suggested that you keep a very close eye on youngsters. There are many exciting and diverse distractions to grab a child's attention and lure them away from the safety of the party and guide. The dangers are very real. The animals are wild and a small child can easily be hurt or killed. It only takes a few seconds for an accident to happen.

COMING OF AGE

*When young Africans between the ages of twelve and fifteen are about to enter adulthood, they go through a series of rituals. These **rites of passage** vary from tribe to tribe and region to region. Sometimes the transition takes months or even years. The boys of the Samburu tribe take great pride in the ceremonies involved in the transition from child to adult. One of the many requirements is the painting of their bodies and hair with red ochre and fat.*

During the courting period youngsters get together and sing and dance into the wee hours of the morning. The dances generally consist of jumping three or four feet straight up into the air for long periods of time. This often induces a trance-like state.

A young man will hold his girlfriend's hand and instead of a kiss he will flick his long red braids into her face. The giggles and flirting could be those of a teenager anywhere in the world; the language is universal!

HAZARDS FOR KIDS

Other less ominous hazards include heat, dust, and insects. If you travel in Kenya you will undoubtedly encounter all three. Try to prepare your children for what is ahead. If they understand and know what to expect, things often go more smoothly.

It is a very good idea to bring mosquito repellent with you for your young ones. Malaria is commonplace in Kenya. The best way to stop your kids from getting it is to keep them from being bitten by the carrier mosquito.

Use a mosquito net over the bed at night if at all possible and keep kids coated in repellent after sundown when the offending insect is about. Burning mosquito coils within a safe distance of where your child sleeps will also help in preventing the mosquito from delivering its nasty bite.

Time spent getting from one sight to another in a vehicle can be a long and arduous ordeal even for the toughest adult. Add thick clouds of dust to any ride and you have a child's nightmare. To help the children deal with it, try making a game out of tying a damp bandanna over their noses "cowboy" fashion.

FUN WITH FLYING ANTS

A favorite game during the rainy seasons of my childhood was to catch the flying ants or termites. During the rains these small little creatures take flight in search of new homesites. It is amazing what fun it can be to use a butterfly net and run through the rain filling it with the insects.

Once the net was coated with hundreds of the winged ants, we would cook them (with supervision) in a dome shaped outdoor African mud oven. The delicate crispy flavor was second only to the pure pleasure of running through the warm cleansing downpour in the Kenyan bush.

If you rent a car or go out with a tour, check to see if it has an air conditioner and that it is in working order. This will often help keep the dust outside the car instead of up your kid's nose. Kenya can get very dusty if there has been no rain. Driving through the dusty countryside is made a little more pleasant with an airconditioned vehicle.

When traveling for long stretches, it is wise to bring your child's favorite toys and games. If motion sickness is not a problem, perhaps children's books with pictures or information on local wildlife are a worthy notion. Out of consideration for others in your party, low-key entertainment is best.

To avoid the exhaustion of traveling by car, choose one game park and fly in. The trip will take far less time and will be more enjoyable. This mode of transport costs more, but will cut down on the wear and tear your children endure.

If you are vacationing at the beach, **sunblock** is a wise precaution. The sun can be strong reflecting off the sand and can cause a nasty sunburn. The sun at the equator is stronger than it is at home and will have more of an effect on your skin in a shorter period of time.

Sometimes the unpredictable currents sweep strong swimmers out to sea. It is advisable not to allow children to swim without supervision. Staying within the safe zones will eliminate potential problems.

An encounter with any of the myriad of ocean dwellers, such as sea urchins or stinging man-o-war, can be extremely unpleasant for a youngster. Use caution and keep an eye out for anything unusual in the clear water.

NECESSITIES

Anything you might need is available in the larger towns. However, the brands you are accustomed to and the variety of choices may be limited. If you are particular, it is better to bring diapers, baby food, or special dietary needs with you in your luggage.

Such things as toys, books, sunscreen, and clothing for children are easy to find in most stores in Kenya. Just ask your guide or driver to take you to the local shop – **duka** – to get what you need. If you find yourself out in the bush, ask your hotel clerk and often they can have the item brought in on the next car or plane coming your way. The "bush telegraph" has a way of getting things done when necessary.

Don't be intimidated by the perilous sounding advice regarding children in Kenya. Caution and common sense when you are in a strange environment should not stop you from having fun.

As always, use the rules of common courtesy and common sense when it comes to your children. Not only will other tourists appreciate your efforts but the children themselves will be happier as they focus on the amazing Kenyan experience.

NUDITY

*It is very common for the Kenyan children to run around naked. The women will often be nude from the waist up and the men may be barely covered with a blanket (**shuka**). Nudity is a perfectly normal occurrence in this part of the world and should not be ridiculed. Prepare your children for this sight so that they can accept this as a way of life in Africa, and so that they do not make the villagers feel uncomfortable with their stares.*

11. KENYA'S BEST PLACES TO STAY

Kenya has some of the most amazing assortments of accommodation for you to choose from. The options vary from grass shacks, basic tents, tented camps, homestays, lodges and hotels. The six places I depict here are worth mentioning for a variety of reasons, but not necessarily because of the facilities or amenities. Things such as location, activities, ambiance, design and history played a part in the selections.

Adapting is all part of enjoying and learning the difference between what we are accustomed to at home and the challenges of being abroad. Accept the task of seeing beyond what's on the surface and try to behold the real beauty of Kenya and its friendly people.

Because the prices of hotels in Kenya vary according to season and market conditions, the rates quoted here are for double occupancy during peak times and include all meals. There are frequent promotional specials and package deals that may be a better bargain at the time you are visiting.

OL MALO RANCH/SANCTUARY, *PO Box 56923, Nairobi, or Muridjo Ltd., PO Box 163 Rumuruti. Tel. 571 661, Fax 571 665, E-mail: francombe@olmalo.demon.co.uk. Ol Malo is a member of Bush Homes Africa Safaris, Tel. 502 491, Fax 502 739. $460 per night for double occupancy. Due to the popularity of Ol Malo, it is necessary to book far in advance.*

Ol Malo is a small privately hosted home up in Kenya's **Northern Frontier District**. The owners, Colin and Rocky Francombe, purchased the 5,000 acres of fragile arid land to build their dream home. In desperate need of some love and attention, the expanse of semi-desert is obviously benefiting from the Francombe's years of ranching experience.

It is called Ol Malo, "place of the greater kudu," because the area is known for its concentration of the rare antelope not often found anywhere else in Kenya. The owners even have a tame female kudu named Tandela that you can pet if she comes around. As a baby, Tandela was saved from an untimely death in the wilds.

The Francombe's spend much of their time taking care of and attracting wildlife to their protected piece of land. As keen conservationists the game always comes first. This is true even if it means going without a bath when there is a shortage of water in order for the animals to drink. For guests, there is a wonderful, new hide down at the waterhole so you can have eye contact with an elephant or two!

Game is not as prolific here as it is in other parts of Kenya, but the animals are learning that this is a sanctuary where they will not be disturbed. More and more gerenuk, kudu, elephant, buffalo, lion, giraffe, leopard and other smaller mammals are making Ol Malo part of their territory.

Getting here can be a bit of a challenge if you decide to drive. The road is rough and in some places almost impassable, but it can be done if you have unlimited time and endurance. The best way to arrive however, is by small plane. Ol Malo has a good landing strip providing it doesn't rain, which it rarely does.

The nine individual structures of the compound are built at the very edge of a high escarpment. Four of these are ensuite guest cottages. All the high pitched roofs are thatched with an attractive local reed. The walls are built from locally quarried, colorful stone found in the area.

Nestled between the rocks along the cliff, the private cottages have the most remarkable bedrooms and bathrooms. The enormous custom made tub offers comforting hot water to soothe the aches of a day-trek through the bush. The grand window extends a view of the cute rock hyrax as they scurry about in search of a tasty morsel.

Enjoying a picture-perfect sunrise while lying in the oversized king bed and sipping tea delivered at your specified time makes you never want to leave. The room decor is tastefully done with charming natural materials and local handicrafts which you can purchase while visiting the nearby town of Maralal. The curve of ancient olive wood adds interest throughout the buildings.

The view from the wide open verandahs is breathtakingly beautiful. A large glass picture window keeps out the gusty winds and the separate living room and dining room are kept warm in the evenings by a crackling fire. The orange, yellow, and red of the ethereal sunset is a sight you shouldn't miss.

Rocky and Colin are warm and friendly hosts who share their knowledge and love of the Kenyan bush while dining with you in the candlelight or sitting in the cozy living room. The large grandfather clock in the corner of the room and the tame African Gray parrot show the care with which the Francome's put this place together; one piece at a time.

A secluded free-form swimming pool is perched cliffside and offers an incredible view to the valley below. The attractively shaped pool is engineered to look like it flows over the side of the precipice. In fact, there are gutters catching and recycling the water, keeping it clean as they skim impurities off the surface.

The grounds and meandering walkways are a pleasant surprise in this desert setting. The rock gardens are full of exotic plants found naturally in the area. Rocky cherishes the local aloe plant which she has used to lovingly landscape the gardens. She has even managed to find and nurture an unknown species.

For your pleasure there are many exciting activities, such as guided nature walks, game drives, visits to an unspoiled local *manyatta* (village), camping near the Uaso Nyiro River, bush picnics, camel rides, game viewing by the watering hole and just relaxing by the unique pool.

The four exclusive and exquisite one-level guest cottages along with the wild beauty of the wilderness are the most romantic settings I have ever seen in all my travels. The very face of Africa is unveiled here with a personal and delightful experience. Ol Malo truly belongs in the fairy tale category!

DIANI HOUSE, *PO Box 19, Ukunda, Mombasa. Tel. 0127 2412, Fax 0127 2391. Diani House is a member of Bush Homes Africa Safaris, Tel. 502 491, Fax 502 739, e-mail aceltd@africaonline.co.ke, www.dianihouse.com. $195 per person per night.*

To get to Diani House you fly from Nairobi to the airport in Mombasa. One of your hosts (either Lulu or John) picks you up there for the ride to **Diani Beach** or a taxi can be arranged. The drive is a pleasant one as your guide points out the various species of trees, places of interest and explains a little local history.

On the way from the airport you must cross the river on a huge passenger and vehicle ferry. This is quite an exciting adventure but can sometimes take a few minutes to board if the line of cars is long. Here you are met by a colorful array of locals who use the ferry to commute to work in the city. There are tasty cashews, peanuts, juicy mangoes, fresh bananas and other goodies for sale.

After the fascinating hour long drive from Mombasa you will be ready for the hideaway at Diani House. Located about half way along Diani Beach, this Arab style home offers a taste of colonial Kenya of days gone by. Here you can rest on the cool verandah with a refreshing coconut water drink or restore yourself with a walk around the garden enjoying the quiet beauty.

Comprised of twelve forested acres of land, the grounds are an impressive array of flowering trees and shrubs. The coconut palms, giant baobabs, bright bougainvillea and fragrant frangipani offer a haven to many birds, bushbabies, monkeys and other wildlife living here in this slice of paradise. A short walk down the lush garden path offers a beautiful view of the white beach and Indian Ocean.

There are only eight beds, which will assure you it will never get too crowded. Each room has its own spacious bathroom done in the large red tile made locally. The shower is oversized and open with a built-in tile seat for your comfort. Complimentary amenities are tastefully arrayed on the wide sink.

Instead of glass, the windows are attractively covered with wrought iron bars, lacy curtains, and an optional mesh roll-down screen, as there is no air conditioning. Instead, the open windows and ceiling fans circulate the cool ocean breeze. The rooms stay fresh and comfortable.

The large Arab style poster beds are skillfully carved antiques. Draped in a mosquito net at night, the dark wood and the intricate details of the bed are pleasing as you drift off to sleep. If slumber eludes you, try a book from the wide selection available either in your room or the picturesque family room.

The house, decorated in colorful local fabrics and crafts, is set back from the beach offering complete privacy. To add to the casual and comfortable ambiance there are scattered rugs, overstuffed pillows, and relaxing music.

The short walk down the grassy slope with adorable dogs at your heels can't prepare you for the memorable view ahead. The sand on the beach is so white and fine it looks like salt and the color of the crystalline ocean is perfectly turquoise. For miles to the left and right all you can see is more pristine beach. You can literally feel the everyday cares of life dissolving as you relax in nirvana.

Food is a special feature of a Diani House vacation, with emphasis on fresh local produce. Fishermen bring fish and shellfish to the kitchen door straight from the ocean. These delicacies, along with the abundant tropical fruit and fresh vegetables, make dining here a gourmet's delight. The fresh sashimi and prawns tempura are delectable!

Diani Beach has hotels, tennis, and squash courts, shops, a casino, night clubs and some excellent restaurants for you to enjoy if you wish. The good thing is that they are close enough if you want them but not near enough to disturb the peace and privacy of Diani House.

As if these things were not enough, the choice of things to do goes on forever. Bountiful fishing; snorkeling; diving; trips to nearby islands on John and Lulu's well equipped boat; windsurfing (with lessons); day trips to Mombasa or local markets for shopping and sightseeing; game viewing of elephant and rare sable antelope in Shimba Hills National Park; spotting a myriad of colorful birds in Jadini Forest; enjoying Tiwi creek's spectacular beauty; or horseback and camel riding on the beach are a few of the amusements available to you.

This idyllic setting is about as close to paradise as you are going to get for a beachside vacation. My only word of caution is to allow enough time to fully enjoy the sights, sounds, and natural beauty of this ocean paradise – and wear your sunblock!

GRAND REGENCY HOTEL, *PO Box 40511, Nairobi. Tel. 211 199, Fax 217120; in the US, toll-free reservations Tel. 800/223-5652. $275 per night for double occupancy.*

The city of **Nairobi** had its doubts about whether this venture would ever actually open. The story behind the luxurious hotel adds a bit of spice to its recent history. Apparently, during construction the ownership changed hands several times due to either politics and money, or perhaps both. With sly smiles the locals will tell you there is much more to the amusing yarn than meets the eye!

Opening day was postponed over and over again. The city's businessmen and hoteliers held their collective breaths. Eventually the building was completed and the big day arrived with much media publicity.

The lavish and modern facility was touted as the absolute best in Nairobi. Scandal, however, was still rearing its ugly head, when along with other coverage on the front page was the story of the Grand Regency Hotel being seized by the Central Bank of Kenya. Interestingly, the owner of the bank is the president of Kenya's son, who now also owns the hotel.

The questionable birth of this ultra-modern hotel is in no way reflected in the accommodations or services offered within. The management takes pride in setting the highest standards of excellence. From the cordial doorman to the friendly room attendants you will be impressed during your stay.

Driving through the entrance to the spacious, cobbled parking area you will be able to tell this is a classy establishment. The trees and flowering shrubs make it look not so much like a parking lot but rather some sort of promenade. If you have a vehicle, you can feel safe leaving it here.

If you start feeling homesick for the comforts of home, the Grand Regency offers lodgings equal to those found in any US city. The added bonus is that it all has the mysterious touch of Africa subtly hidden throughout. At the 240-plus room facility, anything you might need as a business or pleasure traveler is within easy grasp. Nightclubs and other attractions are no further than a short easy walk or cab ride.

The Grand Regency is considered the regional business center of East and Central Africa. Here you can keep in touch with the rest of the world at the business center. A full secretarial staff and state-of-the-art telecommunications services are at your disposal.

The luxury of air conditioning (not often found in Kenya) is just the beginning as you walk into the soaring lobby of the hotel. Intricately designed Masai beadwork is artistically recreated on a towering wall of the multi-storied atrium. In my opinion, this complex design is the highpoint of the decor with shimmering greens, reds, blues, and yellows.

As you ride to your room in the glass elevators the show below is of shiny brass, marble, and granite in the piano lounge, restaurant, and bar. Mirrors, strategic lighting, and green plants add to the feeling of luxury throughout the open areas. Views of the city and Uhuru Park can be seen from any of the surrounding picture windows.

On an outdoor terrace, the Grand Regency boasts a covered, all-weather, heated swimming pool with a fully equipped gym, sauna, Jacuzzi, steam bath and massage facilities. This is a truly great place to pamper yourself either before your bush safari or as a last fling before the long trip home.

The bedrooms are on open levels around the atrium. The mahogany furniture, great panorama, bidet, hair dryer, room safe and satellite TV are marks of elegant sophistication. Once you get settled in the lovely room, you'd be happy to stay for more than a couple of days.

For any last minute purchases, try the shopping arcade where you will find souvenirs, artifacts, sundries, and a florist. If you run out of toothpaste or forgot your eye drops, this is the place to stop.

For a little more excitement pay a visit to the casino or one of the elegant 24 hour restaurants, bars, or cafes. Tender barbecue, delicious breakfast buffets, candlelight dinners, or traditional English high tea are just a few of the appetizing choices. My personal breakfast favorite is the mushroom omelet, pork sausage, baked tomato with curry seasonings, home-made breads and fresh tropical fruit slices.

This new and distinctive landmark located in Nairobi's newest up-market business area is an excellent, if a little pricey, choice. You won't be more pampered or comfortable than at the Grand Regency Hotel.

AMBOSELI SERENA LODGE, *Serena Lodges & Hotels, PO Box 48690, Nairobi. Tel. 710 511, Fax 718103. $208 per night for double occupancy.*

As you check into the Amboseli Serena Lodge the front desk clerk will proceed with all the usual paper work. Then she'll say "here's your key" – as she hands over a Masai club with the room key attached. While you giggle in wonder at this foot-long stick with a knob at the end, she'll continue by explaining that the Masai use these weapons to protect themselves. You can use it to gently fend off the pesky monkeys roaming the grounds.

There are two reasonable ways of getting to the lodge. The first and by far the easiest is to fly in and land at the nearby airstrip. The flight from Nairobi will take a mere thirty minutes. You will be able to enjoy the view and general feel of the terrain below without getting hot, sweaty, and dusty. The second option is to make the 160 mile drive from the city. Depending on the road conditions, this should be a four hour drive.

Amboseli, which means "salt dust" in the Masai language, pretty accurately describes this slowly regenerating barren land. You can contribute to the restoration of the park by planting a tree on the 60-odd acre property and leave a little piece of yourself in this wonderful place.

The 96 room lodge is set almost in the middle of **Amboseli National Park** and is designed to blend with the environment. With the idea of following the Masai construction of a *manyatta* (village), the buildings are camouflaged by surrounding bush. Also like local homesteads, there seem to be no square edges here, but rather smooth curves and rounded rims along windows, doors, and openings.

A favorite part of the hotel is the wooden bridge you must cross to get inside. Gurgling running water under your feet will immediately make you feel cooler. The carefully tended water lilies and enchanting overhanging gardens only add to the feeling of escape from the warm temperatures.

Built of what looks like red mud, the one level connected buildings are tastefully decorated with African animal and Masai themes throughout. Dried hanging gourds of all shapes and interesting sizes serve as shades for the lights.

The halls leading to the rooms are open to the heavens as they meander through dense tropical gardens. Headboards for the beds are made of bamboo-sized sticks and Masai spears hold up the shower curtains. The giant paintings of wildlife give you an exciting taste of what's to come in the real bush safari.

Set in one of the few wet and contrastingly green areas, Serena Lodge has chosen one of the more pleasant surroundings in Amboseli to set up shop. The tall acacia trees are roosting spots for crowned cranes, white pelicans, and other feathered wonders. At night the spotlights reveal elephant families within ten or twelve feet of you as they chomp on the long grass. During the day it is common to see cheeky monkeys or gnu cavorting on the grassy terrace.

Many people make the trip here to see the famous snow-capped **Mount Kilimanjaro**. Unfortunately, the splendor of the Tanzanian mountain can't be seen from the public areas of the Serena. This drawback is offset by the views from the bedrooms. You will either have a view of the looming mountain or the water hole, which is frequented daily by herds of thirsty antelope, elephant, and gazelle. As there are no barriers or fences, anything can happen. The outdoor terraces, the refreshing swimming pool and the main bar overlook the bright green vegetation of the watering hole. Monkeys stealing a piece of fruit right off your table, herds of elephant joining you for tea, or colorful starlings flocking to drink are sights worth the trip.

Meals at Amboseli Serena feel like intimate occasions, as the dining hall is divided into many different size rooms. To reach this area you must cross another charming bridge over running water surrounded by floating gardens and water lilies. Breakfast and lunch are buffet style, while dinner is a romantic candlelight affair. To add to the pleasure of varied meals, oversized windows give the illusion of being outdoors.

Every other night on the terrace below the pool you can choose to participate in the **Masai Exotic Dinner**. For the price, you will enjoy traditional Kenyan fare, a variety of barbecued meats, and an open bar. The waiters look proud in their colorful *shukas* (blankets used for as clothing) as they serve you under the star-filled evening sky.

Aside from the excellent game viewing, there are many activities to keep you entertained during your stay. Masai dancers around the evening camp fire, bird walks, jogging trails, informative and casual culture lectures, local singers and flights over Mount Kilimanjaro in a small plane are a few of your pastime choices.

Each room has its own bathroom which is modern and clean, but be prepared for small bedrooms in this unique Kenya lodge. Amboseli Serena is a most memorable hotel for any number of reasons that make a stay here worthwhile. Its excellent game viewing, the outstanding view of the majestic Mount Kilimanjaro, and the attractive grounds would take me back again and again.

LITTLE GOVERNOR'S CAMP, *Governors' Camps-Musiara, Ltd., PO Box 48217, Nairobi. Tel. 331 871, Fax 726 427. $325 per night for double occupancy. Due to the popularity of the Governors' tented camps, it is necessary to book well in advance.*

Located in **Masai Mara**, the most popular game reserve in Kenya, Little Governors' Camp is just one of four luxury tented camps run by this outfitter. To get to any of the camps it is necessary to fly in to the Musiara airfield, only a short ride from any of the sites. All of the camps are very popular, but the favorite always seems to be Little Governor's.

As the smallest of the tented camps, there is naturally less noise, fewer crowds, and more personalized service. Guests spend time with the staff and each other in a low key and friendly atmosphere. The sense of balance between privacy and communal camping makes you feel extra special.

One of the most remarkable elements of this exciting camp is getting there. The first step of the adventure is to load up in a boat for the trip across the **Mara River**. The boatman pulls you over to the other side along a rope secured on each bank. This is loads of fun but can be a little scary if you stop to think about what might be in the water below you!

Next comes the hike up a steep set of steps carved into the bank. You will need to be moderately fit to climb the stairs and to get around the camp itself, but the effort will be worth it. Once at the top, a short walk down a shady forest pathway will end this portion of your escapade.

Before you is a spectacular sight of seventeen tents looking out over the marsh. This is where you will be spending your nights and the hot hours of your day. Splendid views of the flat, never-ending plains and the high cliffs will show you one of the many wonderful faces of Kenya.

Even though there is no electricity, you will quickly get into the spirit of true camping with the added romance of candles, lanterns, and flashlights provided for you. There is something terribly exciting about not having electric light. You will feel as though you have stepped back to a time when Africa was first being explored. But this will be the extent of the hardships you will have to endure during your stay!

Each canvas tent has a covered outdoor verandah with two well-placed safari chairs and a small wooden table. Inside, the simple furnishings include twin beds, a clothes rack, a dresser and more safari chairs. The tents are comfortable, clean, and more importantly fun!

Adjoining each tent is an exclusive tented bathroom. You will be amazed by the running water, hot showers, flush toilets, and here at Little Governors', even a bidet! In some of the other camps, the showers are traditional and are filled with warm water at your request.

I would be remiss if I did not mention the growing reputation of the camp's excellent food services. Breakfast and lunch offer great selections of buffet-style fare set under tall acacia trees. The outdoor settings with views of the marsh, the hills beyond, and wandering wildlife make meals here delightful. It is astounding how such delicacies can be produced in this rough setting miles from anywhere. Even more amazing is the seemingly endless supply of ice and cold, cold drinks.

Evening meals in the intimate dining tent culminate with outstanding desserts. The flickering candlelight, elegant crystal, and carefully pressed linens somehow go hand in hand with the outdoor setting. For most guests, an after dinner drink around the campfire is the perfect prelude to a good night's sleep.

A balloon ride with champagne breakfast on the plains is worth the effort of getting up before dawn. If you don't feel floating over the bush as the sun rises is worth $350, at least go and watch the take-off. It is definitely worth a picture to see the multi-colored canvas slowly fill with hot air and lift gently in to the sky.

Other worthwhile activities include excellent game drives in open topped vehicles, pre-arranged fishing on Lake Victoria, superior souvenir shopping, an interesting museum, nature hiking or simply absorbing the tranquillity of the Mara River.

Masai Mara is famous for its outstanding array of wildlife. At the unfenced camp, it is not uncommon for hippos to stroll by in the early morning for a taste of the sweet grass growing outside your tent or for the elephant to make an unannounced raid on the camp's larder. Any number of giraffes, birds, monkeys, waterbuck and gazelles can parade past your tent flap at any time. Rest assured – the armed guards patrolling the grounds give a comforting sense of security.

At Little Governors' tented camp the emphasis is on unobtrusive service and high quality in an authentic African setting. Splurging for a stay here will give you a lifetime of unequaled memories in this exotic, game-filled camping experience.

ISLAND CAMP, *Lonrho Hotels Kenya Ltd., PO Box 58581, Nairobi. Tel. 216 940, Fax 216 796. $170 per night for double occupancy.*

How would you like to swim with the crocodiles? Here in the **Rift Valley** at tented Island Camp this can be your reality. **Lake Baringo**, one of only two fresh water lakes in Kenya, is a silt-stained lake full of crocs, tilapia fish, and hippos. The crocs won't mind sharing their cool home with you as you go for a dip, water ski, or windsurf. According to the locals, no one has every been harmed by these reptiles.

Almost as exciting as swimming with the crocodiles is getting to Island Camp. After you leave your vehicle with an *askari* at the end of a rocky track you're in for the ride of your life. A 20 minute run aboard a motorized canoe has you whipping around twitching hippo ears, slithering crocodiles, or perhaps a local Njemps fishing canoe. The wild beauty of the rocky islands and awesome mountain ranges will quickly put you in touch with the majesty of nature.

When you arrive at *Ol Kokwe* (place of rocks) island you are almost at your destination. Clamber out of your boat and restore yourself under the cool shade with a refreshing drink before setting off on the final leg of your journey.

As you begin your climb up the steps and paths to the top of the hill, take time to catch your breath and enjoy the magnificent extinct volcanoes, strings of mountain ridges, outspread trees, and the energetic scurrying lizards that abound. Once you reach the top and you take it all in, you will know this unique beauty is the reason you came.

The perfectly adequate tented accommodations are not in the same class as some of the other camps, but you will feel more than compensated for this by the dramatic play unfolding before you. Shimmering on the water and the surrounding rocks, the light show as the weather changes will entertain you for hours. Varying shades of purple, cobalt blue, and dusky gray mix and blend to cover the land with their cloak.

Each of the 23 tents is positioned for privacy along with a wondrous view. On a craggy outcrop, under a wide tree, or on the side of a hill the canvas rooms are tastefully set up. You won't even know there are other people sleeping within shouting distance.

If you have never had the pleasure of a solar-heated shower, this is your chance. Zip down the flap of your tent and step through the door to the well built bathroom. Here you will find all the conveniences of home, including a flush toilet – which can be rare in the outbacks of Kenya.

To help prolong the life of the canvas, add some protection from the weather, and cool things down, all the tents are covered by an extended thatched shelter. The thatch makes for a comfortable and attractive verandah where you can sit and watch the sunrise or read a book.

During the heat of the day there is nothing more pleasant that sipping a cold drink while lounging around the picturesque pool. From the open-sided thatched lounge and bar an attentive waiter will keep your glass full. You won't even have to budge from under the vine covered arbor. Wonderful traditional English tea with some form of delicious home-made cookies or cakes is served promptly near the pool. Staying slim while on vacation here might present a problem as the food is always plentiful.

Meals are a new adventure in the main thatched dining area. Sitting at the height of the tree tops and looking out from the wall-less structure across Lake Baringo is just the beginning. As the breeze flickers the candlelight you can almost imagine you are Robinson Crusoe living in paradise.

There is much to do here at Island Camp, all you have to do is ask. Set up a long walk with a guide to spot any of the 400-plus species of resplendent birds that make their homes along the shore; hike to the remarkable hot springs at the end of the island; meet a family of local **Njemps tribespeople** as you enjoy ancestral dances or mysterious reed music; take a boat ride into the marshes and up the **Molo River** where you will see hippo, crocodile, and flocks of birds; visit **Lake Bogoria National Reserve** where you'll find kudu and thousands of pink flamingoes – or simply enjoy the sense of space and the stark beauty of this peerless camp setting.

12. NAIROBI

Ngare Nyarobe was the original Masai name of the Nairobi River. *Nyarobe* means a place of cold water – along these banks the people once came for the cool drinking water. In the swamps bordering this river, the first small town sprang up and was called **Nairobi**. In 1899, Nairobi was nothing more than a depot for the **East African Railroad**. No one expected it to become a permanent city, much less the capital of the Republic of Kenya. This was particularly true because of the rampant diseases from yellow fever to the plague and the thick unworkable black cotton soil.

From 1889 to 1902, the settlement suffered severe hardships. The first thing to hit the Masai and Kikuyu stock was a devastating outbreak of rinderpest. Then came a ravaging scourge of locusts wiping out everything in their path.

In 1898, the rains failed, bringing great famine and destruction to the land. The culminating catastrophe of the times came in 1902 with an outbreak of the bubonic plague. At this point, the government ordered the city burned to the ground as a drastic measure to wipe out the epidemic. It worked; and eventually this tenacious town was rebuilt.

Now, less than 100 years old, Nairobi still survives and flourishes. Appropriately, the largest city in East Africa has been nicknamed "City in the Sun" and "Safari Capital of the World," but there is more to it than that. The truth, much like their history, is not all romance. The **Nairobi River** never actually was a river, but rather more like a stream (except during the rainy season when it becomes a raging torrent). And sadly, today no one would dare venture close to the polluted trickle much less drink from it.

Due to the enormous population growth and the influx of people looking for jobs the city has had the very difficult task of absorbing the masses. Unfortunately, Nairobi has been unable to keep up with the expansion and hence the beggars, shanty towns, bad roads, and piles of garbage.

Because of its reputation for being less than perfect, travel agents recommend staying in the city for as little time as possible. I say, live a little and see how the other half lives! As long as you are prepared and have somewhat of an open mind, Nairobi is a wonderful city to visit. Frankly, it is no more unpleasant than some of our cities.

Very much a city of contrasts, Nairobi is the best and worst of all worlds. High rises, office buildings, movie theaters, shopping malls, luxury hotels, swimming pools, taxis, rush hour traffic jams and shanty towns are contrasted by blooming purple jacaranda, nandina flame, and bougainvillea flowers.

In the northern suburbs some of the country's rich and powerful have their homes. Large and beautifully decorated houses are complimented by their attractively landscaped grounds. It is common to see new Mercedes Benz or Land Rover vehicles cruising the streets.

As there is much to experience in and around Nairobi, allow at least three days to get to know the intricacies of its varied peoples, sights, and cuisines. It is a vibrant city with a rich history and will set a great backdrop for your safari. Hopefully, you will come away understanding what makes this such an inspiring city and why visitors return again and again.

CITY PLANNING, NAIROBI-STYLE

When the new street plans of Nairobi were roughly drawn up, certain criteria had to be met. The city designers made sure Kenyatta Avenue (then called Sixth Avenue) was wide enough for a twelve-span ox cart to turn full circle.

ARRIVALS & DEPARTURES

Chances are you will fly into Nairobi as most tourists do. **Jomo Kenyatta International Airport**, *PO Box 19001, Nairobi, Tel. 822 111*, is the main airport in Kenya and a short 11 mile drive from the city.

There are plenty of cabs available to get into town. Taxi is by far the best way to get to your hotel quickly and safely. The fare will be about $16, but make sure you agree on the price before you get in. If possible try to hook up with fellow travelers and share the expense of a cab ride into town.

Another option is to arrange with your hotel to pick you up if they have a shuttle service. Many of the larger and busier hotels offer this assistance as a courtesy to their guests. Depending on where you are staying there is sometimes a small but worthwhile fee. It is wise to inform the hotel in advance of your arrival schedule to avoid having to call from the airport.

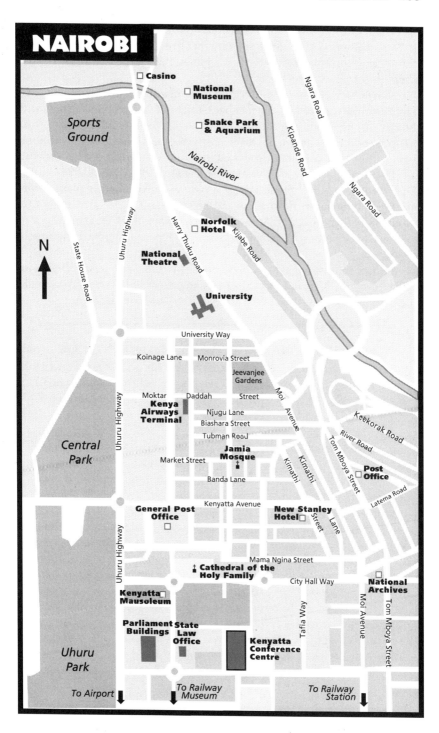

The Number 34 bus will take you in to town, but I don't recommend it. The locals know this bus as the one that brings in new arrivals and it is not uncommon for tourists to be jostled by the crowd and robbed. Not a very good first impression.

Kenya Airways operates a regular bus schedule to and from the **City Bus Terminal** on Koinange Street back and forth between the airport and the city center. If you are coming from the airport, the bus will drop you off at any hotel downtown. If you are going to Jomo Kenyatta, the minibus departs for the 30 minute ride at least four times before and after midday.

The small but busy **Wilson Airport**, *PO Box 19011, Tel. 501 941,* is the departure point for anyone taking a commuter or charter plane from Nairobi to any safari destination. There are daily scheduled flights to Masai Mara, Samburu, and Amboseli. Lamu, Nanyuki, Nyeri, and Eldoret are also on the flight schedule with private operators but not with as much frequency.

Air Kenya, located at Wilson Airport, runs daily and weekly flights to Nyeri, Nanyuki, Masia Mara, Lamu and anywhere in between. As a small operator the airline enforces its weight restriction on luggage.

AIR KENYA FARES & TIMES WITHIN KENYA

*The fares and times listed below are for **Air Kenya** and are subject to change. Other air carriers have the same approximate rates and fly to all the same places. There are scheduled flights to most destinations in Kenya, not only those listed here.*

• *Twice a day at 10:00 am and 3:00 pm, there are return flights departing Wilson Airport for Masai Mara. Round trip $150 and one way $87. Tickets for children under twelve are half price.*

• *Every day at 1:15 pm there is a return flight departing from Wilson Airport for Lamu. Round trip $236 and one way $118. Tickets for children under twelve are half price.*

• *Once a day at 1:15 pm there is a return flight departing Wilson Airport for Kiwayu. Round trip $330 and one way $165. Tickets for children under twelve are half price.*

• *Once a day at 9:15 am there is a return flight departing Wilson Airport for Nanyuki/Samburu. Round trip to Nanyuki $115 and one way $70. Round trip to Samburu $180 and one way $105. The fare from Nanyuki to Samburu is $40.*

• *Once a day at 7:30 am there is a return flights departing Wilson Airport for Amboseli. Round trip $125 and one way $70.*

• *Once a day at 10:00 am there is a flight from Nanyuki to Masai Mara. The fare is $135.*

If you can get enough people together and hire a charter plane, it makes any trip more affordable and you arrange your departure times to suit yourself. To find the best deal, try one of the main private air carriers: **Eagle Aviation**, *Tel. 606 015*, **Skyways Airlines**, *Tel. 506 018*, **Equator Airlines**, *Tel. 501 360*, and **Prestige Air Services**, *Tel. 501 212*.

Kenya Airways runs services to about 30 destinations departing from Jomo Kenyatta. Their offices are located at: *Barclays Plaza, Loita Street, PO Box 41010, Nairobi,, Tel. 229 291, Fax 336 252, or Jomo Kenyatta International Airport, Tel. 822 171/822 288.*

For more information, see Getting Around Kenya and Getting To Kenya sections in Chapter 6, *Planning Your Trip.*

ORIENTATION

South of Nairobi is the Railway Station and Nairobi National Park. A little to the northeast of the park is Jomo Kenyatta International Airport. Most visitors coming to Kenya arrive here and then enjoy the drive into town on the excellent double highway.

To reach town, you will drive through part of the city's industrial center, which includes Firestone tire factory and General Motors assembly plant. Heading in the other direction away from Nairobi's city center will put you on your way to Mombasa.

North of Nairobi is the famous Norfolk Hotel, the National Museum, the University, and the International Casino. Also to the north is one of Nairobi's upper middle class suburbs – Westlands. There is a popular shopping mall here frequented mainly by the Asian population.

It sounds from this description that these places are located far from the city center and Nairobi is spread over a large area; this is not so. Nairobi is a remarkably compact area and most places can be reached in under thirty minutes providing traffic is cooperative.

Northeast of the center of town is the somewhat lower class suburb of Parklands; the location of the Aga Khan Hospital and nearby homes of a large Asian population. Very near this site is the popular guest house simply called Mrs. Roche's. Traveling a bit further east of here is the bus station and the mostly African suburb of Eastleigh.

To the west of the city's center are Central and Uhuru Parks. The commons offer a break of pleasant green in contrast to the color of concrete and asphalt. Further to the west you will find the National and Nairobi hospitals, government offices, the Y's and the better class hotel accommodations. Beyond this and also to the west, are the elegant and widespread suburbs of Hurlingham and Ngong.

> ### NGONG ROAD
> *Just off Uhuru Highway along Ngong Road, you will pass a stone building which is the **Railway Club**. Here in 1899, the first game of cricket was played in Nairobi.*

What is called the city center is bounded by University Way (north), Tom Mboya Street (east), Haile Selassie Avenue (south) and Uhuru Highway (west). This area is roughly rectangular in shape and covers approximately one square mile. Here is where most tourists find themselves walking and shopping. If you count yourself in this number and need a landmark, keep you eye on the 344-foot tall Kenyatta International Conference Center, which can be seen from anywhere.

GETTING AROUND TOWN

In 20 minutes you can easily walk anywhere within the city center. It is safe to do so only during the day. Nairobi is a contrasting city to tour on foot and with a good map you can wander to your heart's content. If you look like a tourist, be prepared to be hustled frequently. Just ignore the followers and they will soon drop away when they don't get a positive response from you.

If you find yourself shopping as the stores are closing and the sun is setting, get a cab. It doesn't cost much but is worth the precaution. For around $3 you can go anywhere within the city. You won't be able to hail a taxi on the street as they do not drive around looking for passengers. Instead, ask the storekeeper to point you in the direction of the nearest stand.

The taxi drivers are often willing to hire themselves out for a specified period of time at a fixed price. Tell the driver where you want to go and what you want to see and let him suggest a price. This way you have your own personal driver. He will drop you off and wait for you at each stop. In my opinion, this is by far the best route to seeing the sights without having to worry about renting a car.

If you are booked on a package safari you will always start out in Nairobi. Your tour might include a day or two in the city or its environs. If this is the case, you will often have transportation provided to the tourist areas. You may want to go somewhere other than where the group is going or, if you are on your own, check with the front desk of your hotel to see if any arrangements for day trips to museums and animal centers or excursions to the game parks can be made. Many of the centrally located hotels will organize these jaunts for you as an in-house request but don't advertise the service for outsiders.

TAXI PRICES AROUND NAIROBI

From the Hilton to Jomo Kenyatta International Airport, $16
Taxi around the city center, $3
Taxi to Safari Park, $13
Taxi to the Casino, $4.50
Taxi to the Carnivore Restaurant, $11
Taxi to The Bomas of Kenya, $14
Taxi to Wilson Airport, $11
Taxi to United Nations Building, $13
Taxi to Westlands Shopping Center, $5.50
Taxi to the Windsor Hotel, $14
Taxi to The National Museum, $4.50

To rent a car for a day or so of sightseeing in and around Nairobi, there are some places such as **Rent a Beetle**, *PO Box 60157, 7th floor, Finance House, Loita Street, Tel. 338 041,* that will offer you a car for around $24 per day. Check around and see if anyone will match their prices or give you a better deal.

For more information on getting around, see Getting to Kenya in Chapter 6, *Planning Your Trip.*

WHERE TO STAY
City Center

GRAND REGENCY HOTEL, *PO Box 40511, Uhuru Highway/Loita Street, Nairobi. Tel. 211 199 or 1-800/223-5652, Fax 217 120. $275 per night double occupancy. All major credit cards accepted.*

This sparkling new hotel is all about comfort and high standards. Whether you are a business traveler or a tourist, this large hotel will cater to your every need.

Located in Nairobi's newest and classy business area the wide variety of restaurants, 24 hour coffee shop, health center, business center, shopping arcade, casino, airport shuttle and heated/glass covered swimming pool offer first class service with a taste of Africa thrown in for good measure.

Perhaps the most impressive thing about the hotel is its soaring atrium. Filled with light, space, mirrors, marble, brass and green plants the open area exudes sophistication. From floor to ceiling along one immense wall is the intricate pattern of a Masai earring done in shining glass pieces. You will only be able to take your eyes off the bright blue, yellow, red and green to enjoy the panoramic Nairobi skyline.

The stylish rooms are furnished with mahogany pieces and include a minibar, TV, telephone and video equipment. In the bathrooms you'll find hairdryers, guest robes, a bath/shower and even a bidet. Selected as one of my best places to stay – see Chapter 11 for more details.

NAIROBI SAFARI CLUB, *PO Box 43564, University Way, Nairobi, across from the University. Tel. 330 621, Fax 331 201. $226 per night double occupancy. All major credit cards accepted.*

Interestingly enough, the hotel has somewhat of a theme. It runs as a kind of "social club" with guests having temporary membership. The feel of the white circular tower hotel with its vertical rows of balconies and windows is one of a traditional London clubhouse.

Everywhere you look there is dark wood paneling, deep leather armchairs, tropical plants, low light lamps and carpets that allow no noise. In the center of the hotel is the Kirinyaga Lounge, a private salon and library in which guests can relax after a day of sightseeing.

The broad white marble steps and shiny brass name plate identify this as The Nairobi Safari Club – an all-suite hotel. The 146 apartments vary in size, but all have dining and sitting areas in addition to the bedroom. Furnishings try to continue the comfortable feeling of a British club. They include a minibar, three telephones, full bathroom and TV.

Although the idea of the hotel is one of a stately English club the pool with its sun terrace and bar, health center, airport shuttle, Safari bar, Kirinyaga restaurant, Brasserie and gift shops all are unmistakably entrenched with an African bush theme, which lends itself to a pleasant stay.

HOTEL INTER-CONTINENTAL, *PO Box 30353, City Hall Way, Nairobi. The hotel is bordering on Uhuru Highway and convenient to Kenyatta Conference Center. Tel. 335 550, Fax 214 617. $195 per night double occupancy. All major credit cards accepted.*

Facilities such as a bank, shopping area, travel agency, spacious conference center, airport shuttle, health facilities, business services, beauty salon and a heated pool for children and one for adults are some of the great options at this seven story, 400 room downtown hotel.

The Six Continental Club Lounge, the coffee shop and the Pool Terrace Restaurant offer food and drinks at all times of the day and night. The Chateau Bar and Restaurant on the top floor of the hotel is popular for its dancing and the birds-eye-view of Nairobi.

The rooms have recently been under much needed renovations. The accommodations now feature many thoughtful and comfortable additions.

NAIROBI HILTON, *PO Box 30624, Mama Ngina Street and Moi Avenue, Nairobi. Tel. 334 000, Fax 339 462. $150 per night double occupancy. Facilities for disabled guests available. All major credit cards accepted.*
The Hilton's 18 story cylindrical tower is a landmark on Nairobi's skyline. The building covers one city block and is currently undergoing extensive renovations. Rows of shops, a beauty parlor, travel agency, doctor/dentist, airline offices and photo shop are just a few of the facilities available to you on the ground floor.

Most of the rooms in the tower have large curved windows which give a great view of the hustle and bustle of daily life in the city. The more spacious rooms open onto the terrace facing the heated pool. Guest bedrooms come with all the standard furnishings in addition to a small refrigerator, minibar, hairdryer and best of all, a programmable electronic safe for your valuables. Interestingly, the hot water that serves the building comes from the hotel's own deep well.

For your enjoyment there are several good but somewhat expensive restaurants and bars to choose from. The Pool Terrace serves international and local cuisine and the Jockey Bar has a popular "taste of Britain night" featuring English dishes and beverages. The Amboseli Grill is a supper club with late night dancing. The Mara Restaurant is a good place to meet for a business lunch or breakfast and the Resident's Lounge is a quiet getaway. At the Pizzeria you can order an assortment of Italian fare.

NEW STANLEY HOTEL, *PO Box 30680, Nairobi. Tel. 333 248, Fax 211 472. Located at the corner of Kimathi Street and Kenyatta Avenue. $110 per night double occupancy. All major credit cards accepted.*
First opened in 1906, the Stanley has a romantic if somewhat tattered reputation. It has become a tradition of travelers to stop here for a visit to the Thorn Tree Cafe where Ernest Hemingway and other famous characters came while on safari. A large live thorn tree is the focal point of the cafe. Traditionally messages pinned to the trunk will be safe for months until the recipient can make it in to claim the note.

Originally intended to cater to the railroad staff, the New Stanley has grown to 400 rooms of various sizes. The owners have plans to proceed with a much needed overhaul of the facilities. In spite of the run-down and dark look that prevails, the hotel is bustling with activity. There is a sense of adventure and excitement as the crowds of visitors browse in the gift shops or simply enjoy being at the heart of things.

From the fifth floor you can enjoy an excellent view of Nairobi or swim laps in the swimming pool. As the main hotel restaurant, the Tate room serves an excellent lunch or dinner menu while the popular Safari Bar allows great people watching and the feeling of being suspended in mid-air.

SIXEIGHTY HOTEL, *PO Box 43436, Muindi Mbingu Street, Nairobi.* *Tel. 332 680, Telex 22513. $70 per night double occupancy. All major credit cards accepted.*

This hotel is rather in need of redoing but will offer you an inexpensive place to stay with adequate accommodations. The ten story, 340 room building was built in 1972 and still manages to keep itself afloat. There is no pool at the Sixeighty but the neighboring Boulevard Hotel allows guests to use their pool.

IQBAL HOTEL, *Taveta Road. Tel. 220 914. $10 per night double occupancy. Shared bathroom facilities. Cash only.*

The legendary Iqbal is very popular among budget travelers. The rooms are clean and the company intriguing. If you are up early you will be able to enjoy a hot shower; later in the day the water will be cold. There is a bulletin board where you can find all sorts of interesting tidbits of information. The storage room is a good place to leave luggage if necessary.

DOLAT HOTEL, *Murigo Mansion House, Mfangano Street, Nairobi. Tel. 222 797. $7 per night double occupancy. Cash only.*

This is probably the best value for the money in this hotel price range. You can feel completely safe here and the staff is very personable. Cleanliness seems to be a priority at the Dolat where the sheets are changed daily, the bathrooms (one with each room) and bedrooms are spotless, and there is water all day long. In contrast to other accommodations in this category it is quiet all night; this place does not double as a brothel.

City Outskirts

THE NORFOLK HOTEL, *PO Box 58581, Harry Thuk Road, Nairobi. Tel. 216 940, Fax 216 796. $255 per night double occupancy. All major credit cards accepted.*

In existence since 1904, the Norfolk has a remarkable history around which has evolved an eclectic weave of buildings with wings, paths, patios, and peaks. The high arches will remind you of the horse and carriage days when legendary people like Theodore Roosevelt came to Kenya to play and hunt.

Stirring with activity, the small lobby and grounds are decorated in dark paneling, local stone and tile contrasting with lively aviaries, tropical gardens, green lawns and cobblestones. Outstanding service and comfort are ensured by the staff/guest ratio of at least one to one. Most of the comfortable and modern rooms form a circle around a lovely central courtyard filled with birds and flowering trees. Due to several extensive expansions and renovations in the guest rooms, some of the old charm of the original hotel has been lost. In its place there is a typical five star hotel.

The swank Lord Delamere Terrace and Bar and the romantic Ibis Grill have reputations for excellent cuisine prepared by world-famous chefs. Both of these restaurants, along with the pool terrace and fully equipped gym, are popular meeting places for local business people and friends.

NAIROBI SERENA HOTEL, *PO Box 46302, Nairobi. Tel. 725 111, E-mail: 62820976@eln.attmail.com, Fax 725 184. $210 per night double occupancy. All major credit cards accepted.*

The 183 room and seven suite Serena has a reputation as one of the world's leading hotels. The lobby is remarkably beautiful with its thick green plants, brass accents, skylights and colorful tiles. A ten minute walk from the center of the city, the hotel is set at the edge of Central Park. The planners carried on the parkland theme with their own lush gardens. Everywhere you look around the patios, balconies, and common areas you'll notice planters full of tumbling flowers and vines.

Throughout the hotel the decor carries an attractive and winning African theme. There are Swahili sofas, low couches, wooden carvings, bright fabrics, tapestries and Kisii stone all tastefully complemented by outstanding service from the staff. From the pool and public areas in the Serena you will be able to see a remarkable vista of the Nairobi skyline. The pool is most attractive with varying colors and textures of tile wrapping themselves in ever-increasing circles around the water — a perfect place for tea. The modern guest rooms have large picture windows with a view of either the city or the gardens below. To match the luxurious accommodations, the hotel offers a business center, gift shops, health club, hairdresser, bookstore and electronic safes.

MAYFAIR COURT HOTEL, *PO Box 74957, Nairobi. Tel. 748 278, Fax 746 826. $100 per night double occupancy. All major credit cards accepted.*

An excellent choice for an equitable price, the Mayfair is located in the upper class suburb of Parklands. Just a short walk away is a variety of shopping and restaurant options, including Westlands Shopping Center. If you prefer to head into the city, seven minutes away by car, there is a complimentary shuttle bus running every hour.

Reminiscent of the original 1930s establishment, the recently remodeled 174 room hotel still retains some of the enchanting ambiance of a bygone era. The bedrooms are simple but spacious, clean and tastefully decorated. The ensuite bathrooms have all the conveniences of home. The glossy Kenya marble floor, cascading plants, and widespread windows add to the intriguing brick, timber, and tile design. Two sparkling outdoor swimming pools, fish ponds, patios, tree-lined walks and gardens enhance the extensive landscaping.

The informal Mischief's Bar or The Oasis restaurant offers a wide selection of above average refreshments. For something different try The

Mayfair Casino and Club, situated in a separate building within the hotel compound or the up-to-date health club. Other amenities include three superior shops, a hairdresser, and conference facilities.

JACARANDA HOTEL, *PO Box 47557, Waiyaki Way, Nairobi. Tel. 335 807, Fax 340 541. $82 per night double occupancy. All major credit cards accepted.*

The Jacaranda is surrounded by attractive gardens in the Westlands suburb and offers a shuttle bus to the city center. It is a pleasant place to stay and has an innovative bar and restaurant. The swimming pool and conference facilities cater to tourists and local business people alike.

PANAFRIC HOTEL, *PO Box 30680, Valley Road, Nairobi. Tel. 333 248, Fax 211 472. $80 per night double occupancy. All major credit cards accepted.*

To get to this budget hotel located near Central Park you must first drive through a gas station. The building itself is a huge unremarkable concrete structure but the facilities are all you could want for: clean and affordable. The modern hotel offers service apartments, suites, regular rooms and a large outdoor pool along with extensive conference amenities. Prices for the rooms include breakfast.

BOULEVARD HOTEL, *PO Box 42831, Harry Thuk Road, Nairobi. Tel. 227 567, Fax 334 071. $70 per night double occupancy. All major credit cards accepted.*

A practical no-nonsense 70 room hotel, the Boulevard is less than a fifteen minute walk from downtown. The hotel gardens overlook the Nairobi River and there are tennis courts and a swimming pool on the grounds. The guest rooms on all three floors have adequate bathrooms and a private balcony. The accommodations tend to be on the small side and those facing the street can be noisy.

FAIRVIEW HOTEL, *PO Box 40842, Bishop Road, Nairobi. Tel. 723 211, Fax 721 320, E-mail: fairview@form-net.com. $63 per night double occupancy (deposit required). No air conditioning. No health spa facilities. Swimming pool available at nearby hotel. No credit cards accepted.*

As a family-owned business since the 1930s, this 130-room bed and breakfast hotel can comfortably accommodate guests on its ample five acre spread. The hospice consists of two garden cottages and an enormous rambling stone house. Inside these buildings there is an odd collection of guest rooms in varied sizes and decors. The unique character of each bedroom makes this place all the more charming, as it adds to the sense of history and individuality.

Even though it is situated just outside Nairobi, on Nairobi Hill, you will feel as though you have escaped to a garden paradise. The grounds are fabulous. The large spreading trees and green lawns attract plentiful birdlife along with a variety of local and international guests. The patio and the dining room cater to business people from the city who come here to sample the traditional African buffet. Some of the rooms share a bathroom and families are welcome in this friendly and relaxed atmosphere. The Fairview has its own water supply and generator in case the city supply of either should run out. All of these things, along with the good value for the money, make the affordable Fairview my choice for the start to an adventure in Kenya.

HERON COURT HOTEL, *PO Box 41848, Milimani Road, Nairobi. Tel. 720 740. $20 per night double occupancy. All major credit cards accepted.*

At the Heron Court you will find everything you need from clean bathrooms with adjoining bedrooms to hot water and twenty four hour laundry services. Small apartments are available for monthly rental and the security is reliable. A swimming pool, store, sauna, and Buffalo Bills (a very popular restaurant) make this a great place to stay. The sheets are changed daily and you will enjoy the friendly staff.

YMCA, *PO Box 63063 State House Road; Nairobi. Tel. 724 070 and 724 116; Ambira Road, Tel. 553 132; Tom Mboya Street, Tel. 722 877;* **YWCA**, *PO Box 40710, Mamiaka Road, Tel. 724 789, Fax 71059.$10.50 with shared facilities, $14 with private bathroom, $38 per month. Includes breakfast.*

The Y's offer clean, safe accommodations with dorm beds and shared bathrooms or private rooms with bathrooms. Meals other than breakfast are $2. In some of the Y's, families and couples are welcome. To stay here you must be a member of the Y or join for a small membership fee of $1.

MRS ROCHE'S, *in the outskirts of Parklands and opposite the Aga Khan Hospital on Third Parklands Avenue off Limuru Road. Tents and vehicles are welcome. $1.20 for a tent per night and $1.60 for bed in a shared room per night. Cash.*

It is the only place to stay if you plan on camping. Flowering trees and colorful shrubs make Mrs. Roche's a lovely place to stay. To get to the camp site, take a matatu from the Oden Cinema at the corner of Tom Mboya Street and Latema Road. A sign in the window will show the destination as the "Aga Khan." Tell the driver where you are going.

The grounds tend to get crowded during the busy seasons, but you can feel safe here. Freshwater showers, clean toilets, and good local food at the Stop 'n' Eat nearby make this a favorite for the low budget traveler.

City Suburbs

GIRAFFE MANOR, *PO Box 15004, Langata, Nairobi. Tel. 891 078. $450 per night double occupancy. All major credit cards accepted.*

Located just eight miles from the city center, the Manor is intended to be a home, not a hotel. The manor was originally built in 1932 by Sir David Duncan. At any given time there are under ten people staying here. If you chose to stay here you will have added your name to an exclusive list, including those of Brooke Shields, Johnny Carson, and Walter Cronkite.

The high point of your stay will be seeing and feeding an endangered Rothschild giraffe or wandering among the varied wildlife in the primeval forest. The giraffe have managed to survive because of the efforts of the family (Jock and Betty Leslie-Melville, and Rick and Bryony Anderson) in starting the African Fund for Endangered Wildlife (AFEW). It is common for the semi-tame giraffe to poke their long necks through the windows of the manor as you eat breakfast in the sunroom.

The grand two story stone home is elegantly furnished with some original Karen Blixen furniture in one bedroom, rich fabrics, and lovely heirlooms. The manor which sits on 120 acres of forested land, has four double bedrooms with either connecting or adjacent baths. Gourmet dining has become a tradition at the manor and will add to the exceptional experience of staying here.

WINDSOR GOLF & COUNTRY CLUB, *PO Box 74957, Ridgeways Road, Nairobi. Tel. 219 784, Fax 217 498, E:mail: bookwindsor@africaonline.com. $184 per night double occupancy. Free shuttle to town. All major credit cards accepted.*

No effort or expense has been spared to build this exclusive, 130 room golf resort. The extensive amenities include a full fitness and beauty center, three lakes for bass and tilapia fishing, tennis and squash courts, croquet lawn, bowling green, walks with an ornithologist, jogging trails, swimming pool and an all inclusive 18-hole golf course.

The grand red-roofed buildings set along the edge of the golf course offer a selection of studios, apartments, or standard rooms – all furnished in traditional English fashion. The lobby and diverse public areas are ornately decorated with resplendent fabrics and one-of-a-kind pieces of art in keeping with the grand Victorian era.

SAFARI PARK HOTEL, *PO Box 45038, Nairobi. Tel. 802 493, Fax 802 477. $150 per night double occupancy. Shuttle bus in to town. All major credit cards accepted.*

Each room in this 60-plus acre resort has a private terrace with a view of the professionally landscaped grounds. Exotic Lamu-style furnishings add a touch of Kenya to the airy light rooms and the bathrooms are outfitted with gold and marble. Constantly growing, the Safari Park has successfully kept a relaxed vacation atmosphere at the same time providing a taste of native Africa in dramatic thatched buildings.

The grander of the two pools flows under little bridges, through lush gardens, around islands and catches its guests as they catapult down the water slide. If this sounds too wild for you, try something else – a massage, shopping, tennis or a sauna; it's all here. Tucked around the grounds amid the native trees, flowering shrubs and twittering birds are at least seven varieties of cosmopolitan restaurants and an up-scale casino. Choose from African to Japanese cuisine or anything in between; you'll never have to eat the same food twice.

UTALI HOTEL, *PO Box 31067, Nairobi. Tel. 802 540. $80 per night double occupancy. All major credit cards accepted.*

The Utali includes a full breakfast in the price of your room, making a stay here great value. The conservative 50 room hotel has attractive gardens and an inviting swimming pool to its credit. A free shuttle to the city, small refrigerators in every room, conference facilities, a boutique and room service are a few other perks.

Nearby Utali College has an arrangement with hotel management to allow students to staff and train at the hotel. With this agreement in place, the guests are thoroughly spoilt by enthusiastic trainees as they prepare for a career in the hospitality industry.

THE KENTMERE CLUB, *PO Box 39508, Nairobi. Tel. 41053. $32 per night double occupancy. All major credit cards accepted.*

Roughly twelve miles outside Nairobi, the 16 room hotel tries to maintain the appearance of a small English inn. Heavy beams, wood paneling, and flower-filled gardens maintain the feeling, as do the far-off fields of green tea.

The inexpensive garden cottage rooms are clean but the decor could use a bit of a facelift. Each bedroom has a full service bathroom, cozy fireplace, and porch. If you want to swim, play golf, or tennis, the nearby Limuru Country Club will welcome you.

WHERE TO EAT

If you are with a group tour going out on safari, this is probably your last chance to eat anywhere other that your hotel or lodge. Once you arrive at your destination in the bush, if you are lucky, there won't be too much else around other than wildlife and nature.

While traveling around Kenya on your own however, the choices will be surprisingly varied. Nairobi has many outstanding places to eat, with Indian and seafood (which is always very fresh) restaurants being particularly good.

To give you some idea of how much it will cost you to eat at any of the places listed below, I have assigned each restaurant one of the following (prices are per person not including beverages and tips):

• **inexpensive** = under $7
• **moderately priced** = $8 to $15
• **high priced** = over $15

IBIS GRILL, *in the Norfolk Hotel, PO Box 58581, Nairobi. Tel. 335 422. High priced. Emphasis on local ingredients. Bar services available. Major credit cards accepted.*

For romance, elegance, and good food, the Ibis Grill won't disappoint you. The award-winning chefs come from all over the world and have given the restaurant quite a reputation. Dinner is often served under shiny silver salvers and the tables are set with silver and rich linens. Candlelight and live piano music set the mood as the ibis' on the wall tapestries seem to come to life.

MANDHARI RESTAURANT, *in the Serena Hotel, PO Box 48690, Nairobi. Tel. 725 111. Reservation suggested. High priced. International cuisine. Bar services available. Major credit cards accepted.*

For fantasy, refinement, and worthy fare this is one of the best places to dine in Nairobi. In Swahili, *Mandhari* means landscape, which is certainly what the management has accomplished with the impressive Kisii stone carving and cascading plants. Heavy linen, china, and silver pay tribute to the superb cuisine.

CHATEAU RESTAURANT, *in the Hotel Inter-Continental bordering Uhuru Highway, PO Box 30353, Nairobi. Tel. 335 550. Reservations suggested. High priced. Continental cuisine. Bar services available. Credit cards accepted.*

The menu offers a variety of choices from chicken to fish to beef. All the selections will come perfectly prepared with succulent fresh Kenya vegetables. If you can afford it, dining here will be delightful. The Chateau Restaurant and Bar will give you whatever you are looking for as far as cuisine goes, and they'll even throw in a little evening dancing. The panoramic Nairobi skyline is easily seen through the wrap-around windows adding to the exotic ambiance.

ZEPHYR, *in Rank Xerox House, Westlands, Nairobi. Tel. 750 055. High priced. French cuisine. Bar services available. Major credit cards accepted.*

Excellent nouvelle cuisine with a Japanese flair. This is an elegant and romantic restaurant.

TAMARIND RESTAURANT, *in the National Bank building on Aga Khan Walk between Harambee Avenue and Haile Selassie Avenue. Tel. 338 959. Reservations suggested. Moderately priced. Seafood. Bar services available. Major credit cards accepted.*

The Tamarind has earned a worldwide reputation for elegant sophistication and outstanding seafood. A relaxed and friendly atmosphere will make you want to come back. Try the prawns Piri Piri, Chilli Crab, or Lobster Swahili for some of the freshest seafood ever. The high standards and consistent service provide real value for the money.

HAANDI RESTAURANT, *PO Box 13855 Westlands, Nairobi. Tel. 448 294, Fax 445 807. Moderately priced. Indian food. Bar service available. Major credit cards accepted.*

As their specialty, Haandi offers Indian delicacies marinated and cooked in clay ovens. Your order will be made to your specifications, whether you want spicy hot or very mild. The food is plentiful and well presented. You can enjoy watching the cooking process through a pane of thick glass. Sometimes they even use a blow-torch!

Their Garlic Chilly Tawa Prawns are fresh queen prawns prepared on a flat iron griddle with lots of onions, tomatoes, ginger, garlic and masalas. If you are a vegetarian, try the Dal Bhukara; black lentils cooked slowly overnight with garlic and green chilies.

FAIRVIEW HOTEL, *Bishop Road, Nairobi. Tel. 723 211. Moderately priced. International fare. Bar services available. No credit cards accepted.*

The Fairview is popular with locals for its traditional African lunch served twice weekly. The dining room has large windows which let in the warm sun and bright light. On the patio, meals are served off a set menu while inside a buffet offers a delicious selection of international foods. Altogether the atmosphere is relaxed and friendly at this English country hotel/restaurant.

ORNA'S, *PO Box 76518, ABC Place, Waiyaki Way, Nairobi. Tel. 445 368. Moderately priced. American fare with emphasis on homemade baked goods. Beer and wine only. No credit cards accepted.*

When you walk in the door you'll feel welcomed and comfortable. Sitting in a cozy booth with mirrors on the wall and flowers on the tables you could be anywhere in the US.

This small cafe is the best place in town to get an excellent Reuben sandwich or fabulous French Onion soup for lunch. Orna's is packed with local business people, housewives and youngsters having a bite. Tourists haven't found this home-away-from-home restaurant yet but they will when they get a hankering for bagels or corned beef. The dinner menu with its lengthy selection includes tasty steaks, fresh salmon, or delicate vegetarian cheese soufflé. When you eat here save room for the exquisite, just-baked desserts. All time favorites are the Orange Praline Meringue Torte or perhaps the New York Style Baked Cheese Cake.

CARNIVORE, *outside Langata near Wilson Airport. Tel. 501 709. Reservations suggested. Fixed moderate price. Bar services available. Major credit cards accepted.*

Everyone who comes to Kenya must try the Carnivore if they are true meat eaters. People flock here to sample the complete meat eating experience from antelope to zebra (all farm raised) and everything in between. Included in the price are salads, breads, desserts, and coffee.

At the Simba Saloon there is a weekly entertainment program, featuring the whole shebang from local to international bands. On Thursdays there is jazz music and disco on other days. This is a great place to take the kids as there is a safe, clean playground just outside where they can spend all that extra energy.

KAREN BLIXEN COFFEE GARDEN, *on Karen Road between Karen Blixen Museum and Karen Club, Nairobi. Tel. 882 779. Inexpensive. Kenyan fare. Major credit cards accepted.*

The garden restaurant is open from 10:00 am to 5:00 pm and offers meals freshly prepared from the best of Kenya's produce. A small shop has unusual gifts and souvenirs.

RICKSHAW CHINESE RESTAURANT, *in Fedha Towers on Standard Street. Tel. 223 604. Inexpensive. Chinese food. Bar services available. Major credit cards accepted.*

The mouth-watering food here is rated highly by the local population, and I agree. With an ample menu and good service, this is a great place to get an excellent Chinese meal.

MARINO RESTAURANT, *on the first floor of the National Housing Corporation Building, Aga Khan Walk just off Haile Selassie Avenue. Tel. 227 150. Inexpensive. Italian food. Bar services available.*

For your seating pleasure you can select from an open terrace or the roomy interior. The menu offers mostly Italian fare plus some continental dishes. The food is above average and worth trying.

TRATTORIA, *on the corner of Kaunda Street and Wabera Street. Tel. 340 855. Inexpensive. Italian food. Bar services available. Major credit cards accepted.*

For a full course meal including soup, salad, dessert (the ice cream is marvelous) and wine, you will have an excellent dining experience at the very popular Trattoria. The a la carte menu has a good range of selections for both lunch and dinner.

Fast Food

The following list of fast food places are all inexpensive with somewhat unremarkable interiors. You will see locals choosing to eat at these places as the food is hot, plentiful, and good. You will find such things as fish & chips (fries), salads, fruit, sausage, chicken, burgers and soups. There will be no need for credit cards:

PRESTIGE RESTAURANT, *in Tsavo Lane just off Latema Road;* **SUPERMAC**, *opposite the Thorn Tree Cafe in the shopping center on Kimathi Street;* **WIMPY**, *located on Mondlane Street, Kenyatta Avenue and Tom Mboya Street;* **NAIROBI BURGERS**, *located across from the end of Latema Road on Tom Mboya Street* and **PIPES RESTAURANT**, *also on Tom Mboya Street.*

Breakfast

If breakfast is your thing, you can try any of the hotels, which offer pretty good breakfast buffets but will cost anywhere from $8 to $25. The Hilton, the Grand Regency, the New Stanley, and the Inter-Continental seem to have the best selections and service.

For a more colorful start to your day, here are a few choices that will more than satisfy your appetite while at the same time show you where the people that live in Nairobi eat their breakfasts. At any of these restaurants you will get cereal, fresh fruit and juices, toast, sausage, yogurt, eggs, coffee, tea, beans, bacon, porridge, *mandazi* (doughy sweet bread), Indian samosas and just about any other kind of breakfast food you can come up with:

ILLIKI CAFE, *on Moi Avenue in the Ambassadeur Hotel;* **GROWERS CAFE**, *on Tom Mboya Street;* **GOLDSTAR RESTAURANT**, *on the corner of Moktar Daddah Street and Koinage Street* and **HONEY POT**, *on Moi Avenue.*

Cheap Lunch

For an inexpensive lunch consisting of such things as pasties, ugali, posho (corn), stew, fish, chicken, curry, beef and other rib-sticking fare, try any of these restaurants. The food is simple but worthwhile and everything is clean. Once again, these places are favorites with the local business crowd and tend to fill up quickly at mid-day:

HARVEST, *on Kenyatta Avenue between Koinage and Loita Streets;* **NEW BEDONIA CAFE**, *on Mfangano Street;* **JAX RESTAURANT**, *on Kimathi Street in the Old Mutual Building;* **THE PUB**, *under the Sixeighty Hotel on Standard Street;* **CABOOSE RESTAURANT**, *at the corner of Haile Selassie Avenue and Uhuru Highway in the Harambee Plaza;* **CAFE HELENA**, *opposite City Hall on Mama Ngina Street;* **CALYPSO**, *downstairs in the Bruce House;* **JACARANDA CAFE**, *in the Phoenix House Arcade between Kenyatta Avenue and Standard Street;* **COFFEE BAR**, *on Mama Ngina Street;* **AFRICAN HERITAGE CAFE**, *with one entrance on Banda Street and the other through the African Heritage store* and **BULL CAFE**, *on Ngariama Road.*

SEEING THE SIGHTS

The National Museum, Snake Park & Aquarium

Before going off on safari, the **National Museum**, *Tel. 742 131*, is a great place to gather your facts and figures and brush up on snake identification. To get there from the center of town, take a cab or stroll the mile uphill to the entrance off Uhuru Highway. Opening hours are from 9:00 am to 6:00 pm daily and the cost is roughly $4. Guided ornithological walks through nearby woods can sometimes be worthwhile.

A little run down compared to the Smithsonian, the National Museum is still worth a visit as the best displays in the country are housed here. The two story building will keep you marveling for at least two hours with its exhibits in the Mahatma Ghandi Hall, Aga Khan Hall, and Lamu room.

NAIROBI MUST SEES

If you only have a short time in and around Nairobi, here are a few places that should be on your "must see" list:
The Railway Museum
Daphne Sheldrick's Animal Orphanage
Karen Blixen Museum
The National Museum and Snake Park
Nairobi National Park

Discover the beginnings of man in the Prehistory Hall with early skeletons, fossilized elephant dung, and great contributions by the Leakey family. See displays describing the traditions of Kenya's tribes. Stare at a traditional pendant worn to ensure fertility or find out why tapping on the ground with sandals was thought to guarantee a safe safari. View musical instruments, gourds, clothing, weapons, woven baskets and other fascinating items of daily tribal life. Take a look at a huge collection of preserved birds, butterflies, fish and wildlife. Imagine the fragrance of the intricate flower paintings produced by Joy Adamson, the famous author of *Born Free* and adoptive mother of Elsa the lioness.

AHMED THE ELEPHANT

*With impressive nine and a half foot tusks weighing over 300 pounds, the now famous elephant **Ahmed** was destined to become a favorite of Kenyatta and a symbol of the war against poachers. He was placed under 24 hour guard until 1974 when he died of old age. The ivories stand today in the National Museum along with a life-size replica of the pachyderm himself.*

The Snake Park and Aquarium, *Tel. 742 131,* are just across the street from the museum. Displays vary, but generally you will see anywhere from 100 to 200 live reptiles. Crocodiles, terrapins, spitting cobras, black mambas, puff adders, tilapia, pythons, tortoises and lizards are the inhabitants of this small and sometimes second class collection.

Kenyatta International Conference Center
There is no admission to this 28 story conference center in City Square. Built in 1974, it is home to the ruling party in Kenya and has an impressive auditorium that can hold 4,000 delegates. Tours are offered Monday through Friday between the hours of 9:30 am and 12:30 pm and 2:00 pm and 4:30 pm.

Take the elevator to the top of the building where you will find a rooftop walkway and an impressive panoramic view of Nairobi. Inside, the hexagonal tower, which claims architectural inspiration from Rome and Africa, are walkways of red tile and fountains. In the gardens outside is a statue of Kenya's champion and first president, Jomo Kenyatta.

Railway Museum
On Ngaira Avenue near the railway station is the **Railway Museum**, *Tel. 21211*. For $4 between the hours of 8:30 am and 4:30 pm every day, you can spend a few hours climbing on fascinating old engines and coaches instrumental in opening up the country on the "Lunatic Line."

One of the most intriguing railcars is the one depicted in the book, *Man Eating Lions of Tsavo*. The historical account tells of lions eating the work crews during the railway construction in 1897. Superintendent Charles Ryall tried to stay awake all night in one of the railway cars in order to kill the man-eaters. Unfortunately, he fell asleep and was consequently dragged through the window and eaten by an old lion. A version of these events was retold in the 1996 movie, *The Ghost and The Darkness*, featuring Michael Douglas and Val Kilmer. The other famous carriage was used in the filming of the movie *Out of Africa*, in which Meryl Streep portrayed Karen Blixen.

Inside what was once a railway station is the memorabilia of the times. Strangely enough, the railway and harbor administrations were once inclusive. This is why the displays lend themselves to some maritime exhibits such as relics from the German battleship *Konigsberg* which sunk in a Tanzanian river in 1917.

Perhaps the most interesting museum display is the cowcatcher with a long low bench attached, representing the best place for celebrities to ride for game viewing. Winston Churchill and Theodore Roosevelt both had the honor of riding through Kenya in this manner.

Jamia Mosque
It is rare that visitors are allowed in the ornate and fabulously floodlit Arab mosque. However, it is worth taking a quick peek inside especially at night. The Islamic Sunni sect constructed the gilt domes, five clocks keeping time for the five daily prayers and an elaborate *mihrab* showing the direction of Mecca.

Parliament Building & Kenyatta Mausoleum

If you have the time, take a free tour of the historic building or take a seat in the public gallery. To set up an appointment call the sergeant-at-arms, *Tel. 21291.*

The outside of the building is not overwhelming, but the interior is worth seeing. A 49-panel tapestry presented by the East African Women's League depicts Kenya's colonial history. Thirty-two pieces of impressive hardwood line the landing and a statue of Kenyatta presides in the central hall. Outside in the gardens is Jomo Kenyatta's mausoleum, attended by an honor guard.

Payappa Arts Centre

The inspirational motto above the door says "Copying puts God to Sleep." Here a collection of painters and sculptors perfect their art forms. There is a gallery where pieces are displayed; some are for sale and others are simply on exhibit. The center is located off Ridgeways Road, *Tel. 512 257*, and has an admissions charge of $2. The hours are Monday through Friday, 9:00 am to 5:00 pm, and 2:00 pm to 5:00 pm on Saturday.

Nairobi Arboretum

A short taxi ride outside the city brings you to the Nairobi Arboretum. The 80 acres of well-kept shrubs, lawns, and carefully identified trees are home to a host of colorful birds. If time allows, this is a great place to enjoy the variety of a lush tropical garden. It is best to go with a group or a guide for safety reasons.

McMillan Library

As Kenya's main library, there are some excellent reference books housed upstairs. The wife of Sir Northrup McMillan donated the library in memory of her husband. McMillan, an American transplant, was knighted for his services to the British Empire during WWI.

Uhuru Park & Central Park

These two parks are one large expanse of grass divided roughly in half by Kenyatta Avenue. Both are popular hangouts for courting couples or local residents. In Uhuru Park there is a small boating lake, while Central Park offers a monument dedicated to President Moi's first ten years of rule. It is not wise to find yourself in either place after dark.

City Park

For under $1, you can get into the first public park in Nairobi. There is a maze, a children's playground in a sunken garden and a bandstand. It is on City Park Road just off Limuru Road about two miles from the center of town. The hours are 10:00 am to 6:00 pm on Monday, 7:00 am to 2:00 pm on Friday, and all other days noon to 6:00 pm.

In the mature 296 acre park, the trees offer a respite from the sun and the lovely gardens will delight your senses. A WWII cemetery holds the remains of 97 East African soldiers who gave their lives for a cause they believed in. Further along is a colorful display of fine orchids.

NIGHTLIFE & ENTERTAINMENT

Movies

The Nation newspaper has an entertainment guide section that features what is currently showing at the movie theaters. Generally, there are three shows a day: matinee, evening, and late night show. If the cinema has two screens there are normally two shows on weekdays and weekends – one at 7:00 pm and the other at 9:30 pm. For a listing of all the cinemas or theaters available, check in the yellow pages. The ones listed below are the best of the selection:

• **Nairobi Cinema**, *Uchumi House, 2nd floor on Aga Khan walk, in the city center, Tel. 226 603*

• **Kenya Cinema**, *Moi Avenue below Zanze Bar, Tel. 226 982 (two screens)*

• **20th Century**, *between Mama Ngina and Standard Street, Tel. 338 070 (two screens)*

• **Fox Drive-In**, *Thika Road, Tel. 802 293*

Clubs/Bars/Casinos

BUFFALO BILLS, *Heron Court Hotel on Milimani Road. Tel. 449 904.*

Famous drinking establishment with reasonable food and prices. Starting at 5:30 pm, the place starts to fill up with all manner of expatriates and tourists who want to have a few laughs and a couple of drinks. Never a dull moment here!

ZANZE BAR, *Moi Avenue, 5th floor of the Kenya Cinema Plaza. Tel. 222 568.*

Good food, drinks, music, and atmosphere. Every Friday the club features a different music group and on Tuesday's and Thursday's it is Karaoke night.

GALILEO'S, *Westlands Road. Tel. 744 477.*

The most exclusive, plush, private members club in Nairobi. The Flashpint Band plays nightly. Hours are Tuesday through Sunday; guests are welcome on Friday nights but it is best to check ahead.

MISCHIEF'S, *Mayfair Court Hotel, Tel. 746 708.*

This modern bar boasts a great music selection from its Databeat system (their state-of-the-art music equipment). Generally filled with groups of rambunctious fun-loving visitors.

THE MAYFAIR CASINO & CLUB, *Parklands Road, Tel. 743 300.*

If you are not expecting the extravagance of Las Vegas, this can be an amusing place to spend an evening trying out your luck with the cards.

THE INTERNATIONAL CASINO, *Westlands Road, PO Box 45827, Nairobi. Tel. 742 600, Fax 742 620.*

Situated in the suburb of Westlands (you can't miss the casino sign), this casino has a reputation for excellence. An exciting place to test your fortune before setting off on safari; the casino offers Blackjack and American Roulette, among other things.

THE JOCKEY PUB, *Hilton Hotel, Tel. 334 000 ext. 0131.*

This traditionally British pub is another favorite local hangout but is rather on the expensive side. Try it for classic English fare, real ale, and lively conversation.

SOCIAL & CULTURAL EVENTS

• *Wildlife Clubs of Kenya. Langata Environmental Education Center on Langata Road near the animal orphanage, offers a monthly lecture on wildlife. Tel. 891 904, Fax 215 969 or write PO Box 62844, Nairobi.*

• *Goethe-Institute. The German cultural center at Maendeleo House along Loita/Monrovia Street has varied activities. Call 224 640 for the latest events.*

• *Kenya Cultural Center, PO Box 43031. Opposite the Norfolk Hotel on Harry Thuk Road, the center offers lunch time concerts featuring The Kenya National Theatre Dance Troupe. For more information on upcoming programs look in the Daily Nation, or call 220 536.*

• *Nairobi Cultural Institute. Located on Ngong Road, the institute offers courses on Kiswahili. For more details, call 569 205.*

• *United States Information Service. Video shows and library services are available here. It is located in the National Bank Building on Moi Avenue. Write US Embassy, PO Box 30143, or call 334 141.*

SHOPPING

The most condensed shopping in Nairobi is in a roughly four-sided section of town. On the west side is Uhuru Highway, on the north University Way, on the south Moi Avenue and on the east City Hall Way. Spend a pleasant day strolling around this area and buying up the many interesting souvenirs.

For a taste of how the locals shop, try the street stalls along **Tom Mboya Street** and **River Road** or **Kariokor Market** near the bus station on **Racecourse Road**. The name of the Kariokor market comes from the

African mispronunciation of "Carrier Corps." Here you will find anything from delicious fresh fruit to rubber sandals, but perhaps it is most popular for its *nyama choma* or roast meat. This is usually goat or beef served with large helpings of delicious African-style mashed peas, beans, and potatoes.

The **City Market** on Mundi Mbingu Street caters to locals as well as tourists. Be prepared to haggle in order to get the price you want; it is expected of you. Of course, there is also a limit as to how much bargaining should go into the purchase. Recognize the point where it becomes rude and offensive and stop before you get there. Allow the merchant to make a living without becoming another impolite tourist.

As you go through the door to the market you will see an impressive array of goods for sale in a maze of stalls. This can certainly look a little intimidating but it will be worth the effort once you walk in. Venture into the main hall where the perfume of roses, orchids, guavas, mangoes and pineapples will delight your senses. If you keep going, the smell of meat and fish will prevail.

ILLEGAL PURCHASES

The sale of game trophies or objects made from them is illegal. You will be offered the temptation of buying a lion claw mounted in gold or an elephant hair bracelet – but don't be fooled – they are not real. The lion claw is a camel's hoof and the bracelet is plastic, cow horn, or woven reed. Please don't support or encourage these scoundrels, whether you believe the goods are fake or real.

Just off the main hall you'll find the bargains you came for. With a little haggling the Kisii soapstone carvings; colorful sarongs; impressive ebony woodcarvings; paintings; menacing spears; hand-made shields and other souvenirs are yours to take home.

The **craft market** behind the **Jamia Mosque** near the city market is a great place to look at the handicrafts in the network of booths. Out the back door is the area where woven goods such as the famous Kenya baskets abound. It can sometimes be discouraging to browse here, as overbearing stallholders pressure you to buy.

Make sure you watch your purse as pickpockets are not unheard of in this part of town. It is unlikely you will use your credit card and safer not to have it with you; leave it in your room or the hotel safe.

Plenty of small change is what you will use the most in the market area. The small stalls offer a range of inexpensive items for sale (the handmade earrings cost no more than fifty cents!) and making change for large denominations can cause a bit of a problem.

Other quality shops, like **African Heritage**, *Banda Ave., Tel. 333 157*; **680 Jewellers & African Art**, *in the 680 Hotel, Tel. 333 900, Fax 213 220*; **African Cultural Gallery**, *Mama Ngina Street, Tel. 333 044*; **Batiks & Jewellery Ltd.**, *Hotel Intercontinental, City Hall Way, Tel. 222 727, Fax 339 874*; **Hand Carvers Den**, *Langata Shopping Center on Langata Road opposite the Carnivore, Tel. 725 645*, line the streets of the city and its neighborhoods. The goods sold in these boutiques are often of better quality and there is no wrangling over prices. In a more sophisticated manner, just simply ask for a discount and you might get it. You will find that some of the shops have a fixed price policy and will not haggle at all.

Unmounted precious and semi-precious stones are a deal in Kenya. Whatever you choose, you can almost be sure it will be half the cost of the same item in the US. The list is long but some of the better buys include jasper, agate, rubies, amethysts and malachite. Some of the most pleasing and rare are tsavorite and tanzanite.

It is best not to make your purchase of stones in the street because the gems may be of questionable quality. If you are interested, take a look in **Kiamathi Jewellers**, *Norwich Union House opposite the Hilton Hotel, Kimathi Street, Nairobi, Tel. 224 754*; or **Rockhound**, *256 Collins Road, Karen, Tel. 882 297*; Karen is a classy suburb of Nairobi.

Also in Karen on Mbagathi Ridge is **Kazuri**, *Tel. 882 362*, a pottery and bead factory. The 150 women who work here offer a wide array of colorful items that make great gifts. An interesting tour is included in the price of your visit.

On the outskirts of the city is **Westlands**. Here in this thriving shopping district look for **Sarit Centre**, *Westlands Road, (PO Box 14474), Tel. 747 408, Fax 747 806*, where the selection of gift items and hand-carved treasures provide a modest profit for some of Kenya's talented craftspeople. The Sarit Centre is a two story mall that contains about ten stores. The upper-class of Nairobi often shop here for fabrics, stationery, and clothing.

At **Utamaduni**, a suburb of Langata, a good representation of all Kenyan goods is displayed. Buying here will save you some travel time, as the collection of souvenirs from different sources are all at one central location. Stop here on your way to or from the **Karen Blixen Museum** and the **Giraffe Centre**.

Back in Nairobi, **The Spinner's Web**, *Kijabe Street, PO Box 52164, Tel. 228 647*, near the Norfolk Hotel, sells all kinds of woven goods such as jumpers and baskets all made out of natural fabrics. The pottery and ornaments are worth seeing also.

EXCURSIONS & DAY TRIPS
AROUND LANGATA
Nairobi National Park & Animal Orphanage
Nairobi National Park, *Tel. 501 081*, is close to the city center and tour operators run groups to the 44 square mile park a couple of times a day, usually early in the morning or later in the afternoon when game viewing is best. Generally, the tour will take three to four hours depending on how long you linger. Altogether allow a good half day to feel like you saw everything and had time to enjoy.

Getting to the park is quite easy if you decide to venture off on your own. The tricky part is knowing where the turnoff is. As you get near, slow down and keep a sharp eye out. Setting out from Nairobi, go south on Uhuru Highway and turn right at the football stadium. You will see Wilson Airport on your left; keep going. The principal entry will be a short distance down the road also on your left. Admittance begins at 6:00 am and ends at 6:00 pm daily.

Outside at the main gate is what is erroneously called the **animal orphanage**, *Tel. 501 081*. In fact it is little more than a run-down zoo and certainly should not be confused with Daphne Sheldrick's Animal Orphanage. At the national park orphanage, many of the animals will never have the option of being re-introduced to the wild. But if you're here anyway, you might as well have a look around for $2.40 or 60¢ for kids. Children on school field trips often stop here to learn about their country's valuable animal resources. Whether you enjoy it or not depends on how you feel about caged animals.

Other entrances besides the main gate are the Cheetah Gate in the far eastern part of the park, the Langata Gate, Banda Gate, Mbagathi Gate to the west, the Masai Gate to the south or the "eastern entrance" in the middle of the northern boundary line. The cost to get into the park is $12 per person plus $1.50 for your car.

The park is supposedly surrounded by a fence, except at the gates where you are likely to see a warden. Not many people are aware however, the park is actually open in some spots to allow migrating animals safe passage. The fences, of course, ensure that animals stay in and poachers stay out. Once upon a time the wardens had time to show people around, but now the park has become an important rhino sanctuary and their time is spent watching out for the endangered beasts; poachers prefer to do their dirty work further afield. As a result of the intense 24 hour a day surveillance, the huge animals are surviving.

INTERESTING FACTS

Nairobi National Park was the first Kenyan national park. It was designated in 1945 and opened in 1946 after being used as a Somali reserve, Nairobi public park, a WWI training base, and a WWII firing range. It is now the headquarters of the Kenya Wildlife Service.

From here you can see the tall Kenyatta Conference Center and hear the planes fly overhead from Jomo Kenyatta International Airport. Here, as in many parts of Kenya, there is a battle between encroaching civilization and wildlife. Without support from visitors like you, this park may well disappear.

The only wildlife you won't see here are elephants, because they are too destructive and too big, and kongoni, which were wiped out during a severe drought. The odds of seeing lion, giraffe, cheetah, zebra, waterbuck, oribi, Thompson's gazelle, wildebeest, impala, buffalo, leopard, hippo, crocodile, jackal, hyena, warthog, baboon, vervet monkey, rock hyrax, all sorts of birds and the elusive rhino are excellent. To be able to see the whiskers on the leopard and the twinkle in the hyena's eye, take your binoculars.

Driving off the well maintained and signed roads is strictly forbidden. If you are caught by the rangers trying to sneak around off the designated tracks, they will not be lenient with you and rightly so. Vehicles present a real threat to both the environment and the wildlife surviving on this small tract of land.

Leaving your vehicle is also taboo except where there are signs telling you otherwise. Once again, this is for the protection of the environment, the animals, and for your safety. In the specifically designated spots you can get out of the car and revel in the vistas. Local visitors bring picnics which they may have to share with the impertinent vervet monkeys.

If you can't manage to get out to the "real" bush, this is a sample of the excellent variety of Kenya's wildlife and terrain six miles outside of Nairobi. In this, the oldest park in the country, there are rivers, bush country, thick forests, open plains and rocky valleys that are home to a wide range of birds and animals. These are still wild animals even though they are in a national park.

To get a head start on game spotting, ask the warden where the wildlife is. Depending on the food situation and the abundance of water, the location of the animals will vary. If there is plenty of both, the animals tend to be spread over a wide area. If the food and water are to be found only around man-made dams along the Athi River, then the game will be localized here.

Daphne Sheldrick's Animal Orphanage

To get to the orphanage, *Tel. 891 996*, go three miles past the gate to the Nairobi National Park and turn left. There is no entry fee but it is hoped you will leave a donation in the box on the porch. Believe me, only those with a heart of stone won't feel like emptying their wallets to help this wonderful lady continue her work.

There are no set hours for seeing the baby elephants or rhinos but the number of visitors is restricted. Usually a small number of people are allowed in during one hour of play time for the babies. Noon is the usual time, but call ahead to verify.

David Sheldrick started the wildlife trust which his wife continues today. The severely traumatized orphans must stay in contact with "family" members 24 hours a day or they will not survive. Africans take on this role, which includes hourly feeding, stool clean up, daily rubs with sunscreen, and a myriad of other absolutely necessary services. Only recently has the milk formula essential to survival been perfected. It takes up to five years for these orphans to be re-introduced to the wild.

The Bomas of Kenya

Heading past Nairobi National Park on the right hand side is this popular **cultural center**. Here you can watch a trained dance troupe perform many traditional songs and dances. Locals feel these performances are not authentic, but it may be the closest you will get to any native cultural entertainment.

For $4.50 for adults and $2.10 for kids, the visit includes the **Harambee Dancers** as well as a walk through what are supposed to be authentic traditional homes or *bomas*. There are daily performances at 2:30 pm during the week and 4:00 pm on the weekend. During the weekend, there is an acclaimed disco following the show and of course there are the standard pesky souvenir sellers and shops. The sound system sometimes leaves much to be desired, as does the circus atmosphere.

Langata Giraffe Center

A favorite with me, the $4.50 is well worth it to spend time with the endangered Rothschild giraffes and warthogs. The **Giraffe Center**, *Tel. 891 078*, is located on Gogo Falls Road near the Hardy Estate shopping center, about eleven miles outside Nairobi. Used as an educational tool for local children as well as a tourist attraction, there is an interesting display of art and information on conservation. Daily hours are from 9:00 am to 5:00 pm.

From a circular raised platform that puts you at giraffe eye level, you can handfeed the beautiful semi-tame Rothschild giraffes with pellets provided in a bucket. The funny looking warthogs gathering around the fence are most grateful for a few morsels thrown their way. In the background you can see the elegant stone structure that is **Giraffe Manor** (see *Where to Stay*, above) where you can spend the night or have an exclusive dinner. Running around on the lawn behind the mansion are guinea fowl, Thompson's gazelle, and other small game.

The center is run by the African Fund for Endangered Wildlife. Since their inception, the number of Rothschild giraffes in Kenya has risen from 100 to about 600. The organization continues to encourage new membership and educate those they come in contact with.

On the grounds, there is a nature trail and a bird and animal sanctuary which is open to the public. Walking along the trail will introduce you to a half a mile of assorted African plant life as well as the occasional bushbuck.

Uhuru Gardens

The park is located four and a half miles south of the city on Langata Road just past Wilson Airport. There is no admission charge and the park is open all hours. *Uhuru* means freedom, so it stands to reason the park was built to celebrate the 20th anniversary of Kenya's independence from Britain. A tall cone-shaped tower depicts two hands of friendship releasing the dove of peace. The gardens in front of the monument are supposedly laid out as a map of Kenya.

AROUND LIMURU
Kentmere Club

To get to the **Kentmere Club**, *Tel. 0154 41053*, take the Limuru Road past City Park and turn left at the Muthaiga roundabout. About four and a half miles further along, turn right on to Limuru Road (Banana Road). The Kentmere is on Limuru Road in **Tigoni**.

This typically English colonists' club is surrounded by expansive tea and coffee plantations, and is subdivided by lush green forests. You can stay at this peaceful getaway and pretend you have stepped back in time or you can simply enjoy a delicious meal in the quintessential British pub with its warm fires, low white ceilings, and dark wooden beams. For more information, see *Where to Stay*, above.

Just a short distance down the road is the **Waterfall Inn**, *Tel. 0154 40672*, which is worth seeing if only for the scenic vista. A lovely fifty foot waterfall, restaurant, pony rides, camel rides, disco and picnic spot will relax you to the point where you decide to spend the night. To get in there is a charge of $4.50 per vehicle; to stay overnight costs about $32 per night double occupancy.

Kiambethu Tea Farm

Follow the directions to the club above. Just under nine miles down the road turn right at the Limuru Girl's School sign (the school was started by Mr. Mitchell to educate his four daughters). Pass the school and turn left into the entry way that is marked "L.G. Mitchell." The drive takes about an hour from Nairobi. Situated at 7,200 feet in a garden of Eden with views of the Ngong Hills and Mt. Kilimanjaro, the farm was home to Mr. and Mrs. Lewis Mitchell. Following Mrs. Mitchell's death in February 1998, her tours are being continued by her daughter and son-in-law, Fiona and Marcus Vernon.

At Tigoni, the **tea farm**, *PO Box 41, Limuru, Tel. 0154 40756, Fax 76230, E-mail: kiambethu@iconnect.co.ke,* will introduce you to the interesting process of tea production (ask for a history booklet to keep as a memento and to introduce you to the fascinating history of the farm and the family). The tour includes drinks and a fine meal for roughly $15 per person, but must be arranged well ahead of time. A walk through the indigenous woods to see wild and shy colobus monkeys, and medicinal flora, is an added bonus and often a favorite part of the day.

A mile down the road from the farm is the church. Also started by Mr. Mitchell, here is where Dr. Louis Leakey and other members of the Leakey family are buried. Lovely stained glass windows were sent from a church in Southwest England, and the arches above the sanctuary are from cypress grown on the farm.

Church of the Torch

In Thogot, near the town of Kikuyu, the little **Church of the Torch** is worth a short visit. Established by Scottish missionaries in 1898, the Presbyterian church is the place Jomo Kenyatta was baptized. Monuments on the grounds pay tribute to those first settlers and the hardships they endured. It is best to stop here on your way back from Kiambethu and Kentmere.

AROUND THIKA

Chania (Queen's Cave Waterfall)

There is nothing left except an industrial wasteland around Thika, once famous for its flame trees due to writings of Elspeth Huxley. It is best to bypass the town and head straight for the falls. The drive from Nairobi takes under 45 minutes to cover 24 miles. The 80-foot **Chania waterfalls** are a popular picnic spot for locals and make for an interesting day trip, especially as this was where Churchill camped in 1907. He was hunting lion and although he heard many, he never got the chance to shoot one.

Chania Falls are at their best just after a heavy rain. Wide plumes of cascading water plunge 90 feet to the gorge below. For a worthy view of the falls, lovely gardens, and a good lunch, try the Blue Post Inn. Just off the Thika Road (A2), the **Blue Post Inn/Hotel**, *PO Box 42, Thika, Tel. (0151) 22241*, attracts a cross-section of Kenya residents who come to spend the day.

The Chania Falls border the grounds of the Blue Post. The hotel was built in 1906 on a point of land where the waters of the Chania and Thika rivers meet to form the Thika and Chania Falls. Early settlers stopped there for tea and talk and to see the falls from the hotel's garden. Today the falls are quite wide at this point but can be a little muddy. The hotel has seen better days, but is still a good spot to view the falls, enjoy the flower gardens, and have lunch.

Fourteen Falls

On the Athi River close to Thika is the 90-foot **Fourteen Falls**, which is also a popular place for family outings. To get there, leave Thika heading towards Kilima Mbogo village along the Garissa A3 Road. Follow the signs to Ol Doinyo Sabuk National Park turning left at the intersection. Take the small track going 2,500 feet to a clearing. Just ahead through the trees are the falls. Ask the locals to watch your car as you climb down the steep path to the water. From the parking area, follow a winding path through the brush to the foot of the falls.

Fourteen Falls looks like one edge of an immense, broken, jagged bowl. Reddish brown water covered with swirling white foam rushes down the precipice between the protruding caramel-colored rocks. Huge boulders jut from the bottom of the basin. It is not uncommon to see a young fisherman perched on a flat rock watching the waters of the Athi River swirling down to the Indian Ocean.

Ol Doinyo Sabuk National Park

A little over a mile further down the road from Fourteen Falls is this seven square mile park. There is no entry fee other than a signature before you head up the 4,067-foot mountain. The park hours are from 6:00 am to 6:00 pm.

Half way up is the resting place of a distinguished gentleman farmer, Sir Northrup, who once owned the land. At the top, the reward will be a wonderful view of the Athi plains and perhaps even Mount Kenya. It is not advisable to wander too far from your vehicle because of the roaming buffalo and for security reasons. You may also catch a glimpse of impala, rhino, leopard, monkeys and other buck. It is particularly pleasant here once the rains come to see butterflies in large numbers.

Murang'a

Once upon a time in the 1900s, the town was nothing more than "two grass huts within a stone wall and a ditch." Today **Murang'a** is the first significant town you will reach on your way north. It is considered the beginning of the Central Highlands and the furthest of excursions from Nairobi. After first driving through Thika, you will arrive at Murang'a, once known as Fort Hall, an administrative outpost. A detail of the King's African Rifles kept the peace with the Kikuyu during the colonial era.

From Nairobi it is a 54 mile drive to Murang'a through ruggedly beautiful country, where crops are grown as far as the eye can see. The busy little town today is a mere 28 miles from Thika on the A-2.

As you stop in Murang'a, the **Church of Saint James and All Martyrs** is the main attraction. The cathedral is located on a hill above the town center. The place of worship is dedicated to the Christians who were killed during the Mau Mau uprising when they refused to take the oaths demanded by the guerrillas. The Archbishop of Canterbury blessed the church in 1955 as a memorial to the thousands of souls (primarily Kikuyu) lost in the fight for independence. Inside, murals painted by **Elimo Njua**, a famous Kenyan artist, depict the Nativity story with an African back-drop. There is no admission charge but you will have to ask the caretaker to open the building.

The chapel looks down from its hilltop perch to the town of Murang'a below. It is worth seeing particularly for the murals painted by the famous Kenyan artist Elimo Njua. It was quite a feat for a black artist to be recognized for his talents in 1955. The fact that he was honored and his art chosen to decorate a memorial to a sad war speaks highly of his work. He was one of the first black Kenyan artists to be accredited in this way.

The murals are particularly fascinating because they are painted and designed from an African perspective. All the people are black, with features bearing a resemblance to the Kikuyu tribe. The Nativity scene includes all African shepherds and women dressed in native attire; all bear gifts to The Baby lying in a Kikuyu manger.

In another mural depicting *The Last Supper*, the hills of (what represents) Golgotha are dotted with the small mud huts of a Kenyan village. Long-necked giraffe stand besides the *banda* (hut) where the meal is spread, and thorny, green acacia trees add a surreal quality. Finally, the Crucifixion scene shows a black Christ surrounded by a very typical Kenya landscape with rolling plains and flat-topped acacia trees. The mural is so unlike anything we see in the US that it opens up a whole new perspective. It certainly gives visitors a lot to marvel at and ponder upon.

AROUND NGONG & KAREN
Denys Finch-Hatton Memorial

To get here, leave Nairobi along the Ngong Road and drive through the town of Ngong. From here the road winds along to the memorial. You will need to ask at the farmhouse for admittance and pay the $4 entry fee.

In 1918, this sociable Englishman organized hunting safaris for those who could afford them. He was immortalized in the movie *Out of Africa* as the boyfriend of the famous author, Karen Blixen. Finch-Hatton was killed in an unfortunate flying accident in 1931.

Ngong Hills

A lovely 16 mile drive from Nairobi, you will really get a feel for colonial Kenya in the **Ngong Hills**. It was here the settlers chose to live because of the fertile soil, temperate climate, and the surrounding beauty. The farms of the day were planted with eucalyptus from Australia and other exotic flora from around the world, but they never quite gave up being English. This is reflected in the style of the homes that you can glimpse through the exquisite gardens.

Known as the "purple hills," the views are marvelous here in the Ngong Hills. There are trails open to the public but the road is only paved as far as the Ngong town. After that you will need a four-wheel drive in the wet season. As a word of caution, be wary if you are out there alone, as muggings have been known to happen.

LEGENDS OF NGONG

*Reaching a height of roughly 8,000 feet, the **Ngong Hills** look like the knuckles on a giant's hand. There are two local legends that explain the creation of the famed hills. The first says a giant tripped and fell, making knuckle-like indentations in the earth. The other states that as God was shaping the earth, he flicked the dirt off his hands and this is where it landed.*

Karen Blixen Museum

The museum was once the home of Karen Blixen, who wrote nine books under the name of **Isak Dinesen** – the best known of which is *Out of Africa*. To get there follow Ngong Road to Karen and look for Karen Road. The entry fee is $3.50 and the hours are 9:30 am to 6:00 pm daily.

Karen was born in Denmark and came to Africa to marry a Swedish cousin, Baron Bror Blixen-Finecke. She loved the coffee farm from the start and gave it all she had to give. It was destined to fail, much like her marriage to the baron. In 1925 they divorced amicably, but things went further awry when she came down with syphilis and the farm was bankrupted.

After her boyfriend Denys Finch-Hatton was killed, she left her house and farm which she cherished so much and returned to Denmark. Today the land belongs to the Kenyan government and is home to an agricultural college.

FURTHER SOUTH OF NAIROBI
Lake Magadi

Actually part of the Rift Valley, this blindingly white (take sunglasses!) and very shallow lake (around four feet deep) is seldom visited by those traveling in the valley system, as it is too far south. That is why I have included it in the Nairobi chapter as a possible day trip on your itinerary. You will be able to enjoy the wonderful bird populations in relative solitude.

There is no public transportation from Nairobi. A railway line runs to Magadi to collect extracted soda or trona from the nearby factory, but unfortunately it doesn't carry passengers. You will need to travel by car on the C58 road. Head out of Nairobi towards Wilson Airport and past the main entrance to Nairobi National Park. Turn left along Mbagathi Road and follow the C58. If the weather is clear as you pass the Ngong Hills, a magnificent view of Mount Kilimanjaro opens up before you.

The Magadi Soda Company contributes to Kenya's largest mineral export of sodium salts, potassium, and soda used in detergents and glass-making. Driving down the hill to the factory you will notice a fine white powder spewing from the plant.

As it is set in a semi-desert area, the lake is quite different than those further north in the Rift Valley. Semi-solid mire and hot springs surround the edge of the soda lake, which is home to large numbers of wading birds and pelicans. Patches of microscopic bright pink algae attract the famous rose-colored flamingos. Some years ago Lake Magadi was put on the map when severe drought threatened the health of young flamingos. Hundreds of thousands of soda-encrusted babies were retrieved from the lake in an impressive rescue operation.

Olorgesailie National Park

Before reaching Lake Magadi on the C58 (Nairobi-Magadi road) you will see a sign on your left for the **Olorgesailie Prehistoric Site**. The park is open from 9:30 am to 6:00 pm and there is an entry fee. This site was once covered by a small lake attracting game and in turn hunters. It was here that Dr. Leakey discovered bones, stone age tools, and a living site of "hand ax" man perfectly preserved in the volcanic ash and lake silt. It is particularly exciting for archaeologists that in the Rift Valley the alkaline soils and mineralized waters faultlessly fossilize artifacts from many thousands of years ago.

Valuable finds like those displayed in an absorbing but modest on-site museum are still brought to the surface today by ground movement and erosion. There are a few basic bandas available for rent (thatched huts), but being popular with Nairobi residents they fill up fast, so book ahead.

PRACTICAL INFORMATION

Banks & Exchanging Money

Possibly the most popular bank in the city of Nairobi is **Barclays**. The branch located at the corner of Wabera Street and Kenyatta Avenue is open Monday through Saturday from 9:00 am to 4:30 pm.

At Jomo Kenyatta International Airport, Barclays Bank is open 24 hours a day, seven days a week. When you first arrive in Kenya, it is most convenient to change some of your money here. There are also other places to change currency conveniently located in the arrival area.

The **Travellers Forex Bureau Ltd.** claims that for every foreign currency transaction with their establishment, you'll get more shillings for your dollars. They don't charge commission and generally offer competitive rates. Located on the lower ground floor of The Mall at Westlands, their office is easy to find. Westlands mall is at the corner of Uhuru Highway and Ring Road near the traffic circle. *For more information, write to PO Box 34535, Nairobi, Tel. 443 866, Fax 446 604.*

Finerate Forex Bureau Ltd. is a money changing firm owned and managed by a competent team of ex-bankers who were in the forefront when the Exchange Control Act was being dismantled. Strategically located around major business, tourist, and shopping centers, the company has a "walk in, walk out" policy and charges no commissions. *Situated safely on the ground floor of Bruce House near 680 Hotel, Kenyatta Avenue, Tel. 250 406, Fax 250 407.*

Crown Bureau de Change, *PO Box 22515; Tel. 250 720, Fax 252 365,* on the ground floor of the Corner House complex along Mama Ngina Street is another reputable and safe place to buy travelers checks or change money. Here you will find a state of the art computer system that displays daily exchange rates on an electronic board.

Beauty Salons

There are any number of hairdressers, beauty salons, and barber shops to choose from. The services offered will vary anywhere from a buzz cut to a full manicure and pedicure. The prices will also vary widely depending on what you are looking for. In general, the prices are comparable to those at home. It is best to call ahead and check prices and availability.

For any kind of beauty regimen, try the **YMCA Hairdresser Salon**, *Kirk Road, Nairobi, Tel. 724 419*; **Westlands Hairdressing Salon**, *Westlands, Nairobi, Tel. 745 069*; and **Ultimate Hair and Beauty Salon**, *Tigori Road off Argwings Khodhek Road, Nairobi, Tel. 714 739.*

Health/Sports Clubs
If you are in the mood for tennis, hockey, cricket, soccer, squash or just a workout, call any of the facilities listed below for their hours, rates and weekly schedules.
• **Parklands Sports Club**, *Ojijo Road, Tel. 742 938*
• **Impala Club**, *Ngong Road, Tel. 568 684*
• **Nairobi Gymkhana**, *corner of Forest Road and Rwathia Road, Tel. 742 804*
• **Nairobi Club**, *Ngong Road, Tel. 725 726*

Hospitals
For any emergency or to call the police, dial **999**. Hopefully you will not need to find medical services while you are on vacation. If you do, these are the best facilities available that will offer the best possible treatment:
• **Gertrudes Garden Children's Hospital**, *PO Box 42325, Muthaiga Road, Nairobi, Tel. 763 474*
• **The Aga Khan Dispensary and Maternity Hospital**, *PO Box 30270, 3rd Parklands Avenue, Nairobi, Tel. 740 000, Telex 22772*
• **Kenyatta National Hospital**, *PO Box 20725, off Mbagathi Road, Nairobi, Tel. 726 300*
• **Nairobi Hospital**, *PO Box 30026, Argwings Kodhek Road, Nairobi, Tel. 722 160, Fax 728 003*
If you are in need of an ambulance, you can call any of the services below:
• **St. John's Ambulance**, *PO Box 41469, Saint John House, Country Lane, Nairobi, Tel. 224 066*
• **Red Cross Society of Kenya**, *PO Box 40712, Nairobi, Tel. 503 781, Fax 503 845*
• **E.A.R.S. Medivac Ltd.**, *Ndemi Road PO Box 59045, Nairobi, Tel. 566 683, Fax 652 695*
• **AMREF**, *PO Box 30125, Nairobi, Tel. 501 301, Fax 506 112*
• **Kenya Africa Air Rescue Ltd.**, *PO Box 41766, Nairobi, Tel. 337 030*

In addition to ambulance services, the last four organizations on the list above offer air rescue, emergency transportation, and clean blood for transfusions.

Laundry

If you should require any dry cleaning or washing services while you are in Nairobi, there are only two places where you might have some success. I suggest you bring clothes that can be roughly hand washed and do not require dry cleaning. As labor is inexpensive in Kenya, most hotels have someone come in daily to do the laundry.

• **Rajputana Laundry**, *Tel. 558 964*
• **Tintoria Ltd.**, *Soin Arc, Westlands, Tel. 448 664, Fax 448 665*

Luggage Storage

The Nairobi railway station has a luggage storage room, where for a small fee you can leave bags you don't want to carry or can't take with you. The office is open from 8:00 am to noon and 1:00 pm to 6:30 pm daily.

Most hotels will also keep you bags for a few days if necessary. Sometimes there may be a small charge for the service. Check before you drop off your bags how much it will be per day and get a receipt for each item. It is advisable not to leave anything valuable in the suitcases if at all possible.

Phone Home

For international telephone and fax services try calling from the **International Call Centre**. If you want to see where the middle class people who live in Nairobi shop, you can combine making your phone call with a little shopping of your own.

The call center is located in The Mall in Westlands at the corner of Ring Road and Uhuru Highway; look for the roundabout and you won't miss the mall. All major credit cards are accepted for payment as is US and Kenyan currency. Hours are Monday through Saturday from 9:00 am to 7:00 pm.

Swimming Pools

For $1.50, you can feel free to use the large pool and diving board at the **YMCA** on State House Road. Almost anywhere you stay, however, will have its own pool or will provide you with one nearby. If you want to go somewhere other than your hotel to swim, you can probably get in to use the pool for around $3.

Water

Sometimes in the city there can be water shortages that may last for a couple of hours or longer. When water, a precious commodity in Kenya, is in short supply it is only turned on for a few hours each day. It is best to be prepared to go without a shower if this happens. Some hotels, such as the Hilton, have their own water supply from a bore hole and are unconcerned with the rationing.

It is hard for us to understand how water, something we take for granted, can be rationed for household use. Out of consideration and in the name of conservation, use water sparingly. While brushing your teeth or soaping up in the shower, don't just let the water run but rather turn it off. Every effort is appreciated by the local populace.

13. THE CENTRAL HIGHLANDS

Mount Kenya and the **Aberdares** are the highlight of this area, with its moody weather and fertile surroundings. The fascination with the **Central Highlands** is in its variety, both in terms of landscape and climate. High in the hills the trout streams have become legendary, as have the life-giving rivers and dramatic waterfalls.

The rough circumference of the Central Highlands encompasses **Murang'a** in the south, the **Aberdares** in the west, **Nyeri** in the center, **Nyahururu** and **Nanyuki** in the north, and **Meru** and **Embu** in the east. Beginning just to the north of Nairobi, the Central Highlands continue upwards forming the eastern wall of the rift valley.

Without traveling great distances, you can experience lush cool forests or acres of open farm and ranch land. On the eastern side of the mountain there are rolling hills covered in verdant crops dipping and rising with the terrain. Del Monte grows almost one-third of the world's pineapples on its fabulously large plantations. Bananas, corn, oranges, and an array of plump vegetables are also grown here for export.

The cultivated fields give way to the famous purple-gray grasslands where sheep, herds of cattle, and wildlife graze in harmony. On the

WHAT'S IN THE SACK?

As you drive around in this region, you are bound to see piles of burlap sacks on the side of the road. The sacks are on their way to market and are filled with produce harvested off small farms. The contents of the bags will vary depending on the altitude – higher up it will probably be tea; in the mid-elevations, coffee; and in the lower regions pineapple, sugarcane, and tobacco. It's a strange sight to see trucks stopping to collect each and every one of these bags.

western side of the Highlands, the land is uniformly level, parched, scrubby and captivating in its own way. It is amazing to be driving along in a fairy glen heading east when suddenly the view before you opens up to what looks like the surface of the moon.

Home to the **Kikuyu**, the Central Highlands are regarded as a sacred part of their history. This belt between 6,000 and 10,000 feet of habitable land is where the new British settlers chose to make their homes. The soil was fertile, disease was uncommon and the climate perfect. African families were often forced to relocate, as large homesteads spread across the landscape.

Many believe this was the cause of the **Mau Mau uprising**. The Kikuyu wanted their land and their country back. Today there are only a few large farms owned by descendants of the colonials. The land has been reclaimed and subdivided into many small subsistence lots owned by Kikuyu families.

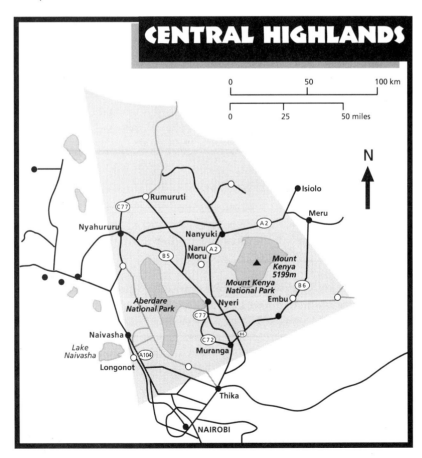

CENTRAL HIGHLANDS MUST SEES

If your time is limited in the Central Highlands, these are the places I recommend as "must sees:"
· **Church of Saint James in Murang'a** *– (See Chapter 12, Nairobi, Excursions & Day Trips – the church is in the Central Highlands but is more easily reached from Nairobi than destinations in this chapter)*
· **Aberdare National Park**
· **Nyandaru (Aberdare) Mountains**
· **Mount Kenya**
· **Nyahururu**
· **Animal Orphanage – Mount Kenya Safari Club**

NYERI

Here in the town of **Nyeri** is where many of Kenya's renowned athletes first came to train. The landscape is rich and highly cultivated. The community itself is an obvious reminder of the colonial past, with a touch of true Kenya in its vivacious market. Nyeri was once the location of yet another military camp during the fight for independence.

It is one of the largest towns in the Central Highlands and can claim the administrative headquarters of the Central Province. Today there are a cathedral, three churches, a mosque, bookshops, hardware stores and a Muslim center that are part of the town.

ARRIVALS & DEPARTURES

By Bus

There are two bus stations in Nyeri from which buses and matatus arrive and depart daily to destinations further north or to Nairobi.

By Car

The drive to Nyeri is a rather unremarkable one. Take the Nairobi-Nyeri road (A-2) which winds its way around the foothills of Mount Kenya. Keep veering left towards Murang'a. Occasionally you will see a brilliant orange flower on a flame tree or perhaps the purple colors of a jacaranda in bloom. Spreading off in the distance are thatched huts and planted terraced slopes as far as you can see.

ORIENTATION

Nyeri has one central road with other arteries running off it. There isn't a whole lot to keep you here and most people only stay for a short time. There are two post offices, one at each end of town, and two clock towers also at each end of the municipality. The Batian Hotel is the southernmost landmark. The Central Hotel as the northern boundary.

GETTING AROUND TOWN

It is possible to get from one end of town to the other on foot or by car. Walking however, is the best option as roads are often rutted making driving slow. Walking is not advised at night.

To rent a car for the day, check at the **Outspan Hotel**, *Tel. 0171 2424*, and the **Aberdare Country Club**, *Tel. 02 216 940*. Usually they rent cars to their guests who want to go to Aberdare National Park, but may be willing to assist you if they're not too busy.

WHERE TO STAY

In this territory, as with most regions in Kenya, the villages or municipalities offer little in the way of accommodations. Sometimes you will be able to find acceptable rooms in the old colonial hotels in town, but the facilities are often worn.

The best hotels are in the outback and include room, board, game drives, and entertainment. You can choose from private ranches, tents, bandas, hotels that appear to be colonial country clubs or lodges hidden deep in the bush.

THE ARK FOREST LODGE, *Lonrho Hotels, PO Box 58581, Nairobi. Tel. 216 940, Fax 219 212, E-mail: ark@form-net.com. $264 per night double occupancy. No children under seven. All major credit cards accepted.*

There is no access to this hotel by private vehicles. You must arrive here from the Aberdare Country Club, which handles reservations and the daily 2:30 pm pickup for the 45 minute drive to the lodge. Built on the western slopes of the Aberdares, the ark shaped resort stands beside a shallow wateringhole and a man-made salt lick. Your first glimpse is of the dramatically curving roof across the valley. Access to the Ark itself is over a long wooden bridge with forests spreading along each side.

The animals are drawn to this place from the surrounding thick woodlands and deep valleys. Game viewing from platforms and bunkers ensures you don't have to leave the comforts of your hotel to see wildlife. Three levels of viewing areas are the highlight of a stay here. A rhino or elephant can be a few feet away and you can smell, see, and hear every movement. A buzzer in each room signals the arrival of game at all hours of the day or night. If you are more interested in sleep, you can turn this off. Bright floodlights shine at night to allow game viewing and picture taking any time. A resident naturalist is available to answer questions.

The rooms themselves resemble tiny cabins with an adjoining bathroom equipped with a shower. Dark paneling makes the 60 bedrooms appear even smaller and gloomy. Inadequate windows don't offer much of a view but the accommodations are certainly functional.

A much frequented bar and long communal dining tables encourage interesting conversation among your fellow guests. Early rising and late nights make the warm fireplace in the main lounge a welcome retreat. Tea and cakes here in the afternoon are a relaxing affair.

SANGARE, *Safcon Travel, PO Box 59224, Nairobi. Tel. 503 265, Fax 506 829. $390 per night double occupancy. All major credit cards accepted.*

To get to Sangare you can drive in, but first you must stop and pick up a gate key at the Aberdare Country Club. Once you use your key to open the gate, follow the steep winding roads and enjoy the magnificent views. Eventually you will arrive at the vine-covered ranch house. A wraparound porch invites you to stay awhile and chat with the Prettejohns who own the estate.

If you don't have time to drive, fly to Nanyuki where the Prettejohns will pick you up. On the return trip to Sangare from Nanyuki you can make your selections of various activities. Watch the great bird and animal populations from your verandah, see the world from horseback, have a catered picnic in the bush, enjoy nighttime game drives or try your hand at some excellent trout fishing.

Everything here at Sangare is meant to afford privacy and the feel of luxury camping for a small group of visitors. The site consists of three simple bandas strategically placed alongside a man-made dam. One structure is a small kitchen where all the meals are prepared from fresh produce grown on the ranch. Another building is the dining room/living room. A crackling fire keeps visitors warm as they enjoy a cup of tea. You can step out onto a terrace which affords a lovely view of the water. The last building is a pleasant, simply furnished, two bedroom banda. Both rooms have their own full bathroom which includes hot water.

Game spotting is rewarding for such things as antelope, buck, leopard, and elephant but unfortunately there are no lions.

TREETOPS, *Block Hotels, PO Box 47557, Nairobi. Tel. 335 807, Fax 340 541. $158 per night double occupancy. All major credit cards accepted. No children under seven.*

There is no access to the hotel for private vehicles. Transportation is provided by the Outspan Hotel at noon. The hotel is located just inside the gates to the Aberdare National Park. Built on stilts in 1952, the resort overlooks a waterhole and salt-lick for optimum no hassle game viewing. Extensive lighting provides easy nighttime animal watching at the waterhole below. As large game such as elephant and buffalo have been drawn here for the salt and water, they have destroyed the surrounding habitat over the years.

This tree-house hotel built in 1932 was inspired by the story of Peter Pan. The original two rooms have grown considerably and today make it one of the most famous hotels in Kenya. The hotel has recently undergone a complete refubishment. Among the most prestigious people to stay here was Princess Elizabeth in 1952. It was here she heard of her father's death and her accession to the throne.

The 50 affordable rooms called "nests" resemble closets. The windows are too small and there are no private bathrooms. Instead, there are communal showers nearby. In the dining room, thick linens line the long tables. Bench seating and dark paneling on the walls seem to contradict the detailed menu by creating a feeling of claustrophobia. The living room, on the other hand, has an enchanting viewing deck on the roof and large bright windows. Live trees grow among the halls, giving the feeling of being in the treetops.

THE ABERDARE COUNTRY CLUB, *Lonrho Hotels, PO Box 58581, Nairobi. Tel. 216 940, Fax 216 796, E-mail: lonhotsm@form-net.com. $126 per night double occupancy. All major credit cards accepted.*

The country club is a slice of jolly old England. The gardens are wonderful examples of horticulture and the views are exquisite. Sitting under the cool shade of a tree on the front lawn, relaxation, and leisure reign. If you are not staying here, you may join the club for a small fee and use the golf, tennis, swimming, riding, walking and fishing facilities. On a clear day, Mount Kenya will allow you to see her peaks from the pool side Karuru Bar.

Built on a sheer incline by the Lyon family in 1937, the country club called "Steep" is much sought by the local populace, who come here to escape the rigors of Nairobi. Plush leather couches, large stone fireplaces, and dark carpeting decorate the living room and bar in the main house. The dining room walls are covered with dark paneling framing the charming view out the large windows.

The first two meals of the day are served buffet style, while the evening meal is chosen from a set menu as candles shimmer in the night. The cuisine at The Aberdare Country Club has a reputation of being excellent, with typical fare like fresh trout. Children under 12 are encouraged to eat early.

A small, private game sanctuary on the grounds will reveal a few members of Kenya's four footed population. Unfortunately, on this 1100 acre sanctuary you will see no lion, elephant, or buffalo, but eland, zebra, giraffe, impala and the like are plentiful.

Behind the original stone building with its red tile roof are 38 ensuite guest cottages. Each cottage has a fireplace, private outdoor terrace, huge windows, and is engulfed in pretty tropical vegetation.

OUTSPAN HOTEL, *Block Hotels, PO Box 47557, Nairobi. Tel. 335 807, Fax 340 541. $112 per night double occupancy. All major credit cards accepted.* The Outspan is a charming old colonial hotel built in 1927 with great views of Mount Kenya. A regular crowd of daily visitors come for tea in the hotel's enchanting gardens before leaving for other destinations. It's strange that few people stay here in the beauty and comfort available.

The facilities and entertainment are excellent. You can choose from a visit to a coffee plantation, trout fishing, Mount Kenya hikes, nature and Chania river walks, golf, tennis, squash, billiards, darts, videos, cards, swimming, Paxtu museum and shopping in the souvenir store.

The history of the hotel is intriguing; Sherbrooke Walker and his wife Lady Bettie wanted to build the first upscale hotel for the first travelers on the new railway line to Kenya. The new hotel boasted the first flush toilets in the area! Outspan (the term used when a team of oxen are unyoked) still reflects the luxury of the day, although some of the furnishings could use a facelift.

Garden cottages and standard rooms all feel open and airy. Fireplaces and overstuffed leather chairs are also standard in each room. Bedroom options include garden access, mountain views, and enclosed patios.

The well tended sweet smelling gardens are beautiful. Built with a taste of Britain, the design accentuates Mount Kenya in the background. A wide contingent of colorful birds, including a vain peacock, parade daily for guests.

Chippendale chairs and crisp linens compliment the outdoor breakfast and lunch buffets. Inside, the cheery bar, sitting area, and snooker room are decorated with dark paneling, brass, warm fireplaces, and sofas in soft colors. Altogether a lovely place to experience a taste of Kenya past.

BATIAN GRAND HOTEL, *in the center of Nyeri town. Tel. 0171 4141. $45 per night double occupancy. Rate includes breakfast. Major credit cards accepted.*

The Batian Grand Hotel is one of the better places to stay in Nyeri, apart from several really low rent dives that I will not recommend. The rooms are clean and nicely furnished, although a bit on the small side. There is a parking area that is guarded 24 hours a day. A bar and restaurant offer standard fare.

GREEN HILLS HOTEL, *a short drive out of Nyeri town. Tel. 0171 2017. $25 per night double occupancy. Rate includes breakfast. Major credit cards accepted.*

The facilities and staff at the Green Hills Hotel are excellent. There is a sauna, spa, two good restaurants, a bar, playground, swimming pool and guarded parking. The 124 rooms are well decorated and furnished. Attractive green lawns surround this mid-range hotel.

ABERDARE FISHING LODGE, *or check in with the Naro Moru River Lodge, PO Box 18, Naro Moru. Tel. 0176 6262, Fax 0176 62211. $5 per night double occupancy. Major credit cards accepted.*

The self-help banda (thatched huts) are very Spartan with cold showers only. You will need to bring along your own bedding, food, and cooking utensils. There are two *askari* (guards) for protection around at all times. Firewood is provided by the guards but it should be noted that getting a fire going in these altitudes can be tough. An exciting place to stay if you prefer a more unique taste of camping in Kenya.

ABERDARE PARK CAMPING, *reservations are required and should be made at the park headquarters in Mweiga. Tel. 24. $1.20 per night per site.*

The park headquarters in Mweiga is located roughly eight miles north of Nyeri. It is best to call in advance, but if you don't, stop by and talk to the rangers. It's more than likely they will be able to help you.

WHERE TO EAT

For the most part, the hotels listed above in *Where to Stay* offer the best restaurants and bars. However, in Nyeri there are a few inexpensive clean places offering good wholesome food and usually a bar or two.

The **WHITE RHINO HOTEL,** *on the northwest side of town heading towards the golf course,* is a popular watering hole for Europeans. It offers a lounge and restaurant. The **CENTRAL HOTEL,** *near Barclays Bank and the post office on the north side of town,* has a good restaurant but is nothing fancy. It has its own bar and a disco on Friday nights. **UPTOWN CAFE** has tasty burgers, steaks and curries. Try the **PEOPLES CAFE,** *near the main post office,* for coffee and snack foods.

SEEING THE SIGHTS

In the center of Nyeri town look for a **stone marker** dedicated to yet more casualties in Kenya's troubled path to independence. The inscription reads, "To the memory of the members of the Kikuyu tribe who died in the fight for freedom. 1951-1957."

NIGHTLIFE & ENTERTAINMENT

For an interesting time, go to the movies at the **Batian Beer Garden/ Restaurant and Cinema,** *Tel. 4141.* The **Rhino Hotel** is popular with the local European population as a common meeting place. There is a terrace bar and lounge where you can get beer and other alcoholic beverages. The **Central Hotel** has a decent bar with a disco on Friday and Saturday nights.

On the outskirts of town, the **Green Hills Hotel,** *Tel. 2017,* has a comfortable bar where you can get a cold drink. At the **Outspan Hotel,** *Tel. 2424,* you can try the **Mount Kenya bar,** which unfortunately doesn't offer a view of the mountain but is set in lovely surroundings. The hotels listed in the *Where to Stay* section above have some of the best bars and restaurants in and around Nyeri.

SPORTS & RECREATION
Game Drives
In the unlikely event you are staying in a hotel or are part of a tour not doing any game viewing in the parks, you can make your own arrangements. To get in to Aberdare National Park and see the wildlife, check with the **Outspan Hotel** in Nyeri. You will be able to join a group into the eastern part of the park for the entire day for a cost of $30 plus park fees. If you wish to see the park on your own, the Outspan will rent you a four wheel drive for $78 per day. At the **Aberdare Country Club**, your alternatives are to rent a vehicle for $162 for half a day or $312 for a full day. For either of these options, there will be a 20 percent charge added to your bill if you are not a guest in the hotel.

Wherever you choose to spend your nights, there are a multitude of activities such as horseback riding, climbing, fishing, visiting native homesteads and night drives for your pleasure. Large quantities of game viewing however, whether during the day or night, should be your host's ultimate goal for your safari.

Gliding Club of Kenya
Just north of Nyeri, **The Gliding Club of Kenya**, *PO Box 926, Nyeri, Tel. 0171 2748*, has its headquarters in Mweiga. If you are interested in soaring over the Aberdares, get in touch with the club managers Peter and Pietra Allmendinger.
Spa
The **Green Hills Hotel**, *Tel. 0171 2017,* outside the township of Nyeri has massage facilities, a swimming pool, and sauna. If you are not a guest, there may be a small fee to use the amenities.

Golf
Across the street from the lovely **Outspan Hotel** is a nine hole golf course, which is open to the public for a small fee.

SHOPPING
Every town you come to will have some sort of market where you can shop for African trinkets and carvings. These places tend to move around or set up on a street corner when the weather is good. Towns usually have one main road lined with shops full of carvings, shukas, jewelry, and the like. If the Africans know tourists are arriving, they will set up a "shop" on

the side of the airstrip runway or on the bank of the road. Most of the tourist hotels have souvenir shops on the grounds or in the lobby. All you have to do is get out of your vehicle and swarms of souvenir sellers will find you. My only advice is if you like it, buy it because you may not see another one quite like it.

Any of the many stores along the main road in Nyeri sell books, hardware, and a wide variety of just about anything you might be looking for. For some interesting shopping try the **Municipal Market** or the **Vegetable Market**. The Municipal Market is located just south of the clock tower on the south east side of town. The Vegetable Market has a tendency to move around. A new market can spring up at any time in any spot. All it takes is some home-grown produce and the ever-present local entrepreneurial spirit. If you ask anyone, they will point you in the right direction.

At the **Spinners' and Weavers' Cooperative**, *set on the grounds of the Presbyterian Church on Mount Kenya Ring Road,* you can watch the women working the local wool and buy well made goods such as shawls, rugs, and sweaters. The hours are Monday through Friday 9:00 am to 5:00 pm and Saturday 9:00 am to 12:30 pm. There is no admission fee.

EXCURSIONS & DAY TRIPS

Lord Baden-Powell Museum – Paxtu

On the grounds of the Outspan Hotel there is a fascinating museum dedicated to the founder of the Boy Scouts. **Lord Baden-Powell**, who was born in 1857, lived in Paxtu, the home built for him, from 1938 to 1941 when he died. Pay $4 at the reception desk of the hotel for admission to the museum.

Lord Baden-Powell's Grave

The famous man is buried at Saint Peter's Church graveyard in Nyeri. Look for the church on Aberdares Road opposite CalTec Garage. Access to the church and tomb are free of charge.

Aberdare National Park

The volcanoes that make up this park are on the eastern side of the Rift Valley and are part of the Aberdare Mountains. This region is damp most of the year and has a reputation for being mostly covered in fog or mist. During the wet season you will need a four-wheel drive vehicle if you want to stand a chance of getting around. If the rains have been particularly heavy, the park closes down altogether.

Why would anyone want to come here, you might ask? Precisely because of the rain, thick forests, and steep hillsides. The area remains unspoiled by humankind. The views, waterfalls, and streams are some of the best you will ever see and the wildlife is abundant. Elephant, buffalo, lion, antelope and leopard are frequently noticed roaming the crags but to see them you will have to stay more than a day. Accommodations in the park are very basic and consist of three campsites. You will have to bring all your own gear and warm clothing (see *Where to Stay* above).

THE ABERDARES

*The **Nyandarua Range** or the **Aberdares** are the second most important part of this region after Mount Kenya. The 37 mile long range has recently been renamed Nyandarua in Kikuyu, which means "drying hide." In the eyes of the Africans they resemble a hide stretched over a drying rack. The new name will take a while to replace the old one.*

In 1884 the mountains were christened after the president of the Royal Geographic Society, Lord Aberdare. The volcanic range with its deep abyss running from north to south proudly reveals Ol-Doinyo Lesatima as the third highest peak in Kenya at 13,000 feet.

The dramatic and beautiful Aberdares are a sought-after escape for the citizens of Nairobi when they need a change of scenery. The highlands resemble a slice of Scotland with the deep alpine moors. Further up are bamboo forests filled with delicate flowers and vines, and climbing still further are thick impenetrable forests.

Enjoy the heavenly feel of the place but don't expect to see much in the way of game, at least in the forests. The elusive bongo, colossal elephant, rhino, and buffalo can be five feet away but the bush will be too thick and the animals will hide when they hear you.

To get to the park start off from Nyeri town and take the Nyahururu Road north for about three miles. Turn left at the Ruhuruini Gate/ Aberdare National Park sign. Turn right at Ihururu village at the sign to Kimathi Secondary School. Keep making right turns until you get to the park gate. Here you will have to honk your horn for the gate-keeper.

In this location you will certainly never feel as though you are part of the tourist crowd. If solitude and uniqueness are your bag, this is the place for you.

Karuru & Gura Falls

The 900-foot high **Karuru Falls** and the 1,000-foot **Gura Falls** can be reached via a foot path. Gura Falls in the Aberdares are the highest in Kenya and were used in aerial shots for the movie *Out of Africa*. Two thin glistening streaks weave their way down the ravine where the Gura and

Karuru rivers meet. The walk there and back is about four miles. If you plan on making this trek, it is wise to take a park ranger with you. The chances of seeing a bongo, black leopard, elephant, or rhino are slim, unless you stay around for a few days. What is abundant in the area is birds – there are hundreds of amazing different species.

Both Karuru and Gura Falls are opposite each other and located in the southern region of the 766 square kilometer **Aberdare National Park**. Gura Falls are Kenya's deepest. The thin white plume of water from Gura Falls cuts an impressive swath through the lush green and impenetrable trees on both sides of the narrow cascade. Two giant steps break the rushing water's downward motion. The gushing flow seems to appear from nowhere at the edge of a vast flat plateau. Karuru Falls eventually merge with Gura Falls and flow into the Gura River heading towards the coast.

To find the falls from Nyeri, head west out of town past the Outspan Hotel and keep going toward Aberdares National Park. Within a short drive, under five miles, you'll enter the park via the Kiandongoro Gate. Turn left or south towards the Aberdare Fishing Lodge until the road veers west. The walk there and back is about four miles.

Italian Memorial Church

Built in 1952, this tiny church is offered by the Italian government as a memorial to those patriots who lost their lives during WWI and WWII. There were many large prisoner of war camps in Kenya, including one near Nyeri. It is quite a stirring sight to see the photos, memorabilia, and hundreds of markers lining the walls.

To get to the memorial chapel, go about three miles north of Nyeri and turn left. The church is open from 8:00 am to 5:00 pm daily. There is no charge, but the keeper will have to unlock the doors for you.

PRACTICAL INFORMATION

Banks

There are three banks in Nyeri; **Standard Chartered Bank**, **Barclays Bank**, and **Kenya Commercial Bank**, which keep Nairobi banking hours. If you need to change money, I would stick with Barclays.

Post Offices

Nyeri boasts two post offices, which both keep Nairobi post office hours. They are situated at opposite ends of the town. You can make phone calls or send parcels home from either one.

NYAHURURU

Nyahururu is best known as one of the highest towns in Kenya at an elevation of 7,742 feet. It is a popular stopping point for tourists moving to and from Masai Mara and Samburu game parks.

Located right on the equator, the captivating colonial town of Nyahururu (also known as **Thompson's Falls**) is surrounded by native conifers and what's left of primitive forests. A young man of 25, **Joseph Thompson** set off from England by order of the Royal Geographic Society to explore Kenya. In 1883 or thereabouts, he gave his name to the Thompson's gazelle and the splendid falls on the **Ewaso Narok River**.

ARRIVALS & DEPARTURES

By Bus

There are any number of matatus and buses coming and going from the station located on the south side of town. You can get to Isiolo, Nanyuki, Thika, Kericho and Nairobi. You will have to check with the station for departure times and fares as they are subject to change.

By Car

Probably the best way into town from Nairobi is to take the A-104 through Naivasha for the 96 mile drive to Nakuru. Turn right and east from Nakuru for the picturesque drive to Thompson's Falls. Scenic panoramas over the Aberdares and miles of fields planted in beans and corn stretch as far as the eye can see.

By Train

Even though you see train tracks running alongside the town, don't get your hopes up and think you can finish your journey by hopping on a rail car. In 1929 there was a train that carried passengers around Kenya through Thompson's Falls, but today this railway line carries freight only. It's rather sad to see this romantic form of transport go by the wayside.

ORIENTATION

The town of Nyahururu basically has one main street to its name running from north to south. Two significant roads bisect the main thoroughfare and run from east to west. All the shops and businesses are along one of these three roads. The railway line is on the east side of the settlement and serves as the town border. In the center of the township is the stadium. Coming in from the north you will find an Esso gas station, while on the west entrance is a BP gas station.

GETTING AROUND TOWN

Leave your car and walk around this small town. Look for someone to watch your vehicle or park in a fenced area. Walking from one side of town to the other takes under twenty minutes.

WHERE TO STAY

THOMPSON'S FALLS LODGE, *Thompson's Falls Lodge, PO Box 38, Nyahururu. Tel. 0365 22006. $25 per night double occupancy. All major credit cards accepted.*

Built in 1931 as a typical highland farmhouse, the inn has a marvelously warm log fire to keep off the night's chill. The rambling brick structure has lovely garden views of Thompson's Falls but small souvenir shacks have taken over the cliff, blocking the scenic panorama. A popular place for a Sunday picnic, the locals enjoy the falls as much as tourists.

Accommodations are either in the main building or in cottages spread around the attractive grounds. Each room has its own fireplace and bathroom with hot water. The shiny wood floors and antique furnishings are a throwback to the charm of colonial days. In the central edifice there is a comfortable bar, lounge, and restaurant.

Camping on the premises is something many people consider as a great alternative. Included in the $2 per person fee you can have all the firewood you need plus access to showers and bathrooms in the main building.

MOKORINDO COTTAGE, *Mokorindo Cottage, c/o C. Aggett, Kifuku Estates, PO Box 2, Rumuruti. $20 per night double occupancy. All major credit cards accepted.*

The setting for Mokorindo Cottage, so called because of the Mokorindo tree at the edge of the water, is one of quiet beauty and solitude. The Laikipia Plateau with its wide open spaces, dozens of birds, and plentiful thorn trees makes a striking setting for the secluded bungalow.

The two room cottage is draped in bougainvillea and blooming golden shower creepers. Inside, the inviting fireplace, large dining room and living room, and fully equipped bathroom provide for the perfect escape from the hustle and bustle of the world. To finish off a perfect vacation you will be spoiled by the attentions of the resident cook.

A dam built in the middle of several thousand acres of working cattle ranch provides a great view from the cottage as well as spectacular bird watching. Look for Egyptian geese, sacred Ibis, ducks, and cormorants as you settle down on the vine-covered terrace. These and any of the other 200 species of birds are the only wildlife you will see in the area.

For entertainment, try catching your supper of largemouth bass in the dam, do a little duck or game bird shooting, paddle around in the dinghy, or go for a long nature hike.

BARON HOTEL, *Tel. 0365 32751. $15 per night double occupancy. Breakfast included. All major credit cards accepted.*

A clean and efficiently run hotel in the middle of Nyahururu, the Baron will provide you with the basic conveniences for a very reasonable price. Each room comes with its own bathroom and there is always hot water.

WHERE TO EAT

The **THOMPSON'S FALLS LODGE** (see *Where to Stay* above) has some of the best fare around. You can choose from the main dining room, where reservations are suggested, or try the outdoor grill where tasty teas or lunches are served. For $6, the full English style breakfast will keep you going throughout the day. For something different, select a picnic lunch from the market and come to the pretty gardens around the lodge.

At the **TROPICAL BAR AND RESTAURANT**, the local style barbecue might be of interest if you feel adventuresome. The Tropical restaurant is right around the corner from the Baron Hotel on the south side of town. At the **BARON HOTEL** on the main drag, you can also find a rib-sticking, affordable meal.

SEEING THE SIGHTS

Thompson's Falls

Perhaps Nyahururu's biggest claim to fame are the 236 foot Thompson's Falls. As part of the **Ewaso Narok River**, these cascading falls tumble to the thick forest below. First seen in 1883 by Joseph Thompson, the most photographed falls in Kenya were appropriately named after him.

There are droves of persistent souvenir sellers waiting to pounce if you set foot around the falls. Some of the carved items sold by them can be quite lovely, but it is best to select carefully.

The one safe route down carved stone steps to the waterfalls can be a little slippery. For safety reasons, it is wise to get a guide to go with you from the Thompson's Falls Lodge.

Nyahururu Mosque

If you have never been to a mosque, this might be your chance. Look for a small but interesting building on the southern end of town. You may not be allowed in if you are not appropriately dressed.

Clocktower

As in any town worth its salt, there will be a clocktower built by the colonials to ensure everyone was running on the same time schedule and to mark the town center. Here in Nyahururu the small clocktower is worth at least driving by for a quick look.

Town Hall

Almost right in the middle of Nyahururu, the Town Hall is reminiscent of days gone by when all decisions were made here by the government's representatives and the residents had an opportunity to be heard.

NIGHTLIFE & ENTERTAINMENT

Every Friday and Saturday night, the modern and clean **Baron Hotel** (see *Where to Stay* above) opens a disco until the wee hours of the morning. Deep snug chairs and a blazing fire invite you to spend an evening in the lively **Thompson's Falls Lodge** bar (see *Where to Stay* above).

SPORTS & RECREATION

Fishing

At Mokorindo Lodge, you can fish from the shore or a dinghy for a lunker large mouth bass. Your options are to return it to swim another day of have it cooked for supper.

Hiking

Arrange to go for a long guided or unguided nature walk around the working Mokorindo ranch. The birds that call this area home are plentiful including the popular sacred Ibis. These same opportunities are available at the Thompson's Falls Lodge near Nyahururu, along with a climb down to the falls themselves.

Bird Hunting

A stay at Mokorindo Cottage will afford you the opportunity of trying your hand at game bird or duck hunting.

SHOPPING

At the edge of the precipice overlooking Thompson's Falls are many unattractive *dukas* who sell souvenirs to tourists. The hawkers will pester you until they realize you're not interested or you buy something. There is nothing wrong with what's for sale, but it's a shame the view to the beautiful falls is hidden by shanties.

In Nyahururu there are two markets that may be appealing if you wish to buy local produce. The **Open Market** and the **Covered Market** are within a short distance of each other near the stadium.

PRACTICAL INFORMATION

Banks

As in all towns in Kenya there is a **Barclays Bank** in the center of town which is (in my opinion) the best place to do business. Two other banks are the **Co-Op Bank of Kenya** and the **Kenya Commercial Bank**. All three are in the same area of town.

Hospital

Located on the road to Nakuru, the hospital is able to take care of the most basic needs. For any serious injuries or treatment a trip to Nairobi is probably in order.

Post Office

There is one post office situated across from Barclays Bank. From here you can send a postcard home or purchase Kenyan stamps.

NANYUKI

The small town of **Nanyuki** is the social center for the prolific farm lands around Mount Kenya's slopes and the Laikipia Plateau/Plains. Nanyuki is used by tour operators as a bathroom or lunch stop for tourists heading to game sanctuaries. Built beside the **Nanyuki River**, the town is a railhead for the surrounding farms and their produce. A permanent company of British soldiers and Kenyan air force personnel live and conduct military maneuvers nearby.

ARRIVALS & DEPARTURES

By Air

In Nanyuki there is a small airfield which is very popular with travel agents in Kenya. To arrive at most destinations north of here and save considerable drive time, the short airstrip is often used by charter flights.

By Bus/Matatu

To and from both Nairobi and Isiolo there are daily buses to Nanyuki. Ever-present minibuses and matatus run every day from Nyeri and Nyahururu. Check at the bus station for details on arrival and departure times and fares. The bus stand is on the northern edge of the park in Nanyuki.

By Car

Nanyuki is a relatively pleasant 121 mile drive on the A-2 from Nairobi. If you have sufficient time, it might be fun to tour all the way. Most people, however, choose to fly.

ORIENTATION

As with most of the small towns in Kenya there isn't much to Nanyuki. The furthest point of interest to the north is the Simba Lodge along the Isiolo Road. To the west and a little out of town is the Nanyuki Guest House marking the border. Another hotel, the Silent Guest House is the southernmost boundary of town and along the far eastern edge is the Nanyuki Sports Club.

GETTING AROUND TOWN

There is one broad, tree-lined main street which is the heart of town. The road can be a little rough if it has been raining but for the most part it is very driveable. It only take as few short minutes to get from one end of town to the other by car.

WHERE TO STAY

BORANA LODGE, *Tandala Limited, PO Box 24397, Nairobi. Tel. 567 251, Fax 564 945. $500 per night double occupancy. All major credit cards accepted.*

Each of the six guest bandas on the private ranch has a setting of its own at the edge of the cliff's rim. The views of the Laikipia Plateau and Mount Kenya are majestic from the enormous windows surrounding the buildings. Even the bathrooms, which are completely private, have deep bathtubs with optimum vistas.

The 35,000 acres of Borana Lodge offer excellent game viewing opportunities and many other exciting activities. Study the wildlife at the water hole below with a birds-eye-view from the swimming pool perched at the edge of a high ridge, take a night or day game drive over the Laikipia Plateau and spot kudu, lion, buffalo, klipspringer, elephant and other plains animals from the open Rover. Fly around Mount Kenya, ride a camel, fish in remote Lake Turkana or simply walk through the bush.

You will be spoiled with attention if that's what you want and surrounded by luxury and refinement. Each banda includes a sitting area with a cozy fireplace for your pleasure, comfortable and oversized home-made beds, and lounge chairs. The natural stone, wheat colored thatch, and polished cedar are pervasive throughout the lovely buildings and the grounds. Sloping paths, rock gardens filled with native plantlife and even lily ponds make you want to stroll forever. Looking over the edge of the vast escarpment, is the gorgeous stone swimming pool. Below is a watering hole that attracts lion, buffalo, elephant and other animals like the shy greater kudu.

The drawing and living rooms are a great place for pre-dinner drinks around either of the two fireplaces as you snuggle down in a plush sofa or chair. When dinner is ready you'll climb the stairs only to be wowed by an extraordinary table made from a hunk of rosewood. The fire and candlelight are outdone only by the excellent service from the dining room staff and the refreshing homemade cuisine.

MOUNT KENYA SAFARI CLUB, *Lonrho Hotels, PO Box 58581, Nairobi. Tel. 216 940, Fax 216 796, E-mail: lonhotsm@form-net.com. $319 per night double occupancy. All major credit cards accepted.*

This huge estate has a most fascinating history, beginning with the love story of Rhoda Prudhomme, a fifty year old woman from New York. Here on safari, the wealthy woman was guided by Gabriel, a handsome young French pilot. They fell in love and were allowed to purchase the land from Mrs. Wheeler, who would only sell to the lovers who had given up everything for each other. In the 1930s, the mansion was home to the "Happy Valley" couple who called it *Mawingo*, Swahili for clouds.

In 1948, the entrepreneur Abraham Block bought the home and turned it into a Hollywood style hotel for the rich and famous. The amazing guest list bears signatures from Conrad Hilton, Winston Churchill, Bob Hope, Lord Mountbatten, Lyndon Johnson and on and on.

Today it is an oasis of comfort and the dream of actor William Holden who stayed here on a hunting safari in 1959 and had to have it – so he bought it! There probably isn't a finer or larger place to stay. Addition after addition has spread over the lush grounds covering almost 100 acres of meticulously maintained tropical gardens. To get around the vast complex you need to avail yourself of provided transportation.

The type of room and location can make a significant difference. You must choose what suits you best. There are luxury villas with their own dining room and Jacuzzi. Riverside bandas have all the indulgences of modern life and then some. Garden suites offer privacy but no view. Standard rooms, studios, and suites are all in the main building where a sense of history prevails. Finally, there are the outstanding William Holden Cottages with fireplaces and breathtaking scenery.

There is plenty to keep you busy here for your entire trip. Take pleasure from the horseback riding, an African museum, tribal dancing, ping pong, tennis, nine-hole golf, spa, souvenir shopping, game spotting or the heated swimming pool. If you are not a guest, there is a small daily membership fee.

An animal orphanage run by the William Holden Foundation is a wonderful place to spend an afternoon. You can see orphaned or sick animals being prepared to return to the wild. The 1,000 acre wildlife sanctuary is home to any number of game including elephant, gazelle, zebra, lion and sacred ibis.

SEGERA RANCH, *Wilderness Trails, PO Box 56923, Nairobi. Tel. 506 139, Fax 502 739. $300 per night double occupancy. All major credit cards accepted.*

Only one group of guests may stay at the ranch at any given time. This allows for exclusivity and luxury during your safari on the 50,000 acre cattle ranch. Options available for your stay include game viewing in an open Toyota Land Cruiser, horseback riding among the plentiful wildlife (giraffe, zebra, antelope, elephant...), picnics in the bush, sundowners (drinks) with a great vista, lounging by the uniquely shaped pool or game walks with a guide.

The main house, where visitors stay, can comfortably house six people. The master bedroom has its own bath and sitting area with fireplace. The other rooms don't have great views of Mount Kenya and share a common bathroom. The decor is a homey eclectic collection of furniture making you feel welcome and at ease. A warm fire is lit each night to ward off the chilly night air.

Wonderfully fresh home-grown vegetables grace your plate at mealtime. All the fare served in the elegant dining room or outside on the terrace is prepared by the accomplished cook and his staff. There is obviously great care and pride taken with such delicacies as made-from-scratch bread or succulent lamb stew.

Nearby, the Prettejohns (the same Prettejohns who own Sangare in Nyeri) who manage the ranch have their own house on the grounds. The area is surrounded by sweeping lawns and beds filled with an array of vegetation from cactus to ancient trees. You are made to feel like you stepped into the middle of the African bush miles from nowhere.

If you plan on driving to Segera, you must either have a four wheel drive vehicle or be aware there is no passable road if it rains. Most people choose to fly in and avail themselves of the airfield on the ranch. If you don't require a host or if you bring your own food (to be prepared by the staff) the cost of a stay here is discounted. Most of the time, visitors are accompanied by their tour operator who acts as a host or an experienced guide is hired for the job.

WINGU KENDA, *Wingu Kenda, PO Box 321, Nanyuki. Tel. 0176 22829, Fax 0176 32020. $300 per night double occupancy. All major credit cards accepted.*

The most interesting piece of trivia about five acre Wingu Kenya, which means "cloud nine" in Swahili, is the fact that it is the home of John Hurt's ex-wife Donna. Here you will share the comfortable but luxurious ranch style home with her and the large collection of Hollywood memorabilia.

Built in the neighborhood surrounded by estates of the rich and famous, you never know who you might see as you engage in the activities around the property. Go for a long walk or ride one of the horses in the woods, play a round of tennis and then plunge into the refreshing pool. You can do pretty much what you want when you want; this philosophy also applies to meals.

A view of the artistically landscaped and terraced gardens comes with breakfast and lunch served on the patio. A gorgeous view of Mount Kenya awaits in the background. Dinner is an elegant but informal affair in the spacious dining room.

Each of the three guest rooms is equipped with a small refrigerator, sliding glass door leading to a patio, and a full bathroom. Around the ranch house you will see stone chimneys, large windows, and custom made wooden furniture. Donna is excited about the adventure of sharing her home with visitors. Her attitude is one of welcome in the usual friendly American way.

OL PEJETA LODGE, *Lonrho Hotels, PO Box 58581, Nairobi. Tel. 216 940, Fax 216 796. $230 per night double occupancy. No children under 16. All major credit cards accepted.*

The 110,000 acre private ranch was once home to multi-millionaire Adnan Kashoggi and used particularly for hunting. All over the walls and rooms of the mansion are trophies and mounts of this bygone era. Today, 23,000 acres are set aside for a rhino sanctuary while the mansion is used as a hotel for safari guests.

In the six luxury suites located in the main house and Buffalo Cottage no more than 12 people are accommodated at a time. It is a toss-up whether the most luxurious suite in the house belonged to Mr. or Mrs. Kashoggi. Both boast enormous custom made beds, outstanding views of famous Mount Kenya and elephant sized baths.

As you explore the house and grounds you will notice everything is done on a grand scale. Nothing is average. Sitting in an enormous chair by a huge fireplace will make you feel like the shrunken Alice in Wonderland. The projection room, video library, two swimming pools, spa, two tennis courts and game blind are just a few of the extravagances at Ol Pejeta Lodge.

Wildlife regularly visits the watering hole and you can even meet a tame rhino up close and personal. Horseback riding will allow you to get nearer than ever to the animals in their own environment, while game drives both during the day and at night are at your behest.

THE MOUNTAIN LODGE, *Serena Lodges & Hotels, PO Box 48690, Nairobi. Tel. 710511, Fax 718103, 62578620@eln.attmail.com. $208 per night for double occupancy.*

It is possible to drive to this hotel from Nairobi in two and a half hours. One of the definite pluses of a stay here is the view from each room. There is no need to join the crowds to see animals. Instead just look out your window or step out to the balcony. This hotel is known as a "tree hotel." If there is a specific creature you want to see, tell the porter, and he will wake you during the night if your animal appears.

The Mountain Lodge, built in 1973, was designed and assembled with game viewing in mind. Built next to a watering hole as well as on a regular path traveled by wildlife, there is much to see. Lion, hyena, antelope, rhino, elephant, leopard, warthog, buffalo and other game are frequent visitors. A viewing bunker connected to the lodge by a short tunnel offers close wildlife viewing. All accommodations (42 rooms) come with a private bathroom but tend to have a somewhat musty smell. Sound has a way of traveling between rooms as the insulation is not what it should be. The dining room and bar make up for this by being warm, merry, and bright. The food, rooms and service get mixed reviews; on some days it's great, on others, not so great.

SWEETWATER TENTED CAMP, *Lonrho Hotels, PO Box 58581, Nairobi. Tel. 216 940, Fax 216 796. $148 per night double occupancy. All major credit cards accepted.*

Two things make Sweetwater Camp a charming place to stay. First, it is secluded and generally off the crowded tourist track; second, while you are safely surrounded by hidden electric fences, the animals can get very close as they come to drink at the waterhole. Nightfall is no obstacle to game watching when bright floodlights chase away the shadows.

Once part of the ranch belonging to famed millionaire Adnan Kashoggi, the game sanctuary now runs under new ownership. Game drives around the 22,000 acres of preserve are worth the effort to see giraffe, protected rhino, elephant, and bountiful plains wildlife. Horses and camels are available upon request to take you into the bush. If you are not in the mood for driving or riding, there is a remarkable view of wildlife from a nearby thatched treehouse.

The dining room is part of an old gate house from the estate. Decorated Arab-style, the living room with its low furniture, fireplace, and wide windows feels warm and pristine. All 25 of the tents face the watering hole in two rows carefully placed one behind the other. The back row is built up on platforms for good viewing, but it is better to stay in the front line if possible. Each tent has a private verandah overlooking a lush green grassy area.

MOUNTAIN ROCK HOTEL, *The Mountain Rock Hotel Group. PO Box 40075, Nairobi, Tel. 335 807 or 540 780, Fax 543 810. $130 per night double occupancy.*

The Mountain Rock hotel is not as accessible as it should be from Nairobi and the hotel itself is rather on the average side. The food, service and rooms get mixed reviews.

If you are interested in climbing Mount Kenya, the hotel at 7,200 feet in the foothills of the reserve will be happy to organize everything but equipment. This hotel also offers gamedrives, walks and horseback riding.

KENTROUT, *just outside the town of Timau. $50-100 per night double occupancy.*

To get to the trout farm and restaurant head towards the towns of Meru and Timau. Look for the sign labeled Kentrout and turn here. A short two mile detour on the side road will bring you to the site. Accommodations are very adequate, clean, and comfortable. The restaurant is a popular place for, of course, grilled fresh trout!

WHERE TO EAT

The Mountain Rock Hotel, has a good restaurant where a full breakfast will cost around $6.50 and an excellent dinner in warm and lively surroundings about $10. For some of the best meals in town along with good service and fair prices, try the **SPORTSMAN'S ARMS HOTEL** restaurant located on the outskirts of town, *Tel. 0176 22598.*

Other than hotels listed in *Where to Stay* above, the selection of eateries which are any good should include the **MARINA BAR AND RESTAURANT** across from the post office and **KENTROUT** farm outside of town in Timau. The fish of your choice is pulled from a tank and served as a special charcoal-grilled trout dish. It is a great place to stop for lunch or tea if you're traveling towards Meru from Nanyuki.

SEEING THE SIGHTS

Settler Store

Built in 1938, the old fashioned colonial shop is the most famous of the stores on the tree-lined streets of Nanyuki.

Equator Sign

Just south of the town, there is a famous sign marking the site of the equator. It is fun to watch water poured through a funnel into a jug swirl one direction in the northern hemisphere and the other direction in the southern hemisphere.

Town Market

The market is fun to visit for a good representation of a typical gathering place for the locals to sell their wares. Here you will find potatoes and other fresh produce grown locally.

NIGHTLIFE & ENTERTAINMENT

Check out the bar and lounge at the **Mountain Rock Hotel** for a tasty drink and lively conversation. At the **Sportsman's Arms Hotel**, *Tel. 0176 22598*, to the southeast of the township, the bar has an upbeat ambiance. Army personnel gather here for drinks during their off-duty hours. It is a pleasant place to spend an evening.

SPORTS & RECREATION

See *Where to Stay* above for more information, addresses, and phone numbers.

Game Drives

At the **Borana Lodge, Segera Ranch, Ol Pejeta Lodge, The Mountain Rock Hotel, Sweetwater Tented Camp** the game drives arranged by the managers/owners can be some of the best in the area. Elephant, gazelle, zebra, lion, giraffe and plentiful bird life are just the start of a long list of animals you should see at these places.

Mount Kenya Safari Club

There is plenty to keep you busy at the Club for your entire trip or an afternoon. If you are not a guest, there is a day membership fee. Take pleasure from the horseback riding, African museum, tribal dancing, ping pong, tennis, golf, spa, souvenir shopping, game spotting or the heated swimming pool.

Horseback Riding

Horseback riding for $15.00 per hour is an entertaining option at the **Mountain Rock Hotel**. On horseback, you will be able to ride close to the animals and get a good feel for the Central Highland area of Kenya.

Fishing

Trout fishing arranged by the **Mountain Rock Hotel** for $6.50 is an excellent day trip if you like to fly fish. The price for fishing includes all tackle and a license.

Guided Walks

The main attraction at the **Mountain Rock Hotel**, after the game of course, is the wide selection of guided walks. If you are a bird enthusiast, ask at the lodge about your walk options. As a climber you may want to head up Mount Kenya. No matter how simple or difficult a trek you want, there is usually one put together by the Mountain Rock Hotel to satisfy your need to climb.

SHOPPING

At the site of the **equator sign** there are a great many souvenir shacks where a multitude of Africans will try to lure you in. The mud can be a bit of a deterrent if it has been raining, but there are some interesting buys such as carvings, masks, spears, and the like.

The **Settler Store** is the most notable of the shops in Nanyuki, although there is a varying range of well-stocked and interesting stores in which to browse. Take a look in the **Cotton Culture** shop on the main street stocked with lovely locally woven and knitted goods.

Nanyuki, once a railhead town, now offers some ideal shopping at **The Spinners' and Weavers' Co-operative/Workshop** on Nyeri Road. It is located on the premises of the Presbyterian Church, across the street from the District Hospital. As the local women knit, weave, spin and dye all the items they sell, it is a noteworthy spot to visit. This women's cooperative produces traditional hand woven items including warm sweaters and is renowned for quality fabrics, rugs, and shawls. The best buys however, are the colorful, inexpensive rugs.

EXCURSIONS & DAY TRIPS

Mount Kenya Safari Club Animal Orphanage

Located on the grounds of the club (see *Where to Stay* above), the animal orphanage is run by the William Holden Foundation as a conservation center, breeding program and education center. If there are children (young or old) in your party, this is a place you should definitely visit. You will be allowed to cuddle bush babies, scratch a giant tortoise on the back, or delight in a rare striped baby bongo. Stephanie Powers, the actress, contributes her time to run the ranch and orphanage. You will often see local school children on field trips learning the importance of guarding the priceless wildlife resources of Kenya.

Mount Kenya National Park, Mount Kenya & Mount Kenya Biosphere Reserve

Mount Kenya, a volcano that erupted over two million years ago, dominates the landscape in the Central Highlands. This is the highest mountain in the country and is the central point of the 227 square mile park. Of the 18 glaciers recorded in 1893, only seven remain. It is estimated they will all disappear within 25 years.

The first European to see the mountain was Johann Krapf in 1849. The German missionary told his peers of the snow covered peaks. He was ridiculed for his claim until 1883, when Joseph Thompson was able to verify his allegation.

The 75 mile base of Mount Kenya straddles the equator. **Batian**, its highest peak, reaches 17,058 feet into the sky making it a popular place for climbers. Its peaks are covered with snow all year round. More often than not these summits are surrounded by clouds, in spite of the equatorial location. The best times of day to see the mountain are first thing in the morning or just before the sun goes down. There are eight accepted routes up the mountain, four of which are used regularly. The most frequented routes are Naro Moru to the west, Sirimon to the north, Chogoria to the east, and Point Lenana for amateurs. For obvious reasons, there is no solo climbing. You may either join an organized group or hire a reasonably priced guide. There is an amazing variety of wildlife and plants to enjoy as you climb and the vistas can be breathtaking.

The **biosphere reserve** includes **Mount Kenya National Park** and of course the mountain itself. In the upper regions there is the common and fascinating mole-rat and rare golden cats. In the mid-regions you will find rock hyrax, duiker, and a type of mouse shrew. In the lower forests look for leopard, giant hogs, black rhino, mongoose, suni, duiker and elephant, if you are patient and have some time to wait.

During your safari up the mountain, you will find many places to stay such as camp sites, lodges, and huts. Many of these places are rustic and self-service. It is best to inquire at the **Naro Moru River Lodge**, *PO Box 18, Naro Moru, Tel. 0176 62622, Fax 0176 62211, E-mail: mt.kenya@africaonline.co.ke*, about their condition and availability before you go. For more information on how to book a camping, hiking, or walking safari up Mount Kenya, see Chapter 9, *Sports & Recreation.*

To get into the Mount Kenya National Park there is an entry fee of $27 in addition to $1.50 per vehicle. Camping charges are $3.20 per person per night. If you have guides and porters you will have to pay for them as well.

PRACTICAL INFORMATION
Banks
On the main drag in Nanyuki you will find three banks. Towards the north of town on the left are the **Kenya Commercial Bank** and the **Standard Chartered Bank**. A short distance away to the south is the popular **Barclays Bank**. Standard Nairobi bank hours apply.

Post Office
The requisite small town post office with all postal essentials is situated towards the south end of town just off the principal road. This is also a good place to make a phone call.

NARO MORU

Naro Moru is the headquarters of the Warden of the Mountain National Parks, and the Guides and Porters Association. The town is most popular as the starting point for a climb up Mount Kenya from the Naro Moru River Lodge.

ARRIVALS & DEPARTURES

By Air

It is possible to fly into Nanyuki airstrip and arrange with the Naro Moru River Lodge to pick you up for a $20 fee. This is probably the easiest way to get to the area. Lodge transfer fees are $78 to the meteorological station and $39 to the Kenya National Park gate.

By Bus/Matatu

There are lots of buses and matatus going back and forth between Nairobi and Isiolo. They will be glad to stop and let you off anywhere along the way including Naro Moru.

By Car

Naro Moru is located 22 miles north of Nyeri on the Mount Kenya (A-2 ring road) on the western side of Mount Kenya.

By Shuttle Bus

Between the Naro Moru River Lodge and Nairobi there is a shuttle bus daily for $73 round trip and $40 one way. The bus leaves Nairobi at 2:30 pm, departing from the lodge at 9:00 am. To get tickets in Nairobi, go to the first floor of College House, University Way, *Tel. 337 501.*

ORIENTATION

There is little to see in the township itself but a few very rudimentary hotels, houses, and tiny stores. The town is predominantly agricultural warehouses full of local produce.

WHERE TO STAY & EAT

NARO MORU RIVER LODGE, *Alliance Hotels, PO Box 49839, Nairobi. Tel. 337 501, Fax 219 212 or PO Box 18, Naro Moru. Tel. 0176 6262, Fax 0176 62211. $114 per night double occupancy. All major credit cards accepted.*

A comfortable hotel whose shop hires out all equipment needed and handles bookings for the mountain huts on the climb up Mount Kenya. Just 10 miles south of the equator, the lodge has developed some lovely lush green gardens set amid cool trees and shaded lawns.

For trout fishing enthusiasts a fly-fishing stream is available a short distance away. They even go so far as to provide the necessary tackle. Other activities include walking by the river, bird watching, tennis, squash, darts, horseback rides and a sauna.

The main dining room and the Point Lenana Bar and Lounge are housed in the original lodge. Near the attractive pool an open and bright bar and excellent restaurant add to the feeling of fun and excitement as guests prepare to face the challenges of the mountain.

Accommodations vary significantly in price. On the outskirts of the lodge are campsites and bunk houses which are rustic. Further in are self-service bandas which can be a good deal if the weather is on your side. The rest of the rooms dotted along the rocky terraces following the curve of the river come with fireplaces, balconies, and bathtubs.

A spacious main dining room and the **Point Lenana Bar and Lounge** at the Naro Moru River Lodge are about the only places to eat around Naro Moru. There are no other restaurants in town and the food selection in the shops is slim.

SEEING THE SIGHTS

To get into Mount Kenya National Park you must first pay an entry fee at the gate, which is at about 8,000 feet. This will be the last point you can access by vehicle if it has been raining. Before reaching the station, you must cross a deep ravine via Percival Bridge. The **meteorological station** is reachable by four wheel drive if the weather has been dry.

NIGHTLIFE & ENTERTAINMENT

The **Point Lenana Bar and Lounge** at the **Naro Moru River Lodge**, *Tel. 0176 6262*, is artistically decorated with signed T-shirts. It has become a fun tradition for climbers from around the world to leave an autographed T-shirt once they have been to Mount Kenya. The wood burning fireplace adds a touch of warmth and camaraderie to groups of climbers coming or going.

SPORTS & RECREATION

For trout fishing enthusiasts, peaceful fly-fishing streams are available a short distance away from the **Naro Moru River Lodge**, *Tel. 0176 6262*. They even provide the necessary tackle and licenses at the lodge. Other activities at the lodge include walking by the river with or without a guide, bird watching, tennis, squash, darts, horseback rides and relaxing in the sauna and swimming pool.

PRACTICAL INFORMATION
Banks

There are no banks in Naro Moru. The nearest bank is Nyeri or Nanyuki. If you are in desperate need of money try your skills of persuasion at the Naro Moru River Lodge.

Post Office

There is one post office in Naro Moru from which would-be mountaineers like to send postcards home.

SHOPPING

There is no shopping to speak of in the village of Naro Moru. There is a string of small stores which offer the absolute basics but nothing worth making a special trip.

At the **Naro Moru River Lodge** you can buy or rent any kind of camping equipment or clothing you might find necessary if you want to climb and/or camp on Mount Kenya. The store is open from 7:00 am to 1:00 pm and 2:00 pm to 8:00 pm daily.

EXCURSIONS & DAY TRIPS
Climbing Mount Kenya

To climb the mountain and stay in the available huts, you must make reservations through the Naro Moru River Lodge as they own all the facilities along the route. A charge of between $7 and $11 for huts and 60¢ for camp sites are the fees depending on where you stop. You might consider joining the **Mountain Club of Kenya**, *PO Box 45741, Nairobi, Tel. 501 747*, in order to get a 25 percent discount. There is no charge for porters or guides. With your own camping equipment you are within your rights to use the trails and camping spots with no problem.

ISIOLO

The dusty little town of **Isiolo** acts as a gateway to the northern frontier. At roughly 4,000 feet, the township has gained a reputation of lawlessness because of the many Somali refugees swarming in. You will notice the local populace looks different than Kenyans elsewhere. This is because many Somali soldiers after WWI moved here to start a new life. Today the town is a lively place to stop and have a look around.

ARRIVALS & DEPARTURES
By Air

Rather than make the long drive to Isiolo, you can fly in to Nanyuki and make the roughly three hour drive to town. If you are staying at Lewa

Downs there is an airfield about an hour and a half drive from Isiolo or Nanyuki. If you can fly in here you will cut down your actual travel time and be able to spend more hours on safari.

By Bus

To take the bus for a seven hour journey to Nairobi, it is best to purchase your ticket ($7 a day in advance) with the Akamba office in Isiolo. The bus leaves three times a day at 7:30 am, 9:00 am and 8:00 pm, but it is best to check on departure times as they may vary. The journey will take you through Nanyuki, Naro Moru, and Thika with stops in each place. If your destination is north to Marsabit or Moyale, the Mwingi bus station will handle your bookings. The service times are very unreliable so it is best to wait until you hear a bus is leaving.

There are two bus stations in Isiolo. The first (Mwingi) is situated at the back of the Bomen Hotel. It is a bit difficult to spot as there are no signs and it looks like the front of a store. The obvious clue it is a bus depot are the buses standing out front. The Akamba bus station office is easier to find, located across the road from the gas station.

By Car

Isiolo is approximately 51 miles north of Nanyuki on the A2/Great North Road. The drive is a somewhat pleasant one with the usual cautions about bad roads in the rainy season.

ORIENTATION

To the south of Isiolo the town market is the furthest border. There is nothing much to the west of town but the boundaries are the Silent Inn and the Jamhuri Guest House – both near the bank. To the north on the right fork of the road is a police check point and on the left fork is the post office. East of the main road there are four streets spreading outwards. Along this boundary you will find the Bomen Hotel as the most significant structure on the edge of town.

GETTING AROUND TOWN

Oddly enough, one of the most remarkable things about the town of Isiolo are the speed bumps. In one area of town there are no less than 21 at the southern entry! Traffic is almost forced to a standstill as it tries to wind its way along the streets.

WHERE TO STAY

LEWA DOWNS, *Bush Homes Africa Safaris, 750 Piedmont Avenue, Atlanta, Georgia 30308, Tel. 404 888 0909, Fax 404 888 0081, e-mail safari@bushhomes.com. Bookings Ltd., PO Box 56707, Nairobi. Tel. 225 255, Fax 216 553. $310 per night double occupancy. All major credit cards accepted.* The entrance to the ranch is about 12 miles past the Meru fork on the Isiolo road if you are driving. It is also possible to fly into the area by booking with local airlines. Known for its combination cattle ranch and wildlife sanctuary, Lewa offers the best of both worlds inside its solar powered electric fences. Walking, horseback riding, camel riding, and day and night game drives will provide you with excellent opportunities to see the abundant wildlife. The rooms are a little run down and could use some maintenance, but the game is spectacular.

Six simple bandas built in pairs and joined by a shared verandah offer accommodation for guests. The rustic and sparsely furnished rooms need some attention – especially the leaky roofs. A lovely fire warms up the communal living room between the two bandas and treats such as popcorn or home-made cheese sticks are delicious. Private bathrooms offer the very basics and would be improved greatly by some hard scrubbing and good lighting.

Sharing home-cooked meals on the outdoor dining verandah and a spectacular view down the ravine to the winding river below is special. Baboons and warthog run amok around the towering yellow fever trees.

Established as a rhino sanctuary, Lewa is one of the few places where you can get fairly close to the guarded animals. Ask to see the video tapes that have been made about Lewa for television; the family tends to be a bit shy about these but they are outstanding!

Nearby, there is a fascinating museum, a shop with nice but over-priced souvenirs, a wood furniture factory and a spinning and weaving cooperative where you can purchase rugs and such. For an additional fee the owner will take you up in his small plane for a closer look at Mount Kenya.

NGARE NITI, *Part of Lewa Downs. Wilderness Trails, PO Box 56923, Nairobi. Tel. 506 139, Fax 502 739. $300 per night double occupancy. All major credit cards accepted.*

Would you like to sleep under the same roof where Denzel Washington and his family once stayed? Well, this is it. After a leisurely drive across Lewa Downs Ranch (61,000 acres) stopping to see elephant, sacred ibis, giraffe, and zebra roaming along the sides of the road, you'll pull up to a large two story house and two cozy cottages nearby.

The thatched roof and exterior of the house are partly covered with sweet smelling creepers and the gardens are filled with brilliant flowers of all kinds. Inside, the decor is definitely African with an English country-side touch and lots of wood for warmth. Up the elegant staircase the main bedroom has its own balcony and grand views in all directions. Downstairs the impressive dining room table, fireplace, and soaring ceiling make this unhosted stay a wonderful experience.

BOMEN HOTEL, *Isiolo. Tel. 0165 2225. $25 per night double occupancy. Full breakfast included. All major credit cards accepted.*

Each room has its own bathroom with hot water available all day. A choice of any of the 40 clean, well situated, and nicely decorated rooms are great value for the money. If you are on your way to Samburu or Buffalo Springs Reserves, the Bomen Hotel offers a good spring-off point and it won't break the bank. You can rest comfortably in the knowledge your car is safe in the guarded hotel lot.

WHERE TO EAT

Perhaps the best place in Isiolo to get a good and very affordable meal is the **Bomen Hotel**, *Tel. 0165 2225.* The hours are a bit restrictive (breakfast from 7:00 am to 9:30 pm, lunch from noon to 2:30 pm; dinner from 7:30 pm to 10:00 pm) but it is still worth the effort.

If you'd like to try a Kenyan meal for under $3, look in on the **Pasoda Lodge**. In the same price range, a delicious curry dish at the **Silver Bells Hotel** will satisfy any appetite. A small cafe at the **Frontier Lodge** offers a limited but tasty selection of home-cooked fare.

SEEING THE SIGHTS

Mosque

The quaint little **mosque** towards the south end of town might be worth taking a look at if you enjoy mosques. Remember to go appropriately dressed in order not to offend.

Town Market

For a taste of how the local people conduct day to day shopping, take a walk down to the **market** at the end of town. It is a short distance from the mosque along the main road. Here you can sample some of the delicious fresh fruit and vegetables grown in and around Isiolo.

NIGHTLIFE & ENTERTAINMENT

At the **Frontier Lodge** in Isiolo, there is a lively bar which is popular with the bar hopping crowd. On occasion, the lodge will have a live band for dancing and entertainment. The **Pasoda Lodge**, also in town, offers its own quiet pub for an evening drink. Try the **Bomen Hotel** for its tastefully decorated and friendly tavern.

SPORTS & RECREATION

Game Drives

Lewa Downs (see *Where to Stay* above) offers day and night game drives to provide you with excellent opportunities to see rhino, elephant, buffalo, gerenuk, gazelle, warthog, zebra, giraffe and perhaps even lion. The wildlife and rhino sanctuary are big attractions around Lewa and worth a visit anytime.

Plane Rides

At **Lewa Downs** the owner (who trained as a cropduster in Georgia in the US) will take you up in his plane from the ranch airstrip for a spectacular view of Mount Kenya. This of course is only available in good weather when the clouds decide to show the great mountain peaks.

Walking

At **Lewa Downs** there are several selections of guided walks. You can opt for a walk down by the river where baboon, warthog, and perhaps a klipspringer will surprise you; or be on the lookout for any of our colorful feathered friends that abound here.

Horse & Camel Riding

Horseback or camel riding at **Lewa** is a special affair and an exciting way to spend a day. The wildlife is so comfortable with the pack animals, there is no fear between them. You can get remarkably close to the shy gerenuk, warthog, baby giraffe, or zebra. The unusual saddles and strange movement of a camel are two things you're not likely to forget.

SHOPPING

The **market** situated at the south end of town offers a great selection of fresh fruit, vegetables, and other products including meat. Towards the center of town, the **standard stores** have canned goods and any household items you might need for your trip. As far as souvenirs go, there are plenty to choose from as soon as the **street vendors** identify you as a potential buyer. The mobs are much worse around your car than if you are on foot. Look for good bargains on brass, copper, and aluminum bracelets or perhaps a short Somali dagger.

PRACTICAL INFORMATION

Bank

Here in Isiolo there is only one bank and that is Barclays. If you are heading further north, this is the last bank you will come to until you reach the northern town of Maralal.

Gas Station

The responsible thing to do is buy as much gas as you can manage here in Isiolo before heading any further north, as there are limited choices north of here until Maralal or Marsabit. The **BP station** is at the north end of town just before the road forks. Outside Isiolo, the prices also go up considerably for obvious reasons. In nearby Baragoi, there are some places to buy the commodity or perhaps a mission station will spare you a gallon if they have a surplus.

Post Office

Going north out of town the road splits in two; at this juncture bear right. The post office will be to your right just a short distance down the road. Here you can make phone calls or handle any necessary postal transactions.

EXCURSIONS & DAY TRIPS

Lewa Downs Museum

In the old family home there is an excellent museum with a wealth of information. The story of Anna Mertz who started the rhino sanctuary and all her lifetime endeavors are interestingly described. The history of man and a display of tools that are half a million years old will capture your attention.

Lewa Downs Sitatunga Blind

At Lewa Downs there is a rare collection – twelve to be exact – of aquatic antelope. That's right, aquatic. The small antelope live in thick reeds growing in swamps. Almost extinct in Africa, the Sitatunga antelope are very shy and hard to see. Sitting up high in the secluded blind at dawn or dusk might afford you the honor of seeing this scarce and delicate creature.

RING ROAD

*Known as the A-2 or **Kirinyaga Ring Road**, this extensive highway covers the entire Central Highlands area and travels all the way north to Ethiopia. On this stretch of road it is possible to make a complete circle from Nairobi around the Central Highlands and back again with very little backtracking.*

MERU

The town of **Meru**, which serves as a popular agricultural center, is surrounded by dense forest. Originally founded as a harvesting center for the Meru Oak, Meru now grows potatoes and *miraa* (a locally grown narcotic plant). Because of the altitude there is damp fog and mist clinging to the entire community. If you are planning a trip to **Meru National Park**, you must stop here first.

The number of trees in and around Meru is remarkable. This is due solely to the Meru people, who have taken to heart the lessons of replanting the felled timber on eroded hillsides. The small trees grow quickly with the plentiful water supply running down the mountain.

GEORGE ADAMSON QUOTE
"My little camp under Mugwongo Hill in the Meru National Reserve was built of palm thatch... I felt a surge of elation as I left the artificial world... for the last time and drove north to Meru. Mugwongo Hill is covered with green scrub and rusty-coloured rocks."

ARRIVALS & DEPARTURES

By Air

Presently there are no scheduled flights to Meru but it can be reached from Nairobi by a combination of the Air Kenya scheduled flight to Nanyuki and a charter flight from Nanyuki to Meru. A chartered flight from Nairobi is also an option. The flight costs start at about $300 per person, round trip, depending on the number of people in the group. It is about a 40 minute flying trip from Wilson airport. At **Elsa's Kopje** in **Meru National Park** there is an airstrip. It actually is part of the camp (owned by Cheli & Peacock) and sits at **Mugwongo Hill**, the site of George Adamson's first campsite.

By Bus

To make reservations for the bus to Nairobi ($5), go to the Akamba bus station office to make the necessary arrangements. Generally there are three departure times at 7:30 am, 9:00 am, and 8:00 pm, but it is best to double check. You will have to make stops at the townships of Chogoria, Embu, and Thika.

By Car

To get to Meru you must drive around the southern side of Mount Kenya along the northeast end of the ring road. The town is south of Isiolo and due west of Nanyuki. On the way you will notice the steep climb, deep valleys, and thick forests surrounding you. The dense fog and low clouds tend to obscure the lovely vistas.

ORIENTATION

Arriving in town from the north, the first sign of civilization you will see is the popular market on your left, roughly two miles from the town. To the west, another market marks the boundary to the tiny village. Driving through Meru to the south end of town, the last thing you will notice is the crowded matatu stand or the bank. Finally, to the west are the Milimani Hotel (about one and a half miles from the center) and the Stanstead Hotel (about one mile from town).

GETTING AROUND TOWN

The town of Meru is actually just a sort of hodgepodge of huts along the main road. It is simple enough to either drive along or walk from the market to the bank.

WHERE TO STAY

ELSA'S KOPJE, *Cheli & Peacock, PO Box 39806, Nairobi, Tel. (254 2)748 327 or (254 2) 748 633, Fax (254 2) 750 225, e mail chelipeacock@attmail.com, www.chelipeacock.com. $230 per night double occupancy. Includes game drives.*

Located in Meru National Park, in the old Northern Frontier District is Elsa's Kopje (which means rocky outcropping). Name by the owners of Cheli & Peacock, the New (1999) lodge is a tribute to Elsa, the orphaned lioness raised by George and Joy Adamson and the rocky outcropping the lodge sits on. Once an adult, the famous lioness was returned to the wilds of Meru. Mugwongo Hill is the site of George's first campsite. It is possible to reach the new camp by road or to fly in to the airstrip at Mugwongo Hill.

The eight private cottages are placed well away from other guests. There is a magnificent view of the surrounding park with it's scattered kopjes and delightful baobab trees. Two of the stone and thatched cottages have twin beds, while the others all boast kings.

The rocks in the hillside are artfully and creatively incorporated into each structure. Each cottage will wow you with its artistic decor and original design. The open floor plans will keep you cool during the hot days as will the refreshing swimming pool.

The animals in the area are shy and not accustomed to people. The uniqueness of this situation offers a more natural opportunity to see how they live. From here there are lots of things to do, fishing, Tana River rafting, visits to Kora National Park, night and day game drives and possible camping.

KINDANI CAMP, *Langwenda Safaris Ltd., PO Box 56118, Nairobi. Tel. 445 797, Fax 443 267. $250 per night double occupancy. All major credit cards accepted.*

To get to rustic Kindani Camp in Meru National Park you can either drive or fly. To drive you must have a four wheel drive vehicle as there are several streams to cross and after a rain the roads get very muddy. Flying is the easiest way to go.

Designed to be a rustic camping experience with the basic comforts, Kindani has outdoor showers surrounded by a low screens, stone buildings for the flush toilets, and hot water! There is no electricity but you really don't seem to miss it as the lanterns are more than adequate. Each of the five thatched bandas comes equipped with mosquito nets, a wash basin, and three beds. Situated at the edge of the Kindani River you will know without a doubt no other tourist will invade your private and natural safari. Game drives, nature walks, and a swim in the pool filled with river water add to the peaceful union with nature you'll experience here.

MERU MULIKA LODGE, *Msafiri Inns, PO Box 42013, Nairobi. Tel. 330 820, Fax 227 815. $76 per night double occupancy. All major credit cards accepted.*

Seemingly deserted, this might just be the place to have a unique safari if you don't mind the somewhat frayed feel of the accommodations. Each cottage and the rooms in the two story building come with a shower or tub, private verandah, and adequate mosquito nets. A small swimming pool, multicolored gardens, and remarkable trees draw you to enjoy the outdoors. The communal areas such as the dining room have outstanding views of the verdant Mulika swamp and picturesque Nyambene Hills.

The swamp is a popular gathering place for wildlife arriving at all hours to quench their thirst and munch on the green foliage. From the lodge it is exciting to see bright birds as well as gazelle, zebra, warthog, and other African game.

LEOPARD ROCK LODGE, *Let's Go Travel, PO Box 60342, Nairobi. Tel. 340 331, Fax 336 890. $40 per night double occupancy. Major credit cards accepted.*

There are ten completely self-sufficient bandas at the Leopard Rock Lodge. Each cabin has hot water, electricity, fully equipped kitchens, and mosquito nets. This is an interesting place for a small group of people to stay and see Meru National Park. If you run out of supplies, there is a store at the site selling the basics such as canned merchandise and beer.

COUNTY HOTEL, *on the main road near the turnoff for the Meru National Museum. $33 per night double occupancy. Price includes full breakfast. All major credit cards accepted.*

Rooms at the County Hotel are both clean and comfortable, with all the necessities of life including hot water and private bathrooms. You can feel safe leaving your car in the secured parking area of the hotel.

WHERE TO EAT

For a taste of local food at bargain prices ($3), try the curry at the **COPPER COIN** restaurant just near the bus station. The **COUNTY HOTEL** offers two restaurants; choose the more upscale one and enjoy a good rib-sticking meal.

SEEING THE SIGHTS

Meru National Museum

Located in the northeast corner of the Mount Kenya ring road, the **museum** is just past the town hall. For $2 you can see inside what was once the District Commissioner's Office. Tiny and faded, the museum houses a rather unpleasant snake park and zoo along with a more remarkable display on the Meru tribe, a representation of a village, and a garden of medicinal herbs. Museum hours are 9:30 am to 6:00 pm daily Monday through Saturday. On Sundays the hours are 11:00 am to 6:00 pm and on holidays it is open from 1:00 pm to 6:00 pm.

Miraa Market

The miraa is grown legally here in Meru. The **miraa market**, to the southeast of town, is worth seeing to watch the local producers bundle the twigs, leaves, and branches in manageable sizes for sale. The internal Kenya market and the sizable international market keep the cultivators busy with orders for the legal narcotic.

Mosque

As in all these small Kenyan towns, there is a **mosque**. If you have developed an affinity for religious edifices you might as well stop and take a quick look.

NIGHTLIFE & ENTERTAINMENT

In the center of town there is a rather loud and basic bar in the **Continental Hotel** where it is possible to buy a cold beer. The **Stanstead Hotel**, *Tel. 20360,* just outside town, offers a clean bar and restaurant with reasonable selections and prices. At the **Milimani Hotel** you can have fun watching locals enjoying disco music.

A little more upscale is the **County Hotel** where the bar is hopping. Five miles outside town to the north is the **Rocky Hill Inn**, which offers a bar and tempting barbecue to its visitors.

SPORTS & RECREATION
Game Drives
At **Kindani Camp** and **Meru Mulika Lodge**, the game drives to see gazelle, zebra, warthog, elephant, cheetah, gerenuk and giraffe can be outstanding. In **Meru National Park** (see *Excursions & Day Trips*, below), how much game you see depends on where you are and how thick the bush is.

From **Elsa's Kopje** (see *where to stay*, above) there are lots of things to do, fishing, Tana River rafting, visits to Kora National Park, night and day game drives and possible camping.

Swimming
The **Forest Lodge**, located just over five miles outside town, advertises itself as a country club. Here there is a swimming pool for guests. Jump in if it's warm enough for a swim. **Kindani Camp** has a swimming pool filled with river water. If you should stay here, this might be an interesting new experience!

SHOPPING
Take a look at the **miraa market** as a matter of interest even if you don't actually buy anything. A short walk down the road from the miraa market is a second market where you might find a few trinkets to take home. On the furthest reaches of town along the main road to the north is yet a third market where locals buy their necessities.

PRACTICAL INFORMATION
Banks
The **Barclays Bank** office is the more popular of the two banks in Meru. It is right next door to the Continental Hotel and one door down from the town's mosque. Further towards the center of town is the **Kenya Commercial Bank**.

Post Office
Situated half-way between the Stanstead Hotel and the County Hotel is the town's post office.

EXCURSIONS & DAY TRIPS
To get to the parks and reserves from Meru, follow these directions: from Meru town at the Meru Country Club it is a short drive to the top of a hill and the crossroads. Turn right towards **Meru National Park**. From here you will cross over the Nyambene Hills to a small village called

Maua. The good road ends and a dirt track goes 19 miles to the Murera Gate into the park.

Next to Meru National Park at the southwest tip are **Bisandani, Kora,** and **North Kitui National Reserves.** Just east of Bisandani and 93 miles north of Mount Kenya is **Rahole National Reserve.**

Meru National Park

Meru is one of the least frequented parks in Kenya. It is located just east of Mount Kenya and over the tall **Nyambene Hills.** There are certain parts of the park that are wilderness areas and off limits to tourists. You are unlikely to spot many other visitors.

Originally, Meru National Park was established as a wildlife rehabilitation center. It was here that Joy and George Adamson trained Boy, the lioness Elsa's son, and Pippah the cheetah, how to hunt and revert back to the wild. **Mugwongo Hill** was the site of the first camp.

With as little rainfall as this park gets, it is remarkable to note that there are thirteen rivers and numerous streams running off nearby mountains. The result is a striped landscape with lush green ribbons flowing through dry brown valleys.

Adamson's Falls, the last of the major rapids and cataracts of the Tana River as it heads out to sea is also the location of **Pippah's grave.** The tomb is marked by a monument of heaped stones in the forest next to the river.

The fertile soil of the Central Highlands along with heavy rainfall make the vegetation lush and thick. For interesting variety, the park offers tall grass, forests, and green swamps while the landscape is dotted with tall doum palms. The wildlife is hard to see due to the thick bush. This doesn't mean elephant, lion, cheetah, Grevy's zebra, gerenuk or reticulated giraffe are not abundant.

Bisandani National Reserve

During the wet season the animals from Meru National Park spill over into the 230-odd square mile park. Wildlife can enjoy the lush feeding in the riverine forests and swamps or meander out to the dry thorny bushland surrounding the trees. There are no safari facilities but the elephant and buffalo are abundant.

Kora National Reserve

Known primarily as a scientific study location the reserve is not known for abundant numbers of wildlife. Elephant, rhino, hippo, cheetah, and antelope however, are indeed plentiful around the fertile river. There are no visitor facilities available.

Unfortunately, the great **George Adamson** who made this park his home was killed here in 1989 by poacher-bandits. It was in rocky parts of the lovely Kora reserve that he chose to reintroduce captive lions and leopards.

North Kitui National Reserve

North Kitui National Reserve is right next to Meru National Park and the **Tana River**, covering approximately 500 square miles. It is an excellent location for hippo and crocodile but offers no guest facilities.

Rahole National Reserve

There are no facilities for visitors on safari in the 508 square mile reserve. Four wheel drive vehicles are essential and so is a reliable guide to lead you over the faint, ever-changing paths. The game viewing is not famous but elephant, Grevy's zebra, and beisa oryx call it home. Scenery is lovely along the **Tana River** but keep an eye out for crocodiles. On the north side of the river among the arid thorn bush, an experiment was conducted to find out how area tribes and wildlife might survive together.

CHOGORIA

The town of **Chogoria** is located on the lower and eastern slopes of Mount Kenya. The only reason you would have to come here is if you were going to try your hand at the scenic Chogoria route up Mount Kenya.

ARRIVALS & DEPARTURES

By Bus

It is possible to take the Akamba bus running between Meru and Nairobi. If you ask, they will stop here and let you off. The drive takes three and a half hours from the capital.

WHERE TO STAY

The selection here in Chogoria is extremely limited and perhaps it would be best to stay in Meru or Nyeri and make this a day trip. The **TRANSIT MOTEL**, *Tel. 96,* is a cheap alternative to sleeping in your car. The accommodations are clean and cost $2!

The cabins at the **FOREST STATION** are probably your best bet. Each of the fifteen cabins comes equipped with fireplaces, hot water, kitchens, and comfortable beds all for under $15.

WHERE TO EAT

The **TRANSIT MOTEL** offers limited selections on their menu but the food is adequate.

Otherwise, try the **LENANA RESTAURANT** or the **FOREST STATION.**

EXCURSIONS & DAY TRIPS

Climbing Mount Kenya along the **Chogoria route** is reputedly the most scenic route up Mount Kenya. The first day's hike is a long one so it is best to set off early in the morning on your day of departure. To make arrangements for guides and porters check at the Transit Motel where the **Chogoria Guides Club** is located.

Depending on the route you select to climb Mount Kenya, your charges for guides, cooks, and porters will vary accordingly. On the Naro Moru route the fee is $4.75, and on the Chogoria route the charge per guide is $4. For the Sirimoni route a cook or guide costs $10 while a porter is $6. A porter will carry roughly 40 pounds for a three day trip, not including his own food and equipment.

EMBU

On the southeastern slopes of Mount Kenya nestled among the hills is the small town of **Embu**. Labeled the provincial headquarters of the Eastern Province, the title gives it its claim to fame. It is an intensely cultivated area and there isn't much to see or do unless you are here for the fly fishing.

ARRIVALS & DEPARTURES

By Bus/Matatu

For the reasons mentioned, it is best not to take a chance with either the bus or matatu. If you must travel this way, buy your ticket at the Akamba bus office on the outskirts of town. The Akamba buses seem to have the best safety record by comparison.

There is one matatu stand in the heart of town that goes to Nyeri. On the east side of town there is a bus and matatu stand servicing Nairobi and places in between. It is best to buy tickets a day in advance and check departure times carefully.

By Car

The road along here is in excellent shape but caution is advised as curves, high bridges, hills, and valleys abound. Also beware of the crazy matatu drivers who kill themselves and all the passengers aboard about once every two weeks.

ORIENTATION

The town of Embu is spread along the highway for quite a distance. The furthest point north is the post office. To the southwest is the Valley View Hotel. To the east is the Kibukubu Lodge.

GETTING AROUND TOWN

It is a good idea to have a car to get around Embu; I surmise you'd have one anyway in order to get here. The Izaak Walton Inn is about a mile and a half outside town and is probably the only thing worth seeing.

WHERE TO STAY

IZAAK WALTON INN, *Msafiri Inns, PO Box 42013, Nairobi. Tel. 229 751, Fax 227 815. $24 per night double occupancy. All major credit cards accepted.*

Located at 5,150 feet above sea level, there is usually at least one of the 42 rooms available should you stop here unexpectedly and decide to stay. Each room comes with a private bathroom.

Once there was a popular nine hole golf course here but the local council decided it would be put to better use by growing corn and beans. Originally a farm house, the inn is set on eight acres of green lawns and tropical gardens. Today it is a popular place to stop for tea.

WHERE TO EAT

The **IZAAK WALTON INN** has the market cornered in Embu when it comes to great places to eat. The food is excellent and often includes delicious trout dishes. If you are just passing through, the inn is a picturesque place to stop for a traditional English tea.

In town, try the **VALLEY VIEW HOTEL**, **KUBUKUBU LODGE** or the **AL-ASWAD HOTEL** for an inexpensive and decent meal.

SEEING THE SIGHTS

Uhuru Monument

In town across from the State House and Police headquarters is the town's freedom or Uhuru Monument with an appropriate inscription.

Institute of Agriculture

Jacaranda trees line the road between the Izaak Walton Inn and the famous Institute of Agriculture.

DANCERS & BEE-KEEPERS

If at all possible try to see the rare dances performed by the Embu people. The dancers dress in black coats and white masks as they perform the routines on stilts. The tribe is also honored for its ability to produce excellent honey from their bee hives.

NIGHTLIFE & ENTERTAINMENT

Up the road from Embu is the **Izaak Walton Inn** with a lovely warm fire crackling in the fireplace and the offer of a hot toddy to keep your insides warm. A pretty cozy place to spend an evening.

SPORTS & RECREATION

Fly fishing is one of the real attractions in and around Embu and is encouraged by the owners of the Izaak Walton Inn. They will supply you with directions and gear if necessary. In this part of Kenya you will find some of the finest fly fishing rivers in the country, filled with colorful rainbow and brown trout.

SHOPPING

There is no shopping to speak of. If you are in need of basic necessities, take a trip back to Nyeri or perhaps Meru.

EXCURSIONS & DAY TRIPS

Mwea National Reserve

The wildlife in the **Mwea National Reserve** consists of lesser kudu, elephant, buffalo, and smaller mammals, but it is not known for great animal sightings. Large baobab trees and plenty of acacia and thorn brush make up the landscape where there is no irrigation. In other spots, rich green fields of rice flourish as the life-giving water of the **Tana River** flows down man-made channels.

PRACTICAL INFORMATION

Banks

The only bank in Embu is **Barclays**. The staff is friendly but don't expect to change too much money at this small town bank.

Post Office

Located at the northern end of town is the traditional small town post office.

Library

Oddly enough, there is a library at the north end of town just before the post office. Perhaps this is because of the eminent Institute of Agriculture nearby.

14. MOMBASA & THE COAST

The spectacular sunny coastal regions of Kenya stretch roughly 300 miles from the town of **Shimoni** in the south to **Boni National Reserve** in the north. Anywhere between the two distant points are glorious white beaches and tourist resorts, particularly popular with Europeans on package tours. The least visited and less populated shores are south of Diani Beach.

A mixture of Arab, African, Portuguese, Hindi and English forms the framework for the Swahili coastal people and their language. Many speak their own local dialects, English and of course the widespread Swahili tongue. Most locals are bewildered by visitors and either shy away or try to satisfy their friendly curiosity.

Mombasa Island, the "capital" city, is connected to the mainland by causeways. Mombasa is a major sea port and hub of the region, and divides the shore into the **North Coast** and the **South Coast**. From Mombasa you must cross **Mombasa Harbor** to go north and **Kilindini Harbor** to go south.

Visitors must use the **Likoni Ferry** to reach the towns of **Msambweni**, **Funzi** and **Shimoni**; **Shimba Hills**; **Wasini Island**; the beaches at **Shelly**, **Tiwi**, **Diani** and **Galu** on the south coast. Waiting for the car ferry to arrive is dusty and hot but also a colorful and fun experience. Vendors try to sell you freshly roasted cashews and refreshing coconut milk. Waiting for the ferry, streams of humanity on foot, bicycles, or pulling carts provide a kaleidoscope of activity and great people watching. It is fascinating to see the blend of new and old. Mixed in among the local Africans dressed in suits it is not uncommon to see a warrior with red hair and lots of beads. The contrast is a reflection of the amazing tribal adaptation.

Once across the dividing waters of Kilindini Harbor, the road follows the shoreline but the picturesque Indian Ocean is out of sight. Tall signs point left down potholed paths towards hidden beachside destinations.

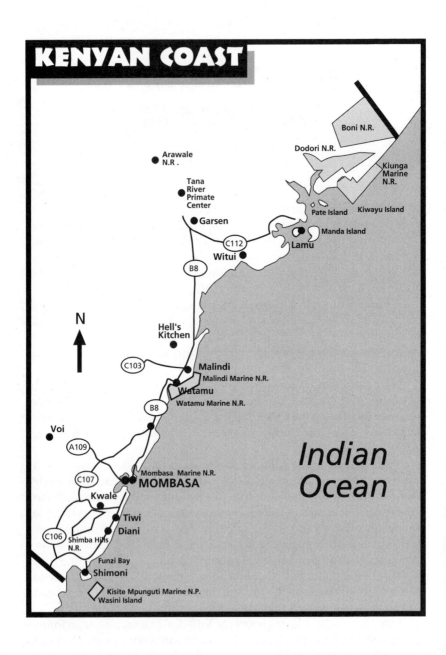

KENYAN COAST

Boni N.R.

Dodori N.R.

Kiunga Marine N.R.

Arawale N.R .

Tana River Primate Center

Pate Island   Kiwayu Island

Garsen

Manda Island

C112

Lamu

Witui

B8

N

Hell's Kitchen

C103

Malindi

Malindi Marine N.R.

Watamu

Watamu Marine N.R.

B8

Voi

A109

Mombasa Marine N.R.

C107

MOMBASA

Kwale

Indian Ocean

Tiwi

Diani

C106

Shimba Hills N.R.

Funzi Bay

Shimoni

Kisite Mpunguti Marine N.P.

Wasini Island

The winding dirt tracks must be traversed under leafy coconut trees, thick mango stands, and even the odd baobab or teak tree. Children, chickens, and brightly dressed women share the roadway as pedestrians.

Going north from Mombasa via the relatively new **Nyali Bridge** is easier than crossing on the Kisauni ferry and encourages the increase of tourist hotels. Between Mombasa and **Kilifi** the resort beaches are **Nyali, Bamburi, Shanzu** and **Kikambala**. The most frequented beach town vacation spots north of the main city are **Watamu, Malindi** and **Lamu**.

No matter where you stay along the Kenya coast you will be dazzled by tropical delights. Green lush vegetation is filled with sweet smells of frangipani and honeysuckle. Brilliant varieties of bougainvillea and hibiscus color the world in contrast with green bush and an azure ocean.

One hundred and fifty miles of ancient coral reefs protect swimmers from harm and the land from erosion. Superbly colorful and prolific marine life abounds all along the underwater rocky ledges, particularly in the marine parks and reserves. Even the sometimes annoying seaweed seems to have a beauty of its own. In this hot and humid Shangri-La, the laid-back population invites you to live by their motto "*haraka, haraka haina baraka*" – literally translated "haste, haste has no blessing."

KENYA COAST MUST SEES
Mombasa Old Town
Watamu & Malindi National Park
Gedi Ruins
Lamu

MOMBASA

The port city of **Mombasa** was recorded as early as 110 AD by Diogenes and again in 150 AD by Ptolemy. Both Greeks noted the wealth flowing in and out of the busy harbor as traders came and went. These same docks are still active, serving many of the neighboring African countries.

As time passed, coastal tribespeople and Arabs intermarried. They settled along the lush coast creating a new culture and Swahili language that has slowly touched all parts of Kenya. At the end of the 16th century, Portuguese explorers and traders brought a garrison to Mombasa and over a five year period the settlers built **Fort Jesus**. Much later during the 19th century the British government took an interest in abolishing the flourishing slave trade and eventually took over the colonization of the country.

Today, the second largest city in Kenya looks a little seedy and run-down, but in my view it is a romantic place with much to offer in the way of diverse cultures and an intriguing population. Seventy percent of the half million people are African. The rest are Asians and a few Europeans. Down the narrow maze of cobbled streets there are eye-popping street stalls, pungent open markets, mosques, and intricate architecture to fill you with awe.

There are no beaches on Mombasa Island and what hotels exist are small and out of date. Tourists on safari prefer to stay elsewhere near the white sand and blue waters of the Indian Ocean. It is common for visitors to come in by car early in the morning and spend the day sightseeing and shopping in the slow Swahili fashion.

ARRIVALS & DEPARTURES

By Air

If you are on your way to Mombasa, **Moi International Airport**, *PO Box 98498, Tel. 433 211*, is where you will land. To get off the plane, there is a steep roll-up set of stairs down which you must descend for a short and usually sunny walk across the tarmac to the terminal. The airport is located just off Nairobi Road about eight miles from the city center.

Kenya Airways runs services to about 30 destinations. Their locations and phone numbers includes: *Savani House, Mombasa, Tel. 21251; Moi Airport, Mombasa, Tel. 433 211; Malindi, Tel. 20237 and Kisumu, Tel. 44056.* Kenya Airways offers four flights daily from Nairobi's Jomo Kenyatta International Airport to Moi International in Mombasa and the same from Mombasa to Nairobi. If you must get back to Nairobi be sure and confirm your booking. Due to frequent overbooking, people are often left standing on the runway and there is nothing you can do about it at this point. I suggest you return to Nairobi the day before you are due to fly out of Kenya, or be very sure your reservation is confirmed. Again, reconfirm, reconfirm and reconfirm!

Air Kenya, *Wilson Airport, PO Box 30357, Nairobi, Tel 501 421,* is a domestic carrier. This airline runs daily and weekly flights to Nyeri, Nanyuki, Masia Mara, Lamu and anywhere in between. As a small operator the airline enforces a weight restriction on luggage.

If you can get enough people together and hire a charter plane, it makes the trip more affordable. To find the best deal try one of the main private air carriers: **Eagle Aviation Limited**, *Tel. 316 054*, **Skyways Airlines**, *Tel. 221 964*, **Equator Airlines**, *Tel. 501 360*, and **Prestige Air Services**, *Tel. 21443*. These carriers also make trips to Malindi and Lamu from Mombasa.

By Bus

If you are in search of a bus office they are pretty much all located along Jomo Kenyatta Avenue. Daily departures for Nairobi are usually in the early morning or late evening. The long journey takes between seven and eight hours with a short break in between for quick meal. Prices vary from $3.65 to $4.20 depending on the carrier – Cat, Mawingo, Malaika, or Akamba. For a little more money go with one of the better motor coaches such as **Malindi Bus**, **Goldline**, and **Coastline**.

Kenya Airways runs a popular **shuttle bus** to and from the airport from the Nkuruman office. Departure times are 10:20 am, 2:20 pm, and 5:40 pm.

If you are heading **south** of Mombasa you must first get off the island via the Likoni Ferry and then catch a bus to your destination.

From Mombasa **north** to Malindi and back, there are several buses departing daily. The three companies operating the run are **Malindi Bus Service**, **Tana River Bus Service**, and **Garissa Express**. They all have offices in Malindi, Mombasa, and Lamu. The ride takes about three hours. In Mombasa they all depart from outside the New People's Hotel on Abdel Nasser Road. The cost is $1.50 per person.

By Car

It is 297 miles from Nairobi to Mombasa along the A109; the main road linking the two. For tourists driving from the interior of Kenya the highway ends here when it meets the coastal road. All the major car rental companies and some smaller ones have offices in Mombasa. To my way of thinking, a car and driver are still the best way to get around if you don't have arrangements with your hotel.

To get anywhere south of Mombasa, you must first cross the **Likoni Ferry**. It can only take 24 cars at a time. From this point on, all you need to do is follow along the main A14 coastal road. Everything branches off this central highway.

Heading north of Mombasa all the way to just north of Malindi is the Mombasa to Malindi road or the B8. Just like the southbound road, everything branches off the highway as it winds its way along the coast. Once upon a time to get to the northern reaches of the coast you had to take a row boat across the harbor; then the crossing was upgraded to a ferry. Today there is a modern bridge spanning the waterway which was partially constructed and funded by the Japanese.

These are the most reliable car rental agencies in Mombasa:

• **Hertz**, *Tel. 316 333/4, 315 079, PO Box 84782, Mombasa* (with a branch at the airport)
• **Avis**, *Tel. 23048, Moi Avenue, Mombasa* (with a branch at the airport)

- **Europcar**, *Tel. 312 461, PO Box 90631, Mombasa* (with a branch at the airport)
- **Budget**, *Tel. 24600, Moi Avenue, Mombasa*
- **Central Rent-a-Car**, *Tel. 20171, 312 070, PO Box 99753, Moi Avenue, Mombasa*

By Shared Taxi

From Mombasa to Malindi or anywhere else in between, you can share a seven-person taxi for $3 per person. They leave early in the morning once they are full from the bus station in town.

By Train

The reservation office at the railway station in Mombasa is open from 8:00 am to noon and 2:00 pm to 6:30 pm daily. The fares to Nairobi on the deluxe service are $40 in first class and $26 in second class. The deluxe train leaves at 7:00 pm and arrives at 8:30 am. This includes dinner, breakfast, and bedding and is better than the regular service. The regular train leaves at 5:00 pm and arrives at 8:00 pm. The advantage of the regular run is that you can see more of the countryside in daylight. Either way, make reservations as far in advance as possible as demand always exceeds supply.

There is a left-luggage service which costs 35¢ per day per bag. Its hours are 2:00 pm to 6:30 pm Monday through Saturday. On Sunday the hours are 7:30 am to 10:00 am and 2:00 pm to 6:30 pm.

Mombasa Railway Station is located away from the harbor at the westernmost end of Haile Selassie Avenue. *For more information, call 312 221 in Mombasa or 221 211 extension 2700/1/1 in Nairobi.* Many of the major hotels and travel agents will make reservations for you providing you pay with a credit card.

ORIENTATION

Most visitors come to Mombasa Island to see the Old Town and its shops and historic architecture. In the older part of town, **Fort Jesus** sits facing the water on the southeastern part of the island. The main thoroughfare through the old town is **Ndia Kuu Road**. It is bordered on one side by water and on the other by Digo Road – the furthest part of the old town.

The rest of Mombasa Island is new, spread out and much like the capital city of Nairobi. A small cross section is referred to as the city center. The main road through the center of town is **Moi Avenue**. Along this avenue you will find the heart of the new city with taxis, hotels, restaurants, travel agents, stores and of course the famous "ivory" tusks.

MOMBASA'S "IVORY TUSKS"

Visitors to Mombasa at some point end up driving down Moi Avenue only to be surprised by the four giant elephant tusks spanning each side of the wide two-lane highway. The tapered ends form an X at the highest point. Local drivers pass underneath the archway made by the tusks whether they are coming or going oblivious to the noteworthy landmark. Don't worry, the tusks are actually aluminum painted white – not ivory! They were erected in 1952 to commemorate a visit by Britain's much loved Queen Elizabeth.

GETTING AROUND TOWN

By Boat

The huge **Likoni Ferry** connects the southern mainland with Mombasa Island. It is free to pedestrians and costs 30¢ per car. It runs all day and all night but the hours vary. Between 5:00 am and 12:30 am it runs about every 20 minutes. From 12:30 am to 5:00 am the crossings are less frequent.

By Bus

There is a public bus running to and from town/airport which you can take for a few cents. The ride is often uncomfortably hot particularly if the bus is crowded. It does however, give you a true feel for the average man's mode of transport in Kenya.

By Taxi

The standard taxi fare to town from the airport is $4.45. Before you get into one of these decrepit old cars, make sure you have agreed to the price up front as there are no meters. To get to places south of Mombasa it is possible to cross over on the ferry and then hire a cab to take you where you are going.

THE OLD PORT

Filled with smells and sounds of a popular harbor, it was once possible to get up close and personal with the Arab crews and their dhows. If a large craft was moored here the often friendly crew shared coffee or perhaps even souvenirs with tourists. Today this practice is no longer allowed by the suspicious port authorities and customs agents. Sadly, the entire port area is strictly off limits to anyone wishing to take photographs.

WHERE TO STAY

Mombasa City Center

OCEANIC HOTEL, *PO Box 90371, Mombasa. Tel. 311 191. $120 per night double occupancy. Includes breakfast. All major credit cards accepted.*

Favoring the style and decor of the '50s, the rambling old hotel looks in need of refurbishment. It touts itself as the largest hotel on the island of Mombasa. A marvelous view of the Indian Ocean and Likoni Bay opens before you from the grounds. It is close to the Likoni Ferry off Oceanic Road but there is no beach here. There is a swimming pool and outdoor bar in a nice garden setting. For meals you may choose from Chinese, Indian, and Italian restaurants.

MANSON HOTEL, *PO Box 83565, Mombasa. Tel. 222 420. $80 per night double occupancy. Includes breakfast. All major credit cards accepted.*

The Manson is a comparatively new facility with its main focus on business travelers. It has all the necessary amenities including ensuite bathrooms. The staff is very willing to make guests comfortable and you will find the overall hotel clean and adequate. If you want a cool room you must ask, as not all 84 bedrooms come with air conditioning. There is no bar and the restaurant serves exclusively vegetarian food.

THE CASTLE HOTEL, *PO Box 84231, Mombasa. Tel. 223 403, Telex 21008. $75 per night double occupancy. Full American breakfast included. All major credit cards accepted.*

While this hotel has a good central location on Moi Avenue in Mombasa, its 60 rooms look like they have been well used. It has been here for some time judging by the frayed furniture and worn look. The rooms have few extras other than the high ceilings, full bathrooms, and air conditioning.

Built in 1908, it was very well liked by the British set. It was run by a Mr. Schwentafsky, nicknamed "Champagne Charlie" because of his interest in women guests. It was renovated by the new owners after a run of bad luck following WWII. There are three bars and a restaurant where visitors to the city should try one of their cold drinks; the most visited is The Terrace.

The Castle is popular with tour buses as a drop-off and pick-up point. Tall potted plants, grand staircases, polished wood floors, and white-washed pillars reveal the hotel's colonial past. The long cool dining verandah is a pleasant place to watch the hustle and bustle on the adjacent avenue.

NEW OUTRIGGER HOTEL, *PO Box 82345, Mombasa. Tel. 220 822, Telex 21368. $65 per night double occupancy. Breakfast included. All major credit cards accepted.*

The Belgian management offers a small hotel with such enticements as excellent French cuisine and a nearby beach. Situated with views over the waters of Kilindini Harbor, the rooms have air conditioning and balconies. A pleasant swimming pool is an added bonus as are the attractive palm trees and tropical plants around the complex.

MANOR HOTEL, *PO Box 84851, Mombasa. Tel. 314 643, Fax 311 952. $40 per night double occupancy. All major credit cards accepted. Price includes breakfast. Ask for the air conditioned rooms.*

This sub-standard castle-like hotel has sadly drifted into disrepair, despite its great potential and interesting history. Once the British Governor's mansion, the only redeeming features are its tall arches, the cool side verandah, garden, view of the typical bustling street life and the friendly staff.

If you stay here you are sure to come away with the smell of moldy towels in your nose, the sound of rattling air conditioners in your ears, and the taste of low-grade food in your mouth. A first impression of the dark lobby with its worn floor tiles is depressing.

HOTEL SAPPHIRE, *Mwembe Tayari Road, Mombasa. Tel. 491 657. $28 per night double occupancy. Diners Club credit cards are accepted. Price includes breakfast.*

Situated near the railway station, the new hotel is some distance from the center of town. The rooms have private bathrooms and air conditioning. Accommodations are simple and clean. Staff is friendly and willing.

Budget

In Mombasa there are many other cheaper places ($15 to $20) to choose from. In some of these hotels the rooms are dirty, service is lousy, and safety may be in question. There are however, some of these less costly accommodations where a night's stay need not be sleepless. Basic clean rooms and adequate service in simple surroundings gives them a passing grade.

Here is a list of some of those places: **NEW PALM TREE HOTEL,** *Tel. 312 169 on Nkuruman Road* – private bathrooms and fan with breakfast; **GLORY GUEST HOUSE,** *Tel. 313 204 on Shibu Road* – breakfast and air conditioned private rooms with bathrooms. Make sure you ask for these rooms as there are more basic ones also. **HOTEL SPLENDID,** *Tel. 220 967 on Msanifu Kombo Street* – private bathrooms and breakfast. The place is old but very clean. Ask for a private room or you may end up sharing!

South of Mombasa

In this part of Kenya south of Mombasa, the real attraction seems to be the beaches – gleaming white coral sand, the prettiest aqua-colored water, and a protective reef. There are many resort hotels and a few more appealing accommodation alternatives.

KAPOK TREES

As you make your way down the highway heading for the southern beaches you will see attractive coconut, mango, cashew, and kapok trees. When the ripe fruit of the kapok tree bursts open, it exposes the black kapok inside which is used to fill pillows and mattresses at many of the hotels. Kapok is also commonly used as a filling for those orange life jackets found on boats.

Shelley Beach

After a ride on the Likoni Ferry, the first beach you'll come to is Shelley. The strand is narrow and unattractive with few places to stay. You will find, however, lots of privacy and few tourists. It is a great place to go for a day picnic from Mombasa providing the seaweed isn't out in force.

SHELLEY BEACH HOTEL, *Shelley Beach Hotel, PO Box 96030, Mombasa. Tel. 451 001, Fax 451 349. $29 per night double occupancy. All major credit cards accepted.*

With its proximity to the ferry and the town of Mombasa, the hotel caters to economical excursion crowds. There are many sightseeing options available from here or you may choose to lounge around the crowded swimming pool. Most guests seem to prefer the pool to the ocean or uninviting beach a few feet away. The hotel offers transportation to town for a small fee.

CPK GUEST HOUSE, *Tel. 451 619. $10 per night double occupancy. Full board.*

The pleasant, full service guest house is some distance from the beach and close to the Likoni Ferry. It is simple, clean, and has all the necessary facilities.

Tiwi Beach

Tiwi remains relatively secluded and unvisited by tourists. The bonus to this is that the vendors and "beach boys" are not as plentiful. However, Tiwi is beginning to develop a reputation for not being entirely safe. Do not walk down the roads or the beaches by yourself particularly at night.

Two or three miles off the main coastal road there are two gravel lanes. One is signposted, the other is not but both head through the seaside scrub for Tiwi beach. All the smaller hotels and self-help bandas have signs on the main road pointing the way. If you don't make reservations well in advance, you won't get a room here. This is particularly true during the high season – January, April to early July, August to early September, and Christmas/New Year.

Along this stretch of beach around the large rocky coral outcrops there are private homes and rental cottages good for groups or families. Many of these places have pools and self-service accommodations with or without local staff. Most of the lodgings along Tiwi are low-key. A few yards from the white sand, the facilities are clean and relatively safe. There is also a favorite thatched watering hole right on the beach where it is easy to strike up conversation with characters who frequent the area.

A beachside campsite is very popular with youngsters from Nairobi who come here on vacation. My family vacationed and camped on Tiwi beach 35 years ago when there were no other facilities. We'd drive down from Kitale and pick out a campsite on the beach.

Down the soft sandy shore there are caves filled with bats and swallows. Accessible during low tide from the shallow water, the underground chambers formed over centuries as the ocean moved down the continental shelf. You can see the different reefs left high and dry over many hundreds of years. Black lizards, mud crawlers, and various kinds of colorful crabs live in the sheer coral cliffs.

FALCON BAY LODGE, *PO Box 2084, Mombasa. Tel. 2553, Fax 2565. $90 per night double occupancy. All major credit cards accepted.*

As yet unfinished, there are currently eight charming cabins with plans for fifty more sometime in the future. The number of guests are pleasantly few allowing the staff to do some real pampering. The accommodations are attractively furnished, air conditioned, and come with in-room bathrooms. When you make reservations be sure to request the ocean-view rooms which obviously have a nicer outlook. There is also a large house available for rent which comes with four bedrooms, a living room/dining room and a patio pool – great for larger groups or families.

The grounds are alive with typical sights and aromas of Kenyan flora and fauna. Bewitching wooden carvings accompany visitors along the pathways leading to the quiet beach or the sand-floor bar and grill. Altogether the lodge offers good value for the money.

Below are some unremarkable but adequate accommodations near Tiwi that may offer an alternative if you find yourself in a bind:

TIWI BEACHLETS, *Tel. 0127 2551* – these small but complete cottages at the top of a rocky bluff go for $13 each. Paved pathways lead down the cliff to the beach. There is also a bar and restaurant.

TWIGA LODGE, *Tel. 0127 2457* – a great place to camp on the beach for a few shillings. A room goes for $7, a cottage for $12 with breakfast. There is a bar and restaurant, catering to an interesting mix of guests.

CORAL COVE COTTAGES, *Tel. 0127 4164* – popular with British/Kenyan youngsters the hotel is right next door to the Twiga and is in the same price range. You may choose from bandas with no facilities to those fully furnished.

TIWI VILLAS, *Tel. 0127 2362* – depending on the number of people, the price varies from $11 (double) to $26 (four guests). There is a pool, bar, and restaurant at the cliff-side facility. The grounds and cottages are attractive and well maintained.

CAPRICHO BEACH COTTAGES, *Tel. 0127 24630* – at these self-service cottages you must either bring or rent your own mosquito nets and sheets. The kitchens are fully equipped. For two people the cost is $15, for six guests it is $30.

SAND ISLAND BEACH COTTAGES, *Tel. 0127 2461* – the prices, facilities, and arrangements are the same as the Caprichio Cottages.

Diani Beach

About an hour from Mombasa, Diani Beach is one of the most lovely stretches of white sand, coconut trees, and blue waters in Kenya. There are many hotels, resorts, and private homes along the shore but thankfully they have all tried to stay unobtrusively hidden. Surrounded by tall trees and abundant flowering green gardens the low-rise buildings blend well with their natural setting. Monkeys, birds, and crabs feel comfortable, although sadly the once abundant leopard is now gone.

DIANI REEF GRAND HOTEL, *Sonotels Kenya Limited, PO Box 61753, Nairobi. Tel. 227 571, Fax 227 585. $220 per night double occupancy. All major credit cards accepted.*

Around the extensive grounds, towering coconut trees and fuschia bougainvillea fill the attractive rock gardens with color and tropical charm. A wide sandy beach caressed by cool ocean breezes invites you to stay a while if you can find a spot among the crowd of visitors.

There is so much to keep you busy at Diani Reef Hotel you may not get to see Kenya if you try to do it all! Personally I prefer something a little less overwhelming and for the same price it can easily be had.

Polynesian, Middle Eastern, African, French, Italian, International and Indian Ocean restaurants are ready to please the whim of your tastebuds. A charming floating dining hall serves a breakfast buffet of fresh fruit and morning cuisine. Gambling, dancing, squash, tennis, archery, jogging, pedal boats and two swimming pools are a few of the options offered.

The staff at the fifteen year old 300 room hotel seems unable to keep up with the mildew problem prevalent at the seaside, but they are aware of it. Therefore, I suggest you check your room carefully or ask for accommodations in the newer wing which is closer to the ocean. Each room comes with a private bathroom and air conditioning.

DIANI HOUSE *PO Box 19, Ukunda, Mombasa. Tel. 0127 2412, Fax 0127 2391, e-mail aceltd@users.africaonline.co.ke, www.dianihouse.com. Diani House is a member of Bush Homes Africa Safaris, Tel. US 404 888 0909, e mail bushhomes@africaonline.co.ke, www.bushhomes.com, Tel. 502 491, Fax 502 739. $187-$290 per person per night. One of the best!*

To get here, you fly from Nairobi to the airport in Mombasa. One of your hosts (either Lulu or John) picks you up there for the ride to **Diani Beach** or a taxi can be arranged. The drive is a pleasant one as your guide points out the various species of trees, places of interest and explains a little local history.

On the way from the airport you must cross the river on a huge passenger and vehicle ferry. This is quite an exciting adventure but can sometimes take a few minutes to board if the line of cars is long. Here you are met by a colorful array of locals who use the ferry to commute to work in the city. There are tasty cashews, peanuts, juicy mangoes, fresh bananas and other goodies for sale.

After the fascinating hour long drive from Mombasa you will be ready for the hideaway at Diani House. Located about half way along Diani Beach, this Arab style home offers a taste of colonial Kenya of days gone by. Here you can rest on the cool verandah with a refreshing coconut water drink or restore yourself with a walk around the garden enjoying the quiet beauty. You'll find 12 acres of land, including coconut palms, giant baobabs, bright bougainvillea, and fragrant frangipani, which offers a haven to many birds, bushbabies, monkeys and other wildlife living here in this slice of paradise. A short walk down the lush garden path offers a beautiful view of the white beach and Indian Ocean.

There are only eight beds (three twin rooms, one double room (with private bathrooms) and a single room with shared bathroom) so you are guaranteed an uncrowded stay. Each room has its own spacious bathroom done in the large red tile made locally. The shower is oversized and open with a built-in tile seat for your comfort. Complimentary amenities are tastefully arrayed on the wide sink. The windows are attractively covered with wrought iron bars, lacy curtains, and an optional mesh roll-down screen, as there is no air conditioning. Instead, the open windows and ceiling fans circulate the cool ocean breeze. The rooms stay fresh and comfortable.

Food is a special feature of a Diani House vacation, with emphasis on fresh local produce. Fishermen bring fish and shellfish to the kitchen door straight from the ocean. These delicacies, along with the abundant tropical fruit and fresh vegetables, make dining here a gourmet's delight. The fresh sashimi and prawns tempura are delectable!

Selected as one of my *Best Places to Stay* – see Chapter 11 for more details.

MUKURUMUJI TENTED CAMP IN THE SHIMBA HILLS, *(part of DIANI HOUSE) PO Box 19, Ukunda, Mombasa. Tel. 0127 2412, Fax 0127 2391, e-mail aceltd@users.africaonline.co.ke, www.dianihouse.com. Diani House is a member of Bush Homes Africa Safaris, Tel. US 404 888 0909, e mail bushhomes@africaonline.co.ke, www.bushhomes.com, Tel. 502 491, Fax 502 739. $195-$221 per person per night.*

While in Mombasa, you may want to venture into the new private, tented camps in the nearby Shimba Hills. A short one hour drive from Diani House this extension will add a marvelous alternative to the beach but still lets you explore along the south coast of Kenya. The camps is on a forested hill in the privately owned "Sable Valley Game Sanctuary" overlooking the Shimba Hills National Reserve.

There are four comfortable twin bedded double tents. Each is covered with palm thatch and has its own verandah and bathroom ensuite — what a luxury to be able to flush your toilet and have a hot camp shower while camping in the wilds of Africa! All the excellent, home-cooked meals are served in the community dining room.

The Shimba Hills National Reserve boasts the only resident population in Kenya of the splendid sable antelope. In addition, there are hosts of smaller animals along with elephant, buffalo, giraffe and a host of butterflies and birds.

SAFARI BEACH, *Alliance Hotels, PO Box 49839, Nairobi. Tel. 337 501, Fax 219 212, E-mail: ahl@africaonline.co.ke. $185 per night double occupancy. All major credit cards accepted.* **Jadini Beach Hotel, Safari Beach Hotel,** *and* **Africana Sea Lodge** *make up the three Alliance hotels along Diani. There is a complimentary shuttle bus connecting the three facilities or you may choose to walk.*

A large thatched circular building serves as an impressive lobby. Behind the reception area are the bedrooms with little or no view of the Indian Ocean. Each of the 186 two story thatched cabins are comfortably furnished with above average bathrooms but a somewhat worn look.

It is a shame the owners did not take advantage of the spectacular setting and place the buildings within view of the lovely beach. An ice cream parlor and big swimming pool are the only facilities near the sand. It makes a pleasant day to sit in a deck chair with something from the snack bar and watch the tide roll in. It is quite a hike around the extensive grounds from the beach to the rooms or the Sportsman's Club.

The well-equipped club is situated further from the beach behind the guest rooms. They offer tennis, squash, exercise machines, a snack bar, and a small pool.

INDIAN OCEAN BEACH CLUB, *Block Hotels, PO Box 47557, Nairobi. Tel. 335 807, Fax 340 541. $180 per night double occupancy. All major credit cards accepted.*

From the moment you arrive you know this place is different. Check-in takes place at individual welcoming tables after a rejuvenating ablution with a scented hand towel. The central buildings are an interesting throwback to colonial Kenya with their red roof tile and wood shutters. Scattered around these main structures are 100 whitewashed guest cottages made to resemble a Swahili village. Whether they have thatched or flat red Swahili style roofs, all rooms face the sparkling Indian Ocean.

Inside the cozy accommodations, management has taken the time to add many extras. Hair dryers, full bathrooms, air conditioning, and direct-dial phones satisfy the basics while stone floors, king-size Lamu beds, thick wooden ceiling beams, cushioned window seats and hand painted tiles add quality and style. The cottages however, do tend to be a little too close together and somewhat on the small side; but not enough to detract from a pleasant stay.

The main dining room, Spices, is located upstairs. It offers exotic views of the vast seascape with its whitecaps, tall leafy coconut trees, and ancient mammoth baobabs. The design feels wall-less and open. Outstandingly delicious cuisine offers home-grown fresh fruit and vegetables along with just-caught seafood. Downstairs is an airy breakfast room overlooking the grand swimming pool which is cleverly planned to flow over its sides. Three additional smaller pools grace the grounds. Perhaps the most outstanding outdoor feature is the huge shapely baobab trees sheltering a 16th century mosque. The club certainly boasts the best seaside location on the coast and as a bonus, is close to the mouth of Tiwi River. Because of a break in the reef there is always surf and water for swimming – even at low tide. It is particularly fun to jump off a high sand bank into the river and float upstream on the salty incoming tidal flow.

Many activities such as snorkeling, sailing, windsurfing, tennis, Tiwi River guided nature walks, squash, golf (at the Nyali Golf Club) and a shuttle to Diani and Likoni are free to guests. For deep sea fishing and scuba diving there is an additional charge. There is also a beauty salon, souvenir shop, and children's club on the grounds.

JADINI BEACH HOTEL, *Alliance Hotels, PO Box 49839, Nairobi. Tel. 337 501, Fax 219 212, E-mail: ahl@africaonline.co.ke. $164 per night double occupancy. All major credit cards accepted.* **Jadini Beach Hotel, Safari Beach Hotel**, *and* **Africana Sea Lodge** *make up the three Alliance hotels along Diani. There is a complimentary shuttle bus connecting the three facilities or you may choose to walk.*

Renovated in 1990, the expansive Jadini Hotel feels bright open and airy. The bedrooms boast high ceilings, large sliding glass windows, and ocean views. Attractive seaside decor compliments the modern facilities in each room.

A small but inviting pool overlooks the cool waters of the Indian Ocean and the sandy beach. Poolside music and dancing is a popular pastime. Around the large complex there is always a cacophony of color and movement as the many guests happily engage in vacation activities. Choose from any of the hotel's restaurants, the nearby ice cream parlor or lobster bar.

This small stretch of beach called Jadini is a continuation of Diani Beach. Interestingly, it is named for the surrounding hardwood forest covering the entire coastline. In some spots there are remnants of the forest but most of it is gone. In these tiny patches of woods there are bush babies, vervet and colobus monkeys, baboons, butterflies and birds.

LEISURE LODGE, *Leisure Lodge, Diani Beach. Tel. 0127 2011. $176 per night double occupancy. All major credit cards accepted.*

Although the hotel, casino, and club forming the heart of this resort have an overwhelmingly German guest list, Americans are also welcome. From the rich looking lobby you can reach an upscale shopping mezzanine and the fun-filled casino where high thatched ceilings and classic Kenya red tiles are a reminder of where you are. Visitors to both the exclusive club and the hotel share the restaurants, tennis courts, golf course, horses (riding on the beach and interior), diving school, and shuttle bus to Mombasa.

The 200 room hotel portion stretches along one side of the complex in multi-story buildings and has its own elegant pool. If you should stay here ask for an ocean view. The grounds at the hotel, while set back from the beach, effuse a sense of first class refinement but the club is even more lavish. Meandering pathways, emerald lawns, and bridges over lily ponds surround the exclusive garden club and its two pools. Filled with luxurious opulence, all 116 rooms and six suites are further still from the Indian Ocean's shore.

LEOPARD BEACH, *PO Box 34, Ukunda. Tel. 1261 2111, Fax 1261 2113. $156 per night double occupancy. All major credit cards accepted.*

The most noteworthy feature at this hotel is the well-planned layout. The resort, now nearly 30 years old, is actually quite large but seems intimate and exclusive because of the dividing levels of construction. Each ledge is amazingly hewn into the rocky cliff with guest rooms having the topmost setting. In descending order follow the lovely cliffside pool and a fun disco. As you climb down the walkways notice the charming view of the bay, hidden rock gardens, and delightful lily ponds. Once you reach the small beach take care where you swim as the coral can be razor sharp.

Magnificent oversized suites are the best choice here. Each attractively decorated suite comes with a small living room, tended garden, and a patio from which the Indian Ocean view is breathtaking. The standard bedrooms look worn and faded. **LAGOON REEF HOTEL,** *Reef Hotels, PO Box 61408, Nairobi. Tel. 214 322, Fax 332 702. $150 per night double occupancy. All major credit cards accepted.*

Three story thatched buildings with oversized windows, balconies and a view of either the pool or the carefully landscaped garden are available for just under 300 hotel guests. You may choose from standard, family, or superior rooms with air conditioning or fans. Naturally, the superior rooms on the third floor have the best ocean vistas.

Catering to tour groups like most hotels along the beach, the Lagoon Reef is situated on 20 acres of remarkably well cared for grounds. All manner of colorful and fragrant plants landscape the hillsides and slopes leading to the beach. Tennis courts nestle amid the natural bush and a lagoon-like swimming pool blends with a tropical island. Monkeys and colorful birds exchange chatter as they flit in and out of the shrubbery-lined pathways. A huge ancient baobab tree defies description.

The sound of water is everywhere from the beach side bar to the lily ponds in the lobby. Wooden bridges and diffused light reflect in the clear pools. A high peaked thatch roof in the reception area keeps visitors and the aviary birds cool.

GOLDEN BEACH HOTEL, *PO Box 31, Ukunda, Mombasa. Tel. 0127 2625, Fax 0127 2321. $142 per night double occupancy. All major credit cards accepted.*

Visitors to the Golden Beach Hotel are usually large groups of vacationing Germans. The tall concrete structure houses 138 rooms, all set far back from the beach. It is quite a walk to the water and the wide sandy shore, which is the reason we are here! The unappealing resort does, however, have adequate facilities, pretty gardens, and a large swimming pool. There is an emphasis on watersports and beachside activities for guests.

AFRICANA SEA LODGE, *Alliance Hotels, PO Box 49839, Nairobi. Tel. 337 501, Fax 219 212, E-mail: ahl@africaonline.co.ke. $130 per night double occupancy. All major credit cards accepted. Jadini Beach Hotel, Safari Beach Hotel, and Africana Sea Lodge make up the three Alliance hotels along Diani. There is a complimentary shuttle bus connecting the three facilities or you may choose to walk.*

Even with much needed remodeling underway in the 158 rooms, I would not choose to stay here simply because the lodgings are too far from the beach and too close together. The accommodations are, however, adequate and clean if unimaginatively decorated. In addition to a small swimming pool for guests, there is a large six bedroom cabin with full kitchen, living room, patio, and garden available for rent with or without staff.

ROBINSON BAOBAB CLUB, *PO Box 84792, Mombasa. Tel. 1261 2026. Reservations are generally made in Frankfurt, Germany. $130 per night double occupancy.*

The downside to staying here is the overwhelmingly loud music, the pervasive mold, and the sheer complexity of getting around the huge network of rooms. With accommodations for 300 people it is hard to find a quiet place. The mostly German clientele are friendly and willing to include everyone in their party.

As the oldest hotel along Diani Beach, the Robinson was constructed in 1974 in a spectacular setting, high on a rocky cliff. From the dining room the wide open view of the Indian Ocean can be breathtaking, particularly at sunset. The grounds are cooled and shaded by established leafy trees and natural vegetation. Inside the public areas unusual Lamu furniture and decor add a touch of Africa.

TWO FISHES HOTEL, *PO Box 23, Ukunda, Mombasa. Tel. 1261 2101. $128 per night double occupancy. All major credit cards accepted.*

With 199 rooms housed in thatched buildings, the large complex exudes an air of unpretentious simplicity. The relaxed atmosphere unfortunately spreads its way to the housekeeping department which seems to be lax in its duties judging by the dirty-looking surroundings. Brown and orange decor extends throughout the public areas crying out to be modernized. An unusual pool in the lounge area flows outdoors where things improve considerably. Popular with kids, the swimming pool is the most striking feature at the hotel. Slender canals of water run under bridges and over a well-used slide into a lower pool.

TRADE WINDS HOTEL, *African Tours and Hotels Limited, PO Box 30471, Nairobi. Tel. 336 858, Fax 218 109. $120 per night double occupancy. All major credit cards accepted.*

A palm-studded white sandy beach is the highlight of a stay here. In spite of a marvelous setting, the hotel does not live up to its potential. Common areas are old and worn and the pool could use some attention. With room for 200 guests, the Trade Winds is a large facility set too far back from the beach.

PARADISE OCEAN VILLAGE CLUB, *Universal Safari Tours, PO Box 49312, Nairobi. Tel. 221 446, Fax 218 686. $115 per night double occupancy.*

Guest rooms consist of small cabins surrounded by natural vegetation including dark pink bougainvillea and gnarled baobab trees. Swooping archways, patios, and whitewashed stucco conform to the Spanish look of the cottages. A joint living room separates the quarters which have a tendency to be gloomy and close. The foyer and check-in areas (set back from the beach) are light and airy adding to the generally casual atmosphere. Included in the cost of your stay are archery, snorkeling, windsurfing, and poolside activities.

A selection of relaxing eateries with beachside dining, homey checkered table cloths, and thatched roofs carry through the informal theme. There is a lobster and seafood grill, a game meat restaurant and a bright juice and fruit bar. As the small facility caters mainly to French patrons, the menus are in French.

SOUTHERN PALMS BEACH RESORT, *PO Box 363, Ukunda, Mombasa. Tel. 0127 3721, Fax 0127 3381. $108 per night double occupancy. All major credit cards accepted.*

This huge new 300 room beach resort awaits you 22 miles south of Mombasa. It claims its two free-form swimming pools are some of the largest in East Africa – they do look cool and enticing. There is an outdoor Jacuzzi and an attractive swim-up bar (Island Palace Bar). Meals can be taken in the inviting bright restaurant with a poolside patio or under grand thatched peaks where you'll find Kenyan cuisine.

Throughout the large complex there is a blend of Arabian and Swahili architecture. Sweeping white domes and clean curving archways compliment intricately woven thatch and hanging lamps. The charming decor loses some of its pull because of the hotel's size; when it's full the numbers can be intimidating. Balconied bedrooms face either the ocean or one of the azure pools. Inside, the decor is simple, clean, and comfortable with Lamu carved furniture. Canopied beds with mosquito nets, large ensuite bathrooms, and air conditioning are standard. If your room is further inland it can be quite a walk to the beach.

Sand from the nearby beach dazzles the eyes as you set off on your windsurfer or try scuba diving lessons. Squash, tennis, and a modern health spa will keep you fit during your stay. The lovely grounds dotted with swaying coconut trees, stone floors, and intricately patterned woodwork invite you to just sit by the water and relax.

KASKAZI BEACH HOTEL, *LTI-Kaskazi Beach Hotel, PO Box 135, Ukunda. Tel. 0127 3170, Fax 0127 2396. $104 per night double occupancy. All major credit cards accepted.*

As a recent addition to Diani (1991), the Kaskazi Beach Hotel has captured the elegance and romance of something out of Aladdin's tales. The complex can be a little overwhelming in its size. Landscapers used the naturally rocky coastline to sculpture attractive rock gardens filled with tropical vegetation and cool pools. Surrounding the garden on three sides, tall buildings produce an Arabic style with graceful arched balconies and white marble forms. In each of the 193 rooms expect to find bright colorful decor, small bathrooms, and air conditioning.

To cater to large groups the management sets up dinner and breakfast buffets either outdoors on the patio, around the free-form pool, or in the main restaurant. From the dining patios, not only is the sparkling Indian Ocean visible but it is enhanced by the mysteriously exotic ruins of a formerly forgotten mosque. If you wish to get away for a more elegant dinner try the Aladdin Grill. For something more casual there are snack bars near the pool and the beach.

Under the lofty thatched ceiling of the reception area, splashes of wondrous colors, a white marble staircase and indoor waterfall give the impression of palatial living. Graceful window arches let in warm sunshine reflecting off the touches of brass and glass in the airy lobby. Lamu style furnishings, rich drapes, and upholstery flow into the colorful Lamu Lounge. Watersports, tennis courts, dancing to a live band, games and tribal dancing are just a few of the constantly changing entertainment options offered by Kaskazi management.

NOMAD, *PO Box 1, Ukunda, Mombasa. Tel. 0127 2155, Fax 0127 2391. $80 per night double occupancy.*

Started as a restaurant 15 years ago, the food and service still live up to the outstanding reputation. The fact that local Kenyans flock here to eat is a true indication of constant quality. Even if you don't stay here it is worth visiting one of the two restaurants for a meal.

To get to Nomad you must first drive past modern looking stores, a disco, and even a high-rise. At the turnoff the route suddenly changes to a fascinating country dirt road. Once you arrive, there is a choice of older bandas or newer cabins (all with electricity) – just a short stroll from the ivory beach and the Indian Ocean.

On Sunday there is a Jazz lunch with curry as the main dish. The larger of the two eateries serves a variety of selections with fresh seafood as its main focus. The gentle ocean breeze, open sides, and tall thatched roof make it very casual and relaxing. Nomad's Beach Bar is even more natural and informal. The floor is beach sand and the woven palm roof is held up by a coconut tree trunk. Sandwiches and seafood are superb.

The cabins are light and bright opening to private patios and the beach. Modern and spacious bathrooms are clean. Large mosquito nets and fans keep the heat and the bugs away. These accommodations are perfect for small groups or families.

In the older bandas the standards are not quite as high, but they are still popular with local Kenyans on vacation from Nairobi. There are no fans but each banda has its own full service bathroom. The wooden structures feel small and dark, particularly when compared to the cabins. The advantage here is you are right on the beach and there won't be more than 50 people staying here!

DIANI SEA LODGE, *Welcome Inns Limited, Kenya, PO Box 37, Ukunda. Tel. 0127 2114, Fax 0127 2287. $55 per night double occupancy. All major credit cards accepted.*
From the central buildings there is a pleasant view of the kidney shaped pool and stretching grass lawn down to the pristine beach at the Indian Ocean. Wooden loungers mark the way offering ring-side seats for the watersports activities. A pool bar which serves snacks, a toddler's pool, and a children's playground make this an inviting place for families with kids. For the grown-ups there is a bar and a disco in the main building; tennis and miniature golf outside.
The German owned hotel caters to large groups in the 145 room facility. One hundred and thirty five air conditioned cabins dot land-scaped grounds back from the beach. Each bungalow has a private bathroom with shower and a terrace. Another ten rooms are available in an apartment block closer to the sea.
DIANI SEA RESORT, *Welcome Inns, Limited, PO Box 37, Ukunda. Tel. 0127 3081, Fax 0127 2287. $55 per night double occupancy. All major credit cards accepted.*
Because it is new, Diani Sea Resort is a good choice among the reasonably priced hotels. Everything is clean and has that new shine, making guests feel special. With space available for over 300 people, there are choices of suites, family, and standard rooms. Accommodations are roomy with private bathrooms (showers), and air conditioning. Bed-rooms open onto a patio or colorful garden adding charm and light. Set back from the ocean, the basically "U" shaped buildings are simply constructed in the no-nonsense German fashion, going for practicality rather than pizzazz.
Protected by the buildings, a large sloping garden filled with tropical delights and twittering birds pleases the senses. From the dining room at the top of the angled garden there is a pleasant view of the goings on below. At the furthest end of the flowerbeds is a sparkling swimming pool where children play with abandon on the island and waterslide. Standard ocean watersports are available to those who are inclined.
FOUR TWENTY SOUTH, *Mrs. M. Martin, PO Box 42, Ukunda. Tel. 2034. $21 per night double occupancy for the better cottages.*
There are several selections of cottages on the grounds which cost less, but those costing $21 are the nicest. This lodge is very popular with local Kenyans from Nairobi – so book ahead. The facilities are self-help with kitchen equipment provided.

Galu Beach
Further south than Diani, the beach at Galu is smaller and even more private. The ocean swimming here can be a little difficult in places because

of patches of sharp coral rock. The relatively unused beach attracts few tourists and has maintained its air of naturalness with dirt roads and native vegetation.

PINEWOOD VILLAGE, *PO Box 190, Ukunda, Mombasa. Tel. 0127 3720, Fax 0127 3131. $230 per night double occupancy. All major credit cards accepted.*

Here at Pinewood you can have the best of both worlds with the privacy of living in your own completely equipped condo, full service personal staff, resort security, organized tours and beach hotel facilities. You may choose to cook your own food in the villa's kitchen or have a steward prepare it. There is a small market on the grounds selling fresh fruits, vegetables, and seafood for just this purpose. For a change of pace, try the delightful restaurant and bar right in the complex.

The 20 two-story townhouses at the end of Galu Beach fuse into a natural setting back from the sand. Flowerbeds, green grass, and Kenyan bush surround the cozy compound. The communal pool with its swim-up bar is a great place to meet like-minded guests or simply relax in the warm sunshine. The outdoor decor is light and bright with flowing archways and fresh whitewashed walls. This feeling of cleanliness continues indoors.

Prepare for your day in the good-sized bathroom with its richly adorned Italian tile. In the evening, step out of the air conditioned upstairs bedroom onto your private verandah and watch the burnished sun disappear over the skyline. Sleep on the large comfortable bed shielded by sheer white mosquito netting. Downstairs, vivid African materials contrast with white walls and ebony furniture.

NEPTUNE PARADISE & NEPTUNE COTTAGES, *PO Box 696, Ukunda, Mombasa. Tel. 0127 3061, Fax 0127 3019. $158 & $145 per night double occupancy. All major credit cards accepted.*

Of the two side-by-side hotels, Paradise is the newer, smaller, and nicer of the two. Altogether there are 250 thatched, two floor bandas surrounded by pretty gardens. Those rooms overlooking the pool can be noisy but have the best view. If you'd rather select quiet, then your outlook will be the back of more rooms. The grounds are long rather than wide, making the walk to the beach more than a few minutes. Inside the newer, brighter accommodations at Paradise, expect to find well supplied amenities. Ensuite bathrooms, telephones, and mini-bars are standard.

An inviting swim-up bar and a thatched dining and bar area next to the beach make for pleasant daytime entertainment. One of the bars is built to look like a boat with dolphin bar stools – very creative!

GHOSTLY GAZI

Just north of Msambweni is the town of Gazi, which holds a particularly macabre background. It seems that in 1895 Sheik Mbaruk made the village his home. From here he antagonized the British whenever possible. When soldiers came to quash his uprising, he fled leaving behind his splendid Arab-style house.

The locals say the village dogs avoid the place at all cost, and so they do. Legend tells of 16 decapitated villagers buried behind the magnificent wooden doors within the foundations. Mbaruk also hid his victims' corpses in the large conical projections built into the corners of the rooms. The ghosts of his prey allegedly wander in search of revenge.

Msambweni Beach

Surrounded by private property, Msambweni (translated to mean "place of the antelopes") remains almost completely unspoiled. Low cliffs and rocky outcrops along with coral reefs add interest to the landscape. To get there you travel down a pot-holed narrow track past coral and mud huts and coconut groves.

SEASCAPES BEACH VILLAS, *Seascapes Limited, PO Box 45541, Nairobi. Tel. 334 280. $80 per night double occupancy. All major credit cards accepted.*

To get away from the crowds of tourists at the large resorts try Seascapes. Enjoy the solitude of an unsullied beach in the condominium/ hotel with a cook and domestic. Simply buy your fresh veggies, fruit, and groceries from the little store on the grounds, give it to the cook and presto – there's dinner.

Intriguingly perched at the top of a cliff on 12 acres of well maintained property, the view is impressive. Walkways criss-cross the healthy looking lawn. Coconut trees and bougainvillea thickets add character and color. The picturesque sandy bay can be reached down a long flight of steps, guaranteeing a "Robinson Crusoe" effect. The 16 two-story villas look out to a small pool popular with those who wish to be sociable. If swimming isn't your bag, take in a game of squash or tennis with your fellow travelers. For an outing there is the popular cafe and poolside bar.

Fans and balconies grace the big three-bedroom thatched apartments. Private bathrooms and a complete kitchen are standard in the Arabesque dwellings. Simple furnishings and whitewash keep things feeling comfortable.

BEACHCOMBER CLUB, *PO Box 54, Msambweni. Tel. 340 331, Fax 336 890. $76 per night double occupancy. All major credit cards accepted.*

The telltale sign of visiting Kenyans once again gives away the specialness of Beachcomber's. Not quite on the deserted beach, the two story guest rooms are faced instead with tropical gardens and tall coconut trees. From the secluded verandahs you might steal a quick glimpse of the blue ocean as the breeze blows the palm fronds out of the way. A sculpted sea shell splashes water into a petite, attractive pool. Inside the decorative lobby all manner of quaint souvenirs wait to be bought.

A set of narrow hewn steps lead down to the sandy cove. Tempestuous waves at high tide sound their warning at the foot of the hotel. To reach the azure ocean at low tide a trek across the life-filled coral is the only way. Jagged rocks, crystalline pools, and hidden inlets invite the adventurer in you to take charge – inspiring and exciting! Beached canoes filled with brightly colored pillows await your return.

At the bottom of the tapering staircase is the cave bar and grill. Colorful cushions, craggy coral walls, and artistic decor are the backdrop to remarkable lunches and cocktails. Sitting here with a view of the ocean's frothy surf – life doesn't get much better than this.

The draw here at the club is the quiet solitude, serene beauty, and outstanding cuisine. Owner Tamsin Corcoran caters to the visitors in her 16 basic, non-air conditioned rooms with welcoming friendliness and a flair for the dramatic. The first and last meals of the day are served in the dining room at the top of the cliff. Magnificent open vistas of the Indian Ocean and sculptured rocks will complete your vacation tales.

Chale, Funzi, Shimoni, & Wasini Beaches

The order of these beaches, as you head south down the coast, is Chale, Funzi, Shimoni & Wasini.

Just after Ukunda and right before arriving at Msambweni along the A14 coastal road, you will come to the beaches of **Chale Island**. This small island south of **Galu Beach** is still pristine with startlingly lovely rock formations, native trees, and quiet sandy beaches. To get across the narrow waterway, you will need to negotiate with the locals to take you over in one of their boats for a few shillings. Sometimes there are swarms of sandflies which can be very annoying, so check with the natives before crossing to see if these biting, flying dots are around.

Funzi beach lies half way between Msambweni and Shimoni further south down the A14. After a careful walk around prolific coral formations along the beach, it is possible to wade across to Funzi Island at low tide. Make sure you know when the tides are low or you may be stranded for the return crossing. Another option is to hire one of the local fishermen to take you across in his boat for a dollar or so.

After leaving Msambweni your safari will take you past green swamps and sugar cane fields. Fifty miles south of Mombasa is **Shimoni**, right out at the end of a small peninsula. This is the site of the first permanent

British settlement on the Kenya mainland. Shimoni means "place of the holes" because of the extensive cave system running underground. Army patrols years ago walked seven miles inland in these underground honeycombs. Slave traders lowered their prisoners into the caves and marched them beneath Shimoni to their waiting dhows. You can still see (with a flashlight) the shackles in the walls. Apart from the coral caves, the area is famous for big game fishing. The headquarters for **Kisite National Marine Park** is here.

Wasini Island is easily visible from shore but not easily accessible. There are no roads, no cars, and no running water. Wasini Island, just off the Shimoni Peninsula, is a perfectly unspoiled forested place as yet untouched by tourism. On the island there are Muslim ruins, coral gardens, a Swahili village, and a fabulous seafood restaurant.

FUNZI ISLAND CLUB, *PO Box 90246, Mombasa. Tel. 225 546, Fax 316 458. $400 per night double occupancy. Minimum three night stay–all inclusive. Closed for the off season.*

Inside the seven tents comprising the camp there are many extras such as large Lamu beds and comfortable furniture. Just outside, wash your sandy feet in thoughtfully placed containers which also keep flocks of bright birds happy. Bush showers add a fun and refreshing touch. Patient and adorable donkeys pull water for the tents. Covered patios provide much needed shade at the height of a hot sunny day. Well out of earshot from each other, the "rooms" are designed to be open and light with privacy a major consideration.

Getting to the island involves an adventure in itself. Precariously balanced in a handsome canoe, guests set off towards a wall of tall mangrove. Trust the operator. Just at the last moment a tree covered passageway opens up. Shortly you land on a pristine beach only to step back in time to a forgotten era.

An old fashioned record player playing a tune in the thatched "lounge" is the first thing to garner your attention. Fascinating books, photos of happy visitors, telling fish trophies, and singular mangrove root tables are a great setting for a drink and the artful humor of your host.

Fishing with experts over the reef for such trophies as marlin, tuna, and sailfish is what most guests are here for. Guided bird excursions, snorkeling, boat trips, and fabulous picnics entertain non-fishing members. Plenty of refreshments and deliciously fresh seafood perfectly complete a lighthearted and easygoing stay in paradise.

CHALE ISLAND PARADISE, *Tel. 0127 3236, 3477, or 3478, Fax 0127 3319. $325 per night double occupancy.*

Thirty small cabins set on the romantic island of Chale make a perfect getaway. Large thatched accommodations overlooking the ocean have private sunbathing beaches. Inside, a bedroom/living room combination and in-room bathrooms are artfully decorated with flowers, rugs, and Lamu furniture.

In an hour you can walk around the pristine isle and the nature reserve. Natural springs, salt lakes, white beaches, and a wealth of animal and bird life blend harmoniously. Canoeing, fishing, diving, boating and snorkeling are just a few of the activities available to keep you busy.

A charming open-air restaurant serves the lunch buffet while dinner and breakfast may be taken in your room. The small library, open sided bar and beach bar are wonderful places to sit, caressed by sea breezes while enjoying the view of paradise.

SEA ADVENTURES, LTD, *PO Box 56, Shimoni. Tel. 12. $300 per night double occupancy – includes big game fishing – rates may vary depending on fishing activities.*

Accommodations with the Hemphill family are either in their comfortable home where you become one of the family or in an adjacent banda. The draw to Sea Adventures is days of deep sea fishing for trophy size quarry. Simon and his father Pat operate two large, well equipped vessels and are willing to meet any requirements you may have, including specials for kids.

PEMBA CHANNEL INN, *Pemba Channel Fishing Club, Limited, PO Box 86952, Mombasa. Tel. 313 749, Fax 316 875. $150 per night double occupancy. All major credit cards accepted. Open only August through March.*

A few plain white cabins dot the grounds on the embankment above the celebrated Pemba Channel, which is world famous for big game fishing. Flower beds, a gorgeous tiled swimming pool, Wasini Island in the background, and fishing boats on the go add a thrill to any visit. The inn is available only for the duration of the angling season from August through March. You take the risk of having your reservation (unfairly?) canceled if you aren't booking a boat.

Huge finned trophies, photos, and record size catches adorn the open-sided lounge. The oversized room manages to feel inviting with shells, sweet flowers, and the lingering karma of those who won. Share the thrill of a day out on the waves with other interested sportspeople – sorry, no kids under eight.

Besides the marvelous angling, be prepared to delight in the manager's gourmet cooking and her effervescent charm. Sandra has made the once ordinary fisherman's lodge a warm and homelike inn. Fans and mosquito nets make the bandas comfortable, while roomy well stocked bathrooms and flowers add a personal touch. Try to get a room with a view of the water.

SHIMONI REEF LODGE, *Reef Hotels, PO Box 61408, Nairobi. Tel. 214 322, Fax 332 702. $122 per night double occupancy. All major credit cards accepted.*

Ten bandas with individual patios and thatched roofs are the heart of this somewhat shabby hotel. Easygoing and serene are two words that best describe the lodge. It caters mostly to scuba divers at its PADI center. The tired-looking pool is set among gardens, coconut trees, and green lawns. An adequate restaurant and bar overlooks the Wasini Channel.

Shimba Hills

Each year the Shimba Hills become more and more popular with tourists who want to escape the sun and surf for a short while. Less than an hour's drive from Mombasa, the hills run parallel to the south shore. The cool green forest is home to small herds of elephant, buffalo, and giraffe. The reserve is probably most distinguished for its rare but hard to see sable antelope.

SABLE VALLEY, *Wilderness Trails Limited/ Bush Homes Africa Safaris, Tel. US 404 888 0909, e mail bushhomes@africaonline.co.ke, www.bushhomes.com, PO Box 56923, Nairobi. Tel. 506 139, Fax 502 739. $280 per night double occupancy. All inclusive. All major credit cards accepted.*

This small farm and private game sanctuary sits at the southern end of the Shimba Hills. Rosemary and Dick Knight oversee an ongoing program to reintroduce wildlife to the area. Any species that has disappeared due to poaching or hunting is reintroduced to the remaining rain forest surrounding the estate. Funds earned are put to good use in this important service.

Two large and well designed bandas with all the necessities cater to welcome guests. Farm-fresh cooking, a pool, and a Shimba Hills sunset cocktail will stay etched in your memory. Other activities include bush and bird walks, game drives, and educational visits to local villages.

SHIMBA HILLS, *Block Hotels, PO Box 47557, Nairobi. Tel. 335 807, Fax 340 541. $118 per night double occupancy. No children under seven. All major credit cards accepted.*

Three of the rooms actually have trees growing through them in this tropical jungle setting. The treehouse atmosphere is encouraged with wooden walkways, open viewing areas, and verandahs facing the watering hole. From the charming open-sided dining room or the aptly named Jungle Bar, guests can observe monkeys and elephants at the water's edge.

The 24 rooms are small but nicely done with twin beds, colorful materials, electricity, fans and oversized windows. Built from stone and wood, the spotless bathrooms and showers are shared by all guests except those in the private honeymoon suite. Even though Shimba Hills does not have a reputation for plentiful wildlife, it is a pleasant change from the heat of the coast. The facility offers dawn and sunset game drives, as well as walks through Cycad forests to Sheldrick Falls and Marere Dam.

North of Mombasa to Kilifi

Between the large city of Mombasa and Kilifi the development of resorts and hotels is prolific. Most of the hotels cater exclusively to British, German, and Italian groups from Europe. The competition is fierce to provide the most comforts, activities, and beautiful surroundings. Generally, however, a stay here loses all sense of what Kenya is about and sadly most guests rarely venture outside this protected environment.

Nyali Beach & English Point

From English Point you can see across the water to Old Town Mombasa. Here at Nyali Beach begins the concentration of northern beaches.

FRERETOWN

Just north of Nyali Bridge, at the corner of the turn-off on the main road to Malindi, is Freretown. It was established in the 19th century by Sir Bartle Frere, a former British governor in India. His intent was to provide the first colony in Kenya for freed slaves. A free standing bell next to the main road was erected by missionaries opposed to slavery. If a slave ship was spotted along the water, the bell rang a loud clear warning.

NYALI BEACH HOTEL, *Block Hotels, PO Box 47557, Nairobi. Tel. 335 807 or 011 471 551, Fax 340 541. $220 per night double occupancy. All major credit cards accepted.*

There is much to see and do at Nyali Beach Hotel for up to 450 guests of all ages. On the 26 acre complex there are seven restaurant selections from casual to fancy, shopping arcades, and a discotheque. Choose from aerobics to deep sea fishing or glass-bottom voyages over the reef.

Opened in 1946, the grand old hotel six miles from Mombasa has been expanded since then, but the history remains intriguing. After the Nyali Bridge was built in 1931 and WWII ended, the government asked Eva and Harry Noon to develop the first coastal hotel in Kenya. After considerable struggles the task was completed and the hotel elegantly stands as a tribute to what can be done with determination.

Open archways, big windows, potted plants, marble and tile greet you in the lobby. Older cabins, rooms in the main building, and accommodations in wings spreading around the well established gardens offer a variety of options. All the choices come with every comfort, including 24-hour room service, air conditioning, bathtubs, and telephones.

Guests cool off or catch the Kenya rays at the beachside tropical Lagoon pool. Others do their laps in the more formal Olympic swimming pool. Inviting lounge chairs and delicious seafood are worth the price of admission! The hotel won the UK's 1996 Thompson Gold Award and hosted a stay by the Duke of Edinburgh, Prince Phillip.

THE TAMARIND VILLAGE, *PO Box 95805, Mombasa. Tel. 471 729, Fax 472 106. $190 per night double occupancy. All major credit cards accepted.*

The detailed and varied design brings alive the 22 individually owned condominiums. Bright pink cascading bougainvillea and flowering creepers contrast beautifully with stark white walls. Multi-level verandahs and hallways, intricate metal work, thatch and wooden beams, and Arabic flavors fill the facility with charm and mystery.

Flowing down the side of the hill along with the staggered apartments are bountiful gardens and award-winning landscapes. Walkways decorated with contoured rocks and flowers fill with fragrance. From the curved pool and adjoining Jacuzzi a harbor view opens up of drifting dhows and shimmering water. Sipping champagne at the swim-up bar adds elegance to a first class stay.

Each of the full service apartments reflects the decor of its owners who are willing to share this treat with you. Choose to enjoy a pleasant staff and/or cook, do for yourself, or experience some of both. On those days when you're on your own, dash next door to the acclaimed Tamarind restaurant. The attractive poolside Lido Bar serves light lunch and breakfast for your convenience.

REEF HOTEL, *PO Box 82234, Mombasa. Tel. 471 771, Fax 71349. $152 per night double occupancy. All major credit cards accepted.*

In this huge facility catering to up to 350 people, you can choose from a private villa with its own pool or a myriad of smaller rooms. The hotel attracts many tour groups and entertains them with videos, bingo, water sports and pool activities. Maybe a good place for kids but not somewhere you can relax in private. The hotel is a concrete jungle of interwoven walkways and monolithic buildings housing guest rooms. It is easy to loose your sense of direction as you wander in search of the elusive beach.

MOMBASA BEACH HOTEL, *African Tours & Hotels, PO Box 30471, Nairobi. Tel. 336 858 or 011 471 861, Fax 218 109. $142 per night double occupancy. All major credit cards accepted.*

All the rooms give the impression of openness with their light and bright decor. Facing the ocean the large five story structures sit on a craggy bluff surrounded by mature trees and seaside gardens. Several staircases lead down to the dazzling sand where guests stroll in search of flotsam. Some of the rooms have great views overlooking the azure waters and the beach. The simple swimming pool is complimented by the fun of a waterpark complete with slides. In addition to the usual Kenya resort holiday pastimes, there is the option of business meetings in one of three conference facilities. A shopping arcade and five reasonable restaurants cater to the many visitors passing through.

Bamburi Beach

This is the next strip of busy tourist haunts heading north. The beach resorts vary from large complexes to small hotels.

WHITESANDS, *Sarova Hotels, PO Box 30680, Nairobi. Tel. 333 233 or 011 485 926, Fax 229 388. $160 per night double occupancy. All major credit cards accepted.*

Popular with conference groups and tourists, the enormous complex can house up to 700 guests. This is somewhat of a drawback, as the buffet lines are long and crowds in public areas around three pretty pools and a fun waterslide are large. If you like to make friends with visitors from all over the world, this is the place for you.

Delightful tropical gardens, meandering waterways, creative wooden bridges, and cool lily ponds criss-cross the grounds. Moving around the far-reaching facility provides one surprise after another. Water gardens and stepping stones lead you through a world of Swahili-style archways and along white marble halls. Swaying coconut trees and white sand offer the quintessential Kenya beach. All quite magnificent!

Management is quite creative in its pursuit of guest entertainment at this, the largest hotel on the Kenya coast. Besides the watersports and disco there are Swahili lessons and coconut tree climbing! Four detached gazebos serve as dining areas and there is also a coffee shop, poolside grill, and reputable full service restaurant.

SEVERIN SEA LODGE, *PO Box 82169, Mombasa. Tel. 011 485 001. $146 per night double occupancy. Children 50%. All major credit cards accepted.*

The rooms here at Severin Sea are set back from the Indian Ocean but as far as rooms go these are better than expected. Thatched roofs and typically whitewashed walls are standard in the two or three floor bandas. Clean modern bathrooms, air conditioning, and attractive Lamu furniture make the rooms comfortable.

Two good sized pools and a creatively thatched open bar are popular with guests. As the largest hotel on Bamburi Beach it is obvious the owners have taken some care to make the place singular. The conference center has modern equipment and looks like a traditional mosque. On a nearby stream floats an enchanting dhow restaurant where Molo lamb, Kilifi oysters, or Malindi sole entice every guest.

NEPTUNE BEACH HOTEL, *PO Box 83125, Mombasa. Tel. 011 485 701. $134 per night double occupancy. Children under 12, 50%. All major credit cards accepted.*

A Disney ice cream parlor and a round swimming pool attract families with kids. For the adults there are several stores near the attractive entrance and a thatched poolside bar. A short distance from the beach, 80 rooms satisfy basic hotel requirements.

OCEAN VIEW BEACH HOTEL, *PO Box 81127, Mombasa. Tel. 011 485 601. $120 per night double occupancy.*

The scuba diving office seems to get more attention than the hotel which looks old and unkempt. Crowds of tourists lie lounge chair to lounge chair on the lawn and the adjacent beach. The unremarkable cement building does not invite you to spend your vacation here.

BAMBURI BEACH HOTEL, *PO Box 83966, Mombasa. Tel. 011 485 611. $96 per night double occupancy. All major credit cards accepted.*

The Bamburi offers adequate rooms with no notable features. As it caters to large tour groups, the small beach is often crowded. There is a nightclub and a good selection of recreational activities.

KENYA BEACH HOTEL, *PO Box 95748, Mombasa. Tel. 485 821. $85 per night double occupancy. All major credit cards accepted.*

With Swiss management, the Kenya Beach Hotel has a reputation for being clean and well kept. A good sized swimming pool and concrete patio sit near the slender strip of seashore. An attractive open dining area overlooking the Indian Ocean serves simple but tasty fare. Several two and three floor apartment buildings contain 100 comfortable guest rooms. Surrounding the moderate facility are pleasant gardens.

TRAVELLERS BEACH HOTEL, *PO Box 87649, Mombasa. Tel. 485 121, Fax 485 678. $80 per night double occupancy. All major credit cards accepted.*

Inside the reception area, the high ceiling and white walls make the hotel feel spotless. Waterways flowing through the lobby add a touch of ingenuity. Narrow blue streams wind between the buildings to four swimming pools. The grounds are spread out and surrounded by lush tropical vegetation. Thatched roofs and palm trees add a genuine feel of Kenya to the 286 room hotel.

Choose from several stores and restaurants (La Pergola, pizzeria; Sher-e-Punjab, Indian; Suli-Suli, fish grill and Vunja-Joto, ice cream parlor) in the long narrow complex which splits in two around a private seashore estate. For nighttime entertainment, try the modern underground "Show Boat" club.

As one of the newer lodges along the beach the guest accommodations are well equipped with ensuite bathrooms, air conditioning, small balconies, and TVs. The only drawback here is the size of the complex.

PLAZA HOTEL, *PO Box 88299, Mombasa. Tel. 485 321. $76 per night double occupancy.*

Not much to write home about here other than an ordinary looking swimming pool. A tall unremarkable building housing guest rooms sits on a narrow strip of land surrounded by basic gardens. If cost is your main concern, the Plaza will do.

Shanzu Beach

At Shanzu there are some major resorts along the distinctive curve of the beach. Compared to the straight beaches of Bamburi and Nyali, Shanzu has a somewhat more interesting coastline. At low tide you don't need to walk far out to find a pool to swim in.

HOTEL INTERCONTINENTAL MOMBASA, *PO Box 83492, Mombasa. Tel. 011 485 811, Fax 485 437. $195 per night double occupancy. All major credit cards accepted.*

More like a city hotel than a beach resort, it is common to see men in business suits wandering the carpeted halls or riding up to the fourth and highest floor. The "U" shaped building sits on eight acres right behind a fringe of coconut trees on the white beach.

Conference rooms, a busy casino, disco, and a variety of restaurants cater to the upper-class clientele. For something more formal try the serious looking Vasco Da Gama Restaurant with its international cuisine. More casual is the Frangipani Cafe and terrace for snacks and light meals.

Like its counterpart in Nairobi, the impressive lobby features distinguishing decor. Tiny octagonal fountains, impressive marble floors, and soaring ceilings with heavy but attractive beams draw your attention. Angled verandahs off each room look down on the gorgeous oversized swimming pool with its swim-up bar and the carefully tended gardens. Red hibiscus, pink bougainvillea, and tall coconut trees dot the landscape. Inside the 192 guest rooms there are ensuite bathrooms, air conditioning, and minibars.

OYSTER BAY BEACH HOTEL, *PO Box 10252, Bamburi, Mombasa. Tel. 485 531 or 485 061, Fax 485 963. $150 per night double occupancy. All major credit cards accepted.*

Sitting rooms with attached bedrooms are the standard accommodations in this new hotel. Lamu style furniture and air conditioning make staying in any of the 35 suites a pleasure. From each room's curving verandah, the shimmering Indian Ocean lapping against the small beach looks like a picture on a postcard. Watersports off the pier and a cool drink from the pool's swim-up bar add interest to any vacation. Striking rock gardens complete with waterfall compliment the starkly white hotel perched at the top of the cliff.

MOMBASA SERENA BEACH HOTEL, *Serena Lodges & Hotels, PO Box 90352, Mombasa. Tel. 254 11 220 732, Fax 241 11 485 453, E-mail: eln@attmail.com. $176 per night double occupancy. Children under 12, 50%. All major credit cards accepted. Courtesy shuttle bus available.*

Over the years the Serena has earned a reputation as one of the leading hotels in the world. This is certainly true when it comes to the impressive public areas, enchanting grounds, and attentive service. The overall design of the 166 room hotel is a perfect blend of flowing water and romantic Swahili architecture. Low lying two and three floor thatched structures house guests on either side of the central buildings. Everything is whitewashed and clean with no sense of overcrowding.

Intricate lattice designs, curving archways, bubbling fountains, and small ponds are surrounded by shiny white marble, meandering walkways, and tropical gardens. You can see the sparkling Indian Ocean and sandy beach from almost everywhere. If it's possible, the tiled free-form pool overshadows all of this with its cascading water and swim-up bar.

Teatime on the beach and champagne for breakfast are standard features. Specializing in barbecue and seafood, the Jahazi Grill (with the upper floor shaped like a dhow including the sails) overlooks the ocean. For cocktails and complimentary hot hors d'oeuvres, there is a cool piano bar. The decor throughout the establishment including the elegant Fountain Restaurant is filled with hanging brass lanterns, brightly colored cushions, and carved Swahili/Lamu style furniture.

Appealing archways, thatched roofs, and verandahs grace all the guest accommodations. Windows, domes, Lamu furnishings, and fancy mirrors follow through on the Arab theme. Closest to the ocean are the older lodgings depicting a Lamu village with the front rooms having a better view. Given the reputation of the facility, it is surprising these quarters are small. The newer rooms are much better with fancier bathrooms and more space.

Kikambala Beach

Eighteen miles north of Mombasa, the straight, long Kikambala Beach offers nothing spectacular for visitors; this includes the accommodations – although some might say that finally there are some places with a Kenya flavor and character.

WHISPERING PALMS HOTEL, *PO Box 5, Kikambala. Tel. 0125 32004, Telex 21018. $145 per night double occupancy. All major credit cards accepted.*

Large numbers of package tour groups pass through this shabby hotel. Dominating concrete buildings make an unattractive attempt to blend thatch with the architecture. Three small pools offer no relief from the noisy crowds.

MOMBASA SUN & SAND, *PO Box 2, Kikambala. Tel. 0125 2621 or 0125 32133, Fax 0125 2133. $124 per night double occupancy. All inclusive. All major credit cards accepted.*

Small thatched bandas with air conditioning set amid lush gardens give the overall impression of a romantic hotel. The expansive grounds are lovely but the rooms and public areas are in need of maintenance. Crowds of tours groups have left telling signs of wear which have not been addressed. There are two pools, one of which is filled with seawater.

LE SOLEIL, *PO Box 84737, Mombasa. Tel. 01251 2195, Fax 01251 2164. $90 per night double occupancy. All major credit cards accepted.*

Catering to families with children, accommodation choices vary from suites and standard rooms to large villas. There are restaurants on the grounds or you may decide to do your own cooking in the full service kitchens. With the general appearance of a townhouse or condominium compound, the rooms are set away from the beach. Already showing wear and tear, the new hotel's rooms are adequate. The swimming pool with its swim-up bar didn't make a great impression.

THOUSAND PALMS, *Club Thousand Palms Limited, PO Box 84, Kikambala via Mombasa. Tel. 0125 32165, Fax 0125 32161. $57 per night double occupancy. All major credit cards accepted.*

Thousand Palms is an inexpensive hotel catering mainly to large groups of package tours. There was nothing spectacular on offer here and the general air was one of second-rate housekeeping.

WHERE TO EAT

While traveling on your own you may not want to eat in restaurants for your entire trip, or if you are staying in one of the self-service bandas you may want to stock up on groceries. For your fruit and vegetables take a walk around the **market** next to the Hydro Hotel on Digo Street. For those items not available here, go to the well stocked **Fort Supermarket** on Nyerere Avenue. If you choose to dine at one of the restaurants in or around town, take the precaution of making reservations if possible. It just avoids potential hassles.

To give you an idea of how much it will cost per person (not including beverages or tips) to eat at any of the places listed below, I have assigned each restaurant one of the following:

- **inexpensive** = under $7
- **moderately priced** = $8 to $15
- **high priced** = over $15

Mombasa

TAMARIND RESTAURANT, *in Nyali overlooking the harbor. Tel. 474 600. Shares a driveway with the delightful Tamarind Village. Major credit cards accepted. High priced. There is also the* **Tamarind Dhow,** *Tel. 229 520 offering the same delightful cuisine while cruising. Reservations strongly suggested.*

It is hard to say which is best, the fresh seafood or the view. The Tamarind restaurants have a reputation for excellence the world over which they strive to maintain with great service and food. The Prawns Piri Piri, Chilli Crab, or Lobster Swahili are the best!

FONTANELLA RESTAURANT, *corner or Moi Avenue and Digo Road. Moderately to high priced. Major credit cards accepted.*

There is a great selection off the large menu. Choose from lobster to local-style fish and chips and anything in between. A no-pressure atmosphere at the shaded courtyard eatery allows you to relax with a cold beer and a sandwich or splurge with fresh seafood.

LE BISTRO, *Moi Avenue near the tusks. Moderately priced. International fare. Open daily for breakfast through to late dinner. Major credit cards accepted.*

A varied menu of seafood, steak, pasta, hamburgers and pizza is served by the Swiss/German owners. The restaurant and bar has a charming low key atmosphere that makes you feel at home.

HARD ROCK CAFE, *next door to Kenya Airways on Nkuruman Road; it's hard to miss. Tel. 222 221. Moderately priced. American cuisine. Major credit cards accepted.*

If you feel homesick for rock and roll and want food named after famous musicians, this is the place for you. It is clean and American-looking with somewhat loud music. It is a popular hang-out for young local business people. It has nothing to do with Kenya and apart from the waiters you won't even know that's where you are.

LA TERRAZZA, *on Mama Ngina Street near the lighthouse. Tel. 312 838. Moderately priced. Italian cuisine. Major credit cards accepted.*

The romantic setting overlooking the Indian Ocean is excelled only by the excellent Italian fare.

CAPRI RESTAURANT, *in Ambala House, Nkuruman Road. Tel. 311 156. Moderately priced. Seafood and continental dishes. It is open for lunch and dinner but closed on holidays and Sundays. Major credit cards accepted.*

This is one of the city's most frequented restaurants. It is French-run with outstanding European and South African wine selections. The cuisine is superb.

HUNTER'S SNACK BAR, *in Ambala House, Nkuruman Road next to the Capri Restaurant. Inexpensive.*

The bar serves light casual finger foods but is most visited for the really cold selection of beer in air conditioned surroundings. A good place to meet friends, take a break from the heat and relax.

ARCADE CAFE, *in Ambala House, Nkuruman Road on the ground floor. It is in the same building as the Capri Restaurant. Inexpensive. Open 8:30 am to 5:30 pm.*

A great place for lunch and lighter fare. The menu offers pizza, hot dogs, meat pies, sandwiches, ice cream, coffee, soft drinks and fruit juices. It is a friendly place with good food.

PISTACCHIO ICE CREAM & COFFEE BAR, *Located near the Hotel Splendid at Msanifu Kombo Street. Tel. 471 771. Inexpensive. Light informal cuisine. Open from 9:00 am to 10:00 pm.*

Owned by the same people who run Le Bistro, the eatery has a return customer following. A limited buffet with good food sells for about $4 while ^ la carte items (such as spaghetti) are also available. Their fruit shakes and ice cream are delicious. Choose to sit at the sidewalk cafe or inside behind large picture windows as the world goes by the heart of Mombasa. The cappucino bar and coffee selections smell wonderful. The ambiance is one of Italy in the 1950s.

CHINESE OVERSEAS RESTAURANT, *on Moi Avenue. Inexpensive. Chinese cuisine.*

Basic Chinese food served in the usual manner and in the usual quantities. The restaurant is clean and the service above average.

RECODA RESTAURANT, *in Old Town on Nyeri Street. Inexpensive. Curbside service. Local foods. Open for supper only.*

Each day there are different local coastal dishes available. Friendly waiters are happy to show and explain what is in the offing. Generally look for delicious beans in coconut, grilled fish and meat, salad, and chapatis.

SWAHILI CURRY BOWL, *off Moi Avenue on Tangana Road. Inexpensive. Closed on Sunday.*

This is the number one spot for ice cream and delicious local coffee. Other Swahili style dishes all appetizingly prepared in coconut milk will keep you coming back for more.

NEW CHETNA RESTAURANT, *under the Cosy Guest House on Haile Selassie Road. Inexpensive. Southern Indian vegetarian food.*

There is outstanding value for a meal here at New Chetna. Masala dosa and idli are two items from their varied vegetarian menu.

South of Mombasa

Most of the resorts, hotels, and lodges south of Mombasa are within a relatively short distance to some sort of food shopping facilities just off the main road. The prices are a little higher but local items are still cheaper than those at home. Fruit and vegetables are always extremely fresh as they are locally grown in Kenya.

Shopping in the markets and supermarkets for light lunch and breakfast foods can save you a tidy sum of money. It is always fun to see how their stores compare with ours. There are however, many delightful places to eat out, including all the resort hotels.

ALI BARBOUR'S, *on the main road near Diani Beach. Tel. 2033. High priced. Seafood. Major credit cards accepted. Located between Trade Winds Hotel and Diani Sea Lodge.*

There is a beach bar and also a cave-style restaurant. The food has an up and coming reputation for excellence.

VULCANO RESTAURANT DA LINA, *at the southern end of Diani Beach off the paved road. Tel. 2004. Major credit cards accepted. Open from 7:00 pm until. Moderately priced. Italian cuisine. Reservations encouraged.*

There is an outstanding selection of both Italian and seafood cuisine with lobster, crab, calamari, and fish as the specialties.

HHNCHEN GRILL & NIGHTCLUB, *along the paved road with a group of restaurants at Diani Beach. Major credit cards accepted. Moderately priced. German cuisine.*

If you are interested in a quiet evening, this may not be the place for you. The predominantly German clientele can get rowdy as they sing along with the German songs emanating from strategically placed speakers.

The atmosphere feels happy and cheerful. The cuisine is authentically German. The spatzen, German egg dumplings, and strudel offer a deliciously delicate flavor.

RESTAURANT MAHARANI, *along the paved road with a group of restaurants across from Ali Barbour at Diani Beach. Major credit cards accepted. Moderately priced. Indian food.*

Not overly fancy, Maharani's is a good place for a genuine Indian meal. With plenty of fresh seafood available along the beach, the cook prepares a great seafood curry Indian style.

TEMURA'S RESTAURANT, *along the paved road with a group of restaurants across from Ali Barbour at Diani Beach. Major credit cards accepted. Moderately priced. Indian cuisine.*

Clean and comfortable, Temura's restaurant is a popular place for an evening meal. If you are not familiar with Indian food and prefer your meals mild, start off with something not too spicy. The Kenya lamb and rice dishes or prawns are excellent.

NOMAD'S, *near Diani Beach. Nomad, PO Box 1, Ukunda, Mombasa. Tel. 0127 2155, Fax 0127 2391. Moderately priced. Seafood.*

Started as a restaurant 15 years ago, the food and service still live up to the outstanding reputation. The fact that local Kenyans flock here to eat is a true test of constant quality. Even if you don't stay here it is worth visiting one of the two restaurants for a meal. See *Where To Stay* above for more details.

GALAXY CHINESE RESTAURANT, *along the paved road within a group of restaurants at Diani Beach. Major credit cards accepted. Moderately priced. Chinese cuisine.*

For those who are not too keen on trying anything unfamiliar, Galaxy serves the usual Chinese fare such as shrimp fried rice. The sweet Kenya vegetables used in the stir-fry retain their fresh flavor and crisp texture.

WASINI ISLAND RESTAURANT, *Located on Wasini Island. Moderately priced. Seafood. Major credit cards accepted.*

From the shore at Shimoni you can see the small island of Wasini, which is home to this attractive eatery. The restaurant has an excellent reputation for the freshest seafood around.

SEEING THE SIGHTS
Fort Jesus National Park

A 17th century Portuguese fort on the Indian Ocean in Mombasa Old Town is the biggest attraction in the city. The large fortification which dominates the harbor entrance is open from 8:30 am to 6:00 pm each day. It costs $2.50 for adults and $1.50 for children under 16 to get in, plus a "tip" for the excellent guides who speak several languages. For brochures and information write to: *Curator, Fort Jesus Museum, PO Box 82412, Mombasa.* There is a historical museum on the site filled with ancient ceramics and artifacts from around the area. In the gift shop there are souvenirs and books for sale.

The displays give a good historical account of the inhabitants' lifestyles during the period. A fascinating cemetery, living quarters and barracks for 100 people, and completely self-sufficient water supply were the design of Italian architect Joao Batista Cairato. Shaped like a human body, the clever configuration made it practically impossible for invaders to conquer. The fort's long bloody history of murder, siege, starvation, shelling and treachery will captivate you for a couple of hours.

Old Town

If you are on your own, I suggest purchasing *The Old Town Mombassa: A Historical Guide*, before you set off. A maze of narrow streets can be confusing if you don't know where you are going. The guidebook shows points of interest and leads you around safely. In Government Square, there is a sign saying photography of the old harbor is prohibited. I can't imagine why, but take note anyway.

The best times to venture forth are early morning or late afternoon when local people are milling about in the cooler temperatures. Old government offices, banks, and businesses have long since moved but their legacy remains. While the buildings are very often not more than 100 years old, the architecture is different than what we are used to. Studded

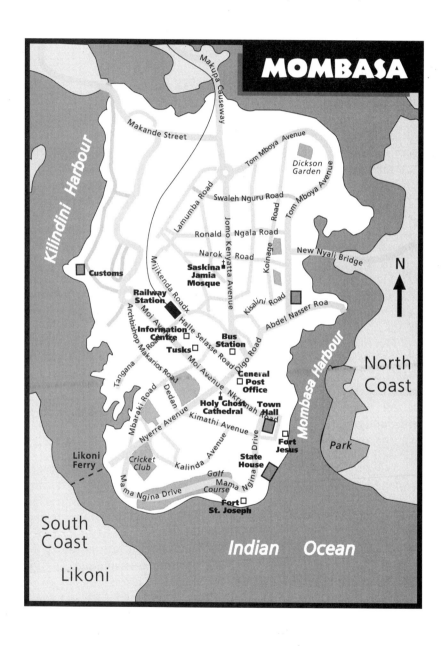

MOMBASA

Makupa Causeway

Makande Street

Tom Mboya Avenue

Dickson Garden

Kilindini Harbour

Swaleh Nguru Road

Lamumba Road

Tom Mboya Avenue

Jomo Kenyatta Avenue

Ronald Ngala Road

Narok Road

Koinage Road

New Nyali Bridge

N

Customs

Saskina Jamia Mosque

Mijikenda Road

Kisalini Road

Railway Station

Abdel Nasser Roa

Moi Avenue

Halle Selasse Road

Information Centre

Bus Station

Archbishop Makarios Road

Digo Road

Tusks

Moi Avenue

Nkrumah Road

General Post Office

Tangana

Mbaraki Road

Dedan

Nyerere Avenue

Holy Ghost Cathedral

Town Hall

North Coast

Mombasa Harbour

Kimathi Avenue

Fort Jesus

Park

Likoni Ferry

Cricket Club

Kalinda Avenue

State House

Mama Ngina Drive

Golf Course

Mama Ngina Drive

Fort St. Joseph

South Coast

Likoni

Indian Ocean

carved doors represent the wealth of the inhabitants. Narrow cobblestone avenues are a contrast of cars and herds of sheep. For the seclusion of Swahili women there are fancy lattice and ornamental enclosures. A blend of Swahili, Indian, and colonial style shows itself in wide shade verandahs, shuttered windows, ornate balconies, and adorned signs.

NIGHTLIFE & ENTERTAINMENT

Nightclubs & Bars

The **Florida**, *Mama Ngina Drive*, is probably the best place in town for a little nightlife. The owners also lay claim to the Florida clubs in Nairobi. Here in Mombasa, the club sits right on the ocean and has its own swimming pool. There is a lively dance floor and three open-air bars. The price of admission is $2.20 for men and $1.10 for ladies.

Casinos

In Nyali (north of Mombasa) and Diani (south of Mombasa) the international casinos, entice visitors to come and play the night away with roulette, blackjack, and slot machines. **Nyali International Casino**, *Tel. 471 551*, is located a short drive across the Nyali Creek Bridge from Mombasa in the complex around Nyali Beach Hotel. **Diani International Casino**, along with a popular disco, is at the Diani Reef Grand Hotel, *Tel. 227 571*.

The **Joker's Bar** at Nyali has a reputation for tasty late night snacks and cocktails.

Diani Beach

All the nightclubs in this section are located along the same general stretch of paved road that runs along the coast and through Diani right near the town of Ukunda. On the main Mombasa to Tanzania highway at the town of Ukunda there is the turning point for Diani Beach. The paved road runs less than two miles to a T-junction which connects to the beach road. This little two lane road runs several miles both north and south along the shore. Within these few miles is everything Diani has to offer.

The best of the few selections for dancing and nightlife other than at the large beach resorts is **Shakatak Disco**, just about next door to the **Hhnchen Grill & Nightclub**, which is situated at the T-junction along the main highway. Admission is free but the drinks are expensive. Getting into the resort nightclubs can prove to be a hassle if you are not a guest. **Bush Baby Nightclub** is opposite the Two Fishes Hotel; **African Papaya Nightclub & Restaurant** is located at the northern end of the paved road near the Diani Reef Grand Hotel and north of Ukunda.

SPORTS & RECREATION

Swimming

The water inside the coastal reef is usually calm and safe for swimming. The temperature ranges between 27-35 degrees centigrade. Strong currents do exist however, particularly outside the coral ridge where there may be sharks, man-o-war, and other potentially harmful creatures.

In case the water is too cold or has receded beyond the reef leaving nowhere to swim, most hotels and resorts have their own pools with the added advantage of beach chairs, bar service, and shady coconut trees.

Camel Rides

It is becoming more and more popular for tourists to ride one-humped camels along the beach. You will see one or two grown camels and perhaps even a baby tagging along under the guidance of their owner. Do not avail yourself of their services if the camels look unhealthy and tell the owners so. It is also wise to ask how much and for how long before you get on.

Dhow Rides & Harbor Cruises

Booking a cruise is a simple matter of making a reservation through your travel agent or one of the tourist hotels. You may make reservations directly with **Tamarind Dhow Safaris**, *Tel. 20990 or 315 569*, but allow a few days as they can be busy. The price varies from $51 for the 6:00 pm evening dinner cruise and $43 for the 10:30 am luncheon departure. For your fare you will get a four hour harbor cruise in a luxury dhow, a marvelous seafood or steak meal cooked on board, live band entertainment and round trip transportation. Alcohol is served from their well stocked bar.

Jahazi Marine Limited, *Tel. 472 213 or 471 895*, has another slightly different offer for $65 anytime Monday through Thursday. Included is transportation, a sunset cruise with cocktails as you sail by Mombasa Fort and Old Town, a barbecue at Bamburi Nature Trail, a safari through the park by flashlight and a stop at the Bora Bora Nightclub and casino. It seems expensive, but if you like this sort of thing it is probably good value for your dollar.

A popular excursion from Shimoni is a day-long dhow trip to the **Island of Wasini** to see the local Swahili village, Muslim ruins, coral gardens, and a gourmet seafood feast at the Wasini restaurant. Book through **Pilli Pipa Safaris**, *PO Box 84045, Mombasa; Fax 0127 2401*.

Fishing

Many of the hotels and resorts cater to avid fishermen, as Kenya's coast produces some of the world's best fishing. Marlin and sailfish, two popular big game fish, are often found near Shimoni in the Pemba Channel. During the fishing season, the waters off Shimoni can get particularly busy with worldwide participants in the deep sea fishing events. It doesn't matter if you are a beginner or a professional, there is room for you.

SHOPPING

In Mombasa there are all the same items that you'll find in Nairobi along with Arabic coffee sets, Lamu chests, and Ethiopian silver. Many of the elegant old residences on **Mbarak Hinawy Road** have banded with the souvenir traders to offer their wares. Around Fort Jesus in the Old Town there are many dark mysterious stores. Look for these along **Ndia Kuu** in addition to Mbarak Hinway Road.

For row upon row of kiosks, stands, shops, and galleries, work your way down **Nyerere Street** and **Moi Avenue**. Wood carvings, soapstone, baskets, drums, paintings and life-like figurines are what you'll mainly see. For beautiful *makonde* carvings (usually depicting groups of people sometimes carved in abstract forms), jewelry, and antiques try **Labeka**, *Tel. 312 232*, on Moi Avenue. You can rest assured the quality of the goods sold here will be above average.

Along **Biashara Street** is the main place to shop for anything made of cloth. A Swahili proverb is usually woven in to the border around the material. Colorful *kangas* or *kikois* are worn by most Kenyan women, sometimes under their austere black robes.

For an entertaining time try the **Jisaidie Self-Help Group**, *Tel. 432 635*, at the **New Magongo Market** just west of Mombasa. Watch the people work their crafts and buy anything from drums to beaded jewels.

If you are approached by locals on the streets, as I'm sure you will be, do not buy any colorful, shapely coral or sea shells. The temptation to purchase a delicate coral souvenir will be hard to resists but let your conscience prevail. It is more than likely they were stolen from one of the marine parks where such things are heavily protected.

Up and down the beaches of Kenya you will find it hard not to meet beach boys and see small stands selling wares of all kinds. Jewelry, wood carvings, colorful kangas, and shells are the usual merchandise. Many of the hotels employ security guards to keep these vendors away from their guests as they can be annoyingly persistent.

EXCURSIONS & DAY TRIPS

Bamburi Quarry Nature Trail

Open from 2:00 pm to 5:30 pm daily, the **Bamburi Quarry Nature Trail**, *Tel. 011 485 729*, includes a crocodile farm, fish farm, reptile pit and plant nursery. Feeding time is at 4:00 pm. The nature trail is just off the main road from Mombasa to Malindi with a signpost pointing the way.

The land was once decimated by cement production activities which ended in 1971. A lot of work was done on the reclaimed property including reforestation. The objective was not only to restore the landscape but to create a small scale replica of the Kenya bush. Once the plants and forests were established, bush pigs, monkeys, birds, oryx, eland, buffalo, hippo and warthog were introduced. The brainchild of agronomist Rene Haller, it is at once a wildlife sanctuary, award winning conservation center, and a working organic farm producing fish, crocodiles, coconuts, and timber.

Mamba Crocodile Village

Crocodile souvenirs and thousands of crocodiles attract hordes of tourists to **Mamba Village**, *Tel. 011 472 709.* Located north of Mombasa on the mainland near Nyali Golf Club, there are streams, waterfalls, and wooden bridges to make the crocodile farm seem more humane. The owners have the best of both worlds, by charging admission and also selling skins to make handbags and shoes. There are a few huge crocs lying around in the sun and lots of babies under five. If you have seen one of these places you've seen them all, but it is fascinating to watch these scary looking reptiles.

Jumba La Mtwana National Monument

This fascinating monument is actually excavated ruins of a 14th century Swahili settlement and slave trading center. The name means "house of slaves." It is located a short distance north along the coast just after crossing the Mtwapa Creek bridge near Kibambala village. Look for the signpost. Grassy slopes down to the ocean and huge old baobab trees add interest to the site. The most impressive remains are those of "the mosque by the sea" – a large worship center with many tombs and wall scripts from the Koran.

Mombasa Marine National Park & Reserve

Located just under five miles from Mombasa, the park within the reserve is opposite the Hotel Intercontinental. This park was established in 1986 for the preservation of the extensive coral reefs and the exquisite fish living there. Fishing is permitted only with a license.

Shimba Hills National Reserve

The closest wildlife refuge to the coast now sports its own tree-hotel. In the 743 square mile park the main game attraction is the unique sable antelope. Sadly it is often killed by poachers for meat. Other wildlife such as warthog, waterbuck, elephant, and roan antelope can be seen. At the Shimba Hills Lodge there is a baited waterhole where you may see leopard. It is possible to arrange day trips into the forest to look for birds, wildlife, and enjoy the lush vegetation. A visit to the 68-foot high **Sheldrick's Falls** also makes for a pleasant outing.

CLIFFS & SUNSETS

All along the Kenya coast there are honeycombed cliffs filled with caves used by slave traders to hide their captives and wait for their ships to arrive. In many of these creepy places the locals believe the spirits of the prisoners remain to shake their chains and haunt the beaches looking for peace or perhaps revenge. The spirits are kept company by baboons or other wildlife who make the caverns home. There is no better vantage point than these sharp coral bluffs to see the spectacular sunsets and sunrises over the Indian Ocean. Because of the proximity to the equator, these dramatic shows only last a few minutes; you must be quick to catch them.

The ancient rainforest, grass plains, and lowland bush of the reserve are an easily accessible ten miles inland. To get there follow the A14 road about half-way between Diani/Ukunda and Mombasa. Turn towards the town of Kwale on the C106 Ngombene-Lunga Lunga Road. The main entrance to the reserve is two miles past Kwale. There is also a small airfield catering to visitors.

Because of the monsoon winds blowing off the Indian Ocean over the eastern hills, there are surprisingly cool and refreshing temperatures in Shimba Reserve. Its maximum elevation is a mere 1,463 feet. When the coast gets too hot and sticky, many people escape the sun's rays in the cloud covered hills.

Kisite Marine National Park & Mpunguti Marine National Preserve

Located close to the Tanzania border, the reserve and the park within have some of the best coral reefs just off Kisite for snorkelers and divers. As an added bonus you might get lucky and see roseate and sooty terns using three of the islands as breeding grounds.

You can either use your own accouterment or rent whatever you need. There are several outfitters with boats ready to help for a price. **Aqua-Ventures Limited**, *at the Indian Ocean Beach Club, Tel. 0127 3730 ext. 179*, will rent all necessary equipment, give you a guide, and even include a five-course lunch! **Kisite Dhow Tours**, *at Jadini Beach Hotel, Tel. 2331,* offers a seafood lunch, guided tour of Wasini Village, morning dhow tour, and snorkeling at the marine park for $65.

If you would rather make your own arrangements check with the park headquarters at Shimoni. To get into the park costs $4. To hire a local boat for the crossing it's $4.90 per person for under 12 people. For twelve or more people it is $1.90 per person. The boats do not sail if the weather is bad and the water rough.

Wasini Island

Wasini Island is easily visible from the shore at the Shimoni Peninsula at the southernmost coastal point but is not easily accessible. There are no roads, no cars, and no running water. Electricity comes from generators.

Wasini Island is untouched by the 20th century. Giant old baobab trees stand amid pristine forests. Men prepare for the next fishing expedition by mending nets and building fish traps; women weave mats. Muslim ruins tell of days past. It is fascinating to wander through strangely shaped ancient coral gardens providing, of course, the ocean isn't flooding them.

PRACTICAL INFORMATION

Automobile Association of Kenya

The AAA, *Tel. 26778*, will be able to help you if you are in need of information on specific road conditions. They have some road maps available if that's what you need. The office is just north of the tourist office on the road connecting Aga Khan Road with the railway station.

They may come and help you if you get into car trouble on the road, but I wouldn't necessary count on it. The phones may not be working and/or their office may not always be open. If you are within the city it will be easier to get help, but if you are out in the country there may be no way of communicating with them. They are best used for road information and maps.

Banks & Money

There is an **American Express** office at **Express Kenya**, *Tel. 312 461*, *PO Box 90631*, on Nkuruman Road.

On Moi Avenue there is a popular **Barclays Bank** where you can easily change your money. Their hours are 9:00 m to 3:00 pm Monday through Friday. On the last and first Saturday of each month they open from 9:00 am to 11:00 am. You will probably get a better exchange rate here but it is usually no problem to change money at the stores and beach hotels.

Embassy

The **US Embassy**, *Tel. 315 101*, in Mombasa is located at Palli House on Nyeri Road.

Hospitals

• **Coast General Hospital**, *Tel. 314 201, PO Box 90231 Mombasa*
• **H.H. Aga Khan Hospital**, *Tel. 312 953 PO Box 83013, Mombasa*
• **Pandya Memorial Hospital**, *Tel. 314 140 PO Box 90434, Mombasa*

Post Office

The main post office is on Digo Road. Hours are 8:00 am to 4:30 pm Monday through Friday and 8:00 am to noon on Saturday.

Telephones & Fax

The city code for Mombasa is **011**. To send a fax or use the telephone, you must use the 011 prefix. **Mombasa International Call Center**, *Tel. 11 475 167*, offers fax and phone services. Located at the Planet Shopping Center on Bamburi Road, the hours are 9:00 am to 7:00 pm Monday through Saturday.

Tides

Along the coast there are significant tidal variations. When the tide comes in at some resorts, the ocean laps at the very edge of the buildings or may leave only a narrow strip of sand. Check with your hotel so you don't get stranded on rocky outcrops or lose your belongings to the water.

Tourist Information

You can't miss the regional **tourist office**, *Tel. 311 231*, located just past the famous tusks on Moi Avenue. Its hours are 8:00 am to noon and 2:00 pm to 4:30 pm Monday through Friday. On Saturdays it is open from 8:00 am to noon. It has tour guide books of Fort Jesus, Old Town Mombasa, and (adequate) maps for sale.

KILIFI

The waters of Kilifi Creek separate Mombasa and Malindi to the north. This is the first major break in the coastline between the two towns. Up until 1991 there was only a car ferry crossing the expanse. Today there is a bridge.

For years now the farsighted colonial Kenyans and astute world travelers have been buying all the property along the water. Beautiful villas and creative homes stretch along the waterway and the ocean. The beautiful beaches along the creek banks have the added bonus of being

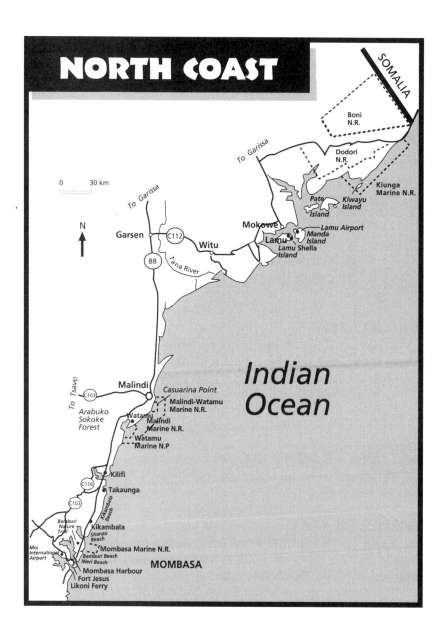

seaweed free. Because they are surrounded by private property, the beaches are relatively inaccessible. The best way to reach them is to take a walk at low tide from the ferry landing.

Kilifi is a popular boating and sailing center to which tourists remain largely unexposed. If you care to find those who boat here, try having an evening cocktail at the Seahorse Inn just off the main road to the left on the northern bank.

ARRIVALS & DEPARTURES

By Bus

The buses passing through Kilifi are usually heading to Malindi and/ or Mombasa. When they stop to pick up or drop off passengers in Kilfi there is rarely any heavy movement either way. The buses tend to stay full so getting on can sometimes be difficult. You are better off hiring a car or cab or risking a ride on the matatus.

By Car

The B8 highway, also known as the Mombasa to Malindi road, follows along the coast passing through all the major towns and villages. Kilifi is no exception.

ORIENTATION

Kilifi is actually divided in two parts. On the Mombasa side is the small village of **Mnarani**, where there is not much to hold your interest. Once you cross the creek to the northern bank you'll find **Kilifi Town**.

North of town is Barclays Bank and south of town is the post office and further still the Kilifi Members Club. The furthest building west is the Shahani Tamu Restaurant. To the east is the Kilifi Cafeteria.

GETTING AROUND TOWN

The easiest way to get about is on foot. It only takes a few minutes to walk around the town.

WHERE TO STAY

TAKAUNGU HOUSE, *Wilderness Trails Limited/ Bush Homes Africa Safaris, Tel. US 404 888 0909, e mail bushhomes@africaonline.co.ke, www.bushhomes.com, PO Box 56923, Nairobi. Tel. 506 139, Fax 502 739. $280 per night double occupancy. All inclusive. Closed for May and the first half of June. All major credit cards accepted.*

The guest house near the ocean was once an old slave trader's house and now wraps around a small swimming pool. Three guest bedrooms with adjoining bathrooms, living room, and dining room feel homey and familiar. Shuttered windows, massive support beams, and whitewashed walls add historic interest. In 1844, the *HMS Stork* sailed by the pristine sandy bay with its craggy rocks and recorded the structure on a map. Takaungu town, the homestay's namesake, is allegedly the oldest slave port in Kenya.

Lush gardens, ancient ruins, and massive baobab trees surround the secluded estate where Phillip and Charlie Mason, your Kenya-born hosts, have lived for 20 years. Their new Arab-style house nearby allows them to make your stay with the family personal and yet completely private. Marvelous dishes of fresh crabs, oysters, prawns, and fish make their way to your table from the local fishermen's daily catch.

As owners of the Swynford boatyard they offer much in the way of water activities. Big game fishing, water skiing, scuba diving, snorkeling and picnics up Kilifi creek are just few of the many choices.

MIRELLA RICARDI'S KILIFI HOME, *Safcon Travel Services, PO Box 59224, Nairobi. Tel. 503 265, Fax 506 824. $150 per night double occupancy. All major credit cards accepted.*

A romantic and secluded setting on the banks of Kilifi Creek is just an introduction to a unique vacation spot. Tall old baobab trees, flowing shrubbery, stairs leading to the private beach, friendly dogs and rubber dinghies add to the festive formula.

Mirella, an author, photographer, and artistic individual shows her affinity for creativity throughout the two guest houses and in her delicious cuisine. In the older of the two homes the decor is new. An open dining and living room offers delightful vistas of blue water and abundant trees.

The newer residence is full of creativity. Intricate metal grillwork in place of windows, carved poles, sweeping archways, and majestic thatched ceilings intrigue recent arrivals. A ladder leads to a cozy bed loft while downstairs are two more bedrooms. Unfortunately, there is only one full bathroom and the mosquitoes can be troublesome.

KILDINI, *Kesana, PO Box 39672, Nairobi. Tel. 749 062, Fax 741 636. $150 per night double occupancy. All major credit cards accepted.*

Not far from the bridge over Kilifi Creek is a home owned by Michael and Jean Skinner. It can be rented with or without them as hosts and with a full domestic staff. The exotic looking house has three bedrooms making it a homey place for a group of traveling companions or a family. The Skinners also own Juani Farm in Molo so they are well versed in the art of hosting and guiding visitors around Kenya.

Down a short flight of stairs is a secluded and pristine beach where swimming in the Indian Ocean is refreshing. Around the pool and house there are beds filled with colorful flowers and exotic tropical trees.

KILIFI BAY RESORT HOTEL & VILLAGE, *DEINSA S.A., PO Box 3092, CH 6901 Lugano or PO Box 156, Kilifi. Tel. 0125 2511, Fax 1252 225 or 0041-091-228 490. $90 per night double occupancy. All major credit cards accepted.*

Charming and roomy cabins typify the best of the Kenya coast with tall thatched roofs and Lamu furniture. Italian owned, the hotel can easily accommodate 85 visitors. Inside the cottages, three rooms decorated with imagination and color appear fascinatingly different and more than comfortable. From the ample patio, tropical vegetation fills your senses with more dramatic color and delight.

Coconut trees sway between the main buildings built back from the beach and the popular pool. The sandy seashore is reached down hewn stone stairs. Stretched out under the thatch or in the warm sunshine all your cares will evaporate – the test of a true vacation.

BAOBAB LODGE, *Baobab Lodge, PO Box 40683, Nairobi. Tel. 222 229, Fax 332 170. $78 per night double occupancy. All major credit cards accepted.*

To get to the coral sand beach from the top of the craggy cliff where the lodge sits you must first take a walk past captivating baobab trees and down a rocky stairway. Covered with pools, crabs, and starfish, the fascinating reef is easily accessible on foot during low tides. The atmosphere at the hotel is laid-back and casual but the setting and accommodations are special. Scattered around the property under tall shade trees are 26 attractive guest cottages with oversized patios. From most of the rooms there is no ocean view; instead they are made distinctive with Masai sketches and African decor.

Small and personal at the top of this cliff in Kilifi, the main lodge has a wonderful swim-up bar at the pool and a panoramic scene of the ocean. The dining room is open on the sides with a tall thatched roof to keep out the hot sun. For your pleasure there are secluded spots in the shade perfect for reading or watching the birds, scuba diving, and glass-bottom boat tours.

SEAHORSE INN, *off the B8 Highway. Tel. 011 485 520 or 0125 22813. $70 per night double occupancy. All inclusive. All major credit cards accepted.*

The picturesque bandas sit amid a copse of coconut trees right on the banks of Kilifi Creek. The water at this point is a couple of miles wide. The attractive mid-range inn is about a mile off to the left of the Mombasa to Malindi road on the northern side of the creek.

Moderate & Budget

There are other acceptable accommodations in the mid-price range near town. Pretty garden settings and clean rooms can be found at these hotels. On the Mombasa side of the creek is the **MNARANI CLUB**, *Tel. 011 485 520,* catering to large package tours from Europe. Close by on the main road is the fairly small **DHOWS INN**, *Tel. 0125 22028*. The simple rooms (with bathrooms and mosquito nets) face the gardens and cost $15. On the northern side of the creek and a ten minute walk from town look for the **MKWAJUNI MOTEL**, *Tel. 0125 22472*. With breakfast, the tariff is $16. The spotless rooms are small but have a verandah with a table and chairs.

In Kilifi Town on the low rent scale there are several places where you can get a room for under $6. If you stay at any of these places, you may have to share a bathroom. **TUSHAURINE BOARDING & LODGING**, *Tel. 0125 22486*, is about the best, followed by **TOP LIFE BOARDING & LODGING**, **KILIFI HOTEL**, **HOTEL 36**, and the **NEW MWANGEA LODGE**.

WHERE TO EAT

The best place in town for a consistently delicious meal is the **SAHANI TAMU RESTAURANT**, *located across from the Mnarani Club*. The restaurant is open daily from 11:00 am to 2:00 pm and 6:00 pm to 10:00 pm except Tuesday. The fare is very good Italian or fresh seafood and will set you back no more than $15 at the top end of the menu. The **MNARANI CLUB** and the **SEAHORSE HOTEL** offer excellent value with their lunch buffets or their ^ la carte dinner menu under $6.

For under $3 try typical Kenyan food at the **Kilifi Hotel** near the bus station. The **KILIFI CAFETERIA**, particularly at lunch time, keeps guests happy for under $5. I suggest however, that you stay away from the **DHOWS INN** where the food can either be very good or very bad. It just isn't worth the risk. The limited menu offers seafood and meats for $3 and the service is usually slow.

NIGHTLIFE & ENTERTAINMENT

A nightly floor show at the **Mnarani Club** usually includes some form of tribal dancing followed by a live African band. There is a $4 charge to get in. At the **Dhows Inn** the bar is usually vivacious and the drinks are properly cold. There are other bars in Mnarani but the drinks aren't cold and they may be a little rough around the edges.

SPORTS & RECREATION

Snorkeling & Diving

All along the coast are marine reserves where snorkeling and diving are permitted. The shapes, colors, and sizes of the fish and coral will amaze you!

Windsurfing

From any of the shores you can often see white foaming breakers beyond the reef. The cool monsoon trade winds blowing inland make ideal conditions popular with windsurfers. Many of the resorts offer lessons and equipment for those willing to take a few falls in the refreshing Indian Ocean. At the **Mnarani Club**, *Tel. 011 485 520*, it is possible to rent windsurfers for $3.90 per hour for non-guests.

BEACH SAFETY

Along many of Kenya's beaches it has become unsafe to venture out at night alone for fear of muggers. During the day, be sure and leave all jewelry and valuables in your hotel safe, unless told by management it is okay to do otherwise. With the advent of tourism, the downside comes in the form of ruffians out to make a quick dishonest buck!

SHOPPING

In the town of Kilifi there is a small but interesting book store, an open air market, and an enclosed fruit and vegetable market. As it only takes a few minutes to get around on foot, take the time to look about.

On the south shore of Kilifi Creek, in the village of **Mnarani**, look for the craft stores. German and Swiss guests staying at the Mnarani Club seem to make up the bulk of their customers. They have a selection of your typical Kenyan souvenirs for sale.

EXCURSIONS & DAY TRIPS

Takaungu Town

Supposedly the oldest slave port on the Kenya coast, **Takaungu** is worth a visit if you have the time. The villagers are very superstitious and don't venture out to the beach at night. If you can get someone to translate for you, there are wonderful stories of mysterious events going back to the time of slavery. You will hardly, if ever, meet another tourist here.

Mnarani Ruins

A short distance outside the town of Kilifi on the Mombasa side of Kilifi Creek are the well preserved **Mnarani Ruins**. They sit at the top of a cliff overlooking Kilifi Creek and the old ferry landing. Fortunately they have not found their way into the mainstream of tourism, but you still have to pay $3.90 to get in if there is anyone there to collect.

The ruins are not as large as those at Gedi but they are just as impressive. The city was once part of a string of Swahili towns dotting the

East African coast. Excavations done in 1954 show the site was occupied from the 14th to the 17th century. Remains indicate the town was destroyed by pillaging Galla tribes.

Remnants of the town wall with its busy gate and an amazingly deep well offer a look into the past. There is a Great Mosque with its delicately carved inscription around a niche (*mihrab*) pointing the way to Mecca, a smaller mosque, and various tombs. One of the burial chambers is actually a pillar tomb.

PRACTICAL INFORMATION

Banks

Both **Barclays Bank** and **Kenya Commercial Bank** in Kilifi are open from 8:30 am to 1:00 pm Monday through Friday and 8:30 am to 11:00 am on Saturday.

Post Office

The small post office does a steady business. Opening hours are 8:00 am to 4:30 pm Monday through Friday and 8:00 am to noon on Saturday.

WATAMU

This major package tour destination is most popular for the snorkeling at **Watamu Marine National Park** (part of the Malindi/Watamu Biosphere Reserve), easily accessible by boat or a lively swim when the tide is out. At this time particularly, the ocean pools are filled with bright fish, sinister sea urchins, and vivid starfish.

Seaweed tends to be heavy along the Watamu beaches and can be bothersome. Underwater, various beautiful shades of leafy green and yellow seaweed fronds gracefully dance to the rhythm of the tides. Filtered sunlight glistens off each visible bough turning the ocean floor into a magical place.

The craggy shore is broken up into three separate coves. Coral outcrops separate the sandy bays and form shallow saltwater pools filled with shells and darting fish. If you feel adventurous, wear protective shoes at low tide and walk out to any of the oddly shaped islands left jutting from the ocean.

The northernmost cove and part of the headland is covered by the rambling Watamu Beach Hotel. Behind it is the actual town of Watamu. The central cove is filled with many resorts but they are not as extensive as those in the southern cove. The most southerly cove is fronted entirely by hotels and a few private homes.

ARRIVALS & DEPARTURES

You will be arriving and departing from **Malindi Town**; this is the same Arrivals & Departures information you'll find under the Malindi Town section below.

By Air

Just eight miles from the Gedi turn-off on the Mombasa to Malindi road is **Malindi Airport**. It is smaller than Moi International in Mombasa but does a steady stream of business bringing tourists in and out of the area.

To find the best deal try one of the main private air carriers, which include:

• **Eagle Aviation Limited**, *Tel. 0123 21258*
• **Skyways Airlines**, *Tel. 0123 20951*
• **Prestige Air Services**, *Tel. 0123 20860*

These carriers make return trips to Malindi from Mombasa costing $29 round trip. The flights take 30 minutes and depart at 8:30 am and 2:15 pm. The offices for these airlines are on the Lamu road in Malindi.

Air Kenya Aviation, *Mombasa, Tel. 011 433 982*, has one flight a day four times a week for $56. **Kenya Airways**, *Malindi, Tel. 0123 20237*, has two flights a day from Nairobi to Mombasa via Malindi.

There is a charge of $1.50 for departure tax. Check-in time is 30 minutes before departure. Be sure and reconfirm. A maximum weight limit of 22 pounds is customary. Excess baggage charges are 20¢ per pound but this is not strictly enforced.

By Bus

From Mombasa to Malindi and back there are several buses departing daily. The three companies operating the run are **Malindi Bus Service**, **Tana River Bus Service**, and **Garissa Express**. They all have offices in Malindi, Mombasa, and Lamu. The cost is $1.50 per person.

Buses from Malindi at the mainland across from Lamu leave at 7:00 am and 7:30 am. The fare for the five hour trip is $4.50. Advance reservations are required.

By Shared Taxi

From Malindi to Mombasa you can share a seven-seater taxi for $3 per person. They leave early in the morning once they are full from the bus station in town.

ORIENTATION

Watamu was once a small sleepy fishing village around which bars, souvenir stores, hotels, and restaurants have emerged. Fortunately and amazingly, the village has retained most of its original atmosphere but now caters almost exclusively to tourists. There are still makuti-roofed cottages, sandy lanes, and tall coconut trees preserving the old ways. It does seem bizarre to see the invasion of tourists in beach attire wandering down the dusty streets.

GETTING AROUND TOWN

The quickest way to get around the village of Watamu is on foot. To venture to other resorts and beaches, try renting a bicycle. In town, next door to the Nyambene Lodge, there's a rental facility where you can get bikes for 50¢ per hour or $2 per day.

WHERE TO STAY

HEMINGWAYS, *PO Box 267, Watamu. Tel. 326 624, Fax 0122 32256. $208 per night double occupancy. Children's facilities available. All major credit cards accepted.*

Dining, drinking, and fishing, not necessarily in that order, seem to be the main attractions at this casual but classy privately owned hotel. Raised up and built over what was once Seafarers hotel, Hemingways was completed in 1988 and is designed to look out over the ocean. Attractive and unusual whitewashed walls contrast with high typical thatched roofs stretching along the seafront.

Two wings can house up to 175 guests. Rooms in the older wing are basic, clean, and small, but have a better view of the water through barred and curtained windows. The newer and larger two and three story wing is much nicer but angles back from the beach. Air-conditioning, safes, showers, mosquito nets and balconies are pretty standard.

Spreading stone patios and two lovely swimming pools are surrounded by tall coconut trees. Out in the ocean unusual rock formations jut out of the bay. Hemingways has a reputation for outstanding and unusual cuisine from set or a la carte menus. Sunday buffets are free to guests. Fresh seafood and delicacies such as tropical fruit and crepes are readily available.

Honeymooners favor Hemingways because of the delightful and secluded setting and the constant pampering. There are candlelight dinners outdoors and vases of dawn-tinted roses. Look for a welcome basket of strawberries in your room and a poem with a rosebud on your pillow. Complimentary tea at 4:00 pm and a picture of your fishing success are some standard amenities.

During the season, full or half day fishing trips in any one of several hotel-owned boats are a common occurrence. Loved ones await their return looking for the catch flags; one for each trophy snared – white means a fish over 30 pounds, black represents kingfish ... More and more, Polaroids vouch for the tagged and released prize left to swim another day. The bar, popular with Kenyans, fills with chatter of the day's adventures. When the bell tolls in Hemingways bar to honor a fisherman's catch, it's his responsibility to pick up the tab until the bell rings again!

BLUE BAY VILLAGE, *Blue Bay Village, PO Box 162, Watamu. Tel. 0122 323 626, Fax 0122 32422. $140 per night double occupancy. All inclusive. Children under 12, 50%.*

Generally catering to an exclusively Italian clientele, it is possible for Americans to stay here in the delightful thatched cabins. The rooms are simple but fulfill the necessary requirements of a comfortable hotel. Many do not have views of the ocean but their garden settings are refreshingly green.

Genuine and excellent Italian cuisine is served in the classy dining room. Don't miss the outstanding panoramic views of the water at sunset. With two beaches on the bay for guests to choose from there is almost never a problem with seaweed. To reach the sand you must first go through a large carved door.

The lobby with its towering roof, quaint stores, and lounges requires a second look to take in all the splendid decor. A central open-to-the-sky square filled with green tropical plants is dominated by the lovely pool. Multi-colored cloth, shiny brass, masterful thatchwork and dark Lamu furniture contrast delightfully with stark whitewashed walls.

OCEAN SPORTS, *Ocean Sports Limited, PO Box 100, Watamu. Tel. 0122 32288 or 0122 320 008, Fax 0122 32266. $120 per night double occupancy. All major credit cards accepted.*

Individuality and casual charm are the working formula at Ocean Sports. Local Kenyans and their families have been coming back year after year since 1957 when it opened as the first hotel in Watamu. They have given it the nickname "Open Shorts"! The bandas stretch along a small hill behind the main hotel. Four of the 29 large rooms are air conditioned and they all have in-room bathrooms.

Each cottage has its own simple but distinct architecture and decor. The patios are the only standard feature where tea is served every afternoon. The sole downside is the location of the rooms across a parking lot away from the beach, but this is outweighed by a super casual, friendly atmosphere. The bougainvillea and frangipani filled gardens and meandering pathways invite guests to enjoy the fresh sea air. If this sounds too strenuous, sit in the lively bar (shaped like an old boat) and chat with the characters propped up there. Or enjoy the dining room with a cool drink or fresh seafood platter and watch the waves lap the sandy beach. A medium-sized pool offers a change from the salty ocean.

A diving school and deep sea fishing are also a continuing tradition for guests. For $19 experienced divers can go to the reef.

TEMPLE POINT VILLAGE, *PO Box 296, Watamu. Tel. 0122 32057, Fax 0122 32298. You must either arrive as a walk-in visitor or book through the Italian office at 1 Viaggi Del Ventaglio, Via de Amicis 43, 20123, Milano, Italy. Tel. 5818644. $100 per night double occupancy. All inclusive. All major credit cards accepted.*

While the beach is quite lovely and the setting equally so, it is not possible to swim off the shore here because of the sharp coral. The hotel offers guests (mostly Italians) a boat ride to nearby private sandy beaches or the option of two turquoise blue swimming pools.

The village is made up of charming two-floor bandas furnished in the traditional Lamu/Swahili fashion with ceiling fans, mosquito nets, and ensuite bathrooms. There are accommodations for 180 people. Tennis and watersports are a favorite with guests, as are the sensational views over the sea and delicious food in the bar and restaurant.

BARRACUDA INN, *Barracuda Inn, PO Box 59, Watamu. Tel. 0122 32061, Telex 21347 BARCDA KE. $100 per night double occupancy. All major credit cards accepted.*

Catering almost exclusively to Italians, it may be difficult to get a reservation. Guests in the 64 room inn enjoy socializing around the big swimming pool. Set at the edge of the Blue Bay Lagoon, the complex offers visitors water sports, tennis, squash, and gymnastics. Whitewashed walls and high thatched roofs attractively dominate the scene. Starting at the waterfront, adequate guest cabins run inland in queues.

TURTLE BAY BEACH CLUB, *Turtle Bay Beach Club, PO Box 457, Malindi. Tel. 0122 32080 or 0122 32622, Fax 0122 32268. $90 per night double occupancy. Children's programs available. All inclusive. All major credit cards accepted.*

The all-inclusive hotel caters to families and tour groups. Watersports such as windsurfing, snorkeling, scuba lessons, and a glass-bottom boat are part of the deal. Throughout the laid-back, 154 room hotel there are all sorts of activities including tennis, darts, a giant African chess set, miniature golf, ping pong and of course the crucial swimming pool.

Surrounded by tall full-grown native trees the view from around the large centrally located pool is postcard perfect. Thatched shelters make it is easy to get out of the burning sun's rays while still enjoying the white sand and crystalline waters of the ocean. Sloping grounds, wide staircases, and meandering pathways full of colorful foliage envelope the white low level buildings. Choose from larger and newer deluxe rooms located in smaller thatched three-story units or select one of the more numerous standard rooms. Each room features ceiling fans, in-room bathrooms, and private balconies. Overall this is an average hotel, but with good dollar value for groups and families.

MRS. SIMPSON'S, *PO Box 33, Watamu. Tel. 0122 32023. $75 per night double occupancy.*

There's no telling who your fellow guests might be in this large homey house. Families with kids, hitchhikers, or students fill the beach house with an uplifting party atmosphere. The frills are minimal with cold showers in sometimes shared bathrooms, a "mozie" net, a lamp, and a bed for everyone. The friendly and welcoming hostess finds it hard to turn anyone away. Because seven is really the optimum number of people, you might even end up sleeping on the roof!

Mrs. Simpson has lived in Kenya since 1923 and been taking guests into her book-filled rambling beach house for over 20 years. Her enthusiastic interest in the environment and marine preservation is contagious. During the communal mealtimes it is fascinating to hear her stories of times past.

Besides great conversation there is much to do for entertainment. Knowledgeable staff members take visitors to the Arabuko-Soke Forest, snorkeling, or out on the sailboat. Everything here feels like an adventure.

Budget

The list of additional accommodations in the area is slim. In front of Watamu village is the expanse of **WATAMU BEACH HOTEL**, *Tel. 0122 32001 or 011 485 520*. The clientele is exclusively German and they don't encourage other guests. Two middle of the road but adequate places to stay are the **PEPONI COTTAGES**, *Tel. 0122 32246*, and the **WATAMU RESTAURANT & COTTAGES**, *Tel. 0122 32062*. Both charge about $20 for rooms and have swimming pools. The Peponi is a two-story balconied thatched building. Small bedrooms have nets and bathrooms. At Watamu Paradise (the nicer of the two) there are a few pleasant cabins with fans, nets and bathrooms.

At the low end of the hotel spectrum, for under $15 there is the **WATAMU COTTAGES**, *Tel. 0122 32211*, **HOTEL DANTE, VILLA VERONICA/MWIKALI LODGE**, *Tel. 0122 32083*, and the **SEVENTH DAY ADVENTIST YOUTH CAMP** where you can pitch a tent if you can get in.

Further down the line are the **BLUE LODGE, SAM'S LODGE**, and the **MAASAI HOUSE**, where I wouldn't recommend staying even if the rates are $10 or less.

WHERE TO EAT

The resort restaurants are generally excellent but can be a little expensive. The best of these is the **WATAMU BEACH HOTEL** buffet, *Tel. 32001 or 32010*, and located at the northern end of the little village near the ocean. For $6.50 it's all you can eat of their large and varied table. In town there is the **HAPPY NIGHT BAR & RESTAURANT**, located at the southeastern end of town closest to the water, where they serve cold cold drinks and Kenyan/British meals. The food and service are always good, but their hours are a bit erratic.

HOTEL DANTE, *Tel. 32243*, next to Happy Night Bar & Restaurant heading west or inland, offers basic home style food but the drinks are warm and you may have to wait for service.

From the roadside store called **FRIEND'S CORNER**, there is a limited selection of tasty African fare. The only other place to eat is **COME BACK CLUB TIM'S RESTAURANT**, which serves less than outstanding meals, located across the village street.

SPORTS & RECREATION

Boat Trips

Ask at any of the major hotels or at the souvenir shacks lining the road about **glass bottom boat** rentals. For $15 per person, a trip to the **reef** is a must.

You can also go to a group of **caves** at the entrance to **Mida Creek**. Most of the hotels organize half day excursions to the mangroves, sandlots, and inlets of the waterway. Schools of giant (7 foot long!) rock cod or grouper accustomed to divers and snorkelers call the underwater coral caves home. To actually see the bottom dwellers, diving gear is necessary. If you don't dive or snorkel, it still makes for an interesting boat tour as you take in the varied bird life and rich landscape.

Dhow Rides

Dhow trips on **Mida Creek** operated by **Ocean Sports**, *Tel. (0122) 32288 or (0122) 320 008, Fax (0122) 32266,* can be booked through any of the hotels in Watamu. As you gently float the day away, keep your binoculars handy to spot any of the dozens of migratory birds. The thick mangrove and tidal mud-flats are also alive with scurrying crabs and other interesting denizens of the deep.

Fishing

Watamu and Malindi along the northern coast are extremely popular with fishermen who come here to enter any of the numerous tournaments. In the rips and mountains under the ocean an up-current brings tasty squid to the surface. Bonito tuna and small skipjack follow them. These in turn are followed by large yellowfin tuna, sailfish, and mighty marlin. **Hemingways**, *Tel. 326 624*, and **Ocean Sports** have eleven boats between them for your fishing pleasure.

SHOPPING

Along the side of the main road in Watamu there are countless souvenir stalls catering to tourists.

EXCURSIONS & DAY TRIPS

Gede National Park

Located just off the Mombasa to Malindi road about two miles from Watamu are the marvelous partly excavated Swahili ruins, surrounded by almost impenetrable woods. To get in to **Gede** or Gedi (which means "precious"), there is a charge of $4 which is worth every penny. Buy the detailed map and guide book at the entrance in order to get the full historical effect. Hours are 7:00 am to 6:00 pm daily.

An ancient city of Islamic origin, Gede is estimated to be from the 13th century. For reasons unknown, the mysterious city was abandoned towards the end of the 14th century. Archaeologists guess the ocean receded and left them high and dry or invading tribes ran them off. Thick forest took over the site but it was re-discovered in 1920.

The large palace is particularly fascinating with all its rooms, halls, and niches. There is even a "safe" for valuables and impressive "bathrooms." Some partial restoration work on the great mosque and the deep wells is making slow progress. It is possible to wander around the 45 odd acres of ruins where it's fun to imagine what the town was like so long ago. Monkeys chatter in the treetops, tiny antelopes or perhaps an elephant shrew may show themselves. Birds, snakes, millipedes, huge ants, lizards and butterflies bask in the sun, sharing the ruins and encompassing forest with you.

The locals stay away at night claiming ghosts haunt the site. Even the archaeologist James Kirkman, excavating the area, says he felt like he was being watched. The entire place is filled with a mysterious and delightfully titillating aura.

Giriam Village

Near Gede is the village of **Giriam**, where tourists are offered entertainment by drummers and supposedly native dancers. The costumes and dancing are well rehearsed and appear contrived. The dancer's attire looks more like a grass skirt getup than anything a Kenyan tribesperson would wear. At Giriam there are many vendors selling cheap souvenirs.

NATURE & FOREST RESERVES

*Many tourists to Kenya don't understand that the more renowned wildlife areas are actually **nature preserves** and not national parks. The important preserves are not as strictly controlled as other areas. Instead, the Forestry Department lets nature take its course.*

Arubuko Soke Forest Reserve

Surrounded by habitation and farmland, the coastal forest is rarely visited considering its close proximity to the ocean resorts. Many unusual animals such as the yellow-rumped elephant shrew and the Zanzibar duiker can be found in this thick and hot lowland forest. Butterflies, monkeys, and rare birds like the Sokoke scops owl call this small patch of timberland home. Sadly, this is the last remaining woodland patch of its kind left in East Africa.

PRACTICAL INFORMATION

Bank

There is a branch of **Barclays Bank** in Watamu. Their hours are 9:00 am to noon on Monday, Wednesday, and Friday.

Weather

The monsoon winds blowing across the Indian Ocean determine the seasons at the coast. During the northeasterly *kaskazi* the winds last from October through March with most of the rain falling in November. From April to September the stronger and colder winds of the *kusi* discourage visitors, but reduce room rates considerably. Generally the coastal weather year round tends to be sunny, humid, and warm.

MALINDI

Malindi, the northernmost tourist resort, is the second largest city on the coast. Many tourists to the southern part of Kenya make the mistake of avoiding the town altogether. If you have any interest at all in Arab or Portuguese history and culture, take some time to explore the steamy, humid town of Malindi. In my opinion it's worth the effort.

The tourist boom hit the 14th century town and helped it grow quickly with wide roads and new buildings. Interestingly, however, it has retained some of the identifiable Kenyan characteristics and remains an important business center. Fishing, cotton growing and processing, and sisal production still bring in significant income.

ARRIVALS & DEPARTURES

By Air

Just eight miles from the Gedi turn-off on the Mombasa to Malindi road is **Malindi Airport**. It is smaller than Moi International in Mombasa but does a steady stream of business bringing tourists in and out of the area.

To find the best deal try one of the main private air carriers, which include:
- **Eagle Aviation Limited**, *Tel. 0123 21258*
- **Skyways Airlines**, *Tel. 0123 21260*
- **Prestige Air Services**, *Tel. 0123 20860*

These carriers make return trips to Malindi from Mombasa costing $29 round trip. The flights take 30 minutes and depart at 8:30 am and 2:15 pm. The offices for these airlines are on the Lamu road in Malindi.

Air Kenya Aviation, *Mombasa, Tel. 011 433 982,* has one flight a day four times a week for $56. **Kenya Airways**, *Malindi, Tel. 0123 20237,* has two flights a day from Nairobi to Mombasa via Malindi.

There is a charge of $1.50 for departure tax. Check-in time is 30 minutes before departure. Be sure and reconfirm. A maximum weight limit of 22 pounds is customary. Excess baggage charges are 20¢ per pound but this is not strictly enforced.

By Bus

From Mombasa to Malindi and back there are several buses departing daily. The three companies operating the run are **Malindi Bus Service**, **Tana River Bus Service**, and **Garissa Express**. They all have offices in Malindi, Mombasa, and Lamu. The cost is $1.50 per person.

Buses from Malindi at the mainland across from Lamu leave at 7:00 am and 7:30 am. The fare for the five hour trip is $4.50. Advance reservations are required.

By Shared Taxi

From Malindi to Mombasa you can share a seven-seater taxi for $3 per person. They leave early in the morning once they are full from the bus station in town.

ORIENTATION

Most of the lodges are scattered along the shore south of the town's center. Hotels in the area tend to be of a more Arabic design or heavily influenced by Italians. Accommodations close to the city are your usual nondescript architecture.

GETTING AROUND TOWN

By Bicycle

Unless you like to walk, I suggest you rent a bicycle from **Ozi's Guest House** (overlooking the beach near the fishing jetty on the foreshore road) or the **Silver Sand's Camp Site** to get around town. The cost is roughly 50¢ per hour or $2 per day.

By Car

On the main street running along the coast near the Blue Marlin Hotel all the car rental agencies have offices. **Glory Car Hire**, *Tel. 0123 20065*; **Hertz**, *Tel. 0123 20069*; **Avis**, and **Europcar** will gladly do business with you.

By Taxi

If you are heading to Gedi ruins or anywhere that far out, try sharing a taxi. For $19 you can pretty much be driven around for at least half a day depending on your negotiating skills.

WHERE TO STAY

There are many many places to stay near and around Malindi. The accommodations below are those at the top end in terms of quality.

INDIAN OCEAN LODGE, *Safcon Travel Services, PO Box 59224, Nairobi. Tel. 503 265, Fax 506 824. $500 per night double occupancy. All inclusive. All major credit cards accepted.*

Wherever you go along the coast, you will be hard pressed to discover anything more stunning than the Indian Ocean Lodge. At any given time there are a maximum of eight people staying inside the walled, four acre, homestead so privacy is optimum. You will find the hosts, Peter and Joanna Nicholas, to be expert sources of intriguing information about the local history and lifestyle. As gracious innkeepers they will escort guests to anything from sailing and shopping, to golf and tennis – at the pool you're on your own.

The grounds and gardens will make you think of Eden with effusions of bright bougainvillea, ancient baobab trees, and fragrant frangipani draped in sunshine. The high peninsula on which the property sits overlooks the sapphire ocean and the sandy beach below. A long stone staircase takes you there.

Gleaming whitewashed walls of the Arab-style guest houses are something out of a fairytale. There are open staircases, tall archways, cozy nooks, and secluded patios filled with sumptuous Swahili furniture and hand woven rugs. Four poster beds give ample bedrooms the feel of a monarch's boudoir. Everything is airy and touched by sunlight.

TANA DELTA CAMP, *Robin Hurt Safaris, PO Box 24988, Nairobi. Tel. 882 826, Fax 882 939. $480 per night double occupancy. Three night minimum. Closed in the off season. All major credit cards accepted.*

Tana Delta Camp truly provides a taste of real Africa. The journey to the camp is an experience you won't soon forget! From Malindi the company vehicle jolts, rattles, and bumps down sweltering dusty roads for more than three and a half hours. Along the way Kenya may reveal topi, waterbuck, or buffalo through dense thorny bush and coastal vegetation. When the vehicle comes to a stop at the Tana River, it isn't the end but rather the beginning of another adventure.

A converted dhow – the "African Queen" – is the next mode of transport. For half an hour the banks change from grassy savannah to mangroves and salt bush. Hundreds of birds take flight as the boat thrusts down the river. Hippo families snort in disgust as their home is disturbed and huge crocodiles sun on the banks. It feels like the Africa of the movies. In fact, *Young Indiana Jones Chronicles* was partly filmed nearby in the Tana forest.

For those with less adventure in their souls it is possible to hire a charter plane to fly you to the airstrip. This cuts two hours off the trip but in my opinion you really miss out on a true safari. Perhaps the answer is to drive in and fly out; the best of both worlds.

A thatched round shelter serves as the main gathering place, dining room, and bar. Renaldo and Jill Retief share their knowledge and experiences of the territory over freshly prepared seafood meals. Keep your eyes peeled for crocodiles, elephants, hippos, bushbucks, lions, baboons and lots of birds as you walk through acacia forests or down miles of isolated beach. Soaking in the natural mud pits helps ease the sting of mosquito bites and does wonders for your skin. Guides happily take you fishing or to nearby fishing villages.

Six simple tents nestle among sand dunes where the river meets the ocean. Untouched beaches on one side and mangrove-lined waterways on the other cradle the pristine camp. Natural bush adds privacy while adjoining bathrooms and cool shade patios give comfort. Creative beds made of mangrove poles and bright materials adorn the canvas interiors.

KINGFISHER LODGE, *Kingfisher Group, PO Box 29, Malindi. Tel. 21168. $200 per night double occupancy. All major credit cards accepted.*

Four deluxe thatched cabins with air conditioning and ceiling fans are the only available accommodations at the inland resort. A luxurious and refreshing swimming pool sits amid well-maintained colorful gardens. Alongside the pool is a round open dining area where guests meet for appetizing home-cooked meals.

Golf, watersports (other than fishing), tennis, and squash come with the price of your stay at the family owned and run business. The colonial clan also organizes upscale deep sea fishing and tented safaris for visitors. From this, their home base, these experienced guides, fishermen, and hosts do everything in their power to satisfy.

CHE-SHALE, *PO Box 857, Malindi. Tel. 20676. $200 per night double occupancy. Closed from the end of April to the middle of July. All major credit cards accepted.*

While it may be a little hard to make reservations through the local Italian owners in Malindi, the final experience and destination are worth the trouble. Each of the ten straw huts assembled on a secluded beach 12 miles north of town offer the consummate upscale camping adventure. Electricity and adjoining bathrooms with safari showers and chemical toilets make things comfortable.

To reach Che-Shale you can either ride there on horseback or in a four wheel drive vehicle. This inaccessibility is exactly what makes the location so appealing. You feel like you've reached the end of the world. It is something out of a romantic novel with remote bays to explore, a warm ocean to snorkel in, birds to watch, and long energetic walks to take in search of treasure.

The rustic shacks offer cool respite from the midday sun under extended verandahs. Lounge on the cushioned divan here and make shapes from the clouds or simply revel in the solitude. The view from each hut varies from the cerulean ocean to shimmering sand dunes.

In those moments when you feel sociable head for the thatched bar. Large brightly covered pillows cover the floor and Lamu cots offer effortless comfort. For meals, join your fellow guests in the dining room as the skilled chef prepares outstanding masterpieces. Savory char-grilled fish, fresh cracked mangrove crab, and deep-fried seaweed are served with an Italian twist.

WHITE ELEPHANT SEA LODGE, *Turisanda: International Tour Operator, Via Poerio 2/A 20129, Milano. Tel. 0123 20223. $200 per night double occupancy.*

Without making reservations through their exclusive Italian office there is no way to assure a room here. If you happen upon it as a walk-in and they have vacancies, you will be given a place to stay. Obviously the guests are 99 percent Italian and all services are geared this way. The buildings are two-story apartment style set in lush gardens. Forty large rooms with air conditioning and Swahili decor cater to upper class customers. There is a swimming pool and game room.

MALINDI BEACH CLUB, *PO Box 868, Malindi. Tel. 20928, Fax 30103. $145 per night double occupancy. All major credit cards accepted.*

Two-story Arabesque-looking buildings, housing 24 new and completely private rooms, are casually placed around the landscaped grounds. Exotic wrought iron grills, charming verandahs, and high archways complete the Swahili architecture. Inside, mosquito nets, tile and wood floors, air conditioning and full service ensuite bathrooms exude luxury.

Tiled walkways lead you to hidden patios, tree lined gardens, and two saltwater swimming pools. The exclusive beach faces Malindi's marine park where watersports of all kinds are available. In addition there are horseback rides on the sand, golf, tennis, gambling and dancing. Throughout the main public areas (club house, lobby, and piano lounge) take in the brass antiques, Lamu chests, and valuable rugs. Italian dishes and fresh seafood are specialties of the fine restaurant.

KILILI BAHARINI, *Francorosso International Spa, Via Veneto, Rome, Italy. Tel. 06 4457055. $145 per night double occupancy. All major credit cards accepted.*

The majority of guests here are Italian but the place is worth visiting for its interesting set-up and unusual style. Three separate collections of three or four villas surround a small pool. These rooms share the secluded setting only with each other making it exclusive.

Each large thatched cottage is filled with quaint Swahili furnishings and bright fabrics. Ensuite bathrooms, thoughtful amenities and comfortable beds are standard. Individual spacious patios are great for lounging. Up above are particularly imaginative lofts reached by stepladder. Flower beds, coconut trees, and bright landscapes add color and character around the villas and down to the public pool closer to the Indian Ocean. Here you will find a casual dining room and bar catering to the European clientele.

AFRICAN DREAM VILLAGE, *PO Box 939, Malindi. Tel. 20442 or 0123 20119, Fax 20119. $140 per night double occupancy. All major credit cards accepted.*

The large resort is popular with European tour groups who come to stay in the tall thatched buildings. There are enough rooms to accommodate up to 120 people in the village at one time. Air conditioned bedrooms complete with ensuite bathrooms are surrounded by gardens filled with indigenous trees and flowering shrubs. There is swim-up bar in the popular swimming pool. All the public areas feel bright and open. A discotheque entertains visitors during the evening hours. Daylight activities include watersports and visits to Malindi Marine Park.

SCORPIO VILLAS, *Scorpio Enterprises Limited, PO Box 368, Malindi. Tel. 20194, Fax 21250. $140 per night double occupancy. All major credit cards accepted.*

On the lush tropical grounds there are three swimming pools and a labyrinth of 17 good sized bandas. Besides being too close together, the attractive cabins are well equipped with bathrooms and kitchens. There is even a cook/steward for each cottage. The furniture is typically Swahili.

There is an excellent restaurant within the complex. A narrow track leads down to the beach and the Indian Ocean.

THE TROPICAL VILLAGE, *PO Box 68, Malindi. Tel. 0123 20256, Fax 0123 20788 or Pan Travel Viaggi Turistici, SA 6900, Lugano, Switzerland. Tel. 091 232043, Fax 091 226 286. $140 per night double occupancy. All major credit cards accepted.*

The main attraction at the village is the open restaurant specializing in Italian and seafood cuisine for the predominantly European guests. An attractive swimming pool and lush gardens enhance the setting considerably. Clean whitewash and tall thatch cover several two story buildings housing guest rooms. Private bathrooms and pleasing Lamu furniture make the accommodations a change from anything at home. You will see The Tropical Village is appropriately named when you walk around the complex under swaying coconut trees, red bougainvillea, and other lush equatorial vegetation.

COCONUT VILLAGE, *PO Box 868, Malindi. Tel. 20938, Telex 21459. $135 per night double occupancy. Children under 12, 50%. All major credit cards accepted.*

The double-story cottages are furnished in traditional Swahili fashion. Dominating the classy Italian vacation spot, the thatched rooms have style. Request a room with an ocean view. Away from the beach are a busy pool and restaurant with a relaxed and casual air about them. Every night there is some form of entertainment for guests.

SILVER SANDS VILLAS, *Silversands Beach Cottages Limited, PO Box 91, Malindi. Tel. 20407 or 0123 20842. $130 per night double occupancy. All major credit cards accepted.*

Set right on the beach, the thatched restaurant and bar are particularly appealing because of the sand floor, checkered tablecloths, and ocean view. Bright gardens and flower beds surround two swimming pools. Further from the sand and water along a narrow strip of land are the guest cabins that can accommodate 62 people.

Inside the rooms at the family run hotel, parquet flooring and air conditioning are standard. Lamu furniture, bathroom bidets, and private verandahs add unique touches to the small resort. There are larger villas such as the "Malindi" available if you have a big group.

EDEN ROCK HOTEL, *Tropicana Hotels Limited, PO Box 350, Malindi. Tel. 20480. $100 per night double occupancy. All major credit cards accepted.*

Most of the clientele at this in-town hotel is German tour groups. The facility has been renovated recently giving it a fresh new feel. The structure itself looks like any ordinary city hotel with ocean vistas from the foyer and some rooms. To reach the beach you must first walk down landscaped terraces, through garden patios, and around two swimming pools.

KIVULINI BEACH HOTEL, *PO Box 142, Malindi. Tel. 20898, Telex 21335. $80 per night double occupancy. All major credit cards accepted.*

A bumpy but not unpleasant drive down a sandy track is your introduction to Kivulini. Surrounding native vegetation allows your imagination to wander back to the days when Kenya was largely unpopulated. A romantic pathway by the ocean and a rocky bay are the setting for the hideaway hotel.

Private patios at each of the 36 round thatched cabins and unique wood furnishings keep guests happy and comfortable. There is an interesting collection of souvenirs in the gift shop and an attractive free-form pool. Only three miles from Malindi town, the quaint hotel caters almost exclusively to Italians.

STEPHANIE SEA HOUSE, *PO Box 583, Malindi. Tel. 20720. $70 per night double occupancy. All major credit cards accepted.*

This is your typical basic beach resort. The rooms have Lamu/Swahili style furnishings and high thatched roofs. Forty bandas built too close together fill mainly with Italians. Unfortunately the accommodations are set back from the beach. The restaurant and pool, however, look down over the water and sand.

BLUE MARLIN, *PO box 54, Malindi. Tel. 20440, Telex 0987/21410. $56 per night double occupancy. All major credit cards accepted.*

Built on the Malindi beach, this regular city hotel offers basic facilities. There are 145 air conditioned rooms and two swimming pools. To get to the sand and water you must first take a fairly long walk through the gardened grounds.

BOUGAN VILLAGE, *Bougan Village, PO Box 721, Malindi. Tel. 21205, Fax in Italy 5242139. $50 per night double occupancy. All major credit cards accepted.*

Lamu furniture equips the cabins and rooms of this 16 acre garden resort. Private bathrooms complete the simple basic accommodations. A central thatched club offers a pool, restaurant, and two bars for the predominantly Italian guests. At night there is a noisy disco. As the beach is far from the guest rooms there is a bus traveling to and from the beach all day long. On the sand, a bar sells drinks and snacks.

DORADO COTTAGES, *Hotel Buildings Limited, PO Box 868, Malindi. Tel. 20252. $50 per night double occupancy.*

The 22 full service whitewashed cabins are under Italian management and usually rented to tour groups. Each banda comes with a bedroom, bathroom, living room, and kitchen. There is a refrigerator but no stove. Rollaway beds can be added. Meals are served in an older cottage with a view of the beach. The attractive thatched bandas do not face the water; instead they are set close together in colorful gardens around two pools. To reach the beach there is a small pathway down the hill.

PALM TREE CLUB, *PO Box 180, Malindi. Tel. 20397, Telex OVERTURCO 21214. $50 per night double occupancy. All major credit cards accepted.*

There are detached bandas or standard rooms to choose from on the widespread grounds. Standard accommodations overlook the pool. The oversized swimming pool is surrounded by the round central building. Room decor is a mix of African carvings, animal skin throws, and stylish Lamu furniture. There are private bathrooms, cool thatched ceilings, and fresh flowers in each bedroom.

To get to the beach, guests must take the continuously running shuttle bus. For those interested in playing golf, the Malindi Golf Course sits next door. In addition, there is bowling, tennis, and horseback riding. The Italian resort frequently shows Italian movies for its European visitors.

THE DRIFTWOOD BEACHCLUB, *The Bunson Group, PO Box 45456, Nairobi. Tel. 337 604 or 0123 20155, Fax 723 599. $50 per night double occupancy. Breakfast included. All major credit cards accepted.*

Very basic bandas, some with ocean views and air conditioning, have been here for some time. The general style at the family run hotel is one of informality and relaxation. This casual air sometimes shows itself in the less than perfect housekeeping. A diving center and swimming pool add interest. The restaurant and bar are favorite hang-outs for the British Kenyan populace who come here to be sociable and enjoy the rib-sticking food. The sea and sand are only a few short paces from the open dining room.

LAWFORDS HOTEL, *PO Box 54, Malindi. Tel. 20440. $50 per night double occupancy.*

Built on the Malindi beach right next door to the Blue Marlin, the regular city hotel offers very basic facilities. To get to the sand and water you must first take a fairly long walk through the grounds.

WHERE TO EAT

GELATERIA BAR, *in the Sabaki shopping center. Moderately priced. Gelati ice cream.*

The range of flavors and selection of ice cream is excellent. The prices are higher than at home but it is worth it on a hot sticky day.

EDDIE'S, *just off Lamu Road. Moderately priced. Tel. 20283. Seafood. Open from noon to 2:30 pm and 7:30 pm to 10:30 pm.*

Choose anything from simple fish platters to lobster delicacies. This is one of the best seafood restaurants in Malindi. The ambiance is particularly tasteful and familiar. Before sitting down to your meal, try the swimming pool for a refreshing dip.

PUTIPU RESTAURANT, *at the Stardust Club in the northern part of town. Outdoor dining. Moderately priced.*

Tasty Italian cuisine, including pizza.

HERMANN'S BEER GARDEN, *north of town. Moderately priced. German and Continental cuisine.*

This restaurant caters to large tour groups – particularly German. The music is loud and the atmosphere jovial. Food is about average.

EL PESCATORI, *south towards the Driftwood Club. Major credit cards accepted. Moderately priced. Seafood. Reservations suggested.*

The upscale restaurant is open-air and serves dinner only.

I LOVE PIZZA, *near the Metro Hotel in front of the jetty. Major credit cards accepted. Moderately priced. Italian cuisine.*

Pizza, pasta, chicken, and seafood seem to be the most popular choices. It is open from noon to midnight every day and stays busy.

DRIFTWOOD CLUB, *at the south end of town close to the water. Tel. (0123) 20155. Major credit cards accepted. Moderately priced. Seafood. Open for lunch and dinner.*

If you are not a guest here you must pay $1.55 for temporary membership. This includes use of the restaurants, bar, showers and swimming pool. The sailfish and shrimp are delicious.

LA MALINDINA, *at the Malindi Beach Club facing the popular marine park. Tel. 20045. Moderately priced. Major credit cards accepted.*

Delicious gourmet Italian fare in an Arabian nights setting.

There are many inexpensive places to eat that are extremely popular with tourists not wanting to stay in their hotels for every meal. **OZI'S GUEST HOUSE**, overlooking the beach near the fishing jetty on the foreshore road, *Tel. 20318*, serves seafood and excellent Indian curry. The **PALM GARDEN** on Lamu Road across from the gas station serves mostly seafood and curry. The establishment is divided in two. The front half serves light snacks such as burgers, and light curries and sausage. The back thatched section is for sit-down meals.

MALINDI FRUIT JUICE GARDEN serves – you guessed it – fruit juices and scrumptious milk shakes. For a light lunch try the **NEW SAFARI HOTEL**, popular with locals. **BAHARI RESTAURANT** in the center of town offers Indian food with an enticing African flair. Near the Portuguese Church in a shopping complex is **TRAVELLER'S CAFE**. There is a choice of true Kenyan or European cuisine.

SEEING THE SIGHTS

Vasco Da Gama's Cross

In the 14th century, Malindi was an important Swahili settlement, rivaling Mombasa and Pat_ for control of the coast and also important as a commercial center. Portuguese sailors and traders opening the sea route to India found a welcome here not offered elsewhere along the coast. This encouraged more visits to trade and settle. Because of the warm reception, **Vasco Da Gama** fashioned (in 1499) a tall simple white cross used as a navigational aid. At the south end of the bay the restored stone pillar can still be seen today.

Ancient Ruins

To the north there are a few scant remains of a palace, a mosque, and a small number of pillar tombs. Closer in there are the partial ruins of a Portuguese church with a painting of the crucifixion still visible. Saint Francis Xavier visited here on his way to India.

NIGHTLIFE & ENTERTAINMENT

Most of the resorts offer some sort of entertainment at night. If you don't want to stay at your hotel for the evening, there is plenty to keep you busy while adding a more authentic Kenyan flavor to your vacation.

Bars/Clubs

At the **Coconut Village**, in the south part of town just off the Tourist Road near the ocean and the Driftwood Club, *Tel. 20938,* there is a popular makuti-roofed disco overlooking the beach which is usually open on Wednesday. There is a small cover charge unless you get there early. The amazing bar is actually a branch of a living tree! The open-air tavern sits right on the sand wrapped around this resilient tree.

Right next door to the Metro Hotel, at the waterfront between Tourist Road and the main jetty, is the **Malindi Fishing Club**. A friendly British clientele shares the bar, its snacks, and the usually old videos. To get into the thatched, informal club there is a membership fee of 75¢ per person.

Perhaps the most frequented bar/disco on the beach is the **Stardust Club** which doesn't get started until about 11:00 pm and goes until the wee hours. The charge to get in is $8 on Saturday and $4 any other night. The Stardust Club is next door to Herman's Beer Garden and Putipu Restaurant heading north along the main coast road. Just to the south of it is Barclays Bank.

For a small association charge, you may join the members at the **Malindi Golf & Country Club**, under two miles north of town, *Tel. 20404,* in their fine bar and restaurant.

Casino

The main draw these days is the relatively new **Casino** on the Lamu road. It is open from noon to 5:00 pm daily and at midnight serves spaghetti free of charge. It has all the usual international games with the bets going as low as 75¢.

SPORTS & RECREATION

Deep Sea Fishing

Most of the resort hotels and the **Malindi Fishing Club** can organize a deep sea fishing trip for $468 per boat for four people. All tackle and equipment is included.

Golf & Tennis

At the **Malindi Golf & Country Club** a few miles north of town, *Tel. 20404,* there is a wide selection of sporting options including of course, golf. In addition, for a small membership fee you may play tennis.

Reef Tours/Glass Bottom Boats/Snorkeling

You will frequently be asked if you are interested in taking a boat to the reef for snorkeling or glass bottom boat viewing. For $18 per person you can do an all-inclusive trip. Round trip taxi to/from your hotel, boat hire, and park entry fee ($7.15) are part of the deal. The park is open 7:00 am to 7:00 pm daily. Masks and snorkels (often ratty!) are provided. Fins can be rented for $1.60 on the beach at the marine park.

Scuba Diving

At the **Driftwood Club** at the **Silver Sands** resort, diving is offered for $39 plus a $7.15 park entry fee. The diving school charges $455 for a course.

SEAWEED & MUDDY OCEAN WARNINGS!

*Throughout the year Kenya's coastal beaches can be affected by long strings of green slimy seaweed. The worst time is during the **kusi** monsoon when swimming or walking on the beach is made difficult by the green pest. Many of the resorts and hotels employ workers to bury or burn what they can gather, but what floats in the water can be disconcerting for would-be swimmers. It tends to be worse on the north beaches, relatively harmless (although very smelly!) and annoyingly unpredictable – here today, gone tomorrow. Don't however, let this stop you from the overall experience.*

During the rainy season large quantities of reddish brown silt drains down the Galana River to the ocean. The visibility in the water is minimal and the lovely blue color is temporarily gone. The rest of the year this is not a problem. To avoid the muddy silt simply move to a beach south of town.

SHOPPING

Malindi offers some interesting shopping with a colorful **outdoor market**, chic stores, and trendy boutiques. Near the mosque along the beach there are at least 25 shacks filled with all manner of Kenyan treasures. Baskets and wood and soapstone carvings are just a few of the dozens of items for sale. The quality is pretty good, but they expect you to bargain at least a little.

EXCURSIONS & DAY TRIPS

Malindi/Watamu Biosphere Reserve

There are actually four separate parks and reserves comprising the Malindi/Watamu biosphere. They are **Malindi Marine National Park and Reserve** and **Watamu Marine National Park and Reserve**. The best time to visit these parks is at low tide when it is easy to see the lifeforms in and around the coral.

The coral reef here at Watamu is even more spectacular than Malindi because it is much less exploited and poached by shell hunters. Many tide pools provide excellent snorkeling. The visibility here is unaffected by silt brought down inland waterways as is the case with Malindi and the Galana River. The Watamu reef is just over one and a quarter miles away. It is easiest to hire a glass bottom boat to get there from any of the hotels or souvenir stalls lining the road for $15 per person. It is certainly well worth it. Nearby at **Whale Island**, the roseate and bridled terns nest from June to September.

Snake Park

Entry to this your standard snake park is $4.50 for adults and $2.35 for kids. It is open from 9:00 am to 5:00 pm every day. To find it, look for the Sabaki shopping center on Lamu Road. It is right behind it.

Falconry

The hours of business and entry fees are the same as the snake park. There are several caged birds of prey, an enormous wandering tortoise, and a chimpanzee on a rope. It all seems rather sad to me!

PRACTICAL INFORMATION

Banks

Both the **Standard Chartered Bank** and **Barclays** have offices in town. Their hours are 8:30 am to 1:00 pm and 2:30 pm to 5:00 pm Monday through Friday. On Saturdays their hours are 8:30 am to noon. When there are few tourists in the off season the banks may not open on Saturdays.

Post Office
In addition to the usual postal services there is an international phone center. Hours are 7:00 am to 7:00 pm Monday through Friday and 8:00 am to 2:30 pm on Saturday.

Telephone
The Malindi fax and telephone city code is *0123*.

Tourist Office
There is a small **tourist information center**, *Tel. (0123) 20877*, on the Lamu road across from the shopping center and next door to the Kenya Airways office. While the staff is willing and wants to help, they really seem to have little to offer in the way of knowledgeable advice.

LAMU ISLAND & THE REMOTE NORTH COAST

Visitors to **Lamu Island**, the most northerly coastal region, are attracted by the thoughts of becoming one with the Swahili culture and exploring historical ruins and monuments. It is the oldest living town in Kenya and is populated almost exclusively by Muslims. Amazingly, it has changed little over the centuries and remains relatively untouched by the 20th century. The women still wear the black somewhat modernized version of the wraparound *buibui* and the men dress in flowing white robes (*khanzus*) and wear small caps called *kofia*.

Dingy stores filled with exotic wares and narrow streets leading past funky drains are all part of a day in Lamu Town. The heavy Arab/Moslem influence is obvious in the unique architecture and design throughout the city. In spite of the thousands of visitors heading this way each year, the center has managed to maintain much of its specific personality and distinctive culture. A slow-paced lifestyle is one of its most captivating features.

North of Lamu are the romantic resorts known for secluded beaches and complete repose with perhaps some watersports thrown in. Tourists usually end up staying either in the town of Lamu or in the neighboring seaside village of **Shela**, where the accommodations are better than in Lamu and so is the beach access. Everything at Shela happens at a very tranquil pace. The beaches are pristine and unspoiled. You won't find many places in the world as relaxing or beautiful.

Off the mainland, in the seas of the Lamu Archipelago, there are many small islands. **Manda Island** is the easiest to get to as it is the closest to the shore. There are also the **Manda Toto**, **Paté**, and **Kiwayu Islands**.

The local people still hold close their way of life and have little regard for tourists. It is important to respect their customs and traditions. They do not appreciate photographers or unsuitably clothed visitors. Try to blend in and avoid shattering their hometown lives.

The population, currently at 12,000 souls, is on the increase. Where will they all live? How will they survive? These are difficult question that will soon need answering. Cash is necessary to maintain employment, restoration, and preservation. These facts of life are slowly forcing the populace to embrace the hundreds of daily visitors bringing in money. Many are even selling their homes to enterprising foreigners for what seems to them like great profit.

It is a "Catch 22" or no-win situation with a strong argument on both sides. How do you embrace and control tourism but still hold on to the traditional ways that bring visitors here?

ARRIVALS & DEPARTURES
By Air
Most visitors heading for Lamu Island first fly to **Lamu Airstrip** on the neighboring island of **Manda**. Once you land, be prepared to be hounded all the way by annoying "beach boys." They want to sell souvenirs, dhow rides, and hotel rooms.

To find the best deal, try one of the main private air carriers, which include:
- **Eagle Aviation Limited**, *Tel. 0121 3119*
- **Skyways Airlines**, *Tel. 0121 3226*
- **Prestige Air Services**, *Tel. 0121 3055*

These carriers make return trips to Malindi from Lamu twice a day. Their offices are all on the Lamu road in Malindi. The flights take 40 minutes and depart at 10:00 am and 4:00 pm. The fare is $83 return.

These airlines also make return trips to Lamu from Mombasa costing $124 round trip. The flights take 70 minutes and depart at 8:30 am and 2:15 pm.

There is no departure tax from Lamu. Check-in time is 30 minutes before take off. Be sure and reconfirm. A maximum weight limit of 22 pounds for gear is the norm. Excess baggage charges are 20¢ per pound, but this is not strictly enforced.

By Boat
To reach the island of Lamu you must cross the Indian Ocean by boat or fly into Manda Island airport. From the airport, visitors usually take a dhow or hire a boat for the short crossing. The price is 60¢.

There is no motorized transport to the island besides diesel powered launch from the mainland jetty. The skiff leaves from the seaside town of Mokokwe and costs 75¢. The district commissioner is the only person who owns a motor-powered boat accessing the islands. From Lamu to Shela the motorized dhows charge the same 75¢ fare.

By Bus

Once you get from Lamu to Malindi there are several buses departing daily. The three companies operating the run are **Malindi Bus Service**, **Tana River Bus Service**, and **Garissa Express**. They all have offices in Malindi, Mombasa, and Lamu. The ride takes about three hours. The cost is $1.50 per person.

Buses on the mainland across from Lamu leave for Malindi at 7:00 am and 7:30 am. The fare for the five hour trip is $4.50. Advance reservations are required.

By Car

To travel north from Malindi, the B8 leads visitors towards the inland town of Garsen. Here you may continue west towards Garisa, but most people turn right onto the C112 road. This route follows the coastline first to Hindi and then to Mokokwe. From here you can cross to the islands in the archipelago.

ORIENTATION

The ancient town of Lamu is a maze of narrow winding streets lined with sometimes smelly open sewers. In spite of the disposal system, the dusty hot village is filled with a special ambiance of times long past. Lamu is filled with dozens of guest houses, hotels, and places to eat. As the town grew, it followed the curve of the seashore to take advantage of the breeze and trading routes.

At the farthest end of town, heading north along the waterway, is the carving workshop. If you keep going from the main jetty straight inland you'll eventually arrive at the village of Matondoni. The Riyadha Mosque is the most remote building southwest of the village. Beyond the outskirts of town, the Civil Servants Club and Shela await you.

CONSTRUCTION TECHNIQUES

Traditional homes in Lamu are constructed with walls made of coral and tall, attractive thatched roofs. The thatch is supported by long mangrove poles. The size of each room in the structure is determined by the length of the mangrove posts used in the ceiling and the floor. The longer the poles the bigger the house!

GETTING AROUND TOWN

By Dhow

For those hard to reach places, it is possible to hire a dhow for a pleasant boat ride. There seem to be more dhows here than anywhere else along this coast. The fares are relatively cheap, particularly if you share the craft with others. The fare to reach the village of Matondoni on the west side of the island is about $13, including a barbecue fish lunch. Motorized dhows shuttle guests back and forth between Lamu and Shela frequently during the day. The cost is a mere 75¢ per person.

WHAT IS A DHOW?

*A **dhow** is a single masted ship with a triangular sail, sharp prow, and raised deck at the stern. They are used in the Indian Ocean as a principal form of transportation. The angled sails were formerly utilized by Portuguese explorers.*

By Donkey

The beasts of burden are the most common form of transport used by the locals on their narrow winding streets. Sometimes there are "traffic jams" with donkeys and herds of sheep or goats meeting in a tight spot. After much yelling and agitation things sort themselves out.

By Foot

Getting around the town of Lamu is easily accomplished on foot. The narrow winding streets have little traffic, making walking safe. The only peril you might encounter is herds of goats or donkeys.

From Lamu to Shela it is a 40 minute walk. You can go overland or along the shore. The overland route can be confusing without a guide due to the many paths criss-crossing the landscape. If the tide is out, the beach trail is a piece of cake. At high tide however, you will do some swimming if you follow this course.

A walk to Matondoni village from Lamu can take up to two hours and may be unpleasant during the heat of the day. I recommend the alternative donkey or dhow ride.

WHERE TO STAY

Lamu Town

The list of places to stay at the bottom end of the list is staggeringly long for such a small town. This makes it almost impossible to mention every room, floor mat, and rooftop where you can sleep. Instead the inventory below includes only those lodgings worth mentioning.

LAMU PALACE HOTEL, *PO Box 83, Lamu. Tel. 0121 3272. $56 per night double occupancy. All major credit cards accepted.*

This Swahili style hotel is conveniently situated along the waterfront close to the city center. As it is relatively new, the large lodge is blessed with air conditioning. There are many small and confining bedrooms with bathrooms available for rent. Sadly, the character does not completely blend with the local flavor making it somewhat of an eyesore. The hotel's restaurant offers a wide variety of entree selections.

PETLEY'S INN, *PO Box 4, Lamu. Tel. in Lamu – 0121 48107 or 3107; Tel. in Nairobi – 29612. $37 per night double occupancy. All major credit cards accepted.*

Recently purchased by Americans, the charming old hostel is getting a much needed facelift. The new owners are adding and restoring many intriguing Lamu touches to the waterfront inn. The second floor is occupied by – of all things – a swimming pool! On the roof is a charming restaurant. Located near the museum, the hotel also qualifies as the depository of a fascinating culture.

YUMBE HOUSE, *PO Box 81, Lamu. Tel. 0121 3101. $32 per night double occupancy.*

A full breakfast is covered in the price of your stay in this historic building. Found in the heart of town, the general character suggests a safe and comfortable lodge. Each simple but adequate spotless bedroom comes with its own full bathroom and mosquito nets. The beautiful four-story traditional Swahili home with makuti roofs and airy patios surrounds a striking courtyard. At the top of the building there's a lounge, from which there is a picturesque view of the harbor and city.

LAMU HOTEL LURES

Many of the hotels pay a commission to local "beach boys" for bringing guests their way. The commission is added to the price of your room. You really don't need an "agent," particularly if you are wise and made reservations in advance. As these pests crowd around you, don't be too shy about telling them you have already made arrangements; they can be pushy!

If there isn't much going on around town, hotels often offer guests a discount for longer stays. Don't pay for your board up front as you may find somewhere else you like better. Once you have paid, it may be difficult to get your money back.

LAMU HOUSE, *Tel. 0121 3246. $27 per night double occupancy. Breakfast included.*

This is an outstanding place to stay if you want some real local flavor. The hotel is a restored 16th century Swahili house in the heart of town. Bedrooms and communal areas are furnished in comfortable local style.

STONE HOUSE, *PO Box 81866, Mombasa. Tel. 223 295, Fax 221 925. $20 per night double occupancy. All major credit cards accepted.*

A big plus for this newcomer to Lamu is its personal water supply. The 18th century remodeled bed and breakfast serves both Swahili cuisine and fresh seafood in its restaurant. The bedrooms have ensuite bathrooms and charming Lamu furniture. The name is derived from the unique architecture and stone construction methods utilized by the locals. You can get away from the hustle and bustle outside while enjoying cordial and unobtrusive service.

Budget Choices in Lamu

The following places are worth looking at because of their offerings of clean, cool and comfortable accommodations at anywhere from $27 to $15 depending on how willing you are to negotiate. **KISHUNA GUEST HOUSE,** *Tel. 0121 3125* – new and away from town, the place has little in the way of local color. **BUHARI HOTEL,** *Tel. 0121 3172* – go for the open upstairs rooms only. **CASUARINA REST HOUSE,** *Tel. 0121 3123* – large airy rooms with good views, clean facilities, and great value. It was once the police station!

WATER ON LAMU ISLAND

Water on the island can be hard to find, making it a very precious commodity. Most of the year there are strictly enforced restrictions. This can mean unflushed toilets and quick showers from buckets. It is part of the charm of staying here but not something hotels (particularly the cheap ones) like to advertise. The precious liquid asset is usually available in the early morning and evening hours only, so plan accordingly.

Shela

The charming village of Shela is where many tourists choose to stay. Whether you stay here or not, it is a pleasant place to wander. The populace originally came from Takwa in the 17th century when that site was deserted. Today they still speak their own version of Swahili; different from the dialect used in Lamu. Perhaps the most interesting building here is the lovely mosque located behind Peponi's.

PEPONI HOTEL, *PO Box 24, Lamu. Tel. 0121 3029 or 33421, Fax 33029, Telex 21471 PEPONI. $220 per night double occupancy. Closed in May and June. No swimming pool. All major credit cards accepted.*

Difficult to translate precisely, the word Peponi describes a serene place of retreat from stress and the daily grind. With only 25 rooms, the hotel couldn't be more relaxing and intimate. In one direction a stroll via walkways and outdoor stairs surrounds you with mature trees and luscious gardens all the way to the tiered bedrooms. On the other side of the central buildings a flower draped sea wall, a green lawn, and coconut palms face the rooms. Blue ocean, sandy beaches, and pink bougainvillea are all you see from each private verandah.

Varying in size, the attractive guest rooms are equipped with ceiling fans and mosquito nets. Elegant Lamu beds and adjoining bathrooms complete the standard features. Older accommodations with dramatic high ceilings are furnished with less artistic flair than the newer, more colorful rooms.

Journeying to the Danish family-owned business is a great part of a stay here. For the last 25 years, the Korschens have welcomed visitors after they unwind with a short dhow ride and a stroll down the hotel's sandy beach. Have your cameras ready for charming shots of waterside homes, exotic gardens, and old Lamu town. Not only has the hotel's first-class reputation for hospitality spread but so has its standing as a special place to dine. If at all possible, go for drinks and/or dinner.

KIJANI HOUSE, *PO Box 266, Lamu. Tel. 0121 3235 or 3237. $124 per night double occupancy. Closed in May and June. Breakfast included. All major credit cards accepted.*

The whole scene is something out of movie. Fishing boats and seasoned fishermen bring the pier to life. Further into the property, three thatched Swahili guest cottages and two pools invite visitors to let their hair down and relax. Flowering shrubbery attracts local bird populations to do the same. Notice the traditional coral construction.

Seven rooms house visitors with comfort and style. Lamu furniture, four poster beds, high ceilings, and fresh flowers in copper pots add charm. Full bathrooms, private verandahs, mosquito nets, and ceiling fans add contentment. Making new friends under the cool thatch of the lounge or dining room is part of the mystery of traveling here.

ISLAND HOTEL, *PO Box 179, Lamu. Tel. 0121 3290. $80 per night double occupancy. No pool. Breakfast included. All major credit cards accepted.*

Basic and clean, the 14 room lodge sits in the center of the small village. Each room comes with a cooling fan and a full private bathroom. In some of the rooms the walls don't meet the ceiling which allows sound to travel freely between rooms. At the top of the hotel there is a quaint and excellent restaurant with partially open sides and picturesque views of Shela Town.

Near Lamu

BLUE SAFARI CLUB, *Bruno Brighetti's Blue Safari Club, PO Box 41759, Nairobi. Located on Manda Island. Tel. 338 838, Fax 218 939. $900 per night double occupancy. All major credit cards accepted.*

Two rows of round grass and thatch cottages follow the shoreline of Manda Island (the best view comes with the front row). Lively colored curtains and bed covers are made from local fabrics. Native Lamu chairs with woven seats furnish the verandahs. Creatively arranged shells and driftwood are Gianna's artful touch. Fans and mosquito nets keep things comfortable in the small bedrooms. Down a short enclosed hallway made of woven grass is the private bathroom with its refreshing cold water shower.

For 20 years now the Italian Brighetti family has enjoyed the seclusion and beauty of this private isle. They share their haven and their dinner table with the well-to-do and possibly famous clientele who come here for solitude and pampering. The club's capacity is 24 people but usually the numbers are far less.

The only way to arrive is by boat over the deep blue ocean which gives the club its name. Young Marco or his father Bruno will pick you up for the exhilarating ride. Your first glimpse of paradise takes in the romance of tall coconut trees and white sandy beaches.

Music and movies in the open dining and living "room" add a touch of civilization. The bar never closes. There are lots of large fluffy cushions scattered for lounging. Unobtrusive staff caters to all your needs with sociable smiles. You set the pace, choosing from sailing, fishing, reef snorkeling, beach walking or any of the other outdoor activities.

KIWAYU SAFARI VILLAGE, *PO Box 55343, Nairobi. Tel. 503 030, Fax 503 149. $380 per night double occupancy. Closed from the middle of April for a few (varying) months. Located on Kiwayu Island. All major credit cards accepted.*

This place is a slice of perfection! It is you, a few fellow travelers, and all the nature you can absorb. Twenty-two large grass, palm, and thatch cottages line the beach. Each is strategically placed for privacy, an exquisite view, and quick access to the ocean. It is rare to see the straw shades drawn over the large openings serving as doors and windows; there is no need.

Honeymooners and fashion models revel in larger-than-king size beds covered with romantic nets and colorful material. Inside full bathrooms (with cold water showers) and a dressing chamber you might easily find a growing tree. The secluded porch comes with hammocks and armchairs laden with bright pillows. Everything blends with the natural surroundings.

In the open-sided dining room and adjoining den more overstuffed cushions, tall thatched ceilings, and unique floor mats offer functionality and fantasy. Gently lapping waves, coconut trees, and distant craggy cliffs set the mood for flights of fancy here at what was once a hunter's camp.

From the nearby airfield it is only a short distance to the hotel where harmony with nature and guest satisfaction are top priorities. There is nothing austere about Kiwayu Village. The menu – mostly fresh seafood – includes such extravagances as delicately prepared lobster or huge crab claws. Besides eating, drinking, and relaxation, there is a wide range of water related sports and activities to choose from.

KIPANGANI SEA BREEZES, *PO Box 232, Lamu. Tel. 0121 3191. $130 per night double occupancy. All major credit cards accepted.*

New management has taken over the charming ten banda hotel with many suggestions for betterment. The resort sits amid coconut trees and ocean breezes on the far shore of Lamu Island. Mosquitoes and scurrying crabs keep guests company as they do at most beach resorts. It can be quite hot if the air is still.

Because of its location, tariff, and idyllic seclusion, Kipangani is popular with newlyweds. The laid-back atmosphere however, does not affect the luscious and plentiful seafood cuisine. A centrally located thatched recreation room seems to be a lounging focal point. Hammocks and large throw pillows invite you to relax and luxuriate in the tropical splendor.

WHERE TO EAT

It is not uncommon to have locals ask you home to be entertained by their families and enjoy a local dinner. For a few dollars, it is a unique look into local family lifestyles. Be sure to politely discuss the terms before accepting, thus avoiding any embarrassment later.

On the island the selection is slim for up-market affordable dining. Try these places where you can feel sure the food meets high standards.

PEPONI'S, *on the harbor waterfront at the far end of Shela Village. Tel. 0121 3029. Fresh seafood. Major credit cards accepted. Moderately priced.*

Exquisite setting and cuisine – a must try restaurant. Seafood is the specialty and Danish/Lamu is the pleasing style of the formal dining room. China from Holland hangs on the white walls contrasting with dark local furniture. There are whitewashed terraces, French doors, and Swahili artwork.

Outdoors, a beach-sand floor and healthy bougainvillea enhance the more casual **BARBECUE GRILL**. Scrumptious salads and barbecued fish or meats are the above-average selections.

BARRACUDA RESTAURANT, *at the Island Hotel, Tel. 0121 3290. Fresh seafood. Moderately priced.*

There is a wide range of selection from simple fare to crab and lobster. The service and food is consistently good.

GYPSIES GALLERY, *across from the waterfront. Snacks & coffee. Inexpensive.*

A fun place to watch the world go by and enjoy a light snack for lunch. Popular with visitors.

Soups, steaks, seafood, and curry are standard fare at most eateries in Lamu. If you know where to look it is easy to find inexpensive and tasty homemade dining.

At **PETLEY'S INN,** *Tel. 48107,* just back from the water near the main jetty near Lamu Museum and Prestige Air Services, the food is excellent and the restaurant opens to non-guests. Try the cheese somosas or the seafood lunch or dinner for a mere $6. **BUSH GARDENS** and **HAPA HAPA RESTAURANT** sit side by side on the waterfront. Both are extremely popular for all meals including breakfast. Fruit juices, lobster, and all manner of fish and crab come with coconut rice and/or fries. If service is slow it is worth the wait – particularly at Bush Gardens. Try the popular waterfront **OLYMPIC (SYNBAD) RESTAURANT** for lunch or dinner. It is an exemplary choice for stuffed pancakes, fresh fish, and homemade soups. It's located at the south end of town just back from the Indian Ocean.

For vegetarian and a more unique selection of chicken dishes, visit the **LABANDA RESTAURANT,** located just a short distance further south from the Olympic. For lighter fare such as shakes and snacks inquire at **KENYA COLD DRINKS,** on the waterfront near the jetty and the Lamu Museum. Investigate the **BANTU CAFÉ** (in the Newcastle Lodge, overlooking the main square and the fort; it's also next door to the colorful market) where with advance reservations you can sample an outstanding selection of local foods. At the **MAZANGIRA CAFÉ** on the verandah of the old fort, watch the people go by and enjoy fresh fruit juice with a very affordable meal.

A few places with a reputation for expensive but not very reliable service are the **NEW MAHARUS HOTEL** (close to the main square by the fort) and the **LAMU PALACE HOTEL,** on the southside of Lamu overlooking the water, *Tel. (0121) 3272.* An inexpensive place to avoid in town is the **NEW STAR RESTAURANT** which gets mixed reviews from it patrons.

GHAI'S at the northern end of town past the main jetty right on the water, seems to have good value but is also inconsistent with its quality. The **CORAL ROCK,** a short distance further north of Ghai's heading towards the door carving workshops, has changed names several times over the years. The marginal meals includes banana pancakes and grilled fish. There is a feeling that customers are a nuisance and this turns me off.

SEEING THE SIGHTS

Lamu Museum

You'll find the museum on the waterfront next door to Petley's Inn and adjacent to Prestige Air services, just back from the main jetty. Entry to the **museum** in Lamu is $1.50 and it is open from 8:00 am to 6:00 pm daily. It takes a couple of hours to see everything and is a great way to discover Lamu. Start with the informative slide show (ask to see it). Then move on to the other displays, which include a Swahili house and various dhow models.

In the museum store you can purchase carefully written books on the history of Lamu and a helpful small leaflet that includes a map. If you plan on staying in Lamu more than a few hours, the map is worth having.

Swahili House Museum

Off to the side of Yumbe House, a local hotel, look for the **Swahili House Museum**. There is a charming courtyard typical to the homes in town. The interior is fully furnished and splendidly renovated to its traditional glory. Hours are from 8:00 am to 6:00 pm daily. There is a charge of $1.50 to get in.

Donkey Sanctuary

Located right at the waterfront, the **donkey sanctuary** is run by the International Donkey Protection Trust of Sidmouth, Devon, UK. Because the Lamu primary form of transport is the donkey, there are any number of these beasts of burden on the island. Any hurt, abused, or simply old donkeys are welcomed here to find protection and asylum. It is a most surprising but worthwhile enterprise that will pull at your heartstrings.

Lamu Fort Museum/Aquarium & Library

The restored and renovated **Lamu Fort** now holds a natural history museum, the island's library, and a marvelous aquarium. The enormous and impressive edifice was begun in 1810 by the Sultan of Pat. Finishing touches were completed in 1823. It was used as a prison from 1910 until 1984. To get here from the main jetty, head inland and you will come to the customs office. Lamu Fort is directly behind this building and adjacent to the local market.

Mosques

Lamu town is filled with at least 20 historic **mosques**. There are few doors or windows onto the street, making them hard to recognize as anything but local buildings made of coral. On the outside the minarets are not outlandish or large. One telltale sign of a mosque is the dozens of shoes piled outside during prayer times. Resounding calls to prayer echo throughout the city as a daily reminder of the Islamic faith.

The mosques in Lamu are small and generally tourists are welcome. If you have never seen a Muslim worship service, I think you will find it interesting. The ornate carvings and detailed woodwork is not only beautiful but fascinatingly ornate. The workmanship is often quite detailed and obviously done over some time with much patience and pride.

The only requirements for visiting are: that your clothing be conservative with no or little skin showing; no shorts or bathing suits or short sleeves; that you remove your shoes before entering; and that you cover your head. The people worshipping in these mosques are sensitive and serious about their religion so please be considerate.

MAULIDI

Maulidi is a revered observance of the prophet Mohammed's birthday. Celebrated by Muslims making pilgrimages from all over Kenya just after Easter, the entire town becomes a bright colorful place. There are time honored dhow races and dancing in the streets. Accommodations are hard to find so book ahead and enjoy the festivities.

Carpenters

Take a walk to the far end of town in the opposite direction from Shela. Once you reach the harbor look for generations of carpenters hard at work. The skills and designs passed down from generation to generation are in danger of disappearing. But if enough visitors buy their intricately carved lintels and doors, the art won't be lost. It is truly amazing to watch the devotion and dexterity going into each stroke of their primitive tools.

In and around Lamu, the **boat builders** reject modern tools and technology to carry out their traditional craft. Instead they prefer to build their dhows by hand with specialized tools used for centuries.

NIGHTLIFE & ENTERTAINMENT

Bars/Clubs

The thatched patio bar open to the public at **Petley's Inn**, *Tel. (0127) 48107,* just back from the water near the main jetty. It is near Lamu museum and Prestige Air Services. This is a charming place to be cooled by the ocean breezes, and is the most frequented place on the island where you can get a really cold drink.

Another place in town to get a truly cold beer is the **Lamu Palace Hotel**, *Tel. (0121) 3272*, on the southside of Lamu overlooking the water. Just behind it is the Lamu Book Center and a little further south is the Olympic Restaurant. Apart from anything else, it a great location for people watching. At the **Peponi Hotel** on the harbor waterfront at the far end of Shela Village, *Tel. 0121 3029,* the drinks are also marvelously cold and the atmosphere irresistible.

The **Civil Servants' Club** outside town on the southside has a disco on the occasional Friday or Saturday night. Look for posters scattered around town advertising the dates of the dance. There is a $2 entry fee.

SPORTS & RECREATION
Dhow Rides/Services
It takes about 15 minutes to ride the **Peponi Hotel** dhow shuttle one way to or from Lamu Town. Departure from the hotel is at 9:00 am and return is at noon.

For $8 per person for less than four people and $4 per person for four or more people you can go out on a dhow for a lazy day. Five is the maximum number of passengers the vessels can comfortably hold; any more bodies and the small craft is just too cramped. Full day or half day trips are the norm, but as competition for your business is fierce, you can negotiate almost any kind of outing. You might even try three or more days!

The cost includes fishing, a fish barbecue (with your catch), and snorkeling. However, the dhows seem to offer their services during the heat of the day (a hat and sun screen are a must!) when fishing is at its worst, so be prepared to catch nothing and eat the fish provided by the captain. The best snorkeling is two hours away so you may not see the most spectacular underwater scenes. As long as you go out with reasonable expectations and an awareness of what you're likely to encounter, it is a fun and memorable outing.

There is a marvelous opportunity to dine on fresh lobster while sailing in a dhow. This special activity takes place during sunny days or at night under the stars; either way it's wonderful.

Snorkeling
The best snorkeling is a couple of hours away from Lamu on **Manda Toto Island**. You must hire a boat to get there which should be no problem. Just inquire at your hotel.

Swimming

From the town of Lamu there is a long beach backed by sand dunes where it is safe to swim. Guests at Peponi can walk to the beach or you can catch a ride with a dhow from the town. It is unwise to bring valuables with you because of theft problems.

When swimming in front of the Peponi, be careful to avoid vessels traveling the waterway and beware of sometimes strong currents. In the evening and early morning, when there is less boat traffic, the appeal to swim here is much greater than at busier times of the day.

SHOPPING

Some of the better shopping on the Island of Lamu is at **Kipangani Village**. It is a pleasant day trip easily arranged to include tea, snacks, and a visit to gorgeous unoccupied beaches nearby. The villages excel in their weaving crafts producing hats, baskets, and attractive mats.

There are several small **markets** in Lamu town serving the local population. It is educational and fun to wander among the vendors looking at (and sampling) fresh produce. Baskets and calabashes used by the sellers make great authentic keepsakes if you can make a good enough argument for them to sell.

EXCURSIONS & DAY TRIPS

Tana River Primate Sanctuary

The **Tana River Primate Sanctuary** is the only remaining 68 square miles of riverside forest on the mainland. Near Kenya's largest river (the Tana) and the Indian Ocean, the trees offer evidence that forests once stretched all the way across the country. All manner of rare animals such as the Hunter's hartebeest struggle to exist. In addition to over 248 different bird species, the sanctuary is home to an unusual collection of endangered primates, including 800 crested mangabeys and the red colobus.

Arawale National Reserve

Almost dead center between Malindi and Lamu, following the coast road (B8) north, is where the Tana River empties into the Indian Ocean. The B8 turns inland and heads toward the northern town of Garissa. The first main town you'll come to is Garsen where the B8 coastal road from Mombasa and the C112 coming from Lamu, meet. Just north along the B8 is the Tana River Primate Sanctuary. Not much past it, on the east bank of the Tana River, is the 213 square mile **Arawale National Reserve**.

Many of the tour and safari organizers tend to overlook the Arawale National Reserve and as such there are no facilities for guests. In the past, there have been operators offering excellent river safaris here but interest seemed to wane for no obvious reason. If you check with the larger hotels, tourist resorts, and travel agents, they may know the present itineraries of any tour companies organizing river safaris in the area.

The hartebeest or kongoni seems to prefer living in this arid thorny region where they have daily access to water.

WHAT IS A BIOSPHERE?

A biosphere is any area of the world that contains unique landforms, landscapes, and systems of land use which are intended to provide large protected areas ideal for scientific study of their unique qualities and interdependencies. Out of 271 in the world, Kenya has four.

Dodori, Kiunga, & Boni National Reserves

Moving northwards along the coast on the B8 you will need to turn onto the C112 heading to Lamu. From Mokokwe head northwest on the minor road until you come to Bodhei. Turn northeast, and you'll arrive at the national parks of Dodori, Kiunga, and Boni in that order.

Kiunga Marine Biosphere National Reserve is about 80 miles north of Mokokwe (which is across from Lamu) on the mainland. The parks sit side by side on this, Kenya's northernmost coast. If you venture a few miles past Boni you will find yourself in the Somali Republic. Kiunga permits swimming, sailing, water-skiing and diving. The coastal preserve includes many spectacular coral formations and offshore islands. Birdlife includes gulls, terns, and other ocean going birds. Along with a large fish population, look for rare green and dugong turtles. Kiunga is an important breeding ground for seabirds during the months of July and October.

Boni is 535 square miles of unusual lowland coastal forest with standing groundwater attracting herds of elephant in the dry season. At low tide the pachyderms cross from Boni to nearby Dodori National Reserve and then over to Elephant Island. Boni is named after a small surviving tribe of Boni hunter-gatherers living in the area. It is thought these early inhabitants are descendants of the African pygmies or southern bushmen.

On one side **Dodori** links to Boni and on the other to Kiunga Marine National Reserve. The 350 square miles of groundwater forests, lowland dry backwoods, and mangrove swamps provide breeding habitat for the shy topi and a host of smaller creatures. It is quite a treat to watch families of elephants help each other across the shallow flats to the island.

Matondoni Village

To reach the village on the west side of Lamu Island you can choose to take a two hour walk, hire a donkey (which takes a little less time), or take a dhow along the coast for $13 (with lunch). The main attraction here is to watch the master craftsmen repair and build dhows. The small village is not equipped to handle overnight guests but there is a cozy cafe where you can purchase fruit juices and local dishes of fish and rice.

Kiwayu Island

This island has a reputation for catering to the rich and famous. It sits at the far northeast end of the **Lamu Archipelago** and is surrounded by the Kiunga National Marine Reserve. The coral reefs on the eastern side of the island are recognized as some of the best in Kenya.

There is an airstrip catering to those wishing to fly in. In the village there is a small general store that sells basic provisions.

Paté Island

After a varied history of power and collapse, today the island of **Paté** remains relatively run-down. It is a shadow of its former glory. It looks like an insignificant semi-inhabited strip of land with no draw for tourists. If you enjoy being truly off the beaten path, this island will be of interest to you. There are some engaging but overgrown ruins called **Nabahani** just outside the small community.

Manda Island

There is a popular dhow trip to **Manda Island** from Lamu for $19. If you ask, the captain may include a delicious fish barbecue lunch. The island is across the channel from Lamu making it easy to get to. Once you arrive after the one and a half hour trip, there are 12 acres of 16th and 17th century **Takwa ruins** to explore. Maintained by the National Museums of Kenya, the entry fee is $1.78. You will have roughly 45 minutes to look around and then you must ride the tide back out to the ocean.

It is important to note that the vessels depend on the wind for speed – no wind, no forward movement – so the trip can sometimes be interminable. Don't be surprised if you are asked to push the dhow if the tide is heading out and the water a little shallow. Access to the island is during the high tide only, up a mangrove studded creek shaded by baobab trees. If you miss the ebb tide, a night on Manda Island with thousands of mosquitoes can be awful.

Manda Toto Island

Manda Toto Island is known for its excellent snorkeling. It is located just off the northeast coast of Manda Island and is accessible by dhow only.

Because of its inaccessibility, the outstanding reefs and undiscovered beaches remain relatively untouched and unvisited.

PRACTICAL INFORMATION

Banks

Be prepared to wait for half an hour or more to cash a check or change money. If the banks are busy, the process can be interminable. The **Standard Chartered Bank** and the **Kenya Commercial Bank** are both located on the harbor front. Hours are 8:30 am to 1:00 pm Monday through Friday and 8:30 am to 11:00 am on Saturday.

Bookstores

It is possible to purchase local newspapers, novels, and international magazines at the bookstore in Lamu. It is located next door to the Garissa Express office. Hours are 6:30 am to noon and 2:30 pm to 9:00 pm.

Guides/Boatmen

In the town of Lamu there are any number of eager guides willing to take you around for the day, an hour, or ten minutes. Many of them speak adequate English but be sure you can understand it. Set a price before you go off on your jaunt and don't pay up front. Going with a guide not only gives you a more accurate and educated overview of the history and hideaways of the town, but also saves you from others pestering to be hired.

Safety

Muggings, rapes, and even a murder or two have occurred along the beaches and byways around Shela and Lamu. The local police have cracked down and practically eradicated the problem, but to avoid any unpleasant or dangerous situations check with the locals before setting off on your own.

Tourist Office

During the busy season there is a small counter set up near the dhow jetty serving as a tourists' information center. Don't expect too much.

15. THE RIFT VALLEY

Visitors to Kenya normally get their first taste of the magnificent **Rift Valley** as they drive north on the excellent Nairobi to Naivasha highway. In the beginning the journey begins with cool conifer forests, until the huge arid fissure opens up before you. To absorb its magnificence you must stop just past the town of **Limuru**; these are the best views. (Don't let the souvenir sellers distract you with their sometimes poorly made wares – you can probably do better elsewhere.) In the distance, towering **Mount Longonot** fills the landscape while 30 miles across the chasm loom purple-blue valley walls.

Millions of years ago, in and around the Rift Valley, volcanic eruptions frequently covered the earth with red-hot lava and fine gray ash. Upheaval deep in the earth's belly ripped the land like cardboard, leaving jagged cliffs and deep valleys that today is the greatest continental fault system in the world. Starting in Mozambique, the amazingly huge crack in the earth runs from Malawi, Tanzania, Kenya, Ethiopia and the Red Sea all the way through the Dead Sea in Israel in the Middle East. Telltale signs of the pure might and enigma of the earth's evolution were left behind for our wonderment in the form of extinct volcanic cones, immense calderas, and half-submerged islands.

Running from **Lake Turkana** (described in Chapter 16, *Northern Kenya*) in the north to **Lake Magadi** (dealt with in Chapter 12, *Nairobi*) in the south the long narrow valley cuts Kenya almost in half. For our purposes the rift begins in the town of **Naivasha** to the south and ends with **Lake Baringo** and **Kerio Valley National Reserve** in the north. The Rift Valley is peppered with soda and fresh water lakes sought after by hundreds of spectacular birds, wild animals, and of course, tourists. Lakes Naivasha, Nakuru, Baringo, Bogoria and Elmenteita are the most visited in that order of popularity. Magadi, Bogoria, and Nakuru are soda lakes while the others are freshwater.

RIFT VALLEY MUST SEES

Mount Susua (Suswa)
Lake Naivasha
Hell's Gate National Park
Green Crater Lake
Eburu Mountain
Lake Nakuru National Park
Lake Bogoria National Reserve
Lake Magadi (best accessed from Nairobi)

NAIVASHA

A popular place for the infamous "Happy Valley" crowd, this area of Kenya was one of the first settled by Europeans. **Naivasha** is a corruption of the Masai words *En-Aiposha* meaning "the lake." Many land tracts around the town are still owned by descendants of the settlers. The most eminent family about is that of Lord Delamere. This family's estate surrounds the town and flows west towards Nakuru.

As a small service center for the surrounding agricultural district, Naivasha doesn't have too much to keep you here, but it is a good place to buy any necessities you may need. Vast farms growing strawberries, flowers, and beans export these goods to Europe and the world.

ARRIVALS & DEPARTURES

By Air

Most of the hotels and lodges have their own private airfields but will arrange to pick you up if you arrive at a public strip nearby. Perhaps you could arrange to drive in and fly out of the area for the best of both worlds.

By Bus

Buses and matatus are easy to find here in Naivasha town if you are heading for Nyahururu, Narok, Nakuru, Nairobi or towns further west. All of these leave from the main bus stand except for the matatus on their way to the capital which depart from the stand on Kenyatta Avenue.

By Car

The main Nairobi to Naivasha road actually goes around the town so you will have to make a slight detour to get here. From the capital it is roughly a one hour drive (53 miles) to Naivasha along the A104 Nakuru Road.

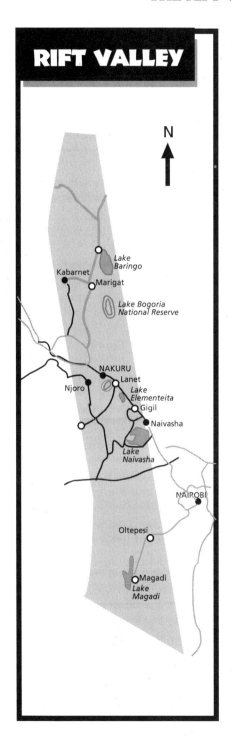

By Train
All bookings are best made before leaving Nairobi. You can reach Naivasha by train but be prepared to disembark early in the morning. Trains to Kisumu and Malaba go through the town in the late afternoon.

ORIENTATION

The town basically consists of two main streets with a few smaller intersecting roads. In the north of the town is the Kenvash Hotel (under construction at the time of this writing). The southernmost buildings are the Naivasha Silver Hotel and Jolly Cafe. On the west side of the village is the railway station and to the east is a matatu stand with service to Nairobi.

GETTING AROUND TOWN

Everything is well within walking distance. Depending on the condition of the roads, you should park and walk. If possible have someone watch your car and your valuables.

WHERE TO STAY

MUNDUI, *Wilderness Trails Limited, Bush Homes Africa Safaris, Tel. US 404 888 0909, e mail bushhomes@africaonline.co.ke, www.bushhomes.com, PO Box 56923, Nairobi. Tel. 506 139, Fax 502 739. $360 per night double occupancy. All major credit cards accepted.*

Near the main house (built in 1926) at Mundui is a second, self-contained home built in 1933 by an Austrian as a hunting lodge for his guests. Deceptively formal looking on the outside, the "cottage" is bright and open on the inside with an enormous fireplace and soaring ceilings in the large ground floor living room. Two comfortable bedrooms with full bathrooms dominate the second floor which is decorated with elegance and charm. It is here that exclusive parties of visitors to the 12,000 acre estate spend their leisure time. Add your name to the impressive guest list including the likes of Ernest Hemingway and the Aga Khan.

Whether you arrive down the long driveway trimmed with bougain-villea or fly into the private airstrip, your first sight of the colorfully landscaped primary household will take your breath away. Large windows and colonial style verandahs offer spectacular distant views of the Rift Valley walls and volcanic peaks. Lake Naivasha, bordered by green lawns and huge shade trees, is a picturesque backdrop. A warm welcome from the Lord and Lady of Enniskillin, Sarah and Andrew Cole, whose family has played a role in Kenya's history, certainly puts the culminating touch on the grand estate.

For entertainment spend a day by the pool or paddle the morning away in a boat on the cool lake. Birds and wild game are varied and abundant on open plains surrounding the property. An early morning walk to see giraffe, cheetah, eland, hippo or zebra works up an appetite for breakfast on the lawn. It is also possible to spend the day at Crater Lake, Elsamere, and other nearby sights.

LOLDIA HOUSE, *Musiara Limited-Governor's Camps, PO Box 48217, Nairobi. Tel. 331 871, Fax 726 427. $326 per night double occupancy. All major credit cards accepted.*

The main guest house, constructed from carved lava rock, was built by Italian prisoners of war in the 1940s under the direction of the current owner's grandfather. From the long shady verandah, picturesque Mount Longonot and moody Lake Naivasha stand out against once ferocious volcanic domes and the felt-green yard. Drink in the colors of flowering bushes, colorful beds, and large wild fig trees as you enjoy a sundowner from a front row seat.

Rather than stay in the home of Rick and Bette Hopcraft who own the surrounding cattle ranch, you will be attended to by the resident manager in the old stone house or a large and elegantly thatched banda a short distance away. Pleasant decor throughout the rooms, private bathrooms, and exceptionally well prepared meals add to the feeling of luxury. Perhaps the most remarkable feature other than dramatic vistas through attractive old windows is the long list of activities.

Lake Nakuru National Park, Hell's Gate, or Lake Bogoria make great day sightseeing trips. Take a picnic lunch and test your stamina with a climb up Mount Longonot. Go fishing off the bow of a sailboat or paddle along the shore in a canoe. Learn about the plentiful birds as your craft glides on Lake Naivasha's waters or walk through the bush with the live-in ornithologist/botanist. Take pictures of buffalo, ostrich and assorted antelope from horseback or once again simply relax in a soft chair by the cozy fireplace.

KONGONI GAME VALLEY RANCH, *PO Box 41759, Nairobi. Tel. 338 838, Fax 218 939. $300 per night double occupancy. All major credit cards accepted.*

The beauty of this private home is you'll never feel you are seeing Kenya as a tourist but instead, as a personal guest of the Italian family of Bruno and Gianna Brighetti. The main long, low stone house built around a central courtyard, unattached guest bandas, or another separate dwelling on the lakeshore are your choices for accommodation. Whichever you pick offers relaxation, fun, and a unique Kenya experience from a settlers point of view.

A French Marquis and his American wife first moved to the roughly 14,000 acre ranch in 1901 after they fell in love with the mystery and beauty of Africa. In a private part of the manicured grounds the couple are buried facing their favorite magnificent vista. Today the Brighettis love this land no less than the previous owners and take particular care of the wildlife, the people, and the land.

To fill the days, there is much to do. Hike, drive, or ride horses among plentiful plains game or down along the fertile lakeshore. Hippos and myriads of pelicans, coots, and herons accompany you on a boat outing around the lake. Back at the ranch in the sun room, pizza, pasta, ice cream, bread and all manner of homemade Italian delicacies are ready when you are.

Simply sit on the wide verandah absorbing the view of Lake Naivasha in the deep Rift Valley below or walk among the manicured lawn's bright English flower beds with breathtaking volcanic vistas and vast grasslands all around you. See if you can distinguish between the flat-topped acacia trees and the forests of euphorbia.

Each of the bedrooms is bright and comfortable with the personal decorating touch of the owners. As the name of the ranch implies, the family is fond of kongoni as you will notice from the hartebeest motif dotted around the home. Look for particularly interesting old fashioned ensuite bathrooms with charming antique fixtures and bidets.

THE WAGON WHEEL, *Safcon Travel Services, Limited, PO Box 59224, Nairobi. Tel. 503 265, Fax 506 824. $290 per night double occupancy. All major credit cards accepted.*

History envelops the Morson family. In 1904 the eminent Lord Delamere encouraged the opening of a sawmill in Limuru by two brothers. Around 1976 they gave up logging but stayed to breed racing horses and grow tea. Kitch Morson and his wife Millicent recently retired to The Wagon Wheel, where lush gardens and valuable historical pieces are available for privileged guests to enjoy. Ask to see the unusual collection of antiques around the farmhouse including elegant china. Some of the antiques were even used on the set of the movie *Out of Africa*.

Two comfortable guest bedrooms in the double story home come with their own bathrooms and private exits to the spectacular gardens. As one of the most beautiful yards ever designed, the English flavor flows from one raised flower-filled bed to another. Winding paths invite visitors to get lost as they take in the sweet fragrances and bright colors. Tall shrubbery and exotic shade trees harbor any number of our feathered friends.

Walking to Lake Naivasha, hiking, boating, bird watching and visits to nearby points of interest can be arranged for Millicent's houseguests upon request.

OLERAI HOUSE, *Oria Douglas-Hamilton, PO Box 54667, Nairobi. Tel. 334 868, E-mail: oria@iconnect.co.ke. $280 per night double occupancy. All major credit cards accepted.*

Often used by residents of Nairobi as a relaxing and casual weekend getaway cottage, Olerai is unhosted except for the well trained and friendly staff. In two of the four bedrooms arranged around a garden terrace, quaint lofts and dormer windows make the rooms unique. Murals add a touch of elegance in some of the individual bathrooms of what was once the family home. Today it is a great place for a group or a family to spend quality time together.

The vine covered homestead is surrounded by lush lawns, tall shade trees, and sweet smelling flowers. Eating under the huge spreading acacia (*olerai* in Masai) for which the place was named is a special treat. Unfortunately there is no view of Lake Naivasha or any acceptable access, but perhaps a postcard perspective of Mount Longonot in the background will make it up to you.

Nearby on the grounds is Sirocco House, the newer family art deco home. Built in the 1930s by Oria's parents, the house offers an unusual hideaway for a sundowner or classic English tea. With a reputation as excellent elephant conservationists, Ian and Oria encourage guided nature walks around the farm or in the scenic hills. Airplane flights around Mount Kenya, ox wagon trips, and visits to Crater Lake are other options for your pleasure.

LONGONOT RANCH HOUSE, *Safaris Unlimited (Africa) Limited, PO Box 24181, Nairobi. Tel. 891 168, Fax 891 113, e-mail info@safarisunlimited.com, www.safarisunlimited.com. $280-320 per night double occupancy.*

Originally built by Martha Gellhorn, one of Ernest Hemingway's wives, today no one actually lives in the hilltop ranch house. However, the hilltop ranch house is fully staffed with a manager, chef, stewards, room staff, askaris, gardeners and grooms for the horses.

Typical of the colonial era, the house has a lovely open central courtyard and cool wrap around verandahs. A large welcoming fireplace and oversized chairs invite guests to stay a while. Bedrooms in the main building and those in an adjoining guest cottage are winningly decorated in bright flowery prints.

Once you leave the shores of Lake Naivasha and head up towards the house with its elevated setting, enjoy the distant vistas and surrounding landscape. On the immediate grounds a natural craggy formation is filled with aloe and cactus plants making a pretty rock garden. Further afield, Mount Longonot, Hell's Gate Gorge, and dramatic volcanic mountains hold your attention.

On the 79,000 acre ranch, horseback riding gets you close to groups of zebra, giraffe, gazelle, antelope and other plains game. Guests at Longonot Ranch have the additional pleasures of riding among the animals (for a fee of $15.00 per horse per hour) or hiking with a park ranger. In tall thorn trees on the grasslands, look for a glimpse of an elusive cheetah. Optional activities include side trips to Elsamere, Mount Longonot, and other nearby attractions.

CRATER LAKE (LAKE SONGASOI TENTED CAMP), *Let's Go Travel, PO Box 60342, Nairobi. Tel. 340 331, Fax 336 890. $220 per night double occupancy. All major credit cards accepted.*

Near Lake Naivasha the small camp is set up inside the encircling walls of an impressive crater within Crater Lake Sanctuary. The camp comes equipped with flush toilets, hot showers, and six simple tents. To get to the campground first you must take an exhilarating hike along steep narrow paths through rocky crags.

The most unusual feature of the camp is the green waters of Crater Lake at the bottom of the extinct volcano. During your stay, walk around the lake where you're likely to see fish eagles, colobus monkeys, and waterbuck. In the simple mess tent, a master chef prepares highly distinguished meals for his lucky guests.

MORENDAT HOUSE, *PO Box 299, Naivasha. Tel. 0311 20041. $210 per night double occupancy. No children under twelve. All major credit cards accepted.*

Giulia Bisleti, owner of Morendat House, likes to persuade her guests that her strategically placed home should be their base while in the area. Set conveniently between lakes Nakuru and Naivasha, the elegant house is minutes off the main road and close to Lake Naivasha.

The whitewashed stone exterior of the main house is enhanced by lush leafy plants along the verandah, fragrant fruit trees, and tumbling flowers in the large garden. Adjacent to the building is an additional full service guest cottage with an inviting swimming pool alongside.

Decor in the spacious rooms is artistic, eccentric, and at the same time genteel. Shiny copper, gentle arches, antiques, and collector's art will fill your head with ideas for your own home as you relax in Giulia's.

LAKESIDE HOUSE, *PO Box 1262, Naivasha. Tel. 02 56742 or 0311 20908. $180 per night double occupancy.*

June Shaw is the owner and gracious innkeeper at Lakeside House where her visitors are treated like part of the household. Sleeping accommodations are either in the main house or a nearby banda. While the grounds may be pretty but unspectacular and the rooms adequate but a little cramped, you won't find more gracious or welcoming hospitality than at Lakeside House. To get to the house take the Moi South Lake Road and once you arrive enjoy a close-up view of Lake Naivasha from the peaceful verandah. Family members of the small residence will help arrange your itinerary including boat rentals, nature walks, and sightseeing to nearby Crescent Island or Hell's Gate.

LAKE NAIVASHA COUNTRY CLUB, *Block Hotels, PO Box 47557, Nairobi. Tel. 335 807, Fax 340 541. $120 per night double occupancy. All major credit cards accepted.*

A favorite with Nairobi residents, Lake Naivasha Club provides a fun, weekend getaway for the capital's population and tourists alike. If you are not a guest of the club, a sizable membership fee is charged to use the facilities.

The club is set on roughly 55 acres of lush gardens and green rolling lawns. Spreading yellow fever and acacia trees shade delicious lunch buffets served outdoors on holidays and weekends. Picturesque views of wading birds, waterbuck, and sunrises are magnificent from a wooden gazebo at the end of a wandering path. Rest on rustic wooden seats under the tall trees or relax on the long cool verandah as birds and wildlife entertain you on the grounds.

Used as a convenient base for the numerous area sights, Lake Naivasha Country Club has several options for your enjoyment. You can take excursions to Crescent Island, get fishing boat and equipment rentals, go on guided lake cruises, bird and nature walks, and visit local attractions. Ferry services, souvenir stores, and adult/children's pools are also available.

Just after WWII, the flying boats of British Airways on their way to South Africa following the Nile, landed here at what was then Kenya's international air terminal. Today, the charming old house with its French doors and wooden floors is only part of the club layout. Small cottages and one story annexes complete the 50 room count, each with their own verandah and garden view. All the rooms have private bathrooms with full facilities. The airy dining room, quaint bar, and elegant lounge areas will keep you comfortable with a romantic fireplace and splendid views.

SAFARILAND CLUB, LIMITED, *PO Box 72, Naivasha. Tel. 0311 20241, Telex 39051 Safarclub. $110 per night double occupancy. All major credit cards accepted.*

As of this writing, the club was in dire need of refurbishment. Management mentioned an overhaul was in the works including additions of a spa and golf course. The club itself can house up to 114 people not including the campsite next door. With ample acreage and a striking lakeside setting, the potential is exciting. For the present time, cottages and a variety of rooms are dotted around the grounds. Facilities that might be considered for an inexpensive day outing at the club include an aviary, boat and horse rentals, a pool, and tennis courts.

ELSAMERE CONSERVATION CENTER, *Elsamere, PO Box 1497, Naivasha. Tel. 0311 30079. $90 per night double occupancy. No children under seven. All major credit cards accepted.*

There are a couple of accommodation options at Elsamere, including the Adamson bedroom in the main house or one of the three attractive cottages facing the lake. All the rooms come with full bathrooms, colorful decor, and a verandah. The only requirement states guests must belong to a conservation society of some kind. Meals at the all-inclusive center are served at long communal tables where conversation with fellow diners is fun and lively.

To satisfy your needs to explore, rent a boat, and set off along the edge of the lake or hike down one of the nearby nature trails. Wildflowers, peaceful lake vistas, and lots of birds will keep you company. In the large aged trees surrounding the conservation center, noisy resident colobus monkeys will keep you entertained for hours.

LA BELLE INN, *Naivasha, Tel. 0311 20116. $23 per night double occupancy. Full breakfast included. All major credit cards accepted.*

In the town of Naivasha itself, La Belle Inn offers clean accommodations with private bathrooms upon request. A friendly staff will take care of all your needs. There is safe parking and a popular bar on the premises. The French cuisine is famous throughout the area.

WHERE TO EAT

Of course any of the out of town hotels or homestays offer excellent places to eat. **LA BELLE INN** in Naivasha town, *Tel. 0311 20116,* is a relaxing place to enjoy delicious and reasonably priced French food. A meal will run you about $4!! It is open daily except Tuesdays. The long outdoor verandah is most popular and offers a view of the busy and dusty street life beyond. For less impressive settings try the clean **JOLLY CAFE** next-door to the Silver Hotel. The food is good and inexpensive and the staff is friendly.

The **NAIVASHA SILVER HOTEL** on Kenyatta Avenue and the **OTHAYA ANNEXE HOTEL** on Station Lane both offer reasonably good restaurants if you like to vary your menu. To investigate true African food for those of you who are truly adventuresome, try the **SUN SET RESTAURANT** towards the south end of town. Outside of town towards the eastern end of Moi South Lake Road, try the **YELOGREEN BAR & RESTAURANT** for a cold drink or tasty fare.

NIGHTLIFE & ENTERTAINMENT

It can be extremely relaxing to sip a cold beer on the much frequented porch at **La Belle Inn** as you watch the Kenyan world go by. An upstairs bar and restaurant at the **Naivasha Silver Hotel** or the bar at the **Othaya Annexe Hotel** sell tasty beer.

SPORTS & RECREATION

Game Viewing/Drives

For safe and excellent game viewing take a trip out to **Crescent Island** where you will find a host of game (excluding cats and elephants). It is possible to walk among the animals with no fear. From the **Safariland Club** a fee of $32 will get four people across to the island. Excursions can also be arranged through the **Lake Naivasha Club** at much the same price.

Birds and wild game are varied and abundant on open plains surrounding **Mundui**. An early morning walk to see giraffe, cheetah, eland, hippo or zebra works up an appetite for breakfast on the lawn. Take pictures of buffalo, ostrich, and assorted antelope from horseback at **Lodia House**. Drive or ride horses among plentiful plains game on **Kongoni Game Valley Ranch**.

Hiking/Walking

Nature walks all around the area are a popular pastime with the guests of the **Lake Naivasha Club**. For a full day of walking (14 miles) through **Hell's Gate National Park** from the lake shore to the lake road turn off at Elsa Gate – carry plenty of water and some food. Check at your hotel for guides and details. If you stay at **Mundui**, it is possible to spend the day walking around Crater Lake or Elsamere. Take a picnic lunch from **Loldia House** and test your stamina with a climb up Mount Longonot. Hike among plentiful plains game on **Kongoni Game Valley Ranch**.

The owners of **Olerai House** encourage guided nature walks around the farm or in the scenic hills. During your stay at **Crater Lake** or **Lake Songasoi Tented Camp** walk around the lake where you're likely to see fish eagles, colobus monkeys, and waterbuck.

Birding

At **Lake Naivasha Club**, guided ornithological walks are a pleasant and educational way to spend a morning. From **Loldia House** learn about the plentiful birds as your craft glides on Lake Naivasha's waters or walk through the bush with the live-in ornithologist/botanist.

Fishing

Fishing on Lake Naivasha is a popular pastime, as it is only 52 miles from Nairobi. A healthy population of fresh water crayfish help rangers keep tabs on the environment around the lake. **Lake Naivasha Club** offers boat and equipment rental. When you stay at **Loldia House**, go fishing off the bow of a sailboat or paddle a canoe along the shore.

Windsurfing & Sailing/Boating

For those of you who are interested in either windsurfing or sailing, check at the **Crescent Island Yatch Club** for availability and rates. Guided lake cruises can be arranged from the **Lake Naivasha Club** for guests and non-guests alike. Rowboats can be rented from **Fisherman's Camp** for $1.10 per hour and motorboats go for about $11 per hour. If you want a driver it will cost you $22 per hour; an $11 deposit is required.

Spend a day at **Mundui** paddling your boat on the refreshing lake. Along the fertile shore around **Kongoni Game Valley Ranch**, hippos, pelicans, coots, and herons accompany you on a boat outing around the lake.

Ox-Wagon Safaris

Cordon Bleu Safaris, *c/o UTC, PO Box 42196, Nairobi,* offers a variety of day and overnight trips for visitors. During the unusual experience, a team of 14 oxen will pull your covered wagon slowly through the bush as you look for animals. Ox wagon trips from **Olerai House** can be arranged for your pleasure. See Chapter 9, *Sports & Recreation*, for more information.

Horseback Riding

The **Safariland Club** charges $15 per hour for horse riding around their property – a great way to see the countryside. On the 79,000 acre ranch horseback riding gets you close to groups of zebra, giraffe, gazelle, antelope and other plains game. On the grassland look for a glimpse of a cheetah. At **Loldia House** among the many activities, it is possible to test your photography skills from horseback as you get close to antelope, zebra, and ostrich.

Swimming

At **Lake Naivasha Club** there is a swimming pool for adults and a children's wading pool. If you are not a guest, expect to pay a membership fee. For $3 the **Safariland Club** allows non-guests to use their pool. The pool at **Mundui** is a great place to while away a sunny afternoon.

SHOPPING

Next to the Lake Naivasha Club, the **Elmenteita Weavers** offer a variety of pretty locally produced handicrafts. Look for hand-woven items such as cushion covers, colorful kikois, and shawls. At **Lake Naivasha Club** there is a souvenir and sundry shop for your perusal if you are in the area. **Elsamere Conservation Center** has a small gift shop for souvenirs.

Just outside the town of Naivasha, with a marvelous view of Mount Longonot on your left, is a convenient stopping point. From here not only is the view lovely, but there are many **dukas** selling carvings, baskets, rugs, and dozens of other keepsakes.

EXCURSIONS & DAY TRIPS
Lake Naivasha

Fresh water **Lake Naivasha** is very popular with residents of Nairobi as a weekend getaway or a vacation spot. There are a variety of places to stay and a lot to see in this, the highest (6,100 feet) of the Rift Valley lakes. Around the lake and its shores are productive vineyards, fertile farms, buoyant papyrus islands, and striking yellow fever acacia trees. Flocks of birds and increasing herds of hippos call the lake home.

Existing controversy continues between conservationists and those in search of the tourist dollar. As the popularity of Lake Naivasha increases so does the ecological interference. So far, whether intentionally or not, nutria (from a fur farm), sports fish, crayfish, and aquatic plants have been introduced.

Interestingly, the levels of the lake unpredictably rise and fall as semi-submerged farm posts attest. In the 1890s the waters just about disappeared completely, only to return with a vengeance. The waters rose 50 feet above the previous waterline covering a large tract of arable land. Since then, however, the lake level has receded and settled at a respectable 43 square miles.

From 1937 to 1950, flying boats took the four-day trip from England and landed at Lake Naivasha, then Nairobi's airport. At the Lake Naivasha Hotel, passengers climbed off the flying boats and onto waiting buses for the trip to the capital.

Crater Lake Sanctuary

To get into the serene isolated sanctuary (entrance fee is under $1), there is an entrance fee well worth it for the lovely views. In the heart of the extinct volcano an intensely emerald lake captures your attention as does the thick green plantlife. As it is necessary to cross through gates on private land, please make sure the gates are closed behind you.

Green Crater Lake is in Crater Lake Sanctuary just west of Lake Naivasha off the North Lake Road. Getting to the secret and beautiful spot can be somewhat of a challenge if you are on your own but the view of the green lake below from the crater's rim is worth a few hours of searching. Take a knowledgeable guide with you in a four wheel drive vehicle down the Lake Road from Elsamere.

Go five miles to the police post on your left and continue on for another four and a half miles to two large iron gates and a Coca-Cola sign. Go through the right hand gate and drive 380 yards where you must make a sudden right turn. Climb the small hill and follow the track almost to the crater's rim. Walk to the edge and lose yourself in the wonderful view of the dark green lake.

If you decide to make the difficult climb down to the emerald-green water, notice the delightful smell of the camphor (moth ball) bush and the pretty pink mistletoe flowers. Walking along the water's edge there is no need to fear crocodiles as there are none, but it is said oversized pythons inhabit the area. The Masai claim the waters have miraculous medicinal powers for their sick cattle.

Crescent Island

To get to **Crescent Island** it is best to take a boat, although it is possible to walk across a muddy causeway when the lake dries up. The small patch of land in Lake Naivasha is a private game sanctuary, where it is safe to walk among the animals. Zebra, giraffe, hippo, antelope and waterbuck are often seen grazing on the stubby grass. There are no large cats or elephant on the island which was once an active volcano. Today only the outer rim of the extinct dome is visible above the mysteriously fluctuating water level of the lake. There is an attractive yacht club on the island catering to sports enthusiasts.

Elsamere Conservation Center

Once home to famous author Joy Adamson who wrote *Born Free*, the 57 acre site is now a residential conservation center. Open to visitors from 3:00 pm to 6:00 pm, there is a small entrance fee of $2.20 which includes tea on the lawn. It is no wonder Joy wanted to retire to this serenely beautiful lakeside setting. Sadly, she was murdered in 1980 and never got to fully enjoy her lovely home. It is possible to see *The Joy Adamson Story* movie, visit the memorial room or do a little shopping in the gift shop. Afternoon tea on the lawn or pre-arranged luncheon at the center are pleasant options for day guests.

To make arrangements, write to **Elsamere Conservation Center**, *Moi South Lake Road, PO Box 1497, Naivasha, Tel. 0311 30079*.

Hell's Gate National Park

From the Moi South Lake Road just to the south of Lake Naivasha, it is under two miles to the main gate (Elsa Gate) into **Hell's Gate National Park**. There is another entrance on the west side of the park called Ol Karia Gate. It costs $27 per person to get into the park plus $1.50 per vehicle.

After paying the usual entrance fee, take a hike between steep red cliffs. Make the ambitious climb up **Fischer's Tower**, an 80 foot high volcanic outcropping named after a German explorer. If these suggestions sound too exhausting, simply enjoy the fabulous scenery in **Njorowa**

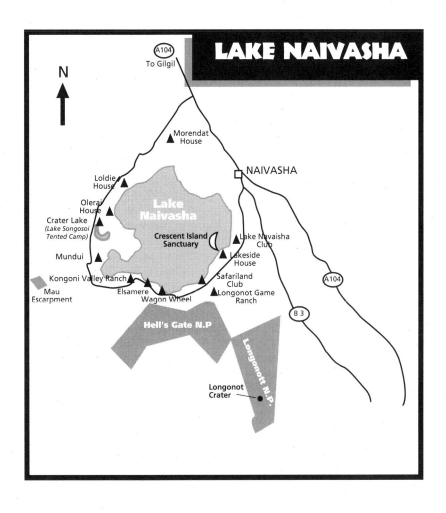

LAKE NAIVASHA

N

A104
To Gilgil

Morendat House

NAIVASHA

Loldie House

Olerai House

Crater Lake
(Lake Songosoi Tented Camp)

Lake Naivasha

Crescent Island Sanctuary

Lake Navaisha Club

Mundui

Lakeside House

Kongoni Valley Ranch

Safariland Club

Mau Escarpment

Elsamere

Wagon Wheel

Longonot Game Ranch

A104

B 3

Hell's Gate N.P

Longonot N.P.

Longonot Crater

Gorge, more commonly known as **Hell's Gate**. The deep chasm with its ochre colored cliffsides, isolated volcanic domes, and a geothermal project at one end are interesting from a geological point of view. Easily seen from all around the park, tall plumes of steam rise into the air from **Ol Karia Geothermal Station**. Much of Kenya's electricity is produced here with the scorching (300 degree Celsius) underground water.

Assortments of succulents such as aloe punctuate the landscape while birds of prey such as eagles, owls, and buzzards soar above. The rocky crags are home to cute families of rock hyrax and plentiful bird species. Off in the distance, spreading grasslands are speckled with game such as zebra, antelope, gazelle, baboon, leopard and cheetah. In Hell's Gate, walking is allowed – take advantage it.

Mount Longonot Mountain Park

Home to a varied population of wildlife and birds, **Mount Longonot** thrusts its way straight up out of the Rift Valley floor. The local African name *Oloonongot* perfectly defines the area as "the mountain of steep ridges." The dormant (some say extinct) volcano in the 61 square mile park is on the southern side of Lake Naivasha. To get into the park be prepared to pay $12. If you are with a group, check to see if the entry fee is included in the price of your tour.

In 45 minutes it is possible to take a pathway to the summit where stunning vistas await you. All the way around the rim of the volcano takes about another three hours. If your energy is still intact, climb down inside the crater all the way to the bottom where a permanent population of buffalo reside. It is best to go with a guide for safety reasons; leave a local to watch your car in the parking area.

Mount Susua (Suswa)

With four wheel drive it is possible to drive all the way to the rim of the seven-mile-diameter **Mount Susua** volcanic crater. The Masai and their children who call this place home will soon find you as you wander around. If you leave your car make sure someone is watching it, or your valuables will disappear. As always, go with someone whom you trust to guide you carefully through the dangerous passages and around holes in the pathways.

At 7,734 feet, the dormant volcano is one of the more unique sights in Kenya, filled with both fascinating features and wildlife. Inside the caldera look for leopard, baboon, gazelle, kongoni, eland, reedbuck and klipspringer who are easily seen if you proceed quietly through the seemingly uninhabited thick cedar forests.

In my opinion, neighboring Mount Longonot, which draws many more visitors, does not offer as much excitement as Mount Susua. Here there are miles of hidden caves, lava tunnels, huge rooms, and a 1,200 foot deep moat around which you will rarely see another tourist. The water-filled moat is particularly captivating because it separates a central lava plateau and the outer wall of the crater. It forms an unmatched phenomenon.

Eburu Mountain

Comparatively easy to get to, it is hard to understand why tourists are never taken to visit "steam mountain." There are breathtaking vistas of the entire area from the mountain peak. There are steam jets and old volcanic craters to explore and wildlife is plentiful. Ask your travel agent or hotel to get you a guide familiar with the territory.

The wilderness of Eburu Forest is around **Eburu Mountain**, where buffalo, lion, zebra, and gazelle carry on their lives. It is possible to climb down a narrow path to the floor of one of the smaller craters on the mountain. As you get near (you don't need a four wheel drive) you will pass the Harambee Secondary School which was once a British settler's farmhouse and some old scaffolding and odd looking buildings. The farmers and settlers harnessed the steam from the mountain to dry pyrethrum flowers, which in those days were used as insecticide.

Naivasha Vineyards

On the eastern shore of Lake Naivasha are the famous vineyards that use the lake's waters for irrigation purposes. The wine tends to be a little tart but is worth trying. Take a bottle home as a souvenir of your trip as you enjoy a tour around the wine-producing estates.

Bees Herb Garden

With advance arrangements it is possible to visit this educational herb garden.

Olorgesailie National Park

This park is actually part of the Rift Valley but is more easily accessed from the capital. See Chapter 12, *Nairobi*, section on Further South of Nairobi.

Lake Magadi

The lake is part of the Rift Valley and is popular with residents of the city for weekend getaways or day trips. You will not see many tourists in the area. See Chapter 12, *Nairobi*, "Excursions & Day Trips Further South of Nairobi."

LELESHWA LEAF

*The Masai are a very clean people but often lack the opportunity of bathing or using western deodorant. To combat unpleasant under-arm smell, the innovative tribespeople use the **leleshwa leaf** found growing in abundance around Mount Longonot Mountain Park near Lake Naivasha. With the handy leaf tucked under their arms the odor problem is easily overcome.*

PRACTICAL INFORMATION

Banks

On Moi Avenue, which is the main street in Naivasha, you will find two banks. Hours for both **Barclays Bank** and **Kenya Commercial Bank** are standard.

Post Office

Just north of the railway station on Moi Avenue is the standard village post office, offering the usual services such as telephones and stamps.

GILGIL

There is not much for tourists in the small town of **Gilgil** between Nakuru and Naivasha, other than a place to stop for a quick freshen-up or perhaps a round of golf. The one-street town grew out of a small market center and today remains a run-down relic of days past.

ARRIVALS & DEPARTURES

By Car

Seventeen miles outside of Naivasha, the Nairobi/Nakuru Road winds through dense copses of acacia trees to the town of Gilgil.

WHERE TO STAY

RIVER HOUSE, *Bunson Travel Services, Limited, PO Box 45456, Nairobi. Tel. 221 992, Fax 723 599. $140 per night double occupancy. All major credit cards accepted.*

As the name implies, the private home sits on 49 forested acres at the edge of a sparkling river. Around the grounds, manicured green grass hugs prolific flower-filled beds and sun dappled walkways. In well tended vegetable gardens, home-grown produce will soon take its place on visitors' plates after being deliciously prepared by Nann, the owner and master chef.

The Barrat home stands ready to welcome you to the family with its crackling fire, family portraits, and friendly dogs. Visitors are lulled into a sense of security as they listen to the friendly chatter around the table. A comfortable bed in one of the two guest bedrooms with ensuite bathrooms cradles you throughout the night.

LAKE ELMENTEITA LODGE, *PO Box 70559, Nairobi. Tel. 224 998, Telex 22658. $180 per night double occupancy. All major credit cards accepted.*

As a new hotel this might be a good choice. Management explains there is a sauna, tennis courts, and swimming pool to service the 30 cottages and suites. With everything being freshly built, the hotel will probably enjoy a good bit of popularity at least to begin with. Views from the hilltop site down to Lake Elmenteita should be awesome as flamingos and other wildlife wander along the shore. Game walks, horseback riding, and ox wagon safaris will be offered between this hotel and its sister lodge, Lake Nakuru Lodge.

DELAMERE CAMP, *PO Box 48019, Nairobi. Tel. 335 935, Fax 216 528. $176 per night double occupancy. All major credit cards accepted.*

To spend the night at this magnificently beautiful site you have two choices of accommodations. The first and most exclusive is a four bunk treehouse with no electricity or in-room bathrooms. Instead you are blessed with a battery powered spotlight for splendid game viewing at the waterhole below and an open terrace on the roof.

Your second choice just four and a half miles away is one of the twelve tents spread along the hillside down to the lake. Each tent is set on a wide concrete landing with sizable full-service bathrooms attached at the back. Inside, the furnishings are comfortable with twin beds, wardrobes, shelves, and a desk. On the verandah, snuggle into a cozy hammock or safari chair.

The primary concrete and wood building houses a bar at one end and dining room at the other. One side is completely open with views of the shimmering lake in the foreground and soaring volcanic peaks in the distance. In the center of the lodge surrounded by woven sofas and chairs is an inviting fireplace.

The splendor of the location lies in the fact that it is a mere hour by road from Nairobi, is on the private estate (Soysambu Wildlife Sanctuary) of the current Lord Delamere, and is one of the most naturally gorgeous and sequestered spots in Kenya.

Nearby game blinds afford excellent views of the shyer animals and offer great photo opportunities. Spend a few hours in the bush with a guide to learn about the uses and fables surrounding local trees, plants, and shrubs. Take a night game drive and look for aardvark, bush babies, and other nocturnal wildlife. Go for a picnic or sundowners in the hills overlooking pristine Lake Elementeita.

WHERE TO EAT

The **RIVER HOUSE** just outside of Gilgil, *Tel. 221 992,* is an excellent place to stop for a first class lunch. The superb meal is prepared by one of the owners who happens to be a master chef.

SEEING THE SIGHTS

Gilgil Commonwealth War Cemetery

Less than two miles out of the little village is the **Commonwealth War Cemetery** where 200 victims of the Second World War are buried. One of forty such cemeteries in Kenya, this one (and the others) are meticulously maintained by the Commonwealth War Graves Commission. It is a sadly moving sight to see all the lives lost to war.

SPORTS & RECREATION

Game Viewing

From **Lake Elmenteita Lodge** and its sister hotel **Lake Nakuru Lodge**, there are guided game walks to see the flamingos and other birds along the lakeshore. At the exclusive **Delamere Camp**, hidden game blinds let the wildlife get unknowingly close to you. Night game drives to see unusual denizens of the dark are easily arranged from camp.

Ox Wagon Safaris

There are plans to offer ox wagon safaris to guest between the **Lake Elmenteita** and **Lake Nakuru Lodges**. It is presently possible to arrange for a full day or overnight safari in a wagon pulled by a team of at least fourteen enormous oxen. The slow and relaxing journey lets you see giraffe, zebra, gazelle, buffalo and other game from a unique perspective and pace.

Golf

Three short miles outside of Gilgil is the **Gilgil Club** where the traditional game of golf is played on what is jokingly called the "browns." The brown grass and rough fairways offer those who enjoy a wonderfully challenging game of golf the opportunity to play nine holes in the remarkable Kenya highlands. The club buildings carry an air of golden colonial days.

EXCURSIONS & DAY TRIPS

Soysambu Wildlife Sanctuary /Lake Elmenteita

On the shores of saline **Lake Elmenteita**, deep in the heart of the Rift Valley, the **Soysambu Wildlife Sanctuary** is a birder's paradise with thousands of greater and lesser flamingos, pelicans, storks, and plovers gathering along the banks while other game congregate in the nearby bush.

Hippo once called the lake home but after the last dry spell around 1985, they gave up and moved to more welcoming surroundings. As the smallest lake in the Rift Valley, it is common for the waters to dry up completely, if only temporarily. When this occurs, there is nothing here but a dry and dusty patch of ground.

The sanctuary is located within the vast estate of Hugh, the Fifth Baron and current Lord Delamere. Most of the shallow soda lake is on this private land. There are no entry fees but lots of hard-to-climb fences.

Kariandusi Prehistoric Site

There isn't a whole lot to see at the excavation site itself but the small **museum** offers interesting insights and a look at stone tools from the Acheulian dig. A ten minute walk from the main road, the caretaker charges $2 as an entry fee. The hours are 8:00 am to 6:00 pm daily. In the 1920s, Louis Leakey began the easily accessible dig located off the signed main Naivasha to Nakuru Road. Stop by if you are in the area and have the time.

Kariandusi Diatomite Mine

Still a working mine and not technically a tourist attraction, the gatekeeper may allow you in if they are not too busy. For fifty years men have been using picks and shovels to remove the **diatomite**. A white chalky rock, it is made up of millions of compressed silica skeletons of millions of microscopic sea organisms or diatoms. Diatomite serves two very different purposes. The first is as an effective but non-poisonous insecticide in grain silos. The second is for filtration in the brewing industry.

Because of the digging there are tunnels and deep pock marks covering the site with paths crisscrossing the sides of the excavations. Deep in the bowels of the dark underground passages live thousands of admirably adaptable bats.

PRACTICAL INFORMATION

Post Office

The post office in the town of Gilgil is open Monday through Friday from 8:00 am to 1:00 pm and 2:00 pm to 5:00 pm.

NAKURU

The noisy, dusty, and chaotic town of **Nakuru** is the fourth largest in Kenya and the farming capital of the Rift Valley Province. Derived from the Masai word *Enakuru*, the name means "place of the swirling dust." The town is of interest mainly to those who have jobs at the nearby fertile vegetable and fruit farms or cattle ranches.

The rich farming town has a substantial population of 75,000 and some would say is quite pleasant. When shallow Lake Nakuru's water levels drop, the soda crystallizes along the shore in a blinding white strip (you'll need sunglasses) of fine dust particles. When this happens, soda whirlwinds and baby tornadoes cover everything in sight with the fine powder. Life becomes difficult.

ARRIVALS & DEPARTURES

By Air

If you have reservations, many of the hotels around Lake Nakuru will arrange round-trip transportation to and from **Lanet airfield**. The small airfield is east of Lake Nakuru and east of the A104 Road. It is a short ride from the air strip to the town of Nakuru.

By Bus

Departures by bus for Nyahururu, Nairobi, Naivasha, and most places west of here are frequent. The crowds of people milling about outside the bus stand make it difficult to miss.

By Train

As always, it is best to make any reservations in advance while you are in Nairobi. Otherwise you might not get a seat. The trains have a tendency to be crowded and arrive and depart at odd hours of the night. Daily trains from Nairobi come in at 2:25 am and from Kisumu they arrive at 12:30 am. Malaba trains pull in at 8:45 pm on Tuesday, Friday, and Saturday. In Nakuru the railway line splits; one offshoot goes to Kisumu on Lake Victoria and the other to Malaba on the Ugandan border.

ORIENTATION

The busy railway line borders the town to the east running parallel to Geoffrey Kimali Road. On the west side of town West Road borders the downtown area while to the south is Ronald Ngala Road. An interesting local market borders the east of town along with the railway terminal and bus and matatu station.

GETTING AROUND TOWN

If you are energetic, you could possibly walk all the way around town but it probably isn't worth your while. If you don't have a vehicle of your own, get in touch with **Jomina Tours & Travel Limited**, *4th Floor, Spikes Building, Kenyatta Lane, Nakuru, Tel. 212 956*, and see what they have to offer. If this doesn't work out for you, take a taxi. Depending on where you want to go, the charge should be very reasonable. Arrange the fare before you get in the car.

WHERE TO STAY

LAKE NAKURU LODGE, *PO Box 70559, Nairobi. Tel. 224 998, Fax 22658. $160 per night double occupancy. All major credit cards accepted. Transfers to the lodge can be arranged from the nearby Lanet airfield.*

Game walks, horseback riding, and ox wagon safaris will be offered between this lodge and its sister hotel, Lake Elmenteita Lodge, adding interest to a stay here. The wildlife walks right up to the short rock wall along the edge of the grass, almost as curious about us as we are about them. Bright pink flamingos mingle along the lakeshore while colorful birds compete with flowering brilliance in the garden.

Older bandas surrounded by flower beds and walkways have seen better days both in terms of cleanliness and maintenance. The cabins are small and the beds hard. Newer deluxe suites are bigger, private, and have better facilities. There are a total of 60 rooms. Panoramic vistas of Lake Nakuru National Park from the suite's individual verandahs can fill hours of leisure time at the hilltop resort.

The community areas around the swimming pool, dining room, and viewing terrace are popular with tour groups who frequent the lodge. There are three restaurants and 23 bars. With scenic backdrops down the hill to the water, it isn't difficult to spend days lounging while game wanders in plain sight.

DELORAINE, *Wilderness Trails Limited/ Bush Homes Africa Safaris, Tel. US 404 888 0909, e mail bushhomes@africaonline.co.ke, www.bushhomes.com, PO Box 56923, Nairobi. Tel. 506 139, Fax 502 739. $160 per night double occupancy. All major credit cards accepted.*

On the 5,000 acre working farm, horseback safaris are the main interest of Tristan and Lucinda Voorspuy – although, those who don't ride are also welcome to their home. Polo ponies are available for outings into picturesque hills or neighboring fields. Besides running a homestay facility, the Voorspuys use some of their 40 horses to operate an "Offbeat Safaris" outfit. It is possible to organize day trips to Lakes Baringo, Nakuru, and Bogoria from the centrally located estate.

Built in the 1920s by Lord Francis Scott, the impressive two story residence boasts a croquet lawn, tennis court, and well kept flower gardens. From the edge of manicured grass, sweeping steps take you up to lofty carved stone arches. Above these, a porch wraps itself around the second floor of the colonial mansion.

Inside Deloraine, six bedrooms with their own bathrooms cater to small and exclusive groups who become part of the family during their stay. Over the years a stream of royalty and famous personalities graced the table in the ample dining room. An ongoing facelift is revitalizing the interior to accentuate high timbered ceilings, an oversized fireplace, and a grand living room.

SAROVA LION HILL, *PO Box 30680, Nairobi. Tel. 333 248, Fax 211 472. $136 per night double occupancy. All major credit cards accepted. Transfers to the lodge can be arranged from the nearby Lanet airstrip.*

The Sarova Lion Hill Lodge caters to large tour groups and offers basic rooms set in lovely surroundings. Duplex accommodations with private balconies and bathrooms trail down the hillside around the main building. From the Rift Valley Bar or Flamingo Restaurant you can luxuriate in views of Lake Nakuru National Park and the lake at the bottom of the hill. Lush tropical gardens and a pool help to add interest to the utilitarian site as do a troupe of local dancers.

JUANI FARM, *Kesana Limited, PO Box 39672, Nairobi. Tel. 749 062, Fax 741 636. $116 per night double occupancy. All major credit cards accepted.*

Everything around the self-sufficient farmhouse has a decidedly English touch. Dense with colorful flowers, rows and rows of beds edge the thick green lawns. Whenever possible, traditional colonial meals are served outdoors where you are surrounded by the garden's natural beauty and the Rift Valley's distant cliffs.

Translated to mean "a place in the sun," the hospitality of Michael and Jean Skinner lives up to the name with its warmth and courteous service. Vases of flowers, hot water bottles, drinking water, and hand cream are at your disposal in the bedrooms. Their inviting settlers' home is the last of its kind in the Molo area as lands have slowly been turned over to Africans.

A hodgepodge of construction over the years has added outdoor halls joining rooms to the main farmhouse. A roaring fire keeps off the evening chill inside the comfy living room. Bathrooms and fireplaces add country charm to three spacious guest bedrooms.

WATERBUCK HOTEL, *corner of West Road and Government Avenue, Nakuru. Tel. 211 516. $26 per night double occupancy. Including breakfast. All major credit cards accepted.*

The balconied rooms here offer good value for the money. Full bathrooms, a delicious breakfast, and guarded parking makes this a good choice if you are on your own and on a tight budget.

MIDLAND HOTEL, *Nakuru. Tel. 212 123. $15 per night double occupancy. Including breakfast. All major credit cards accepted.*

A top-end hotel for Nakuru town, all the rooms have their own bathrooms and are clean and comfortable. The establishment is old and the word "rambling" perfectly describes its old glory.

WHERE TO EAT

Certainly the place with the best reputation in town is the **TIPSY RESTAURANT**, on Gusil Road across from the Nakuru Club, which includes curry, fresh fish, and Western food on its menu. Two more excellent eateries serving Indonesian, Western Chinese and Tandoori dishes are the **OYSTER SHELL** (upstairs at the corner of Club Road and Kenyatta Avenue in the center of town, *Tel. 40946*) and the **KABEER RESTAURANT**, which also has an excellent Indian breakfast available as well as lunch time takeout.

The **WATERBUCK HOTEL**, at the corner of West Road and Government Avenue west of town, *Tel. 211 516*, prepares a tasty fare of curry and barbecue in its restaurant and bar. A friendly staff happily serves the patrons. One indoor and one outdoor restaurant are the standard at the **MIDLAND HOTEL**, at the corner of Geoffrey Kamati Road and Moi Road, *Tel. 212 123*. Excellent beef curries or barbecued chicken make this a favorite lunch spot, and you don't want to miss the popular Long Bar.

For a quick snack or savory coffee, try the **KENYA COFFEE HOUSE**, on the corner of Moi Road and Kenyatta Avenue. At the **STEELE INN BAR & RESTAURANT**, a small cottage on Kenyatta Avenue next door to the Esso gas station, you can sample rib-sticking colonial type food (mostly basic chicken dishes) as you sit outside on the verandah and look out over pretty gardens. From the **RIFT VALLEY BAR** or **FLAMINGO RESTAURANT**, located at the Sarova Lion Hill hotel on the eastern side of Lake Nakuru Park, *Tel. 333 248, Fax 211 472*, you can have a drink or meal with a spectacular view beyond.

SEEING THE SIGHTS

Agricultural Show

In June each year one of the country's main **agricultural shows** is held in Nakuru. Displays of the fine crops and livestock are displayed and judged. It is a fine example of a colonial country fair.

NIGHTLIFE & ENTERTAINMENT

Most of the restaurants and hotels in the area have some sort of saloon or lounge where they serve beer. Try the bar at the **Waterbuck Hotel** if you are looking for a quiet place to have a drink. The **Midland Hotel** boasts three adequate taverns, the best of which is the Long Bar.

There are two discos in Nakuru; **Illusions** on Kenyatta Avenue and one above the **Oyster Shell Restaurant**. Illusions is open Wednesday, Friday, Saturday, and Sunday nights while the Oyster Shell is open every night. There is a cover charge of $1 to get in.

SPORTS & RECREATION
Game Viewing
Game walks, horseback riding, and ox wagon safaris will be offered back and forth between **Lake Nakuru** and **Elmenteita Lodges**. From the viewing terrace at Lake Nakuru Lodge, the wildlife is easy to see. Giraffe, zebra, and other game come right up to the edge of the lawn. Colorful birds and pink flamingos are abundant along the lakeshore.

Horseback Riding
If you are a guest at **Deloraine** you will surely participate in a horseback safari through the nearby plains and hills. If you're not a guest and a special request is made for a day of riding on the farm, it may be arranged in advance. However, only skilled riders need apply. The game is accustomed to seeing the horses and allows riders to get close. There's no telling what adventures will come your way.

Swimming
A delightful pool is the focus of the community areas at **Lake Nakuru Lodge**, where it is easy to spend the day enjoying the sun's rays and the wildlife at the same time. Tropical gardens surround the pool at **Sarova Lion Hill**, adding a bit of interest to the practical hotel.

Hiking/Walking
On the other side of Nakuru town rises the gigantic extinct volcano known as **Menengai**. A pleasant walk to the top takes a couple of hours with small shacks about halfway up selling food and drinks. All the hotels and lodges in the area offer guided nature and ornithological walks that are worth your time and effort.

GREATER OR LESSER FLAMINGOS?
With a good pair of binoculars it should be easy to tell the two species of pink flamingos apart. The more common of the two is the lesser, which is unique to the Rift Valley. The lesser flamingo is much smaller than its counterpart and has a lot more salmon-pink covering its body. The greater flamingo tends to be whiter and larger.

SHOPPING
At the **Kenya Coffee House**, corner of Moi Road and Kenyatta Avenue, you can buy a bag of roasted coffee beans to take home. The shops in town are filled with souvenirs for tourists. Look for kikois,

carvings, beads, and some leather goods which might catch your eye. The local market is always a colorful place to find local Kenyan wares, as well as the freshest fruit and vegetables possible.

Kikois are colorful pieces of woven cloth worn as clothing by the local people. Generally the bright red or orange fabric is wrapped around their waists or chests and tucked in at one end. What an easy and comfortable way to dress every day!

EXCURSIONS & DAY TRIPS
Lake Nakuru National Park

The 80 square mile **national park** is often a lunching place for tourists on the road as it is safe, accessible, and there's plenty to see. As this is a national park, it is not possible for tourists to walk around freely. You must safari in a vehicle, either on your own or in a tour bus. However, visitors may get out at certain designated spots along the shore. From Nairobi a full day tour costs about $40 per person. If you wish to include Lakes Bogoria and Baringo as well for a two day tour, the price is roughly $150 per person. From the town of Nakuru a tour of the park in a taxi will cost about $15 for three hours. Park entry fees are $27 per person plus $1.50 per vehicle. Check to see if these are included in the price of your tour.

For starters, Rothschild giraffe, hippo, warthog, gazelle, leopard, buffalo, reedbuck, waterbuck, and pelicans make excellent photo opportunities in the surrounding grasslands and rocky cliffs. Delight your eyes with the pink gathering from the top of **Baboon Cliffs**. To protect the black rhino population brought in from elsewhere, the park is equipped with a solar electric fence.

All around the park the forests of cactus-like euphorbia and acacia trees offer respite to over 400 species of birds stopping over on their way to and from Asia and Europe. Of all the birds, bright pink greater and lesser flamingos have the most widespread reputation and attract the most visitors. Lake Nakuru in its time has seen up to two million flamingos on the lake all at once. If the birds are startled they take flight in one giant wave of dawn-tinted color.

The salmon hue of the flamingos beautifully contrasts against the emerald blue-green of the water. The shade of green changes according to the water level, general environmental factors, and the accumulation of microscopic blue-green algae. More precipitation in the shallow lake encourages the plant's growth which in turn produces a deeper greenish-blue coloration. This algae is food for insects and flamingos. Fish feed on the insects and they in turn feed the millions of birds. To provide added food for pelican colonies, wildlife experts have introduced tilapia fish to Lake Nakuru.

In 1986, Nakuru National Park was one of the first parks to be designated as a **rhino sanctuary** and research station. Armed guards posted at nine mile intervals along the electric fence manage the herd of 19-plus rhinos and keep murdering poachers at bay. More rhino sanctuaries are planned by Rhino Rescue, but it takes a lot of time and, as always, money. If you are interested in helping, contact **Rhino Rescue**, *PO Box 1, Saxmundham, Suffolk, 1P17 3JT, United Kingdom.*

Menengai Crater
Outside Lake Nakuru National Park rises **Menengai**, which in Masai means "the place of dead spirits." The gigantic extinct volcano is just five miles north of Nakuru town. Drive to a lookout point at the very top (7,467 feet) where you can see the impressive black lava inside the huge caldera. From the summit enjoy awe-inspiring vistas of Lakes Nakuru and Bogoria and scenic green farms in the distance. The deepest point inside the crater is 1,585 feet down from the rim.

Two hours of walking should get you to the top if you choose not to drive. There are stores at the halfway mark where refreshments are for sale. It is best to hire a guide to keep an eye out for puff adders, muggers, and possibly even ghosts!

MASAI GHOSTS

Around 1854, two groups of Masai tribes fought a fierce battle in the area. The victors celebrated their win by ruthlessly tossing captives to the bottom of Menengai Crater. Hundreds of human skeletons remain where they fell – bleached and broken. The whining wind over the crater's rim is said to be the spirits of those killed looking for revenge. To this day, the locals refuse to go inside the deep caldera – you're on your own here.

Hyrax Hill Prehistoric Site
The remains of a stone hillside fort and the rock hyrax that live there give the site its name. To get in it will cost you a mere $1.60 and of course a tip for your guide – if you want one. A visit will be much more rewarding if you have someone tell you a little of the fascinating history. Open from 9:00 am to 6:00 pm daily, the excavation site is just outside Nakuru town. The small farm house now turned museum is at the north end of Hyrax Hill. It proffers guide books and displays of ancient finds such as beads, tools, and pottery.

The surrounding area is rich with artifacts buried over time and excavated by Louis Leakey, starting in 1937. Of the three settlements found here so far, the most recent is from about 250 years ago and the earliest about 3,000 years ago. Interestingly, there are many *bau* boards carved into the rocks around the site. The ancient African board game was played for the exchange of cattle for women.

Human bones and coins are just a few of the riches unearthed. In one burial pit some of the 19 male skeletons were found inexplicably decapitated. Unfortunately through the years the digs, including this one, were plundered and the treasures stolen. Perhaps the most fascinating and curious pieces are the six Indian coins. One is 500 years old and the others date from 1918 and 1919. Today, some of the excavations are overgrown but it is still worth stopping, if only for the view of Lake Nakuru from the top of Hyrax Hill.

Molo Town

A short drive from Nakuru is the town of **Molo**. Set in lovely green meadows and fertile high country, the town is known for its flocks of sheep and mutton. Molo lamb is renowned throughout Kenya for its excellent flavor and quality.

TANGANYIKA BOILER

*Around much of Kenya hot water is readily available from an ingenious set-up called a **Tanganyika boiler**. Water from a nearby supply such as a well fills a 55 gallon steel drum set up horizontally on blocks. A wood fueled fire burning underneath keeps the water boiling until a faucet turns on inside the house. Voila – very hot water!!*

PRACTICAL INFORMATION

Bank

Also on Kenyatta Avenue are two banks, the **Standard Chartered Bank** and **Barclays Bank**, within a short distance of each other.

Gas Station

Look for the **Esso Station** on the west side of town on Kenyatta Avenue.

Post Office

Along Kenyatta Avenue is the standard Kenya post office with regular hours and services.

KABARNET

Because **Kabarnet** is the home town of President Arap Moi and the administrative headquarters of the Baringo district, there is an exceptional road from the nearby village of Marigat. Carefully placed atop the Kamasai Massif, the town has awesome views in all directions. The Kerio Valley drops away on one side while towards Lakes Bogoria and Baringo the Rift Valley stretches for miles.

ARRIVALS & DEPARTURES

By Air

If you don't want to drive, it is always possible to avail yourself of the small airfields around the area. Most of the hotels and camps will provide transportation to their lodges from the airstrip if they don't have their own landing site.

By Car

Only three hours from Nairobi, the Kabarnet area is a popular retreat from city to country life. The ordinary small town is surrounded by lush green farms growing vegetables and fruit for local consumption and export. Just east of Kabarnet after Marigat and south of Lake Baringo, a magnificent highway climbs 4,500 feet of the Rift Valley's western escarpment. The road turns and twists for 35 miles with frightening hairpin bends and sharp drops, but it is one of the best highways in the country.

ORIENTATION

Part of Kabarnet straggles down the slopes on either side of the Kerio Valley ridge. Most of the development, however, is stretched along the top of the rise making for a long narrow shape.

WHERE TO STAY

ISLAND CAMP, *Lonrho Hotels Kenya Limited, PO Box 58581, Nairobi. Tel. 216 940, Fax 216 796. $170 per night double occupancy. All major credit cards accepted.*

Located at Ol Kokwe Island on Lake Baringo, one of only two fresh water lakes in Kenya, the camp sits on a silt-stained lake full of crocs, tilapia fish, and hippos. The crocs won't mind sharing their cool home with you as you go for a dip, water ski, or windsurf. According to the locals, no one has every been harmed by these reptiles.

The tented accommodations are not in the same class as some of the other camps, but you will feel more than compensated for this by the dramatic play unfolding before you. Shimmering on the water and the surrounding rocks, the light show as the weather changes will entertain you for hours. Varying shades of purple, cobalt blue, and dusky gray mix and blend to cover the land with their cloak.

Each of the 23 tents is positioned for privacy along with a wondrous view. On a craggy outcrop, under a wide tree, or on the side of a hill the canvas rooms are tastefully set up. You won't even know there are other people sleeping within shouting distance.

During the heat of the day there is nothing more pleasant that sipping a cold drink while lounging around the picturesque pool. From the open-sided thatched lounge and bar an attentive waiter will keep your glass full. You won't even have to budge from under the vine covered arbor. Wonderful traditional English tea with some form of delicious home-made cookies or cakes is served promptly near the pool. Staying slim while on vacation here might present a problem as the food is always plentiful and tasty.

There is much to do here at Island Camp, all you have to do is ask. Set up a long walk with a guide to spot any of the 400-plus species of resplendent birds that make their homes along the shore; hike to the remarkable hot springs at the end of the island; meet a family of local Njemps tribespeople as you enjoy ancestral dances or mysterious reed music; take a boat ride into the marshes and up the Molo River where you will see hippo, crocodile, and flocks of birds; visit Lake Bogoria National Reserve where you'll find kudu and thousands of pink flamingoes – or simply enjoy the sense of space and the stark beauty of this peerless camp setting.

Selected as one of my best places to stay – see Chapter 11 for more details.

SARUNI, *Chartered Expeditions Kenya Limited and Utalii Tours and Safaris Limited, PO Box 61542, Nairobi. Tel. 333 285, Fax 228 875. $130 (subject to change) per night double occupancy. All major credit cards accepted.*

To get to Saruni, which means "a place of rescue," you must take a pleasant boat ride from the mainland jetty to the island site. The rustic tented camp truly allows visitors to be "rescued" from all forms of civilization and experience the bush in its natural state.

All eight tents come equipped with sun-heated showers, fun-to-use lanterns, comfortable long-drop toilets, and colorful furnishings. With lots of screen covered openings the "rooms" and "bathrooms" feel light and airy. The most remarkable things about camping at the end of Ol Kokwe Island are the privacy and the superb mountain and lakeside views.

The manager willingly takes guests to the nearby hot springs as he points out the many species of birds in the area. For great excitement and titillation it is possible to swim in the hippo and crocodile filled waters of Lake Baringo. Excursions by boat build up an appetite for one of the camp's delicious homecooked meals. Under the shade of a large spreading acacia tree, strategically placed tables and chairs serve as an outdoor living room. Alongside the thorn tree, a thatched hut with screen sides houses a plain dining room and bar. Over 100 lanterns romantically light the way safely down the paths at night.

LAKE BARINGO CLUB, *Block Hotels, PO Box 47557, Nairobi. Tel. 335 807, Fax 340 541. $100 per night double occupancy. All major credit cards accepted.*

The 68 rooms at Lake Baringo Club are basic but adequate. There is a main building in the center with an original wing of rooms on one side near the refreshing swimming pool. These quarters tend to be a little on the dark side with low ceilings but have large bathrooms with tubs. On the other side of the central structure is the new wing where the bedrooms are brighter with high ceilings. Fans and verandahs are standard features.

The unassuming buildings are covered with a blazing kaleidoscope of bougainvillea and surrounded by tall brightly blooming trees. Hidden lake and mountain views are not missed as all your attention is drawn to the flamboyant equatorial gardens. Wooden tables and chairs scattered around in the shade are perfect for watching the 400 resident bird species.

Camel rides, boat trips, visits to a Njemps fishing village, hillside hikes, bird walks, trips to Lake Bogoria, hippo and crocodile spotting or shopping in the local store will keep you busy until you wonder where your vacation time has gone.

LAKE BOGORIA LODGE, *Tel. 037 42696. $120 per night double occupancy. Prices vary depending on accommodations – regular rooms or cottages. All major credit cards accepted.*

A mere one and a half miles from the northern entrance to lovely Lake Bogoria, this secluded lodge offers the perfect getaway from the usual tour groups. You can choose a normal guest room or go for the more exclusive cottages surrounded by succulent flower-filled gardens. Each room comes with its own full service bathroom and tasteful decor.

Often overlooked, the lodge has a central location for visits to the bubbling thermal springs, flamingo-covered Lake Bogoria. If you're lucky, you'll spot the elusive kudu and klipspringer.

KABARNET HOTEL, *African Tours & Hotels, PO Box 30471, Nairobi. Tel. 336 858, Fax 218 109. $34 per night double occupancy. All major credit cards accepted.*

Located in the town of Kabarnet, the 30 room impressive modern hotel offers a conference center and a pool. Dramatic vistas over the Kerio Valley are the only remarkable feature of this relatively new hotel, although the food in their restaurant is quite delicious.

WHERE TO EAT

The **LAKE BARINGO CLUB**, *Tel. 335 807,* offers a great place to eat breakfast or dinner. For the morning meal, expect to pay $6 and dinner will be in the range of $11. Children eat for half-price.

Try a tasty meal at the grand looking **KABARNET HOTEL**, *Tel. 336 858.* **ISLAND CAMP**, *Tel. 216 940,* offers an excellent and traditional English tea and dining in the tree tops.

SEEING THE SIGHTS

Mosque

Apart from the post office, bank and Kabarnet Hotel, the large green and white **mosque** is the only other building of significance in the town. As always, be polite when visiting the place of worship as the people can be sensitive to improper attire or disrespectful tourists.

NIGHTLIFE & ENTERTAINMENT

Lake Baringo Club is just about the only place around where you can get a really cold beer. It is fun to stick around for the evening (7:00 pm) slide show and talk about the extensive birdlife in the vicinity.

Island Camp on Ol Kokwe Island has two bars worth visiting once you arrange the boat trip over.

SPORTS & RECREATION

Game Viewing

At **Island Camp** or **Saruni** on Lake Baringo the dik dik, bushbuck, and a plethora of birds make nature walks an exciting way to spend your vacation. **Lake Bogoria Lodge** enjoys a great central setting for seeing flamingos, kudu, and klipspringer.

Boat Rides

From the **Lake Baringo Club** it is possible to take a boat tour around the lake for $40 for a minimum of seven people. Ask the locals in Kampi-Ya-Samaki village to point you in the direction of the boat ramp over to **Ol Kokwe Island** where Island Camp is set up. To get across will cost roughly $7 round trip.

Once there, exciting boat trips around the lake go for $22 per hour. Boat trips up the **Molo River** and into the **Mukatan Swamp** are very rewarding. Warblers, herons, crakes, storks and gallinules are just a few of the bird treasures found here. On Gibraltar Island in Lake Baringo, live the amazing 5-foot tall Goliath herons.

Swimming

The **Lake Baringo Club** charges a daily membership fee and $2 per person per day if you wish to use their pool facilities and you are not a guest. In addition, you can play badminton, ping pong, darts, and use the library.

Over on Ol Kokwe Island, **Island Camp** has a lovely swimming pool which is delightful during the heat of the day. From Island Camp fulfill your sense of adventure with a swim in Lake Baringo with harmless (so they say) crocodiles. I survived the dip and live to say it is exhilarating!

Water Skiing

If you wish to do a little skiing, make arrangements at **Island Camp** for $45 per hour. You will certainly stay up on your skis when you think of hippos and crocodiles below you – a once-in-a-lifetime experience!

Hiking/ Walking

For $4 per person plus $2 if transport is included, the **Lake Baringo Club** has a worthwhile guided bird/nature walks. From **Island Camp** you'll get your exercise hiking to nearby hot springs or walking to a traditional Njemps village.

Camel Rides

Take a half hour camel ride from the **Lake Baringo Club** for $2. This is an exciting and inexpensive way to while away a morning.

SHOPPING

If you join a group from the Lake Baringo Club visiting the nearby **Njemps village**, there are home-made handicrafts for sale by the villagers. Be firm with them if you are not interested in buying as they can be very persistent. As you are with the tour, taking photos and walking around has been pre-arranged and approved by the chief.

EXCURSIONS & DAY TRIPS

Lake Bogoria National Reserve

Long, narrow, and unspoiled, **Lake Bogoria** in the 44 square mile park is a 30 foot deep soda lake fed by hot sulfurous springs. These springs along with thermal steam jets, geysers, and bubbling streams make fascinating attractions. As a precaution, take note: the soft ground sometimes collapses along the edges and the water is boiling hot.

The reserve was originally formed in 1981 to protect the greater kudu who calls this area home; but it is also possible to see klipspringer, baboon, jackal, hyena, buffalo, dik dik, cheetah, warthog and impala. Vervet monkeys and baboons are often seen sharing the fig trees at the south end of the lake. Colorful lizards, mongoose, and the occasional snake enjoy the peaceful isolation of the national reserve.

Depending on the algae growth, there are sometimes thousands of flamingos bordering the lake like a giant pink boa. Oddly enough, the lake supports no fish life because of a high build-up of salts and minerals. Without an outlet, the only escape for the water is through evaporation; this results in the build-up of these inorganic substances.

Dominated by high steep hills on the western side of the Laikipia Escarpment, the park consists of typical African bush and riverside vegetation except further west where it is rocky and barren. There are two gates to get in; Mogotio at the south end and Loboi at the north. Take the north entrance near Marigat town as the razor-sharp lava at the south entry will destroy your tires.

You must tour this park in a vehicle, either your own or a tour bus, as it is a National Park and walking is prohibited. From Nairobi a full day tour costs about $40 per person. If you wish to include Lakes Nakuru and Baringo as well for a two day tour, the price is roughly $150 per person.

Lake Baringo

Freshwater **Lake Baringo** gives a sense of untamed beauty and calm detachment. Roughly ten miles from the town of Marigat and a little more from Kabarnet, the lake is filled with all kinds of wildlife.

Hippos hide in the cool water to escape the extreme heat or the local fishermen. Njemps tribesmen fishing in flimsy rafts made out of branches of the Ambatch tree are a common sight on the water. The enormous hippos wander along the grassy banks during the cool nights to forage on the lakeside plants. Swimming with supposedly harmless crocodiles in the 40 foot deep waters only adds to the melodrama of being here. For bird watchers, the lake is a cornucopia of over 448 species of birds including hornbills and majestic eagles.

The severe arid landscape blends well with craggy islands, dramatic distant mountain ranges, and cinnamon-like silted water. The thoughts of contracting malaria (as this is a malaria area) is the only possible drawback – take precautions.

Tugen Hills

From the town of Kabarnet, take a hike through the beautifully scenic **Tugen Hills**. There are several fairly accessible routes to choose from. They vary in what they have to offer and will reward you with a pleasant day of sightseeing. Walk through cool forest to the picturesque 8,210 foot peak of **Saimo**. Guides are readily available if you should want one.

Kerio Valley National Reserve & Kamnarok National Reserve

Kerio Valley (25 square miles) and **Kamnarok** (34 square miles) reserves are fairly new and unspoiled nature reserves in the confines of Kerio Valley. Looking like Kenya's own Grand Canyon, the valley plunges over 3,500 feet in just a few short miles.

Kamnarok lies about 13 miles from the bridge over the Kerio River on the road to Kabarnet and Tambach. Its purpose is to protect the bird life on the tiny Kamnarok Lake. Thirteen miles from Kabarnet, the Kerio Valley Reserve safeguards the famous and beautifully scenic Kerio Gorge.

Keep an eye out for some of the most magnificent and impressive termite mounds in the country as you take in the natural wonders. The locals commonly harvest honey from the bee hives carefully encouraged in hollowed out acacia tree trunks.

WHERE DO THE BIRDS GO?

Visitors on safari come all the way to the lakes in the Rift Valley because they know what a spectacular sight the thousands of birds make. When erratic yearly fluctuation in water levels deplete food and habitat, the birds move elsewhere – it isn't possible to predict their movements. Be prepared to see no birds as they sometimes migrate to smaller and less accessible lakes. Mostly it's an ornithologist's dream. At other times, there are few birds because of random changes in the lakes.

PRACTICAL INFORMATION

Bank & Post Office

The only buildings of any significance in the town of Kabarnet are the relatively new **post office** and the **bank**. Both have been constructed to try and encourage growth and expansion in the "presidential town" but this does not seem to be having much success.

Gas Stations

To fill your vehicle with gas or diesel stop at the **Lake Baringo Club**. This will be the last place between Marigat and Maralal where you will find the rare commodity.

16. NORTHERN KENYA

The **Northern Frontier District** as it is commonly referred to, is another demonstration of Kenya's fabulous geographical and climactic varieties. There are miles and miles of sun-drenched plains, relentless desert, dramatic escarpments, towering rock formations and contrasting stretches of green bush at river's edge. The wildlife surviving here in northern Kenya frontier district includes the rare greater kudu and the graceful gerenuk along with buffalo, elephant, leopard, rhino, blue-legged ostrich, Grevy's zebra and several types of gazelle.

Most people are not aware that the less popular northern regions make up more than a third of Kenya's land mass. Forty miles past Isiolo in the Central Highlands the paved road ends. Here begins the rugged, dry, and beautiful scrub desert. The most northerly town is the unremarkable and unvisited **Lokitaung** near the shore of Lake Turkana. Also in the north are the famous fossil sites in **Sibiloi National Park**. To the west is remote **Lokichokio** town, which offers nothing to tourists, and the growing town of **Lodwar**. In the east, **Marsabit** offers respite from the desert heat. To the south, are the villages of **Maralal**, popular with tourists, and **Wamba**, a one-street town.

NORTHERN KENYA MUST SEES

As you head off into the arid lowlands and the remote north, these are the sights I recommend as must sees.

Shaba National Reserve
Buffalo Springs
Lake Turkana
Central Island
Sibiloi National Park
Marsabit National Reserve
Mt. Kulal
Gof Sokorte Guda crater lake

Tour operators often include **Samburu**, **Shaba**, and **Buffalo Springs National Reserves** in safari itineraries. **Lake Turkana** and **Marsabit National Park** are also favorites. Other than these places, the north and northeast are only for those who have a keen sense of adventure and perseverance. You must be willing to brave the frustrations of flat tires and heat in offbeat northern Kenya. It will reward you with joys of extraordinary vistas, crimson sunsets, and calming solitude.

LODWAR

As the administration center of the Turkana district, the fast growing town of **Lodwar** was once used by the British government as a detention center for those involved in the Mau Mau uprising. Because of the Turkwell Dam, oil exploration, and increased tourism, the town has grown significantly over the last few years. It is from here that you will take any excursions to the west side of **Lake Turkana**.

ARRIVALS & DEPARTURES

By Air

Near Turkwel Dam there is a relatively new airfield that can be accessed by small planes. Now that the town is connected with Nairobi by air, there is no telling how fast this now significant community will grow.

By Bus

The bus service to and from Lodwar is extremely unreliable. The standing schedule is supposed to be at 10:00 am and 2:00 pm to and from Kitale but the truth of the matter is this is rarely the case. If you must take a bus, you should stand around and wait until one shows up.

By Car

Follow along the Trans-African Highway north from Kitale and you will arrive at the town of Lodwar in due course. The paved road from the south has put Lodwar firmly on the map.

WHERE TO STAY

As with all lodges, hotels, camps, and places offering accommodations anywhere outside Nairobi, the tariffs are all-inclusive. This means three meals, entertainment, and game drives are included in the costs quoted unless otherwise specified.

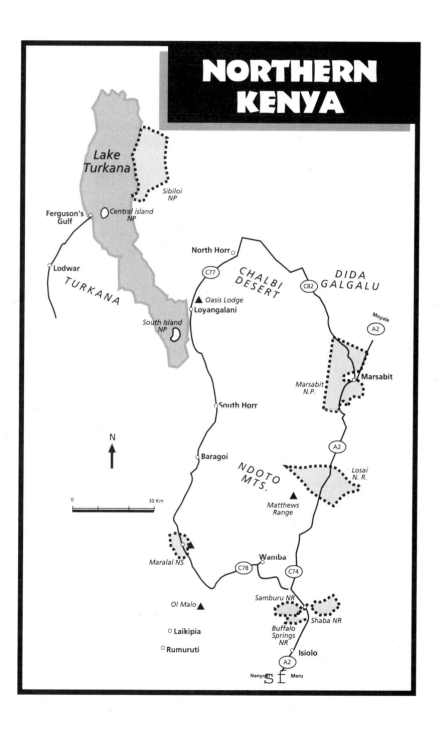

LAKE TURKANA LODGE, *PO Box 74609, Nairobi. Tel. 760 226, Fax 760 546. $150 per night double occupancy. Closed until mid-1997. All major credit cards accepted.*

Located on the west shore of Lake Turkana, the cottages are not the best in the world. Generally popular with fishermen and bird watchers, the accommodations are run down. There is hope however, as they are currently in the process of being sold which may mean a facelift. All the bandas face the water, have good lake access, and hippo are easy to watch from your verandah. For entertainment other than fishing and birding, there is a swimming pool and arranged trips to Central Island and Koobi Fora.

TURKWELL HOTEL, *in town, Tel. 21201.*

The Turkwell is new and as such is currently the town's focal point. A simple room with fan and shared bathroom costs under $5. Perhaps not the best choice of places to stay, but certainly offering a decent meal such as steak, fries, sausage, and eggs.

WHERE TO EAT

In the town of Lodwar there are several small motels where the food is above average. At the **MOMBASA HOTEL**, near the JM bus office, try the doughnut-like *mandazis* for breakfast before setting out on a day of sightseeing. **MARIRA BOARDING & LODGING** has an outstanding fish and chips dish that will not leave you wanting.

Try either the eggs and sausage breakfast or the steak and fries dinner at the **TURKWEL HOTEL**, *Tel. 21201,* if you're looking for rib-sticking food. **LAKE TURKANA LODGE** (see above) offers a good menu selection for either dinner or lunch in the hotel restaurant.

NIGHTLIFE & ENTERTAINMENT

The bar at the **Turkwel Hotel** is a popular place for local gatherings and seems to be the social center of town where you can find cold beer.

Lake Turkana Lodge has a decent bar where a cold drink is forthcoming along with a friendly game of darts. Interestingly enough, the bar terrace was once in the water but because of the receding water levels it now sits high and dry 250 feet from the lake.

SPORTS & RECREATION

Fishing

At **Lake Turkana Lodge**, you can make arrangements for hours of fishing in Lake Turkana. Try your luck at catching fighting tiger fish or Nile perch among the 40 different species of fish in the lake. As the waters recede, the fish population suffers but fishermen still bring home enough for dinner.

Birding

Bird watching is a popular pastime at Lake Turkana. Ask at the **Lake Turkana Lodge** for more information of what species are wading during your visit. Look for broad-billed sandpipers, black-headed gulls, flamingos, and storks just to mention a few.

Swimming

For entertainment other than fishing and birding there is a swimming pool filled with lake water at **Lake Turkana Lodge** which can be used by non-guests. Check in at the reception first.

SHOPPING

At the **Diocesan Craft Shop** take a look at the intricately made mats and baskets which come in a variety of sizes and colors. In the town of **Kalokol**, three miles from the Lake Turkana Lodge, look for all manner of Turkana souvenirs at reasonable prices. Just south of Lodwar in the nearby township of **Lokichar** is a Turkana cooperative. Here the baskets, beads, carvings, and jewelry are an excellent value with fixed prices.

EXCURSIONS & DAY TRIPS

Lake Turkana

The far reaches of the north Kenya border near **Lake Turkana** are a sensational spot for a vacation. Formerly known as Lake Rudolph, today it is named after one of the tribes living on its shores. Stretching roughly 155 miles from end to end, the lake is encompassed by volcanic rock and semi-desert where the temperature sometimes reaches 140 degrees Fahrenheit. The high salinity at the southern end of this soda lake prevents anything but a few scrubby thorn trees from growing. Fed by the Omo River in the north, Lake Turkana is much less briny at this end. The lake is most famous however, for its unique blue-green color. Hence, it is commonly called the **Jade Sea**.

The lake is noted for the largest population of **Nile crocodile** on earth. As the lake was once a source of the Nile about 10,000 years ago, it explains the still flourishing pockets of Nile perch and crocs. Lake Turkana is most famous for these sharp-toothed reptiles. There are also colonies of gregarious hippo, feisty tiger fish, huge perch, and large flocks of bright birds.

Roughly 15,000 years ago the lake covered four times its current area. Sadly, the level of the lake is falling at a rapid rate due to naturally shifting plates below the earth and climatic changes. Man-made alterations in the water flow caused by the Omo and Turkwel dams have added their share of pressure to the current situation.

Turkwel Dam/Gorge

The French/Kenyan hydroelectric plant project is said to be the largest man-made lake in Kenya. It is destined to supply the dense highland's population with electricity. With its dramatic rock surroundings, airstrip, and paved roads, it is hoped this will become an important tourist destination. To draw the crowds there will be fishing, sailing, and other water sports.

Lokichar

Just south of Lodwar is the nearby town of **Lokichar** famous for its **baskets**. Prices are fixed here, making this a pleasant experience. Influenced by the local mission church, the local Turkana cooperative offers a great selection of souvenirs, including such items as beaded aprons, wrist knives, wooden bowls, and jewelry.

South Turkana National Reserve

South Turkana is one of the least visited reserves in the country because poachers from Somalia have all but wiped out the once prolific game. Thick forests along the river banks and thorny bush were home to kudu and elephant. With the help of the game department these wildlife populations are being re-established. The 430 square mile park mainly consists of two small forested mountains reaching an altitude of 8,925 feet. They are surrounded by dry desert-like plains where Turkana herders use the land to graze their skinny livestock.

Nasolot National Reserve

Just to the west of South Turkana National Reserve is **Nasolot** which again, due to heavy poaching, has little to offer those in search of large numbers of wild game. The thorny bushland just outside the Uganda border covers 36 square miles with no recognizable roads. A small group of rhino once called Nasolot home but they have since been killed. Small herds of elephant and kudu still remain but are understandably shy.

Kalokol

From Lake Turkana Lodge, inquire about walking to the village of **Kalokol**. The short three mile walk will invigorate your sweat glands, but once you arrive the promise of Turkana trinkets and souvenirs will make you forget about the heat.

Lokichokio

This is possibly the most remote town in the country. There is nothing to do here but you will be able to say you have seen the ends of the earth in Kenya (if that's something you want to be able to say!). The population of roughly 25,000 people is made up of locals, aid workers, and oil exploration teams. The village made headlines in 1989 when the town was bombed (supposedly by Ugandan planes) and several Kenyans died.

Ferguson's Gulf

On the western side of Lake Turkana is **Ferguson's Gulf**, the most accessible part of the lake shore. To arrive here it is easiest to travel along the paved road from Kitale in the west, but the vistas are not nearly as breathtaking. Due to a severe drought in Ethiopia, the water levels have dropped significantly. In order to actually reach the water you will have to walk quite some distance. There is a spectacular and varied bird population including skuas, sandpipers, and slender-billed gulls among other waders. Along with ever-present hippos who come out at night to feed, crocodiles nest along the grassy shore. It is best to check with the locals to see if swimming is currently safe.

Central Island National Park

At Lake Turkana Lodge you can arrange to visit **Central Island** as a day excursion. An impressive population of 12,000 crocs live in the craters of the barren but scenic and still active volcanic island. Occasionally steam, smelly gas, and smoke come pouring forth but it is nothing to be too concerned about. In the months of April and May you may see the tiny croc babies hatching or scurrying to their water haven. Scorpions, impressive lizards, large numbers of birds, and hippos share the two square mile park as their home.

Tour prices are high but I think you will find the view worth the cost once you arrive. For an eight person covered cruise, it is $52 and for the four person open cruise you'll pay $39. It might be possible to hire a local fisherman to take you on the eight mile cruise, but it is best to check the boat out thoroughly before leaving. The dangers are very real if you get caught in an infamous squall.

UNPREDICTABLE WEATHER

Both on Lake Turkana and throughout the desert north, the climate can change from calm to magnificently furious with no warning. Many El Molo and Turkana tribespeople have been killed when vicious squalls shatter the silence with violent thunder and lightning, taking everything in their path. Amazingly, the peace is restored within minutes leaving behind clear skies, clean air, and sometimes immeasurable destruction.

PRACTICAL INFORMATION

Bank

As with the post office, there is only one bank in Lodwar: the **Kenya Commercial Bank**. I imagine as the village grows more banks will move into reap the benefits from commercialism.

Car Essentials

A four wheel drive vehicle is a must in this part of the country. Do not leave your rental agency without first checking your equipment. This must include a high-rise jack, sand ladders, a shovel, extra fuel and a long rope or chain. The chain/rope is used to pull you out of soft sand by willing herdsmen and their camels, for a fee of course.

Post Office

To date, there is one post office in town which is closed on Saturday. With new business arriving in town all the time, this is very likely to change.

WAMBA

Short of being billed as the provincial headquarters for the area, there is nothing in the one street town of **Wamba** but it is a typical Samburu village. It is from this village that John Hillaby, author of *Journey to the Jade Sea*, began his famous camel trek to Lake Turkana.

In the foothills of Matthew's Range, it is possible to see eagles riding on the thermals in search of prey in the valleys below.

ARRIVALS & DEPARTURES

By Air

It is possible to fly into a local airfield which services all the lodges and hotels in the area. As the number of people on safari increases, so does the use of the airfield near Wamba. Flying in, in my opinion, is the best way to get to this destination.

By Car

From Nairobi to Wamba you must cross 300 miles of rough African roads and dusty terrain, but it can be done. It is wise to have a guide with you who can point out the most viable approach. There are not many signs around other than a few rocks painted yellow to mark the way. To the untrained eye, the "road" can sometimes be indistinguishable from the desert.

WHERE TO STAY & EAT

KITICH CAMP, *Supoko Limited, Kitich Camp, PO Box 14869, Nairobi. Tel. 444 288, Fax 750 533. $250-300 per night double occupancy. Closed in April. All major credit cards accepted.*

If you drive to Kitich camp in Matthew's Range, it is best to go through Isiolo and then Wamba for the 300 mile trip from Nairobi. For those more pressed for time or not willing to endure the dust there are two options; fly into Wamba or the landing strip near the camp itself. The staff will arrange to pick you up for the drive to camp.

Home grown vegetables served for dinner are also a favorite of the elephants who raid the garden regularly. Birds, butterflies, buffalo, leopard, gerenuk and other hardy wildlife share the picturesque beauty of the surroundings with the tented riverside camp.

The Ngeng River sets the stage for tranquillity in the lush Ngeng Valley contrasting with the hills and desert scrub beyond. Spend your days hiking through the remote splendor, play Tarzan and swing from a rope into a natural river pool, or simply enjoy the feeling of communing with the universe.

The small ten-tent camp has undergone a facelift but the accommodations are still those of real African camping. Each tent sits alongside the river with no electricity or running water. Instead, the management provides safari showers and long-drop toilets. Twin beds in every tent, chairs on the private verandah and an open sided dining/bar offer the basic comforts of home.

There are no roads in this remote part of the Mathews Mountain range to allow for game drives. Therefore, the staff organizes walking and hiking. Take a hike for 40 minutes to the swimming hole or stroll for 20 minutes to the fishing hole where barbel and catfish abound.

SAMBURU SERENA LODGE, *Serena Central Reservations, PO Box 48690, Nairobi. Tel. 71051, Fax 718 103, E-mail: 62578620@eln.attnet.com. $182 per night double occupancy. All major credit cards accepted.*

Wild cats, marabou storks, and crocodiles share a provided meal of raw meat at the river bank, so close you can see each feather and ivory tooth. Elephant make a habit of walking along the edge of the water to cool off or simply while away the time. At night, floodlights outline the amazing markings on a leopard's coat as he relishes the bait strung up for him. During meals in the open-sided dining room, impudent monkeys and birds are kept away from the buffet by watchful tribesmen. Game drives, hot air balloon rides, and wildlife lectures add to the pleasure of this safari destination.

Multiple levels of game watching terraces and an attractive pool have an ample selection of lounge chairs and safari seating. Rock gardens, lily ponds, thick shade trees and bright flowering vines blend beautifully with the landscape as they shelter you from the desert outside. Tasteful murals and Samburu artifacts decorate the lodge in a most interesting fashion.

Guest bandas have two standard bedrooms, a full bathroom with shower and a small verandah. Very clean with whitewashed walls; creativity and color in the rooms comes from the bright fabrics.

LARSEN'S TENTED CAMP, *Block Hotels, PO Box 47557, Nairobi. Tel. 335 807, Fax 340 541. $178 per night double occupancy. No children under ten. All major credit cards accepted.*

Each of the 17 classy tents has a bird name such as curlew, bateleur, hornbill, or swift. Situated on platforms facing the reddish-brown flow of the Uaso Nyiro River, each green tent has its own bathroom with hot water and a private deck. Well trimmed emerald lawns spread between the canvas reception, bar, and dining tents. Doum palms and acacia trees shade the walkways and the canvas from the sun. In the evenings, hanging lamps light the winding paths giving the true feel of camping in the Kenyan bush.

Larsen's has developed quite a reputation for its excellent cuisine and non-intrusive but elegant service. Dinner is a special occasion with candlelight, china, and silver in the open-sided mess tent. Breakfast and lunch are buffet style or you may choose a traveling picnic for your midday meal. Piles of wildlife books and safari decor make the bar a cozy place to enjoy the sounds of the night; or, you might prefer to stare into the nightly campfire reliving the excitement of the day.

Upon arrival you are greeted with a refreshing drink while friendly staff acquaint you with meal, hot water and game drive times. The crocodile infested river attracts animals of all kinds to drink. Elephants, monkeys, Grevy zebra, gerenuk, oryx, ostrich and plentiful birds are seen here drinking or crossing the river; seemingly there to entertain you.

SAMBURU INTREPIDS CLUB, *Prestige Hotels Ltd., PO Box 74888, Nairobi. Tel. 338 084, Fax 217 278. $170 per night double occupancy. All major credit cards accepted.*

One of the 25 extravagant tents nestled among the shade of large African trees and sweet smelling gardens will fulfill your safari dreams. Inside, ceiling fans, poster beds, and mahogany furniture add a touch of comfort. The bathrooms come equipped with everything, including double sinks. Situated at the edge of a sandy river bank in Samburu National Reserve, the central buildings of the lodge are a delightful mixture of wooden walkways, thatched peaks, open rooms, tree-shaded corridors and wonderful river views. Built to feel like a tree house, the theme continues as you lounge around the pool under vine covered bowers. In the club stores, pick up some of the locally made souvenirs.

Enjoy excellent dinner fare as romantic light filters down from hanging gourds. For breakfast and lunch try the outdoor buffet before setting off on a nature walk, camel safari, or game drive in the semi-desert surrounding the club. To get to Samburu Intrepids, it is possible to fly to the nearby airstrip and arrange for a transfer.

SAROVA SHABA LODGE, *Sarova Hotels Limited, PO Box 30680, Nairobi. Tel. 333 248, Fax 211 472. $160 per night double occupancy. All major credit cards accepted.*

Water, water, and more water seems to be the predominant theme throughout the beautiful lodge. The Ewaso Nyiro river and the flowing natural springs provide water for colorful lily ponds, dainty fish pools, serene waterfalls, trickling streams and the impressive swimming pool. In the center of the azure pool is a romantic hideaway perfect for a honeymoon couple to lounge away an hour or two. The seemingly endless and secluded bays are enhanced by shapely rocks and bright colors of bordering flowers.

After a long drive over dusty jarring roads and black lava desert in the Shaba Reserve it is such a pleasure to find this oasis ready to welcome you with its festive atmosphere and architecture. A gas station can fill your tank as your batteries recharge from the trip in the comfort of the cool lodge. A high thatched roof, a room on stilts, palms growing through the ceiling, exotic views of Samburu herdsmen, and rocky hills are what you can expect during mealtimes in the wall-less dining room.

Cheerful fabrics and natural materials flow throughout the lodge creating a sense of oneness with nature. Each of the 85 guest bedrooms built in two storied thatched chalets face the river and the dry desert beyond. Although there is no air conditioning, the ceiling fans keep you comfortably cool. Full bathrooms with marble vanities and bathtubs are standard facilities at the Sarova.

A variety of evening entertainment, crocodile feeding, nature hikes and exciting game drives to see eland, zebra, and klipspringer await you. A great place to stay and enjoy Kenya!

SAMBURU LODGE, *Block Hotels, PO Box 47557, Nairobi. Tel. 335 807, Fax 340 541. $144 per night double occupancy. All major credit cards accepted.*

Located in a prolific game area of Samburu National Reserve, the busy and popular tourist lodge sits on the edge of the Ewaso Ngiro River bank. Tall thatched roofs and shiny stone walls are the construction materials of the central building. From here the guest cottages spread along the water's edge in various sizes and settings for quite a distance. Each banda has its own bathroom but verandahs are not standard.

Seemingly hanging over the water is the notable Crocodile bar from which you often see game. For further entertainment take a game drive out into the reserve, watch (20 foot long) crocodile and leopard baiting, enjoy a bird or nature walk, shop in the gift stores, cool off in the pool or get your spirits up with a Samburu dance. If you have driven in, there is a gas station on the property.

BUFFALO SPRINGS LODGE, *African Tours & Hotels Limited, PO Box 30471, Nairobi. Tel. 336 858, Fax 218 109. $120 per night double occupancy. All major credit cards accepted.*

The lodge has a prime location with outstanding views of the Buffalo Springs Reserve and the famous crystalline waters. Cool and open at one end, the main building offers a good place to enjoy the rocky desert panorama. From here, visitors can saunter down to good game sighting spots near the springs where the animals come to drink. A swimming pool and restaurant/bar overlook a natural spring where wildlife can be observed in comfort.

As the only lodge in the reserve, it can only be classified as passable. Small concrete cottages have replaced the original 40 tents that once stood on the site. Without much effort, the owners could turn this place around, making it one of the loveliest places in the area. It is a shame to see such a breathtaking setting go to waste.

SPIDER'S WEB

During the night, large African spiders come out of hiding to make their tablecloth-sized intricate weavings between the acacia trees. As you get out of bed and begin to wander around your camp or lodge, beware of the sticky webs which tend to cling to your face and arms as you walk by.

SPORTS & RECREATION

Game Drives

All the lodges and hotels listed offer game drives for their guests. If room is available or arrangements are made in advance, it is possible for someone who is not a guest to join the daily excursion to see wildlife. At **Samburu Serena** and **Sarova Shaba Lodges**, bait is set out for leopard and crocodiles under bright floodlights; other wildlife share the leftovers. Game drives leaving from here will fill your mind with the sights and sounds of Africa.

From **Larsens Tented Camp** and **Samburu Lodge**, the spectacular view of elephants and other animals crossing and drinking at the river is rivaled only by the classy setting and daily game drives.

Hiking

At **Kitich Camp** the hiking through the Kenya bush and experiencing the grandeur of the country along with butterflies and birds is something worth anticipating. You can look forward to great guided walks from the

Samburu Intrepid Club and **Sarova Shaba Lodge** into the surrounding semi-desert. All hotels in the area offer supervised nature treks and bush hiking. The distance and terrain covered will be designed to match your skill and interests.

Swimming

Swing from a thick rope and drop into the pool below; tell your friends back home you actually swam in a real Kenyan river. The **Samburu Serena Lodge** pool is surrounded by rock gardens and cool shade – a lovely place to spend a hot noontime. Green flowering vines continue the tree house theme around the welcoming pool at **Samburu Intrepids Club**. The most impressive pool of all is at the **Sarova Shaba Lodge** where flowing water sets the stage wherever you wander on the grounds.

Hot Air Balloon Rides

Although they are a bit expensive, how many times is your life will you ride above Africa in a balloon? You can do so from the **Samburu Serena Lodge**.

Camel Safari

Camel safaris are an interesting side trip offered by **Samburu Intrepids Club**. The trips are set up to satisfy your basic desires depending on how long and far you wish to travel. Check to see if you actually get to ride the camels.

SHOPPING

In the town of Wamba, there are several small stores that carry a surprisingly good stock of basic supplies if you should run out of anything essential. At **Samburu Intrepids Club** and **Samburu Lodge** there are several souvenir shops where a fair selection is there for the visitor.

EXCURSIONS & DAY TRIPS

Matthews Range

Named after the general Sir Lloyd Matthews, the forested hills are rarely visited by tourists. To get to the range by car, pass the turnoff signs for Maralal and Wamba and drive another nine miles. Turn right here and follow the track running alongside the Ngeng River until you see a bridge to your left; cross and follow the road to Kitich Camp.

The hillsides attract heavy, wet rain clouds which dump their load here. Slopes covered with succulent vegetation and flowing streams vouch for the effective system. Hidden deep in the bush is a guarded herd of rare black rhino. Sharing the cool jungle as an escape from the desert heat are buffaloes, elephants, lions, and other wildlife.

Samburu National Reserve

A popular place for visitors, **Samburu National Reserve** offers a wide selection of places to stay. A short flight from Wilson airport and only 213 miles from Nairobi, the reserve is beginning to compete with Masai Mara for notoriety with tourists. Just 23 miles from Isiolo, the Archer's Post Gate is where most people enter the park. Look for a large and obvious granite outcropping, **Lololokwe**, to use as a landmark.

Most of the time there is excellent game viewing close to the **Ewaso Ngiro River**. The "brown" river meanders through the reserve attracting elephant, buffalo, giraffe, leopard, crocodile, hippo, all kinds of birds, dik dik and smaller plains game.

The landscape here includes attractive river vegetation such as doum palms, lush tamarind, and flat-topped acacia trees. Further from the water are dried river beds, rocky hills, lava rock bluffs, red termite hills and plenty of thorny bush.

KAREN BLIXEN ON SAFARI LIFE

"There is something about safari life that makes you forget all your sorrows and feel as if you had drunk half a bottle of champagne... bubbling over with heartfelt gratitude for being alive." – **Karen Blixen**

Shaba National Reserve

The towering **Shaba Massif** rises elegantly and alone above the park, protecting the game from the elements. The panoramic vistas are outstanding but getting there can be a little rough if it has rained. The reserve is south of the Ewaso Ngiro River and across the road from the Samburu National Reserve. Untouched wilderness covered with sensational terrain encompasses everything from thick river forests (20 miles long), grasslands, and swamps to steep rocky crags and dry bush.

The **Najorbe Gate** is about three miles south of the **Archer's Post**. Turn at the sign for the **Sarova Shaba Lodge** and go about four miles to the entrance. It is also possible to fly into the small plane landing strip just two minutes away. The least visited of the three parks, this is perhaps the one with the most pristine game viewing and the most undisturbed vegetation. Sadly, this is the site where Joy Adamson, author of *Born Free*, was killed by poachers in 1980 while returning a young leopard named Penny to the wild – a sharp reminder that this is still untamed Africa.

Buffalo Springs National Reserve

Named for the crystalline **Buffalo Springs** running through the area and the once prolific buffalo herds, the reserve is across the Ewaso Ngiro

River and just south of Samburu National Reserve at roughly 3,000 feet. In 1960, the British Army dynamited this 40 foot wide hole which promptly filled with water from underground springs. As it is so close to Samburu and Shaba National Reserves, naturally the spectacular terrain is much the same but no less beautiful or special. The one difference here is the inclusion of lowland plains covered with thick rich grass.

There are two gates to get inside the 50 square mile park. The first, **Isiolo Gate** or **Gare Mare Gate**, is 12 miles north of Isiolo; the second, **Buffalo Springs Gate**, is a mere three miles before the Archer's Post. Crossing between the three reserves is no problem during the day but to spend the night there are required fees in addition to entry charges. Swimming in the cool pool is considered safe, as a low wall keeps out crocodiles and elephants.

PRACTICAL INFORMATION
Hospital
Wamba has a small hospital to handle any minor health issues but for anything more, a trip to Nairobi is essential. Check out the services of the Flying Doctor's as a wise precaution.

Park Fees
To enter Samburu, Buffalo Springs, or Shaba parks is $27 per person in addition to $1.50 per vehicle. Even though they are seemingly one large continuous area, you must buy an entry pass for each reserve.

Police Station
While there is no bank or post office as yet in Wamba, there is a good sized police station. Hopefully you won't run into any trouble or need the services of the law. Remember to stick with a group as there is safety in numbers.

MARALAL
Maralal, a colorful Samburu town set in refreshing, treed highlands, is half-way between Nairobi and Lake Turkana. The **Lerochi Plateau** lies below the town which holds the title of regional headquarters. Popular as an overnight stop for tour companies on their way to Lake Turkana, the town has a way of captivating visitors with its bizarre ramshackle atmosphere.

In 1934, the town got its name from the first shack built with a tin roof as it reflected the sun's rays. In Samburu language the word *maralal* means "glittering."

ARRIVALS & DEPARTURES

By Air

The exclusive and private ranches in the area have good landing strips for small planes. If the weather has been wet, you may have to delay your flight in until things dry out a little. Landing on a slippery runway takes skill from the practiced Kenyan bush pilots and makes for an exciting adventure.

By Bus

Yare Safaris is the most popular provider of bus transportation to Maralal. If you are not with Yare or any tour group, there is a bus arriving and departing every other day for Isiolo in front of the New Garden Hotel. A ticket costs $6.50. The New Garden Hotel is at the north end of Maralal across the street from the post office and the market. Look for a dusty patch of ground in front of the hotel and there you'll find the buses. Isiolo, approximately 100 miles to the south, is the nearest large town from Maralal.

By Car

Getting to Maralal by car can be the experience of a lifetime, one I'm not sure I'd want to endure. The advantage is you will certainly get to see the countryside in its entirety. The five to six hour drive from Nairobi (five through Nyahururu and Rumuruti or six through Nanyuki) will take you through dusty towns and along pot-holed tracks. Truck drivers making the 220 mile journey from Nairobi make it a two day trip by spending the night in Nyahururu.

WHERE TO STAY

OL MALO, *Wilderness Trails Limited/Bush Homes Africa Safaris, Tel. US 404 888 0909, e mail bushhomes@africaonline.co.ke, www.bushhomes.com, PO Box 56923, Nairobi. Tel. 506 139, Fax 502 739, e-mail francombe@olmalo.demon.co.uk. $460 per night double occupancy. All major credit cards accepted. Book far in advance.*

Ol Malo is a ranch owned by Colin and Rocky Francombe, who purchased the 5,000 acres of fragile arid land to build their dream home. In desperate need of some love and attention, the expanse of semi-desert is obviously benefiting from the Francombe's years of ranching experience. It is called Ol Malo, "place of the greater kudu," because the area is known for its concentration of the rare antelope not often found anywhere else in Kenya. The owners even have a tame female kudu named Tandela that you can pet if she comes around. As a baby, Tandela was saved from an untimely death in the wilds.

The Francombe's spend much of their time taking care of and attracting wildlife to their protected piece of land. As keen conservationists the game always comes first. This is true even if it means going without a bath when there is a shortage of water in order for the animals to drink. Game is not as prolific here as it is in other parts of Kenya, but more and more gerenuk, kudu, elephant, buffalo, lion, giraffe, leopard and other smaller mammals are making Ol Malo part of their territory.

The nine individual structures of the compound are built at the very edge of a high escarpment. All the high pitched roofs are thatched with an attractive local reed. The walls are built from locally quarried, colorful stone found in the area.

Nestled between the rocks along the cliff, the private cottages have the most remarkable bedrooms and bathrooms. The enormous custom made tub offers comforting hot water to soothe the aches of a day-trek through the bush. Enjoying a picture-perfect sunrise while lying in the oversized king bed and sipping tea delivered at your specified time makes you never want to leave. The room decor is tastefully done with charming natural materials and local handicrafts which you can purchase while visiting the nearby town of Maralal. The curve of ancient olive wood adds interest throughout the buildings.

The view from the wide open verandahs is breathtakingly beautiful. A large glass picture window keeps out the gusty winds and the separate living room and dining room are kept warm in the evenings by a crackling fire. The orange, yellow, and red of the ethereal sunset is a sight you shouldn't miss. A secluded free-form swimming pool is perched cliffside and offers an incredible view to the valley below. The attractively shaped pool is engineered to look like it flows over the side of the precipice. The grounds and meandering walkways are a pleasant surprise in this desert setting. The rock gardens are full of exotic plants found naturally in the area. There are many exciting activities, such as guided nature walks, game drives, visits to an unspoiled local manyatta (village), camping near the river, bush picnics, camel rides, game viewing by the watering hole and just relaxing by the unique pool.

A new addition to Ol Malo is a wonderful hide down by the watering hole. From here you will often be given the obvious privilege of coming eye to eye with elephant and other thirsty game. For the more adventurous, it has bunk beds, a shower under the stars and an elephant jaw bone as a loo seat! The fun of the hide is a steep stair climb down the cliff where, once there, peace reigns.

The four exclusive and exquisite one-level guest cottages along with the wild beauty of the wilderness are the most romantic settings I have ever seen. The very face of Africa is unveiled here with a personal and delightful experience. Ol Malo truly belongs in the fairy tale category!

Selected as one of my best places to stay – see Chapter 11 for more details.

MUKUTAN RETREAT, *Gallman Memorial Foundation, PO Box 45593, Nairobi. Fax 521 220. $460 per night double occupancy. All major credit cards accepted.*

Ol Ari Nyiro Ranch is owned by the author of *I Dreamed of Africa*, Kuki Gallman. Set at the edge of the Laikipia Plateau facing the Great Rift Valley, the cottages scattered a good distance from each other, accommodate only six people. Each cottage is designed artistically with native materials. Papyrus roofs, local stone, twisted olive tree trunks and cedar planks will give you creative ideas to bring home. Lamu furniture, detailed wood carvings, huge stone bathrooms and double fireplaces make the place magical. All the rooms come with a lovely open verandah with views of the Mukutan Gorge.

The property is a working cattle ranch where wildlife and domestic animals live in harmony with each other and nature. Horseback riding, fishing, game drives and walks are a few of the entertainment options available.

MUGIE CAMP, *Cheli & Peacock, PO Box 39806, Nairobi, Tel. (254 2)748 327 or (254 2) 748 633, Fax (254 2) 750 225, e mail chelipeacock@attmail.com, www.chelipeacock.com. $375 per night double occupancy. Includes game drives.*

Tucked away on 46,000 acres of a private ranch, Mugie Camp sits within the 9,000 square kilometers of Laikipia Plains. There are six spacious tents that can accommodate two very comfortably. The tents come with a shower, toilet and complete privacy and solitude. To reach the camp, there is the nearby Mugie airstrip.

Around twilight, a resident leopard sometimes appears to entrance guests with grace and elegance. Along with abundant wildlife such as the elusive reticulated giraffe and Grevy's zebra, you might learn to tell the difference between a civet and a genet.

The camp's service to its guests is a priority with the staff. Sundowners over the vast valley surrounding you are a spectacular event. Life doesn't get much better than sitting under the wide African sky around a huge bonfire warding off the evening chill. Camel riding, horseback riding, guided walks, night game drives and donkey treks will keep you busy if that's what you're after.

COLCHECCIO RANCH, *PO Box 50, Rumuruti. Tel. 749 280, Fax 882 521. $350 per night double occupancy. All major credit cards accepted.*

For those comfortable on horseback, take a ride through the 18,500 acre ranch and see giraffe, klipspringer, lion, buffalo, leopard, kudu, elephant and zebra. Perhaps you'd rather trek to Crocodile Jaws and see where the river vanishes only to reappear as a raging whirlpool 120 feet further down the trail. Nature walks, bush picnics, game viewing at the waterhole, night and day game drives, a lovely swimming pool and tennis courts await your pleasure at Colcheccio.

Recently refurbished by Luisa, daughter of Count Carletto Ancilotto, the ranch can house only 10 guests at a time in the exclusive cottages perched on the edge of a high precipice. All the rooms have a remarkable view from cliff-hanging verandahs. On a clear day you might even spot Mount Kenya in the background. Inside the bandas look for bidets in the bathroom, cedar closets, high thatched ceilings and colorful local decor.

In the main building housing the card room/library, living room, and dining area, get comfortable with your binoculars or snuggle next to the warm fire. Inspiration comes easily from the never ending beauty of a Kenyan sunset or the vastness of the bush.

MARALAL SAFARI LODGE, *PO Box 45155, Nairobi. Tel. 211 124, Fax 214 261. $112 per night double occupancy. All major credit cards accepted.*

For your convenience, the lodge has its own small airfield to eliminate the rigors of driving. If you wish to get here by car, take the Nyahururu and Rumuruti route from Nairobi.

Located in the Maralal Game Sanctuary, the lodge offers plenty to keep its guests entertained. Visit an authentic Samburu village, go for camel rides through the bush, or peek through the walls of a leopard blind for a glimpse of an elusive cat. At the waterhole (the only permanent one in the area) and salt lick, warthog, eland, buffalo, impala, zebra and baboons gather for their communal drink. Thirty feet of open space is all that separates you from the game as you enjoy a tasty meal in the dining room. All twelve of the guest bandas have fully equipped bathrooms, French doors opening out to colorful gardens, a fully functional fireplace, soaring ceilings and best of all; no fences to keep wildlife out of the lodge grounds.

WHERE TO EAT

In the heart of Maralal, the **HARD ROCK CAFE** probably offers the closest thing to American food in the area. The **BUFFALO LODGE** offers inexpensive and tasty meals and is the best of the cheap motels around. Outside of town, the **MARALAL SAFARI LODGE** caters to visitors in its comfortable restaurant. Breakfast in any of these establishments runs about $4 and lunch or dinner roughly $9.

SEEING THE SIGHTS

Kenyatta House

Visit the hillside home of **Jomo Kenyatta** just outside Maralal. Under house arrest, he was held prisoner here for seven years before becoming the first president of Kenya.

Market

A trip to the market will reward you with the knowledge of how the local Samburu people conduct the business of buying and selling their produce. The market is small but remarkably interesting and lively.

NIGHTLIFE & ENTERTAINMENT

In town, there is a **Hard Rock Cafe**, where the drinks are cold and the food tasty, making it the most frequented place around. For more basic local entertainment check the **Buffalo Lodge** where there is a video room and bar. Sometimes there is a disco here on Friday or Saturday nights. The bar at the **Maralal Safari Lodge** outside town offers excellent cold beer and game viewing from the terrace; a lovely way to while away an afternoon.

SPORTS & RECREATION

Game Drives

At both **Ol Malo** and **Maralal Safari Lodge** the game drives can be rewarding. Take your binoculars and scan the hillsides for buffalo, eland, klipspringer and other northern game. The precious water holes at the hotels are also great game spotting sites for elephant, leopard, and monkeys among others. A private game park at the lodge has a large herd of curious eland.

At **Colcheccio Ranch** enjoy a day or night game drive to spot elephant, giraffe, gerenuk, eland, klipspringer and buffalo roaming the huge spread. Perhaps you would rather take a horse instead of a vehicle. This is easily arranged by the ranch staff and will get you even closer to the wildlife.

Walking

Hiking and walking through miles of semi-desert bush and attractive hills is one of the best ways to see Kenya. Your guide will point out useful and native plants while you sneak up on game that would be long gone at the sound of a vehicle. Both **Ol Malo** and **Maralal Lodge** will arrange walking, hiking, or camping during your stay. Carefully strolling through the semi-desert on your way to the waterside and Crocodile Jaws will fill your day with excitement at **Colcheccio**. Look out for snakes living in the rocks; they don't like to be startled.

Swimming

Swimming pools at the lodges are almost a requisite these days as people with children find them an excellent source of entertainment for the kids during "down time." It is almost worth visiting Ol Malo just for a look at the spectacular cliff-side pool.

Camel Safari

At **Ol Malo** camel rides are available for your pleasure. Let Rocky or Colin know how far you want to travel and for how long. Camel safaris arranged by Yare Safaris and leave from the **Maralal Lodge** regularly. See Chapter 9, *Sports & Recreation*, for more information.

Lake Turkana Safari

If you are interested in a safari to Lake Turkana, Yare Safaris have scheduled departures from Maralal by truck. These safaris can be crowded and rough but you will meet all sorts of interesting travelers. Be prepared to help out with camp set-ups and anything else they might need. Ask lots of questions before you sign up to make sure you know what's involved.

Maralal International Camel Derby

This annual charity event attended by people from all over the world is held on the third Saturday in October. Money raised helps supply medical facilities for the Samburu. Ten thousand dollars in prize money is given out in the professional, semi-professional, and amateur races. Camels, and if necessary handlers, are available for hire. Camels are inspected daily by a vet and monitored by a KSPCA officer.

Information on entry fees, regulations etc. are available from **Maralal International Camel Derby (MICD) Secretariat**, *PO Box 47874, Nairobi.*

SHOPPING

Try shopping in the **market** among the kaleidoscope of colors for tin cups, blankets, fruit, and fresh vegetables used and eaten by the locals in their daily lives. Maralal is a popular place to buy Samburu crafts and carvings at reasonable prices.

At the **Maralal Lodge** outside town, there are a couple of souvenir stores that might be worth seeing if you're heading this way. The local Samburu will always spot a tourist and inundate you with offers of endless souvenirs.

EXCURSIONS & DAY TRIPS

Maralal Game Sanctuary

Just outside the town is the **game sanctuary** where impala, zebra, buffalo, warthog, hyena and eland can be seen from the road leading to Maralal.

Losiolo Escarpment

One of the most breathtaking scenes in all of Kenya is that of the **Losiolo Escarpment**. You stand at the edge of a giant escarpment and see forever across and down to the **Suguta Valley** below.

PRACTICAL INFORMATION

Bank

If your safari is taking you further north, it would be wise to get any banking taken care of here at the **Kenya Commercial Bank** on the west side of the square. The next available bank won't be until you reach the town of Marsabit. In Maralal the bank is only open for four hours a week. There was some discussion about changing this, so check it out beforehand.

Gas Stations

There are two gas stations in Maralal where you can fill up on reasonably priced gasoline. The first is **Shell** in the center of town and the other is a **Total** station almost directly across the street. Going further north you might find a supply of gas in Baragoi or Loyongalani but prices will be much higher.

Post Office

To mail a letter or make a phone call, the Maralal post office should be able to satisfy your requirements. The staff have a reputation for being extremely helpful and friendly.

SOUTH HORR

The village of **South Horr** consists mainly of a very large Catholic mission and not much more other than spectacular landscapes and vistas. The colorful gardens at the oasis are filled with a parade of dainty butterflies and birds. Surrounded by Mount Nyiro, Porale, and Supuko, the one street town is nestled in the fertile green valley below where papaya and banana crops grow in the rich soil.

ARRIVALS & DEPARTURES

By Air

Between the towns of Baragoi and South Horr there is a small airstrip available for those wanting to avoid using the subsidiary road. You will need to arrange with someone to pick you up here as there is no public transportation available – try the **Desert Rose Lodge**, *Tel. 228 936, Fax 212160.*

By Car

South Horr is nestled on a secondary Kenya road (C77) between Mount Nyiru, Mount Supuko, and Mount Porale. Because the soil in the valley is rich with nutrients, fruit (bananas, papayas, lemons) and vegetables are grown by the local populace along both sides of the dirt road.

Heading northwards, the short distance between the town of Baragoi and South Horr is filled with lush glens and gorges. It is a pleasant relief after the usually hot, dusty road and plains before Baragoi.

WHERE TO STAY

Other than the Desert Rose, the other hotels in town are very, very basic and I can't recommend them unless you want to tell your friends you found a hotel for under a dollar a night (you'll get no hot water and may have to share a room).

DESERT ROSE LODGE, *PO Box 44801, Nairobi. Tel. 228 936, Fax 212 160. $400 per night double occupancy. All major credit cards accepted.*

To get to Desert Rose Lodge, situated between South Horr and Baragoi, there is a convenient airstrip nearby. From the hotel it is possible to combine your stay with an exotic camel safari run by the managers Emma and Yoav Chen. Hiking, bird watching, and panoramic views are what this place is all about, as the game in the cedar forest reserve is minimal.

Solar power provides electricity for the four double guest rooms with full bathrooms. The A-frame buildings are tastefully done with local brick and cedar. An enormous rock is the focal point of the old hunter's camp and is now one wall of the dining room. Between the living and dining rooms, a large open fireplace keeps off the evening chill prevalent in the hills at 4,500 feet. The quaint bar and verandah overlook the pool and a stream below. The swimming pool built into the rocks is filled from a natural water supply.

WHERE TO EAT

In the town of South Horr there are two places that will come up with a basic Indian meal if given a two hour advance notice. Try the **GOOD TOURIST HOTEL** first, and if they can't comply then go to the **MOUNT NYIRO HOTEL** and check there. At either place, tea is always plentiful and readily available.

NIGHTLIFE & ENTERTAINMENT

To get a taste of the local lifestyle stop by the **Serima bar** on the main road. The beer is served warm – the Kenyan way.

SPORTS & RECREATION

Camel Safari

Arrange with the managers of **Desert Rose Lodge** to take a ride through the forest and enjoy the cool shade, plentiful birds, and breath-taking vistas from on top of a camel.

EXCURSIONS & DAY TRIPS

Elgeyo-Marakwet Escarpment

The view from the **escarpment** is one of the best in the country. A sheer drop of about 8,000 feet to the valley below offers a dramatic moonscape vista. The mist and clouds are the only thing standing in the way of your viewing pleasure if they choose not to lift when you arrive.

Mount Nyiro

For anyone who is extremely fit, a climb up the scenic **Mount Nyiro** is worth every broken fingernail. From the 9,000 foot peak you will be able to see **Lake Turkana** in all its splendor and **Telekis volcano**. For safety it is wise to take a guide with you as the lush mountain forests are home to elephant herds and unpredictable buffalo.

Baragoi

The small mission station of **Baragoi** is of recent interest to paleontologists but has nothing much to offer the average tourist. If ancient fossils and human remains are why you came to Kenya, however, this may be a place to consider.

LOYONGALANI

The small village of **Loyongalani**, which means "place of the trees," is on the east side of Lake Turkana and consists of a Catholic Mission and fishing station. Attracting the usual string of township necessities, Loyongalani offers plenty of relaxation and not much more.

ARRIVALS & DEPARTURES

By Air

The airfield at Loyongalani is a good central location to start off your explorations of the furthest northern reaches of Kenya. Tell your travel agent this is where you would like to begin this leg of your journey and work your way back down towards Samburu.

By Bus

There is no public transportation to Loyongalani and no bus station in town.

By Car

As you drive from Maralal to Loyongalani you'll notice the terrain changing, from thick forests to dry arid flat land with scattered green spots where mountains and crevasses manage to keep a little moisture in the soil. Towards the end of the ride, the desert once again changes to dark plains of lava rock with a moon-like terrain.

WHERE TO STAY

THE OASIS CLUB, *Muthaiga Travel Limited, PO Box 34464, Nairobi. Tel. 750 034, Fax 750 035. $150 per night double occupancy. All major credit cards accepted.*

Removed from civilization, the club encourages you to divest yourself of the trappings that come with the responsibilities of society. Let your hair down within the confines of the refreshing refuge where the basics are all you need. Off in the distance the jadestone color of Lake Turkana is incongruous with the surrounding arid desert.

To keep you entertained the owners will take you bird watching, prospecting for crystals and precious gems, perch fishing in the lake, sightseeing on South Island, impressive crocodile viewing, flying to Koobi Fora or visiting with an El Molo tribe. During the heat of the day, try relaxing in one of the two pools filled from a natural spring or take a walk in the thick green forest.

In the thatched and stone dining area and bar, your catch may appear as the evening meal along with tasty German fare. One of the 24 unsophisticated but adequate concrete bandas will be assigned to you for your visit. Overlook the lack of air conditioning and instead sit on your private verandah and delight in the exceptional adventure.

EL MOLO CAMP, *PO Box 34710, Nairobi. Tel. (02) 724 384. $80 per night double occupancy. All meals are included.*

In addition to the camp site, there are 20 self-service bandas on the grounds. The facilities are clean, safe, and run by a friendly and helpful staff. Take a dip in the pool or try the attractive restaurant and bar where the drinks are cold and the food delicious. At 9:30 pm, the electricity is turned off but kerosene lanterns continue to light the camp.

WHERE TO EAT

For truly outstanding local fare stop in at the **EL MOLO CAMP** where the hour long wait will be worth your while. Other than this or the German food in the thatched and stone dining room at the **OASIS CLUB**, look for the standard **teahouses** on the main street of Loyangalani.

SEEING THE SIGHTS

Native Dancing

Take a walk down the main street in Loyongalani and you'll find yourself surrounded by curious children vying for your attention. Their innocence can be captivating. They will try to coerce you to see local dancing later in the evening. The dances can be fun and entertaining, but some people don't think they are authentic and instead view them as stage productions.

NIGHTLIFE & ENTERTAINMENT

If you want a cold drink, head for the **El Molo Camp**. This is the only place for miles around where you can actually find a cold refreshment to quench your thirst.

SPORTS & RECREATION

Game Viewing

Take a boat ride to look at the vast numbers of fascinating crocodiles on **South Island**. Game at **Mount Kulal Biosphere Reserve** includes elephant, cheetah, lion, black rhino, leopard, giraffe, zebra, ostrich, crocodile and gazelle. Arrange with your tour organizer for a guide to take you up the mountain and into the forest of Mount Kulal. In **Sibiloi National Park** you can see hippo, oryx, Grevy's zebra, gerenuk, tiang, hyena, cheetah and of course, crocodiles.

Hiking

To arrange a trip up scenic **Mount Kulal** check in with the Oasis Club. The tour will include both driving and walking through the forest to get to the summit.

Fishing

Casting bait for Nile perch or ferocious tiger fish can be a rewarding experience. These fish are good fighters and, if you keep them, good eating. Stop in at the **Oasis Club** where they can prepare your fishing expedition.

Birding

Birding here can be a special affair if you know where to go. It is best to allow the **Oasis Club** to make the necessary guide arrangements for you.

Visit to El Molo Tribe

A visit to a local **El Molo tribe** can be arranged through the Oasis Club, but some guests find the local tribe to be corrupted by the tourist industry and their original lifestyles changed dramatically. Go prepared to pay for any photos you want to take, if it is possible to take photos at all.

Flights to Koobi Fora

It is possible to reach **Koobi Fora** (see *Excursions* below) by road from here, but by the time you get there you won't want to do anything but rest. It is much more pleasant to allow the Oasis Club or your tour operator to arrange a comfortable flight for you.

Swimming

At the **Oasis Club** there are two lovely spring-fed swimming pools available to both guests and visitors. If you are not staying at the lodge a $15 fee is charged for use of the facilities.

Prospecting

Many people come here to see if they can strike it rich with the crystals and semi-precious gems found in the area. A few of your options around **Mount Kulal** are amethyst and onyx.

SHOPPING

No doubt while you are in Loyongalani, someone will offer you semi-precious and precious stones such as onyx or amethysts which are acquired on Mount Kulal. No doubt the stones are genuine, but make sure you know what you're looking at before you buy.

EXCURSIONS & DAY TRIPS

Chalbi Desert

Once a branch of Lake Turkana, the salt desert is sometimes reclaimed by the lake when rainfall is heavy. Interestingly, the area becomes a shallow sea covering thousands of square miles. The road crossing the desert is impassable even after light or moderate rains. If you intend to come this way, make sure you have the proper equipment and the necessary guide to enjoy the challenge of making it alive. On a good day windswept sands, tire-ripping lava, and mirages will be your companions in this stark land.

South Island National Park

Sightseeing on **South Island** is not nearly as impressive as the more northerly Central Island. However, an impressive crocodile population might entice you to visit. Feral goats also live on the ancient ash-covered volcano tip. From shore, glowing vents on the 15 square mile island are a testament to the rumblings below.

To cross the four mile stretch of water, make arrangements with the Oasis Lodge.

Mount Kulal Biosphere Reserve

One of four in Kenya and 271 in the world, the **biosphere** at Mount Kulal provides for scientific studies of its unique flora and fauna and how they interact. Game in the park includes elephant, cheetah, lion, black rhino, leopard, giraffe, zebra, ostrich, crocodile and gazelle. Vegetation covering the reserve encompasses every possibility on earth from bush, rain, mountain, evergreen and mist forests to saltbrush, desert, and grasslands.

To arrange a trip up scenic Mount Kulal check in with the Oasis Club. The tour will include both driving and walking through the forest to get to the summit.

Sibiloi National Park

Part of Kenya's extensive national park system established in 1970, the 600 square mile **Sibiloi National Park** is a good place to get away from the hordes of tourists in Kenya. As there are not many places to lodge nearby, tour groups tend to keep away from the desert sands and yellow spear grass found on the eastern shores of Lake Turkana. Hippo, oryx, ostrich, Grevy's zebra, gerenuk, tiang, lion, hyena, cheetah, leopard and of course crocodiles find this park as good a place as any to live their lives. For permission to enter or stay here, contact the **National Museums of Kenya**, *PO Box 40658 Nairobi, Tel. 742 131, Fax 741 424.* I recommend flying in as the drive can be arduous and long.

Often called the "cradle of mankind," it is here **Richard Leakey** unearthed the famous Homo Habilis skull of our ancestor. A concrete post marks the site where "1470" was actually found. In addition to hundreds of spectacular finds, you can see the remains of a fossilized forest. Large petrified tree trunks evidence what was once a lush and fertile region.

Koobi Fora Museum

Koobi Fora, the museum displaying some of the prehistoric finds in Sibiloi National Park makes for a fascinating and humbling stop. Over 600 fossils and prehistoric remains came from this area, including a three-toed ancestor to the horse, a human skeleton over three million years old, and a one and a half million year old elephant.

If you want to stay in a self-service banda or get into the museum, you must first get written permission from the **National Museums of Kenya**, *PO Box 40658, Nairobi, Tel. 742 131, Fax 741 424.*

THE CHANGING FACES OF KENYA

The tribesmen living in and around civilization have adapted to western ways by learning English, dressing in a suit and tie, catering to tourists, using cash instead of trading and on and on. As a fiercely proud people however, they refuse to give up their traditions. In a typical African fashion, they have found a way to satisfy both worlds by changing with the times. It is not uncommon to see a tribe member in town dressed in city clothes speaking English, only to see him hours later walking along the road in his tribal costume conversing in Swahili. Such an unpredictable and wonderful people!

MARSABIT

"Place of cold" is the translation of **Marsabit**, where night-time temperatures can get downright frosty. Native Rendille tribes make colorful contrast to the green bush with their bright earrings, multi-colored beads, animal skins, and red shukas as they make their way through the small town. Quickly taking care of business is a priority so they can get back to their valuable camel herds.

ARRIVALS & DEPARTURES

By Air

The safest and best way to get to Marsabit is to avail yourself of the services provided by the small local airport just north of the town.

By Bus

It is possible to arrange for a bus to Marsabit but I don't recommend this mode of transport, as it is highly unreliable and a long uncomfortable six hour trip.

By Car

To reach Marsabit by car, follow the A-2 highway past Samburu. The seemingly endless, arid, flat landscape eventually becomes a cool green oasis high in the hills. To travel in this part of the country it is necessary to hook up with a convoy of some kind to lessen the chances of being attacked by bandits (*shifta*).

ORIENTATION

On the south side of Marsabit the first sign of civilization you'll see is the park gate and signs for the camp site. Shortly afterwards the **District**

Commissioner's Office will be on your left. West of town is the **Esso Gas** station and east of town is another park gate and the prison. To the north is the airstrip and towards the center of the township is the **Shell Station** and bus stand.

WHERE TO STAY

MARSABIT LODGE, *Msafiri Inns, PO Box 42013, Nairobi. Tel. 330 820, Fax 227 815.$64 per night double occupancy. All major credit cards accepted.*

For someone on a budget, this is an acceptable place to spend a night or two inside Marsabit National Park. The bedrooms and public areas are in need of a facelift but the site of the lodge is spectacular. The lodge overlooks Sokorte Dika, an impressive crater lake or *gof.* Oversized windows in each guest room face the watering hole and the varied game below.

WHERE TO EAT

For a good cup of tea and snack foods including *mandazi,* go to the **BISMILLAH TEA HOUSE** across from the Catholic Technical School. At the **KENYAN LODGE** the food is outstanding Ethiopian native cuisine.

Out of town, try the scenic **MARSABIT LODGE** which caters to the safari crowd (see *Where to Stay* above).

NIGHTLIFE & ENTERTAINMENT

On Friday and Saturday nights, the **Marsabit Highway Hotel** has a popular disco and during the week the bar sells beer until midnight. In addition to good food, the **Kenyan Lodge** has a clean and friendly bar open to travelers.

SPORTS & RECREATION

Game Drives

Populations of kudu, oryx, buffalo, cheetah, giraffe, zebra and jackal live deep in the forests of **Marsabit National Reserve** but move to the plains when rainfall is plentiful. There are over 350 noted species of birds including eagles, hawks, and falcons nesting in the reserve. With patience all the wildlife hidden here can be spotted.

Hiking

Explore with a guide one of several extinct volcanic craters in **Marsabit National Park**. Take a 656 foot walk down to the floor of grassy bottomed **Gof Redo** and rest under the shade of the trees growing there.

EXCURSIONS & DAY TRIPS

Marsabit National Reserve

Most famous for the largest elephant tusks in Africa, **Marsabit National Reserve** is a photographer's dream. It is suggested that the ivories are large due to the high mineral content in the soil around the mountain. Populations of kudu, oryx, buffalo, cheetah, giraffe, zebra and jackal live deep in the forests but move to the budding plains when rainfall is plentiful.

If you went to the Nairobi National Museum you saw a replica of Ahmed, the tusker protected by Kenyatta with personal bodyguards. Marsabit was his home until he died a natural death at 65.

The high peak of **Mount Marsabit** is the center of the 1,300 square mile reserve where crater *(gof)* lakes dot the landscape and thick forests break up the monotony of the lower flat countryside. It is a stark and at the same time beautiful place well worth visiting. From the communications tower in the hills above Marsabit town, the panoramic view is awesome. The nature show of moss-draped juniper trees and mist-covered bush will take your breath away.

Gof Bongole with its six mile rim is known as a nesting place for raptors. **Gof Redo** is the place to go if you are on the lookout for kudu. **Gof Sokorte Guda** (Lake Paradise) however, is the most spectacular of the craters and should definitely be a stopping point on your safari. Covering most of the crater floor, it is a piece of tropical heaven right in the middle of the African bush.

To get inside the park will cost you $27 per person plus $1.50 per vehicle. Park hours arc 6:00 am to 7:15 pm daily.

IT'S A BIRD'S LIFE

Marsabit National Park is home to a large population of over 350 species of birds. The rare and elusive **lammergeyer** *(bearded vultures) seems to have established a colony here. To enjoy a favorite meal, the birds have interestingly learned to soar to great heights with a bone only to drop it on the rocks below. Once the bone shatters, the marrow is easy to reach.*

Dida Galgalu Desert

From Marsabit National Reserve take a trip over to the border of the desert where you may well see a grand looking Somali ostrich or perhaps even an aardwolf. If nothing else you will witness the impressive vastness that is a real desert and understand why it was called **Dida Galgula** – "plain of darkness."

Singing Wells of Ulanula

For a rich photographic opportunity, at a price of course, come to the wells where the Rendille bring their cattle for water. As the human chains of men hand dig to the depth of water their habit is to sing and chant; hence the name singing wells. Once the hole is deep enough, water is passed from hand to hand in calabashes to troughs above ground.

Losai National Reserve

Under the necessary and strict guidance of the Kenya Wildlife Preserve, this national park has been placed off limits to visitors for safety reasons. Elephant and rhino once called the impenetrable forest of the reserve home. Perhaps they will again one day.

In the center of an inaccessible lava plateau is a pretty little mission with its own airfield. The 698 square mile park is made up of a variety of terrain including forests, volcanic cones, the **Kaisut Desert** and mountainous regions. In the **Ndoto Mountain Range**, the peak of **Poi** is considered Kenya's most technically difficult climb.

Moyale

The town of **Moyale** lies across the Dida Galgalu Desert from Marsabit. Very few people have the desire to set foot here but crossing the desert in the required convoy can satisfy a certain craving for recklessness.

Other than basics such as a post office, gas station, market, and a few stores, the only thing worth seeing here is the houses which are still built in the traditional fashion. A frame made from wooden poles covered with very thick mud keeps the interior cool no matter what the outside temperature may be.

Garissa

There is almost no reason to venture to this town unless you are traveling with a group going the back route to Lamu. A gas station and bank are the only signs of civilization other than a few questionable hotels. It is unsafe to travel through the area alone because of roaming *shifta* (bandits).

PRACTICAL INFORMATION

Bank

The **Kenya Commercial Bank** is the only bank in Marsabit. You will find the staff friendly and willing to help.

Gas Stations

Heading into town from the west, you will see the **Esso** gas station on your right. **Shell** has its station a little closer to the center of town. With two gas stations in town, the prices for gasoline stay relatively competitive.

Post Office

As with all towns in Kenya, this one has the requisite post office located on the main artery running through town. Here you can make phone calls or send mail home.

17. WESTERN KENYA

Fortunately or unfortunately, depending on your point of view, **western Kenya** is not on the usual tourist circuit. This is slowly changing as visitors try to escape from the minivans and crowds of foreigners doing the same thing they are. If you are into birds or wildlife, this area of Kenya has great and unique varieties of both. Many of them you won't find elsewhere in the country or the world.

It is a very productive area agriculturally with gently rolling hills, vast tea holdings in the south, and fertile farmlands in the north. Consequently the west is the most populated region in Kenya. The roads are well maintained and plentiful because of the need to move people and produce such as sugar cane, wheat, fruit, pyrethrum, coffee and vegetables quickly and efficiently. Matatus and buses abound.

The towns don't have much to hold the interest of tourists other than a couple of the markets and museums. These will entertain you for roughly half a day. Outside the towns, there are other things to intrigue visitors. Safaris through swamps, over mountains, and through tropical rainforests in western Kenya are planned and executed in an authentic manner, particularly if you have a good guide. **Lake Victoria** is a wondrous sight and there are outstanding (and different) places to stay. Personally, I think the area is often overlooked but I might be biased, as this is my part of the country. A few days taking in the sights will reward you with marvelous memories and photos.

The Western Highlands and Lake Victoria make up this portion of Kenya. In the northern reaches are **Mount Elgon** and my home town – **Kitale**. At the region's center is **Kakamega**, pretty much the last point of civilization before venturing west over vast areas of thick bush to Uganda's border. Towards the east you'll find **Eldoret** and southwards are **Kisumu**, **Kisii**, and **Kericho**.

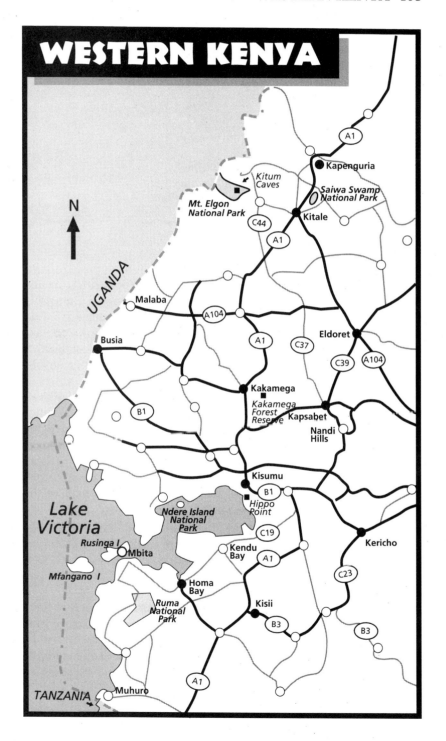

WESTERN KENYA

WESTERN KENYA MUST SEES

Spend a little time in Western Kenya and take in some of the less frequented but no less wondrous must see sights:

Lake Victoria
Kisumu
Kisii
Kericho
Mount Elgon
Saiwa Swamp National Park
Kakamega Forest

KISUMU

Kisumu sits on the gently sloping shores of Kenya's piece of **Lake Victoria**. It is the third largest town in the country (population around 160,000) as well as the regional capital. Once a busy, growing township due to its **Uganda Railway** terminal, today it has somewhat of an abandoned air about it. When the international ferry shut down on Lake Victoria and the flow of travelers to Uganda disappeared, it lost much of its reason for being. You can still see rusting ships in the water, shabby empty warehouses, and abandoned cargo trains.

When it was founded in 1901 as a railhead for the **East African Railway**, Kisumu was considered the worst assignment in the British Empire. The heat, humidity, and diseases such as bubonic plague, dysentery, malaria, black water fever and sleeping sickness took their share of colonizers.

Today as it struggles to survive, there are still a couple of reasons why a tourist might head for Kisumu. Because of its appointment as the headquarters of **Nyanza Province** and a foray into industry, it looks like the community might have a second chance. The passenger rail services are still excellent as are the connections to eastern parts of Kenya.

ARRIVALS & DEPARTURES

By Air

Any of the eleven weekly flights to and from Nairobi take only an hour and cost $44. If you pay in shillings you will save quite a bit. To make your reservations, call **Kenya Airways**, *Kisumu, Tel. 44055/6.* If you wish to make a booking in person go to the Alpha building on Oginga Odinga Road. The local airport is a short ride outside town, going west.

By Bus/Matatu/Taxi

On Kenyatta Avenue on the east side of town is the bus station and the matatu stand. This is a noisy place filled with the smells and activity that accompany bus travel. Coast Bus and Akamba Bus are the operators of choice as they run a regular and prompt schedule. To get to Nairobi the buses travel at night. Akamba charges $4.45 and Coast charges $3.80 per person for this daily trip. For $8 you can share a Peugeot taxi to Nairobi. There is no schedule for the vehicles; they leave when they are full.

The Nissan Matatus are the most reliable and hopefully have the safest drivers. Departure times vary, so check when you buy your ticket. Prices and destinations are as follows:

Destination	Price
• Nairobi	$4.45
• Busia	$1.55
• Homa Bay	90¢
• Isebania	$3.35
• Kakamega	90¢
• Kitale	$2.90
• Malaba	$1.80
• Nakuru	$2.65

By Car

From Nairobi to Kisumu it is 215 miles, making it a driveable distance if you can afford to take a day out of your vacation for car travel. Depending on the condition of the roads and your fellow drivers, the trip can be pleasant or not. It is much more practical while on vacation to fly into Kisumu and rent a car or arrange transport with your hotel.

On Jomo Kenyatta Highway, look for a red-roofed building across the street from the Hotel Royale and the Reinsurance Plaza where you will find **Kamba Travel**, *Tel. 28131*. You can rent a car here for visiting the local area sights.

By Ferry/Boat

The jetty for the ferry is very close to the railway station on the shores of Lake Victoria. Now that the international ferry is closed you will only be able to book passage to Mfangano Island, Kendu Bay, Homa Bay and Asembo Bay. These days the ferries are rarely full, so a second or third class seat is fine. On the *MV Tilapia* and the *MV Alestes,* only second and third class are available. On the *MV Reli* you can choose from any of the three classes.

The *MV Alestes* leaves Kisumu at 9:30 am on Tuesdays and returns on Saturday at 5:30 pm. It stops at Homa Bay, Mfangano Island. If you get off here, your only choice is to stay for four nights.

From Kisumu you can catch the *MV Tilapia*, on Tuesday, Friday, and Sunday to any of the following ports of call:

Destination	Arrival Time	Departure Time
• Kisumu	–	9:00 am
• Kendu Bay	10:50 am	11:10 am
• Homa Bay	2:00 pm	2:30 pm
• Asembo Bay	5:00 pm	8:00 am the following day
• Homa Bay	10:35 am	11:00 am
• Kendu Bay	1:55 pm	2:10 pm
• Kisumu	4:00 pm –	

The *MV Reli* has services to the following places on Sunday and Wednesday:

Destination	Arrival Time	Departure Time
• Kisumu	–	9:00 am
• Kendu Bay	10:50 am	11:00 am
• Homa Bay	1:55 pm	2:25 pm
• Asembo Bay	5:00 pm	8:00 am the following day
• Homa Bay	10:35 am	11:00 am
• Kendu Bay	1:55 pm	2:20 pm
• Kisumu	4:00 pm –	

Fares from Kisumu to these destinations are as follows:

Destination	1st	2nd	3rd Class Fare
• Kendu Bay	90¢	65¢	35¢
• Homa Bay	$1.55	$1.20	55¢
• Asembo Bay	$2.10	$1.65	65¢
• Mfangano Is.	$2.80	$2	$1

By Train

The railway station is a five minute walk from Oginga Odinga Road. For a booking to Nairobi it is best to make reservations well in advance. The station office is open from 8:00 am to noon and 2:00 pm to 4:00 pm daily.

ORIENTATION

The main drag is **Oginga Odinga Road**, which appears to run almost horizontally through the center of town. **Jomo Kenyatta Highway** cuts the town in half vertically. The railway station and jetty are close to each other on the outer west side of town along the lakeshore. North of the city center is the road to the airport and closer in is the small hospital. The **Kisumu Museum** holds the furthest point of interest to the east. To the south is Nzola Road leading to **Hippo Point**.

ACCESS TO LAKE VICTORIA

The best access to Lake Victoria is actually at the small village of **Dunga** *just two miles southwards along Nzola Road. Ask anyone to point you in the right direction or just follow the signs once you are outside Kisumu (see Hippo Point excursion below).*

GETTING AROUND TOWN

The town of **Kisumu** seems to stretch for miles in all directions when you look at a map. The truth is, walking should be no problem at all. This is especially true as everything you might need is concentrated around Oginga Odinga Road.

If you prefer not to walk, you should be able to get around town by taxi for next to nothing. For reference, to go for the two mile ride to Hippo Point will cost you $2.20. It is always best to make arrangements before getting in. I always like the idea of hiring a taxi and driver for the entire day. This way you can come and go as you please and see the sights without any exertion. Make the best bargain you can, but reasonable rates are anywhere between $8 and $10 for the day. Be sure and pay either at the end of the day or half up front and half when you're finished sightseeing.

WHERE TO STAY

MFANGANO ISLAND CAMP, *Governor's Camp-Musiara Limited, PO Box 48217, Nairobi. Tel. 331 871, Fax 726 427. $900 per night double occupancy including fishing and plane flight. All major credit cards accepted.*

Enormous Nile perch and tasty tilapia swim in the waters of Lake Victoria. They wait to fight anyone who dares throw a hook overboard. Bright canoes, imaginative dhows, or speedy fishing boats escort you from the pier to nearby bays or hidden coves.

Getting to Mfangano Island normally includes flying in from a hotel in Masai Mara. Once you land, an exciting boat ride whips you away to the nearby camp. Attractive brownish-red clay is the building material of choice for the six roomy bandas and open hillside dining room. Banana leaves accentuate the thatched roofs. It is impossible not to watch the sun go down or otters at play from any of the large cottage windows.

Attractive stone walks lead you to your accommodations. A lot of thought and careful planning are evident inside and outside the discreetly placed cottages. Once inside, notice the details – Kenyan art, fresh flowers, local crafts, and imaginative decor. This is certainly a classy place to stay where they outdo themselves with discrete service, mouth-watering cuisine and one of the loveliest sites around.

Craggy hills, natural vegetation, scary caves, green lawns and impressive fig trees invite you to leave your cares behind and enjoy the escapade. If you are not into fishing but like the sounds of the camp, come anyway and feed a fish eagle, visit a local village, or take in the impressive bird life around the island.

RUSINGA ISLAND CAMP, *Lonrho Hotels Kenya Limited, PO Box 58581, Nairobi. Tel. 216 940, Fax 216 796. $800 per night double occupancy including fishing and plane flight. All major credit cards accepted.*

Tourists usually come to the camp for half a day of spectacular Nile perch fishing. The drill usually begins early from the Mara Safari Club in Masai Mara. The plane makes its round trip from door to door effortlessly in one day. Once you step off the small aircraft at Rusinga Island you simply walk a few yards to the shade of a magnificent, huge fig tree. You have arrived.

Follow the thick green lawn to the edge of Lake Victoria. From here you can take inventory of the fishing boats, impressive tackle, the pier and of course the scale waiting to weigh your 300 pound catch. Remember, no swimming no matter how inviting it looks because of the bilharzia parasite.

Under more massive trees are three basic bandas with screened-in porches, full bathrooms, electricity, and accommodations for up to six people. The thatched roof adds charm to the rustic but pleasing setting. Relaxing in the comfortable open living room you can sometimes see otters, enormous monitor lizards, and hundreds of birds basking in the warm sun.

Take a walk to the souvenir shop or go further afield to explore the dig where Mary Leakey discovered Proconsul Man. Watching the sun rise and set with Lake Victoria as a backdrop can be spectacular if you decide it's worth staying for a full day of kicking back and fishing – or should I say catching!

SUNSET HOTEL, *African Tours & Hotels Limited, PO Box 30471, Nairobi. Tel. 336 858, Fax 218 109. $50 per night double occupancy. Breakfast included. All major credit cards accepted.*

The Sunset Hotel in Kisumu has one of the best lake and sunset views from each room. Bedrooms are clean and well kept while the service is friendly and prompt. The swimming pool and excellent restaurant add to a pleasant stay. To get to the hotel it is a short taxi ride down Achieng Oneka Road to the affluent suburban setting.

KERICHO TEA HOTEL, *African Tours & Hotels Limited, PO Box 30471, Nairobi. Tel. 336 858, Fax 218 109. $48 per night double occupancy. Includes breakfast. All major credit cards accepted.*

Ruefully, this hotel is another example of the faded glory of the British colonial era. The historic building was built in the 1950s by the wealthy Brooke Bond tea company. The bedrooms are enormously spacious but in need of some attention. There are ensuite bathrooms with showers and hot water. The two suites in the back of the building overlook the lush fields of tea. On the ground floor is a sprawling bar/lounge area which spills out to the terrace and into the lovely well-kept garden. This is a popular hangout for local residents.

Surrounding the Kericho Tea Hotel are lush green symmetrical fields and hills covered with tea bushes. If you follow the path via the grounds behind what was once the service station and through the back gate you will come to the worker's huts. If you are fortunate, you may be able to see some actual picking. Try to arrange a tour with the hotel through the plantation and processing plant.

IMPERIAL HOTEL, *PO Box 1866, Kisumu. Tel. 41485. $46 per night double occupancy. All major credit cards accepted.*

As a new addition to the hotel selection in Kisumu, you might want to try the more than adequate five star Imperial Hotel. Choose from less expensive rooms or go for the more costly apartments and suites. The facilities are clean and the service excellent. There is a tiny swimming pool but unfortunately it is hemmed in by the building. A pleasant choice of two restaurants and a colorful rooftop bar add to any stay.

HOMA BAY HOTEL, *Tel. 0385 22070, Homa Bay (or write to Msafiri Inns, PO Box 42013, Nairobi, Tel. 330 820, Fax 227 815). $25 per night double occupancy. Breakfast included. All major credit cards accepted.*

The Homa Bay Hotel has a very pleasant setting right on the shores of Lake Victoria. Ask for a room with a lakeside view where you can recuperate from the rigors of travel. The rooms are clean and have their own bathrooms with all the necessary amenities.

WHERE TO EAT

Out at **Hippo Point** at the campground, on Nazola Road about two miles south of town, there is a pleasant and relaxing restaurant where an excellent fish and chips meal is served for $2. You will also find cold – instead of the usual warm – drinks for sale. Also at Hippo Point is **DUNGA REFRESHMENTS,** *Tel. 42529,* where the Indian curries are good and more importantly you can eat outside at the edge of the water. Call the restaurant manager to arrange free transport with the understanding you will try a delicious (inexpensive) meal and wonderful sunset.

In town there are lots of places to choose from where the service is great and the food delicious. Two of the best are the **HOTEL ROYALE,** on Jomo Kenyatta Highway at the south end of town near the town hall, *Tel. 44240,* or the **IMPERIAL HOTEL** (which has two restaurants), on Jomo Kenyatta Highway in the center of town and is next door to the

CHICKEN PALACE, *Tel. 41485*. An outstanding lunch or dinner meal of steak, chicken, or fish will cost between $6 and $10.

A basic breakfast of freshly squeezed juice, sweet papaya, fresh eggs, toast and hot coffee is $1 at the **NEW VICTORIA HOTEL**, just off Otiena Oyoo Street at the corner of Kendu Lane and Gor Mahia Road close to the waters of Lake Victoria, *Tel. 2909;* **MONA LISA RESTAURANT**, on Oginga Odinga Road across from the post office; or the popular **TALK OF THE TOWN COFFEE HOUSE**, just off Oginga Odinga Road in the center of town. Talk of the Town is popular with colonials as well as Peace Corp and other volunteer personnel. The restaurant seems to be busiest for breakfast but it is open all day.

At the **LAKE VIEW HOTEL**, on Kendu Lane just across the railroad tracks from Lake Victoria, the restaurant offers – what else – good food and a pretty lake view. The facilities are clean and the staff friendly. The **GULFSTREAM HOTEL** is less conveniently located just outside Kisumu to the east, *Tel. 43927,* but has a very respectable bar and restaurant if you can find transport there and back. Personally I'd rather go for something in town closer to the water.

The new **SUNSET HOTEL**, on the southern edge of town off Jomo Kenyatta Highway on Impala Lane, *Tel. 41100*, has a great value lunch or dinner for $9. For fast food, try the Chicken Palace (see above), **RAFIQ REFRESHMENTS & FAST BURGERS**, or **WIMPY**, all located on Jomo Kenyatta Highway.

SEEING THE SIGHTS
Kisumu Museum
Interesting and highly recommended, it will cost you a mere $1.10 to get into the **Kisumu Museum**, *Tel. 4004*. A short walk of less than a mile east from the center of town, the museum sits on Nairobi Road. The hours are 9:30 am to 6:00 pm every day. For a couple of shillings the caretaker will show you around and point out the most interesting displays. Some people go so far as to say it is the best collection in the country.

The area is home to the **Luo tribe**, which accounts for the third largest group in the country. A traditional Luo homestead is set up outside the museum. The husband's mud hut is surrounded by a house for each of his wives. Also outside is a cramped enclosure for sad looking crocodiles and tortoises.

Inside the museum, take a look at the array of stuffed animals, including one of a lion perched on the back of a wildebeest. The most interesting exhibits are those of common items used by tribes in the area. Weapons, clothing, furniture, musical instruments, farming tools, cooking utensils and traps are all part of the collection.

Kisumu Market

The large **market** in Kisumu is one of the better ones in the country. It is located along Nairobi Road in front of the bus/matatu station and a ten minute walk from the center of town. Because western Kenya is not generally on the tourist circuit, you will find the market to be genuine. There won't be the usual gaggle of trinket sellers following you. Generally friendly vendors will stare, as you will seem a little out of place.

Mosque

As you travel around Kenya you are bound to see a **mosque** in each town. This is one of those things that make great photo collections – all the mosques in the little towns you pass through.

NIGHTLIFE & ENTERTAINMENT

Most of the hotels in Kisumu have a quiet and comfortable bar where you can get a cold drink and relax in the evening. The rooftop bar at the **Imperial Hotel** on Jomo Kenyatta Highway is one of the best. Here you can take in a wonderful view as you chat with the bartender about the goings on in town.

If you are looking for more than that, head for the **Octopus Night Club**. Located on Ogada Street, the complex has an excellent disco/bar/restaurant combination. The three creatively named bars are the **Fisherman's Wharf**, the **Captain's Wives** and the **Pirates Den**. You can dance, talk, eat, drink and be thoroughly entertained by the odd assortment of goings on. The **Kericho Tea Hotel** is a popular place for local residents to relax in the lounge or on the terrace overlooking well-kept gardens.

SPORTS & RECREATION

See *Excursions & Day Trips* below (and *Where to Stay*, above, for information about camp activities) for directions and more details.

Game Viewing

At **Rusinga Island Camp**, a walk along the shore will present you with a wonderful view of hundreds of birds, otters, and monitor lizards. At **Hippo Point** near Kisumu (out Nzola Road), relax with a cold drink and see if the hippo will allow you a quick glimpse of a wide open mouth or twitching little ears. From the camp on **Mfangano Island**, take pleasure in throwing a lunch of fish to the graceful fish eagle or quietly sit by as otters play among the reeds.

On the scenic island of **Ndere** look for impala, dik dik, and gazelle, just to mention some of the prolific wildlife. At **Ruma National Park** you can see roan antelope, Jackson's hartebeest, hyena, zebra, buffalo, Rothschild giraffe, vervet monkey, waterbuck, leopard, impala, jackal, topi, reedbuck, warthog and oribi.

Fishing

Many tourists come to Lake Victoria for the sole purpose of landing a 400 pound Nile perch or enjoying the battle with a tilapia fish. Both at **Rusinga** and **Mfangano Island Camps**, the facilities are some of the best to fulfill your fishing fantasy.

To try your hand at fly-fishing in some of the wonderful mountain streams, ask at the **Kericho Tea Hotel** in Kericho. If this does not pan out, try the **Kericho/Sotik Fishing Association**, *PO Box 281, Kericho*. For a small membership fee, the association will welcome you with maps and directions to hidden honey holes.

Boat Trips

From Kisumu it is possible to take several ferry rides or boat trips to nearby islands on Lake Victoria. Ask your tour agent or your hotel for information on two hour boat trips from the pier around **Kiboko Island**. A four to six hour trip takes you to the island of **Ndere** where you can spend time hiking and enjoying nature.

Swimming

The **Imperial Hotel** has a small swimming pool with not much of a view due to the building surrounding it. You can, however, cool off in the water or keep your kids entertained as they splash and play the heat of the afternoon away.

Tea Tour

Inquire at the **Kericho Tea Hotel** in Kericho for a tour of the processing plant and the plantation itself. This plantation is the one closest to the town and was once owned by the Brooke Bond company. It is also possible to arrange a guided tour through the **Kenya Tea Development Authority**, *Rahimtullah Trust Tower, Moi Avenue, PO Box 30213, Nairobi, Tel. 221 441.*

SHOPPING

Near the town hall on Jomo Kenyatta Highway is the **Wananchi Craft Shop**. The cooperative sells arts and crafts made by local women. There are some interesting woven items worth taking a look at. The **city market** is always fun to wander around whether you want to buy fresh fruit or local cloth.

Check out the booths set up along the sidewalk near the **British Council Library** on the north side of Oginga Odinga Road. This is one of the best places to purchase Kisii soapstone carvings of all shapes and sizes. In the nearby town of **Tabaka**, you can watch the artists carving the soap stone and buy directly from the workshop at reduced prices.

EXCURSIONS & DAY TRIPS

Lake Victoria

Kenya shares the shallow 26,828 square mile **Lake Victoria** with Uganda and Tanzania. It is not part of the Rift Valley lake system. It is, however, a major geographical feature of the region and more impressive for its size than loveliness. Because of constant cloud and haze, the water's color seems to stay a battleship gray for most of the year.

In 1858 John Hanning Speke, an early explorer, had a theory that Lake Victoria was the source of the White Nile river. He was laughed at and ridiculed until 1875 when H.M. Stanley proved him to be correct. Let thoughts of exotic papyrus swamps, quixotic islands, and the promise of teeming fish lure you to the legendary waters.

Tilapia, colorful cichlids (sunfish), tiger fish, and the giant Nile perch are food for the Luo tribes who live along the shore. The Nile perch was introduced in the 1960s and is steadily decimating the other marine life with its voracious appetite. Wildlife around the huge freshwater lake includes hippo and the occasional crocodile. Beautiful bays will tempt you to swim in the huge freshwater lake, but absolutely do not venture in. The bilharzia parasite causes extreme discomfort, not to mention possible death!

Hippo Point

Located at **Dunga** where there is the best lake access, it is easy to find **Hippo Point** and the cafe known as Dunga Refreshments. Follow Nzola Road and the signs south of town for about two miles. It is possible to take a taxi from town for $2.20, or you can walk for about an hour. Even if the wandering hippo are not in sight when you visit, it is still a pretty place to call on – especially for the sunsets and sunrises.

If you want to camp, this is the only site around Kisumu. Camping costs $1.80 per person but there isn't much in the way of shade.

Kendu Bay

To hold your interest in **Kendu Bay**, look for the impressive Kendu Bay mosque, the ferry jetty about a mile along the shore and terns, waders, flamingos and other water birds flocking here to feed. Besides these attractions, the only other point of interest around the small lakeside village is an odd volcanic lake a few miles from town. **Simbi Lake** has an interesting legend surrounding its 17 square miles of stagnant soda. Locals don't go near the place because they say there is a swamped village at the bottom of the lake. The story tells of a woman who was refused hospitality in the community. For revenge she called forth a torrential rain that drowned the population and left the lake as a reminder.

Ndere Island National Park

The easiest way to get to the tiny park is by hiring a boat from the Kisumu Yatch Club. From start to finish expect a six hour round trip including time on the tiny island. If this doesn't fit your idea of traveling in Kenya, drive 25 miles west of Kisumu to Kaloka Beach. For a small fee you can hire a canoe to the island. There is no entry charge into the park.

While on Ndere Island you can walk about with no restraints or restrictions, but keep a sharp eye out for reptiles and wild animals as you enjoy the lovely vistas. Hippo, crocodile, impala, snakes and a wide variety of birds call the isle home.

Homa Bay & Ruma National Park

The people in the ordinary looking town of **Homa Bay** are busy scurrying to the waterside so their produce will make it to Kisumu. The peculiar shape of **Mount Homa** on the horizon and **Ruma (Lambwe Valley) National Park** are the only two spots of interest in the bay area. Most people take a ferry ride to get to the busy township and then drive southwest (20 miles) to get to the park.

Climbing to the top of the 5,740 foot Homa mountain will make you sweat, but views from the top are worth the effort. At the base of Mount Homa is an interesting lime quarry supplying much of the building industry's requirements.

Ruma National Park is accessible (particularly after rain) with four wheel drive vehicle only. But don't dismiss the 48 square mile park yet as the game is prolific and visitors rare. There is no charge to get in and the hours are 6:00 am to 6:00 pm daily. It is marvelous to drive the six miles from the shore of Lake Victoria and have the entire world to yourself !

The main attraction is a herd of over 200 roan antelope who hide in the plentiful grasslands and acacia thickets. Other wonderful (and imported) wildlife includes Jackson's hartebeest, hyena, zebra, buffalo, Rothschild giraffe, vervet monkey, waterbuck, leopard, impala, jackal, topi, reedbuck, warthog and oribi.

Rusinga Island

Rusinga Island and the town of **Mbita** are connected to the mainland by a causeway about an hour's drive from Homa Bay. Matatus and the ferry are two means of transportation to the island. If you are staying at **Rusinga Island Camp** you will delight in the peace and isolation of the place.

The only "sights" are Mary Leakey's **dig site** where Proconsul Man (millions of years old!) was discovered, and the **mausoleum of Tom Mboya** on the northern end of the island. Rusinga was Tom Mboya's birth place in 1930, and he was brought back to rest here after he was shot and killed in 1969. Murdered for his political savvy and outspokenness, the Luo tribesman may have had designs on the presidency after Kenyatta.

Mfangano Island

Jutting black rocks, steep forested hills, driftwood, and secluded Luo fishing villages line the shores of this solitary island. Giant fig trees shade the villagers as they scrub their washing on big boulders along the water's edge. Fishing trips, sunrises, and island hopping from the **Mfangano Island Camp** make a trip here worthwhile.

Kisii

This fast-growing commercial center is where the famous **Kisii stone** is mined, but oddly enough it is not sold here. Because visitors are rare, there is no profit in setting up stores to sell the soft stone. The friendly people will stare at you with curious eyes as they wonder what you are doing here. The quarry makes for an interesting attraction and so does the colorful town market. The region is known as the **Gusii Highlands** and home to one million Gusii people. From Nairobi, the trip to Kisii takes about eight hours by bus and a little less by car.

The town of Kissi has a few adequate hotels, the best of which is the **Kisii Hotel**. The gardens and grounds are well taken care of and come with a flock of resident turkeys. There is also a BP gas station, hospital, post office, police station, two banks (Chartered and Barclays) and an East African Road Service office. All these touches of civilization are centrally located in the middle of the small village.

It is a four hour drive from the mosquito-free town of Kisii to **Manga Ridge**, where your reward is magnificent views of Lake Victoria, Kisumu, and the rolling tea fields of Kericho.

KISII'S PART IN WORLD WAR I

*The **Gusii people** were forcefully persuaded to join the fight as part of the British Army. Here in Kisii the warriors participated in the first Anglo-German confrontation in Africa. The town was in German hands for a short time until the British recaptured it.*

Tabaka

Just eleven miles west of Kisii is the small village of **Tabaka**. Turn left off the Homa Bay Road seven miles beyond Kisii. Follow the road for another four miles to the center itself. There is nowhere to stay and the only attraction is the **soapstone cottage industry**. On the far side of the hill, three quarries work from 8:00 am to 5:00 pm Monday through Friday. Each of the quarries employs about 50 people.

Women carry the stone in sacks from the quarry to the cooperative office. In Tabaka the soft stone is carved by men only. They buy a truck load of rocks which lasts three months and turn out between six and ten pieces a day. Ask around and someone will take you to the workshops. You can watch the villagers plying their trade and buy directly at a much reduced price. Each house in the village has a small array of carvings for sale outside the front door.

SOAPSTONE CARVING

*It is said the people of **Tabaka** are the most artistic in Kenya, producing vases, ashtrays, trinket boxes, animals and birds at a remarkable rate. As the soft rock is exposed to air it hardens, making it more difficult to carve. Water is used to keep the stone soft until the design is complete. Natural colors vary from white through pink and orange. The pink or rose colored stone is the hardest. Some of the people carve for a living; others only supplement their agricultural incomes when necessary.*

Nandi Hills

Driving through the **Nandi Hills** where the magnificent red-blooming Nandi tree originates is a gratifying experience. Unfortunately, the forest that once covered the area has been reduced to less than 15 square miles due to logging, overpopulation, and agriculture. Animal inhabitants are reduced to the odd leopard and zebra.

Legend has it this was the home of the elusive and mysterious Nandi bear. The Nandi people living in their hillside huts claim this is still true.

KERICHO

Kericho gets its name from **Ole Kericho**, an old Masai chief. The headman was killed by Gusii tribesmen in a land battle in the 18th century. Today the wars in the tiny village are over and the people live peacefully surrounded by **tea**. Famous for its estates, the area around Kericho is made up of miles and miles of lime-colored fields of tea. The tea bushes look oddly smooth and uniform in size and color; almost like an enormous felt-covered pool table.

Moi is the main road through town and here you will find the post office, two banks (Standard Chartered and Barclays), the **Tea Hotel**, police station, town hall, Caltex, Kobil, and Shell gas stations. A very short distance to the south of town is a Hindu temple and the town hospital. Northwest of the center are the cheap hotels, the matatu stand, and the ever-present local market. It is possible to fly to the nearby airstrip to begin your trip around western Kenya.

If you want to have a good lunch or dinner buffet, play the grand piano available to guests, or enjoy the garden terrace and lounge, try the Tea Hotel. This is a popular gathering place for residents. It is also worth taking a tea plantation tour if you can work it out with the manager. Try to go at a time when the crop is being picked.

Pickers, who are almost always women, squeeze their way between closely planted tea bushes. Each tender shoot plucked by their adept hands gets thrown inside a large woven basket on their backs. Thick plastic aprons in the Brooke Bond colors protect the workers from being scratched and cut. Be prepared with rain gear as every afternoon you can count on heavy cloudbursts – just what the crops need.

BUS TRAVEL IN WESTERN KENYA

If you decide to travel in western Kenya by bus or matatu, allow plenty of time for sudden changes in the driver's itinerary! When the vehicle empties out and the driver sees there are few passengers, he is likely to decide that's the end of the line for everyone – including you. Perhaps he will choose a different destination depending on where the majority of travelers are headed. With a paid ticket, the driver will arrange for your trip to continue with another bus. You will eventually arrive at your destination. It may just take a little longer than you planned.

PRACTICAL INFORMATION

Banks

Across from each other on Oginga Odinga Road are the **Standard Chartered** and **Barclays Banks**. Both establishments will offer competitive rates when changing your US dollars into local currency. Allow plenty of time for the transaction as a slow pace and long paper trail will try your patience otherwise.

Bookstore

Just opposite the post office on Oginga Odinga Road is the **Sarit bookshop**. This is the best bookstore in town with a good selection of books on Kenya and other assorted topics.

British Council Library

To catch up on the news head for the library on – you guessed it – Oginga Odinga Road. There is a good selection of magazines and newspapers for you to choose from. The hours are 9:30 am to 1:00 pm and 2:00 pm to 5:00 pm Monday through Friday. On Saturday the library is open from 8:30 am to 12:45 pm.

Climate

The climate in and around Kisumu is considerably more humid and hot than at the higher elevations towards the eastern part of the country. Whatever the temperature in Nairobi, you can always add a couple of degrees and know what its like in the township. That is not to say it is unpleasant but it can take a few days to adjust to the steamy air.

Immigration Office

If for some odd reason you should need to renew your visa, it will only take five minutes to do so here. Amazingly, there is no fee and no photos are necessary! The friendly and helpful staff will ask to see your ticket showing a departure date, but they are not too strict about this either.

The office is located at the corner of Jomo Kenyatta Highway and Oginga Odinga Road on the first floor of Reinsurance Plaza. Look for it right behind Deakons Supermarket.

Post Office

Almost in the perfect center of town, the **post office** is on Oginga Odinga Road. It is open Monday through Friday from 8:00 am to 5:00 pm and on Saturday's from 9:00 am to noon. For international calls, buy a phone card at the post office and use the cardphone outside.

ELDORET

As a fairly recent addition to the town of **Eldoret**, the **university** attracts a great deal of new business and development. If this keeps up, Eldoret will surpass Kisumu in size. The town doesn't have too much to offer the journeyer, but it is a good central location for touring the western highlands or the Cherangani Hills.

Migrating Boers in ox wagons founded the townsite; it remained nameless for some time. As the residents needed to call it something they referred to it as "64." This was the number of the land plot where the post office would stand. Later in its history, a newspaper incorrectly spelled its given name *Eldaret*; meaning river, and it is called Eldoret to this day.

Because of the way it came to be, Eldoret has been regarded as an eccentric town with odd stories clinging to its name. For example, local legend says the bank was built around the spot where the safe fell off the wagon. It was too heavy to move!

ARRIVALS & DEPARTURES

By Air

At the time of this writing, small plane travel between Nairobi and Eldoret was suspended. Check with the local airlines to see if service has been restored. If necessary you can still fly into Kisumu or any of the many other airstrips dispersed around the area.

Eldoret now has one of the newest and more modern local airports around. This makes air travel a much better proposition when it's available. The new strip supports Eldoret as it becomes one of the fastest growing towns in Kenya.

By Bus/Matatu

Peugeots, buses, and matatus leave all day long at varying times. Their destinations include Kisumu, Nakuru, Naivasha, Nairobi, Kitale and Kericho.

By Car

To travel by car from Nairobi to Eldoret is a trip of about 195 miles on the smooth and relatively straight A104 Road. If you are interested in seeing more of unexplored Kenya and are not opposed to spending time driving, take the A104 to Nakuru and from there take the B4 towards Marigat. At Marigat turn left towards Kabarnet and the Kerio Valley and finally to Eldoret. This is a lovely scenic drive that will open up more of Africa to you.

By Train

The train service to Nairobi runs on Wednesday, Saturday, and Sunday at 9:00 pm. Arrival time for the overnight trip is at 9:30 am the next morning. You won't be able to see much unless there is a full moon, but it will save you daylight "touring" hours if you sleep and travel at night.

ORIENTATION

Bordering the north side of town is Eldoret's railway station. The post office claims a prominent position on the western border of town on Uganda Road. On the south side of town along Nandi Road is Gilmas Restaurant. To the east is New Church, also on Uganda Road. There is a decent library near the town hall in the center of the township.

GETTING AROUND TOWN

Getting around the central part of Eldoret on foot is little trouble. Everything you need will be within walking distance. If you should want to venture about, hire a taxi for the day on a prearranged fare or rent a car. If you'd like to rent a car, look for **Eldoret Travel Agency**, *Uganda Road, Tel. 33351*; Kenyatta Street dead ends into Uganda Road almost in the center of Eldoret.

WHERE TO STAY

SIRIKWA HOTEL, *African Tours & Hotels Limited, PO Box 30471, Nairobi. Tel. 336 858, Fax 218 109. $60 per night double occupancy. Includes breakfast. All major credit cards accepted.*

As with many of the hotels owned and run by African Tours, it is commonly heard that the food is mediocre and the accommodations shabby. The 105 room high-rise at the corner of Oloo and Elgeyo Roads in Eldoret doesn't seem to be an exception. You can, however, find an adequate room and place to stay should you need to. The swimming pool and conference area are part of the facilities.

KAKAMEGA GOLF HOTEL, *Msafiri Inns, PO Box 42013, Nairobi. Tel. 330 820, Fax 227 815. $40 per night double occupancy. All major credit cards accepted.*

When you stay at the Golf Hotel in Kakamega town you automatically become a member of the neighboring sports club and can use their facilities at your leisure. The rooms in the three story hotel are satisfactory but plain, with not much to write home about. A golf course and attractive flower gardens are the highlight of a visit.

As the choice of places to stay in the area is limited, it is best to make reservations well ahead. The lodge fills up with conference attendees and birders. Even if you don't stay here, have a cold drink in their attractive and relaxing bar. The restaurant and barbecue area offer an excellent meal for $7 per person.

RONDO RETREAT, *The Reverend Godfrey Dawkins, PO Box 14369, Nairobi; or PO Box 2135, Kakamega. Tel. 0331 41345, Fax 0331 20145 (Monday through Friday). $40 per night double occupancy.*

Giant Elgon Olive trees surround the main house in the well-tended and colorful gardens. History tells us that in the 1920s a local sawmiller built the home for his wife whose only request was that it be at the base of the biggest tree in the Kakamega forest. She got her wish.

To get to the retreat run by the Trinity Fellowship Project, you should have a four wheel drive vehicle in case it rains. The drive will take you fourteen and a half miles outside of Kakamega town and into the heart of the forest. The refuge has recently opened to guests after once serving as an orphanage and a youth center. The movie *The Kitchen Toto* was filmed on the grounds.

Shoes must be removed before entering the main building. No smoking is permitted indoors and no alcoholic beverages are served. All the comforts of home are provided excluding a telephone. A generator produces electricity for the entire center.

In the charming dining hall, silver compliments the exceptional meals carefully presented to a maximum of 24 guests. Traditional English tea is served outside on the verandah and, after dinner, coffee marvelously appears by a crackling fire in the lounge. Equally delightful is the decor in the rooms of the main house or the guest cottages dotted around the premises. Look for local crafts, paintings, remarkable antiques, and bright fabrics. Each cottage has its own kitchen and sitting room decorated with class.

Rondo Retreat serves as the perfect getaway where rest, relaxation, and peace are interrupted only by swooping butterflies and the chattering of playing monkeys or exotic chirping birds. Many of the species are found only here in Kakamega Forest. Wander down one of the many forested paths (with or without a guide) to restore your spirit and take in this wondrous piece of nature. Be prepared however, for a few hours of rain which falls every afternoon.

WHERE TO EAT

The **SIRIKWA HOTEL** and the **ELDORET WAGON**, at the corner of Oloo Road and Elgeyo Road close to the railway station, *Tel. 62270*, offer great meals in the usual British style. These two restaurants are probably the best around in Eldoret. At Eldoret Wagon, memorabilia from the colonial days fills the bar/restaurant with an old world charm. Once there was a pleasant verandah which has now been enclosed.

GILMA'S RESTAURANT on Oginga Odinga Street on the south side of town will also be a good choice for good food. For something resembling what we call fast food, try the popular **SIZZLERS CAFE**, at the corner of Kenyatta Street and Nandi Road on the south side of town and right next door to the Eldoret Travel Agency. It is sought out for its tasty sandwiches, steaks, fries, and burgers. Food is always served promptly by friendly staff.

For lighter breakfast or lunch fare, try either the **SPARK MILK BAR** or **OTTO CAFE**, on Uganda Road across from the National Bank of Kenya. Otto Cafe is a popular place for the lunch time crowds; typical items on their menu are steak, fries, chicken, sausages and eggs. At the **GOLF HOTEL**, the restaurant and barbecue has a reputation for excellence at very reasonable prices.

NIGHTLIFE & ENTERTAINMENT

Unfortunately Eldoret is sorely lacking in the way of nightlife and entertainment. The best there is to offer is the **Sirikwa Hotel** restaurant and lounge. The once lovely open verandah at the **Eldoret Wagon Hotel** is now enclosed but you can still enjoy authentic colonial memorabilia on the walls and a cold beer in the bar. Hours for the establishment are 11:00 am to 2:00 pm and 5:00 pm to 11:00 pm in true British fashion. Even if you don't stay at the **Golf Hotel** in Kakamega town, take the time for an ice-cold drink in the fine bar.

SPORTS & RECREATION

Game Viewing/Birding/Hiking

Wildlife in the **Cherangani Hills** is plentiful in the thick bush and surrounding forests. In particular look for baboon, buffalo, antelope, elephant, monkey and hundreds of birds. To book an ornithological or hiking safari, contact Jane or Julia Barnely at **Barnley's House/Sirikwa Safaris**, *PO Box 332, Kitale,* for guided game viewing. The hot humid jungle is perfect for ethereal butterflies, plentiful insects, uncommon reptiles, dazzling birds and small mammals.

In **Kakamega National Forest Reserve**, look for monkeys, porcupines, squirrels and birds at their feeding times in the early morning or late evening.

Golf

The Kakamega **Golf Hotel** offers a golf course popular with locals as well as golfing enthusiasts who are visiting Kenya. If you are not staying at the hotel, you will be charged a small membership fee to play.

Fishing

Fishing for rainbow and brown trout is a delightful prospect in and around the **Cherangani Hills**. The cool temperatures and cold waters surrounding the upper and lower reaches of the **Morum River** produce perfect conditions for trophy-size fish. Even if you don't catch anything, the scenery and terrain will make the trip worthwhile. When booking your trip inquire with your travel agent for available guides or check with the reception at your hotel.

Swimming

The **Sirikwa Hotel** in Eldoret has a pleasant swimming pool where you can spend the day lounging in the sun. At the Kakamega **Golf Hotel** you can keep fit in the sports club or work off the extra vacation pounds with a few laps in their swimming pool.

SHOPPING

In town, try a walk through the smells and sights of the **open market** where you can buy delicious produce for next to nothing. In the **stores** along the main roads you will be able to find an array of Kenyan souvenirs and trinkets to take home.

A half a day's walk along the old Sigor-Tot Road near Sigor is the **Pokot Trading Center**. Pottery, calabashes, metal work such as snuff boxes, and other interesting crafts can be found here where the Pokot people live.

EXCURSIONS & DAY TRIPS

Kakamega

The colorful **daily market** and the impressive **Hindu temple** are worth a detour to the town. Other than these two things you will find the usual post office and a couple of banks. If you are on your way to Kakamega Forest (most people are), this is the last place to pick up supplies.

To get to Kakamega follow the A1 either 30 miles north of Kisumu or 71 miles south of Kitale. The only reason to spend the night here would be if you are too late to walk or get a vehicle to Kakamega National Forest Reserve.

Kakamega National Forest Reserve

Once upon a time about 400 years ago, Kakamega was part of a rainforest stretching all the way to the Atlantic Ocean. Today, **Kakamega National Forest Reserve** is Kenya's only remaining patch (39 square miles) of virgin equatorial forest. This little strip of precious vegetation is surrounded by massive bands of agriculture.

To get to the park take the A-1, Kisumu-Kitale Road, and choose one of two access roads to the reserve. The first is about 12 miles north of Kakamega and the other is 6 miles south of the town. There is no admission charge to the national forest at the moment.

Animals not normally found anywhere else in the country hide inside the thick, dark growth. Colobus, blue- and red-tailed monkeys, bush tailed porcupines, flying squirrels and blue turacos can be seen with patience and a good pair of binoculars. It is certainly worth taking an early morning or night guided tour along the tropical nature trails to feast your eyes.

The Forest Department runs a large tree and shrub nursery in the 92 square mile reserve. The plants are used all over the country for ceremonial occasions and re-planting. There is also a charming but basic four-room rest house (**Kakamega Rest House**) available for $1.50 per person. You must bring your own sheets and food. Each room has a full bathroom. For more information write to: *Forest Ranger, PO Box 88, Kakamega.*

HAMMER-HEADED FRUIT BAT

*In Kakamega National Forest Reserve lives the enormous **hammer-headed fruit bat**, among other nocturnal creatures such as bush-babies and tree pangolins. Fascinatingly, the wingspan of one of these magnificent bats is over three feet from tip to tip! There is no need to be afraid however, as they feed exclusively on forest fruit and occasional insects.*

Cherangani Hills

Cherangani Hills, Marich Pass, Elgeyo Escarpment and Kerio Valley share some common links with Chapter 15, *Rift Valley*, and Chapter 16, *Northern Kenya*, as they are part of the extensive **Rift Valley System**. The geographical line defining north, west, and the Rift parts of Kenya are not exactly straight or conclusively divided. Because of this, some towns or attractions could actually be placed in any of several regions. This can get somewhat confusing if you are reading various books at the same time.

The **Cherangani Hills** are Kenya's only fold mountains. These hills boast dramatic landscapes and forest scenery. The range stretches for 37 miles with the best access from either Eldoret or Kitale. It is a great place to use up extra energy with vigorous hikes, gentle walks, or hard climbs. Choose to spend anywhere from a few hours to a week exploring the countryside with pre-arranged outfitters.

In **Marich Pass** is the **Marich Pass Field Studies Center** along the Wei Wei River**, where it is possible to find basic accommodations for those wishing to spend some time in a remote part of Kenya. Along certain stretches of the river bank are breeding grounds for the very poisonous mamba snake. If you plan on swimming, check with the locals first for a safe spot.

For the most part, groups of students studying botany, zoology, geography, conservation etc., stay at the center. The bandas cost $7 for two people and there are cheaper camp sites with facilities. Wildlife in the area is plentiful in the thick bush and surrounding forests. In particular, look for baboon, warthog, buffalo, antelope, elephant, monkey and hundreds of birds.

The Cherangani Hills rise up 6,000 feet to form part of the western wall of the **Elgeyo Escarpment**. The incredibly steep and beautiful hillsides should be attempted on foot or with a four-wheel drive vehicle only. They can be particularly dangerous after rain because of the very slippery road conditions. Situated above the **Kerio Valley** you will see some magnificent waterfalls and vistas.

DRIVING ALERT IN THE CHERANGANI HILLS

*To explore the **Cherangani Hills** region you must have a four wheel drive vehicle and a plentiful supply of gasoline. Low gear is a given when touring the rough secondary roads taking you to the most spectacular spots. This, combined with the thin air, quickly consumes generous quantities of precious gasoline.*

PRACTICAL INFORMATION

Banks

On Uganda Road in the middle of town are the **Standard Chartered Bank** and **Barclays Bank**. Their hours are 8:30 am to 1:00 pm Monday through Friday and 8:00 am to 11:00 am on Saturday.

Post Office

On the western edge of town on Uganda Road is the post office with its traditional friendly services. Post office hours are from 8:00 am to 5:00 pm Monday through Friday and 9:00 am to noon on Saturday.

Weather

Be prepared for a heavy downpour anywhere in this productive region. This happens every afternoon like clockwork. The crops are abundant and healthy because of the nutrient-rich rain they get every day. Take your rainwear with you whenever you leave your hotel to see the sights.

KITALE

In its heyday back in 1925, **Kitale** was connected to the life-giving railroad which kept the settlers and the town alive. Today this service has been discontinued and the town has taken a decided turn for the worse. It has become another agricultural service town where fruit, vegetables, and cereal are distributed.

It is still a great central location for tourists who wish to travel north, west, or east and see the surrounding sights. Throughout the township (population 30,000), you can see vestiges of glorious colonial days.

ARRIVALS & DEPARTURES

By Air

It is possible to fly into Kitale's local airstrip and begin your exploration of the western regions of Kenya from here.

By Bus

There is an Akamba Bus station on Moi Avenue across the street from the Town Hall and the Law Courts. The daily trips to Nairobi cost $4.80. The bus and matatu stand is west of town around the market area. Pandemonium and chaos seem to reign here but ask and someone will point you in the right direction.

By Car

The quickest way to get to Kitale from Nairobi is via the A104 road. This route will take you northwest through Naivasha, Nakuru, and Eldoret on a reasonably good road. From Eldoret it is only 43 miles to Kitale. The entire drive can be done in one day, but in my opinion it is better to fly in and rent a car once you arrive or arrange to be picked up by your hotel.

ORIENTATION

North of town is the standard railway line and station. The furthest point west are the two markets and south is the Star Lodge and the town hall. To the east is the Kitale museum and nature trail.

GETTING AROUND TOWN

As with most of the small villages and towns around Kenya, there is no problem getting from place to place if you don't mind a short walk.

WHERE TO STAY

LOKITELA FARMS, *PO Box 122, Kitale. Tel. 884 091 (Nairobi), Fax 325 20695 (Kitale) or 882 723 (Nairobi). $330 per night double occupancy. All major credit cards accepted.*

Welcome to a real working Kenyan farm with the accompanying sounds, smells, and animal menagerie. Warm hospitality starts with tail-wagging dogs and purring cats while the parrot says "hello." On the 865 acres, Tony and Adrianne Mills grow maize (corn), milk cows, and accommodate guests. The three guest bedrooms have ensuite bathrooms and comfortable furnishings.

Delicious fresh home-grown produce graces the family table at mealtimes. Farming trophies hang on the walls and the decor has seen better days, but you won't find more personable folk to stay with anywhere. When not out having a good time, you are invited to join the others around the warm fireplace or on the verandah. If you need a little peace and quiet, choose your own private guest lounge or the pretty garden with its flowering flame trees.

Safaris to Mount Elgon, Kakamega Forest, and any of the nearby sights are easily arranged as are horseback rides, game/bird viewing or cow-milking lessons.

KITALE CLUB, *PO Box 30, Kitale. Tel. 20036. $55 per night double occupancy. All major credit cards accepted.*

To use the facilities at the elegant club, a small membership fee is included in the price of your room. Take in a wonderfully relaxing sauna, refresh yourself in the pool, or try your hand at a round of golf. Accommodations consist of two groups of cottages; some new and some old. If at all possible, request the newer rooms as they come equipped with fireplaces. The newer bedrooms are also a little more comfortable than their older counterparts.

As one of the oldest full service clubs in the country, the locals are frequent guests. The club offers an excellent English-style restaurant and popular bar. If you stop by for a drink, it is likely you will end up in conversation with some of the more interesting residents of Kitale.

MOUNT ELGON LODGE, *Msafiri Inns, PO Box 42013, Nairobi. Tel. 330 820, Fax 227 815. $50 per night double occupancy. All major credit cards accepted.*

The most impressive part of a stay at the Mount Elgon Lodge is the lush gardens and the marvelous old building. With so much potential and once obvious colonial pride it is a shame the proprietors have let the place fall into disrepair.

The home once competed with nearby Mount Elgon for attention. Today the mountain wins hands down. Sadly the restaurant is not much better than the tatty decor and there is no swimming pool. What this place needs is a loving owner!

BARNLEY'S HOUSE/SIRIKWA SAFARIS, *PO Box 332, Kitale. No telephone or fax. $40 per night double occupancy.*

The old settler's house is home to Jane Barnley and her daughter Julia who will make you feel glad to be there with their entertaining conversation. A pack of six friendly dogs cavort and play on the green lawn. Surrounding the residence is a striking English flower garden filled with sweet smells and bright colors.

Inside the snug abode, the living room and warm fire invite you to choose a good book from the wide selection and stay a while. The two comfy bedrooms set aside for visitors come with their own fireplaces and twin beds. Home-cooked meals and good company are a specialty at Barnely House. Candles and lamps light your way during the dark nights as there is no electricity. Showers are an adventure among the hanging plants.

If you are on your way to Lake Turkana, this is a good place to stop for a night and catch up on your sleep before continuing on your journey.

To find the beautiful farmhouse look for the green concrete posts and the sign on the right side of the road just a few miles past the entrance to Saiwa Swamp National Park.

WHERE TO EAT

If you are in the area and can make arrangements ahead of time, stop at **BARNLEY'S HOUSE** for a delicious English meal. If you are off on a trip ask Jane to prepare one of her special and delicious boxed lunches for your journey.

In Kitale town, the best place to eat is **ALAKARA HOTEL** on Kenyatta Avenue or the **BONGO HOTEL** on Moi Avenue. The simple but tasty meals here will probably be standard British fare of chicken, fries or rice, and beef stew.

SEEING THE SIGHTS

Market

The little town of Kitale boasts two **markets** both on the west side of town. One of the markets is more permanent and covered while the other is open-air. Both markets are busy, colorful, and worth wandering around in for an hour or so.

Kitale Museum

The museum, also known as the **National Museum of Western Kenya**, was founded by Colonel C.T. Stoneham, a budding ornithologist and butterfly collector. When it was established in 1972, the collection included medals, odds and ends found by farmer Stoneham, and a great butterfly display. Unfortunately his compilation of butterflies has been removed.

Located on Kisumu Road, there is a charge of $1.10 to get in. The hours are 7:30 am to 6:00 pm Monday through Friday, 8:00 am to 6:00 pm on Saturday and 9:00 am to 6:00 pm on Sunday. You will find both indoor and outdoor exhibits.

The interior displays seem to focus mostly on fascinating artifacts from Turkana, Pokot, Luo, and Masai peoples and their lifestyle. Most interesting is the showcase of medicinal cures for syphilis, nose bleeds, and bone cancer. Outside are life-size traditional homesteads and another sorry-looking penned tortoise. Go through the indoor presentations first and get the small nature trail guide book from the craft store.

Behind the museum is a small stretch of unspoiled forest through which there is an excellent **nature trail**. With the nature trail guide book, you can stop at each of the carefully numbered signs explaining the points of interest. Follow the stream to a pretty picnic site.

Slave Stones

In the center of the parking lot at Kitale Club is a circle of stones, serving as a reminder of Kitale's somewhat dubious history. Originally the town was founded as a slaving station on the main caravan route between Uganda and Tanzania. To prevent their escape at night, slaves were chained to a ring at the center of the rock circle.

SPORTS & RECREATION

Game Viewing

Walk through **Saiwa Swamp** (see *Excursions* below) to see black and white colobus monkeys, lots of birds, and perhaps even a rare sitatunga antelope. This is a spectacular place and as yet undiscovered by tourists. Safaris to Mount Elgon, Kakamega Forest, and nearby sights where game and birds are plentiful are easily arranged at **Lokitela Farms** by expert guide/owner Tony Mills (see *Where to Stay*, above). You can choose from one day to one week or more with horses or open vehicle for transport.

Birding

Inquire at **Barnley House/Sirikwa Safaris** for a guide to the nearby swamp where bird watching can be spectacular. **Lokitela Farms** in Kitale offers outstanding personalized birding safaris with the possibility of seeing over 1,000 species.

Walking/Hiking

From **Lokitela Farms** or **Barnley House/Sirikwa Safaris** walks of a few hours or a few days up and around Mount Elgon or the scenic Cherangani Hills can be arranged with little trouble.

SHOPPING

At the **Kitale Museum**, you can buy the usual assortment of tourist paraphernalia and local crafts in the little gift shop. In town the shops are stocked with some local crafts. On the west side of town take a stroll through the **open food market** or the **covered market** for a look at what the local residents have to choose from.

EXCURSIONS & DAY TRIPS

Saiwa Swamp National Park

This small sanctuary is home to an even smaller population of **sitatunga**, an aquatic antelope – yes, aquatic! Both sexes have white spots or stripes on their gray-brown upper bodies and the males have long twisted horns. These deer have specially adapted hooves allowing them to swim under water and move about easily in the soupy vegetation. The unusual and much endangered antelope prefer to stay in the water with only their eyes showing until early afternoon or morning when it is time to feed. Serving as the antelope's larder there are swamp plants, woody vegetation, and grass pastures.

In the ecologically unusual park there are also colobus monkeys with stunning white capes, vervet and de Brazza apes, leopards, bushbucks, baboons, otters, lizards, civets, mongoose and a colorful array of birds. With a competent guide you will probably see eagle owls, cranes, hornbills, turacos and an assortment of waterbirds.

Saiwa National Swamp is fed by a constant year-round supply of life-sustaining water running off Mount Elgon. The only way to get around in the 500 acre bog is on foot. To make the trip a little easier, the park department constructed elevated blinds and wooden paths which can get very slippery when it rains each afternoon. It is necessary to note some of the towers are safe but a bit wobbly. As with all wildlife, you must sit quietly and with much patience to see anything. Be sure to bring good binoculars.

Located three miles off the main road and eleven miles north of Kitale, the park is open daily from 6:00 am to 6:00 pm. There is no admission fee at this time.

Mount Elgon National Park

Fine open walking and hiking up the extinct volcano are just a few of the pleasures at **Mount Elgon National Park**. Spectacular cliffs will take your breath away all the way up to the top at roughly 14,000 feet. Because of the lower altitudes compared to Mount Kenya, the weather at the top reaches of the park are less severe. In my opinion, this is a definite plus for those of us who like to climb but don't want to die doing it.

Hot springs in the heart of the crater are part of the excitement of a visit to the mountain, which straddles the border between Kenya and Uganda. Technically, travel through the park is by vehicle only. Everyone is hoping this will change with the trails and huts being set up by the Mount Elgon Conservation and Development Project.

Bats by the thousands and elephants come to the maze of caves in the park for completely different reasons. The bats live in the caverns, while the pachyderms dig for nutritious salts and minerals. Of all the caves, **Kitum** is the most popular and one of only three open to the public. The other two are **Mackingeny** and **Chepnyali**. Make sure you have a flashlight with good batteries if you plan on spending any time in the dark. Varied wildlife other than bats and elephants also call the park home. Those most frequently seen are Sykes and colobus monkeys, buffalo, forest hog, and bushbuck.

For anyone interested in flora the park is a veritable paradise. At the top are the unusual giant lobelia and groundsel plants among the alpine mooreland. In the mid-range you'll find fantastic bamboo, while at the base of the mountain is typical tropical rainforest. At all the elevations there are many kinds of colorful flowers blooming year round.

As the 68 square mile park is not very busy, it is best to let the ranger know you are there if you enter through one of two unmanned gates. The main entrance and the one usually open is Chorlim Gate, nineteen miles west of Kitale on the C45 road. You must pay the entry fee at the gate and sign in. There is primitive camping available within the park. Get permission from the ranger to walk around.

PRACTICAL INFORMATION
Banks
There are three banks in Kitale; **Kenya Commercial Bank** on Moi Avenue, **Barclays Bank** on Kenyatta Street, and **Standard Chartered Bank** also on Kenyatta Avenue. The hours are the same as the banks in Nairobi.

Post Office
Kitale has the standard **post office** which keeps typical hours. From here it is possible to make long-distance phone calls but these tend to take some time as you must go through the operator in Nairobi. Be prepared to wait.

18. SOUTHERN KENYA

Along Kenya's southern border with Tanzania are some of the most magnificent wildlife areas in the world. This territory south of Nairobi is where the majority of the country's tourists come to stay and revel in the breathtaking scenery and plentiful game.

Most of this zone is designated as reserve or park land and as such is off-limits to agriculture, livestock, and development. In an effort to preserve what is left of the flora and fauna unique to Africa, no more tourist hotels or camps are being built in southern Kenya.

In this part of the nation there are no towns to speak of. Instead, the land is divided into manageable wildlife reserves. Southwest of Nairobi is **Masai Mara National Reserve**, the most famous of all Kenya's parks. Almost directly south of the capital over flat dry plains is soda-filled **Lake Magadi** and the **Nguruman Escarpment**. Heading down towards the coast along the border are **Amboseli**, **Chyulu Hills**, and **Tsavo National Parks** in that order. Nestled between the western and eastern portions of Tsavo National Park is the exclusive and privately run **Taita Hills Wildlife Sanctuary**.

On the other side of the border with Tanzania lies the renowned Serengeti National Park, extending inside Kenya's Masai Mara. Also on the other side of the border is **Mount Kilimanjaro**, Africa's most distinguished mountain. Many of the lodges and hotels have outstanding views of the picturesque peaks when they decide to be gracious and show themselves. The lava rock and moonscape beauty of the Rift Valley ends between Amboseli and Masai Mara.

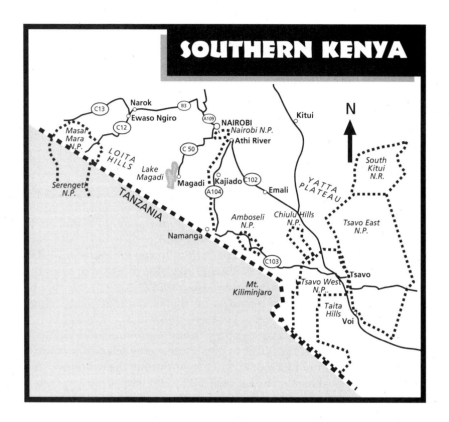

SOUTHERN KENYA

Narok
C13
Ewaso Ngiro
B3
A109
NAIROBI
Kitui
N
Masai Mara N.P.
C12
Nairobi N.P.
Athi River
C50
LOITA HILLS
South Kitui N.R.
Lake Magadi
Serengeti N.P.
TANZANIA
Magadi
Kajiado
C102
Emali
YATTA PLATEAU
A104
Amboseli N.P.
Chiulu Hills N.P.
Tsavo East N.P.
Namanga
C103
Tsavo
Mt. Kiliminjaro
Tsavo West N.P.
Taita Hills
Voi

MASAI MARA NATIONAL RESERVE

From the top of any of the high ridges or rocky outcroppings in Masai Mara you can look down on the 645 square miles of rolling plains, peppered with clumps of trees and patches of thick bush. In the language of the local people, *mara* means dappled or spotted and appropriately gives the area its name. Natural boundaries for the park include the **Mara River** and the **Oloololo** or **Siria** escarpment.

This national reserve is by far the most popular in Kenya with the best game viewing opportunities around. Hundreds of thousands of game animals roam the plains and form the perfect circle of life intended by nature.

Perhaps the favorite time to visit is between July and August when the famous wildebeest migration from the Serengeti to lush Masai Mara takes place. Millions of the comical looking beasts gather grunting, snorting, and pawing to make the annual journey. This magnificent show presented by mother nature will certainly make you feel honored to be a spectator

---

SOUTHERN KENYA MUST SEES

Visiting Kenya can be an overwhelming prospect if you don't have unlimited time. It is difficult to choose where to go and what to see. If you only have a short vacation, here are a few suggestions of places I consider must sees when touring southern Kenya.

Masai Mara Reserve
Tsavo West
Mzima Springs
Lake Chala

---

at this ancient and instinctive ritual. It is not uncommon for tourists to come away with misty eyes – from the dust no doubt!

Through the Mara, as it is referred to locally, run the **Mara** and **Talek rivers** adding to the lush vegetation and riverside forests that keep the wildlife alive. The game numbers are astonishingly high in this slice of Kenya due to human encroachment on the surrounding land, which forces them into the preserve.

Wildlife however, is not confined inside the boundaries of Masia Mara National Reserve but is free to wander unencumbered. The animals do not completely understand it is safer to stay within the confines of the park to avoid poachers or hungry villagers. The park service spends a great deal of time protecting the area and its four-footed inhabitants.

The Mara belongs to the **Masai** who graze their cattle on the sparse grasslands around their homes. Technically, no new human settlement is allowed in the park but the struggle between the natives and the animals continues as the pressure of reduced grazing land increases. The people complain the wildlife encroaches on them even outside the park; killing their crops and sometimes their families. This, along with the damage produced by tourist minivans, leaves eternal doubt as to the future of this garden of Eden.

RESERVE OR NATIONAL PARK?

*Many visitors ask about the difference between a national park and a game reserve. In a **national park**, a specified piece of land is designated solely for the animals with no changes allowed to the natural environment. In a **game reserve**, the local people are permitted to graze their livestock. In case of animal attacks they may kill the troublesome beast.*

ARRIVALS & DEPARTURES
By Air
Many tourists arrive at the Mara by plane where they land at any of several small strips in the area. The camps at further reaches from the capital are almost always accessed by small commuter plane. You must add the cost of transferring to your hotel or lodge to the price of the fare.

The one way fare from Wilson Airport in Nairobi to the Mara on Air Kenya Aviation is $83. The flights leave the capital at 10:00 am and 3:00 pm daily. From the Mara the departure times are 11:00 am and 4:00 pm.

By Bus
Ever-present minibuses coming in from Nairobi usually concentrate in the southeastern part of the reserve. The rainy season makes the tracks almost impassable – particularly where there is vehicle-trapping black cotton soil. There is no public transportation outside of the town of Narok. If you get yourself to the village, which is the closest township to the Mara, it is another 62 miles to the game park.

By Car
The drive from Nairobi usually takes about six hours. It is long, dusty, and bumpy but certainly cheaper than flying. Spectacular views along the road are worth it if the thought of being hot and grimy doesn't deter you. Perhaps driving in and flying out might be a good option. Follow the A104 Road north out of Nairobi towards Ewaso Ngiro. Branch off onto the B3 road. From here choose either the C13 towards the western gates of the Mara or the C12 to the Taleki Gate.

ORIENTATION
The most popular part of the park is on the eastern side around the **Talek Gate, Sekenani Gate**, and the **Olemutiak Gate**, which are most easily reached from Nairobi. If you are looking for the park headquarters you'll find them at the Sekenani Gate.

The western border of the park is the magnificent **Oloololo Escarpment** where the game is most prolific. Access is available through the **Oloololo** or **Musiara Gates**. Because of the difficult wet and swampy terrain (Olpunyatta and Musiara swamps) however, it is not too easy to move around the western portion of the park – particularly after rainfall. Along the Tanzania border on the C12 road is the less frequented **Sand River Gate**.

The **Talek** and **Mara Rivers** provide a large portion of the drinking water for the animals in the reserve. Along the banks of the rivers is a popular place for campsites. The game is plentiful and the vegetation a pleasing green.

GETTING AROUND

There is no public transportation provided to or within the Masai Mara, so do not plan on coming here without arranging for a four wheel drive vehicle first. It would be almost impossible to get around in anything other than off-road transport.

In the park, it is prohibited to drive off the main tracks so as to preserve the balance of nature. The dirt roads can be difficult to see at the best of times. I suggest you hire a knowledgeable guide for everyone's safety.

WHERE TO STAY

OL DONYO LARO, *PO Box 44924, Nairobi. $1,000 per night double occupancy. Includes game drives.*

Stretching from the Rift Valley floor through dry thick bush and changing terrain to high rainforests of the Nguruman Escarpment, the vast luxury camp caters to the rich and famous. Every whim and want is fulfilled in the particular Kenyan style of host Dougie Arnold.

Ol Donyo Laro (Mountains of the Buffalo) is a complete and unusual safari experience. In no particular order you will travel from a fly-in camp to three fixed luxury camps. Not only do the accommodations change but so does the weather, terrain, sights, sounds and vegetation. The experience offers a taste of all Kenya's interior has to offer. In the private wilderness sanctuary however, the game is hard to see in the bush.

For a minimum of four days and nights only one group of up to ten visitors at a time are accepted at the exclusive safari resort. This ensures complete satisfaction from the homegrown fruits and vegetables to mahogany flooring, eiderdown bed covers, spring-fed drinkable running water and extravagant service. It is possible to fly into the airfields near the camps, but the management encourages visitors to make the drive from Nairobi where you are collected from the airport.

The trip to the camp and between camps must be undertaken in a four wheel drive vehicle to ensure safe arrival. First you will venture through the scenic Ngong Hills – the home of Karen Blixen – on well traveled, excellent roads. Soon, you reach the picturesque soda Lake Magadi and then the distant peaks of the Nguruman Escarpment. Eventually the paved road ends and the bush adventure begins. Crossing waterways, breathing dust, swatting tiny flies, hot humid air and long rough paths are free of charge – and part of what Africa is all about!

If you stop first at **Kisidai** campsite, don your tropical jungle attire. Butterflies dance in the tall fig trees. Giant tamarinds shade the streamside mess tent and cool swimming hole. Inside the large green canvas guests tents, polished wood and yards of screening make you feel you're

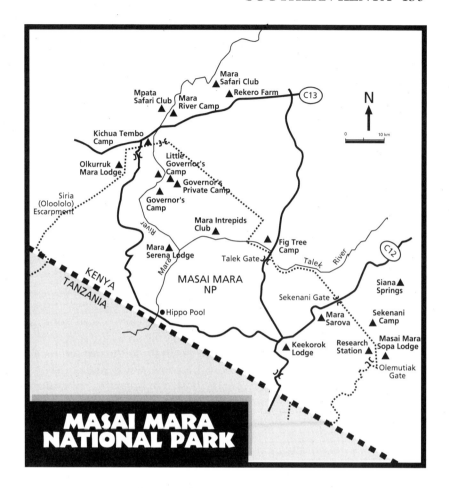

living among the leafy standing timber. Modern ensuite bathrooms cover all the amenities, from toothbrushes to mirrors, essential to the opulent permanent camp.

Usually saved for last, the camp known as **Laro** is more spectacular than the others; if that's possible. Travelers palms welcome you to Eden. Colorful bougainvillea and other garden delights enhance the elegant setting. Tall hills act as the tent backdrop, steep valleys guard the sides. As a setting for the magnificent swimming pool, the Rift Valley spreads to the horizon. Before bed, hot toddys under the moon and tall tales around a crackling fire set the mood for ambrosial dreams.

African mahogany steps lead you to the verandah of your canvas guest "bedroom" set on stilts. Sweet smelling flowers, delicate rugs, shiny wood, gleaming brass, candles, mirrors and elegant handmade furniture entice you to stay indefinitely.

After the fly camp, which could be set in the rainforest or the arid bush of Ol Donyo Laro, the only camp left to mention is **Ol Duvai**. A floodlit tennis court is available for those who want to play a little night game. Afterward, take a dip in the chilly spring water of the stone swimming pool. Look out across the Rift Valley at the never-ending inky sky. From this high perch you'll see more stars than you ever thought possible.

The comfortable canvas tents blend with local stone walls. High peaked canvas ceilings bring class to camping. Fully equipped, roomy bathrooms come with oversized showerheads and lots of mirrors. The screened windows offer views across the border to neighboring Tanzania.

MPATA SAFARI CLUB, *PO Box 58892, Nairobi. Tel. 217 015, Fax 217 016. $680 per night double occupancy. Includes game drives.*

Located 40 minutes outside the Mara, this classy and pricey resort caters to those who want pampered luxury. Private outdoor Jacuzzis and kitchenettes in the suites, Kenyan chefs trained in Tokyo, fresh flowers everywhere and thick terrycloth bathrobes are just the beginning.

Owned by the Japanese, the club offers an interesting perspective on the African experience. From individual strategically placed concrete buildings high atop the Oloololo escarpment, the views are spectacular. The Mara plains and the Mara River spread as far as the eye can see far below. Hike to the bottom and back with a professional guide or choose to end your day with sundowners in the bush. For breakfast, try a sunrise picnic before setting off in the long search for game. At midday, a swim in the lovely pool will help you keep off the extra pounds encouraged by the gourmet meals.

To get to any of the 22 rooms in the complex, there are wandering walkways made from locally quarried stone. Along the paths, colorful native plants and trees help blend the structures with the bush. Inside, curved walls separate the various portions of guest quarters. Wide-angle vistas of the flaxen grasslands are the focus of the rooms. This picture is what greets you from your comfortable bed.

Not only is the outside remarkable, but the festive designs continue throughout the central clubhouse. Unusual and artistic decor on any of the various levels blends well with natural wood and stone.

Bright paintings and exotic looking chairs are everywhere. An open atrium filled with plants, an extensive library, a cozy fireplace and curved bar simply invite visitors to stay forever.

GOVERNOR'S PRIVATE CAMP, *Governor's Camps-Musiara, Ltd., PO Box 48217, Nairobi. Tel. 331 871, Fax 726 427. $650 x 2, as four must book for a minimum of three nights. Includes game drives and bar services.*

The site at Governor's Private Camp can accommodate from a minimum of four to a maximum of sixteen people at a time. The groups booked sometimes use the tent facilities for business meetings and/or parties. If you are particular about your meals, it is possible to plan a menu with the executive chef. The food at all the Governor's Camps however, has a long-standing reputation for excellence. Should you decide to leave it in their capable hands, you will have the culinary delights of professional safari planners.

There are no fences to keep you in or animals out, but an armed *askari* patrols day and night. Daily game drives or entertainment is planned according to your likes, dislikes, and time preferences. The guides are skilled and more than happy to share their vast knowledge about Kenya and the game. Land Rovers with open roofs are the vehicle of choice for travel through the bush; they allow the maximum viewing pleasure.

There is no electricity, but candles, flashlights, and lanterns are provided for each guest. The overall effect is one of a true romantic safari. Simple tent furnishings, flush toilets, showers and a covered but open verandah will make your stay under the cool leafy-green of the Mara forest a memorable one.

REKERO, *Wilderness Trails (K) Limited/Bush Homes Africa Safaris, Tel. US 404 888 0909, e mail bushhomes@africaonline.co.ke, www.bushhomes.com, PO Box 56923, Nairobi. Tel. 506 139, Fax 502 739 REKERO. $440 per night double occupancy. Includes game drives and walks.*

Three twin bed, private cottages accommodate guests at Rekero – my preference is the single cabin with the double bed as opposed to the duplex with single beds. Built from all natural materials, the bandas are basic and adequate with private bathrooms, hot water (Tanganyika boilers) and electricity. The exterior walls are attractive red mud while the inside is white plaster. Both are decorated with artistic animal renderings placed to surprise and please you. (In addition and upon request, a traditional, mobilized, tented camp is an option with accommodations available for 4 to 12 guests.)

The bedrooms and a newly built dining area face the watering hole where elephant, buffalo, and lion often come to drink. It is marvelous to sit on your verandah in the warm sunshine waiting for wildlife to wander by. At night, a guard escorts you from your room along the stone pathway to the main house.

The Beaton family opens their home to guests and willingly shares many adventures of their lives in Kenya. Delicious homemade dinners, outdoor breakfasts and lunches, tea and cocktails are served whenever you are ready. Drinks around the fire with the clan and the friendly household pooches offer the perfect opportunity for storytelling.

Their working farm is located just outside The Mara National Reserve within a conservation area. The number of other tourists you'll share the safari with are few because of the exclusive nature of the homestay. Game drives, guided walks, sundowners on the plains, bush picnics, manyatta visits and hot water bottles offer a taste of real Kenya.

BUSHTOPS, *Glen Cottar Safaris, PO Box 44191, Nairobi. Tel. 882 408. $400 per night double occupancy. Includes game drives and walks.*

Flying into the nearby airstrip in 30 minutes certainly beats a six hour drive from Nairobi to Bushtops outside the Mara. The simple house (up to four people can stay comfortably) is completely private. A full staff does laundry, cleans, and cooks simple but delicious English-style meals.

Inside the basic home, functional furnishings offer comfort and relaxation. The papyrus ceiling is home to adorable geckos found in any self-respecting house in the country. Solar power heats water and provides electricity for the two guest bedrooms. Full service bathrooms include flush toilets.

The best feature of staying here is the view from the hillside where the green iron roofed building sits. Game is drawn to the natural salt lick and seems unafraid as they enjoy their basic dietary treat. Impala, zebra, elephant, gazelle and other wildlife frequently roam the area. For your safety, an *askari* stands guard when the daylight disappears.

Game walks with a Masai guide or a ride through the bush are entertainment options at hand. The pace is slow, you are in charge, and the animals are plentiful. Glen and Pat Cottar, the hosts, encourage their guests to feel free to do as they wish.

MARA CAMP, *Cheli & Peacock, PO Box 39806, Nairobi, Tel. (254 2)748 327 or (254 2) 748 633, Fax (254 2) 750 225, e mail chelipeacock@attmail.com, www.chelipeacock.com. $375 per night double occupancy. Includes game drives.*

The semi-permanent luxury camp is located on Koyiaki Group Ranch adjoining the Masai Mara National Reserve just west of Nairobi. IT can be reached by the Ngorende airstrip a short drive away. Cheli & Peacock have artfully recreated the safari camp of "Out of Africa". Your every comfort is assured, your every need catered to.

The great thing about this camp is that at the end of the tourist season, when the tented camp is broken down, there is hardly a sign that it was ever there in the first place. The surroundings and the serenity found here remain undisturbed.

Six spacious double tents with ensuite toilets and canvas showers face out into the wilds of Eden in Kenya. There is hardly anything more pleasant of fulfilling than sitting on your private verandah while anticipating the next surprise.

Anything from bush breakfasts, sundowners, and roaming herds of wildlife will be there when you're ready. Every whim and fancy is taken care of by the thoughtful yet unobtrusive staff.

GOVERNOR'S CAMP, *Governor's Camps-Musiara, Ltd., PO Box 48217, Nairobi. Tel. 331 871, Fax 726 427. $375 per night double occupancy. Includes game drives.*

Each one of the 38 canvas tents sits alone somewhere along the banks of the twisting Mara River. A cement foundation ensures comfort as does the private bathroom with its hot shower, bidet, and flush toilet. When making your reservation ask for a tent with a good view of the river, perhaps number 23, 22, or 19. Avoid those near the parking area.

This camp opened in 1972 on the site of Teddy Roosevelt's Mara Camp and was the first of its kind in Masai Mara National Reserve. It is perhaps the most popular and well known camp in the Mara with American visitors. Sometimes when all the tents are full, the camps may seem a little crowded.

Statuesque shade trees filled with twittering birds or monkeys and any number of wildlife visitors wander freely through and around the unfenced camp. There is no need to panic when you wake up one morning to find hippo munching on the lawn right outside your tent!

Flying into the airfield and driving over to the reception area built from local stone is about as pleasant a travel experience you can have in Kenya. Once inside the building you can enjoy photographs and bronze sculptures in the small museum.

Dinner in the large dining tent, which seats 100 guests, might look intimidating. The flickering candlelight, a la carte menu and excellent service makes you relax as you feel the intimacy and privacy of the shadows. When the weather permits, lunch and breakfast buffets are served in a clearing along the riverside. Open on three sides, the lounge calls you to sidle up to the log-built bar.

LITTLE GOVERNOR'S CAMP, *Governor's Camps-Musiara, Ltd., PO Box 48217, Nairobi. Tel. 331 871, Fax 726 427. $325 per night double occupancy. Includes game drives.*

Due to the popularity of the Governor's tented camps, it is necessary to book well in advance. As the smallest of the tented Governor's camps, there is less noise, fewer crowds, and more personalized service.

There is no electricity, but you'll enjoy the romance of candles, lanterns, and flashlights provided for you. But this will be the extent of the hardships you will have to endure during your stay! Each canvas tent has a covered outdoor verandah with two well-placed safari chairs and a small wooden table. Inside, the simple furnishings include twin beds, a clothes rack, a dresser and more safari chairs. Adjoining each tent is an exclusive tented bathroom. You will be amazed by the running water, hot showers, flush toilets, and here at Little Governor's, even a bidet!

The camp features excellent food. Breakfast and lunch offer great selections of buffet-style fare set under tall acacia trees. The outdoor settings with views of the marsh, the hills beyond, and wandering wildlife make meals here delightful. It is astounding how such delicacies can be produced in this rough setting miles from anywhere. Even more amazing is the seemingly endless supply of ice and really cold drinks. Evening meals in the intimate dining tent culminate with outstanding desserts. The flickering candlelight, elegant crystal, and carefully pressed linens somehow go hand in hand with the outdoor setting. For most guests, an after dinner drink around the campfire is the perfect prelude to a good night's sleep.

A balloon ride with champagne breakfast on the plains is worth the effort of getting up before dawn. If you don't feel floating over the bush as the sun rises is worth $350, at least go and watch the take-off. It is definitely worth a picture to see the multi-colored canvas slowly fill with hot air and lift gently in to the sky. Other worthwhile activities include exciting game drives in open-topped vehicles, pre-arranged fishing on Lake Victoria, superior souvenir shopping, an interesting museum, nature hiking or simply absorbing the tranquillity of the Mara River.

It is not uncommon for hippos to stroll by in the early morning for a taste of the sweet grass growing outside your tent or for the elephant to make an unannounced raid on the camp's larder. Any number of giraffes, birds, monkeys, waterbuck and gazelles can parade past your tent flap at any time. Rest assured – the armed guards patrolling the grounds give a comforting sense of security.

Selected as one of my *Best Places To Stay* – see Chapter 11 for more details.

GOVERNOR'S PARADISE CAMP, *Governor's Camps-Musiara, Ltd., PO Box 48217, Nairobi. Tel. 331 871, Fax 726 427. $325 per night double occupancy. Includes game drives.*

At Governor's Paradise camp, the 20 tents are set up each year after the rains are gone. The new site is located near the other Governor's camps and the traditionally delicious cuisine is quietly brought in.

There is no electricity and the canvas tents are pitched on the ground as opposed to cement platforms. Staying here is closer to the way things were when camping safaris were in their infancy except, perhaps, for the bathrooms and flush toilets. Bathing and washing water is carried in with buckets. Upon request, hot water can be provided for your gravity shower.

Twisting and turning, the Mara River is never far away but may be invisible through the uncleared bush surrounding your natural campsite. As with the other Governor's locations there are no fences to keep game out. If you sit quietly for long enough you are bound to see peeping eyes just as curious about you as you are about them.

MARA SAFARI CLUB, *Lonrho Hotels Kenya Limited, PO Box 58581, Nairobi. Tel. 216 940, Fax 216 796. $308 per night double occupancy. Includes game drives.*

Located outside the national reserve, the hotel is able to offer guided walks, sundowners on the plains, and evening game drives in one of their 16 Land Cruisers. Masai dancing and talks by the resident naturalist fill your evenings. A warm fire keeps the chill at bay in the lounge. Apart from the lounge, the huge lodge includes a bar, dining room, gift shop, and reception area. Masking the looming size and tendency towards darkness are split-level floors, artistic symmetry, open spaces, and surrounding decks.

Looking down from seating areas on the open porch you notice the Mara River molding to the shape of the main lodge. In the water below, hippos wallow and wiggle their tiny ears. They seem to want to show off for onlookers by opening their enormous pink mouths and uttering odd grunts and snorts. Hippo families are everywhere!

A short stroll from the lodge down stone walkways takes you to the guest accommodations. Forty tents pitched on wooden decks overlook the river and of course, more enormous hippos. An electric fence and steep banks keep the hippos from grazing around the bush surrounding each campsite – nothing to worry about.

Bright colors in the rugs and bed canopies make staying here fun. The completely functional bathrooms even offer thick complimentary bath-robes to use during your visit. Electricity stays on all night. I must say it is nice to get up for a bathroom break and not have to fumble for a flashlight.

After landing on the all-weather runway, wash off the rigors of travel in the heated pool. Lunch on the stone deck, shaded lounge chairs, and a cold drink from the poolside bar are a recipe for the perfect first day.

SEKENANI CAMP, *Chartered Expeditions Kenya Limited and Utali Tours and Safaris Limited, PO Box 61542, Nairobi. Tel. 333 285, Fax 228 875. $300 per night double occupancy. Includes game drives.*

To get to the camp it is necessary to arrange for a transfer from the nearby airstrip. The campsite itself is roughly four miles from the Mara entry gate. As Sekenani is outside the national park, you can get out of your vehicle and walk around in the untamed Kenyan bush.

The climb to the campsite takes you through thick underbrush and a leaf-canopied riverbed. Eventually you arrive at the site at the top of a grassy rise. The setting is breathtaking with distant views and privacy.

A mere 15 extra large tents pitched on elevated platforms make up the camp. The management and staff spare no extravagance or indulgence for the guests. You won't even notice the lack of electricity as you soak in your private bathtub filled with steamy water from a gas heater.

It is difficult to miss the deep oversized tub complete with brass fittings, in the middle of the ensuite bathroom. Enhancing the feeling of luxury are shiny wooden floors and white rugs.

Deluxe tent decor includes hand-carved and painted lockable chests, white bed covers, bright hurricane lamps, and large windows. From your private deck or through one of the many oversized screened openings you might see distant hills, rich swampland or game covered plains. One thing's for sure – there are no bad views from here.

A short distance away across a bridged chasm is the log and canvas dining area. Open ends and a peaked roof make the structure feel light and airy. On the stone terrace there is a nightly campfire under the star-filled sky. The food and personal service at Sekanani are remarkable, particularly considering the remote location.

MARA INTREPIDS CLUB, *Prestige Hotels Ltd., PO Box 74888, Nairobi. Tel. 338 084, Fax 217 278. $256 per night double occupancy. Includes game drives.*

When you touch down at the airfield look for a tall lookout tower nearby. With a drink in one hand and binoculars in the other, this is the perfect place to watch the sun go down as wildlife gets ready to change shifts.

Perhaps the most awesome aspect of the Mara camp is the wooden suspension foot-bridge over the river and the simple metal strips of the vehicle bridge. You will never forget the adventure of a shaky crossing to the camp.

With a Mara river tributary to the west and Talek River to the south, it almost feels like the groups of three or four tents are on an island. Each of the 27 canvas shelters are equipped with rustic but far from rudimentary furnishings. Barrel tables, lanterns, colorful rugs, canopy beds and long vertical mirrors only add to the mystery and romance of the occasion. Completely functional in-room bathrooms and private verandahs add finishing touches to the charming safari camp.

Traditional sit-down dinners served in an open tent are a change of pace from buffet style breakfasts and lunches. After early morning tea on your personal verandah, the first two meals of the day are usually under the shade trees or on the deck by the river. Mealtimes are never boring with twittering birds and naughty monkeys wanting a share of the feast.

After a day of game drives in an open Land Rover, relax in comfortable leather chairs around the bar. To stretch your legs, wander down the stone path to the riverside deck. Fresh bait on the opposite river bank is floodlit to bring in an elusive leopard.

KICHWA TEMBO CAMP, *Windsor Hotels International, PO Box 74957, Nairobi. Tel. 219 784, Fax 217 498. $242 per night double occupancy. Includes game drives.*

The name of this camp, *Kichwa Tembo,* means "elephant head" in Swahili. Throughout the large facility you will notice the elephant theme. The permanent-looking site is popular with American visitors who enjoy the choice of 45 tents or six cabins. If all the accommodations are filled, it can be noisy and a little too public.

The easiest way to reach the grounds is via the nearby airstrip. A five minute drive down a tree shaded dirt track introduces you to clamorous birds and monkeys – a taste of game viewing to come. Daily, one or all of 25 Land Cruisers head to the Mara from the bordering camp.

Surrounding the oddly shaped pool are interesting oversized boulders and well-tended grounds. Cacti, palms, and drought-resistant plants fill the healthy-looking flower beds. Green manicured lawns run right up to the encircling fence. Beyond the boundary are equatorial forests or stretching plains where zebra, ostrich, and lion roam.

Inside each large "bedroom", the bedspreads and rugs continue the elephant motif. Full bathrooms with hewn stone floors are standard. Early morning tea delivered to your door on the private verandah is yet another enduring service. Public areas such as the lobby and dining room are serene and cool. Thatched peaks, heavy beams, and polished stone floors add interest to the round buildings. High standards are evident at the first-class tented camp – a great place for the family.

SIANA SPRINGS, *Windsor Hotels International, PO Box 74957, Nairobi. Tel. 219 784, Fax 217 498. $242 per night double occupancy. Includes game drives.*

Throughout the camp the management has tried to preserve the true nature of the Kenya bush. There are no thick lawns or planted flower beds. Acacia trees and thorny thickets grow where they will. Natural springs bubble up across the property giving the camp its name. The only "unnatural" addition is the small swimming pool.

Game drawn by the promise of water around Siana Springs is often plentiful. This can be a plus for visitors wanting to cut down on drive time to and from the Mara. The Sekenani Gate into the national park is some distance away. It can be annoyingly busy and slow at peak hours.

Because Siana is outside the park, dinner on the plains, sundowners, night game drives, and nature walks are all available for your selection. The on-staff naturalist is knowledgeable and friendly. On foot he will take you near game and point out useful native plants.

Siana Springs is built on the same spot where the renowned Cottar's Camp once stood. (The original wood and stone dining area is still used.) Due to its proximity to Nairobi, the campsite is most popular with guests who choose to drive. A surrounding electric fence gives visitors peace of mind from foraging wild animals. The nightly campfire might keep other nocturnal visitors away.

Forty one en suite tents divided into three groups are spaced around the property. Some can be quite a hike from the public areas – if this bothers you, check before you are assigned a site. A steward in each group takes care of any miscellaneous needs such as shoe cleaning, extra towels, and cold drinks. Each tent has its own verandah.

Inside the spacious canvas tents, electric fans keep things cool. Chunky but comfortable furniture is home-made and obviously built for durability from tough Blue Gum trees. Oversized bathrooms are equipped with "showers built for two" and private toilets. The overall effect is genuine camping in comfort.

PARADISE MARA CAMP, *Paradise Safaris Limited, PO Box 41789, Nairobi. Tel. 229 262, Fax 228 902. $240 per night double occupancy. Includes game drives.*

Popular with tour groups, the entire camp is based around a picturesque bend in the Mara River known as Hippo Point. Obviously, hippo tend to be the focal point of a visit to this particular part of the Mara but other game is plentiful. All the buildings face the river and the rambunctious hippo living there.

Stone and thatch are the main building materials of the dining patio, lobby, and Lookout Bar. The lobby opens onto the cloudy, swirling water filled with beady eyes. The bar and eating area are attractively placed over the river for the best possible ringside seats. Watching the hippo snort and play-fight is better than anything on TV!

Bait is set out across the river each night to attract leopard and a fire competes with the stars after dark. Other animals come to the river to drink, so it is not unlikely that elephant or lion will wake you from your sleep in the wee hours.

A line of double-story guest *bandas* built along the shore come with their own verandah facing the water. The thatched rooms have connecting full-service bathrooms with showers. The accommodations are clean and adequate.

Vegetarian Indian cuisine is the specialty of the chef at Paradise Mara Camp. Other delicious meals are prepared to your specifications with something for everyone.

SIRATA SURUWA, *Bush Homes Africa Safaris, Tel. US 404 888 0909, e mail safari@bushhomes.com, www.bushhomes.com, PO Box 56923, Nairobi. Tel. 571 647, Fax 571 665. $230 per night double occupancy. Includes game drives.*

From Nairobi it is a pleasant hour and a half drive to the Melepo Hills camp near Kajiado. Located half way between Nairobi and the Tanzanian border, Sirata sits on the slopes of the Melepo Hills. These hills divide the Amboseli basin at the foot of Mount Kilimanjaro, from the Great Rift Valley. The A-104 road built for the vice president, who takes this route frequently, is excellent all the way. During the ride you will spot giraffe, zebra, and ostrich feeding or moving within easy viewing distance.

Sirata Suruwa means "glade of elands" in Masai and is the home of Mike and Judy Rainy, their daughter Jessica, her husband Jeff and an assorted pack of loving, tail wagging dogs. The family is often involved in the education of American university student groups. The kids benefit from 25 years of experience while staying in the camp and learn about animal behavior, East African culture, and conservation efforts. This unique community conservation effort on over 7,000 acres has seen poaching almost come to standstill and wildlife numbers increase four fold.

You too can partake of their extensive knowledge of Kenya and share in their love of the land and game if you choose to stay at the relaxing tented camp. You won't find a colder drink anywhere in the country or feel more welcomed by the outstanding hosts. Mealtime at Sirata in the open-sided thatched community building is something special if you want to try local cuisine, fresh fruit, and healthy living. Sitting around a small portable charcoal fire with an after dinner drink and excellent company is a memory you won't soon forget.

As there is no electricity, lanterns emitting soft romantic light line the pathways to three spacious, green canvas tents. Inside there is a vestibule with two safari chairs, a small night stand, an attractive table and a low cushioned seat. The floors are impeccably clean and covered with woven mats. In the sleeping portion of the tent are two sturdy comfortable twin beds and a night stand. Fresh pink, white, and fuscia wildflowers add color and charm.

A short walk away is the open-roofed, safari shower — a thin reed wall encircles two trees. Inside, a table holds the soap and a basin for face washing. A bucket on a rope serves as a gravity safari shower. To fill the bucket with hand-carried warm water the rope is lowered. A tap at the bottom of the bucket opens the showerhead; there's plenty of water even for hair washing. (Bathing al fresco – ahh!). A little further along the path is the long-drop toilet with a view of distant mountain peaks and the game-filled valley below.

Activities are as strenuous or laid-back as you choose. Enjoy a morning game count for gerenuk, ostrich, giraffe, eland or buffalo. Walk to the top of a high ridge where eagles soar. See if you can identify towering Mount Kilimanjaro, visit a nearby *manyatta* (village), or simply drink in the magnificent tranquillity.

MARA SERENA LODGE, *Serena Lodges & Hotels, PO Box 48690, Nairobi. Tel. 710 511, Fax 718 103. $208 per night double occupancy.*

There are several upsides to staying at the Mara Serena Lodge. The most striking is breathtaking vistas across the golden savanna of the surrounding Masai Mara and the two well-used watering holes. Zebra, buffalo, elephant, gazelle and other plains game are wonderful to watch with binoculars.

Rows of 76 small rooms extend from the main lodge. Surrounding pathways and sweet smelling colorful flower beds welcome you. Inside however, the bedrooms are undersized with no patio. If the tiny windows were bigger, the open views would be remarkable. In trying to make up for its shortcomings, each room is done in earthy and bright orange-yellow colors. A full private bathroom finishes off the accommodations.

The outdoor swimming pool is strategically placed to allow the full impact of Kenya stretching to the horizon. On a hot day after a sunrise game run, it is very relaxing to sit by the pool with a cold drink and snooze in the sun. Other than swimming, the lodge offers a fun filled breakfast alongside the hippo pool, balloon rides, Masai dancing, and nature movies.

Designed to conjure up images of a local village, the central building is full of authentic native artifacts, lighted hanging pots, spears, hand-woven fabrics and tropical plants. The staff is friendly and willing and the food simple but tasty.

OLKURRUK MARA LODGE, *African Tours & Hotels, PO Box 30471, Nairobi. Tel. 336 858, Fax 218 109. $180 per night double occupancy.*

Throughout the lodge, a pied crow (a distinctive black and white patern) theme winds its way from leather wall hangings to rugs and bedspreads. If you ask, you'll find out *olkurruk* in the Masai language means "pied crow" – hence the delightful crow motif in the 19 bandas.

Designed to look like an African village, the guest accommodations and public areas are constructed from natural materials. Painted floors strewn with handmade rugs, walls made from reeds, and unfinished timbers add fitting touches. A round room with inviting central fire serves as a public gathering place. Depending on the sometimes cool weather, you may choose to eat in either the inside or outside dining room.

Surrounding most of the rooms, thick bush keeps out the chilly fingers of the wind as it tries to blow through. While its purpose is noble, the thickets prevent the sunlight from reaching the darker corners of your bedroom. This vegetation combined with nippy winter mists make the magnificent views from the craggy hillside hard to see.

The lodge is perched at the edge of the steep rocky cliffs of the Oloololo escarpment. Because of its location, distant views of the Mara are spectacular from the Out of Africa bar. In the movie of the same name, the Denys Finch-Hatton funeral scene filmed here is the hotel's claim to fame.

An electric fence keeps unwanted visitors out of the sheltered lodge. For your comfort, electricity is on all day and solar panels provide free flowing hot showers. The nearby airfield makes visiting Olkurruk a fairly simple affair, but getting inside the Mara can be time consuming. All day or at least half day trips into the reserve in one of the six Land Cruisers available are the norm.

MASAI MARA SOPA LODGE, *Kenya Holiday Management Services Limited, PO Box 72730, Nairobi. Tel. 337 410, Fax 331 876. $180 per night double occupancy.*

The most amazing feature of the lodge is the tremendous thatched roof covering an equally large circular lobby and dining area. (It is amazing to think of the labor involved in the thatching process.) To reach either of these places you must first face steep, dark stairs downward into the heart of the foyer. Follow along the rust colored floor and curved walls to arrive at a delightful open patio.

The water hole below the high ridge where the hotel sits and the picturesque outlook are the two best parts of a visit to this particular corner of the Mara Reserve. Warthog, lion, buffalo, Thompson's gazelle, eland and wildebeest frequent the small, life-giving pool during their favorite early morning hours.

Facing this magnificent view, 60 thatched *bandas* follow the edge of the rocky ridge. Native plants grow amid rocks along the walkway connecting the rooms. Sadly, the interiors need a facelift and some scrubbing. The adjoining bathrooms were not much better.

The Sopa Lodge is very popular with the budget safari outfitters and tends to stay busy. The staff canteen is a good place to buy warm beer, cheap meals, and plenty of friendly company.

SAROVA MARA CAMP, *Sarova Hotels, Limited, PO Box 30680, Nairobi. Tel. 333 248, Fax 211 472. $176 per night double occupancy.*

Manicured lawns, lush flower beds, pools filled with lilies and pathways made of wood meander their way around the large campsite. If it weren't for the stretching plains of Masai Mara in the background, you might feel you were camping in your backyard.

Seventy-five large, basic canvas tents cover the grounds. Each abode has its own complete bathroom built on an adjoining pad. From your "door" you may see grassy savannas or tended shrubbery. Either way, you'll meet your neighbors and their kids as you trek to and from the main buildings or the popular pool.

A tall splendid thatched roof dominates the large lobby. Interesting African artifacts decorate the light, open, reception area. Indoor dining is pleasant when the weather turns ugly, but for most of the fine days try the outdoor patio. Sarova Mara Camp offers safe camping in Africa without any of the hardships.

FIG TREE CAMP, *Mada Holdings, PO Box 40683, Nairobi. Tel. 221 439, Fax 332 170. $150 per night double occupancy.*

Fig Tree Camp is located outside the Mara at the Talek Gate. The large site sits halfway along the eastern boundary of the national reserve right on the Talek River. In fact, to reach the camp there is a charming wooden covered footbridge to cross.

Each of the 30 cabins and tents offer the most essential facilities. However, there is around-the-clock electricity as a bonus. With apparently no sense of planning or consideration of the lovely river views, accommodations are mish-mashed together. Without fencing, the close grouping makes visitors feel safe from wild predators.

Along the river the game is plentiful, particularly the noisy monkeys and bright birds. It is absolutely marvelous to eat breakfast outdoors while watching starlings and doves vie for position. If you hear noises outside your tent at night, it could be anything from a hyena to a lion. Any of the offered activities such as game drives, picnics under the stars, or bush hiking cost extra. The swimming pool, of course, is free. The staff is welcoming and the overall feeling is one of a carefree and spontaneous adventure.

MARA RIVER CAMP, *PO Box 48019, Nairobi. Tel. 335 935, Fax 216 528. $140 per night double occupancy.*

For the price, Mara River Camp isn't a bad place to stay. The staff is friendly and willing to serve you in any way they can. It is, however, 20 minutes from the Musiara Gate to the Mara and has no pool. There is electricity.

Each of the 27 tents are pitched near or along the banks of the Mara River. Some have river views while others simply benefit from tall shade trees and green lawns. The location of the camp is perhaps its most favorable feature. The river is enchanting and captures Africa right down to the ornery hippos.

There are no fences to keep game out of the campsite – so don't wander off alone. You can take advantage of the on-staff ornithologist who will gladly take you bush-walking. Enjoy a game drive in or outside the national reserve.

A charming and partially covered dining area encourages gatherings of birds and monkeys. For relaxation, stretch out in a safari chair and take in the view across the river or up the nearby, steep crag. In the evening you might look forward to music and entertainment by the staff band.

KEEKOROK LODGE, *Block Hotels, PO Box 47557, Nairobi. Tel. 335 807, Fax 340 541. $124 per night double occupancy.*

With over 84 en suite bedrooms, there is something for everyone here at Keekorok, which has seen the likes of Henry Kissinger in its VIP house. To overcome the crowded feeling at the busy whitewashed lodge, solid wings stretch in unusual configurations and the black roofline reaches towards the sky. All accommodations come with ensuite bathrooms and attractive furnishings. There are no fences to obstruct the animals or the view. From most rooms (either from the bed or the patio) the panoramas of surrounding Masai Mara plains are postcard-perfect.

The lodge, built in 1965, is set at the top of a small hill inside the reserve. Pololet River winds its way through rich riverine growth and lofty trees within sight of the hotel. The name *keekorok* means the "place of black trees" in the local language and gives the lodge its name. Along the river there is an abundant show of game. Hippo, monkey, buffalo, and elephant think nothing of grazing on the hotel grounds.

Getting to the lodge from Nairobi is simple enough. Arrive either by small plane to the nearby airstrip or in any of the many minivans heading this way. The lodge is located at a well-traveled roadway intersection. Popular with tour groups or individuals with their own transportation, the hotel only has one van available for sightseeing.

At the bustling main building however, there is always something going on for entertainment. Nature slide shows, video room games, environmental lectures, Masai dancing, balloon rides, an extensive souvenir gift shop and attractive swimming pool are just a few of your choices.

Colorful flowers and green manicured lawns surround the swimming pool for privacy. Stretching from the pool, a stone patio furnished with hefty wood chair and table groupings converges on the open dining room. The river and widening plains take the opposing direction. Down by the river, wooden paths follow the water. It is possible to watch the day-to-day lives of hippo and birds from the small and attractively thatched bar at one end of the walkway.

WHERE TO EAT

Each of the lodges and hotels in and around Masai Mara Game Reserve is equipped to feed its guests, as there are no free-standing restaurants around. The general rule is you eat where you stay.

The exception is in the townships; in this case **Narok**. Popular with the tour operators, **KIM'S DISHES** does a good business. It is catty-corner from the Agip gas station and serves inexpensive fast food such as sausages and fries. It is possible to stop in for meals at any of the hotels if you are driving through and are not an overnight guest.

SEEING THE SIGHTS

Visit to a Masai Manyatta

Generally it is possible to spend half a day visiting a local manyatta or village from any of the camps or hotels. The Masai people living in the manyatta will welcome you but remember to be polite. Often, you will be invited to enter their homes. There may even be very young livestock sharing the one or two room dwelling. Do go in. Don't be put off by the smell or the size of the quarters. These people don't deserve our pity as they are happy living this way. In fact, they feel sorry for us!

Near the Olemutiak Gate there is a Maisa village open to tourists for $3.50. It is perfectly acceptable to use your camera and walk around at will. The upsetting part is it will be you and fifty other nosy outsiders. It is a most unpleasant experience in my opinion, unless you can arrange to be the only ones there. At a place like this, you can also expect to be badgered to buy homemade souvenirs.

QUESTIONS FROM THE HIGHLY RESPECTED MAMA

Once, when my husband and I were invited inside the mud hut of the chief's first wife, we were asked many questions through our interpreter. The powerful lady wanted to know how many children we had? What did we do for a living? How many cows did we own? How many wives did my husband have? She was astounded to find out there was only one wife; we both worked; and had no children and no cows!

NIGHTLIFE & ENTERTAINMENT

At many of the camps, including **Governor's**, it is not uncommon for Masai warriors to dance and chant their way into camp. Their red ochre covered bodies glisten in the firelight as they test their warriorhood and stamina with high vertical jumping. Just about every evening at **Kichwa Tembo Camp**, the Masai dancers strut their stuff for guests. Don't be alarmed when you hear them coming – it is not an attack!

If for some reason you end up at **Masai Mara Sopa Lodge**, take a walk down the path to the disco. Here you are bound to meet fellow travelers staying in one of the 70 rooms along the ridge.

SPORTS & RECREATION

Game Viewing

No matter where you stay it is likely you will go on at least two game drives a day. Early morning and late evening are best as this is when the animals usually feed. There will be lots of wildebeest, giraffe, jackal, hyena, warthog, lion, gazelle, antelope, zebra and ostrich wandering through the rich, wheat-colored plains in and around Masai Mara National Reserve. Harder to spot will be elephant, cheetah, and the very rare rhino.

For the lodges and camps inside the Mara there are strict regulations to be followed. All vehicles must be off the roads and plains by dark and no walking/hiking or night game drives are permitted within the national reserve. Any accommodations outside the park don't have to follow these rules and therefore offer more varieties of game tracking to their guests.

A favorite pastime of mine is to simply turn off the engine and sit with a drink in peaceful solitude. It is amazing how much curious game will come out of hiding to investigate the intruders. There is no need to rush off in pursuit of the next Kenyan fantasy. Instead, slow down and let a brilliant sunset, inquisitive dik dik, or arrogant warthog come to you.

The abundance of predators and wide open spaces will almost guarantee you see a lion kill providing you are patient and quiet. Here in the Mara the wealth of game between July and August (the migration) is quite astonishing. There are one and a quarter million wildebeest and a quarter of a million zebra. With these numbers, it stands to reason that the concentration of meat-eaters here is the highest in Kenya.

JOSTLING FOR POSITION

With the now controlled eruption of new places to stay, there are often too many tourists and minibuses in the Mara. It is customary for drivers to exchange location information by radio when game is spotted and all head for the area. You may be in one of six vans jostling for position around an uninterested but still dangerous animal. An experience of this kind takes something special from the game viewing adventure.

Flying Safaris

The latest in adventures is to take a flying safari from Masai Mara to Mfangano or Rusinga Island in Lake Victoria. The hour-long flight in a single engine plane will afford you the pleasant opportunity of seeing farms, fields, forest, villages and wildlife from the air. As you cross western Kenya to the lake, thoughts of an enormous Nile perch at the end of your line will keep your level of excitement high.

Swimming

A swimming pool surrounded by unique rock formations at **Mara Intrepids Club** provides relief and entertainment during the heat of the day. At **Kichwa Tembo Camp** it is fun to check-out board games from the staff. After a dip in the pool, play a few games of checkers or cards. A heated swimming pool in Africa? Yes! At the **Mara Safari Club** you can do laps in their warm pool even when its chilly. The pool at **Siana Springs** is not quite as remarkable as some of the others but will keep the kids happy for hours.

At midday, a swim in the lovely pool at **Mpata Safari Club** will help you keep fit. A run down swimming pool and sports area at **Masai Mara Sopa Lodge** was in dire need of attention. If you are traveling through the area and want to stop for a swim, the **Keekorok Lodge** allows day-trippers to use their pool for a small fee.

Walking/Hiking

At most of the hotels and lodges including **Sekenani Camp**, guided walks through the bush are options worth the effort. Inside the Masai Mara National Reserve there is no walking permitted but treks outside the reserve can easily be arranged. Some of the resorts charge extra for the service.

Balloon Rides

If you can afford the pricey $300 or more tag for a balloon safari; do so. Takeoff is before dawn; usually from Little Governor's Camp which **Mara Balloon Safaris** calls home. Depending on the weather the ride should last an hour. After silently watching the game below, it is touch-down on the plains. A "traditional" breakfast with champagne adds a final classy touch to the event.

People who had bad experiences say: the animals are scared of the balloon and hide until it passes; depending on the pilot, you may fly too high to see anything but moving dots below; if the wind shifts your ride can be cut down to ten minutes with no possibility of a refund; and the rip-off breakfast won't satisfy a mouse. Make sure you cover these topics before committing!

SHOPPING

Many of the tour operators do not encourage buying from the villagers as this upsets the economic balance of their lives. If you want to purchase anything, check with your guide first. He will usually be able to take you to a market or makeshift shop on the side of the road.

At **Governor's Camp** there is a small souvenir boutique with above average selections of local carvings and beads. **Mara Intrepids Club** has a sundry/souvenir shop where you can buy local wares. Near **Sekenani Camp**, overlooking a marshy pond, is a small stone building with a covered deck. It is a pretty place to watch birds and game come to drink or do a little Kenyan craft shopping inside. An oversized store at **Kichwa Tembo** is filled with a few necessities and Kenyan trinkets.

In the town of **Narok** the number of curb-side stands and stores selling souvenirs will astound you. Expect to be surrounded by vendors in a matter of minutes. You should be able to satisfy your cravings for mementos without any problem.

EXCURSIONS & DAY TRIPS

Narok

Narok is the last place to fill the gas tank, mail a letter, make a phone call from the post office, or exchange money from the **Barclays** or **Commercial** banks. The small provincial township is the main access point to Masai Mara and as such is heavily visited by tourists in minivans. Other than shopping and last minute supplies, there is nothing to do or see in the village.

Lake Magadi

Lake Magadi is part of the Rift Valley and southern Kenya. I dealt with it in Chapter 12, *Nairobi*, because it is a great day trip from the capital. The lake also makes a wonderful trip from Masai Mara but it takes time away from seeing the wildlife. From Lake Magadi it is possible to traverse the Rift's Nguruman Escarpment to Masai Mara (see below).

Nguruman Escarpment

Crossing the **Nguruman Escarpment**, the western wall of the Rift Valley, is possible only with a four wheel drive vehicle and a whole lot of endurance. Because dirt tracks and maps tend to vary widely due to the constantly changing terrain, it is wise to go this way only in the company of an experienced guide. This area includes the **Loita Hills**, with its fabulous vistas, as you emerge through changing, unspoiled landscapes of African bush and forests.

PRACTICAL INFORMATION

Gas Stations

If you didn't fill up in **Narok** and find yourself about to run out of gasoline, you may buy some at **Mara Sarova Camp**, **Mara Serena Lodge**, or **Keekorok Lodge** for a premium price. They don't encourage selling it to non-guests but won't deny you.

Medical Attention

At **Governor's Camp** there is a staff doctor available primarily to the guests. A registered Clinical Officer is a permanent member of the personnel at **Kichwa Tembo Camp**.

Park Fees

To enter Masai Mara you must pay a park fee. Check with your lodge or hotel to see if this is included in the price of your stay. The entry fee to Masai Mara Game Reserve (and to all national parks) is $27 per person per day for non-residents and $1.50 for residents. There is also a $1.50 per vehicle charge. Children's entry fees are $1.35 for non-residents and 55¢ for residents.

Photography

Your first time out in the Mara will make you go crazy with your camera. There is so much beauty and game. Try to be patient however, as one better photo opportunity after another will present itself. If you happen to run out of film tell your host or lodge manager. With some finagling it is usually possible to get more within a day or so from a neighboring hotel.

Weather

During the early morning and late evening it can get quite chilly in and around Masai Mara. It is best to be prepared with warmer layers of clothing you can remove or add as the day goes on. Game drives at dawn with wind whipping about your face can be particularly uncomfortable.

Picturesque rain showers through the yellow rays of the sun usually last only for a short time but can cause havoc with the dirt roads.

AMBOSELI NATIONAL PARK

Local Africans call the site *amboseli*, which in the Masai language means "salty dust" because of the desert-like nature of most of the landscape. Other than dead trees and fine dust, Amboseli boasts five different forms of wildlife habitat. This includes three healthy swamps, thick riverine forests and some of the best views of nearby **Mount Kilimanjaro**.

Even though it is technically not in Kenya, Kilimanjaro, the highest free-standing mountain in the world, attracts a lot of attention from visitors with its spectacular snow-capped peaks. The perfect caldera is covered with one-fifth of all the ice in Africa. Made great by Hollywood movies because of the mountain, Amboseli is second only to Masai Mara when it comes to tourists.

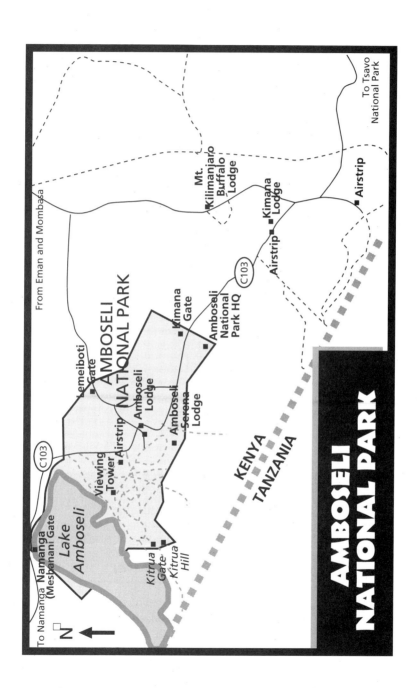

The national park is also known for the large herds of **elephant** roaming and grazing within its boundaries. In 1948 when the land was set aside for Kenya's first game sanctuary, the elephants numbered in the thousands. Those numbers have dwindled significantly due to poaching, drought, food shortages, and tourists. Today there are only about 600 elephants left. It is still possible however, to see the magnificent pachyderms as they move from feeding grounds to water holes.

Besides elephants you are most likely to see the elusive and endangered **black rhino** in Amboseli. Count yourself lucky if you do. The wide open flat spaces make animal spotting a little easier in certain parts of the park. Warthog, gazelle, wildebeest, jackal, baboon, giraffe, zebra, buffalo, hyena, lion and cheetah also call the small sanctuary home.

Between elephants killing trees and minivans destroying the miles of arid savannas, Amboseli has a hard time coping. Only time will tell if recent regulations can turn back the ecological clock for all the wildlife in the park. Today, driving off designated tracks is strictly prohibited.

In 1961 Amboseli was turned over to the Masai and in 1970 a sanctuary around Lake Amboseli was created for wildlife only. In 1977 the area became a national park. Thirty years ago, a lady by the name of Cynthia Moss, left a promising career at *Newsweek* and set off to study elephants in Africa. In 1972 she founded the **Amboseli Elephant Research Project**. Over the years it has become the longest-running African elephant research project in the world.

From her camp in the shadow of Mt. Kilimanjaro, Cynthia studies over 1,600 elephants. She dutifully records the births, deaths, social relationships and other dramas of the elephant's lives. With her presence and help from the Masai this group of elephants represents the largest group in Africa with an intact social structure. Her contributions are invaluable in educating the world.

She is affiliated with the and sponsored by the **African Wildlife Foundation**, *1400 Sixteenth Street, N.W., Suite 120, Washington D.C. 20036, Tel. 888/4-WILDLIFE, 202/939-3333, Fax 202/939-3332, E-mail: africawildlife@awf.org, www.awf.org*, which most people living in Kenya belong to. For those whose hearts are touched by the plight of the animals in Kenya, I would strongly suggest joining and contributing to this very worthwhile organization. It was founded in 1961 and is the leading international conservation organization working solely in Africa. Based in Washington D.C. AWF supports more than 35 field projects in Africa.

Dust swirls around seasonal **Lake Amboseli** during the dry months and erosion takes its toll on the vegetation, but according to scientists there is hope. The water table of the lake is rising and the dry bed more frequently holds water than in times past. In turn, the additional water attracts pink flamingos and other wildlife. Nature in all her glory takes the dead twisted tree trunk sculptures made by elephants, returns them to the soil, and begins the natural regeneration process.

ARRIVALS & DEPARTURES

By Air

Flying to any of the hotels or lodges in Amboseli is easily arranged as most of them have private or shared airfields. When making your reservations check to make sure someone can make the transfer from the strip to your lodge.

For $65 one way, **Air Kenya Aviation** will get you from Wilson Airport in Nairobi to Amboseli in an hour. The daily flights leave at 7:30 am from the capital and 8:30 am from the park.

By Car

Most people going to Amboseli arrive via the town of **Namanga** at the northernmost point of the park. From Nairobi, follow the A104 to Namanaga which is the main border post between Tanzania and Kenya. Turn left onto the C103 which will take you to and all the way through the national park.

You will be lulled into a false sense of security by the good condition of the A104. The 46 mile track (C103) to the **Namanaga Gate** will rattle your bones and destroy your vehicle's shocks. Altogether, the drive is about four hours long.

ORIENTATION

Amboseli is located in the **Rift Valley Province** in the district of **Kajiado** northwest of Mount Kilimanjaro. As I said above, the most popular gate is Namanga but this is not the only gate. To the east is **Meshanani Gate**, then **Lemeiboti Gate**, and further south is **Kimana Gate**. The park headquarters is in the furthest southeast corner of the reserve near Kimana.

The entire west side of Amboseli is covered by the often dry Lake Amboseli. Moving east you'll find the **Sinet** delta, river and swamp in the middle of which is **Observation Hill**. Right in the center of the park is a well-used airstrip. The next patch of green is the **Olokenya Swamp** stretching a good distance across the reserve.

GETTING AROUND

The C103 road runs right through the heart of Amboseli. Throughout the park there are dirt tracks along which it is possible for four wheel drive vehicles to travel. Game wardens prefer visitors to stick to these designated pathways. If you are on your own, check with the park rangers at the gates; sometimes they have maps showing the roadways.

The small park (by Kenyan standards) can and usually is easily covered in a day by the minivans filled with tourists.

WHERE TO STAY

COTTAR'S KILIMANJARO CAMP, *Glenn Cottar Safaris, PO Box 44191, Nairobi. Tel. 882 408. $400 per night double occupancy. Includes game drives.*

The camp is located outside Kimana town between Amboseli and the Chyulu Hills. It is possible to take pleasant day trips to either of these places from Cottar's Camp. Fishing in a cool stream near the campsite or guided game walks/drives are enjoyable pastimes for guests.

One cabin and four basic canvas tents share a picturesque spot on the banks of the stream. Facilities are simple and include flushing toilets and twin beds. The accommodations are set out of sight of each other under magnificent yellow fever trees. In the early morning it is relaxing to watch small colorful birds hop from branch to branch as the sunrise tints the world with orange.

TORTILIS CAMP, *Cheli & Peacock, PO Box 39806, Nairobi. Tel. 254 2 748 633, 254 2 748 327 or 254 2 751 073, Fax 254 2 750 225 or 254 2 740 721, chelipeacock@attmail.com, www.chelipeacock.com. $264 per night double occupancy.*

The Acacia Tortilis tree typifies Kenya and the natural wonders that abound. Tortilis Camp is named after the flat-topped tree in one of the few remaining areas of Amboseli forest. The owners and managers run the camp as an important conservation project involving reforestation, wildlife protection, and distribution of revenues to the native Masai – a great way for your dollar to go further than just your vacation.

Canvas guest tents on attractive wood and flagstone platforms offer the best in luxury camping, except perhaps the "rooms" are a little close together. Tightly woven thatch covers the canvas and extends over stone steps to make attractive verandahs. Wicker chairs, hand-woven rugs, locally made wooden beds, and tables pleasantly furnish your accommodations. Large screens keep the bugs out while allowing the cool breeze to caress you in your sleep. Fully equipped state-of-the-art bathrooms have spotless facilities and hot showers for your pleasure.

In the hilltop open-sided lounge, bar, or dining room, there is nothing more spectacular than watching the mist rise off distant Mount Kilimanjaro and the red-orange sunset. Laze away the hotter parts of the day with a cold drink and a lounge chair by the unfenced swimming pool. You'll feel like one with nature here. Cheerful birds, zebra, elephant, and wildebeest wander around the camp enjoying the cool shade of the leafy greenery. They seem unaware of the 17 luxury tents and their inhabitants.

Gourmet Italian cooking is a specialty of the house – watch out for the pasta, homegrown herbs, and vegetables – they're good! Attended with outstanding service, it is easy to put on a few extra vacation pounds. The friendly staff helps you work it off by taking you out into the park on foot. If this sounds too strenuous, day or night game drives are available.

OL KANJAU CAMP, *an extension of Sirata Suruwa, Bush Homes Africa Safaris, Tel. US 404 888 0909, e mail safari@bushhomes.com, mjrainy@thorntree.org, www.bushhomes.com, PO Box 56923, Nairobi. Tel. 571 647, Fax 571 665. $230 per night double occupancy. Includes game drives.*

An extension of Sirata Suruwa in Amboseli, Ol Kanjau (Camp of the Elephants) is a great opportunity to visit a 20 year elephant research project. This camp combines ecotourism and conservation in a special way that allows visitors to play a part in securing a long term future for these elephants in the greater Amboseli basin. Wild dogs and cheetahs co-exist with the other wildlife.

The tented accommodations are exclusive to groups of 12 visitors or less hosted by Mike and Judy Rainy. All the necessary amenities are provided. In addition, there are bush walks, bird watching, visits with a baboon troop and Masai settlements.

AMBOSELI LODGE, *Kilimanjaro Safari Club, PO Box 30139, Nairobi. Tel. 227 136, Fax 219 982. $210 per night double occupancy.*

On the down side, this lodge shares a rather unattractive entryway with its sister lodge, Mount Kilimanjaro Safari Club. The hotel caters to large groups of tourists in its 118 rooms, making a stay here potentially noisy. The hotel as a whole needs some attention and refurbishment.

On the up side, a new lobby and admittance building are a step in the right direction as far as upgrading goes. Well-kept grounds with spreading lawns and flower beds are an attractive step off from the terrace. From here Mount Kilimanjaro offers itself as a photographer's model for the perfect snow-capped peak. An oversized swimming pool is a great place to spend a sunny afternoon.

AMBOSELI SERENA LODGE, *Serena Lodges & Hotels, PO Box 48690, Nairobi. Tel. 710 511, Fax 718103. $208 per night double occupancy.*

You know you're in for an interesting stay as the receptionist hands over a Masai club with the room key attached. While you giggle in wonder at this foot-long stick with a knob at the end, she'll continue by explaining that the Masai use these weapons to protect themselves. You can use it to gently fend off the pesky monkeys roaming the grounds.

The 96 room lodge is set almost in the middle of Amboseli National Park and is designed to blend with the environment. With the idea of following the Masai construction of a *manyatta* (village), the buildings are camouflaged by surrounding bush. Also like local homesteads, there seem to be no square edges here, but rather smooth curves and rounded rims along windows, doors, and openings.

A favorite part of the hotel is the wooden bridge you must cross to get inside. Gurgling running water under your feet will immediately make you feel cooler. The carefully tended water lilies and enchanting over-hanging gardens only add to the feeling of escape from the warm temperatures. Built of what looks like red mud, the one level connected buildings are tastefully decorated with African animal and Masai themes throughout. Dried hanging gourds of all shapes and interesting sizes serve as shades for the lights.

The halls leading to the rooms are open to the heavens as they meander through dense tropical gardens. Headboards for the beds are made of bamboo-sized sticks and Masai spears hold up the shower curtains. The giant paintings of wildlife give you an exciting taste of what's to come in the real bush safari.

Set in one of the few wet and contrastingly green areas, Serena Lodge has chosen one of the more pleasant surroundings in Amboseli to set up shop. The tall acacia trees are roosting spots for crowned cranes, white pelicans, and other feathered wonders. At night the spotlights reveal elephant families within ten or twelve feet of you as they chomp on the long grass. During the day it is common to see cheeky monkeys or gnu cavorting on the grassy terrace.

From your bedroom, you will either have a view of the looming mountain or the water hole, which is frequented daily by herds of thirsty antelope, elephant, and gazelle. The outdoor terraces, the refreshing swimming pool, and the main bar overlook the bright green vegetation of the watering hole.

The dining hall is divided into many different size rooms. To reach this area you must cross another charming bridge over running water surrounded by floating gardens and water lilies. Breakfast and lunch are buffet style, while dinner is a romantic candlelight affair. Every other night on the terrace below the pool you can choose to participate in the Masai Exotic Dinner. For the price you will enjoy traditional Kenyan fare, a variety of barbecued meats, and an open bar. The waiters look proud in their colorful *shukas* (blankets used for as clothing) as they serve you under the star-filled evening sky.

Activities include Masai dancers around the evening camp fire, bird walks, jogging trails, informative and casual culture lectures, local singers and flights over Mount Kilimanjaro in a small plane, and of course excellent game viewing.

Selected as one of my *Best Places To Stay* – see Chapter 11 for more details.

MOUNT KILIMANJARO BUFFALO LODGE, *Kilimanjaro Safari Club, PO Box 30139, Nairobi. Tel. 227 136, Fax 219 982. $190 per night double occupancy.*

To offset the fact the lodge sits 20 minutes from the closest gate into Amboseli National Park, the management has several interesting sightseeing offers for guests. Choose from day-long picnics to Mzima Springs, Taita Hills, or Chyulu Hills; guided nature walks; visits to a Masai manyatta; camel rides; meals in the bush or plane flights over Mount Kilimanjaro.

High ceilings, dark wood and native stone are the predominant building materials of the 23 year old lodge. It is however, in need of renovation and remodeling. The *bandas* scattered around the property are perfectly adequate but heavy use by over 200 guests at a time eventually takes its toll. The highlight of a stay at Kilimanjaro Buffalo Lodge is the view of its namesake from the popular swimming pool or the Hemingway Tower Bar. The famous mountain looms in the background with a herd of elephant grazing in the foreground – what a sight!

KIMANA LODGE, *Kilimanjaro Safari Lodge, PO Box 30139, Nairobi. Tel. 227 136, Fax 219 982. $170 per night double occupancy.*

Set just outside the town of Kimana, the 112 room lodge has little to remark on other than the charming dining room and bar. An appealing waterfall allows your mind to wander as you sit on the patio and listen to the rushing cascade. The swimming pool entreats young guests to take the plunge. Accommodations are wooden units jammed together around the tiny garden and parking zone. It seems the main clientele are tourist groups heading this way from the seaside.

OL TUKAI LODGE, *Block Hotels, PO Box 47557, Nairobi. Tel. 335 807, Fax 340 541. $170 per night double occupancy. All major credit cards acc*epted. Game drives daily, Masai talks, nature walks.

Located in the heart of Amboseli National Park, Ol Tukai (which means palm tree) welcomes children of all ages. Most of their bedrooms are easily large enough to accommodate an extra bed. A children's menu and early supper is available and security guards allow parents to enjoy their dinner by listening for pillow fights or a wakeful baby.

Ol Tukai is lovely. The entire area is fenced (electric) to keep the game out but the animals come right up to the wire. It is wonderful to sit on your verandah with Mount Kilimanjaro looming in the background and elephant a short distance from your door. Cottage-style accommodations (mostly duplexes) spread out around the grounds, all with private bathrooms. The clean cottages make staying here feel like you are alone. High peaked ceilings, mosquito nets, lights all night, hot showers and attractive Kenyan touches make for a very comfortable stay.

A swimming pool, set off the ground on a rise, is surrounded by beautiful yellow and orange blooming trees and shrubs. The tile and stone combo along with the figure eight shape make for a great place to spend a few hours. A stone's throw away are wildebeest, zebra and other game. Stone floors, giant woven "people" in the restaurant, enormous chandeliers made of spears and parchment, water-filled moats, carved doors, an elephant skull, long wooden walkways, high lofts in the lounge and magnificent views of Mount Kilimanjaro will make you want to run home and redecorate. All around the grounds are yellow fever trees and vervet monkeys. They are ever so cute and seem to pose when a camera points their way. It is best to resist the temptation to feed these little pests. They are not tame and will bite. At meal times you will notice a guard with a sling shot keeping the noisy monkeys away.

KIMANA LEOPARD CAMP LIMITED, *Kimana Leopard Camp Limited, PO Box 16004, Nairobi. Tel. 732 125, Fax 732 462. $80 per night double occupancy.*

A short drive outside the town of Kimana is a second class camp servicing tour groups. The campsite is at the edge of a river but does not necessarily take full advantage of the location. The tents are very small and are furnished with metal cots. There are flush toilets nearby. Each night a leopard is baited to provide entertainment (see sidebar below).

BAITING WILDLIFE

Baiting wildlife is becoming more and more common at hotels and lodges catering to large numbers of tourists. Each evening, a carcass of meat hangs a safe distance from the hotel. The smell of food attracts hungry, meat-eating predators. At night, floodlights brightly illuminate the feeding spectacle. The practice usually involves leopards but not exclusively. Crocodiles, lions, hyenas, baboons and any number of other animals join in for their share.

Many conservationists condemn the practice as it changes the natural order of the food chain. The animals become dependent and after a few generations, soon forget how to hunt and fend for themselves. Others claim it cheapens the safari experience and turns it into a circus or a zoo. After you come face to face with the practice, voice your own opinion to hotel management.

SEEING THE SIGHTS
Observation Hill

From the top of the hill you can see miles of acacia forest, thick patches of bush, green swamps, and flat plains of Amboseli National Park.

With your binoculars, check the area around the swamps for giraffe, impala, hippo, waterbuck and zebra among others looking for food. Be prepared for bold vervet monkeys and baboons trying to get in the car window to steal anything they might consider good to play with or eat.

Masai Village

From within Amboseli National Park it is possible to visit an authentic and friendly Masai village. As part of an ongoing effort to include and involve the inhabitants in the tourist industry, the villagers are encouraged to be hospitable to their guests. This effort only adds to their already sociable nature.

SPORTS & RECREATION

Game Viewing

Most of the land in the dry eastern part of Amboseli tends to be flat and popular with desert-loving animals such as Grant's gazelle. In the center of the park where there is more water, game concentrations of zebra, lion, eland, wildebeeste, buffalo, elephant and birds gather to feed and drink. **Lake Amboseli** in the west is beginning to fill again and form a shallow soda lake popular with cranes, pelicans, and myriad birds. Game viewing in Amboseli is second only to the Mara. You should have no problem seeing wildlife if your lodge or hotel knows what it's doing and takes you to the right places.

Around the swamps of Amboseli it is common to see buffalo carrying their symbiotic friends, the colorful ox pecker which keeps them free of ticks. White cattle egrets, golden weavers, and kingfishers also abound along the shores.

Swimming

The swimming pool at **Kimana Lodge** entices visitors to use their pent up energy as they travel between Kenya's two main cities. From the popular pool at **Kilimanjaro Buffalo Lodge** there is a spectacular view of Mount Kilimanjaro in the background. The water theme at the utopian setting of **Amboseli Serena Lodge** is carried through all the way to the enticing swimming pool. The large swimming pool at **Amboseli Lodge** surrounded by green grass can be a pleasant spot to while away a lazy afternoon.

OL-DOINYO OROK

Just outside the town of Namanga is the sacred rock/mountain of Ol-Doinyo Orok. Orok means "black," and is the good side of the two-faced Masai god Enkai. Conversely, "red" is the angry side of the deity. Here in this holy place, a wise-man/witch doctor is buried with stones strategically piled at the head of his resting site. Supposedly, the rocks draw to him the first and most beautiful rays of dawn.

SHOPPING

The quoted prices of Masai handicraft, such as swords and beads, are completely outrageous when you first ask. Be sure and bargain firmly until you get what you think is a reasonable price for the item in question. Refer to the Souvenir Price Chart sidebar in Chapter 7, *Basic Information*. The shopkeepers in **Namanga** town always hope you'll pay their first asking price. It helps to have small change and shillings.

EXCURSIONS & DAY TRIPS

Kimana

Kimana is a small village between Amboseli National Park and the Chyulu Hills. The tiny village, close to both Kimana Lodge and Kimana Leopard Camp (see *Where to Stay* above). A trip to Kimana might produce some good souvenir hunting off (really off) the beaten path. If you safari this way, it is about 18 miles to Amboseli and 80 miles on dirt tracks and roads to the center of Tsavo West.

PRACTICAL INFORMATION

Camping

If you plan on camping or leaving your vehicle, make certain you don't leave any food in your tent or car. The baboons and elephants are notorious for finding and stealing foodstuffs. You might think this is cute, but I assure you, they will destroy your belongings and may not be too gentle with you if you try to interfere.

Gas Station

In **Namanga** town there is a gas station offering the golden liquid at premium prices. If you are driving, I suggest you try and bring your own gas in containers or fill up before arriving at the park. Many of the lodges and hotels might be willing to sell you some if you are in dire straights.

Park Hours & Fees

The park is open daily from 6:00 am to 6:00 pm. It is 150 miles from the capital and can be accessed by road and air. Check to see if the access charge is included in the cost of your accommodations. The entry fee to Amboseli is $27 per person per day for non-residents and $1.50 for residents. There is also a $1.50 per vehicle charge. Children's entry fees are $1.35 for non-residents and 55¢ for residents.

TSAVO NATIONAL PARK WEST

Tsavo National Park is divided into two halves (referred to as east and west) by the well-traveled Mombasa/Nairobi Road and the railroad. Both sides of the park are covered with over 1,000 miles of dirt tracks, which are used as fire and poaching deterrents. Tsavo as a whole is the largest national park in Kenya.

The western portion is 3,280 square miles and includes the **Ngulia Mountains** and some of the **Chyulu Hills**. For the most part the volcanic landscape is rocky, rugged, and wild. For contrast, the arid plains are broken by bush thickets and huge, free-standing stone monuments.

Once covered with thick green forests, Tsavo West is now plains and grasslands. The drastic change took place over the last century as foraging elephants destroyed the trees and consequently the ecosystem. Today these grasslands are beginning to return to young forests and scrub bush as restoration and conservation efforts go forward.

In 1960, the **elephant** populations numbered more than 50,000, only to be reduced by poachers to a mere 5,000. In addition to poaching reducing the tusker's numbers, there was a devastating drought in 1970 and 1971 which decimated the population to about 4,500. At the beginning of the 1990s when the elephants were last counted, about 6,700 remained in the huge park.

Severe anti-poaching regulations and enforcement has brought the elephant and rhino numbers in the park back from the brink of extinction. In 1969, **black rhino** totaled about 7,000 but were massacred down to less than 100 by 1981. Remaining rhinos are kept in a fenced area near Ngulia Hills and still have a long way to go before they are considered out of danger.

Tsavo National Park is where hunters such as Denys Finch-Hatton and Baron Bror von Blixen came to find record setting elephant ivory.

ARRIVALS & DEPARTURES

By Air

Inside Tsavo there are over 30 airstrips from which to make an entrance. Most hotels and lodges have their own or will pick you up at the one closest to their facilities. Sometimes there is an extra charge for the transfers.

By Car

Getting to Tsavo is simply a matter of following the A109 all the way from Nairobi. The road is good and can easily be traveled in an average car. Once you decide to get off the paved road and head to any of the lodges other than Kilaguni or Ngulia, be prepared to destroy the vehicle unless it is a four wheel drive.

From Nairobi to Mombasa is about 297 miles; Tsavo is a little over half way at 170 miles. It takes about four hours to make the trip. From the south of Amboseli to Tsavo is 56 miles; roughly a two hour drive over rough tracks.

ORIENTATION

Tsavo National Park is divided into Tsavo East and Tsavo West by the Mombasa to Nairobi A109 road and the railroad. The most used gate is the **Mtito Andei** at the north end of the park. There is a campsite here at the park's headquarters. Further along the A109 is the **Tsavo Gate** and another camping spot.

Arriving from the coast there is the **Maktau Gate** accessible after crossing through Taita Hills on the A23. Following along this road you'll come to the westernmost gate of **Mbuyuni** near the Tanzania border.

GETTING AROUND

Do not even think of driving around Tsavo in anything but a **four wheel drive**. The main paths may be accessible but the smaller routes are impassable in a normal car. The underside will be torn apart by the jagged edges of the lava rock. On the most traveled tracks, conical heaps of stones serve as markers and are numbered to make getting from place to place relatively easy.

WHERE TO STAY

OL DONYO WUAS, *Richard Bonham Safaris Limited, PO Box 24133, Nairobi. Tel. 882 521, Fax 882 728. $440 per night double occupancy. Includes game drive and guided walks.*

"The Spotted Hills" is the English translation of *Ol Donyo Wuas*, the home of Richard Bonham in the Chyulu Hills. For the best possible stay, try to make reservations when he will actually be there to act as host. If you are interested, it is possible to arrange bird shooting from July to October and horseback riding through the bush.

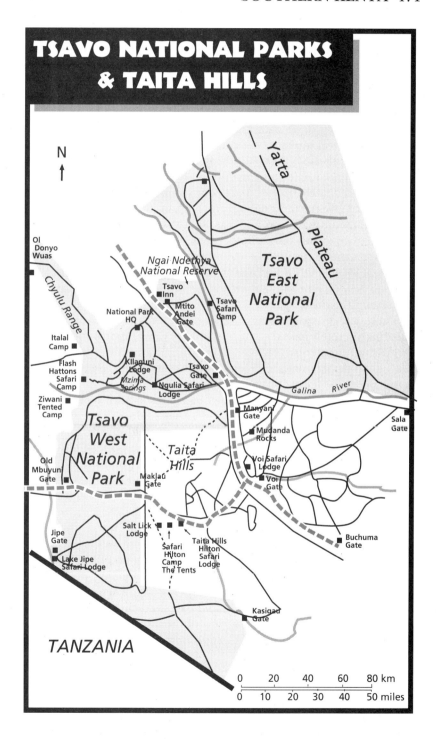

TSAVO NATIONAL PARKS & TAITA HILLS

N

Yatta Plateau

Ol Donyo Wuas

Chyulu Range

Ngai Ndethya National Reserve

Tsavo East National Park

Tsavo Inn

National Park HQ

Mtito Andei Gate

Tsavo Safari Camp

Italal Camp

Flash Hattons Safari Camp

Kilaguni Lodge

Mzima Springs

Tsavo Gate

Ngulia Safari Lodge

Galina River

Ziwani Tented Camp

Tsavo West National Park

Taita Hills

Manyani Gate

Mudanda Rocks

Sala Gate

Old Mbuyun Gate

Maklau Gate

Voi Safari Lodge

Voi Gate

Jipe Gate

Salt Lick Lodge

Safari Hilton Camp The Tents

Taita Hills Hilton Safari Lodge

Buchuma Gate

Lake Jipe Safari Lodge

Kasigad Gate

TANZANIA

| 0 | 20 | 40 | 60 | 80 km |

| 0 | 10 | 20 | 30 | 40 | 50 miles |

Each of the four guest cabins (two are up on stilts) have electricity, a fireplace, wonderful verandah views, and adjoining bathrooms with flush toilets and hot showers. (As water must be carried from below for the flush toilet, it is requested that when feasible, you use the long-drop instead. You'll enjoy the distant and open view from here!) Thick trees and African bush separates the cottages for seclusion and privacy. Colorful interior decor is tastefully done with beaded leather Masai bed covers, bright material, and local wares.

Whenever possible, the chairs, beds, windows and open areas face the magnificent panoramic vista of Mount Kilimanjaro. While building, Richard used thatch, stone, and wood found locally to keep down expenses and give the most natural and enchanting African effect. In the central living/dining room and bar, there is an irresistible fireplace. Surrounded by captivating photographs, the overstuffed comfortable furniture encourages you to sit and listen to the adventures of a lifetime.

FINCH-HATTON'S SAFARI CAMP (Tsavo West), *Future Hotels, PO Box 24423, Nairobi. Tel. 604 321, Fax 604 323, E-mail: finchhattons@iconnect.co.ke. $376 per night double occupancy.*

There are 35 spacious and lavish guest tents pitched on wooden platforms discretely placed along the banks of three hippo pools. Bridges cross the water and observation landings offer flawless viewing. Around the spring-fed pools, natural vegetation is preserved wherever possible to ensure a genuine feel of bush camping.

Just as the camp's namesake brought crystal and a phonograph record of Mozart's music to the wilds of Tsavo, so does the owner of this upscale hotel. Guests must dress for dinner and children are not encouraged. Leather furniture, shiny brass, classy antiques, wooden floors, kilim rugs, oversized mirrors, ensuite stone floor bathrooms and shaded verandahs are the minimum standards set for each guest quarter. As if this weren't enough, views of Mount Kilimanjaro far over the horizon add the finishing touch to a perfect safari.

Hippos graze around the tents at night. Elephants wander down the lava rock paths and there is nothing to stop a lion from walking anywhere within camp. Tall Kenyan guards escort visitors to and from the main building to assure safety. The kidney shaped swimming pool is surrounded by attractive rock formations and raised to keep wildlife out.

The thatched roof, stone walls, and oversized chimney of the main lodge is complimented by a great view of the mountain from the open patio. Expect admirable food and an upscale gift shop – only the best will do, says proprietor Peter Frank.

ILTALAL CAMP, *Iain McDonald Safaris Limited, PO Box 59224, Nairobi. Tel. 503 265, Fax 506 824. $160 per night double occupancy. Includes game drives and guided walks.*

The small Iltalal Camp sits at the edge of the Chyulu Hills, almost hidden between copses of fig trees. On either side of the campsite Masai villagers carry out their daily living. It is possible to organize visits to the Masai manyatta where you will meet curious children and shy adults.

The tents themselves are small and sparsely furnished with two twin metal beds. Adjoining the canvas is a thatched bathroom containing flush toilets and showers. The overall feel of the campsite is one of musty neglect.

There are two ways to arrive at the camp: you may either fly and land at the nearby airfield or drive across the Shaitani Lava Flows of Tsavo West. Along the way you are bound to see elephant, giraffe, zebra and other plains game.

KILAGUNI LODGE (**Tsavo West**), *African Tours & Hotels, PO Box 30471, Nairobi. Tel. 336 858, Fax 218 109. $144 per night double occupancy.*

The focal point of this "new" lodge is the watering hole, easily seen from the open-sided bar, dining room, and the separate central lobby area. From dawn to dusk, there is a constant parade of wild animals vying for first position at the water's edge. Elephant, baboon, zebra, buffalo and innumerable others take a turn drinking and casually entertaining visitors. This was the first luxury lodge in Kenya, built in 1962, but today, it is hardly recognizable after the needed upgrades and renovations. (To get here you can fly into the nearby airfield.) A new VIP *banda* and wing of guest quarters added to the 53 standing rooms now makes Kilanguni a sizable hotel. Simple but attractive locally made furnishings compliment the basic rooms and their adjoining bathrooms. High thatched ceilings and airy openness add charm to the public areas in this utopian setting.

A panoramic view of Chyulu Hills and Mount Kilimanjaro as a backdrop to breathtaking gardens will overload your senses. Semi-tame hyrax scurry about the rocky beds and lizards bask in the sun. Cascades of fluorescent bougainvillea blend with fluttering weaverbirds. The sparkling water of the swimming pool adds a finishing touch.

NGULIA SAFARI LODGE (**Tsavo West**), *African Tours & Hotels, PO Box 30471, Nairobi. Tel. 336 858, Fax 218 109. $144 per night double occupancy.*

Almost in the heart of Tsavo national park, this 52 room, two-story hotel opened in 1969. Unfortunately the accommodations are somewhat used-looking and are in need of refurbishment. Twin beds, mosquito nets, and verandahs are standard. The in-room bathrooms are particularly rundown. If you end up here, don't despair but rather be amazed by the wonderful setting.

The pristine pool and main lodge sit on two flat stone terraces carved out of the hillside; a remarkable feat! A plummeting precipice to the scenic Yatta Plateu below protects one side of the site. From the dining room and viewing terrace there is a marvelous wildlife parade to the waterhole – popular with animals and tourists. Each night, floodlit bait is left to entice rhino and leopard.

The real downside to staying here is you must have your own vehicle for game drives. The Ngulia Safari Lodge has no transportation set aside for bush driving with guests!

ZIWANI TENTED CAMP (Tsavo West), *Prestige Hotels Limited, PO Box 74888, Nairobi. Tel. 338 084, Fax 217 278. $126 per night double occupancy.*

Many of the visitors coming for a stay at the serenely peaceful camp drive in from the coast. Personally, I'd rather use the landing strip nearby and avoid the road travel. A cool wet drink and a damp washcloth await your arrival no matter what form of transport you choose. The effect is immediate and rejuvenating.

Observing a common African practice, cooking at Ziwani is done over homemade charcoal and baking is achieved in metal trunks. It is almost miraculous that the delicate flavor of a full English breakfast complete with toast comes out of such rudimentary equipment. The Kenyan cooks are skilled and have much practice at the delicate art.

There is no electricity in the 16 tent camp, so shimmering lantern light illuminates the way during the dark hours. Neatly thatched roofs keep the tents cool at midday and offer shade on spacious and attractive verandahs. Slabs of concrete afford a stable foundation for all the sites, which tend to be a bit too close together.

The canvas accommodations come with plenty of screened windows making the space light and airy. Woven rugs, straw mats, comfortable twin beds, and wood furniture make for a pleasant stay. Basic long-drop toilets and safari gravity showers take their place behind each "room."

The Sante River and a natural looking dam close by are home to myriad ducks, storks, eagles, and other active birdlife. Food is plentiful for them. Towering trees shade the banks, and papyrus reeds grow in the shallows. Green, well-cared for lawns extend from the waterline to the lodge. As an undeveloped portion of the Ziwani Sisal Estate, it is unfortunate the tents don't overlook this or any other noteworthy view.

In the open-sided bar and dining area, green plants cascade out of hanging clay pots. Monkeys chatter in the trees above and if you walk along around the dam you may see hippo and crocodile in the water. Impressive Mount Kilimanjaro peeks out of the clouds on the horizon. A pretty setting, helpful and friendly service by the staff and the hosts, nighttime leopard baiting across the river, game walks and the proximity to wildlife makes this a pleasant place to spend a day or two.

LAKE JIPE SAFARI LODGE, *PO Box 31097, Nairobi. Tel. 227 623, Telex 25508. $126 per night double occupancy.*

With all the other possible choices in the area I would not decide to stay at this lodge. The flies and mosquitoes are uncommonly bad and the food is not much better. To get away from the bugs, the lodge was built some distance from the water. There is a view of the beautifully pictur-esque lake and Tanzanian Pare Mountains from the pool patio but not from the rooms.

A large building serves as the dining and lobby area. For some odd reason stickers from various tour groups are plastered over the windows obscuring what panorama there is. Thatched guest cabins are so close together that any thought of privacy is lost.

The best part of an excursion here besides the pool and its vista is lovely Lake Jipe. (I suggest a day trip.) You must first drive to the nearby lakeshore. From here, it is possible to take a boat ride across the water. With the mountain as your backdrop, the setting is captivating. Check out the boat for leaks and ask if drinks are included – if not, make sure to bring your own.

HUNTERS LODGE (Tsavo West), *Mada Holdings, PO Box 40683, Nairobi. Tel. 221 439, Fax 332 170. $20 per night double occupancy.*

Established by the eminent game warden John Hunter, the lodge is a popular rest stop when traveling to/from Nairobi and Mombasa. The lodge is at the far north end of the park but has easy accessibility to the A109. There is a pump where you can refill your gas tank.

If you don't want to stay in one of the twenty simple guest rooms, perhaps a quick lunch in the well-regarded restaurant will restore you for the rest of your journey. To stretch your legs, take a walk over the picturesque bridge and around the dam. Prissy peacocks will keep you company in the colorful garden.

WHERE TO EAT

On the road to or from Nairobi to Mombasa, the **HUNTERS LODGE** offers a much frequented restaurant with tasty food, cold drinks, and a pleasant setting. Otherwise, the lodges provide meals.

SEEING THE SIGHTS

Roaring Rocks

A short drive inside Tsavo West from the Mtito Andei Gate is the amazing attraction of Roaring Rocks. Climb up the dark volcanic rock steps to the top. On a warm day it may be a laborious 330 foot climb with a little sweating involved but the panorama is worth the effort. When the wind blows across the exterior of the rocks it produces a most disconcert-ing roaring sound – hence the name.

SPORTS & RECREATION

Game Viewing

To see all of Tsavo you will need to allow more than the usual two or three days allotted to game parks. Other than elephants in the reserve keep an eye out for antelope, hippo, rhino, giraffe, gazelle, ostrich and eland. Around the three permanent rivers flowing through the park, expect to see high concentrations of game, particularly during the drier seasons.

Bird Watching

The birdlife of Tsavo is a prolific as the game. The park is a mecca for those who love our feathered friends. Storks, starlings, and vultures are just a few of the 400 species found here. There is an important migration passage from Europe to Russia crossing over the heart of Tsavo West. Hundreds of thousands of birds take a break and stop to rest here. Ornithologists gather to band and identify the travelers before releasing them to continue the centuries-old journey.

Lake Jipe, with its flat bank and dense rushes, is a haven for birds and bird lovers. Cormorants fish for dinner and kingfishers dart among the reeds. In the background sit the picturesque Pare Mountains of Tanzania.

Dhow Rides

On Lake Jipe take a **dhow trip** across the scenic lake or to **Grogan's Castle**. These rides are popular with day-trippers and can be easily arranged. The North Pare Mountains make a charming framework for the water.

Bird Shooting

At **Ol Donyo Wuas** it is possible to do a little bird shooting from July to October with prior arrangements.

Horseback Riding

Horseback riding through the Kenya bush at **Ol Donyo Wuas** can be an exciting adventure; particularly if you manage to have Richard (the owner) as your guide. He is well-known for putting together all manner of horse safaris, including fly camps.

Swimming

Raised and enclosed by carefully placed rocks, the kidney shaped swimming pool at **Finch-Hatton's Camp** is intended to keep animals out of the unfenced site. The dazzling water of the swimming pool at **Kilanguni Lodge** is a fun way to while away a hot afternoon watching the cute rock hyrax nearby.

The small, enticing pool at **Ngulia Safari Lodge** and the chiseled flat patio it sits on are a testimony to man's ingenuity. **Lake Jipe Safari Lodge** has an inviting swimming pool with amazingly beautiful mountain vistas. Using the pool however, can be unpleasant if the lake flies and mosquitoes are out in force.

SHOPPING

The gift shop at **Finch-Hatton's Safari Camp** has authentic souvenirs and local crafts for sale. Prices may be steep but you can avoid the hassle of bargaining with crowds of sellers.

EXCURSIONS & DAY TRIPS

Mzima Springs

In Tsavo National Park West, waters draining down from Mount Kilimanjaro gather to form a marvelous oasis and clear pools. Mombasa gets much of its drinking water from this life-giving flow.

Underground rivers appear in the arid dust of Tsavo offering a haven for birds, crocodiles, hippo, and other thirsty wildlife. Rich, green plant life flourishes around the water, contrastingly obvious against the arid surroundings. Sykes and vervet monkeys, kingfishers and baboons frolic in the flat-topped acacia, fig, and palm trees.

To attract visitors, the park service constructed a popular underwater viewing area (for hippo) and patrolled walkways. The huge submersible beasts have caught on and tend to gather at the far end of the pool. The plentiful fish populations, however, remain undisturbed and don't mind being watched in the murky waters.

Lake Jipe

With its flat bank and dense rushes, **Lake Jipe** is a haven for birds and bird lovers. To get to the lake turn six miles from Taveta towards the Jipe Sisal Estate. The small lake sits right on the Tanzania/Kenya boundary and is famous for its serenity. From here, dhow trips across the scenic lake or to **Grogan's Castle** can be organized with little effort.

The late Ewart Grogan built a medieval castle here at Lake Jipe on his sisal plantation. The structure is not a castle but rather a rambling old farmhouse. Since Grogan's Castle, nicknamed **Grogan's Folly**, was constructed by the unpopular individual, it has fallen into disrepair. It seems he was an unscrupulous and sometimes dishonest businessman in the 1930s. He was disdained by the British residents because of his character and questionable ethics. Colonel Grogan founded Gertrude's Garden Children's Hospital in Nairobi and to date, he is the only person who can claim to have walked from the Cape to Cairo. The story alleges the trek was for the sake of a woman he loved!

Apparently, the property is currently being considered for renovations. The new Greek owners are thinking of turning it into a tourist lodge.

Lake Chala

To get to the crater lake sitting on the border with Tanzania, take the Voi road for about five miles. Turn left at the next track and drive for eight miles. Look for and take another left on an uphill dirt path. You can either park at the bottom and walk for ten minutes up to the crater's rim, or ride to the top in your four wheel drive vehicle.

The lake can be hard to find but persevere and you will be rewarded. You must be right at the edge to see the blue waters below. If you're lucky and it's a clear day, Mount Kilimanjaro will be your stunning backdrop. According to local fishermen, the crocodile populations have moved elsewhere. The fish populations, however, are still prolific.

The water levels remain curiously constant even if the feeder rivers off Mount Kilimanjaro are running full. In the late 1950s, Royal Navy divers discovered an underground river here. They put dyes in the waterway to see where it discharged. Much later, 250 miles away in Zanzibar, the water was oddly discolored!

CHYULU HILLS NATIONAL PARK

The volcanic ridges of the superb national park are seldom visited. Deep valleys and lush green slopes have spreading vistas in all directions. As some of the youngest mountains in the world, the Chyulus date back between four and five centuries. To reach and explore the expanse, a four wheel drive vehicle is an absolute necessity.

When it rains, the fresh beauty of the verdant hills shines even brighter. The hard to follow dirt tracks are often washed away during the wet season, so a knowledgeable guide is an excellent idea. Underground rivers materialize on the surface becoming a potentially serious hazard to visitors.

Near the Chyulu Gate of Tsavo Park West is the dark **Shaitani** (or Shetani) **Lava Flow**, **caves** and **nature trails**. The threatening, desolate land on the eastern side of the range was a by-product when the hills themselves formed. These lava formations are worth exploring, but caution is advisable and so is a flashlight. Inside one of the caves is the skeletal remains of a baby rhino that probably got lost. The bat droppings can be slippery in **Shaitani Cave** as you hike in one side and out the other. Climbing the **Chaimu Crater** near Kilaguni Lodge is a pleasant way to get out into nature.

SHAITANI LAVA FLOW

*In Swahili, **shaitani** means devil. Because of the sharp, black, dangerous pumice rock, the name aptly describes the ominous territory. Legend has it that anyone climbing to the very top of the relatively new and eerie configurations will disappear forever.*

PRACTICAL INFORMATION

Information Center

At the **Kilaguni Lodge** there is an information center dispensing the latest animal sighting data. It might be worth the effort if you are in the area and want to know where the game is hanging out at the moment. Also inquire at the entry gates for information on road closures and animal sightings.

Park Hours & Fees

Tsavo is open daily from 6:00 am to 6:00 pm and there is a daily admissions charge. The entry fee to Tsavo is $27 per person per day for non-residents and $1.50 for residents. There is also a $1.50 per vehicle charge. Children's entry fees are $1.35 for non-residents and 55¢ for residents.

Weather

Less than 20 inches of rain falls per year in this dry region, making rainwear unnecessary. However, the temperatures can still get quite cool during early morning and evening, requiring a sweater and socks to keep the chill away.

TSAVO NATIONAL PARK EAST

Tsavo is Kenya's largest national park but is not quite as popular as other parks because it is hot, semi-desert. **Tsavo East** (4,600 square miles) is largely made up of 200 miles of lava known as the **Yatta Plateau**. This, the longest lava flow in the world, once acted as a natural barrier for traders and explorers hoping to reach the interior. It starts near the Kenyan capital and eventually ends near the coast. The long lava obstacle is only broken in one spot – where the B7 crosses it outside the park to the north. This portion of the national park tends to have a reputation for being flat, empty desert and as such is less frequented. Magnificent views and thick African bush make this a dramatic part of Kenya, where beauty is strictly in the eye of the beholder.

There are two other reasons why there is a lack of tourists in Tsavo East. First of all, much of the area north of the **Galana River** is closed to visitors for security reasons. Poachers like the remoteness of the park where they feel they can carry out their dastardly deeds in private. Happily, the anti-poaching authorities are gaining the upper hand, but in the meantime the rhino counts are down to 200. Second, wildlife is hard to see because of enormous ranges, thick grass, and thorny bush.

To break up some of the stark volcanic landscape, there are rich green oases thriving along the banks of the **Athi**, **Tiva**, **Tsavo**, and **Voi Rivers**. It is to these oases much of the wildlife in the area comes for water and sustenance.

In the southern section of Tsavo East are the rocky gorges of **Lugard Falls**, where over time the Galana River has worn away the stone. The murky waters rush down a narrow canyon and squeeze through a crevice in the granite rocks. A wild river filled with swirling, uprooted trees and bloated carcasses is an alarming sight during the rains. The crocodiles living down stream long for those days of torrential rains when dinner simply surges their way!

Still further south in the park is a natural catch basin at **Mudanda Rock**. It is safe for you to leave your vehicle here and clamber to the top of the granite knoll. Beyond the sheer drop on either side of the small hill is a popular watering hole for wildlife.

ARRIVALS & DEPARTURES

By Air

Inside Tsavo there are over 30 airstrips from which to make an entrance. Most hotels and lodges have their own or will pick you up at the one closest to their facilities. Sometimes there is an extra charge for the transfers.

By Car

Getting to Tsavo is simply a matter of following the A109 all the way from Nairobi to the **Manyani Gate**. The road is good and can easily be traveled in an average car. Once you decide to get off the paved road and head to any of the camps in Tsavo East, the path won't be so gentle with your vehicle. The dirt road (C103) bisects the park following along the Galana River and exits at the far **Sala Gate**.

ORIENTATION

The main entry from the south is at **Voi Gate** just off the Mombasa to Nairobi Road. The park's headquarters is situated here as is the game-rich **Kanderi Swamp**. The less used **Buchuma Gate** is the closest entry from the coast. Further north, very near the **Tsavo Gate** on the west side of the park, is the **Manyani Gate**.

Access to the further reaches of the park officially end at the **Galana River**, which stretches horizontally from boundary to boundary. At the easternmost edge along the river is the **Sala Gate**.

GETTING AROUND

Only the southern third of Tsavo East is open to the public. The **Voi River** neatly cuts this third of the park in half. Built across the river is the **Aruba Dam** where wildlife is prolific and usually undisturbed by tourists. Stop in at the park headquarters and see if you can prevail upon a warden to take you around the less visited park or at least let you buy a map of the tracks. As always, it is best to take along an experienced guide in your four wheel drive vehicle.

NIGHT GAME VIEWING LODGES

*There are five night game viewing lodges in Kenya – The Ark, Treetops, and Mountain Lodge near Mount Kenya; Shimba Hills at the coast; and **Salt Lick Lodge** in the Taita Hills. All these hotels have turned game tracking around; instead of you looking for wildlife, you let animals come to you! Some nights you get lucky and the spotlit animals are plentiful; other times you might only see a wandering buffalo. Either way, you get to relax and enjoy the show all night.*

WHERE TO STAY

SALT LICK HILTON SAFARI LODGE (Taita Hills Private Reserve), *Hilton International, PO Box 30624, Nairobi. Tel. 332 564, Fax 339 462. $290 per night double occupancy.*

The tall white buildings of the lodge look like clumps of giant mushrooms growing around an expanse of water. The spacious 96 room hotel is constructed on stilts above a wateringhole – a perfect vantage point for wildlife viewing. Isn't this what Kenya is all about?

On the lower and upper levels there are viewing terraces where you can easily see game coming to drink. As you cross over the drawbridge (raised at night), wander along outdoor hallways, or stand at the wide bedroom window, chances are buffalo, elephant, zebra, warthog or gazelle will look right back at you. To get even closer, amble down the underground tunnel to the waterside blind. Now you stand so close you can count whiskers.

The round two story towers are connected with open bridges and capped with pointed thatched ceilings. Large curving bedrooms and adjoining bathrooms are adequately furnished with twin beds and easy-chairs. The top floor rooms are even more enticing because of the thatched peaks finishing them off and slightly more spectacular views.

To help you stay awake all night, hot drinks and snacks are always at hand. When the brisk night air starts to chill your bones, step indoors to the amazing stone fireplace which stretches to the roof. The unique lodge provides a remarkably exciting experience.

SAFARI HILTON CAMP–THE TENTS (Taita Hills Private Reserve), *Hilton International, PO Box 30624, Nairobi. Tel. 332 564, Fax 339 462. $290 per night double occupancy. All three of the Hilton properties in the Taita Hills Wildlife Sanctuary mentioned below are easily accessible by car or small plane from Nairobi and Mombasa.*

Each of the 24 luxury tents at this camp are pitched on platforms somewhere around the James Stewart House. The dwelling was built for the movie *A Tale of Africa*, starring Jimmy Stewart. Today it serves as the perfect camp setting for a crackling fire, hot toddys or tea and Kenyan style barbecue.

The thick forest camouflages each tent and muffles the happy sound of flowing water from the Bura River. Meandering walkways take you over small bridges and through natural bush, eventually leading you back to The House. Nocturnal and diurnal wildlife sounds blend with musical notes from local musicians. Moonlight and lamplight bring a true sense of oneness and peace with nature.

The roomy tents are furnished with twin beds, a nightstand, dressing table, and private bathroom. A flush toilet and hot and cold running water provide the comforts of home. Outside, the wide covered verandah is perfect for bird watching and a hot cup of coffee with the sunrise. Tall green trees are the playground of bright butterflies and monkeys. As a precaution, an *askari* and an electric fence keep unwanted visitors out of the camp.

TAITA HILLS HILTON SAFARI LODGE (Taita Hills Private Reserve), *Hilton International, PO Box 30621, Nairobi. Tel. 332 564, Fax 339 462. $224 per night double occupancy.*

Interestingly, the lodge was built from sandbags (cemented together to make walls) dating back to WWI. Flowering red vines cover all but the doors, oversized window, and balconies of the large three story hotel. Surrounding the central structure, colorful gardens and green lawns blend together in harmony with nature. Tennis courts, a soccer field, a basketball court, mini-golf and an enticing swimming pool are signs of civilization.

Whether you fly in to the private airfield or drive to the wildlife sanctuary to check in at any of the three Hilton managed hotels, you must first stop here. The two floor open lobby is full of interesting African furnishings and natural accessories. A rock fireplace soars from a central sunken room. Stone seats go together well with carved paneling depicting local lifestyles. Scattered everywhere are hand-woven tapestries and rugs.

Breakfast is a buffet set-up with views of mature trees and colorful sunny gardens on three sides. Fresh fruit and home-baked pastries cover the tables. International and local cuisine is usually served for lunch and dinner by well-trained staff in the large Chala restaurant. A bartender serves cold drinks from the cozy lobby bar. Native dancers or musicians present lively evening entertainment.

Each of the 60 rooms have their own bathrooms and verandahs. Depending on which way you face, the view changes. It might be distant mountain ranges and green plains flecked with wildlife or perhaps attractive garden walkways. If this isn't enough, try a camel ride around the grounds, a champagne breakfast, or a bush picnic.

TSAVO SAFARI CAMP (Tsavo East), *Kilimanjaro Safari Club, PO Box 30139, Nairobi. Tel. 227 136, Fax 219 982. $170 per night double occupancy.*

Thirty canvas tents and six cabins built along the Athi River make up the 28 year old Tsavo Safari Camp. Local British expatriates traveling to the coast or simply in need of company either fly or drive in. The objective is to spend a few hours or an entire night visiting with manager Lionel Nutter in the famous thatched bar. Comfortable, casual, and carefree are three excellent words to describe the overall ambiance.

The lush oasis along the river can only be reached by crossing the water in a supplied rubber boat. You must leave your vehicle in the parking area, entrusting it to the attendant and the multitude of birds inhabiting the fertile belt. Early morning is a twitcher's fantasy down by the waterside (a "twitcher" is a bird lover or ornithologist. Hornbills seem to be the most prolific of the birdlife around Tsavo Safari Camp. Other game in the surrounding dryness of Tsavo however, is not as plentiful even on offered game drives (which cost extra).

The accommodations here in what was once a hunting camp are up to the job of making you comfortable. Basic furnishings, large adjoining bathrooms with solar heated showers, and flush toilets come with every "room." A refreshing swimming pool, well-cared for tropical gardens, and spreading shade trees complete the African safari setting.

VOI SAFARI LODGE (Tsavo East), *African Tours & Hotels, PO Box 30471, Nairobi. Tel. 336 858, Fax 218 109. $144 per night double occupancy.*

It is possible to fly in to the airstrip near the town of Voi and drive two miles to the lodge. The road to the hotel is well traveled by visitors driving between Nairobi and Mombasa. In need of a place to stop for lunch, the British style restaurant is a favorite.

Also favored with tourists are the spectacular numbers of elephant, buffalo, antelope, and baboon easily visible at the waterhole from the pool, patio, dining room and guest rooms. All the buildings follow along the edge of ochre colored rocks at the top of the cliff. Inside, the bar is busy with people as well as birds looking for handouts and baboons peeking curiously through the skylight.

Hewn stone makes curious patterns in the floors and on the walls throughout the lodge. Locally made artifacts such as gourd lights and wooden animal carvings decorate the public areas. Rock gardens and pathways surround the swimming pool at the edge of the precipice.

With such a spectacular setting, it is a shame the 50 guest bedrooms are not more inviting. Other than a full wall of glass on one side, there is nothing remarkable to write about – although you could call home from the phone in the shower!

TSAVO INN (**Tsavo East**), *Mount Kilimanjaro Safari Club, PO Box 30139, Nairobi or PO Box 20, Mtito Andei. Tel. 227 136, Fax 219 982. $80 per night double occupancy.*

This 30-room inn at Mtito Andei has excellent access from the Nairobi to Mombasa road. The rooms are very basic but get the job done if you must stop for the night. A small garden-side pool and a good restaurant are your choices if you just need a break from the drive.

WHERE TO EAT

As I've said before in this chapter, each lodge and hotel has at least one restaurant open to guests and non-guests alike. If you find yourself in the town of Voi, take a look at the **VOI RESTPOINT HOTEL** which has three reasonable restaurants, one of which is on the roof. The prices are excellent and the food acceptable, if simple.

As you travel by road from Mombasa to Nairobi, the British-style **VOI SAFARI LODGE** restaurant is a popular eatery for cold drinks and fabulous vistas. It's very likely you'll see large herds of elephants wandering by. **TSAVO INN** has a worthy restaurant if you just need a break from the drive between Nairobi and the coast.

While staying at any of the hotels in the area, expect to enjoy sweet home-grown fruit and vegetables at all your meals. Many of the lodges

BREAKFAST WITH THE ANIMALS

Over the years, wildlife has come to know there is food where there are people. This secret is now passed down from one generation to another with each group getting bolder than the one before. It is enthralling to have monkeys, hornbills or starlings, rock hyrax, squirrels and perhaps even mongooses steal a piece of fruit from your table and then scamper away to enjoy the morsel. This is one of my favorite parts of a safari in Kenya!

offer barbecues under the stars, cocktails on the plains as the blazing sun sets over Mount Kilimanjaro, or romantic sunrise champagne breakfasts. I highly recommend all of these experiences.

SEEING THE SIGHTS
Aruba Dam
Built by the national parks authority to contain the seasonal flow of the Voi River, the dam and man-made lake offer thirst-quenching water to the animals. It is common to see giraffe, ostrich, buffalo, leopard, lion, gazelle and cheetah drinking side by side. The water on the 210 acre lake stays an ochre-red color all the time due to constantly moving red silt.

Lugard's Falls
In 1890, an anti-slaver named Lord Frederick Lugard traveled this way; the scenic falls were named after him. A small fissure in the rocks forces the muddy river water to boil through in a fight to reach the bottom. Once upon a time tourists were told they could stand astride the mad flow. The results were not pretty to anyone but the crocs below. If you hear this nutty claim, ignore it.

Mudanda Rocks
A great place to see the vast plains below, **Mudanda Rocks** is also popular with the local predator population. Be on the lookout for lions and other meat-eaters who use the site to search for easy prey below.

Located not far north of Voi town, it is relatively safe to leave your car and hike to the top of the rocky hillock. Looking down past the steep crevasses on each side, you'll see a small watering hole where animals come to drink. Mudanda Rocks is the perfect spot to commune with nature one on one.

NIGHTLIFE & ENTERTAINMENT
Out here in the African bush, don't expect too much in the way of sophisticated nightlife. Instead, most of the hotels and lodges try to reproduce authentic **native dancing** to drum music. As the locals dance, they often chant or sing and make their own mesmerizing musical rhythms.

SPORTS & RECREATION
Game Viewing
There is much game in the Taita Hills area and the scenery is spectacular. In the former hunting grounds and unsuccessful sisal plantation, the 42 square miles of game sanctuary are ever popular with the

wildlife; they know it's safer here. Warthog, gazelle, giraffe, elephant and buffalo frequent the man-made watering holes at (**Salt Lick Taita Hills** and **Taita Hills Hilton Safari Lodge**) especially during the hotter and drier months of the year.

Hiking/Walking

If you are traveling southward, turn right in the town of Voi towards the village of Wundanyi in the heart of **Taita Hills**. Here you will find what is often referred to as "Africa's Switzerland" – a popular place with hill walkers and hikers. For safety reasons go with a guide or a group. The Wataita people who grow maize, bananas, and fruit in these rolling hills will be happy to point you in the right direction if you stray.

Sports Facilities

At **Taita Hills Hilton Safari Lodge**, there are many sports activities readily available for guests to indulge in such as tennis courts, a soccer field, a basketball court, and mini-golf.

Swimming

The swimming pool at **Taita Hills Hilton Safari Lodge** is bordered by mowed green lawns and a thick hedge; the only thing between you and wild Kenya. **Tsavo Safari Camp's** swimming pool, amid bright gardens and tall shade trees, is a good place to refresh yourself. From the cliffside swimming pool at **Voi Safari Lodge** you can appreciate the vastness of Tsavo. A small pool in the gardens at **Tsavo Inn** is a refreshing respite from the drive between the coast and Nairobi.

EXCURSIONS & DAY TRIPS

Taita Hills

Surrounded on three sides by Tsavo National Park, the Taita Hills provide a striking backdrop for the **Salt Lick/Taita Hills Game Sanctuary**. The 42,000 acres of privately owned land was once a sisal plantation. Today you'll be able to enjoy undulating and sometimes steep hills, magnificent grassland valleys, thick forests, cascading waterfalls, abundant game and luxurious all-inclusive accommodations.

Hilton International holds a long lease on the land where it built three first-class lodges. Part of the contract includes responsibility for game management which is carried out by 18 full-time staff wardens. Wildlife including buffalo, waterbuck, impala, elephant, gazelle and zebra is tracked and guarded with unobtrusive fervor.

Because of plentiful water and rich feeding in the hills, wildlife crosses over from Tsavo West via a natural game corridor. The animals can enjoy the feast in relative safety. Here in Taita Hills, visitors are more likely to come across elusive game. Using portable radios, attentive wardens notify drivers of the games' whereabouts. Long hours of driving are cut short. Because it is a private preserve, the number of vehicles out on game drives is limited. This makes the safari effect more genuine and pleasant.

Voi

Just south of Taita Hills is the somewhat unremarkable town of **Voi**. The town is beginning to grow as tourism expands in that direction. There is a **Kenya Commercial Bank**, a **post office**, a **Caltex** and **BP gas stations** and the ever-present town **market**. Near the Caltex look for fast-food restaurants, a bar serving truly cold drinks and a hodgepodge of miscellaneous stores.

If you follow the railroad a little beyond Voi, you come upon the tiny village of **Taveta**. Taveta is Kenya's southernmost town, linked to Voi by railroad in 1924. This and the fact it was a major player during the years of WWI are its claim to fame.

During the Great War, when Tanganyika (now Tanzania) was a German colony, Taveta (then British) was the site of a fierce battle between the British and the Germans. This clash began just eleven days after the war broke out. It seems everyone wanted possession of the little border town because the railway was strategically important. The Germans won the fight, however, and for the next four years, this region was a central zone of the warfare in East Africa. Much later, when the Germans retreated, they continued to harass the British with guerrilla tactics. The stronger British forces eventually won the war.

MACABRE CAVE

Near the town of Taveta it is said there is a cave full of exhumed skulls where it is possible to communicate with the deceased's ancestors. There are other remote caverns in the banana growing region also filled with ancient bones. However, this macabre cave near the small village is the most accessible. It is interesting to note that the Taita people's practice of consulting their ancestors using exhumed skulls still continues today.

Ngai Ndethya National Reserve

This is a small strip of land connecting Tsavo East and Tsavo West. It is used primarily during the magnificent migration. Game uses the corridor to cross from one side of Tsavo to the other. The primary vegetation here is giant **baobab trees** and menacing **thornbush**. There are no visitor facilities.

South Kitui National Reserve

Located north of the Tsavo East border, **South Kitui National Reserve** is closed to tourism. The bushlands, grasslands and acacia woods are home to gerenuk, gazelle, lion, elephant, cheetah, zebra and giraffe to name just a few.

PRACTICAL INFORMATION

Park Hours & Fees

Tsavo is open every day from 6:00 am to 6:00 pm. There is a daily admission charge of $27 per person and a couple of dollars per vehicle. At this park, only the southern third is open to the public. North of the Galana River is closed, as it may not be safe for tourists owing to bandits and poachers.

Tsavo East is 4,600 square miles in size. For information on the road conditions and animal whereabouts, check in at the warden's office near the Voi Gate.

Fire

Because of the long, dry and hot summer it is not uncommon for fires to break out spontaneously and quickly burn through the dry scrub brush.

Guided by the honey-guide bird, the Akamba use smoke to collect honey from bee hives. Sparks from their "smokers" may sometimes start crackling brush fires. To help control these dangerous situations, there are roughly 1,250 miles of dirt paths used a firebreaks.

Dust

Because the park tends to get little rainfall, there is a lot of fine red dust which covers and gets into everything. Even the wildlife found in the undulating hills isn't overlooked by the red film; you will notice the elephant herds appear to have a bad dye job!

INDEX

THINGS CHANGE!

Phone numbers, prices, addresses, quality of food, etc, all change. If you come across any new information, we'd appreciate hearing from you. No item is too small! Drop us an e-mail note at: Jopenroad@aol.com, or write us at:

Kenya Guide
Open Road Publishing, P.O. Box 284
Cold Spring Harbor, NY 11724